DIVORCE BOOTCAMP

For Low- and Moderate-Income Women

By Anna T. Merrill, Esq.

5th Edition

v5.2

A Step-by-Step Legal Guide to Navigating Your Divorce

www.seraphim-press.com

This is the 5th Edition of this book. Prior editions were published in 2002, 2006, 2007, and 2009.

This book may be purchased for educational purposes.

Cover image 'We Can Do It' by J. Howard Miller.

ISBN-13: 978-1480101265

ISBN-10: 1480101265

Available through most book distribution platforms.

M.S.R.P. $25.00

LEGAL DISCLAIMERS

This book does not constitute legal advice and is written for informational purposes only. It provides a general overview of common issues low and low-moderate income women often experience during divorce. This book is intended to help the reader plan for the impact of divorce on their lives and contain their legal costs, not replace legal counsel. Legal issues are complex matters. Your best source of legal advice is always a flesh-and-blood attorney who practices in your local courthouse.

The author is licensed to practice law in Massachusetts. Laws and theories of property division may vary somewhat from state to state. If you are not from Massachusetts, you will need to visit your state court website (references included) to download your courthouse-specific forms. Use of this manual is not meant to constitute legal advice as to the laws of another state or the unauthorized practice of law. No attorney/client relationship exists between the author and the reader.

This book is not intended to be an advertisement for legal services. The author will not accept individual client case inquiries made because of this book. Chapter Nine makes suggestions on how to find your *own* legal counsel.

This book may not be copied or distributed in any way without the express written permission of the author.

Any advice, legal or otherwise, contained within this manual must be weighed carefully as to whether it would be helpful in your individual situation. If it doesn't make sense, don't do it! Laws change faster than books can be updated. Caveat emptor!

ARE YOU TOO BROKE TO BUY THIS BOOK?

I wrote this book to help women *not* get chewed up and spit out by the courts, not get rich. If you feel you need this book and are *truly* too broke to buy it, please send an email to the publisher's website at:

bootcamp_manual@seraphim-press.com

Write a two paragraph (or more) explanation stating how you heard of this book, why you cannot afford to purchase it, and how you think it will help you plan and implement your divorce. If your explanation is reasonable, they will e-mail an electronic copy of this book to you (limited to year 2013) in a .pdf file.

You will need to give your email address, but your name and contact information will be kept confidential. You are welcome to use a pseudonym and set up a temporary email address at a vendor site such as Yahoo or Hotmail.com. It is your story I wish to hear so I can be sure the next edition of this book remains useful, not necessarily to know who you are. If your husband is still living with you, I suggest you access the website from a friend's house or library internet portal.

ACKNOWLEDGMENTS

To all the fine family court judges who wade through work every day with a manure shovel and hip-waders on, especially those who took the time to gift insight into the thinking that occurs inside their brilliant minds. May all your pro se litigants understand your gavel is not a magic wand and actually *learn* something about the laws and procedures they're asking you to interpret on their behalf.

To all the tireless staff and public defenders at the Committee for Public Counsel Services who endlessly tilt at windmills for the poorest of the poor and get no appreciation and little pay. Especially my first mentor, Bill C.

To my wonderful husband, who patiently humors my pro bono efforts and writing addiction. And to my kids, who put up with being cross-examined about who colored on the wall with Sharpie marker.

To my wonderful focus group, who helped me edit this latest revision to make sure the information was still useful, relevant, and readable by real (i.e., non-lawyer) people. June, Joyce and Nancy … you know who you are. Thank you!

To all the wonderful volunteers, staff and clients at WE CAN, Inc. who help low- and moderate-income clients navigate the wood chipper known as family court after Legal Services has no choice but to turn them away. Visit their website at www.wecancenter.org

To the Women's Bar Foundation Family Law Project for Battered Women, who teach attorneys about the separate track of justice for women who can't afford an attorney. Especially my first mentor, Cindy B.. Visit their website at: http://www.womensbar.org

And to all the women who've attended my on-your-feet workshops over the years, read this book, and taken the time to provide feedback so the next revision could be improved. *You* are the people this book was written to serve.

WOULD YOU LIKE ATTORNEY MERRILL TO DO HER DIVORCE BOOCAMP SEMINAR AT -YOUR- NONPROFIT SERVICE AGENCY?

Anna T. Merrill, Esq. has developed a four-hour on-your-feet Divorce Bootcamp seminar geared for Low- and Moderate-Income Women. The curriculum includes a lecture/overview of divorce law and strategy, on-your-feet sample trial hearings where participants take turns role-playing actual court hearings (including a 'good' and 'bad' restraining order hearing), and a question-and-answer session at the end.

Attorney Merrill will conduct this seminar free of charge (during 2013) for any non-profit women's service court program or women's service agency (including informal groups such as public health departments, libraries or other groups) in any under-served community that lies within the Commonwealth of Massachusetts (schedule permitting).

Due to nationwide restrictions on state-by-state attorney licensing, this seminar can only be performed 'live' outside of Massachusetts if a local attorney assists with the question-and-answer session. Many attorneys who do not have time to put together a presentation, but who wish to provide follow-up services for prospective clients, may be willing to co-present. A stipend sufficient to reimburse out-of-state travel expenses will be necessary unless Attorney Merrill happens to be in the area on other business (it never hurts to ask).

For more information, contact her via the publisher at:

bootcamp_manual@seraphim-press.com

HOW TO USE THIS BOOK

This book is the result of more than a decade serving people the legal system has abandoned. What started out as a one-hour workshop and packet of photocopied forms to help low-income women extricate themselves from a bad marriage morphed into a four-hour seminar and this book. Women told me what they needed and it was incorporated into the next edition. As word got out about my workshop, middle-class women began to attend after they ran out of money for legal fees and their attorneys 'fired' them. I saw horror story after horror story of well-educated women with $30,000, $40,000, and even $60,000 legal bills, forced to go on welfare or driven into bankruptcy.

I finally said ... enough!

There are many fine legal self-help books, but they tend to fall into two categories: 1) fill-out-the-form books by lawyers who assume that you and your spouse are rational, fair-minded adults; and 2) divorce survival books by therapists or other people who were mistreated by the legal system and wish to tell their story. Both are useful and I recommend you read as many as you can get your hands on. But this is the only self-help book written by someone who was *once in your shoes,* who later went back to school to become an attorney!

THIS BOOK DOES NOT ADVOCATE 'DOING IT YOURSELF!' Going it alone should be a *last* resort, not a first. However, sometimes you don't have a choice. If you don't have a spare $5,000 to $15,000 laying around for a retainer and your husband is making your life a living hell, what are you supposed to do? Get chewed up and spit out by the courts? After years of watching desperate women put themselves through the wood chipper, I decided it was time *somebody* spelled things out.

SECTION ONE of this book seeks to do the following:

1. Educate you about all the reasons you need to be prepared to financially stand on your own two feet and how to go about doing that;

2. Cut your unrealistic expectations down to size about what the court can, and cannot do for you so you do not waste time and money tilting at windmills;

3. What documents you need to gather to get a fair property division;

4. Estimate how much child support and alimony you might be entitled to receive;

5. Help you figure out what property you're entitled to receive ... and should ask for;

6. Warn you about ways vindictive ex-spouses, unscrupulous attorneys, and a mindless legal bureaucracy can screw you over. Examples of real-life dirty tricks are highlighted so you can see problems coming:

   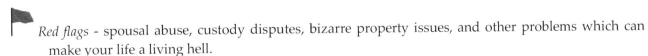 *Red flags* - spousal abuse, custody disputes, bizarre property issues, and other problems which can make your life a living hell.

    Spouses Behaving Badly– real life horror stories.

Dirty Lawyer Tricks– dirty tricks attorneys pull on unwary litigants.

 Smart Woodland Creature Tips– places where an ounce of prevention *now* can head off problems later if your spouse decides to fight dirty.

Legal Mumbo-Jumbo – sneaky lawyer words that sound innocuous but can be a hangman's noose!

$ *Ka-ching!!!* Things that drive up your legal bill.

7. How to find a good full-service attorney, if you can afford one, or piece together legal services to fill in the gaps if you cannot. Includes an overview of mediation ... benefits and pitfalls.

8. Teach you how to dig up information your spouse wishes to hide (discovery) like an attorney does. Includes tips about documenting your spouse's *real* income and assets.

9. Provide sample hearing scripts to familiarize you with common hearings you may be summoned to attend ... and the purpose of those hearings.

10. Sample boilerplate motions, court forms, and separation agreements are dissected and explained ... so you have someplace to look things up when that scary-looking legal pleading comes in the mail.

Preparation is where most legal self-help books fail!

SECTION TWO helps you use the knowledge gained in Section I to negotiate a fair divorce, material many legal self-help books cover. Because you will have a realistic grasp of your legal rights and your net worth after completing Section I, you're much more likely to reach a fair negotiated agreement.

SECTION THREE goes beyond other books. Although posited as 'fiction' because your case will likely be in a different jurisdiction and have factors different than the hypothetical case, it is a nuts-and-bolts, form-by-form approach. This is the only self-help book that shows you what a low- or middle-income woman's case might look like if her divorce becomes contested and she cannot afford to hire a full-service attorney. We will walk by Jane Doe's side as she navigates the legal system ... from filing her own divorce to launching her own trial ... what forms she needs to file ... what hearings she needs to attend ... what she needs to do to prepare for each hearing ... and ways she gets what she needs. The hypothetical case proceeds in Massachusetts as that is where I practice law, but thanks to the Federal Rules of Civil Procedure, *some* version of the tools our heroine uses to navigate the legal system are available in all fifty states.

The purpose of this journey is to educate you about tools attorneys use to solve common problems so you can choose your weapons wisely. By understanding what each tool can, and cannot do, it will make you an educated consumer about whether that tool will benefit *your* divorce. It will help eliminate that sense of panic most clients feel when a 'boilerplate' motion or hearing-notice arrives in the mail. It is my hope that by being a more knowledgeable consumer, you will be able to prioritize legal services and work with an attorney to make this journey *with* you at the lowest possible fee.

If you do not have limitless money to fund litigation, then you don't have the luxury of hand holding, excuses, or denial. You need to know the enemy you're up against, what weapons he has to use against you, what weapons you have to defeat him, and a battle plan to win the war. This book is blunt and to the point. If it offends anybody, I apologize in advance.

STOP SIGNS

This book is organized for a reader who purchases a book to survey the landscape and gather information before proceeding with their divorce. It has a heavy emphasis on gathering information, strategizing, and getting your financial and emotional house in order *before* you file. Sometimes, however, readers may already be in crisis when they pick up this book. Depending upon what your crisis is, you may want to read chapters out of order. Therefore, I will outline a few red flags which commonly require immediate action (this list is not all-inclusive):

 If you or your children are being physically abused, call 9-1-1. As soon as you have sought protection from the police, read Chapter Two: Safety Planning. The restraining order judge usually has the power to order temporary child support. *Then* come back and read the rest of the book.

 If you have just been served with divorce papers, you need help immediately. Read Chapter Nine: Piecing Together Legal Services. Once you have spoken to a flesh and blood attorney (even if only a courthouse lawyer-of-the-day) come back and jump right into Section III: Contested Divorces before coming back to the first section to do damage control. The court is very strict about returning paperwork on time. If you fail to do so, you could jeopardize your legal rights.

 If your husband has moved out of the house and is refusing to support you, read Chapter Five: Child Support if you have minor children, or Chapter Six: Alimony if you do not have children. The court cannot retroactively order alimony or child support if you wait. You must go to court to get these things. Chapter Nine: Piecing Together Legal Services tells you how to find an attorney or, if you cannot afford one, Section III: Contested Divorces gives you a general overview of how to file your own divorce so you can get a court order.

 If your husband is threatening to take custody of your children, read Chapter Fourteen: Child Custody immediately to get a rough idea as to whether his threats have any merit. Then, read Chapter Nine: Piecing Together Legal Services to help you find an attorney.

(This page left intentionally blank)

DIVORCE BOOTCAMP FOR LOW- AND MODERATE-INCOME WOMEN

(This page left intentionally blank)

TABLE OF CONTENTS

LEGAL DISCLAIMERS.. iii

ACKNOWLEDGMENTS v

HOW TO USE THIS BOOK vii

CHAPTER 1 - INTRODUCTION TO DIVORCE.. 1

So You're Thinking of Getting a Divorce?.. 1

The Judge Ain't Gonna Watch Your Back 2

But Don't I *HAVE* to Have an Attorney to Get Divorced? 2

Been there, done that… 3

Prior Preparation Prevents Poor Performance.. 4

My Husband Just TOLD Me that –HE- WANTS A DIVORCE 5

Divorce is Not a Somebody Done Somebody Wrong Song!.................................... 8

Don't Kill Each Other Over a Lousy 10% 9

Who Gets Custody of the Kids does NOT Affect the Bottom Line!!! 10

Can't We Just Work This Out Ourselves? 11

Am I –Ready- to File for Divorce?... 11

    1.   I can't afford an attorney:... 11

    2.   I can't survive without my spouses income:.. 11

    3.   We're staying together for the children's sake:... 11

    4.   I'm hoping to work things out in marriage counseling:......................... 11

    5.   Can't we just separate?.. 12

    6.   My husband moved out of the house because he needs 'to think.' 12

    7.   Can't we just annul our marriage? 12

I Spoke to an Attorney and They Have a Different Opinion 12

What About Same-Sex Marriage?.. 13

Division of the Marital Friends 13

The Devil You Know 14

What if I Change My Mind? 15

Why Y'All Lawyers So Dodgy About Answering QuestionS? 15

    Red Flag Issues.. 16

    Chapter One Summary 18

CHAPTER 2 - SAFETY PLANNING 19

    What is a Restraining Order? 20

    The Restraining Order 'Recipe' 21

        1.   In fear of 21

        2.   Imminent 22

        3.   Serious physical harm 23

    A Hypothetical Restraining Order Scenario 23

        On-Your-Feet Exercise 2-1: A "Botched" 209A Restraining Order Hearing 24

        On-Your-Feet Exercise 2-2: A "Better" 209A Restraining Order Hearing 25

    The So-Called "Father's Rights" (a.k.a. "Batters Rights") Movement 27

    How to Help the Judge 'Get' Your Case in 5 Minutes or Less 28

    Immigration Issues and Restraining Orders 31

    Chapter Two Summary 32

CHAPTER 3 - GATHER YOUR ACORNS 33

    1.   The past 3 years of tax returns. 34

    2.   The past 3 years of tax bills and real estate tax assessment sheets. 34

    3.   The past 3 years of bank statements. 34

    4.   The past 3 years of investment accounts. 34

    5.   the deed to your house and all other real property. 34

    6.   Copies of titles to all motor and recreational vehicles and excise tax bills for them. 35

    7.   Past 3 years of credit card statements and other consumer debt/personal loans. 35

    8.   Past 3 years of utility bills. 35

    9.   Health Insurance. 35

    10.   Life Insurance. 35

    11.   Past paystubs. 35

    12.   Pension information. 36

    13.   Make a list of all major belongings. 36

    14.   Copies of your spouse's business records. 36

    15.   Obtain both you and your husband's social security report sheet from the Social Security Administration. 36

    16.   Documentation regarding any other asset, liability, or collectible you have which may be valuable. 37

    How Should I Organize All This Information? 37

1. Start building an expense notebook: 38

2. Start building an asset valuation notebook. 38

Worksheet 3-1: Acorns Checklist 39

How Much Are My Acorns Worth? 40

Worksheet 3-2: Sample Valuation Worksheet...41

1. Valuing your house and other real estate:...42

2. Valuing Motor Vehicles:..42

3. Valuing Retirement and Pension Plans: 43

4. Valuing Your husbands business equipment, power tool collection, and/or hobby supplies:.........45

5. –Don't- Value Clothing: 46

6. Valuing Furnishings, electronic equipment and other big ticket items: 46

7. Valuing Other assets and collectibles:...46

Additional Steps You Should Take Right Away 47

Case Study – Introduction to Jack and Jane 49

Chapter 3 Summary...50

CHAPTER 4 - THE COURTS FINANCIAL STATEMENT 51

Financial Statements as a Bootcamp Financial Planning Tool...................52

Save Yourself $50 Right Now!..52

Where Do I get –MY- State's Version of This Form?..................................53

Anatomy of a Financial Statement..54

Table 4-1: Gross Weekly Income Calculator...57

Table 4-2: Expense Conversion Chart 59

Table 4-3: Breakdown of Expenses 60

Chapter 4 Summary...64

CHAPTER 5 - CHILD SUPPORT...65

Table 5-1: 50-State Listing of Child Support Websites.........................66

Who is Obligated to Pay Child Support?..68

How Long Can I Expect to Collect (or Pay) Child Support? 68

Table 5-2: States That Cut Support Off Upon Graduating High School 69

Table 5-3: States That Continue Child Support Through College...............69

Jane Doe-Rayme Hypothetical Child Support Guidelines...........................70

Example 5-1: Jane Doe Online Child Support Calculator 70

You Want me To Support My Kids on *WHAT*??? 71

My Husband has Kids from a Prior Relationship 71

    Example 5-2: Hypothetical Prior Families Child Support Reduction 72

Sneaky Tricks Your Husband Uses to Hide Money 72

    1.   Legitimate business expenses which should count for child support purposes: 72

    2.   The mysterious sudden drop in income: 72

    3.   Using pay stubs from the slow season: 73

    4.   Under-reported tip income or cash bonuses: 73

    5.   Demanding to be paid in cash the moment you file for divorce: 73

    6.   Under-the-Table Side Jobs: 74

    7.   Bartering: 74

    8.   "Going Underground": 75

    9.   Funneling Household Expenses through the Business Accounts: 75

    10.   Shacking up with parents or a new girlfriend: 76

    11.   The chronically unemployed or under-employed husband: 76

    12.   A long term pattern of lying about his income to the IRS: 76

The Burden of Proof is On *YOU* to Show How Much He Really Earns 77

Beware the IRS 77

Sympathy *FOR* the Self-Employed Husband 78

HIDING MONEY: ACT 1 - HOW TO SPOT B.S. IN A FINANCIAL STATEMENT.............79

    Example 5.3: Jack's Income (Self-Employed) 80

    Example 5.4: Jack's Payroll Taxes/Deductions 80

    Example 5.5: Jack's Weekly Expenses 81

    Example 5.6: Jack's Liabilities 81

    Example 5.7: Jack's Fishy Personal Loan 82

    Example 5.8: Jack's Legal Fees 82

    Example 5.9: Jane's Quicken Expense Report 83

HIDING MONEY: ACT 2 - SPOTTING FISHY DEDUCTIONS IN A SCHEDULE C 84

    Example 5.10: Jack's 1040 Income 85

    Example 5.11: Jack's Schedule C Income 86

    Example 5.12: Jack's Schedule C Expenses 87

    Example 5.13: Jane's Proposed Schedule C Expense Exclusions 90

    Example 5.14: Jane's Proposed Child Support Income Basis for Jack 90

    On-Your-Feet Exercise 5-1: Contested Hearing on Child Support 91

Leverage the Might of your State Child Support Enforcement Division..................................93

    1.   Get a court order for enforcement: 93

    2.   Have their official application all filled out and ready to go:....................93

    3.   Mail or hand-deliver your paperwork: 94

    4.   Follow up: 94

    5.   Financially prepare for the 6 week delay:...94

    6.   More follow-up:..94

    7.   Check for 'holds': 94

My Husband Won't Contest Custody if I Agree to Waive Child Support 95

Chapter Five Summary 96

CHAPTER 6 - ALIMONY 97

The 1/3 - 1/3 - 1/3 Guesstimate 98

    Table 6-1: Hypothetical 1/3 – 1/3 – 1/3 Alimony Estimate (no child support)......................98

    Table 6-2: Hypothetical 1/3 – 1/3 – 1/3 Alimony Estimate w/ child support 98

    Table 6-3: Hypothetical 1/3 – 1/3 – 1/3 Alimony Estimate..99

TYPES OF ALIMONY 100

    1.   General Term Alimony: 101

    2.   Rehabilitative Alimony: 102

    3.   Reimbursement Alimony:..102

    4.   Transitional Alimony:..103

ALIMONY INCOME..103

What is Alimony Need? 103

    Table 6-4: Hypothetical Jane Doe 'Economic Need' Computation 104

Can I Get Both Alimony and Child Support? 104

    1.   Example 105

    2.   Example:..105

Tax Implications of Alimony vs. Child Support..105

    1.   The Recipient pays the taxes on Alimony 105

    Table 6-5: Hypothetical Jane Doe Alimony Tax..105

    2.   The Payor pays taxes on Child Support:..106

    Table 6-6: Hypothetical Jane Doe Child Support Tax 106

    3.   If you get part Child Support and part Alimony, you pay taxes on each portion accordingly..106

    Table 6-7: Hypothetical Jane Doe Alimony + Child Support Tax 106

Can –I- Be Ordered to Pay My Husband Alimony? 107

   1.   Example: 107

   2.   Example: 107

   3.   Example: 107

When Does Alimony 'End?' 107

Life Insurance and Alimony 108

Health/Dental Insurance and Alimony 108

What if my Former Husband Gets Remarried? 109

What if –I- Get Remarried or Get a New Boyfriend? 109

Can I Waive Alimony in Exchange for an Asset? 110

   Exhibit 6-8: Sample Contested Hearing SCRIPT on Alimony 111

The Massachusetts Alimony Reform Act of 2011 (a proposed nationwide model) 112

Hiding Money 112

Chapter 6 Summary 113

CHAPTER 7 - PROPERTY DIVISION 115

What is 'Property?' 116

Which Property is Subject to Division? 117

What About Gifted or Inherited Property? 119

The Burden of Proof is on the Person Claiming it's Separate Property 119

Inside a Judges Head - How Property Division Happens in Court 120

   Table 7-1: Common Divorce 'Factors' 120

What Happens if We Go to Trial? 121

   Table 7-2: Sample 50:50 Property Division 121

   Table 7-3: Sample 60:40 Property Division 122

   Table 7-4: Sample 60:40 Property Division *after* Attorney Fees 122

   Table 7-5: Sample 55:45 Property Division *after* Attorney Fees 124

   Table 7-6: Sample 55:45 Property Division *after* Mediation 125

What if You Don't Own a Home? 125

   Table 7-7: Low-Income Hypothetical 50:50 Property Division 126

What Happens if One Party Wishes to Keep the Marital Home? 127

   Table 7-8: Sample 50:50 Property Division (Wife keeps house) 127

"Buying Out" the Marital Home 128

1.   Wait until your kids graduate high school and buy him out then, or agree to sell the house then and split the proceeds:...128

2.   You have enough money in other assets (including ones' often overlooked) to buy out your husbands' share...129

3.   Swap a retirement account for the marital home 129

4.   Swapping a pension for the marital home 130

5.   Swapping alimony for the marital home..130

6.   Refinance the house into your own name and give your husband a second mortgage –..........130

⚑ The Tax-Man Cometh 131

HIDING MONEY – PART 3: DIGGING FOR GOLD 133

2.   Hiding Money from Creditors 134

3.   Mad Money...134

4.   Hiding money from –you- in anticipation of divorce..135

Which Assets Should I Ask For?...136

1.   Appreciating Asset 136

2.   Depreciating Asset –..136

3.   Stable-Value Asset 136

4.   High-Maintenance Asset...136

Table 7-9: *YOUR* Proposed 'Dream' Asset Division 138

Chapter 7 Summary..138

CHAPTER 8 - MARITAL DEBT...139

Table 8-1 – Jack and Jane's Secured Debt Allocation Worksheet.................................140

Marital Debts Are *Not* Always Divided 50:50..142

Table 8-2 – Jack and Jane's 2/3 – 1/3 Unsecured Debt Division 143

Anomaly Spotting When Listing Liabilities...143

Table 8-3 –Jane Doe's Mortgage Payment 144

Table 8-4 – Jack and Jane's Mortgage Payment 144

Table 8-5 –Jane Doe's Car Payment..145

Table 8-7 – Jack and Jane's Assets..146

Can I Offer to Pay off a Debt to Keep an Asset?...147

From Table 8-6 – Jack and Jane's 2/3 – 1/3 Unsecured Debt Division..........................147

Table 8-7 – Jane's Projected Weekly Living Expenses/Debt Payment Worksheet.........148

Table 8-8 – *YOUR* Projected Weekly Living Expenses/Debt Payment Worksheet.........149

The Judge's Gavel is Not a Magic Wand..149

CHAPTER 9 - PIECING TOGETHER LEGAL SERVICES ON A 'REAL' PERSON's BUDGET 157

Do I Really Need an Attorney?..158

How to Find an Attorney 158

Setting Up Your First Appointment..160

Preparing for Your First Appointment..160

Have Realistic Expectations About What an Attorney Can Do 161

Interviewing Your Prospective Attorney 163

    1. Does this attorney appear to be knowledgeable about family law?.............163

    2. Does the attorney readily admit the limits of his expertise? 163

    3. Personality is important...163

    4. What credentials does the attorney have 164

    6. Does the attorney perform any pro bono or sliding-fee-scale work 164

Getting Your Spouse to Loan You Money to Hire An Attorney.......................165

    Example 9-1: Sample Motion for Attorney Fees Pendente Lite 165

Keep Your Attorney On A SHort LeasH!!!..166

Mediation/Arbitration/Collaborative Law 167

The Mediator is not 'Your' Attorney 168

Court-Ordered Mediation/Arbitration/ADR 169

Legal Services/ Legal Aid 169

Courthouse 'Lawyer-of-the-Day' Programs 170

The Court's Family Services Department And Self-Help Clinics......................170

Non-Profit Legal Clinics and How-to Classes 171

Do-it-Yourself Books and Document Preparation Services..............................172

Your Own State Courts Website 173

    Table 9-1: 50-State Listing of Free Self-Help Divorce Websites 176

Use the Same Legal Resources Your Lawyer Does...178

Intermission 179

    Table 9-1: Activities to Save Money on YOUR Legal Bill 181

Chapter Nine Summary..182

CHAPTER 10 - UNCONTESTED DIVORCES..185

Negotiated (Uncontested) Divorces ... Pro and Con.......................................186

Advantages (PRO) 186

Disadvantages (CON) 187

Before You Break the Bad News 188

Put Together a Proposed Separation Agreement Package 190

Protect Your Credit Rating 192

Example 10-1: Sample Credit Card Cancellation Worksheet 192

Example 10-2: Sample 'Hard close' request follow-up letter 194

Example 10-3: Sample 'Rollover' request follow-up letter 195

Breaking the Bad News to Your Spouse 197

Who Will Stay in the Marital Home? 198

Example 10-4: Sample Temporary Separation Agreement 201

What Courthouse has Jurisdiction to Grant My Divorce? 202

What Paperwork Must I File to Get an Uncontested Divorce? 203

Example 10-5: Sample Joint Petition for Divorce 205

Sneaky Lawyer Words: Merger and Survival 205

'Official' and 'Unofficial' Marriage Certificates 207

Example 10-6: Sample 'Official' Marriage Certificate 207

Example 10-7: Sample 'Unacceptable' CHurch-Issued Marriage Certificate 208

Example 10-8: Sample 'Unacceptable' TOWN-Issued Marriage Certificate 208

Example 10-8: Sample Affidavit of irretrievable breakdown 209

Example 10-9: Sample Form Disclosing Other Court Proceedings That May Involve Your Children
(Or Sometimes Yourselves) 209

Example 10-10: Registry of Vital Statistics Change Form 211

Example 10-11: Military Affidavit 211

Example 10-12: Request for a Final Hearing 212

Example 10-13: Cover Letter to the Clerk 212

The Final Hearing on an Uncontested Divorce 213

On-Your-Feet Exercise 10-1: Typical uncontested divorce hearing 214

Chapter 10 Summary 215

CHAPTER 11 - SEPARATION AGREEMENTS 217

Separation Agreement Checklist 218

Exhibit 11-1: Sample Separation Agreement Checklist 219

Scrounging Up a Sample Separation Agreement 221

Exhibit 11-2: States with Model Separation/Dissolution/Consent Decrees Available Online 222

Anatomy of a Separation Agreement 223

The Preamble..224

Exhibit 11-P-1: Sample Court-Model Preamble...226

Exhibit 11-P-2: Sample Attorney-Drafted Preamble 227

Exhibit 11-P-3: Sample Court-Model Preamble (cont'd)..228

Exhibit 11-P-4: Sample Attorney-Drafted Preamble (cont'd) 230

Exhibit 11-P-5: Sample Attorney-Drafted Preamble (cont'd) 231

Exhibit 11-P-6: Sample Attorney-Drafted Preamble (cont'd) 232

Exhibit 11-P-7: Sample Attorney-Drafted Preamble (cont'd) 233

Exhibit 11-P-8: Sample Attorney-Drafted Preamble (cont'd) 235

Exhibit 11-P-8: Sample Attorney-Drafted Preamble (cont'd) 236

EXHIBIT A: BOILERPLATES RELATING TO CUSTODY, VISITATION AND RELATED MATTERS
....238

Exhibit 11-A-1: Sample Court "Schedule A – Child Related Matters"..239

Exhibit 11-A-2: Sample attorney-drafted "standard" agreement where Mom gets physical custody, Mom & Dad Share Legal Custody 240

Exhibit 11-A-3: Sample Shared Physical Custody (50:50) Agreement...242

EXHIBIT B: CHILD SUPPORT 243

Exhibit 11-B-1: Sample "Child Support" portion of court'S "Schedule A - Child Related Matters" 243

Exhibit 11-B-2: Sample Attorney-Drafted Child Support Boilerplate 244

EXHIBIT C: ALIMONY BOILERPLATES 246

Exhibit 11-C-1: Sample Court Alimony Boilerplate..246

Exhibit 11-C-2: Sample Generic Alimony Obligation Boilerplate...247

Exhibit 11-C-3: Sample Waived Alimony Clause...248

Exhibit 11-C-4: Sample Waived Alimony, Exceptions to Survival Clause 249

EXHIBIT D: BOILERPLATES ADDRESSING THE CHILDREN'S EDUCATION 250

Exhibit 11-D-1: Sample Boilerplate Addressing the Children's Education 251

EXHIBIT E: BOILERPLATES DICTATING WHO PROVIDES HEALTH INSURANCE AND PAYS UNINSURED HEALTH-RELATED BILLS...252

Exhibit 11-E-1: Sample Court "Health Insurance for the Parties" boilerplate 253

Exhibit 11-E-2: Sample Court "Schdeule A - Medical Insurance for Children" boilerplate 254

Exhibit 11-E-3: Sample Attorney boilerplate on Health Insurance and Expenses...........................255

Exhibit 11-E-4: Sample Alimony Waiver-Driven Agreement About Health Insurance 257

EXHIBIT F: BOILERPLATES ADDRESSING WHICH SPOUSE GETS WHAT ASSET..........................258

  Exhibit 11-F-1: SAMPLE Court Boilerplate Addressing Assets 259

  Exhibit 11-F-2: SAMPLE Attorney Boilerplate Addressing Assets...........................260

  Exhibit 11-F-3: Sample Property Division Worksheet 262

  Exhibit 11-F-4: Sample Motion Requesting the Court Approve a QDRO...........................263

  Exhibit 11-F-5: Sample QDRO...........................264

EXHIBIT G: BOILERPLATES DICTATING REPAYMENT OF DEBTS...........................266

  Exhibit 11-G-1: SAMPLE Court Boilerplate Addressing Debts...........................266

  Exhibit 11-G-2: Division of Debts and Liabilities 267

  Exhibit 11-G-3: Financial Statement Addendum G-1: Unsecured General Liabilities Allocation Worksheet 268

EXHIBIT H: TAX AGREEMENTS 269

  Exhibit 11-H-1: Sample Court Boilerplate Addressing Tax Dependents 269

  Exhibit 11-H-2: Sample Tax Boilerplates 270

EXHIBIT I: ATTORNEY FEE BOILERPLATES...........................271

  Exhibit 11-I-1: Legal Fees and Expenses 271

  Exhibit 11-I-2: Sample for Ongoing Litigation - Legal Fees and Expenses 272

EXHIBIT J: LIFE INSURANCE BOILERPLATES 273

  Exhibit 11-J-1: Sample Court Life Insurance Boilerplate for Each Other 273

  Exhibit 11-J-2: Sample Court Life Insurance Boilerplate for the Children...........................274

  Exhibit 11-J-3: Sample Flat Rate Boilerplate - Life Insurance...........................274

  EXHIBIT 11-J-4: Sample Stepped Life Insurance Obligation Computation to Meet a Child Support Obligation...........................275

  EXHIBIT 11-J-5: Sample Stepped Life Insurance Obligation Computation to Meet an Alimony Obligation (No Children Scenario)...........................275

  Exhibit 11-J-6: Sample Flat Rate Boilerplate - Life Insurance...........................276

PRELIMINARY 'SCRATCH-COPY' TO ROUGH OUT A PROPOSED SEPARATION AGREEMENT277

  Exhibit 11-K-1: Sample Blank Boilerplate Separation Agreement -With- Minor Children 277

  EXHIBIT 11-K-2: Sample Blank Boilerplate Separation Agreement -Without- Dependent Children 311

  Chapter 11 Summary...........................336

CHAPTER 12 - CONTESTED DIVORCES 339

  Should I File an At-Fault Divorce? 340

  Countdown to Filing Day 341

Table 12-1 - Countdown to Filing Day Checklist 341

Contested Divorce Checklist 343

Table 12-2: Forms That Start Your Divorce (Complaint for Divorce) 343

Table 12-3: Forms Filed With or Shortly After Filing for Divorce 344

Table 12-4: Forms A Smart Woodland Creature Prepares in Advance...................345

Table 12-5: Documents You -Must- File On Time 345

Table 12-6: Forms Your Spouse Is Supposed to Get Back to You 346

Table 12-7: Sample Docket File Organization Chart 347

Exhibit 12-1 - Sample Docket File Document Control Sheet 348

How to Fill Out the Complaint for Divorce 348

Exhibit 12-2 - Sample Complaint for Divorce 349

Where Do I File (Jurisdiction)? 350

What If I Need to File in a Hurry and Don't Have a Certified Copy of My Marriage Certificate On-Hand? 350

Exhibit 12-3: Sample Motion for a Late Filing of a Marriage Certificate 351

What If I Can't Afford the Court's Filing Fee? 352

Exhibit 12-4: Sample Affidavit of Indigency 352

The Automatic Restraining Order..353

The Sheriff's Summons 353

Chapter Twelve Summary 354

CHAPTER 13 - TEMPORARY ORDERS 355

Exhibit 13-1: Sample Motion for Temporary Orders 356

Exhibit 13-2: Sample Certificate of Service and Notice of Hearing 358

Supporting Affidavits 359

Exhibit 13-3: Sample Affidavit In Support of Temporary Orders 360

What Do I Do If My Spouse Files First? 361

Exhibit 13-4: Sample Counter-Claim for Temporary Orders 362

How to Dress and Act in Court 364

If Available, Use Your Court's Family Services Department 365

Exhibit 13-5: Sample Family Services Session 366

Exhibit 13-6: Sample Family Services Stipulation 368

Exhibit 13-7: A Sample Temporary Orders Hearing 369

Exhibit 13-8: Sample Temporary Order..371

Exhibit 13-9: Sample 'Form' Order for Support & Health Care Coverage 372

Child, Spousal and Medical Support...372

Payment Information 372

Health Care Coverage Provisions 372

Past Due Support/Costs...372

Chapter Thirteen Summary 373

CHAPTER 14 - CHILD CUSTODY...375

Types of Custody 375

Who Is the Primary Caretaker of the Children? 376

Exhibit 14-1: Some Primary Caretaker Criteria 377

CUSTODY DEFECTS...377

Defect #1 –Your Child has a Clear Preference for Your Husband 378

Defect #2 – Your Husband Cares for Your Children 50% of the Time 379

Defect #3 - Drug or Alcohol Addiction 380

Defect #4 - Mental Illness 381

Defect #5 – DCF has found you guilty of neglect or abuse 382

Defect #6 – You Have a Criminal Record 383

Defect #7 – You Suffer From a Physical Disability 384

Defect #8 – You Are Having an Affair 385

I Want to Hire a Lawyer to Handle My Custody Dispute, but Who?...................386

How Much Should I Tell My Kids About the Divorce? 386

Post-Divorce Dating and Children 388

Who Gets Custody of the Children Is Usually Decided First...............................389

Parent Education Classes 389

Parenting Plans..389

What do I do if my husband contests custody and I want somebody to look into it (Guardians Ad Litem)? 389

Exhibit 14-2: Motion to Appoint a Guardian Ad Litem (GAL) 391

Exhibit 14-3: Limited Waiver of Privilege..392

What If I Need to Move Out of State with my Child? 393

Exhibit 14-4: Sample Motion to Remove Minor Children from the State 394

Exhibit 14-5: Sample Contested Child Custody Hearing 395

My Spouse Took my Kids Out-of-State and Filed for Custody There! 398

Chapter Fourteen Summary 398

CHAPTER 15 - DISCOVERY 399

Exhibit 15-1: Documents You Generally Owe Your Husband at the Time You File Divorce or Within 45 Days 402

Exhibit 15-2: Documents Your Husband Generally Owes You Within 45 Days 403

Exhibit 15-3: The Attorney 'Discovery' Toolbox 404

Exhibit 15-4: Sample Request for Financial Statement 405

Exhibit 15-5: Sample Reminder Letter – Court Financial Statement 406

Exhibit 15-6: Sample Motion to Compel Filing of Financial Statement 407

Exhibit 15-7: Sample Notice of Hearing On A Motion to Compel Filing of Financial Statement 408

Exhibit 15-8: Sample Request for Mandatory Self-Disclosure Documents 409

Responding to Your Spouse's Request for Mandatory Self-Disclosure 410

Exhibit 15-9: Sample Cover Letter for Jane Doe Self-Disclosure Documents 410

Exhibit 15-10: Sample Mandatory Self-Disclosure Compliance Affidavit 411

Document Requests 413

Exhibit 15-11: Sample Request for the Production of Documents 414

Answers to Document Requests 417

Exhibit 15-12: Sample Aanswer to Request for the Production of Documents 418

Requests for Admissions of Fact 422

Exhibit 15-13: Sample Request for Admissions of Fact 423

Answering Requests for Admissions of Fact 424

Exhibit 15-14: Sample Answer to Requests for Admissions of Fact 424

Interrogatories 425

Exhibit 15-15: Sample Interrogatories 426

Answers to Interrogatories 430

Exhibit 15-16: Sample Answers to Interrogatories 430

Expert Interrogatories 435

Exhibit 15-17: Sample Expert Interrogatories 436

Answering Expert Interrogatories 437

Exhibit 15-18: Sample Answer to Expert Interrogatories 437

Depositions 438

Exhibit 15-19: Sample Deposition Subpoena 439

Exhibit 15-20: Sample Motion to Quash Deposition 441

What is Privilege? 442

    Exhibit 15-21: Motion to Quash Subpoena - Privileged Information 444

What Do I Do If My Husband Ignores My Discovery Requests? 445

    Exhibit 15-22: Sample Reminder Letter RE: Discovery Requests.................446

    Exhibit 15-23: Sample Cover Letter RE: Motion to Compel Discovery 447

    Exhibit 15-24: Motion to Compel Discovery and for Sanctions.....................449

    Exhibit 15-25: Affidavit In Support Of Motion to Compel Discovery 451

Chapter Fifteen Summary..452

CHAPTER 16 - THE PRE-TRIAL CONFERENCE 453

Scheduling the Pre-trial Conference..453

    Exhibit 16-1: Sample Request for Pre-Trial Conference 454

The Pre-trial Conference Order..455

    Exhibit 16-2: Sample Pre-Trial Conference Order 455

Your State Divorce Statute Property Division Factors...456

    Exhibit 16-3: Common Property Division Factors.....................................457

A Legal Writing Exercise: The "Dear Judge" Letter...457

    Exhibit 16-4: Sample 'Dear Judge' Letter...458

Mandatory Meeting Before the Pre-trial Conference:...459

The Pre-trial Memorandum...460

    Exhibit 16-5: Sample Pre-Trial Memorandum 461

The Pre-Trial Conference Hearing...465

    Exhibit 16-6: Sample "in chambers" Session at Pre-Trial Conference 466

    Exhibit 16-7: Sample "Joint Motion to Convert to an Uncontested Divorce 467

Chapter Sixteen Summary...468

CHAPTER 17 - PREPARING FOR TRIAL...469

What You Don't Know You Don't Know...470

What is my Theory of the Case? 471

Which Facts Support (or discredit) My Theory of the Case? 473

    Example 17-1: Sample Method of Weighing Facts In Case 474

How do I Get My Evidence Before the Judge? 476

    Exhibit 17-2 – Sample Evidentiary Issue Analysis 477

Direct Examination - The Proper Way to Ask Your Witness Questions 478

Example 17-3: Direct Examination Questions 479

Example 17-4: Jane Doe Gathers Impeaching Evidence 480

Example 17-5: Focus of a Hypothetical Direct Examination Script 482

Exhibit 17-6: Sample Direct Examination of Building Inspector 483

Exhibit 17-7: Sample Direct Examination of Building Inspector (cont'd) 484

Exhibit 17-8: Sample Direct Examination of Building Inspector (cont'd) 485

What Facts is my Husband Likely to Offer to Undermine My Theory of the Case and Support His Own? 486

Asking Your Husband Leading Questions and Cross-Examining Your Husband's Witnesses 488

Exhibit 17-9: Sample Direct Examination of Party-Opponent Husband 490

Exhibit 17-10: Sample Cross-Examination of Husband's Witness 491

Subpoenas 492

Exhibit 17-11: Sample Subpoena 493

Trial Notebook(s) 494

Chapter Seventeen Summary 496

CHAPTER 18 - TRIAL 497

Exhibit 18-1: Jane's Opening Statement 499

Exhibit 18-2: Jack's Opening Statement 500

Exhibit 18-3: Jane's Testimony About Jack's Earning Capacity 501

Exhibit 18-4: Jane's Testimony About Jack's Secret Stock Account 502

Exhibit 18-5: Jane's Closing Argument 503

Exhibit 18-6: *My Cousin Vinny* Fun Trial-Prep Exercise 503

Chapter Eighteen Summary 505

CHAPTER 19 - FINAL DISPENSATION 507

Final Dispensation for a Settled divorce 507

Exhibit 19-1: Sample judgment of Uncontested divorce nisi 508

Final Disposition for a Contested Divorce After Trial 509

Exhibit 19-2: Saample Judgment of Contested Divorce Nisi 510

Appeals – What Can I Do If I Think the Judge was Wrong? 511

Chapter Nineteen Summary 512

CHAPTER 20 - CONTEMPT 513

    Exhibit 20-1: Complaint for Civil Contempt 515

    Exhibit 20-2: Plaintiff's Motion for Attorney's Fees and Costs 516

    Exhibit 20-3: Affidavit of Plaintiff's Attorney Regarding Contempt Costs...........517

    Exhibit 20-4: Contempt Notice of Hearing and Affidavit of Service 518

    Exhibit 20-5: Contempt Hearing Sample Script...519

    Exhibit 20-6: Second Contempt Hearing Sample Script (AKA 'The Three O'Clock Speech) 520

CONCLUSION 521

INDEX...523

ABOUT THE AUTHOR 527

(This page left intentionally blank)

SECTION I

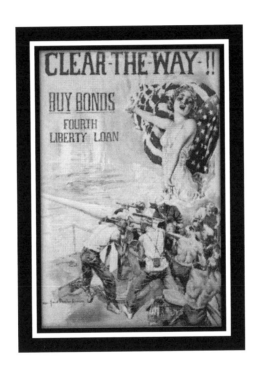

KNOW WHAT YOU'RE GETTING YOURSELF INTO

(This page left intentionally blank)

CHAPTER 1

INTRODUCTION TO DIVORCE

The art of war is of vital importance to the state.
It is a matter of life and death,
A road either to safety or to ruin.
Hence under no circumstances can it be neglected.

The Art of War by Sun Tzu

SO YOU'RE THINKING OF GETTING A DIVORCE?

Being trapped in a bad marriage is like being a small woodland creature caught in a steel trap. Eventually, the evil trapper is going to come along, club you over the head and skin you alive. The small woodland creature (you) is usually aware of only two choices: (1) hope the evil trapper takes pity on your sad eyes and sets you free (forget it!!!), or (2) desperately gnaw off your own leg and hobble into the woods, hoping you don't bleed to death.

Once upon a time, attorneys took pity on small woodland creatures such as yourself and allowed you to pay-as-you-go or pay a reduced fee. You'd end up with a few crushed bones that would eventually heal. Unfortunately, due to the length and complexity of modern divorce cases and reluctance of courts to let lawyers withdraw if you stop paying, most lawyers won't represent you unless you pay up front. Once clients have their divorce in hand, the *last* person they want to pay is their attorney.

If you can't afford to pay the retainer, it's up to *you* to find a stick, shove it between the bars of the steel cage, and get *yourself* out of the trap with a minimum of mangled flesh. The result will *never* be as good as hiring a full-service attorney, but if you have no other option, there are ways to minimize the damage.

THE JUDGE AIN'T GONNA WATCH YOUR BACK

"In the uncertainty of punishment following crime,
Lies the weakness of our halting justice."

Judge Isaac Parker aka 'The Hanging Judge'

People ask, 'is there justice in the courthouses of this country?' That depends. Outcome depends upon your ability to hire a good attorney and fund discovery, investigation, preparation, and expert witnesses to bring their experience to bear upon your case. In other words, if you're wealthy enough to outspend the other person, you'll find your own brand of justice. Otherwise, the Goddess of Justice got the hell out of Dodge a long time ago.

Most self-represented women wander into the courthouse and become embroiled in a blur too complicated to navigate. Even represented women have an appalling lack of understanding about the hearings they're summonsed to attend. Going to court without a lawyer is like playing Russian roulette with 5 bullets in the chamber. If you don't know what you're doing and can't come up to speed on the rules of litigation fast enough to focus on the issues the court *can* help you with, you're in deep trouble.

If you don't know what you're entitled to receive, the judge isn't going to watch your back. Don't get me wrong, judges are some of the most even-minded, compassionate folk I know. But if you don't understand how the game is played, you're shooting yourself in the foot. Without an attorney, you'll *never* get as good of an outcome as you would if money was not a problem. The judge is too busy to watch your back, so starting right now you'd better start watching it yourself.

BUT DON'T I *HAVE* TO HAVE AN ATTORNEY TO GET DIVORCED?

It's possible to get divorced without stepping foot inside an attorney's office. You have a Constitutional right to represent *yourself* in any matter, in any court, for any reason. Family law. Criminal law. Civil disputes. Big disputes or small. Not just small claims court, but the U.S. Supreme Court if your case is interesting enough for them to want to hear. You can't legally represent *somebody else* without a license to practice law, but you can represent yourself.

> *Whether or not that's advisable is a different story.* There's a reason attorneys make so much money. The law is convoluted. A seemingly minor procedural error, such as failing to meet a deadline or object to a piece of evidence, can mean the difference between winning a case and getting taken to the cleaners.

Why has access to justice become so difficult? You're not going to pay my paralegal $85 per hour to photocopy your old bank statements, something you can do yourself for 10¢ per page at Staples, if you're not quaking in terror at the thought of going to court. That's why. Courts and legislative bodies are overpopulated by lawyers who used to be partners at big law firms. Partners at big law firms care about how many billable hours they can get out of you before you go bankrupt.

Whenever somebody walks into court without a lawyer, every person in that courthouse groans. You don't know what you're doing. You don't understand the rules of the game. You have unrealistic expectations of what the court can and cannot do for you, or what you're entitled to receive. Your case goes to trial when it should have settled because you don't understand the law. Worse, because you don't understand how your case got messed up, you come back for a second bite of the apple. And a third … and a fourth … fifth … sixth … seventh.

In other words, courts forgot their sole purpose for existing is to provide access to justice for people like *YOU*, the taxpayers who pay their salaries, and not the wealthy lawyers who swim through their hallways like great white sharks!

Until recently, courts threw up every obstacle they could because then you'd go to Legal Aid or hire a lawyer. It made everybody else's life easier. But then Legal Aid got cut to the bone and the American middle class outsourced to China. It doesn't matter *how* frightened you are. If you don't have any money and need to extricate yourself from a bad marriage, you're going to grit your teeth and jump into the wood chipper. The courts finally figured out taxpayers are subsidizing wealthy lawyers when they make routine divorces difficult to obtain. The pendulum has finally started to swing in the opposite direction.

Some states *still* throw up obstacles. They don't standardize forms or procedures. They write statutes that are impossible to understand. They don't tell you about programs that help routine cases settle long before they go to trial. And they're sticklers about minor details to punish you for wasting their time. But don't *ever* let somebody convince you that you're too stupid to solve your own problems. You have the right to take on as much of your own legal case as you feel competent to handle.

Notice I said *as much of* and not *all*… Most of the time it's not *advisable* to do it *all* yourself. But somewhere between the continuum of plunking down a $5,000 to $15,000 retainer to hire a full-service attorney or going it alone lays a whole range of options to get divorced on a budget. This book is written to help you figure out where that line *is* and use what you've learned to work with your attorney as a *partner*. Not your savior.

BEEN THERE, DONE THAT…

"Experience is the name everyone gives to their mistakes."

Oscar Wilde, playwright

So, you might be asking yourself. How does *this* lawyer know what I'm going through?

I married the first guy who asked. By the time I realized I'd made a mistake, I had a daughter. I stayed as long as I could stand it, eight years. When the urge to go back to school and make something of my life became strong enough to stand up to him, he threatened to stab me with a screwdriver. That's how I was introduced to the wonderful world of divorce.

He could afford a lawyer, I couldn't. He was a dual-citizen of another country and threatened to take my daughter. I did whatever it took to appease him. We'd bought our house during the 1980's market peak. I assumed what we'd paid for it was the value, so I never had it appraised. I had no idea he wasn't doing me any favors 'giving' me a house worth $30,000 *less* than we owed on it, or that I was entitled to have him pay half the marital debt (which were in my name because he had lousy credit) or keep *one* of our four cars (all titled in his name).

In 'exchange' for my child and a negatively mortgaged house, I handed him everything we owned. He walked away with tens of thousands of dollars' worth of contractors' tools without including them in the marital kitty. I slept in a pile of clothing on the floor until a friend took pity and gave me an old mattress. I walked to work until I saved enough to buy a clunker which wouldn't work when it rained. I did every odd job I could to make ends meet, including baiting fish 'chum' onto nets in the middle of the night. In other words, I got screwed...

I remember my first family law class in law school. I got so angry I ran into the ladies room to cry. Looking back through the eyes of a lawyer, I really don't mind that I had to sleep on the floor, walk to work, or put fish guts onto hooks to survive. I wanted to be rid of him and I'm glad he's gone. What bothers me is I signed away $50,000 worth of assets and assumed debt because I didn't know what I was doing. In 2012 dollars that would be $90,000. With my fair share of the marital kitty, my life would have been easier. At the $7.25 per hour I earned back then, I computed I had to work an additional 6,900 hours just to keep my head above water. That's 173 additional 40-hour work weeks, or 3.3 work-years of my time taken *out of my kid's hide* because I was too naive to talk to an attorney!

My goal in life is to help people of modest means gain access to the courts. I like men. I represent men. I have a *Divorce Bootcamp* manual written for men and have helped men take custody away from a crummy mother. My goal is to educate women about the process so they can get a *fair* divorce. There's no such thing as a 'good' divorce.

How can this Bootcamp Manual help you? When I was a single mother, Santa Claus didn't come with a sleigh full of money to pay my bills. Neither did my family, friends, neighbors, or society. No knight on a white horse appeared to carry me off into the sunset. The only men who seek out struggling single mothers are pedophiles. Others will pay you a wide berth until you get you life in order. I had no magic wand to wave away my problems. No matter how much I closed my eyes and visualized the utility bills paying themselves, the only way they ever got paid was to work extra hours and write a check.

No matter how much I wished I could have gotten a judge to undo mistakes I made handling my own divorce, I was stuck with it. No lawyer can correct your past mistakes. What I *can* do is teach you how to extricate yourself with as little pain as possible. If you want to get from point A to point B, *you need to help yourself.*

PRIOR PREPARATION PREVENTS POOR PERFORMANCE

Most women feel it's immoral to strategize for a good outcome *before* letting the other partner know they want out of the marriage. "I don't want to play games," they say. That attitude is ridiculous! Planning for a secure future for yourself and your children is *not* immoral.

When you were in high school, a guidance counselor helped you plan which classes you needed to get a job, learn a trade, or get into college. For four years, you busted your hump to get good grades. Were you being immoral then? Of course not!

If you went to college, you spent years studying for the SAT's, gathering brochures, touring colleges, filling out applications, interviewing recruiters, and applying for financial aid *before* you finally selected a school. Was that immoral? No!

When you bought a house, you researched what town, school system, and neighborhood you wanted to live in before you negotiated a deal. When you had a baby, you planned what name to give it, whether or not you needed to move to a better neighborhood, who would babysit while you worked (or what niceties you would give up to stay home), and what would ensure the little one gets into college someday.

Why wouldn't you take those same steps to make sure you walk away from a bad marriage with your fair share of the assets? And a solid custody or alimony agreement so you can feed yourself, keep a roof over your head, and ensure your peace, sanity, and well-being? Don't YOU deserve the same self-preservation planning that you'd do for your aging parents, children or pets? We'll discuss ways to do this in coming chapters.

A well-planned divorce is a divorce where the woodland creature gets out of the trap with a minor limp.

Woodland creatures with young are *especially* vulnerable. Their only defense is to plan ahead so they don't resort to gnawing off their own leg. If a woodland creature is damaged escaping the trap, the young will go hungry. Literally … because of too few resources. Emotionally … because their mother is too distraught to nurture them. Or financially … because their mother works too many hours gathering food.

Worse, an even nastier trapper called the Department of Children and Family Services may step in and take away your vulnerable young because mom is stretched too thin to care for them. Don't let your little ones starve because some foolish person convinced you preparing for a divorce is a game!

MY HUSBAND JUST TOLD ME THAT –HE– WANTS A DIVORCE

*"Yesterday, Dec. 7, 1941 – a date which will live in infamy –
the United States of America was suddenly and deliberately attacked…"*

Except of President Franklin D Roosevelt's Pearl Harbor Speech

71% of all divorces in this country are initiated by women. The tone of this book reflects this fact, urging women to prepare before they tell their husband they want a divorce. But what if *you* are the one who just got bushwhacked? If you've been caught unprepared, you need to *immediately* do some damage control so you don't get chewed up and spit out by the court.

Get thee to a family law attorney with all deliberate haste lest thee find thyself out on the street, penniless, and without custody of your children or possession of your pets!!!

I can't tell you how many women wander into my office weeks, even months after their husband has had free rein with their finances and dragged them kicking and screaming into court. Many, in fact, don't seek legal help until *after* the first court Temporary Orders hearing, after their legal rights have been irrevocably damaged. Denial is not your friend! If you've ever taken survival training or watched a survival show such Survivorman or Man vs. Wild, you know you need to move quickly to survive.

Getting 'dumped' is never pleasant. While your mind is reeling with uncertainty and your heart is breaking, you are in a very poor position to negotiate a fair divorce. *Especially* if your husband has been using his time planning to hide joint marital assets and artificially reduce his income instead of documenting assets so he can divide them fairly. Therefore, before you read any further, you need to *immediately* take the following triage steps:

1. The moment your spouse leaves the house, quickly take stock of what you have:

    a. Take a camera and go through every room in your house (and garage), taking pictures of everything you have.

    b. Make a backup copy of any financial software you may have, such as Microsoft Money or Quicken to a flash drive or CD.

    c. Grab your checkbook registers, latest bank statements and utility bills and make photocopies.

    d. If you have receipts or warranty information for any big-ticket items in your house (such as your car, that new plasma television, etc.), grab those and make a photocopy as well.

2. Call any credit cards you hold in which your husband is either a joint-cardholder or an authorized user and ask them to revoke his authorization to use that card;

    a. Skip ahead to Chapter 10: Uncontested Divorces and read the sub-heading entitled 'Protect Your Credit'

    b. Chapter 10 shows you how to gather credit card information, create a list to help you keep track of who you did and did not call, what to say to them, how to document it, and has sample boilerplate follow-up letters. Take these steps!

    If your spouse wracks up the credit card bills and your name is on it, you –will- be held responsible for repaying it! It will be extremely expensive to go to court and make your husband reimburse you. Usually, he won't. Or he'll pay late, ruining your credit and leaving you in debt. Don't delude yourself into thinking your spouse will act responsibly. Most *don't!* An ounce of prevention is worth a pound of cure!

c. Most credit card companies have a 24-hour hotline. Since you're probably too upset to sleep, this is a good task to do into the wee hours. The simple act of taking action will give you some piece of mind.

Make sure you leave yourself at least –one- credit card to use until you have a chance to obtain a new one entirely in your own name. If you have a little-used credit card where you are a joint credit card holder (versus just you are the cardholder and your husband an authorized user) with favorable interest rates, that would be the best card to use until you can establish credit on your own.

d. Come back to this checklist when you are done! You're not done doing damage control yet!

3. Bright and early tomorrow morning, go to the post office and get a P.O. Box. If you anticipate staying in the marital home, simply ask your credit card companies and banks to start sending all future statements there until further notice. If you think you may be forced to leave your house, put in a 'change of address' form and get *all* of your mail sent there.

4. If you don't already have one, go to the bank and open a checking and savings account solely in your own name. Get the statements sent to your new P.O. Box.

a. If your husband has actually served you with divorce papers, you cannot take any more than a few hundred dollars out of your existing joint marital accounts to open a new account;

b. If your husband has *not* served you with divorce papers, you may take up to one-half out of your bank accounts and put it in your own account against your anticipated share of the joint marital assets, but you *must* disclose this fact to your husband.

Weigh carefully whether or not this would be wise. It will anger your husband and make bill-paying inconvenient, especially if you have automatic bill pay. If you don't leave enough in your joint marital checking account to cover checks you have already written, you will end up with bounced check charges and damaged credit. On the other hand, it will protect you from having your husband squander money on things you don't approve of. You will be obligated to write him a check for half of every bill that comes in. *Only you* can decide which course of action will better protect you.

c. Most courts *will* allow you to remove enough money from joint marital funds to pay a retainer to hire an attorney, whether or not you have an automatic restraining order in place.

5. If your paycheck or any other recurring payment goes into your joint marital checking account, call and ask them to immediately start depositing the money into your own exclusive account or to start cutting you a check. It may take a full pay cycle for this to go into effect.

6. If you have any small, valuable items which might disappear, lock them up in a safety deposit box and give a list of what you've put in the box to your husband.

7.   Come back to this chapter when you are done.

Whew! No grab some tissues, wipe your tears, and start reading. It is critical you read through to Chapter Three: Gather Your Acorns as quickly as possible. There are additional steps you need to take to do damage control. This book will continue from the viewpoint of the 71% of women planning their divorce (versus the 29% who are blindsided by one), but my heart goes out to you. I know your pain only too well! I, myself, have a permanent pre-lawyer imprint in my posterior from the Wile-E-Coyote Acme Boot-kicker!

DIVORCE IS NOT A SOMEBODY DONE SOMEBODY WRONG SONG!

The judge's job is to interpret the law as written in your home state, not give you 'justice.' He can't make your marital kitty larger than it already is. He can't give you, or your spouse, a bigger share than your state legislature says you're entitled to receive. He can't allow evidence to come into play which the law says he's not *allowed* to consider, and he can't wipe out all of the debts you accumulated during the marriage with a single bang of his magic gavel.

In other words … the only people who win when you and your spouse fight about things the judge has little power to change are the lawyers handling your case…

The judge doesn't care which somebody done somebody wrong in the marriage because, unless you file for a costly at-fault divorce (something almost *nobody* does anymore because they're so expensive to litigate); it's irrelevant. Under modern no-fault statutes, most bad behavior is viewed as a *symptom* of a failing marriage, not the cause of it. The judge dreads hearing you whine about your husband's emotional put downs, his general bad habits, or why you've decided to split. If you think you're going to get up on the witness stand and pontificate about what a rotten no-good rat your husband is, you are sadly mistaken.

I will repeat this. *You're will not receive emotional vindication from the court no matter how much of a rotten, no-good louse your soon-to-be ex-husband is!!!*

Since most people need to hear things three times to get it, I will repeat it again…

You will never, never, never get any emotional satisfaction whatsoever, not a smidgeon, not a speck, from any judge, anywhere, anytime, ever, telling you that you are 'right' and your husband is 'wrong,' or that you are 'good' and your husband is 'bad,' no matter how much time, money, or effort you or your attorney spend proving what a dirty, scum-sucking amoeba your husband is!!!

The judge only cares about your husband's gambling habit if you can show, using bank records, he took 'X' out of the marital estate. Even then, the judge can't make money squandered through poor spending habits magically reappear. All he can do is divvy up what's left. Bad behavior only gives you a few extra percentage points on the marital property division. *Usually* not enough to offset the cost of having your lawyer argue about it at trial.

The judge doesn't want to see you get abused and will give you a restraining order *if* you're in fear of physical harm, but other than that, everything else is simply a feather on the scales of justice. As painful as divorce is, the court views it as a *financial* division little different than if you divided up the assets of a business. This book is about cutting your unrealistic expectations down to size so you don't get taken to the cleaners. Not vindication.

When you walk through the courtroom doors, cut your unrealistic expectations down to size and leave your emotional baggage at home. Any lawyer who tries to sell you vindication will be laughing all the way to the bank. *He-said … she-said* has no place in family court.

DON'T KILL EACH OTHER OVER A LOUSY 10%

Divorce laws differ from state to state, but routine property division for most low- and middle-income couples (absent an inheritance, trust fund, pre-marital agreement or other unusual asset which could be ruled *separate property*) tends to be remarkably similar. Judges start with a 50:50 split and vary from that formula only slightly for factors such as how much one spouse put into the finances of the marriage, raised children, have affairs, or abuse, but *rarely* more than 60:40.

In other words … most people pay their lawyers tens of thousands of dollars to kill each other over, at *most*, an extra 10% of the marital kitty.

Say *what?*

You heard me. If you're a typical middle class family with a house with modest equity in it, two financed cars, two small IRA's, and a few thousand bucks in savings and you're *stupid* enough to go to trial, you're throwing good money after bad. Let's see how I might fund my kids college education at *your* expense?

TABLE 1-1: THE HIGH COST OF UNREALISTIC EXPECTATIONS

Asset	Fair Market Value	Loans/Liens	Equity
House	$295,000	-$250,000	45,000
Husbands Pickup Truck	$15,000	$12,000	3,000
Wife's Car	$8,000	$2,000	6,000
Husbands IRA	$22,000	$0	$22,000
Wife's IRA	$3,000	$0	3,000
Savings	$2,000	$0	$2,000
Value of Husband's Contractor Tools	$12,000	$0	$12,000
Stock Account	$4,000	$0	$4,000
MARITAL KITTY			**$97,000**
50:50 Split (*each* gets)			÷2 = $48,500
60:40 Split if you go to trial: Spouse A (gets) - Spouse B (gets) -	$97,000 x .6 = $97,000 x .4 =		$58,200 $38,000
Increase/Decrease in Marital Kitty Spouse A (gain): Spouse B (loss):	$58,000 - $48,500 = $48,500 – 38,000 =		+ $9,700 -$10,500
Attorney fees (EACH person)			EACH -$15,000
NET LOSS: Spouse A: Spouse B:	+$9,700 - $15,000 = -$10,500 + -$15,000=		-$5,300 -$25,500

Yep! That's right! Even the *winner* ends up thousands of dollars in the hole. As for the loser, if you paid your lawyer to fight things tooth and nail, you lose even bigger because not only did you get less money, but now you're also on the hook for attorney fees. Does this mean you should just throw in the towel and take it on the chin? Of course not! There are ways to minimize your legal fees so you're not throwing good money after bad. If you understand the most you have to lose is usually 10%, you can ask your lawyer hard questions about the return-on-investment for depositions and expert witnesses. Keep your eye on the bottom line so you're not betting on a losing horse. We'll talk more about Property Division in Chapter Seven.

WHO GETS CUSTODY OF THE KIDS DOES NOT AFFECT THE BOTTOM LINE!!!

That chart I just showed you? The one where I spell out how *stupid* it is to launch World War III over a lousy 10%? Guess what? Who gets custody of the kids doesn't change that spreadsheet one bit!

There's this great fallacy that whoever gets custody of the kids 'gets everything.' Although paying or receiving child support will affect your finances until they become emancipated, unless your children are listed on the deed to your house, who gets custody *will not* affect the property division. Your children do not *own* the house, the car, the 401K, or the diamond earrings your mother gave you. Nor will getting custody help you get a bigger piece of the pie. The government is not allowed to seize your assets without just compensation in *any other* situation, so why would a court hand your lifelong savings to the partner who gets custody of a child?

If a wife wants to keep the house so the kids can stay in the same school system, a judge *might* order the husband to take liquid and frozen assets (the furniture, tools, his pension). Or … there may be assets the court excludes (i.e., the trust fund his parents set up for your children) from the joint marital pot. Or he may order less alimony to compensate for a bigger share of some other asset that's not easily divided. Or … sometimes you can *mediate* assigning property to your children outside of court. But when you add up the dollar value, it will still be close to a 50:50 split. Never more than 60:40 unless one of the parties engaged in *egregious* behavior.

Courts have exact mathematical formulas, called Child Support Guidelines, to determine how much income you're entitled to receive (or will have to pay) to help you meet your expenses while raising your children. We'll cover Child Support in Chapter Five.

If you fear your spouse might try to get custody of your children, or he asks for 50:50 shared physical custody, it will affect your ability to procure child support and possibly result in *you* having to pay child support to *him*. If you've been the primary caretaker of your children and lack some defect (such as drug addiction) which might call into question your ability to parent, the evil trapper's threats are probably without basis. However, there are red flags you should watch out for which are covered in Chapter Fourteen: Custody Disputes.

CAN'T WE JUST WORK THIS OUT OURSELVES?

It –is– possible for two people to sit down and work out their own divorce. In fact, if you can do so, I strongly recommend it. However, before you can reach a fair agreement, both parties must understand what they're entitled to receive and the range of fair outcomes a court might give them.

If you're able to work that closely with your spouse, this is the wrong book. Get thee to a marriage counselor and do what you can to save your marriage because it's not beyond hope. Otherwise, you'd be a fool to do anything but plan for the worst while hoping for the best. Alternatives to litigation are covered in Chapter Nine. Negotiated/uncontested divorces are covered in Chapters Ten and Eleven.

AM I –READY– TO FILE FOR DIVORCE?

When I meet with clients, they're often on the fence. Most fear they can't survive financially, followed by concerns about how divorce will affect their children. Misery prompts them to consult with an attorney, but they're not yet ready to divorce.

Doing the financial exercises outlined in this manual before you take another step is the best gift you can give yourself. Some attorneys will engage in high-pressure sales tactics to convince you to file *now*. Resist! If you're not being abused, absent some dire situation which could compromise your legal rights, it's prudent to take stock of your life and figure out where you want to go before jumping into something you're not ready to handle. Striking out on your own should be a well-planned journey, not a leap of faith.

Here are some common issues:

1. I CAN'T AFFORD AN ATTORNEY: Ways to pare down your legal costs by doing some of the preparatory work, forcing your spouse to loan you money to hire an attorney, and piecing together legal services is covered in Chapter Nine.

2. I CAN'T SURVIVE WITHOUT MY SPOUSES INCOME: Until you know exactly how many assets and how much child support or alimony you might receive, you don't *know* whether or not you can survive. The first one-third of this book was written to help women like you answer these questions.

3. WE'RE STAYING TOGETHER FOR THE CHILDREN'S SAKE: Staying in a bad marriage because you have children is unwise. Being raised in a household with parents who can't stand each other usually outweighs the stress of parents separating –if– parents minimize the financial and emotional impact on the children. We look at this more in Chapter Fourteen: Child Custody and Custody Disputes.

4. I'M HOPING TO WORK THINGS OUT IN MARRIAGE COUNSELING: Before you enter marriage counseling, you need *leverage*. "The fact is that it is predominantly men who bring about the conditions that lead to divorce." GORDON B. HINKLEY, PRESIDENT OF THE CHURCH OF JESUS CHRIST OF LATTER-DAY SAINTS. Men care how things affect them *financially*, not emotionally. It doesn't matter

how many times you say he hurt your feelings, unless there's a price tag attached to his behavior, he has no motivation to change. This book can help you estimate that price tag.

5. CAN'T WE JUST SEPARATE? If you move out of the house without a legal framework to define your new relationship, you *will* be held responsible for your husband's mistakes. "Complaints for Separate Support" are not covered, but if you have religious objections or other reasons for separating such as military benefits or a physical disability, the mechanisms for property division and separate support are similar to a full-blown divorce. You just can't get remarried. Any competent family law attorney can negotiate a legal separation, but if your motivation is a lurking military benefits or disability issue, find a specialist *after* doing the preparation exercises outlined in Section I of this Bootcamp Manual.

> *If you move out of the house without a written agreement, it may constitute 'abandonment!'* A sample Temporary Separation Agreement is shown in Chapter 10: Uncontested Divorces.

6. MY HUSBAND MOVED OUT OF THE HOUSE BECAUSE HE NEEDS 'TO THINK.' What does your gut instinct tell you? What do your friends say? More likely than not, the evil trapper has a girlfriend sitting in the wings. Ouch! Blunt, but wake up!!! You deserve better! While his 'little brain' is doing the thinking, gather every acorn you can because his guilt will subside and his new girlfriend will start pressuring him to get rid of you. It's coming, so you'd *better* be prepared!!!

7. CAN'T WE JUST ANNUL OUR MARRIAGE? Couples occasionally ask courts to declare there was never a valid marriage. Annulment is not covered in this manual.

You will not like the cold hard reality which emerges from the financial planning exercises outlined in this book, but only the truth will give you the foundation to coordinate your divorce and survive. In other words, before you ask an attorney to serve your husband with divorce papers, *do your Bootcamp exercises first!!!*

I SPOKE TO AN ATTORNEY AND THEY HAVE A DIFFERENT OPINION

Throughout this book, I repeatedly urge readers to consult with an attorney. Most attorneys are perfectly happy to let you pick their brains and earn an hour's fee without making you retain them. If used properly, spot-advice is money well spent. But what if you gather your paperwork, rough out a proposed property division, and then an attorney tells you it's hogwash?

> *Always give greater weight to the flesh and blood attorney who practices law in the district in which you live!* We'll discuss working with an attorney more in Chapter Seven.

There's a good reason lawyers make so much money for what they do. Law is an intricate and difficult practice. It changes on a daily basis ... far faster than a book can be updated. Subtleties such as the state you live in or personal viewpoint of the judge sitting on the bench that day can change the way your case might turn out. This Bootcamp Manual is meant to be a general overview and guide to family law for non-lawyers, not a bible.

> *If you're getting this 'advice' from your spouse's attorney, you should view it with a baleful eye!*

What if your *gut instinct* tells you the flesh-and-blood attorney has no idea what they're talking about? Get a second opinion. A *good* general practitioner will tell you "this is the limit of my experience." Always ask what specialized training your attorney has received and how long they've practiced family law. We'll cover how to find, and work with, a mediator and/or attorney in Chapter Eight: Piecing Together Legal Services on a Budget.

WHAT ABOUT SAME-SEX MARRIAGE?

I happen to practice law in Massachusetts, the first state in the nation to allow same-sex marriages. Because we were first in the nation, thousands of LGBT couples came here to get married and then returned to live in less progressive states, leaving them in the un-enviable position of being considered married in some states, but not married in others. In Massachusetts, the court is supposed to treat your divorce like any other married couple. If you're from a state *other* than Massachusetts, consult an attorney familiar with LGBT issues. States have come up with all manner of ways to divvy up your assets (and children).

Do your Bootcamp Manual exercises first to figure out how you'd stand in your home-state if you were a 'traditional' couple, then consult an attorney to see how badly discrimination will affect your case. Your divorce will be more complex if you live in a state where the legislature has stuck their heads in the sand and pretended you and your life-partner did *not* accumulate assets and have children. The *good* news is the LGBT community is very active and has many fine attorneys who can advise you on the nuances of the law in *your* state.

DIVISION OF THE MARITAL FRIENDS

There's one division that happens during divorce which has nothing to do with the law. Because I get frantic phone calls from clients who just found out their best friend was really not their friend and it will have negative repercussions, I'm including it. It's called *division of the marital friends* and you'd be foolish not to anticipate what's going to happen the moment you announce you're leaving your spouse.

There are many kinds of relationships you form over your lifetime. First is your relationship with your own family. If you get along with them, they'll generally remain neutral or on your side during your divorce. If you *don't* get along (i.e., you have an in-law who says nasty things behind your back), your husband might be able to get them to backstab you. Eliminate unreliable family members from your planning.

There are friendships formed *outside* the orbit of the marital relationship. These friends know your husband just enough to know he's a jerk, or barely know him at all. Your best friend since the second grade is a strategic ally, but others should be kept in the dark. Think of it this way, it wasn't the sleazy stock-brokers or brilliant prosecutor who put Martha Stewart in prison for insider trading, but the testimony of her trusted assistant.

There are friendships which form around your children's activities. These are the other soccer moms or baseball coach dads. Although you may go to each other's kiddie birthday parties and even plan a camping trip together, don't make them privy to your escape plan. They're attached to your *family unit*, not you. They'll 'help' by letting the cat out of the bag. Chat over soccer practice about the price of bread, but avoid discussing your divorce.

Then there are 'couple' friendships. You might do lots of things together, but they're connected to the *marital unit*. Not you, personally. If you confide in these people, they *will* blab. Once you're single, they'll have nothing in common with you anymore and you'll feel betrayed. Expect the worst and, if after the dust settles some are still friendly, be pleasantly surprised.

Be careful who you confide in because anything you say can and will turn around and bite you in the ass!

THE DEVIL YOU KNOW

No matter *how* bad your marriage gets, even an abusive husband can feel preferable to that void that just opened up in your schedule. While you were still together, at least you had the *illusion* of somebody to lean on. Now you discover half your friends aren't *real* friends at all. There's an old adage. *"It's a lucky man who can count his friends on one hand."*

Your best emotional survival strategy is to start forming *new* friendships *before* you file for divorce. Become involved in church activities. Volunteer at a local shelter or the Red Cross. No matter how bad it gets, somebody else has it worse. It's a great way to thicken your resume, make important business contacts, and polish people skills that may have become rusty.

Take a self-improvement class. Brush up on computer skills. Many small craft and specialty shops offer free or low-cost craft classes. Once you learn to turn a piece of yarn into clothing or a scrap of fabric into a quilt, your whole manner of thinking changes. The people you meet in these classes will stimulate your creativity and intellect.

Most home improvement centers offer free 'how to' classes. Your house isn't going to stop needing maintenance simply because you've given your husband the boot. Learn how to fix things yourself.

Become involved with a grass roots political campaign. It pays to be politically well connected. Learning how to put a new law on the books can help you in other areas in your life.

Join your local Community Emergency Response Team (CERT), Citizens Police Academy, Citizen Fire Academy, Amateur Radio Emergency Service (ARES), or Citizen Sheriff's Academy. Not only will you learn self-preservation skills, but there's nothing like being on a first-name basis with all the cops in town to scare off an abusive ex-spouse.

Nurture different aspects of your personality that were cast by the wayside during your marriage to fill the void left by his departure. Over time, new social ties will blossom into so many new friends, opportunities, and activities that you won't have *time* to miss your ex-husband.

WHAT IF I CHANGE MY MIND?

When you consult with an attorney, many will pressure you to move forward with your divorce. Although perhaps you really *do* need to move quickly ... spousal abuse, assets being squandered, or certain issues such as inheritance or alimony could be ticking time bombs ... there is often no harm in waiting while you take stock of your life and figure out where you stand.

Once you tell your spouse you want a divorce, you've made an open declaration of war. Opportunities to position yourself for a better outcome will be lost. Once your spouse is on the defensive, every attempt to save your marriage will be met with hostility, suspicion and distrust.

The beauty of the *Divorce Bootcamp* method is that, by quietly preparing to tackle your divorce emotionally and financially beforehand, you'll be in a stronger position to demand change. Think back to when you were in school. If you studied hard for an examination, you walked into class confident you would get a passing grade. You ticked off answers with ease, thinking 'that wasn't so bad' once you were done. Your classmates noticed your self-confidence and asked 'Why was taking that exam so easy for you?' It was easy because you went into the examination prepared. When you're prepared to follow through on a threat of divorce if your spouse doesn't shape up, your self-confidence will show. You can logically point out the costs of *not* working on your marriage without becoming defensive, falling prey to empty threats, or even uttering the evil magic words 'I spoke to a divorce attorney.'

And then there's the fact most marriages break down due to financial pressure. If you take my advice on cutting your budget and putting your financial house in order before announcing you want a divorce, much of the stress that's causing your marriage to fail may simply disappear.

There's nothing wrong with being ambivalent about ending your marriage. Do your *Bootcamp* exercises, make the preparations I recommend, and keep your mouth shut while you make plans in case you change your mind. Also, while doing your Bootcamp exercises, I suggest you read "*Too Good to Leave, Too Bad to Stay: A Step-By-Step Guide to Helping You Decide Whether to Stay in or Get Out of Your Relationship,*" by therapist Mira Kirshenbaum. It can help you analyze whether the problems in your marriage are too intractable to change, or can be aided by marital therapy. The nice thing about the *Bootcamp* method is you can quietly change your mind...

WHY Y'ALL LAWYERS SO DODGY ABOUT ANSWERING QUESTIONS?

Now if I've done my job right, some of you might be asking yourself, *'how come she keeps telling me to consult with an attorney? I bought this book so I wouldn't –need- to hire an attorney!'*

No matter *whose* legal self-help book you read, tiny differences in the law can make a huge difference in your case. A state legislature passes a law. The judge gets a case that doesn't quite fit that law. The judge carves out an exception to get a fair outcome called a 'precedent' which we lawyers then have to follow. After a while, the laws begin to resemble Swiss cheese. There's a *reason* lawyers get paid so much money. Some bizarre exception not covered in a book might make your case turn out completely different.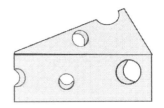

Self-help books such as this are a compromise. We give you a general overview of 'The Cheese' so you can make plans, but there are many holes which could trip you up. It's up to *you* to decide at what point gambling with the outcome of your divorce on advice contained in some impersonal book that tells you it's not meant to be legal advice gets uncomfortable. If by reading this book you spot trouble coming down the pipeline, prepare better financially, or reduce your legal fees because you understand the process, you're that much better off. Don't hurl yourself into a divorce without knowing what you're getting yourself into!

This book is geared for low- and low-moderate-income women who the legal profession has been failing due to enormous legal fees. Women are being denied access to justice. They're burning through their meager savings at the beginning, when self-education could enable you to handle much of the process *yourself*, and forced to complete their divorces alone towards the end, something few civilians should ever navigate alone. There is only *one* piece of legal advice an author can legally give you:

 *Legal advice - when in doubt, seek it out…*

⚑ RED FLAG ISSUES

Throughout this book, we focus on taking time to *plan* before you make that big leap into your new life so your transition from married woman to single one will go as smoothly as possible. However, there are some potential problem areas I wish to make clear from the outset you need to speak to a flesh-and-blood attorney as soon as possible, even *before* you start 'gathering your acorns.'

⚑ ***You bought this book because your husband just announced he wants a divorce.*** Skip ahead to the portion of Chapter 10: Negotiated Divorces titled 'It was My –Husband- who Just Broke the Bad News to –Me-' and take those triage steps before coming back to read Chapter Two. You will not have the luxury of time.

⚑ ***You or your children are being physically abused.*** We cover restraining orders in Chapter Two. If you feel you qualify, speak to an attorney or, at minimum, make an appointment with your local battered women's shelter to speak to an intervention specialist.

⚑ ***You fear there may be a custody dispute*** and your husband's allegations might have some basis in reality. Custody disputes are covered in Chapter Fourteen.

⚑ ***Your husband is a citizen of another country and might abduct your children.*** Custody disputes are covered in Chapter Fourteen, but the issue of child abduction goes beyond the scope of this book. Consult with an attorney if you fear this might happen.

   If your children have passports, immediately lock them up someplace out of your house and contact your local State Department to find out how to put a 'red flag' on your children's record. This will increase the likelihood they'll be stopped if he tries to leave the country with them.

You are an immigrant to this country and here on a conditional visa, or have applied for permanent residency and not yet obtained your green card. Speak to an immigration attorney *right away!* Filing for divorce could fatally impact your plans to remain in this country. You might be deported if you do not take all the right steps *prior* to separating from your husband! Do not go to the Immigration and Nationalization Service for help. Only go to an immigration lawyer. Immigration law goes beyond the scope of this Bootcamp Manual.

Most family law attorneys are NOT also immigration attorneys! A client walked into one of my free legal clinics wanting me to look over her pre-trial memorandum (paperwork for a special hearing held near the end of a divorce that often results in a judgment). She'd been handling her own divorce and seen several previous free volunteer courthouse attorneys over the course of a year. Not one of them had warned her the moment she got her divorce in hand, her visa based on marriage to a U.S. citizen would be invalid!

Your husband is liquidating your joint marital assets and hiding them. We discuss ways to document your assets in Chapter Three.

Your parents are elderly and/or ill or have indicated they wish to gift you/leave you some money. This issue goes beyond the scope of this Bootcamp Manual. Speak to an attorney knowledgeable about both estate planning and family law as soon as possible or they may simply be handing half their hard-earned money to your soon-to-be ex-spouse.

Any other issue which makes you feel like you've got a guillotine perched above your neck. If you feel anxious, follow up on that gut feeling and speak to an attorney, even if it's only a 5-minute consultation with a courthouse volunteer lawyer-of-the-day.

1. Don't gnaw off your own leg to escape a bad marriage.

2. The judge isn't going to watch your back.

3. You have a legal right to handle your own divorce without a lawyer.

4. Prepare, prepare, prepare.

5. Focus on getting your fair share of the money, not emotional vindication.

6. Most attorney fees are racked up fighting over a measly 10% of the marital pie. Assets (and debt) tend to be divided close to 50:50, but rarely less than 60:40.

7. Getting custody of the kids doesn't increase your share of the marital kitty.

8. It –is– possible to negotiate your own divorce. You're more likely to do so if you understand what you're entitled to receive.

9. Make sure you're ready emotionally and financially *before* you file for divorce.

10. Seek the opinion of a licensed attorney in your jurisdiction. Do *not* believe statements from your husband's attorney unless your own research and/or attorney seconds that opinion. Ask attorneys how much experience they have handling your type of case. The opinion of a neutral flesh-and-blood attorney should always be given more weight than this Bootcamp Manual.

11. Same-sex divorce outcomes vary wildly nationwide. Consult an attorney up on the most current GLBT trends in your state.

12. Many of your friends are going to "bail" the minute you file for divorce. Keep your plans to yourself.

13. Make *new* connections in your community. They'll serve you well as you move into your new life.

14. Watch out for red flag issues!

15. When it comes to legal advice, 'when in doubt, seek it out…'

CHAPTER 2

SAFETY PLANNING

The very first thing any woman must ask herself before letting her soon-to-be ex-spouse know she's thinking of serving him with divorce papers is this: "Am I going to get the ever-living crap kicked out of me?"

Only *you* know how your spouse reacts to upsetting news. An announcement that you want a divorce is the single most upsetting nuclear warhead you can drop on your partner, ever. Even good-natured men will react with anger. If your spouse has a propensity for violence, you need to do some safety planning before you take the next step. If your spouse has never hit you, but *threatened* to hurt you, you should create a safety plan. Clever little woodland creatures dig numerous escape tunnels to dive into if a predator happens by. You would be wise to do the same.

Contact your local battered women's service agency and ask for a referral to a safety planner to discuss your options. They will generally ask you a few questions and then refer you to literature, a battered women's counselor, support groups, or other appropriate services. You can usually find such agencies listed in the yellow pages under "Women's Service Agencies," "Battered Women's Agencies," "Crisis Intervention," "Domestic Violence," or "Shelters."

The National Domestic Violence Hotline can be reached at:

(800) 799-SAFE (7233)   http://www.ndvh.org

WHAT IS A RESTRAINING ORDER?

Restraining orders are *civil* court orders mandating the batterer not to abuse you that have *criminal* sanctions if the batterer violates the order. Thanks to federal legislation, every state has some form of restraining order. The means and criteria to obtain one are fairly similar. They must be honored no matter what state you travel through. Most allow judges to include provisions about child support, visitation, and how far to stay away from you or your place of employment.

If your spouse is off the wall, the threat of jail will not stop him from kicking in the front door and beating the crap out of you or kidnapping your children. Restraining orders are only *part* of a comprehensive escape plan.

Put aside 6 weeks living expenses and stow them at a trusted friend's house. The purpose of this is not to hide money from your spouse (you must disclose it when you go to court), but to have money to survive if things turn ugly.

Make a backup copy of all assets, liabilities, and other important documents listed in Chapter Three and store a copy at a friend's house. They'll vanish when you request a restraining order. If you need to make an emergency exit, you can use your backup copies to call credit card companies and freeze your bank accounts. Otherwise, you'll discover your bank accounts have been emptied and credit cards maxed out.

The movie "Sleeping With the Enemy," starring Julia Roberts, portrays a sociopath whom others find difficult to believe is abusing her. Take note of how thoroughly the heroine plans her escape.

If you want to see what *not* to do, watch "Enough" starring Jennifer Lopez. She doesn't get a restraining order or document abuse with the police, doesn't file for divorce before skipping town with their child, and doesn't go to a hospital and get her injuries documented. Pay attention to what the lawyer tells her when she finally seeks legal advice. She had her abusive husband by the short hairs and she blew it! When she later tries to claim he hired people to kill her, nobody believes her because he's done a good job of discrediting her. The movie ending is implausible … you are *not* going to be able to beat up your spouse! But the movie is worth viewing from a legal standpoint because the protagonist makes things unnecessarily difficult for herself.

It's a wise woodland creature who digs a safety burrow (place you can crash with your kids for a few nights where he won't look for you) for herself and her offspring to dive into should things turn ugly.

Always take your children with you and don't abandon them to the batterer! It will undermine your claim that your spouse is abusive and/or should not get custody of the children.

Get an emergency restraining order or file for divorce right away or he might accuse you of 'abandoning' the marriage, jeopardizing your property rights, or kidnapping your children!

THE RESTRAINING ORDER 'RECIPE'

Abuse prevention orders are not meant to get your pesky soon-to-be ex-husband out of the house so you don't have to deal with him. Nor are they meant to "restrain" your husband from uncomfortable arguments about who's to blame for the demise of your marriage or which spouse is entitled to what asset. To get an abuse prevention order, you must *demonstrate a substantial likelihood of immediate danger of abuse.*

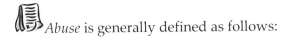*Abuse* is generally defined as follows:

a. Attempting to cause or causing physical harm;
b. Placing another in *fear* of imminent serious physical harm;
c. Causing another to engage involuntarily in sexual relations by force, threat or duress.

If your husband hit you or the police stopped him just as his fist was about to make contact with your face [abuse definition (a)], demonstrating there's a substantial likelihood he's going to do it again is a no-brainer. But what happens if, like *most* women, the definition of abuse you fall under is that he placed you *in fear of imminent serious physical harm*? Reading a statute in its natural form is like having your kid announce, "Mom … I promised my teacher you'd bake a chocolate cake with buttercream frosting for the PTA bake sale tomorrow."

If you've never baked a cake, the task can seem daunting. However, once you've learned recipes are simply lists of ingredients to be purchased at the supermarket, mixed together and baked, it's possible to cook an endless variety of tasty meals. To get a restraining order, you must have all the ingredients.

Like any recipe, it's helpful to list each ingredient separately.

1. *In fear of -*
2. *Imminent -*
3. *Serious physical harm –*

Three simple ingredients. When your husband tries to prevent you from getting a restraining order, he's going to say you're missing one of the ingredients. A Russian friend once sent me her favorite recipe for stuffed aubergine. Being an American, I'd never *heard* of aubergine. Was it meat? Cheese? A pastry? I finally stumbled across a French cookbook. Eggplant. I'd had them growing in my garden all along and never knew they had another name. When baking your restraining order recipe, know which ingredients grow in your garden of marital discord.

So how *do* you prove you have all of the ingredients to get a restraining order?

1. IN FEAR OF – Fear is subjective. What makes one person quake in their boots might make another person laugh. The judge, on the other hand, is required to be *impartial.* While it might be appropriate for a 5'1" woman to be afraid of an angry 6'4" ex-green-beret, most reasonable people would agree a 6'4" ex-green-beret probably isn't *really* afraid of being physically harmed by an angry 5'1" mother of three young children. Therefore, to help guide his decision making, judges have this fictitious little person living in their head named Mrs. Reasonably Prudent Person.

A reasonably prudent person is the combined wisdom of people the judge speaks to when he goes home from work and complains about all the wacky legal cases that come across his bench.

When the judge tries to figure out whether or not your fear is reasonable, he'll ask Mrs. Prudent what *she* thinks. Mrs. Prudent needs to feel your husband made a *direct* threat. Failing that, she wants to see he's been engaging in an *escalating pattern of behavior*. Think of the problem as having a recipe which calls for brown sugar, but all you have on-hand are granulated white sugar and molasses. Violence is brown sugar. Implied threats of violence are lesser ingredients you can combine to make Mrs. Prudent shout 'this tastes like brown sugar!'

When your husband gets angry, does he raise his voice? Raise it to the point the dog runs behind the bed and the kids cry?

  a. Does he block your escape with his body? Chase you down the hall? Lock you in a room? Rip ignition wires out of your car so you can't leave? Steal your checkbook and hide it? Call every 5 minutes and demand you come home?

  b. Does he clench his fists? Make a motion of hitting one hand with the other implying he wants to punch somebody? Does he ever tell you you're lucky he doesn't hit you, or another man *would* hit you?

  c. Does he punch the table or wall? Punch near your head or body? Smash objects to smithereens? Throw things at you?

  d. Does his face turn red? Is he so close spit sprays onto your face while he's threatening you? Do veins bulge out of his forehead?

  e. Does he abuse your pets or children when he's angry at you? Do you ever lock yourself in a room or have you ever been afraid to go home?

I once watched an episode of "Happy Days" where the cool ruffian Fonzie taught the nerdy Ritchie how to deal with a gang. Nobody ever messed with Fonzie even though he never raised his voice or hit anyone. Fonzie taught Richie that by projecting the *threat* of harm, you never actually had to *do* harm. Just by moderating his voice when using his trademark statement, "hey," one knew whether to talk to Fonzie or pay him a wide berth. "Hay-eh-ey?" meant "what's up?" "Hey!" meant "whatcha doin' moron?" "HaY!!!" Meant "I'm gonna kick your ass." Fonzie avoided fights by projecting subconscious intimidation.

Learn to spot deliberate intimidation - I study martial arts. Were you aware Fonzie's bow-legged, broad-armed walk is a classic martial arts fighting stance? It's *deliberate* behavior to intimidate an opponent!

You must be able to point out subtle intimidation to the judge and convince the Mrs. Prudent who lives in his head that, given the escalating pattern of behavior, your husband is *most likely* going to do something to hurt you.

2. IMMINENT – Imminent means now or the near future. Mrs. Prudent needs to believe, the next time you cross paths with the Evil Trapper and don't have a handy policeman around to protect you, he will probably do something violent or stupid.

3. SERIOUS PHYSICAL HARM – This is where most small woodland creatures screw up getting their restraining orders. The harm threatened must be *physical* harm. Hitting. Kicking. Biting. Strangulation. False imprisonment. Or some other harm that *violates the body*. The harm cannot be emotional or economic harm, fear of litigation, or embarrassment. We'll cover this in the hypothetical restraining order scenario that follows.

> *Never lie to a judge about being physically harmed if it's not true!* Not only could you go to jail for perjury, but next time you go to court they won't believe a word you say. Every time a woman lies to gain an unfair advantage, it makes the judge less likely to believe a woman who really *is* being abused. There are other ways to get the court to order your husband to leave the marital home. Motions to Vacate the Marital Home are covered in Chapter Thirteen: Temporary Orders.

A HYPOTHETICAL RESTRAINING ORDER SCENARIO

Husband and wife have an argument. Husband hits the wife or does something which leads her to fear she's about to be physically harmed. Husband storms out of the house. Wife calls a friend, who convinces her to call the police. The police ask the wife what happened, fill out a police report noting any red marks, bruises, or damaged property, and decide whether they believe the Wife will be physically harmed if they leave.

If the police witness enough to get a temporary restraining order, they'll send her to the nearest courthouse. If the courthouse is closed, they'll call a judge and get him to issue a temporary order over the phone. Either way, the Wife will have to fill out an affidavit stating what happened, the judge will ask a few questions, and usually issue a temporary order telling her to come back in a few days for a full hearing on the merits.

By the time the second hearing rolls around, the Husband has called the Wife's friends, neighbors, and even her own family and convinced them she's a head case. Fear makes you scattered, while anger makes you clear-headed. Your spouse will focus on one goal, discrediting you and 'proving' he's not a batterer. To her horror, the Wife often finds her own family and friends siding with the Husband and refusing to believe he's capable of such acts. Everyone tries to convince her to work it out for the kid's sake. He'll apply economic pressure by emptying out the bank accounts and refusing to pay the bills. It's a brave woman who fights to keep her restraining order.

> *Never let old-fashioned or well-intentioned family members or friends talk you out of getting a restraining order.* If you're afraid, your fear is valid. Never let anyone convince you otherwise.

> *Don't get conned into dropping your restraining order!* If you get a temporary restraining order but get either bullied (via threats) or conned (via empty promises) into dropping it, you will have a hard time getting a judge to give you one a second time. Once you've got it, keep it. If you hope to work things out, ask the judge to craft a restraining order which allows your husband to meet you at a marital therapists' office while also attending an anger management program. *–If-* he jumps

through all the appropriate hoops, *then* go back to court and ask the judge to drop it *because* he's met all the conditions.

I spend a great deal of time sitting in the back of the courtroom watching other people's hearings. It's sad to watch fearful, distraught women face their abuser alone or lose their restraining orders because they don't understand what information the judge needs. To educate you what a typical restraining order hearing might be like for a woman who's not represented, I'm including a summarized script of a *real* restraining order hearing I once witnessed.

ON-YOUR-FEET EXERCISE 2-1: A "BOTCHED" 209A RESTRAINING ORDER HEARING

Magistrate:	I call the case of Jane Doe-Rayme versus Jack Rayme. Could you please state your names for the record?
Jane Doe-Rayme:	I'm Jane Doe-Rayme.
Jack Rayme:	I'm Jack Rayme.
Magistrate:	Raise your right hand? Do you swear the testimony you're about to give is the truth, the whole truth, and nothing but the truth, so help you God?
Jack and Jane:	I do.
Judge (reading Jane's affidavit)	Jane, you claim in your affidavit that on the afternoon of January the 5th your husband came home, threatened to kill the dog, and you called the police, is that correct?
Jane:	Yes.
Judge:	Could you please tell me what happened?
Jane (her voice shaking):	He'd been out drinking and came home in a bad mood. For no reason, he kicked the dog and threatened to empty the bank account and leave.
Judge:	Did he hit you?
Jane:	No.
Judge:	Did he threaten you in any way?
Jane (beginning to cry):	He was drunk and he said he was going to take the kids and the car away from me and I'd get nothing.
Judge (to Jack)	Is this true?
Jack (calm and collected):	Not exactly, Sir. I stopped off for a beer after work. When I got home, I saw the dog had peed all over the rug. I made him sniff it and hit him in the haunches. Jane started screaming and throwing things.
Judge (to Jane):	Is that true? Did you throw something at him?
Jane (getting angry):	He's lying!!! I was trying to protect the dog!!!
Jack (rolls up sleeve and points to scratch)	First she threw a glass at me. Then she scratched me. See, I have the marks right here.
Judge:	Did you threaten to kill the dog?
Jack (even calmer):	No, sir. I told her if it peed on the rug one more time I was taking it to the Humane Society.
Jane (interrupting, angrily pointing at Jack):	That's not true!!! He kicked the dog! He did! He threatened to kill the dog and leave me penniless!
Bailiff (stepping towards Jane):	Step back, ma'am.
Judge:	I'm going to extend the temporary restraining order for thirty days, at which time it will come up again for review.

Analysis: Jane focuses on the abuse to the dog and not the implied threat against *her*. The judge may think sticking the dog's nose in a puddle of urine is perfectly appropriate. Her second mistake is focusing on the verbal *economic* threats and not the implied *physical* threat towards *her*. Her biggest mistake, however, is letting her emotions take over. In a good restraining order hearing, the judge will grant the order for a full year, not thirty days.

Spouses Behaving Badly - I spoke with the real 'Jane Doe' this script is based upon after her hearing (she had no lawyer). 'Jack' had been drinking 3-6 beers per day and came home from work each night drunk and verbally abusive. Although he'd never hit her, he punched holes in the wall and pulled the wires out of her car. To outsiders, Jack was a calm, likeable guy who never raised his voice, whereas Jane wore her emotions on her sleeve. With no money and few marketable job skills, the threat of going hungry was easier for Jane to articulate than the fact Jack abused the dog to imply he would do the same to *her*.

Never allow your spouse to turn an abuse prevention hearing into a property dispute!!! Focus on the issue the judge can help you with at that hearing, ending the abuse. You can argue about the other issues later, at your Temporary Orders hearing (covered in Chapter Thirteen).

Many battered women's shelters have volunteers who'll help you focus on which events led you to believe you were 'in fear of imminent physical harm.' Some will even come to court with you to stand by your side. Call your local battered woman's shelter for information about what assistance they can give you to get, and keep, a restraining order. However, at the end of the day, it's up to *you* to give the judge the information he needs to make a good decision!

A "better" hearing based on the same fact pattern follows:

ON-YOUR-FEET EXERCISE 2-2: A "BETTER" 209A RESTRAINING ORDER HEARING

Magistrate:	I call the case of Jane Doe versus Jack Doe. Please state your names for the record?
Jane Doe-Rayme:	I'm Jane Doe-Rayme.
Jack Rayme:	I am Jack Rayme.
Sally Samaratin (stands between them)	I'm Sally Samaratin. I'm just here for moral support.
Magistrate:	Raise your right hand? Do you swear the testimony you're about to give is the truth, the whole truth, and nothing but the truth, so help you God?
Jack and Jane:	I do.
Judge (reading Jane's affidavit)	Jane, you claim in your affidavit that on the afternoon of January the 5th your husband came home, threatened to kill the dog, and you called the police, is that correct?
Jane:	Yes it is.
Judge:	Could you please tell me what happened?
Jane (glancing at a checklist she's prepared)	Almost every night my husband stops after work with his co-workers to have a few drinks. I didn't object at first because he always came home in time for supper. But lately, he's been coming home at 10:00 at night so drunk he can barely stagger in the front door.
Judge:	Has he ever hit you?
Jane (looking at her checklist):	Three times in the past month, we've argued about his drinking and Jack punched a hole in the wall. I have the pictures… (Jane offers the pictures to the bailiff).
Jack (interrupting):	That's not true!!! One of those holes was when I slipped and fell, and the other two I accidentally bumped the wall!!! That's just like her, always making a mountain out of a mole hill!!!
Sally Samaritin:	Shhh… (takes Jane's hand)
Jane: (looks at checklist)	Your honor, if I may clarify? The time Jack slipped and fell into the wall, he was running down the hall after me during an argument. I was so scared I ran into the bathroom and locked the door. The other two times, he punched the wall and said "any other man would

	beat you to a pulp." He's also ripped the ignition wires out of my car on two occasions to prevent me from leaving.
Judge:	Tell me about the dog.
Jane (beginning to cry):	Whenever Jack gets angry, he takes it out on the dog. The dog is so scared that every time Jack raises his voice he pees on the floor. That's what happened the night I called the police. Jack yelled, the dog peed, and Jack beat it half to death.
Judge (to Jack)	Is this true?
Jack:	Nooo… I came home and saw the dog had peed all over the rug. I made him sniff it and whacked him in the haunches a couple of times. Jane started screaming and throwing things.
Judge (to Jane):	Is that true? Did you throw something at him?
Sally Samaratin:	(squeezes Jane's hand and whispers in her ear "stay calm. If he upsets you, he wins…")
Jane (takes a deep breath, refers to her checklist, counts to three, then calmly speaks):	After several minutes of him kicking the dog in the ribcage, I finally threw a water glass against the wall and told him I was calling the police. He came after me and said if I *did* call, he'd take the kids and I'd never see them again.
Jack (losing it):	She's a liar!!! She threw a glass at me! Then she scratched me. (Rolls up sleeve) See, I have the scratch marks right here!
Bailiff:	Step back, Sir… (steps towards Jack)
Judge (to Jane):	Did you scratch his arm?
Jane: (cries, but keeps her cool).	I'm not sure. If I did, I didn't mean it. After I told him I was calling the police, he punched the dog in the face and said he was going to kill it. I grabbed his arm and begged him to stop.
Judge (to Jack):	Did you threaten to kill the dog?
Jack:	No, sir. I told her if it pissed on the rug one more time I was going to take it to the Humane Society!
Sally Samaratin:	(squeezes Jane's hand)
Jane (looking at list):	(Jane shakes her head "no" so the judge can see) Your honor … if I might add one more thing. Two of our three children witnessed my husband beat the dog. They were so scared they cried for hours afterwards.
Judge:	I'm going to extend the temporary restraining order for one year, at which time it will come up again for review. You'll only be able to see your children at times and places designated for visitation.

Analysis: Our hypothetical Jane Doe comes to court prepared. Sally Samaritan (usually a trained abuse prevention specialist) is not allowed to speak as she's not an attorney, but she creates a physical buffer to reduce the subtle physical intimidation and reminds Jane to stay focused. Jane was honest with herself about the rotten things Jack might say about her and was ready to refute Jack's claim she threw a glass and scratched his arm.

Jane puts Jack's drinking in context of an *escalating pattern of behavior.* Jane's testimony about the hole punched into the wall while chasing her down the hall gives the judge enough information to fear she may be in imminent danger of physical harm, the pictures are icing on the cake. Notice when Jane testifies he threatened to take the kids and she'd never see them again, she made no mention of his threat to take her money. Last but not least, Jane testifies two of their three children witnessed Jack's violent outburst and were harmed by it.

Judges care a lot about kids witnessing domestic violence! So do police and social workers. If your husband abuses you in front of the kids and you do nothing, Social Services could take your kids away from you. It's *your* job to shield your kids and get a restraining order.

Before your court hearing, rehearse what you're going to say and what lies your spouse might say about you. Use the sample scripts to create your *own* script and practice answering the questions with a non-judgmental friend or in front of the mirror.

 Always bring a friend or relative to the courthouse with you for moral support.

THE SO-CALLED "FATHER'S RIGHTS" (A.K.A. "BATTERS RIGHTS") MOVEMENT

In response to legislation criminalizing beating your wife, batterers have banded together to 'fight' restraining orders. When they complained about being the 'victims' of 'cry wolf restraining orders,' people avoided them like the bubonic plague. Being obsessive little schemers, they learned to use the courts to turn the issuance of a restraining order into a property or custody dispute. By renaming themselves 'father's rights (propaganda analysis = good, stable, loving, knows best) advocates instead of 'batterer's rights advocates (bad, evil, abusive) and using their children as leverage, they gained traction convincing legislators, judges, and the general public that they are victims of a court system 'biased' against men.

Reality check here ... most judges and legislators are male...

If you beat your wife and she gets a restraining order, you are forbidden to call her, talk to her, or force her back into the abusive relationship. You get one bite of the apple in court and don't get a second chance to disprove the restraining order until it is reviewed in another year. However, if you turn it into a custody or property dispute, not only do you increase your chances of beating the restraining order, but you can use the courts and various state and local administrative hearings to force your terrified spouse to lose days out of work to attend bogus 'hearing's where you can put her on the hot seat under the guise of 'cross examination.' You'd be amazed at how gullible government entities are about allowing themselves to *repeatedly* be used to legally violate restraining orders.

These groups bear innocuous-sounding names such as "Parent and Child" or "Fatherhood United." Members help each other fill out bogus motions and affidavits, recommend additional ways to punish the wayward wife, and teach how to get as many court and administrative hearings as possible to maintain contact despite a restraining order. They act as 'expert witnesses' for one another, creating false or slanted testimony. Eliminating child support is the most common goal, but also to punish the victim and make her life miserable.

If you suspect your spouse has hooked up with one of these groups, *educate yourself immediately*. Bring it to the courts attention *before* your spouse convinces a judge you should lose custody of your children because you're being investigated by 17 state agencies for fraud (complaints all filed by him). Here are some resources available on the internet:

- *High Conflict Divorce or Stalking by Way of Family Court? The Empowerment of a Wealthy Abuser in Family Court Litigation: Linda v. Lyle - A Case Study*, by T. J. Sutherland, R.N., B.S.N., P.H.N., J.D., www.mincava.umn.edu/documents/linda/linda.html

- *Beaten, Raped, Robbed and Left for Dead: Unmasking the "Father's Rights" Movement,* by Kathleen Parker, www.thelizlibrary.org/liz/kathleen.html

- *Stalking Through the Courts,* by Janet Normalvanbruecher, 1999, www.thelizlibrary.org/liz/FRtactic.html

- Website *"Survivors Zone"* www.angelfire.com/in4/sez

- *Father's Rights Groups, Beware their Real Agenda,* by Kathleen Woods, Michigan National Organization of Women (NOW), http://www.now.org/nnt/03-97/father.html

HOW TO HELP THE JUDGE 'GET' YOUR CASE IN 5 MINUTES OR LESS

Restraining order hearings typically last five minutes or less. During that brief period of time, the judge has to read your affidavit, supporting police reports, witness affidavits, hospital records, examine any visual bruises or photographs of damaged property, and listen to each of you tell your side of the story. If your husband rants and raves about how *you* hit him first or why you're not credible, those precious get eaten up even further. Knowing how the court weighs evidence and also non-formal, visual cues is critical to winning your case.

Make a list of talking points - The handwritten, tear-stained affidavit you filled out the day you requested your temporary restraining order is probably a confused, jumbled mess of relevant and non-relevant facts. Be prepared to testify or produce evidence about each component of your husband's behavior which, as a whole, led you to believe you were 'in fear of imminent physical danger or harm.' A bulleted list of facts to check off as you introduce them reduces the likelihood of objections by the other side throwing you off-track.

Neatly assemble documentary evidence. Having credible, neutral, third-party evidence will increase your credibility and the weight of your testimony.

Get copies of any police reports backing up your claims! The Rules of Evidence give heavy weight to police reports. If you go to the police station where the incident happened and tell them you need a copy for a restraining order hearing, they will usually give you a copy of the police report for free or for a nominal fee (usually $.10 cents per page). Sometimes the incident which spawned the police report is clear-cut. Neighbors called the police because they saw your husband hit you and you told the police you'd been hit. Other times, the evidence is less clear cut. Neighbors called the police to report a disturbance because they feared you were being hurt, but when the police got there, you covered for your abuser and told them you were okay. Judges are trained to recognize women may be reluctant to have their husband arrested, but be ready to explain *why* you didn't ask the police for help if you covered for him.

Go to each doctor or hospital you may have visited after being abused in the past and obtain copies of your medical records. If you told the doctor your injury was a result of abuse, he will have noted it on your medical record. The Rules of Evidence give heavy weight to medical records. However, even if you didn't tell your doctor you were injured because you were abused, but you were treated, it can bolster your testimony. For example, if you went to the hospital to have a splint set on a sprained finger, but were afraid to tell the ER doctor he bent your finger back so hard it caused the sprain.

Widespread misunderstanding of HIPA Confidentiality Laws – frequently when you go to your doctor and try to get your own medical records, some ill-informed clerk will claim they can't give them to you because of HIPA Confidentiality Laws. By law, you are entitled to a copy of your own (or your minor children's) medical records for a nominal fee. Keep asking to speak to that person's supervisor and explain the situation until you get somebody educated enough to know what you're talking about. They are supposed to make you sign a 'HIPA Waiver' form and give them to you. If they still refuse, ask them to put their refusal in writing so you can sue them for any damages which arise as a result of their misinterpreting the law.

If somebody reported your spouse to DCF, let the judge know: If the Department of Children and Families (Social Services) conducted an investigation, there will be a Child Abuse Allegation report and also a Child Abuse Investigation report. *You* will probably not be able to get copies, but most judges will make a phone call. Social Services reports carry independent weight above and beyond your testimony. If you are currently working with a social worker, it's a good idea to call them and give them a heads-up you are trying to get your abuser out of your house.

Be wary of how much you tell DCF! Giving your social worker a heads-up you're going to court and they might be getting a phone call from a judge is prudent. Crying on their shoulder is not. Having represented clients whose families became entangled with DCF, my impression is they are a well-meaning, but ineffective bureaucracy which can often cause more harm than good.

Get witness affidavits: If anybody ever witnessed your husband abusing you, get a sworn affidavit. It doesn't have to be notarized, but the person must write "affidavit of" at the top, list their name and address, explain what they personally saw happen, sign it, date it, and write 'sworn under the pains and penalties of perjury of law' just before they sign their name. If you wait until the day before the restraining order hearing, your husband may intimidate them into not getting involved, so get the affidavit as soon as possible! Even if the person agrees to come to court with you to testify, get a sworn written affidavit *right away.* You'd be surprised how many people promise to help in the heat of an emergency, then decide they don't want to lose a day out of work. If the witness testifies live before the judge, so much the better, but no matter what, always get a sworn affidavit.

Hearsay – the court can only consider testimony your witness saw or heard *directly*, such as "I personally heard John threaten to kill Jane and then saw him shove her to the floor." It *cannot* consider testimony such as "my neighbor said he heard John threaten Jane and then shove her to the floor." This rule is called *hearsay* as in 'if I hear *you* say that *she* says, it's hearsay."

Take photographs: Cuts heal and bruises fade. Enlist a friend to take photographs the day after the incident (when bruises tend to become visible). Get them developed right away to ensure you have the evidence you need to convince the judge. The type of lighting (incandescent, fluorescent, or natural sunlight) and shadows cast can highlight or obscure what you photograph, so don't be afraid to experiment. Indirect, bright natural sunlight from a north-facing window is best for photographing bruises. It's common to fill an entire digital card to get a convincing photograph of one or two bruises, so snap away. If you take a particularly convincing photo, spend a few extra dollars and get it enlarged. You will need to tell the court who took the picture (you, or a friend) and swear it '*truly and accurately depicts* what you're about to describe. You will then have to explain what the photograph means.

Truly and accurately depict is a key phrase out of the Federal Rules of Evidence. Whenever a lawyer has a witness introduce a sketch or photograph, they'll ask them, 'does this photograph truly and accurately depict the scene you are about to testify about' before they then have that witness go on to testify why the photograph or sketch is important.

Bring damaged property with you, if possible: If your husband damaged any property, bring it with you (if reasonable) or take a photograph. Use correct lighting (such as moving a lamp to cast the shadow in the best direction) and angle, you can highlight a hole in the sheetrock left by your husband on his last drunken rampage or dent left in the hood of your car when he punched it. If he smashed your favorite porcelain angel lobbing it at your head, put the broken pieces in a large, clear Ziploc bag or clear plastic Tupperware container and bring it to court with you.

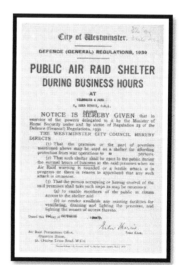

Gather evidence of –other- things your spouse did in the past: If you ever paid to get damage repaired, bring copies of the receipts. Bring your Auto Zone receipt for new ignition wires to bolster your claim he once ripped the ignition wires out of your car to prevent you from leaving. Or the contractor receipt to repair that hole in the sheet rock (or Home Depot receipt for joint compound). Although the incident may have gone un-reported for many years, having receipts supports your testimony he's damaged property to intimidate you in the past.

Dress appropriately for court: Appearances count!!! Never wear excess jewelry, flashy clothing, or short skirts. Cover tattoos, remove body piercing or jewelry which portrays a religious affiliation, and *tone it down*. Wear neat, crisply ironed clothing you would feel comfortable attending a job interview in, but nothing expensive or blatantly designer. A feminine dress, pastel cardigan, demure hairstyle and understated makeup (think librarian) will get you more traction than the most expensive attorney. A frightened demeanor (deer in headlights) will win more points than a warrior queen. Be proud and fearless *after* you get your restraining order in hand. Until then, a pink floral dress and quivering lip are your best weapons.

IMMIGRATION ISSUES AND RESTRAINING ORDERS

In general, police will not report a woman to the Immigration and Naturalization Service (INS) if she reports her spouse abuses her so long as she has no criminal record. Nor will the Probate and Family Court. Their top priority is preventing abuse. However, if you live in one of the states that has been cracking down on undocumented aliens, some person within that system may take it upon yourself to report you to INS for deportation. If you are in the country illegally and your spouse retaliates by reporting your whereabouts to INS, the state court has no power to *stop* the federal INS from becoming involved in your case. Therefore, the moment you have your restraining order in hand, speak to an attorney who specializes in immigration law.

Do not go to INS for help! They might detain you and institute deportation procedures.

If your spouse is a US citizen, there are exceptions which may enable you to stay. But if you're here on a conditional visa and you file for divorce before your status has been lifted, the timing could have a devastating impact on your immigration status. Contact an immigration lawyer as soon as you have your restraining order in hand. You might qualify for political asylum if you can prove authorities in your home country would not protect you from your abuser.

Very few family law lawyers are also immigration attorneys! Be wary of well-meaning advice which might not apply to you. *Hire an expert!*

CHAPTER TWO SUMMARY

1. If you think filing for divorce will push your spouse off the deep end, do some safety planning.

2. If your spouse makes you think he might hurt you, go to court and get a restraining order.

3. Think of statutes as recipes. To get a restraining order, either your spouse has to hit you, or put you *in fear of + imminent + serious physical harm.*

4. The judge has a nice little old lady named Mrs. Reasonably Prudent Person living in his head. It's up to *you* to convince Mrs. Reasonably Prudent Person your fear your husband is about to hurt you is reasonable.

5. Never let your spouse turn an abuse prevention hearing into a property dispute.

6. Ask a battered women's advocate or trusted friend to come to court with you.

7. If your spouse has hooked up with the batterer's rights movement, educate yourself about ways to fend off his vendetta.

8. Gather documents, affidavits, and witness statements. Make a list of talking points. Dress appropriately for court.

9. Police and judges will generally not ask if you're in this country legally when you ask for a restraining order. However, state policies have no impact on federal immigration law. Consult an immigration specialist as soon as you have your restraining order to find out your rights.

10. Arrange a 'safety burrow' (friends' house where he won't think to look) just in case…

CHAPTER 3

GATHER YOUR ACORNS

Any prince that has thoroughly fortified the city in which he resides …
Will not be readily attacked.

The Prince, by Niccolo Machiavelli

Divorce is 90% property division and 10% other factors, such as who was an abusive jerk or having an affair. Child custody is treated as almost a separate issue. Therefore, although you're consumed by anger, fear and sadness, dealing with emotional fallout is the *least* important aspect of planning your escape. Your top priority is ensuring you have the resources to survive while you lick your wounds.

'But I want to divorce my husband,' you might say, *'not spend several months combing through my finances!'* Judges don't have magical mind-reading properties to prove the truth of your unsupported allegations there should be more money. Before you can get a fair share of the assets, you must first prove they exist. Remember the cute little woodland creature, busily gnawing off its own leg? If you don't do your homework, not only will your divorce be unnecessarily expensive, but you'll spend the rest of your life hobbling along on three legs. Smart woodland creatures know how many acorns they need to gather to get them through the winter and where those acorns are stashed so they can avoid starvation.

The court will make you produce the past three (3) years of most documents, so gather them *now* and save yourself a costly archeological dig later. Getting enough information to file a credible financial statement may take weeks, but don't despair! You're a smart woodland creature, planning your escape from a larger foe. You're ensuring the economic survival of yourself and your offspring. In short, as far as nasty chores go, even though you'll find yourself longing for more pleasant tasks such as re-grouting the tile in your bathroom or weeding out poison ivy in your back yard, you must gather the following documents:

1. THE PAST 3 YEARS OF TAX RETURNS. (1040, W2, 1099's, and all schedules) If you can't find them, contact the IRS. When computing child support or alimony, the court sometimes adds back into gross income items your spouse may legally deduct as a business expense, such as costs related to his car, business use of your home, and the business portion of the utilities. The Schedule H (rental income) can also be adjusted if he's renting out part or all of a property to a relative for less than market value. Having these documents provides a baseline for claims of a sudden drop in income most men experience upon the filing of divorce.

2. THE PAST 3 YEARS OF TAX BILLS AND REAL ESTATE TAX ASSESSMENT SHEETS. (Real property, automobile excise taxes, recreational vehicles, etc.). If you didn't save them, go to your town Tax Assessors Office and request them. Under the Freedom of Information Act, you have the right to get copies for a modest cost, usually around 10 cents per page. You do not have to disclose why you want them.

   A real estate tax assessment sheet is not the same as the annual tax bill. Both are useful. The tax bill gives you a rough market value (usually outdated) and amount of tax you pay each quarter. The tax assessor's sheet is helpful when a realtor computes the fair market value of your home.

   If your spouse owns vehicles registered in his business name and the business is located in a different town, make a second trip to *that* town hall. Many towns tax businesses not only for the value of the property the business sits on, but also for equipment and goods for sale stored inside that location. Lists of goods are frequently grossly understated, but the listing provides a start.

3. THE PAST 3 YEARS OF BANK STATEMENTS. (Checking, savings, CD's, money market accounts, etc.) You can obtain statements from them for a cost if you didn't save them. Many banks let you access the past year on-line for free. If your husband is self-employed or you think he's been hiding money, you will need these. *His* attorney will demand *yours*.

4. THE PAST 3 YEARS OF INVESTMENT ACCOUNTS. (Company 401K plans, IRAs, stocks, investment account statements, etc.) You *will* have to produce these! If your husband usually stashes invoices or statements before you see them, start watching the mail for them and photocopy them before he can hide them.

   Spouses Behaving Badly: a client once bagged her husband steaming open her personal mail.

   Spouses Behaving Badly: a client noticed the seal on envelopes appeared ragged, but was still sealed. She finally realized her husband was opening her personal letters, reading them, and then gluing them shut again so she wouldn't know he was snooping.

5. THE DEED TO YOUR HOUSE AND ALL OTHER REAL PROPERTY. Make copies whether owned by you, your spouse, or your spouse's business owns. Also make a copy of all mortgages, home equity loans, and other liens against the property. These are kept at the Registry of Deeds in the county where the property is located. Go to the book and page number and make a copy of the deed. If navigating the registry of deeds intimidates you, go after lunch when the clerks may have more time to assist you, or ask somebody who seems to know what they're doing for help. Some counties make transcripts available online for a modest fee.

6. **COPIES OF TITLES TO ALL MOTOR AND RECREATIONAL VEHICLES AND EXCISE TAX BILLS FOR THEM.** If you've lost one in your name, file for a duplicate title at your state motor vehicle registry. If titled in your spouse's name, write down the VIN number on the dashboard. You'll need detailed information such as the make, model number, year, and details such as the engine size and special features to value the vehicles. Ask your town clerk for all auto and recreational vehicle excise tax bills under both you and your spouse's name. Sometimes the excise tax bill may be the only credible valuation you can obtain.

7. **PAST 3 YEARS OF CREDIT CARD STATEMENTS AND OTHER CONSUMER DEBT/PERSONAL LOANS.** You can obtain missing statements from the credit card company for a fee. Some companies keep the statements on line for several months. Who incurred the debt, the date incurred, and whether it benefited the marriage often becomes an issue. If you're in the habit of throwing out bills after paying them, just locate as many bills as you can (you can access the past years online) and save them from now on. At *minimum* your spouse's attorney is going to demand the last three months.

8. **PAST 3 YEARS OF UTILITY BILLS.** (Telephone, heat, water, gas/oil, etc.) If you toss them after paying them, start saving them from this day forward. Most utilities compare your average KWH or energy costs against last year. You can use the KWH to get a rough idea of your annual utility costs. You must back up your court financial statement as *economic need* is important to get alimony.

9. **HEALTH INSURANCE.** Get copies of your policy, including policy number. By law. You also need copies of all *uninsured* medical expenses for the past three years. Children must be covered until emancipated. Child Support and Alimony will likely be adjusted to reflect who is paying the premiums (we'll discuss this in Chapter Five: Child Support and Chapter Six: Alimony).

  The insured spouse has to keep the other on an existing policy for so long as it is available until remarriage of either party, an order of the court, or an agreement saying otherwise.

10. **LIFE INSURANCE.** There are two types of life insurance, term and whole life. Term expires each year and accumulates no cash value. Whole Life insurance generally has a surrender cash value and that cash value is considered a joint marital asset.

  Make sure your husband doesn't remove you as beneficiary while your divorce is pending. If you will be collecting child support or alimony, you may want to negotiate remaining on that policy in exchange for less child support/alimony or in exchange for another asset. Otherwise, if your spouse dies, you could be left out in the cold.

11. **PAST PAYSTUBS.** Save as many of your own paystubs from here on in as you can find. Save copies of your spouse's paystubs if you can get your hands on them. If your spouse habitually works "x" number of hours overtime every week to make ends meet, the court will sometimes include that when computing child support.

12. PENSION INFORMATION. If you or your spouse work as a teacher for a public school system, or work for a city, town, county, state, or the federal government, chances are there is a pension lurking. Careers covered by pensions include policemen, firefighters, town employees, civil servants, and military personnel. Some older, well established companies, such as Raytheon or IBM, also have pensions. Even if your spouse has not worked at the job long enough for the pension to 'vest' (i.e., he's eligible to start collecting), it has a cash value. Get as much information as you can so you can have it valued (we will cover valuation of pensions later in this chapter). A pension may provide enough leverage to keep your house, the IRA, or the car!

13. MAKE A LIST OF ALL MAJOR BELONGINGS. Go through your house with a camera and take lots of pictures. Make a list of all the big-ticket items such as furniture, expensive jewelry, collectibles such as antiques or coins, electronic equipment, tools, movable appliances (such as microwave ovens and washing machines), and anything you think might be valuable. Write down the model, serial numbers, and take photographs.

Spouses Behaving Badly: My own ex-husband emptied every stick of furniture and belonging we owned, leaving nothing but my clothes dumped into the middle of the floor. Not only did he steal the food and light bulbs, but he also unscrewed the face plates from all the electrical outlets!

Spouses Behaving Badly: A client's contractor-husband removed his tools from their garage, then later tried to claim they were only worth $2,000. Luckily … she took pictures. We were able to reconstruct a credible estimate of the larger tools.

The moment you tell your husband you want a divorce, stuff is going to disappear. Make sure you document it so the court can make you whole!

14. COPIES OF YOUR SPOUSE'S BUSINESS RECORDS. If you have accounting software such as Quicken or Microsoft Money, make a backup copy. Have a techie friend teach you how. Update your backup to a flash drive every week. If your spouse is self-employed, try to obtain a backup copy of his business accounts as well. Even if your spouse has a business partner, his share of the business is still a joint marital asset.

If possible, and note what tools or equipment he has or at least take pictures. That arc-welder or set of Snap-On wrenches may not seem sexy, but the tools of his trade could be worth more than the equity in your house, car, or the IRA. Write down make, model, year and serial number information on all big ticket items and/or take photographs.

15. OBTAIN BOTH YOU AND YOUR HUSBAND'S SOCIAL SECURITY REPORT SHEET FROM THE SOCIAL SECURITY ADMINISTRATION. Every year, social security mails you a statement projecting how much you've paid into the system and how much they project you could collect when you retire at age 67. Although Social Security is not a marital asset subject to division, this statement is a rude wake-up call. By comparing social security entitlements, you can see spelled out in dollars and cents how little you contributed while sacrificing your career to raise your children. If you did not save these, you can go to the nearest social security office with two forms of identification to request your own. You'll have to watch the mail for your spouses.

If you're part of that growing group of women over the age of 50 getting divorced after a long-term marriage, knowing your Social Security entitlement will be a critical part of your financial planning.

If you were married for more than 10 years, you may be able to elect to collect social security at your husband's higher rate rather than your own. Visit the Social Security Administration site to see if you qualify: http://ssa-custhelp.ssa.gov/app/answers/detail/a_id/299/~/qualifying-for-divorced-spouse-benefits

16. DOCUMENTATION REGARDING ANY OTHER ASSET, LIABILITY, OR COLLECTIBLE YOU HAVE WHICH MAY BE VALUABLE. If in doubt, document it. I know of a case where the couples spent three years in court fighting over the value of an old "Wizard of Oz" book given to the wife by her grandparents. The husband claimed it was an original copy from the 1800's. The wife thought it was just a fairly worthless old book whose only value was sentimental. The couple ran themselves into bankruptcy (literally) fighting over the value of a book which turned out to be worth $60.

Wasn't that *fun?* How long did it take you to gather all this stuff? Four hours? Eight? More? Think of it this way. You're documenting tens of thousands of dollars' worth of assets your husband would otherwise walk away with. Remember that 'stuff' I told you I was too stupid to get valued way-back when I was a single mother with a high school diploma? The stuff that almost caused me to have a seizure my first day of family law class? The stuff I later went back, dug through my old records, computed to be worth $50,000 dollars, and then used cost-of-living increases to come up with a 2012 value of $90,000? You are, quite literally 'paying yourself' by taking the time to do this research. Documenting your own 'stuff' helps moderate-income woman level the playing field.

Now go get a nice, hot mug of the highest-octane coffee you can possibly brew. We're not finished yet!

HOW SHOULD I ORGANIZE ALL THIS INFORMATION?

Documenting and valuing your assets is a huge chore. To keep things in perspective, if it gets contested *after* you file for divorce, you'll pay an attorney $300 per hour to do this nasty chore *for* you. The court *will* make you produce these documents if the other side insists upon it and *will* sanction you if you can't produce them. This is where attorneys earn a large percentage of their legal fees.

Get two thick 3-ring binders and several packs of 5-tab or 8-tab dividers. Label one notebook '*EXPENSES*' and the other '*ASSETS.*' If you have a lot of a certain type of asset or expense, feel free to create additional notebooks. Some people prefer to use a box of hanging file-folders instead of a 3-ring binder to sort their information. This might be easier when initially sorting old statements and bills, but put it in a 3-ring binder for your attorney because it's easier to digest. *Convenient* for them translates into *save money* for you!

1. START BUILDING AN EXPENSE NOTEBOOK: Create an 'expense' slot for each class of document I suggested you gather earlier. Suggested tab-dividers are:

- Rent or Mortgage (PIT)
- Homeowners/Tenant Insurance
- Home Maintenance and Repair
- Heat
- Electricity and/or Gas
- Telephone
- Water/Sewer
- Food
- House Supplies

- Laundry and Cleaning
- Life Insurance
- Medical Insurance
- Incidentals and Toiletries
- Motor Vehicle Expenses
- Motor Vehicle Payment
- Child Care
- Other Expenses
- Laundry and Cleaning

2. START BUILDING AN ASSET VALUATION NOTEBOOK. Get two 3-ring binders. Label one and create tab dividers for each class of asset:

- Real estate
- Motor Vehicles
- Pension/Retirement Accounts
- Stocks/Bonds
- Savings/Bank Accounts
- Business Assets

- Furniture
- Home Electronics
- Appliances
- Tools
- Other Assets
- Furniture

We'll begin valuing your assets in a little while. For now, sort through your paperwork, put it in order by account, type and date, and figure out what you still need to scrounge up. For example, if you have three separate Bank of Spank accounts, file each account number under a separate tab.

What if you you've diligently gathered your acorns paperwork, put it in order, and you realize you're missing some of it? Don't despair. Include a sheet of loose-leaf paper on the front of each topic-heading and write down which ones you are missing. Some attorneys will insist you contact your bank or brokerage firm and pay to dig them up. Others will take a 'wait and see' approach. If vanished funds are not an issue and the other side isn't insisting you pay your bank $15 per page to get copies of three-year-old bank statements, you may never need to produce them. Use your common sense.

To help you keep track of what you've found versus what you still need to get, I've created a handy 'Acorns Checklist' to photocopy and use on your archeological dig through the icky spider closet:

WORKSHEET 3-1: ACORNS CHECKLIST

Type of Statement	Period I Need	Who has them	Statements I Have	Statements I Need to Get
State and Federal Tax returns	Past 3 years			
Tax assessments and appraisals on all real and personal property	Current tax bills			
Bank statements: - checking - savings - CD's - money market	Past 3 years			
Investment & retirement accounts: - 401k - IRA - Roth IRA - Stocks - Bonds - Etc.	Past 3 years			
Mortgages, Deeds, and Liens	Since purchased			
Titles to all motor and recreational vehicles	Since purchased			
Credit card statements and consumer loans (including student loans)	Minimum past 3 months or back to incurrence of loan			
Utility bills: - gas/oil - electricity - telephone - cell phone - water bill - trash removal - etc.	Past 3 months to past year			
Health Insurance	Current policy			
Life Insurance	Current policy and cash value			
Paystubs	Past 3 weeks to past 3 years			
Pension Information	Current policy and valuation			
List of household belongings	Photograph and make a list			
Business records and inventory	Past 3 years			
Backup of bookkeeping software	Current copy			
Social Security statement	Most recent statements			
Other valuations	Most recent valuations			

If some of the documents you need are in your husband's control (i.e., he has a stock brokerage account in his name alone) or you suspect he may have been funneling money out of the marital account to hide it, there are tools lawyers use called 'discovery' to force your husband to cough up information. Discovery is covered in Chapter Fifteen.

Discovery – the process of 'discovering' information you don't know using formal requests for information such as Requests for the Production of Documents, Requests for Admissions, Depositions, and Interrogatories.

HOW MUCH ARE MY ACORNS WORTH?

Not knowing the true value of an asset (such as *your* Mass Teachers Pension) can sabotage your escape plan. Don't assume the evil trapper will be too ignorant to value an asset. *He* might assume the latest excise tax bill is accurate, but if he hires a lawyer, the *lawyer* will have the current value appraised. That value may be higher or lower (to your detriment) than you thought. Most legal fees are incurred because people let their lawyers argue about how much something is worth rather than agreeing on a source they both trust (such as a trusted realtor or Kelley Blue Book) to value things for them.

Some classes of assets, such as your savings account or stock portfolio, are fairly easy to value. Whatever the current value is listed on your latest statement, that is the value. Other assets require a bit of legwork. Things such as your house need a broker or appraiser. For other items, I've included a Sample Valuation Worksheet to help you value each big-ticket (>$1,000) item.

Create a new worksheet for each asset. Write down the make, model, year, serial number, and any other identifying information. Take a photograph and paste it to the page. If you still have original receipts or warranty information, staple it to the back or immediately after it. The easiest way to value things is online auctions such as E-Bay or specialty online resellers of similar of used items. Find the most similar item possible. Find quotes from several resellers, print them out, and attach the estimates to the back of the valuation worksheet page.

Now if you're like most people, you've probably accumulated a lot of 'stuff' over the years that you'd rather haul to the dump rather than do this icky valuation chore. Use your common sense.

Start with your 'big ticket' items first and work your way down to less valuable ones, skipping ones you'd just assume donate to charity. Don't nickel and dime the piddling stuff if it's not worth the effort, but don't skip this step or you'll regret it when it comes time to play liars poker in the property division.

This is the perfect time to haul 'stuff' not worthy of valuation to the dump or donate it to a local charity. Be sure to get a donation receipt to deduct off your taxes!

A sample valuation worksheet follows:

WORKSHEET 3-2: SAMPLE VALUATION WORKSHEET

Asset:___Table Saw_____
Make: _Sears Craftsman_____
Model: _portable_____
Year Manufactured: _2002_____
Serial Number: _XBZ2002350073_____
Description: _3.5 horsepower table saw_
with wide carriage and collapsible legs

Year Purchased: __2002_____
Purchase Price $__295.00_____
(Staple copy of original receipt and warranty
information if available)

Special Features/notes:

Staple photograph here

Current value of a similar, brand new model at retail stores: (attach copies of sales flyers if available)
Store:___Sears/Hyannis_____ Date advertised:___1/17/07___ Price: $__325.00____
Store:_____ Date advertised:_____ Price: $_____
Store:_____ Date advertised:_____ Price: $_____

Current value of similar used items at second-hand stores: (attach copies of sales flyers or quotes if available)
Store:___Ellie's fleamarket_____ Date seen: _2/13/07___ Price: $__150.00____
Store:___Jack's Tool Shop_____ Date seen: _1/14/07___ Price: $___183.50___
Store:_____ Date seen:_____ Price: $_____

Current value of similar used items advertised in newspaper "items for sale" ads, Want Ads, or final bid on E-Bay: (attach copies of advertisement or web page if available)
Store:_E-Bay_____ Date seen: _2/15/07___ Price: $__195.00____
Store:_E-Bay_____ Date seen: _2/16/07___ Price: $__167.50____
Store:_Pennysaver Newspaper___ Date seen: _1/27/07___ Price: $__150.00____

Appraisal from dealer, appraiser, or appraisal websites: (attach copies of appraisal estimates, affidavits, or appraisal website webpage if available)
Appraisal source:___friend's husband_____ Date Valued:_12/29/06_ Price: $_~$175.00__
Appraisal source:_____ Date Valued:_____ Price: $_____
Appraisal source:_____ Date Valued:_____ Price: $_____

(Note: My friend Susie's husband Jack, a licensed general contractor, said he and his contractor friends usually pay around $175.00 for a used table saw.)

Estimated value for Financial Statement: $__175.00_____

Justification/Notes on Value: *I used Jack's estimate of value because he is a contractor in the field generally using this equipment. He said he burns through a table saw every year and will often pick up a good used one if he can find one. He looked at our saw and said it is in good condition. His estimate appears to be in line with the range of estimates I got from other used table saw vendors. Jack's affidavit is attached.*

Value might change once you learn more information, but knowing your approximate net worth before you announce you want a divorce empowers you to make hard decisions *now*, before you've committed yourself to an all-out war. I note 'dirty lawyer tricks to help you understand positions attorneys take when valuing each asset.

1. VALUING YOUR HOUSE AND OTHER REAL ESTATE: The single most valuable asset  most people accumulate during their marriage is their home and any other real property they may buy. You must appraise the current fair market value. Town property tax bills are a start, but most towns lag behind the market. Get it appraised!

How do you do this? The easiest (and cheapest) way is to call a reputable real estate broker, explain to them you're thinking of getting divorced, wonder how much your house might be worth if you decide to sell it, and ask them to do a fair market value appraisal. Most will do this free of charge because they hope you'll later hire them. Ask them to point out things to make your home more appealing to buyers and don't be insulted by their comments. They want to see you get as much money as possible. Some repairs, such as weeding the garden, eliminating clutter, or repainting the house, can make a huge difference in the selling price for little money. Schedule them to come when your husband won't be home.

I advise clients to call in three separate brokers to do analyses and to treat their appointments as though conducting a job interview, even if they hope to keep their home. Ask questions about what they plan to do to market your house if you *do* decide to put it on the market and how long they think it will take to sell. That way, if you decide your house is not worth the hassle, you already know who you'd like to hire. The best way to find a broker is use one a friend recently used and was satisfied. If you've refinanced your house within the last 3-6 months, that appraisal may be sufficient.

Dirty Lawyer Trick: When a client wants to keep the house and buy out their husband's share, some lawyers will use the *lowest* appraised value (often the town valuation) on the financial statement.

Dirty Lawyer Trick: The lawyer representing the spouse who *doesn't* want the house will use the *highest* appraised value. Be aware of this dirty trick if you wish to buy out your spouse's share of the house.

Equity is the fair market value of the house *minus* any mortgages, liens, levies, or home equity loans you have against the property

If your house needs repairs, gather estimates from contractors. If you wish to keep your house, demonstrate that $450,000 appraisal is contingent upon repainting, replacing the deck, a new roof, or having mold removed from the basement and how much the contractor says it will cost to make those repairs. Don't get stuck eating repairs on a run-down house!

2. VALUING MOTOR VEHICLES: To value your car or truck, the following websites are acknowledged to be fairly accurate:

www.kellybluebook.com
www.edmunds.com

You need the make, model and year number. The condition it is in, size of the engine, and amenities (such as anti-lock brakes, air conditioning, or moon roof) all play a part in the market value of your car. Print out the appraisals from both websites for further reference. Edmunds.com tends to value cars slightly lower than Kelly Bluebook.

Dirty Lawyer Trick: If a client wants to *keep* a car, some lawyers will view every nick, ding, and rattle with a baleful eye and list it as being in poor condition on the website auto-prompts. They'll use whichever appraisal is lowest (often the state excise tax bill) on the financial statement so their client gets a bigger piece of the pie.

Dirty Lawyer Trick: If a client expects the *other side* wants to keep a particular car, some lawyers will list the car as being in 'above average' condition in the website auto-prompts and list whichever appraisal is highest on the financial statement so the opposing party has to give up more property in order to keep their car.

Kelly and Edmunds don't value many recreational vehicles, so to value your boat, ATV, trailer, or motor home you'll need to do a bit of legwork. Start with your excise tax bill, but I've found these values to be inflated (for example, a utility trailer you paid $450 for brand new at Home Depot is always valued at $1500, no matter what). In other cases, for very old cars, the state doesn't differentiate between the mint condition 1955 Chevy with the original 30,000 miles on it and the rusted 1955 Chevy abandoned in your back yard with a tree growing up through the engine block.

Local newspaper ads, Want Ads, Craig's List or E-bay are good places to get a rough idea of value. Or you can take the vehicle to a local dealer and ask how much they think it would sell for. Ask about broker's fees and how long it would take to sell. Three months is a good sales benchmark for selling these items.

3. VALUING RETIREMENT AND PENSION PLANS: There are two kinds of retirement assets: *Defined contribution plans* (such as an IRA or 401K) which are plans you put money into and receive a statement as to value each year, and *defined benefit plans,* such as the pension a firefighter or soldier will get when they retire based on how many years they worked and how much they earned instead of the cash value of what they put into the plan (sometimes in place of social security). Although both kinds of plans often have both the employee and the employer contribute, how the two types of retirement plans are valued in a divorce are different.

Defined contribution plan – a retirement account you invest money into which follows the ebb and flow of the economy like a brokerage account. Generally, the burden is upon *you* to decide how much you wish deducted from your paycheck each week for retirement savings and *you* to direct the benefit administrator which investment vehicles you wish to park your money in long-term. IRA's, 401(k)'s and many deferred compensation plans are defined contribution plans. If you don't save enough to last the rest of your life once you retire, your money will run out, but you can leave any leftover funds to your spouse or children because it is *your* money.

Cash value for a *defined contribution plan* (IRA, 401k) is the cash value listed at the bottom of your quarterly statement. If the market is experiencing a drastic fluctuation in one of your investment vehicles, call your plan coordinator to get a more current value.

Defined benefit plan – this is what most people think of as a 'pension.' Your employer usually makes contributions to this plan on your behalf. When you retire, how much you are entitled to collect is usually via a formula which includes your last few years of salary and how many years you worked for the company. You will usually collect these benefits from the day you are eligible to retire until you die regardless of how much you paid into the system, but once you die, you generally cannot leave any leftover money to your heirs.

Cash value for a *defined benefit plan* (traditional pension) is harder to calculate. The value listed at the bottom of the annual statement often has little to do with the value that would be assigned to it in a divorce, especially if the pension has not yet vested. If the pension was used in place of social security, only that part of it over and above what would have been contributed to for social security is a joint marital asset.

Vested means you've met the threshold contribution requirements to collect your pension once you're old enough to retire. Often a set number of years of service at the same employer.

Dirty Lawyer Tricks: Some lawyers will contact the benefits administrator at the employer (current or former) and ask them to send a statement of present cash value.

The cash value listed on an employer's benefits statement will usually be quite low and is not the valuation to be used for your divorce!

There are services who can tell you of how much that pension may be worth for a few hundred dollars, money well spent to value an asset potentially worth a million dollars. Visit their websites find out what information they need. Here are a few I've used in the past for informational purposes only, but I cannot vouch for them:

Law Data, Inc.
P.O. Box 650549
Vero Beach, FL 32965
(800) 368-8086
www.lawdatainc.com

Pension Appraisers, Inc.
P.O. Box 4396
Allentown, Pa. 18105-1580
(800) 447-0084
www.pensionappraisers.com

Generally, you (or he) will be entitled to approximately 50% of the that amount of the pension accumulated during the length of the marriage *over and above what would have been contributed to Social Security*. In other words, if you worked as a teacher for 27 years and have been married the last 6, he's entitled to around 50% of what accumulated during the last 6 years.

Do not overlook or underestimate the value of a pension, either your husbands or yours!!!

Pension valuation is an inexact science. You could die before you collect it and never receive a dime. You might die a few years after starting to collect it and get less than your coworkers who live a long life. You may work in a line of work which causes you to have a shorter life expectancy than other professions. Inflation might go up faster than expected, or slower. There are multiple sources which will place a value on a pension. Make sure you understand the possible range of valuations and which method your pension valuation service used before you choose one. If you have a large pension lurking in your property division (his or yours), hire a lawyer experienced in pension division or you could be leaving enormous sums of money on the table.

Dirty Lawyer Tricks: If the pension belongs to *their* client, some lawyers will go for the lowest possible appraised value (called a 'lowball' estimate) so their client gets to keep that asset *and* walk away with a bigger share of the other assets.

Dirty Lawyer Tricks: If the pension belongs to *the opposing party*, some lawyers will go for the highest possible appraised value (called a 'blue sky' estimate) so they can force concessions from the pension-holding spouse.

Pay the extra $50 or so to have the pension valuation expert do a social security offset analysis. That deducts the portion of your (or his) salary each year that *should* have been going towards social security if your employer wasn't paying into social security as well. That portion of a pension should *not* be counted as an asset. Most judges *do* allow an offset because it's not fair for one person to have a social security retirement account exempt from being counted as a marital asset, but the other person's social-security replacement pension is dividable. Get the exact amount! Not a 'guesstimate' at the eleventh hour!

If the retirement benefit is yours, don't stick your head in the sand and hope the evil trapper doesn't think it's an asset. He may not think of it, but his lawyer will! Even if not vested, the court presumes a reasonably prudent person would continue to work at the same job in order to keep their pension (which is often worth more than their salary). Value pensions in the planning stages or you could get blindsided … or robbed!

4. VALUING YOUR HUSBANDS BUSINESS EQUIPMENT, POWER TOOL COLLECTION, AND/OR HOBBY SUPPLIES: If your husband (or you) owns a business, you need to have it valued by a business valuation expert. Do not buy into the evil trappers claim he doesn't earn any money and the business isn't worth anything. I've found millions in omitted assets of so-called 'worthless' businesses. Most self-employed persons either genuinely underestimate the value of equipment and goodwill accumulated over the years, or lie through their teeth to avoid paying taxes (often a little of both). Your spouse may try to claim items are valueless because they've been fully depreciated in his tax records, but those items still have a value (often a very high value). The onus is on *you* to do your homework.

Do not underestimate the value of all the power tools, pieces of lumber, and spare car, truck, boat, or snowmobile parts your husband may have collected over the years to do his "side job!!!" Make a list of potentially valuable items, along with make, model, age, serial number, and any other identifying information, and photograph them. The power tools and shed full of lumber your husband has squirreled away to do his weekend handyman job may be worth more than your car, his truck, and your IRA combined!!!

Even if your husband doesn't use the equipment for work, but has a basement full of power tools or other hobby equipment (such motor vehicle repair equipment to pimp out his "classic car"), chances are he's sitting on a pot of gold and doesn't even know it.

5. –DON'T- VALUE CLOTHING: Regular clothing is usually not considered an asset, but if you happen to own Captain Kirk's original uniform from Star Trek, Marilyn Monroe's dress from the Seven Year Itch, or you have a slew of original designer gowns from your Aunt Vera Wang, then you'll need to value them.

6. VALUING FURNISHINGS, ELECTRONIC EQUIPMENT AND OTHER BIG TICKET ITEMS: Nothing drives up legal fees faster than the bickering over who gets what item. Photograph, document, and find the fair market value of your 'stuff.' Find out how much a similar used item sells for at a used furniture store or E-bay. If you think something might truly be an antique (and not just old), bring it to an antique dealer to get an appraisal. You're going to discover most of the stuff you paid a lot of money for brand-new is now practically worthless, but some items you might have given away may be quite valuable. This exercise will give you a good idea of which items to ask for.

7. VALUING OTHER ASSETS AND COLLECTIBLES: By now, you should be a pro at documenting and valuing your assets. Coin and similar collections can be brought to a dealer for valuation or you can research their value at the library or on line. Expensive jewelry should be brought to a jeweler for appraisal, something you should do periodically anyways for insurance purposes. Furs should be appraised through a dealer. If you have collectibles such as Bearstown Bears or Precious Moments, research the value online.

The court generally doesn't want to hear you fight about items worth less than $1,000. Group items into 'collection's worth $1,000 or more. Often, your husband will deny his 2,000-piece antique train collection is worth anything, but insist your childhood unicorn collection is worth a gazillion dollars. By grouping them, perhaps you can get the judge to do something besides roll his eyes and declare it's too insignificant for him to care. The judge doesn't care about a single Hummel statue, but an entire china cabinet full of them might be a different story.

Dirty Lawyer Trick: Lawyers will often use the *lowest* estimate if it's an asset their own client wants to keep, but the *highest* estimate if it's an asset the opposing party wants to keep.

We'll discuss which assets to ask for in Chapter Seven: Property Division, but first you must gather your acorns before we start talking numbers. *Please* do this exercise. Gnawing off your own leg and bleeding to death in the woods because you were too lazy to find out what your stuff was worth is dumb. Don't let your cute fuzzy offspring starve because you didn't do your homework. You *will* get caught with your pants down around your ankles! I promise this nasty valuation chore will be well rewarded, even if it's never introduced as evidence in court.

The moment you plunk down your neatly indexed 'valuation notebook' listing everything you own, it's fair market value, and credible quotes from at least three sources, his *attorney* will advise him to cut the crap and stop playing games.

ADDITIONAL STEPS YOU SHOULD TAKE RIGHT AWAY

No enterprise is more likely to succeed,
Than one concealed from the enemy until it is ripe for execution.

The Prince, by Niccolo Machiavelli

The moment you announce you want a divorce, your husband's attorney will advise him to freeze your joint marital bank accounts and credit cards so you can't treat yourself to a vacation to Hawaii. This means you won't be able to put gas in your car or pay the rent. If you've allowed your husband to handle the finances over the years, you may have ceased to exist from a credit standpoint. The following steps are sound financial planning.

1. *Open your own P.O. Box.* For a modest fee, you'll have someplace to send mail you don't want your spouse reading and also ensure you have a safe address to forward the rest of your mail to if things turn ugly.

2. *Open your own checking and savings account* at a different bank than your marital accounts. Have the statements sent to your new P.O. Box.

3. *Get a credit card which is solely in your name.* Mail statements to your new P.O. Box. If you have bad credit, you can get one by putting $500 in a security escrow account. Make a $15 - $20 charge to the account each month (auto-pay a small utility bill) then pay the bill in full immediately to start building credit.

4. *Get a safe deposit box.* If you have small valuable items which could disappear, such as jewelry, U.S. Savings Bonds, coin collections, stock certificates, etc., open a safe deposit box and put those items in it for safekeeping. Make a list as you will need to disclose contents to the court. Have renewal notices sent to your P.O. Box.

5. *Start a rainy day fund.* Put a little money into your new checking and savings account every week. Save a minimum of 6-12 weeks living expenses. It takes 6-8 weeks to file for divorce, get him served, and get a temporary orders hearing to define who will pay which bills. If you have children, it will take another 2-6 weeks for the DOR to garnish his wages and get you the money.

As surely as the sun rises in the East and settles in the West, the first thing your spouse will do is cut you off financially and refuse to pay the bills. Plan accordingly. Putting aside a nest egg will take time, but by being clever and pinching pennies, you can quietly funnel money away.

6. *Outfit an emergency supply pantry.* The local governmental disaster plan for H5N1 bird flu is *the government can't bail everybody out.* Have 6 weeks food and supplies (such as diapers, toilet paper, etc.) on hand at all times. As things go on sale, buy an extra 6 week buffer (increase that to 12 weeks if you think you'll be chasing him for child support) until you have enough to tide you over in an emergency.

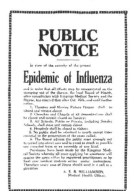

A disaster buffer is additional security against your own, personal disaster if your divorce turns ugly. If your husband pays his bills, maintain your 6 week buffer for a natural disaster such as pandemic flu. But if he plays games, at least you'll be able to eat while you wait to get into court on a contempt motion. And please don't forget to include supplies for your pets! The number of pets who get surrendered to shelters because their owners experience an economic downturn is heartbreaking! If your plan is to take the kids and leave because of domestic violence, figure out how much food, diapers, etc. you use in a week and budget enough in your escape plan for your new household.

For more detailed emergency planning skills for non-Uzi-toting/non-paranoid 'real' people, read my upcoming book, *The Cheap Yankee Guide to Being a Sane Suburban Prepper.*

7. If you need to order things such as past tax returns from the IRS, send them to the P.O. Box. Some places might refuse to mail things to P.O. boxes, but if you *can* do it without a fuss, do so. It's easier than explaining to your husband why you're getting tax returns from three years ago.

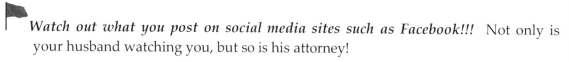

⚑ **Watch out what you post on social media sites such as Facebook!!!** Not only is your husband watching you, but so is his attorney!

Spouses Behaving Badly: A husband claimed he couldn't pay his child support. His wife set up a false account under a pseudonym with a false image of an attractive female and 'friended' him. At the contempt hearing, we produced printouts of his Facebook page where he bragged about custom tires he'd bought for his SUV, a new satellite radio, and a vacation he'd booked to a distant NASCAR race.

Remember, you **must** disclose the contents of any secret safe deposit boxes, checking, or savings accounts, or credit cards you opened on the court's financial statement when you eventually *do* file for divorce. *The purpose of this exercise is not to hide money.* You need to be financially responsible enough to recognize you're about to go through a 6-12 week period when your husband might cut off his nose to spite his face. Be sure you have enough money to continue paying your bills so your marital estate doesn't suffer. If you don't plan for the time it takes to get into court, the evil trapper *will* financially starve you out of your comfy woodland burrow.

CASE STUDY – INTRODUCTION TO JACK AND JANE

Lawyers use 'hypothetical client's to help them wrap their brains around a case. In the last chapter we accompanied Jane to court to get a restraining order against her husband. We'll continue to use Jack and Jane as an example throughout this book. Jack and Jane own a house and consider themselves to be middle class. They get by, but have little equity in their house or cars. Like most moderate-income couples, every penny they earn goes to maintain their middle-class lifestyle, leaving little left over for savings.

The moment they separate, Jane will drop out of the middle class…

Jane earns too much to qualify for free legal help through Legal Services, but does not earn enough to hire an attorney. If she empties out her IRA, she'll incur hefty tax penalties. She's skeptical about taking out a loan because she has no idea how she'd pay it back. Because Jane is proactive and eager to learn, we'll walk her through different steps she can take to ensure an outcome that, although not as good as what she would get with a full-service attorney, at least ensures she'll walk away with a minimally secure future.

We'll pretend prior to the incident over the dog, Jane consulted with an attorney at a free legal clinic about her rights. She attended a women's support group where the other women warned her to put aside a little money. Jane gathered many documents she needs to make her case in court, but she's not confident she got everything. She came across a stock account she didn't know existed. Other documents, such as bank statements, are incomplete. Jane started putting aside money to tide her over in case Jack plays games, but her escape plans were cut short by the restraining order.

I'm *not* recommending you go it alone! But by using a hypothetical, I'm hoping it will help the lay-reader grasp what steps Jane must take to piece together a fairly decent divorce on her own.

CHAPTER 3 SUMMARY

1. Before you file for divorce, take stock of how many acorns you have, where they're located, and ways to get more if you don't have enough to last you through the winter.

2. The court will force you to gather your last three years' worth of financials, so do it in advance and save yourself time and money.

3. There are certain steps you can take to position yourself to financially survive a divorce.

4. Document and get valuations on *everything!!!* Your husband's lawyer will hate you and try to convince you that you're crazy or don't know what you're doing, but don't believe them.

5. Create a valuation workbook. Photograph and document everything about every asset you own. Attach copies of sales flyers, web pages, classified advertisements, appraisals or affidavits if you can find them. Value smaller items into "collections" of $1,000 or more.

CHAPTER 4

THE COURTS FINANCIAL STATEMENT

To guide decisions regarding child support, alimony, and property division, courts make you fill out a detailed financial statement outlining your income, assets, liabilities and expenses. I use Massachusetts' form as an example because that's where I'm licensed to practice law, but the information courts look at doesn't change much from state to state.

You must fill out a fresh financial statement every time you go to court. Therefore, I urge you to photocopy the sample blank financial statement at the end of this chapter and fill out your *own* information as you read, even if you're missing things, so you learn to fill it out right. Once we're done, you should go back and fill in the gaps.

Don't guess! Use actual bills and checkbook records gathered in the Acorns chapter. Your husband's attorney will crawl through your financial statement with a microscope, especially if child support or alimony come into play. He may paint you as a liar because you forgot to include something. I know –I- do that with opposing clients. Cross-examining your opponents lying soon-to-be-ex-spouse in front of the judge is *lots* of fun!

- 'Where's the $50 you earn under-the-table each week cleaning your neighbor's house listed?'

- 'You state here your income is only $400 a week, but your weekly expenses say you've been spending $850. If your income is so low, how do you maintain your lifestyle?'

- 'You're a landscaper, right? It says here you're only earning $250 per week, but last year you earned $70,000. Wouldn't it be more accurate to say you earn $1350 per week and just happen to be earning less because it's January?'

- 'I have here a copy of a stock account statement worth $40,000, but it's not listed on your financial statement. Why did you try to hide it from the court?'

- 'You say your income is only $150 per week, but you're a waitress, aren't you? Where's your tip income listed?'

- 'You claim you've been out of work for the past six months, but you posted on your Facebook page pictures from your recent trip to Hawaii. How did you pay for that trip?'

- 'You're a self-employed general contractor, aren't you? How come you earned $80,000 per year every single year for the past five years, but on January 15th, the day your wife filed for divorce, all of a sudden you can't find work?'

- 'I want you to look at this financial statement. Is this your signature at the bottom? Where you signed you filled out this statement under the pains and penalties of perjury of law?'

Whoopee!!! Lawyers just *love* it when we get to prance around the courtroom like a television prosecutor and make you look like a liar!

FINANCIAL STATEMENTS AS A BOOTCAMP FINANCIAL PLANNING TOOL

The courts' financial statement is a good financial planning tool in its own right. It helps you nail down your *actual* living expenses, which are usually far greater than most people *think* they are.

Keep a separate piece of paper as you fill out this form and note anomalies in your spending habits. If you're squeezing your household budget to build a 3-month financial buffer, note this on your personal copy so you get an accurate picture of how much you *really* need to survive. We'll cover ways to bring your post-divorce expenses in line with your post-divorce lifestyle in Chapter Eight.

SAVE YOURSELF $50 RIGHT NOW!

Some people will read through this chapter and say, 'ohmigod … this is so complicated … I guess I *do* want to hire an attorney!' If so, I have one piece of advice that will recoup you the price of this book.

 Fill out your own financial statement before you go to the lawyer's office.

No matter what state you live in, if you speak to an attorney, they're going to hand you some version of this form. Go online, download it, fill it out yourself, and make a photocopy to hand to them the moment you walk in their office door.

Don't skip this chapter because filling out forms is about as interesting as getting your teeth cleaned! Getting your teeth cleaned is a necessary, if boring, part of good oral hygiene so you don't get rotten teeth. So is learning how to fill out your own legal forms so you don't get rotten legal advice. Every client who walks into one of my free legal clinics asks this *same* information over and over again. Gathering information on-the-spot wastes, on average, 10-15 minutes of our half-hour appointment. That means, if you *don't* fill it out, you're going to be paying your attorney $300 an hour to watch you fumble with a pencil. Do you *really* want to pay your attorney $300 an hour to watch you fill out a simple form?

Rough Draft Financial Statement: $300/hr x 10 min/.0167 = $50

Why does your attorney charge you when you don't fill out the financial questionnaire they send you in advance? Think of it as a 'stupidity charge.' Without this information, we can't give you good legal advice. You're paying us to answer questions about *your* finances and we can't provide answers without it. *You can do it!* Fill out this nasty little legal form *before* you go see a lawyer and save yourself a wad of cash!

WHERE DO I GET –MY– STATE'S VERSION OF THIS FORM?

Although family courts nationwide seek nearly identical information about what kind of assets you and your spouse may have accumulated during your marriage, each state has their own unique financial statement. Some states break down information *more* than we do here in Massachusetts (for example, neighboring New Hampshire not only asks you about how much it costs to heat your house, but also breaks it down into gas, oil, coal or wood), while others lump expenses together further.

The courts financial statement is the single most important document you can prepare yourself in your divorce. To get *your* states' form, visit your local courthouse and ask for a copy of it (there may be a small fee to obtain one).

You could also download it from your state court website. These days, most states post their financial statements online because they want you to come to the courthouse prepared. Type one of the following search requests into your internet browser:

"___(state name)___ family court financial statement"

"___(state name)___ family court financial affidavit"

"___(state name)___ family court divorce forms"

You may need to hunt a bit to find it, but doing so is worth your effort as not only will it make your trip to court easier, filling it out in advance will make seeking legal advice (whether through a private attorney or a free consultation with a volunteer courthouse lawyer-of-the-day) much more efficient (i.e., less expensive). We're going to be using the court's financial statement as a financial planning tool to help you compute potential child support and alimony in the coming chapters.

If you're unable to dig up *your* state court form right this moment, simply follow along with the sample form using a sheet of plain lined paper. Or … you could always use the Massachusetts nifty fill-in-the-blank interactive form which does all the math *for* you ☺ until you can dig up your own states official form. It can be found at:

http://www.mass.gov/courts/courtsandjudges/courts/probateandfamilycourt/documents/cjd301shortform.pdf

There's a 50-state listing of state court self-help websites in Chapter Nine: Piecing Together Legal Services on a Budget that lists links to helpful state websites.

ANATOMY OF A FINANCIAL STATEMENT

Since I practice in Massachusetts, I'll use their form as an example, but the information the forms are looking for doesn't differ much from state to state. In a nutshell, the court is looking for the same basic information any financial planner would ask questions about, so although the order the questions are asked will differ from state-to-state, the actual *information* they seek will vary little. Massachusetts has two separate types of financial statements. I will only cover the short form in this book as that is the most common form you will see nationwide.

We'll go back to our hypothetical divorcee, Jane Doe-Rayme, and go through her financial statement section-by-section so you understand how to fill out your own financial statement.

Commonwealth of Massachusetts
Division **Barnstable**　　　　The Trial Court　　　Docket No. **12D-9999-DV1**
Probate and Family Court Department
FINANCIAL STATEMENT
(Short Form)

INSTRUCTIONS: If your income equals or exceeds $75,000 you must complete the LONG FORM financial statement, unless otherwise ordered by the court.

Jane E. Doe-Rayme　　　v.　　　**Jack T. Rayme**
Plaintiff/Petitioner　　　　　　　　Defendant/Petitioner

At the top left-hand side of the paper is a blank and the word "Division." Write the name of the county where you will be filing your divorce. On the top right-hand side is a words "Docket Number." No matter *which* state you file in, you will be assigned a docket number. This is the courts own tracking number to track all cases statewide. Leave this information blank as it's a number the court will assign once you file your divorce. The Docket Number is a code. It says what year your case was filed (12 = 2012), what courthouse it's in (D=Barnstable), which case number in that courthouse that year (number 9999), and what kind of case it is (DV = divorce).

Next are the blanks _____ v. _____ where you fill out the names of the Plaintiff and the Defendant. Since Jane will be the one filing this divorce, she has put her full legal name (i.e., Jane E. Doe-Rayme) in the blank which says "Plaintiff" and her husband's full legal name in the blank which says "Defendant" (Jack T. Rayme). It's important to put your full name as there may be a Jane B. Doe, Jane G. Doe, and a Jane F. Doe with divorces filed in the same courthouse.

---

1. PERSONAL INFORMATION

Your Name _Jane T. Doe-Rayme_____ Social Security No. _999-99-9999____
Address _100 Any Street, North Anytown, MA 02652_____
          (Street address)   (City/Town) (State) (Zip)
Telephone Number _(508) 867-5309_ Date of Birth _4/4/70_ No. of Children living with you _2_
Occupation _Registered Nurse___ Employer _Home Nurses-R-Us_____
Employer's Address _200 Commerce Lane, Big City, MA_____
          (Street address) (City/Town) (State) (Zip)
Telephone Number _(508)555-1212_ Do you have health insurance coverage? X Yes   No
If yes, name of health insurance provider _____Husbands' BC/BS_____

Personal Information tells the court where they can find you, at work or at home, and gives the judge important information about you family situation in a single glance.

Why do they ask for your social security number? The moment you get divorced, your tax status will change from 'married' to 'single.' This helps the court report this information to the proper state and federal tax authorities. Your spouse's attorney is also entitled to receive this information as, if they suspect you're hiding assets, they may run a credit and asset check on you to see if you're hiding anything. It's also a way for the court to dig up other information should the whim so hit them, such as digging up your prior criminal record, prior restraining orders, or reporting you to the IRS if the judge discovers you've been engaging in tax fraud for many years.

⚑ *Courts –do- report you to the IRS if they find out you've been evading paying taxes!!!*

⚑ *If the court has issued a court order impounding your address due to a restraining order, do not fill out your address on this form. Your spouse is entitled to receive a copy of this Financial Statement. Instead write 'address impounded' and speak to the clerk about giving them an address where you can be served paperwork directly from the court!*

The next question is whether or not you have health insurance. If you are currently covered under either yours or your husband's health insurance plan, check the Yes box and fill out the name of the health insurance provider and the policy number. If the insurance belongs to your spouse, write 'Husband's policy' next to this information. If you have none, write 'none.'

In Massachusetts, the court uses pink paper for these forms to help them pull them out of the case file if laypeople ask to read it because all court records are public information and this form includes your social security number. Find out if the courts in *your* state have a preferred color. They will *usually* accept it on plain white paper if you have no other choice, but you risk having your most intimate financial information inadvertently disclosed to the public by doing so.

2. **GROSS WEEKLY INCOME/RECEIPTS FROM ALL SOURCES**

a)	Base pay from ___ salary X wages	$ 445.00
b)	Overtime	$ 0.00
c)	Part-time job	$ 0.00
d)	Self-employment **(attach a completed schedule A)**	$ 0.00
e)	Tips	$ 0.00
f)	___ Commissions ___ Bonuses	$ 0.00
g)	___ Dividends ___ Interest	$ 0.00
h)	___ Trusts ___ Annuities	$ 0.00
i)	___ Pensions ___ Retirement funds	$ 0.00
j)	Social Security	$ 0.00
k)	___ Disability ___ Unemployment insurance ___ Worker's compensation	$ 0.00
l)	Public Assistance (welfare, A.F.D.C. payments)	$ 0.00
m)	X Child Support ___ Alimony (actually received)	$ 308.00
n)	Rental from income producing property **(attach a completed Schedule B)**	$ 0.00
o)	Royalties and other rights	$ 0.00
p)	Contributions from household member(s)	$ 0.00
q)	Other (specify)	
	_____	$ 0.00
	_____	$ 0.00
	r) **Total Gross Weekly Income/Receipts** (add items a-q)	$ 753.00

Gross Weekly Income asks what types of income you may receive, both earned (salary/wages), unearned (investments), and other forms of income such as child support, alimony and public assistance. Here in Massachusetts, the court asks you to break down all your income, expenses, and debt payments into *weekly* amounts (other states may differ). Read the form carefully and make sure you use the correct breakdown (weekly, monthly or annually).

A *salary* is a stable income you receive every week based on a specified annual base salary. For example, an administrative assistant might be contracted to earn $28,000 per year, payable once every two weeks at $538 per week. She might work late and earn overtime once in a while, but she knows, on average, she'll receive $538.

A *wage* is work you earn according to how many hours you put in. Some weeks you may earn more than others. An example of a wage-earner would be a waitress whose hours fluctuate according to season.

You can compute your 'true' averages as follows:

TABLE 4-1: GROSS WEEKLY INCOME CALCULATOR

How Often Paid		How to Compute
Weekly	=	Fill in "before tax" wages from your paycheck
Bi-weekly (every two weeks)	=	Divide "before tax" wages by 2. A good practice to note with an asterisk that you get paid bi-weekly.
Bi-monthly (twice per month)	=	Multiply "before tax" wages by 24, then divide by 52. It's good practice to note you get paid twice per month with an asterisk as the first thing your spouses' lawyer is going to do is look at your paycheck and assume you get paid weekly or bi-weekly.
Monthly	=	Multiply "before tax" wages by 12, then divide by 52.
Annually (once per year)	=	Divide by 52
Freak overtime and/or seasonal income	=	Divide your total gross W2 wages (including overtime) from you federal tax return by 52 weeks and note what you did using an asterisk

 Do not deliberately understate how much money you earn or things could go very badly in court! Once you lose a judges trust, your case is shot to hell.

What are you to do if you're a seasonal employee and happen to be in your 'busy' season when you file the financial statement? Or you have some other income situation which does not easily fit into the form? Add up all your money (for example, 'tips') for the entire year, divide that amount by 52 weeks, and then put *that* amount down on your financial statement. Hand-write an asterisk in easily legible ink (such as blue) and note a blurb along the lines of 'seasonal job from May 15 to September 15 … averaged annual average ÷ 52 weeks' or 'husband is 5 weeks behind on child support.' That way, the judge knows you're making every effort to be honest in your disclosure

---

3. ITEMIZED DEDUCTIONS FROM GROSS INCOME

a)	Federal income tax deductions (claiming __3__ exemptions)	$	35.60
b)	State income tax deductions (claiming __3__ exemptions)	$	22.25
c)	F.I.C.A. and Medicare	$	37.82
d)	Medical Insurance	$	0.00
e)	Union Dues	$	0.00
	f) Total Deductions (a through e)	$	95.67

4. ADJUSTED NET WEEKLY INCOME   2(r) minus 3(f) $ 657.33

Itemized Deductions - the court wants to know about your normal and routine payroll deductions to get an idea of how much money you *really* bring home. You can find these on your paystub if you receive a salary or wage. If you're self-employed, you're going to have to do a little archeological dig through last years' tax return and figure out how much you paid in federal, state, social security and Medicare taxes and divide that number by 52 weeks.

If you pay health insurance through some other method than payroll deduction (i.e., you pay it monthly yourself), multiply your monthly (or other periodic) premium to get your annual amount, and then divide it by 52 weeks. The same with union dues if you are self-employed and belong, for example, to the International Brotherhood of Electrical Workers and pay an annual membership fee.

Adjusted Net Weekly Income is simply your income after deducting taxes, health insurance and union dues.

5.	**OTHER DEDUCTIONS FROM SALARY/WAGES**		
a)	Credit Union ___ Loan repayment ___ Savings	$	0.00
b)	Savings	$	0.00
c)	Retirement	$	0.00
d)	Other-Specify (i.e., Child Support, Deferred Compensation or 401K) _____	$	0.00
	e) Total Deductions (a through d)	$	0.00
6.	**NET WEEKLY INCOME** 4 minus 5(e)	$	657.33
7.	**GROSS YEARLY INCOME FROM PRIOR YEAR** (attach copy of all W-2 and 1099 forms for prior year)	$	23,140.00
	No. of Years you have paid into Social Security __25__		

Other Deductions is where you document automatic payroll deductions, such as to a savings account or retirement plan. It is another tool for helping the court figure out where your money goes. Fill the information out using your paystub. If you get paid on a time period other than weekly (i.e., every other week) you will need to divide the amount so it comes out to the weekly amount. You'll notice that like most working mothers today, our hypothetical client, Jane Doe-Rayme doesn't have any extra money left over to save.

Net Weekly Income is the total Deductions from your Adjusted Weekly Income.

Gross Yearly Income from Prior Year – the court compares what you earned last year to what you're claiming right now. This lets the court know if you (or your spouse) are earning to your full potential, or if you may be understating your income to gain an unfair advantage over your spouse. You are expected to list your total income from all sources from last year. You *must* staple a copy of your 1099 or W-2s from last year.

> *Many men (especially self-employed men) try to avoid attaching their tax forms to their financial statement in order to avoid having their income attributed properly. Don't let him get away with it!*

It also asks how many years you've paid into Social Security. This section really isn't helpful for most modern women, who work part-time low-wage jobs while raising kids. It *looks* like you paid in the same number of years as your husband, but if you pull the social security retirement benefits statement I suggested in Chapter 3, you'll see you lag far behind your husband in retirement benefits.

8. WEEKLY EXPENSES

a)	Rent or Mortgage (PIT)	$ 542.00	l)	Life Insurance	$	0.00
b)	Homeowners/Tenant Insurance	$ 0.00	m)	Medical Insurance	$	0.00
c)	Maintenance and Repair	$ 0.00	n)	Uninsured Medicals	$	14.00
d)	Heat	$ 27.00	o)	Incidentals and Toiletries	$	10.00
e)	Electricity and/or Gas	$ 23.00	p)	Motor Vehicle Expenses	$	65.00
f)	Telephone	$ 24.00	q)	Motor Vehicle Payment	$	117.00
g)	Water/Sewer	$ 0.00	r)	Child Care	$	115.00
h)	Food	$ 75.00	s)	Other (explain	$	
i)	House Supplies	$ 5.00		Cable TV	$	18.00
j)	Laundry and Cleaning	$ 7.00			$	
k)	Clothing	$ 5.00				
			e) Total Weekly Expenses (a through s)		$	1052.00

Weekly Expenses - the court wants to know about your Weekly Expenses. Unfortunately, except to justify 'need' for alimony, your expenses generally will not get you more money. This section is more for the judge, or your husband's attorney, to scrutinize your living expenses and see if your stated income matches up with your real life living expenses (remember I warned you earlier not to understate your income?).

The court is used to thinking of income and expenses on a week to week basis. Unfortunately, most bills are paid by the month or even the year. How do convert your bills into accurate financial data the judge can understand?

TABLE 4-2: EXPENSE CONVERSION CHART

How Often Bill Paid		How to Compute
Weekly	=	Write amount down as is.
Bi-weekly (every two weeks)	=	Multiply the expense by 26 units. Then divide by 52 weeks.
Bi-monthly (twice per month)	=	Multiply by 24 units. Then divide total by 52 weeks.
Monthly	=	Multiply by 12 units. Then divide total by 52 weeks.
Annually (once per year)	=	Divide by 52 weeks.
Quarterly (four times per year)	=	Multiply by 4 units. Divide by 52 weeks.
Periodic expenses that add up (such as property taxes, water bills, or car repairs)	=	Add up your total expenses from last year. Divide the total by 52 weeks.

Weekly Expenses (or whatever number is assigned to Expenses in your state) are further explained below:

TABLE 4-3: BREAKDOWN OF EXPENSES

a)	Rent – Mortgage (PIT)	Write the *weekly* average you pay. (PIT) refers to "principal, interest and tax", so if your bank collects as part of your mortgage your town property taxes, just fill out your monthly payment on the form. If you pay monthly, you will need to divide that payment by 4.3. You may need to add several amounts together to get the total. If you pay your *own* property taxes, than you will need to look up how much you paid in property taxes total last year and divide that amount by 52.
b)	Homeowner's/ Tenant Insurance	Add up the policy premiums you paid (including interest, if applicable) over the past year, then divide it by 52.
c)	Maintenance and Repair	This refers to maintenance and repair on your home. Since most home repairs are sporadic, you want to figure out how much you pay on an average year for things such as painting your trim, repairing the roof, having an appliance repairman fix your dishwasher, etc. If you know you have a major repair coming up which shouldn't be put off, such as replacing that drippy roof, include the contractor's estimate. Then, divide the total amount for all repairs over the past year by 52 weeks. If you rent, unless maintenance is part of your rental agreement, write zero.
d)	Heat	Fill out how much you pay to heat your home per week and write the fuel source in the blank after Type. Since your fuel costs are probably high in the winter and low in the summer, you will need to figure out the total for the past year and divide it by 52. If you rent and heat is included as part of your rental agreement, note "included" under type and write zero.
e)	Electricity and/or Gas	If you use gas to heat your home, write your gas costs in the column above. If you use gas or liquid propane only to run your oven and hot water heater, include it here. As both can vary widely by season, add up the total years expenses and divide this by 52.
f)	Telephone	Include both your base land phone and cell phone here. If your husband has a separate cell phone with a completely separate cell phone bill (i.e., not one of those multi-phone family plans), exclude his personal phone. Otherwise, since most of these bills are multi-year contracts and you are probably going to be the one stuck with the same bill whether or not your spouse hands you back his phone, include it.
g)	Water/Sewer	You want to add up your total water and sewer bills from the town last year and divide this by 52. If you have a septic tank and regularly have it pumped as part of your maintenance plan, include that as well, but divide the annual amount by 52 weeks and note with an asterisk "includes septic maintenance."
h)	Food	How much you spend on average per week.
i)	House Supplies	The average you spend for house supplies such as toilet paper, Kleenex, plastic bags, bug spray, kitty litter, and whatnot. Don't include personal care items such as shampoo and razor blades.
j)	Laundry and Cleaning	This includes not only the cost of laundry detergent and bleach, but the cost you pay to go to a laundry mat and do your laundry if you don't own a machine. If you bought a machine on credit and are making a monthly payment include the weekly payment amount, but put an asterisk and note "includes monthly installment payment for washing machine and dryer."
k)	Clothing	How much you spend per year on shoes and clothing for yourself and your children, but do not include your husband. Add up your total costs per year and divide it by 52 weeks.
l)	Life Insurance	Fill out how much you spend per year for a life insurance policy for yourself and your children, but do not include your husband if he has a separate policy. Add up the annual cost and divide by 52.
m)	Medical Insurance	Write how much health insurance your family pays per week for a family plan, whether or not it is you or your spouse who pays the premium. If you also have a family dental plan or vision plan, include these amounts as well, but note with an asterisk "includes dental and vision insurance"

n)	Uninsured Medicals	Add up all of the medical bills, regular dental bills, co-pays, prescription medicine and co-pays, eyeglasses and eye exams, therapy sessions, chiropractors, orthodontic bills and similar expenses which were not covered under your health/medical/dental insurance policies and divide it by 52. If this expense is unusually high due to expenses such as extraordinary medical care or your kids braces, note it with an asterisk "includes child's braces."
o)	Incidentals and Toiletries	Things to make you and your children look pretty and smell nice, such as shampoo, makeup, soap, etc. Also non-prescription medication such as all the aspirin and antacids you buy to help you deal with your spouse. As there is usually no other place to list things such as haircuts, perms, or sculpted nails for you and your children, I have my clients include these here as well. I wouldn't mention unless directly asked that you get your hair set or nails done weekly as it will make you appear frivolous.
p)	Motor Vehicle Expenses	This includes your average weekly cost to purchase gas for your car as well as you annual maintenance costs such as changing the oil, rotating the tires, and repairs. It's also the most appropriate place to list your annual car insurance premium, including interest if applicable, but note with an asterisk "includes auto insurance." *Do not forget to add in the cost of your motor vehicle excise tax, license renewal fees, and registration fees.* If you are paying for your husband and/or teenaged children on your policy and/or paying for their cars, include that as well, but note such with an asterisk. However, if your spouse's policy is separate, do *not* include it.
q)	Motor Vehicle Loan Payment	This is for your motor vehicle loan payment (or lease payment), including interest, if applicable. If you have a lease agreement, there may have been an up-front cost you paid when you got the car within the past year in addition to your monthly payment which you should include (averaged over 52 weeks), or an excess mileage cost you paid at the end.
r)	Child Care	This includes your weekly daycare bill to work, for pre-school if you don't work but send your child there to socialize them (note "*preschool" if you don't work), and for extraordinary babysitting you may pay for on a regular basis to attend class or a support group. Average the cost over a year if sporadic. *If you have a quote of how much more it will cost once your spouse is out of the house but have not yet started, note it with an asterisk.*
s)	Other	This is where you list all the other expenses you incur over the course of a year and divide it into a weekly amount. If there are a lot of them, you should attach a separate piece of paper, list all the "Other" expenses, and then put the total in this column, noting with an asterisk "see addendum."

Be sure to include all those sporadic expenses in the "other" column most people lose track of, such as renewing your drivers' license, paying your life insurance premium, pumping out your septic tank or paying for your annual boiler maintenance. The idea is to add everything up to how much on average you pay per year then divide it into 52 weeks. If necessary, write in a footnote to 'other' and then staple an additional page to your financial statement listing unusual expenses. You do not need to, however, list every single expense. I ask clients to break down anything more than $15 per week.

9. COUNSEL FEES

a)	Retainer amount(s) paid to your attorney(s)	$	0.00
b)	Legal fees incurred, to date, against your retainer(s)	$	0.00
c)	Anticipated range of total legal expense to litigate this action	$ to $	Unknown

Counsel Fees is your chance to explain the $8,000 your husband is screaming you 'embezzled' from your joint marital savings account went to pay your attorneys' retainer to represent you there in court that day. The judge will be very happy you took money out of the savings account to hire an attorney instead of muddling your way through his courtroom pro se. Your husband will not.

It's also a chance for the judge to get an idea of how much of a time-consuming pain-in-the-neck your case is going to be based on how much your attorney asked for a retainer. Unfortunately for poor Jane Doe, she's broke. She doesn't have any money for a retainer, so she would write zero.

10. ASSETS (attach additional sheet if necessary)

a) Real Estate
Location _100 Any Street, Anytown, MA_
Title held in the name of _joint_
Fair Market Value $ _375,000_ - Mortgage $ _229,150_ = Equity $ 145850

b) Motor Vehicles
Location _Anytown, MA_
Fair Market Value $ _18,500_ - Motor Vehicle Loan $ _17,500_ = Equity $ 1,000
Fair Market Value $ _12,500_ - Motor Vehicle Loan $ _0_ = Equity $ 12,500

c) IRA, Keogh, Pension, Profit Sharing, Other Retirement Plans:
Financial Institution or Plan Name and Account Number
Merrily-Merrily Retirement $ 15,000
(IRA)
Vanguard (IRA) $ 2,500
$

d) Tax Deferred Annuity Plan(s) $ 0

e) Life Insurance: Present Cash Value $ 0

f) Savings & Check Accounts, Money Market Accounts, Certificates of Deposit-which are held individually, jointly, in the name of another person for your benefit, or held for the benefit of your minor child(ren):
Financial Institution or Plan Name and Account Number
Big Bank – Checking - 000010020345 $ 1,500
Son's UGTMA savings account (money gifted by grandmother) $ 6,000
$

g) Other (e.g. stocks, bonds, collections)
husband's power tools, trailer, 4-wheeler, boat, furniture, $ 17,000
collectible trains, etc. (see attached asset breakdown)
$

h) Total Assets (a through g) $ 202980

Assets is where you list your major assets. If you haven't had a chance to have a broker value your house, pencil in whatever the town says is the fair market value of your house and circle it so that you remember you still need a professional valuation. To get the present cash value of your life insurance, if a whole life policy and the surrender value is not listed, call your insurance company and ask. List all individual and joint bank accounts, stocks, whole life insurance, cars, and collectibles which are held either in your name alone or jointly with your spouse. Include bank accounts you set up for your children which are in your name, but note that it is held in trust for a child. List all of your motor vehicles, including motorcycles, mopeds, go-carts, snowmobiles, ski mobiles, boats, four wheelers, motor homes or travel trailers, boat or utility trailers, or other motorized, recreational, or utility vehicle you own which either has a motor or must be registered to go over the roads. Lastly, include in "Other" such assets as your husband's extensive tool collection (i.e., "power tools") or expensive toy train or coin collection.

11. LIABILITIES (Do not list expenses shown in item 8 above)				
	Creditor	Nature of Debt	Date Incurred	Amount Due	Weekly Payment
a)	See Addendum A	See Addendum A	See Addendum A	See Addendum A	See Addendum A
b)				$	$
c)				$	$
d)				$	$
e) Total Liabilities	*(transferred from Addendum A)*			$283,150	$582

Liabilities is where you list all liabilities, including your mortgage, car loan, credit card bills, personal loans, and other such bills. Since most American's live far beyond their means, you will probably have far more debt than the four spots allocated on the financial statement. If that's the case, note "See Addendum" in lines a-d, fold a plain sheet of paper into five columns and write the same captions at the top of each column as are listed on the financial statement, and list all of your debts. Note that Jane's mortgage payment is essentially listed twice, once under 'Expenses' and a second time under 'Liabilities.' Fill out your court financial statement literally. What's important is to not count information twice in the same *section* as that is how judges interpret information. If you're worried about the judge misconstruing your financial information, hand-write an asterisk and add a footnote.

ADDENDUM A TO WIFE'S FINANCIAL STATEMENT				
	Creditor	Nature of Debt	Date Incurred	Amount Due	Weekly Payment
a)	Big Mortgage	Mortgage	2001	200,000.00	300
b)	Little Bank	Home Equity Loan	2006	29,150.00	60
c)	Big Bank Card	Credit Card	Ongoing	$7,000	55
d)	City Smitty Card	Credit Card	Ongoing	$3,000	$22
	Dr. Orthodontist	Sons braces	2012	$4,500	$11
	Nurses University	Wife's student loan	2000	$2,000	$24.00
	XYZ HVAC repair	Loan to replace boiler	2011	$5,000	$10.00
	Learn'M Tutors	Daughters out-standing tutoring bill	2011	$15,000	$25.00
	Car Loan Central	Car loan – H's truck	2008	17,500	75.00
e) Total Liabilities	*(transferred from Addendum A)*			$283,150	$582

Addendum (optional) – If you have more debts than will fit in the official Liabilities (or any other) section, attach an extra piece of paper with expenses broken down exactly as was done in the section before. Include any debt which you are aware of which is in your name only, jointly, or in your spouse's name which you are partially responsible for incurring (i.e., a credit card for which you are an "authorized user" or an orthodontist bill for your children which comes in your husband's name, but is for your children). The financial statement seeks to ascertain both your total indebtedness and the minimum weekly payment you must make to remain current on each bill, so you will need to divide your payments into a weekly amount using Table A.

CERTIFICATION

I certify under the penalties of perjury that the information stated on this Financial Statement and the attached schedules, if any, is complete, true and accurate.

Date_____   Signature_____*Jane Doe*_____

The *Certification* states the financial statement is accurate to the best of your knowledge and that you're signing it under the pains and penalties of perjury. In other words, you understand if you lie or omit something deliberately, you will be going to jail. Don't assume you can lie and get away with it! I *have* seen judges report litigants to the district attorneys' office for prosecution! Sign and date it.

CHAPTER 4 SUMMARY

1. If you fill out your own official state-court financial statement before ever going to see an attorney, you'll save yourself at least $50.

2. You must disclose all income, assets and expenses as honestly as possible or you are committing a crime called perjury which could cause the court to send you to jail. Once you lose the trust of a judge, he's going to make your divorce a living hell.

3. The court is used to thinking of finances on a week-by-week basis. If you get paid on a schedule *other* than weekly, you'll need to do a little math to average your costs and income over the course of one year and then divide that number by 52 weeks.

4. Monthly expenses such as your mortgage payment or electric bill should be divided by 4.3 weeks because there are 30 days in a month (4.3 weeks). Not just 4 as people tend to think.

5. The courts' financial statement is a wonderful financial planning tool in its own right. We'll look at how to use this tool to help you bring your budget in line with your expenses in Chapter Eight.

6. This Bootcamp Manual has a 50-state listing of state-court sponsored websites to download official forms in Chapter Nine.

CHAPTER 5

CHILD SUPPORT

Nine times out of ten, an enemy has been destroyed
because his supply lines were severed.

General Douglas MacArthur, August 1950 to the Joint Chiefs of Staff

Child Support Guidelines are a mathematical formula set by your state legislature to determine how much your husband should contribute to support his children. Although *amount* varies slightly from state to state, *obtaining* and *enforcing* a court order is fairly uniform due to federal mandates. Judges are required to apply the Guidelines when determining child support and must make written findings explaining why the Guidelines shouldn't apply if they vary by more than 10%. Judges don't like doing this because it's a lot of work. Unless you have an unusual situation there's a good chance you can figure out approximately how much child support you can count on *before* you file for divorce.

Finding this magical number is easy. A rough rule of thumb is the government will make him pay approximately 25% of his *before tax* income as child support for a family with two (2) children.

$_____$ (H's income) x .25 = $_____$ (rough guesstimate)

In this chapter I'll explain what happens in Massachusetts, since that's where I'm licensed to practice law. However, why *guess* how much you're entitled to receive or pay an attorney $300 an hour to guess this rough number for you when obtaining the actual amount is so easy?

A wise woodland creature doesn't pay a lawyer for information they can get for free!

Go to your state's official Child Support Guidelines website, click on the link that brings you to whatever worksheet your state uses to calculate child support, plug in your financial information, and compute your number. Some states make you download a .pdf packet, manually do the math and look up the number on a chart. Others have interactive websites that do the math for you.

A 50-state listing of websites follows. It will probably be easier to type "X-State Child Support Guidelines" into your internet browser than manually type these URL's. Compare the website I recommend with what comes up so you go to the correct one so you're not giving away your social security number to some identity thief in Nigeria.

"_____(State Name)_____ Child Support Guidelines"

Always be careful when using a website that is not an official government website!!! Government websites usually end in .gov or .us. Not only could a private website's information be out-of-date, but they may request personal information which could be used to steal your identity … such as your social security number. Always go to the source!!!

TABLE 5-1: 50-STATE LISTING OF CHILD SUPPORT WEBSITES

State	Official Child Support Website
Alllaw.com *Caveat!	http://www.alllaw.com/calculators/childsupport *Private* portal that will automatically calculate a rough number for you for all states. Does not ask for personal information, but might *not* be current if your state had a recent update.
Alabama	http://www.alacourt.gov/ChildSupportInfo.aspx
Alaska	http://www.alacourt.gov/ChildSupportInfo.aspx
Arizona	http://www.azcourts.gov/familylaw/ArizonaChildSupportGuidelines.aspx
Arkansas	https://courts.arkansas.gov/aoc/acs_guidelines.cfm
California	http://www.childsup.ca.gov/Default.aspx
Colorado	https://childsupport.state.co.us/siteuser/do/vfs/Frag?file=/cm:home.jsp
Connecticut	http://www.jud.ct.gov/Publications/ChildSupport/2005csguidelines.pdf
Delaware	http://courts.delaware.gov/SupportCalculator
District of Columbia	http://csgc.oag.dc.gov/application/main/intro.aspx
Florida	http://dor.myflorida.com/dor/childsupport/guidelines.html
Georgia	http://www.georgiacourts.gov/csc
Hawaii	http://hawaii.gov/jud/childpp.htm
Idaho	http://www.isc.idaho.gov/icsg_cov.htm
Illinois	http://www.childsupportillinois.com/general/calculating.html
Indiana	http://mycourts.in.gov/csc/parents
Iowa	https://secureapp.dhs.state.ia.us/childsupport/changechildsupport/asppages/CSChdEst.asp
Kansas	http://www.kscourts.org/rules-procedures-forms/child-support-guidelines/default.asp
Kentucky	http://chfs.ky.gov/dis/cse.htm
Louisiana	http://www.dss.louisiana.gov/index.cfm?md=pagebuilder&tmp=home&nid=150&pnid=0&pid=137
Maine	http://www.ptla.org/calculating-your-child-support *Pine Tree Legal Assistance website

Maryland	http://www.dhr.state.md.us/CSOCGuide/App/disclaimer.do
Massachusetts	https://wfb.dor.state.ma.us/DORCommon/Worksheets/CSE/Guidelines.aspx
Michigan	http://courts.michigan.gov/scao/services/focb/mcsf.htm
Minnesota	http://www.childsupport.dhs.state.mn.us/Action/Welcome
Mississippi	http://www.mdhs.state.ms.us/csemdhs.html
Missouri	http://www.dss.mo.gov/cse
Montana	http://www.dphhs.mt.gov/csed/packet/guidelines.shtml
Nebraska	http://www.supremecourt.ne.gov/forms/supreme-court-child-support-forms.shtml
Nevada	https://dwss.nv.gov/index.php?option=com_content&task=view&id=56&Itemid=129
New Hampshire	http://www.dhhs.nh.gov/dcss/calculator.htm
New Jersey	http://www.judiciary.state.nj.us/csguide/index.htm
New Mexico	http://www.hsd.state.nm.us/csed/guidelines.html
New York	http://www.nyc.gov/html/hra/html/directory/child_support_calculator.shtml
North Carolina	http://www.state.sc.us/dss/csed/calculator.htm
North Dakota	http://www.ndcourts.gov/chldspt
Ohio	http://www.franklincountyohio.gov/commissioners/csea/pdf/CSX2-10.pdf
Oklahoma	http://www.okdhs.org/onlineservices/cscalc
Oregon	http://www.oregonchildsupport.gov/calculator/index.shtml
Pennsylvania	https://www.humanservices.state.pa.us/csws/home_controller.aspx
Rhode Island	http://www.cse.ri.gov
South Carolina	http://www.state.sc.us/dss/csed/calculator.htm
South Dakota	http://dss.sd.gov/childsupport/services/obligationcalculator.asp
Tennessee	http://www.tn.gov/humanserv/is/isdownloads.html
Texas	https://www.oag.state.tx.us/cs/index.shtml
Utah	http://www.utcourts.gov/childsupport/calculator
Vermont	http://dcf.vermont.gov/ocs/parents/guidelines_calculator
Virginia	http://www.dss.virginia.gov/family/dcse_calc_intro.html
Washington state	https://fortress.wa.gov/dshs/csips/ssgen
West Virginia	http://www.legis.state.wv.us/wvcode/code.cfm?chap=48&art=13
Wisconsin	http://dcf.wi.gov/bcs/guidelines_tools.htm
Wyoming	http://dfsweb.state.wy.us/child-support-enforcement/index.html

Child Support Guidelines don't vary much from state to state, but how states apply them to different situations (sole custody, shared custody, etc.) *does* differ. Read the explanations available on your state's website so you know what to expect. Or … make an appointment to go speak to a local attorney.

Each state assigns Child Support collection and enforcement to a state agency whose job it is to help you chase down your deadbeat ex-husband if he doesn't pay. In most states, the collecting agency is the Department of Children and Families, but other states (such as Massachusetts) collect the money directly through their state Department of Revenue, the courts, or another agency. Find out who'll be doing your collecting for you and get to know them. They're going to be your business partner for a long time.

WHO IS OBLIGATED TO PAY CHILD SUPPORT?

Both parents must contribute to the support of their un-emancipated offspring. If one parent assumes primary custody of the child (i.e., your child lives with you approximately 70% or more of the time), the court understands *somebody* needs to be home to get your kids off the bus. This limits your career choices and means you can't work overtime to meet budget shortfalls. Therefore, the non-custodial parent will be obligated to contribute some percentage of their income towards their child's support.

If you are *not* the biological parent and did *not* legally adopt your partner's child, generally you will *not* be obligated to pay child support.

HOW LONG CAN I EXPECT TO COLLECT (OR PAY) CHILD SUPPORT?

You must support your child until they become emancipated. *Emancipated* means different things in different states. From a non-divorce standpoint, the day your child turns 18 years old, he's legally considered an adult. He can join the Army, sign a contract, and move out of the house if he so chooses. However, since most children turn 18 while still in high school, states extend that period of time until your child graduates from high school (or drops out).

*Emancipated* means your child is no longer legally dependent upon you for support.

What happens after your child graduates high school varies by state. Approximately 2/3 of states believe the day Little Susie flips the tassle on her high school graduation cap, you're both done. Little Susie is perfectly capable of getting a job and making her own way through the world. As of the time of writing, the following states tell your kids 'sayonara:'

TABLE 5-2: STATES THAT CUT SUPPORT OFF UPON GRADUATING HIGH SCHOOL

Arizona	Kentucky	New Jersey	Tennessee (sometimes)
Arkansas	Louisiana	New Mexico	Utah
California	Maine	North Carolina	Vermont
Colorado	Maryland	North Dakota	Virginia
Delaware	Minnesota	Ohio	West Virginia
Florida	Mississippi	Oklahoma	Wisconsin
Georgia	Montana	Pennsylvania	Wyoming
Idaho	Nebraska	Rhode Island	
Kansas	Nevada	South Dakota	

The other 1/3 of states feel Little Johnnie couldn't *possibly* get a job without first going to college, so they prolong the period of time parents are obligated to support him until he graduates a four-year college *or* turns 23. Whichever happens first. Should Little Johnnie graduate high school and get a job, the obligation to support him ends. However, should Little Johnnie decide to go to college, you will both need to keep supporting him. Even if he decides a degree in fine arts is the career path he wishes to take and you do not agree that is a productive investment of $60,000 per year in tuition, but your husband thinks it's just nifty.

⚑ *When your child goes off to college, your child support will be adjusted downwards to account for any tuition your husband pays directly to the college. Plan accordingly.*

TABLE 5-3: STATES THAT CONTINUE CHILD SUPPORT THROUGH COLLEGE

Alabama	Illinois	Missouri	South Carolina
Alaska	Indiana	New Hampshire	Tennessee* (sometimes)
Connecticut	Iowa	New York	Texas
District of Columbia	Massachusetts	Oregon	Washington
Hawaii	Michigan		

Here in Massachusetts, we take the latter view. Our economy is based on technology. Technology jobs require diplomas and judges are overwhelmingly in favor of forcing *both* parents to encourage their children's college aspirations. *Your* state may differ. To find out for certain, browse your state Child Support website. Failing that, speak to an attorney.

🦨 *If you have a child with special needs, most states have exceptions to hard cutoff dates. These exceptions are too varied to cover in this book. Consult a local attorney, PAC, or special needs advocate.*

JANE DOE-RAYME HYPOTHETICAL CHILD SUPPORT GUIDELINES

Remember our heroine, Jane Doe? Jane gathered her acorns in Chapter 3 and knows how much money she and her soon-to-be ex-husband, Jack, earn. She went online to her state's official Child Support website and located their child support guidelines calculator.

Jane is lucky she lives in Massachusetts, where the government figured out if they invest money in creating easy-to-use self-help forms, ordinary people will *use* those forms and save the taxpayers lots of money by not clogging up the courts with stupid questions. Using the information from the financial statement Jane created in Chapter Four, Jane now plugs in the numbers.

EXAMPLE 5-1: JANE DOE ONLINE CHILD SUPPORT CALCULATOR

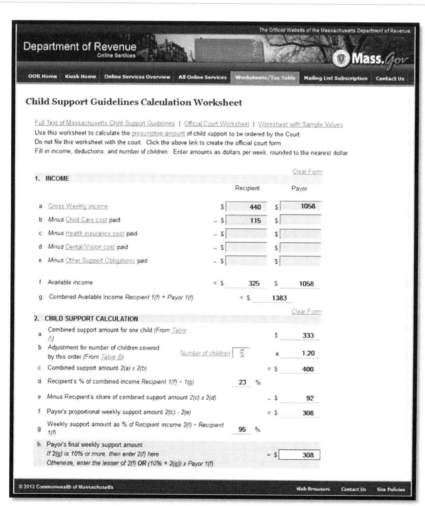

If your state doesn't have a fill-in-the-blank calculator, bribe a friend who's good at math to help you compute your anticipated child support order. It's coffee for your friend or $300 an hour for an attorney? Personally, I'd rather save money for when I –really- need an attorney's advice, plowing through that byzantine draft Separation Agreement you just negotiated in mediation and figuring out if it says what you think it says!

YOU WANT ME TO SUPPORT MY KIDS ON *WHAT*???

If you just did what you were supposed to do (go to your state Child Support Guidelines website and compute your estimated child support), you're probably pulling out your hair. Good... Do your screaming at home, where it's not going to cost you $300 an hour to rant. If you *didn't* compute your state estimate, stop! Go back, find your state's official website, and compute *your* estimated Child Support order.

Child support formulas are deeply flawed. Although they provide a reasonably fair assessment to a family comprised of *two* middle-class wage earners *each* earning above the national median income of $46,000+ per year from traditional 9 to 5 salaried jobs with health, retirement, pre-tax flexible child care spending account benefits and children ranging from age 6 to age 18 in a school system that doesn't nickel-and-dime the parents, as soon as you start deviating from that assumption, things get skewed. Try explaining to a government official that half of the population lives on *less* than $46,000 per year! They can't comprehend the problem of *one* person living on less money than that, much less support little human beings who need food, medical treatment, and can't simply be locked in a closet while you work overtime to pay your expenses! For all the Fathers' Rights movements yowling against child support, the fact is, the modest percentage of their paycheck which goes to supporting their children is usually far *less* than their share to actually *raise* them. *You* are forced to make up the difference.

Unfortunately, there's nothing any lawyer can do to help you solve this problem. We're part of that top tier of wage-earners who are too retarded to fathom what it's like to get by on $46,000 per year, never mind *less* than that. Our idea of pinching pennies is to forego a *second* trip to Europe this year. There's nothing you can do to fix the formula for your own purposes today, but *please write your state Congressmen and complain!*

MY HUSBAND HAS KIDS FROM A PRIOR RELATIONSHIP

If your spouse has children from a previous marriage and the first ex-wife already has court-ordered child support, ex-wife #1 is entitled to collect child support from your husband's income before ex-wife #2. Since the court can't legally take more than 50% of your husband's salary no matter *how* many 'litters' of unwanted offspring he's sired, this leaves you with whatever crumbs are left over. If your spouse has other kids lurking in the picture, be prepared to get the short end of the stick. Here's how to estimate the impact on what *you're* entitled to receive:

EXAMPLE 5-2: HYPOTHETICAL PRIOR FAMILIES CHILD SUPPORT REDUCTION

Husband's Weekly Gross Income:	$1,058
50% of that amount:	$529
First wife's child support order (2 kids)	$308
Amount available to pay you:	$221
What *would* be your child support order (2 kids)	$308
Reduction due to prior orders ($308 – $221)	-$87
Amount you'll *actually* receive	$221

SNEAKY TRICKS YOUR HUSBAND USES TO HIDE MONEY

As if the news the government is clueless about how much it costs to raise a child isn't gloomy enough, now comes the *truly* fun part. Your ex-husband thinks *you* should support them because, after all, you just 'took everything,' greedy little witch that you are, and only collect child support to buy Louboutins, eat caviar, and take expensive vacations to Hawaii. Therefore, he's going to do everything possible to minimize, disguise, or outright *lie* about his income so he doesn't have to pay you.

Outlined below are ways I've seen non-custodial parents hide money. It's up to *you* to prove how much money your spouse *really* earns, including business expenses, under-the-table side jobs, and the cash value of bartering he does to reduce his living expenses. Document every penny he makes, whether cash or non-cash, so you can get as much child support as possible to meet your children's needs.

1. LEGITIMATE BUSINESS EXPENSES WHICH SHOULD COUNT FOR CHILD SUPPORT PURPOSES: The IRS allows small business owners to deduct many expenses, such as a home office, business use of a car, and depreciation for assets which are still functional. However, what is perfectly legal for *tax* purposes is supposed to be included for *child support*. Examine the last three years of Schedule C's and search for line items to point out to the judge that you think should be added back in. There's a helpful trade manual published by James Publishing called *The Determination of Income for Child Support,"* by forensic accountant Nicholas L. Bourdeau, which you may be able to borrow through inter-library loan.

2. THE MYSTERIOUS SUDDEN DROP IN INCOME: The moment you file for divorce, your husband will suddenly lose his job or take a cut in hours. The onus is on *you* to demonstrate your family relied on overtime to meet your expenses over the years or he *chose* to voluntarily quit his job. Use past tax returns (three years is best) to show how much should be added back into the bottom line. If the judge isn't receptive to your argument that the job loss was voluntary, request he order your husband to conduct a job search and report to the probation department weekly until he finds a *new* job.

Spouses Behaving Badly: A client came to me after she'd gotten a restraining order and court-ordered child support to get a divorce. Three days before the hearing, the husband filed a motion requesting elimination of child support because he'd been fired from *both* of his jobs. I subpoenaed business records from both former employers showing the reason he'd stopped showing up for work the day the restraining order was issued. The secretary at one of those jobs provided a witness affidavit stating when she'd called the husband to inquire if he was ill, he'd screamed into the phone, "I'm not going to work to support my #@¢β-ing ex-wife!"

3. USING PAY STUBS FROM THE SLOW SEASON: If your husband is self-employed, he may attempt to use a lowball earnings estimate from the slow season (such as the dead of winter here in tourist-driven Cape Cod) as his average paycheck. Obtain copies of the last three years IRS Schedule C and bring them to court. If you point out his total annual income, you can usually get the judge to use *average* income, not last week's.

4. UNDER-REPORTED TIP INCOME OR CASH BONUSES: If your husband works at a job that

depends heavily on tips, such as a waiter, bartender, or hair stylist, his tip income probably far exceeds his salary. Large employers usually pool tips and divide them amongst their staff, issuing a tax report, or report bonuses issued to the IRS, but many smaller businesses do not. It's up to *you* to do an archeological dig through your household living expenses and show the math doesn't add up unless you add in all those cash deposits into your checking account or cash-receipts for goods.

5. DEMANDING TO BE PAID IN CASH THE MOMENT YOU FILE FOR DIVORCE: Another trick self-employed persons do is stop including cash income in their business records and use the last few months of income (not including cash) as their base child support income. The last three years of tax returns can act as a baseline for the court, but it's helpful to subpoena in their checkbook register and demonstrate that, somehow, while he had no income coming in, he wrote large checks to his suppliers for jobs he was supposedly *not* doing. We'll cover how to obtain records in Chapter Fifteen: Discovery and how to subpoena other documents in Chapter Seventeen: Preparing for Trial.

Spouses Behaving Badly: A self-employed general contractor claimed he'd only been earning $7,000 per year for many years. Just before things went to hell in a hand basket, his wife went into his business safe, photographed $11,000 cash he had in there, the outside of each envelope listing which 'job' it was from and receipts from suppliers, and then counted and photographed how much money was in each envelope. Her photographs were a game-changer. I pulled them out and asked the opposing attorney if he *really* wanted me to put my client on the witness stand to testify about how much cash the husband *really* earned in front of a judge known for reporting tax cheats to the IRS.

6. UNDER-THE-TABLE SIDE JOBS: If your spouse does "side-jobs" such as helping his carpenter brother every other weekend or fixing cars in your garage, you'll need to do some legwork. Photograph him carrying a ladder or other tools of the trade onto a jobsite or the mini auto repair shop set up in your garage. Comb through past bank records, circling deposits he made from these cash side jobs. Gather the past years' worth of bills and receipts (including cash purchases if you saved them), put it in a spreadsheet, and show the judge the math doesn't work unless you account for the $150 per week your husband earns doing side jobs.

Spouses Behaving Badly: A client's husband worked for a local gas station pumping gas and doing auto vehicle inspections at a modest salary. He also did under-the-table 'side jobs' for that same gas station repairing the cars that failed inspection, which was the bulk of his *real* income. The client gathered up their household checkbook register, credit card bills, and receipts and convinced the judge what the husband's real income should be.

Judges tend to be more amenable to adding side-job income if you can't meet your basic living expenses and/or your husband works less than 40 hours per week. If he took the time and effort he puts into moonlighting and worked an above-the-table second job, he'd have more money to support his children. Go to your state Department of Employment Security website, find out how much an entry-level car mechanic or handyman (whatever his "hobby") earns, multiply it by the number of hours he usually moonlights, and put that figure before the court.

7. BARTERING: If your spouse barters to offset expenses or procure certain goodies, it's up to *you* to prove how much, on average, your husband increases his buying power. For example, if your husband is a web designer who earns 80% of his income through his job, but consistently earns another 20% by trading web design services to get things he needs, such as his car repaired, the roof fixed on your house, or gift certificates to restaurants, that 20% extra is 'income' for child support purposes. You will need to piece together evidence to show barter is a consistent source of income and not simply a one-time exchange.

Spouses Behaving Badly: A self-employed contractor husband requested a reduction in child support claiming he couldn't find work. An examination of his Financial Statement showed his living expenses, especially his rent, far exceeded his claimed income. Under cross-examination, the husband admitted he'd been making repairs on the rented home in exchange for living there for free. The judge added the fair market value of that rental into his base income for child support calculation purposes.

8. "GOING UNDERGROUND": Having tangled with the so-called "Fathers' Rights" (a.k.a. batterers' rights) movement, I learned a great deal about their favorite method of avoiding child support. They call it "going underground." The scenario goes something like this. Mr. Wifebeater smacks his wife around, she gets a restraining order, and subsequently files for divorce. After being dragged back to court a few times for contempt because he didn't pay his child support, the judge gives the dreaded speech (known by lawyers as "*THE* speech") where he tells the husband he has until 3:00 that day to come up with the money or he's going to be taken into custody. Either the husband pays, pays part and promises to pay the rest next week, or goes to jail for a few days, but the moment he's out of jail, he disappears.

Not only does the batterers' rights movement teach members to "go underground" and promote it on their websites, but they have set up entire networks of employers willing to pay them under the table and people willing to help them cash checks and pay their living expenses without ever leaving a paper trial for the collective state Child Support Enforcement Bureaus (who cooperate through federal databases designed for this purpose) to pick up on during one of their broad nationwide computer dragnets.

Your lousy no-good lout doesn't have to belong to one of these groups to pick up this dirty trick. If he works at a cash business (such as contractor or tradesman such as a plumber), he can throw his tools into the back of his pickup truck and relocate to another state with no forwarding address. *Good luck* hunting him down!

9. FUNNELING HOUSEHOLD EXPENSES THROUGH THE BUSINESS ACCOUNTS: Some small business owners funnel household expenses through their business accounts. I'm not talking about *legal* deductions allowed by the IRS which you can get a court to add back in, but those deductions which go beyond legal into outright tax fraud.

Spouses Behaving Badly: A small business owner wrote off every can of coffee, cream, and sugar as a business expense. Her husband pointed out these expenses were written off on 100% of their household food receipts (he had the receipts) and the amount matched the Wife's Schedule C. He got the judge to add 30% of that business expense back into the marital kitty (around $1500). Using the mileage estimator on Mapquest and mileage claimed on her Schedule C, he showed the wife claimed the 90-mile commute from their house to her business as a business expense (around $8,500). She stored inventory at the house and wrote off 1/6th of their household overhead as a business expense, but the husband brought in photographs and blueprints to show the 'room' was a 3'x6' closet which took up 1/17th of their floor space. He went through her business credit card and store invoices and matched up charges for items paid for by the business that had been gifts for the wife's mother and sister. He went through her business checkbook register and testified one of the cell phones written off as a business expense was used by the children. Going down the Schedule C, he got the judge to add $16,000 back into the wife's income and reduced his child support by $60 per week.

10. SHACKING UP WITH PARENTS OR A NEW GIRLFRIEND: If your husband lives rent-free or

pays far below the market rate because he lives with his new girlfriend or parents, document the average cost of renting a similar room in your area (newspaper ads are good) and ask the judge to 'attribute' that as income. Not all judges will go for this, but some will if your ability to work is hampered by small children. You can't take your three kids and go couch-surfing if you can't make your rent or mortgage payment, but your single husband can.

11. THE CHRONICALLY UNEMPLOYED OR UNDER-EMPLOYED HUSBAND: Unlike a husband who suddenly stops working, what are you supposed to do if your husband has chronically failed to provide for your family, getting fired from every job he's ever had, quitting as soon as he

has a disagreement with his boss, or is just too lazy to look for one? Or what if he chooses to work part-time, a few days a week, so he can pursue some more interesting hobby such as his art or bird watching? When computing child support, barring disability or reaching the full social security retirement age, the court assumes both parties are capable of working 40 hours per week. If you have pay stubs from a period of time when he *was* working and can convince the court he's *capable* of working, the judge can base his child support obligation on a 40-hour workweek.

12. A LONG TERM PATTERN OF LYING ABOUT HIS INCOME TO THE IRS: If your husband is self-employed and you suspect he doesn't claim all the money he earns on your tax returns, you can often show your spouse earns more. Many self-employed business owners are not smart about hiding cash earnings from scrutiny. Subpoena his business records to the courthouse the day of the hearing (Chapter Seventeen) or obtain them through a discovery request (Chapter Fourteen). Red flags are lots of questionable deductions, charges on your credit cards to pay for items for the house which he deducted as a business expense, or expenses exceeding what he claims he earns.

Spouses Behaving Badly: A client had an electrician husband. The client honestly believed her husband when he told her he only earned $9,000 per year. This didn't ring true as it just so happened my cousin had paid him $6,000 a few weeks earlier for a few days' work. I asked a contractor friend if *they'd* ever used him and learned he'd subcontracted four $12,000-$15,000 jobs in the past year. Doing a little more investigation, we estimated he pulled in $250,000 per year under-the-table after legitimate business expenses. Enough to justify referring the wife to a 'bigger gun' at a downtown law firm with an army of accountants on staff to crawl up his rectum with a microscope.

You'll often need to hire an accountant as an expert witness to prove your husband is hiding money. If he's hiding a *lot* of money, this might be worth your while, but your best bet is to gather your *own* evidence as the clients above did and use *that* to slam him in court. But don't count on the judge giving your evidence the same weight that you do. If it's a lot of money and you need it to survive, talk to an attorney. A good doctor knows when a specialized surgery is beyond his training and makes a referral to a specialist, and a wise little woodland creature knows when to get someone else to spring the steel trap.

THE BURDEN OF PROOF IS ON *YOU* TO SHOW HOW MUCH HE REALLY EARNS

The court assumes your husband is telling the truth unless *you* prove otherwise. It's not enough to claim he earns more. You must *prove* he earns more. It's up to *you* to assert a bigger income should be attributed for child support purposes. *You* must comb through his business records, tax returns, bills and receipts and lay them out in an organized, logical way to support your claims. *You* must document (with photographs, witness testimony, business records, and invoices) how much he really earns. The judge isn't going *believe* your husband earns more simply because you need more, nor does he have time to do your archeological dig *for* you. You must *prove* it by a preponderance of the evidence and *disprove* any lame excuses he makes about why his income is suspiciously low.

BEWARE THE IRS

If your husband has been lying about his income on your joint tax return and you've been signing it, the IRS could come after *you* to pay his past-due taxes. There's no such thing as an innocent spouse exception for husbands who evade paying their taxes. Judges are forever having to cut their courts' budget because the legislature says the taxpayers are out of money. They enjoy nothing better than reporting a scumbag like your husband to the IRS. If you suspect this is the case, consult with an attorney and ask them to include proper tax indemnification verbiage in your Separation Agreement (covered in Chapter 11) to cover your backside if the IRS shows up at your door. It won't spare you an audit. But it will give you recourse to haul him back into court and reimburse you if the IRS comes after you.

Sympathy for your self-employed husband is rampant. No matter how many times I explain the homemaker wife simply cannot *afford* to pay $5,000 for a forensic accountant to come to court as an expert witness to prove her husband is a rampant tax evader, getting a judge to look at a balance sheet and do a simple math equation to see things don't add up can be like pulling teeth. If judges wanted to do math, they'd have gone to MIT and become engineers. You tear out your hair and cry "he earns more!" Your husband waves his hands and cries "the economy stinks!" The judge, often being a man,

 believes your husband despite evidence to the contrary. Lowball child support orders happen. You need to go into court prepared to *overwhelmingly* prove your husband isn't really out of work or you may get a disappointing result.

To prove your case, you must photograph your husband working at numerous jobsites over a lengthy period of time, subpoena in customers to testify about how much they paid him, and show numerous discrepancies about how much money he spends versus what he claims he earns. Most cases I win through investigation *aren't* because the judge believed my client, but because my client's husband didn't want to risk getting nailed for perjury or tax fraud after we photographed him in the act and his lawyer made him file an honest financial statement.

If you know who his suppliers are (restaurant supply warehouses, lumberyards, etc.), you can subpoena in their records of sales to give a rough estimate of his income based upon how many pounds of beef or sets of kitchen cabinets he's purchased. However, be warned suppliers are tight-lipped about their customers. Getting information out of them will be like pulling teeth. Many customers pay cash and leave no record at all.

Spouses Behaving Badly: I had a case where the *only* issue at trial was whether or not the husband was still working as a general contractor. A few weeks before each hearing, the husband would get a minimum wage job then quit as soon as the hearing was over. This happened 5 times over the course of the yearlong divorce. The day of trial, the idiot showed up at the courthouse with his 20 foot construction trailer, tools and all, attached to his pickup truck and parked it in the grass median strip of the courthouse parking lot. It was clearly visible from the courtroom. When I asked him about it during cross-examination, he said he figured he'd go back to his house after the trial and do some work on it.

Say what?

He's unemployed. He no longer owns a business. The truck and trailer are garaged at his house. He rolled out of bed the morning of his divorce trial, where the only issue in dispute was whether or not he was still working as a self-employed general contractor, and decided to hook up his 20 foot construction trailer to go for a ride? We're not talking about taking the *dog* for a ride here! He took his construction trailer for a ride. The judge only attributed another $2,600 per year to the guy for income, not the $80,000 per year we had evidence indicating he earned! These are the kinds of outcomes that leave lawyers banging their heads against the walls going "W-H-AT did I FAIL to MAKE the judge *SEE...*" until they pass out from loss of blood.

 *As a humorous side-note, his lawyer disappeared with him after the trial. I overheard one bailiff comment to another bailiff that his attorney had dragged him out into the back alley of the courthouse to beat the crap out of him ...*

Don't let this discourage you from documenting your husband's surreptitious behavior. Think of each failed attempt as a feather on the scale of your husband's credibility. Picture a down comforter. Is it light? No. A single feather has little weight, but a bunch of them add up to keep you toasty warm. When you ask the judge to attribute extra income to your husband, you're asking him to do extra work making written findings as to why he thinks your husband lied and the child support guidelines shouldn't apply. If the judge doesn't have something *concrete* to write about, he's not going to do something your husband's lawyer could overturn on appeal. Many times, even if the judge doesn't have enough hard evidence to help you in *one* area, he'll find some *other* area where he has more discretion to rule in your favor.

If your husband is less than credible, it's worth the effort to educate the judge. For every bad decision, I've had judges turn around and order more than my client could have dreamed possible. Even if you don't get everything you deserve, $50 extra per week translates into $2600 extra dollars per year, every year, until your child turns 18 (or graduates college), potentially tens of thousands of dollars over time. Always make the effort to ensure your children receive every penny of support they are entitled to receive!

HIDING MONEY: ACT 1 - HOW TO SPOT B.S. IN A FINANCIAL STATEMENT

One way self-represented women often fall flat during a hearing to set child support or alimony is they aren't familiar with ways to ferret out b.s. (bull$#!T) in a Financial Statement to show your husband is *really* earning more money than he claims. However, if you point out inconsistencies to the judge, sometimes you can get him to add that money back into the bottom line he uses to compute how much the evil trapper must pay for support (both alimony and child support). I can't promise a judge will buy your line of thinking even if you *do* point inconsistencies out, but if you're in court anyways, there's no harm in trying. *Maybe* it will get you a little more money?

If your husband's attorney is going to be scrutinizing YOUR financial statement for these same inconsistencies. The sword cuts both ways!

EXAMPLE 5.3: JACK'S INCOME (SELF-EMPLOYED)

3. GROSS WEEKLY INCOME/RECEIPTS FROM ALL SOURCES

a)	Base pay from ☐ salary X wages	$	0.00
b)	Overtime	$	0.00
c)	Part-time job	$	0.00
d)	Self-employment **(attach a completed schedule A)**	$	750.00
e)	Tips	$	0.00
f)	☐ Commissions ☐ Bonuses	$	0.00
g)	☐ Dividends ☐ Interest	$	0.00
h)	☐ Trusts ☐ Annuities	$	0.00
i)	☐ Pensions ☐ Retirement funds	$	0.00
j)	Social Security	$	0.00
k)	☐ Disability ☐ Unemployment insurance ☐ Worker's compensation	$	0.00
l)	Public Assistance (welfare, A.F.D.C. payments)	$	0.00
m)	☐ Child Support ☐ Alimony (actually received)	$	0.00
n)	Rental from income producing property **(attach a completed Schedule B)**	$	0.00
o)	Royalties and other rights	$	0.00
p)	Contributions from household member(s)	$	0.00
q)	Other (specify)		
	_____	$	0.00
	_____	$	0.00
	r) **Total Gross Weekly Income/Receipts** (add items a-q)	$	750.00

In Example 5.1, we see that Jack claims he earns $750 per week from his self-employment income (for this first example, it doesn't matter whether he's a wage-earner or self-employed). However, if we look at Jack's claimed expenses, we see the following:

EXAMPLE 5.4: JACK'S PAYROLL TAXES/DEDUCTIONS

3. ITEMIZED DEDUCTIONS FROM GROSS INCOME

a)	Federal income tax deductions (claiming __3__ exemptions)	$	210.00
b)	State income tax deductions (claiming __3__ exemptions)	$	39.00
c)	F.I.C.A. and Medicare	$	127.50
d)	Medical Insurance	$	0.00
e)	Union Dues	$	0.00
	f) **Total Deductions** (a through e)	$	376.50

4. ADJUSTED NET WEEKLY INCOME   2(r) minus 3(f) $ 373.50

In Example 5.2, Jack has itemized how much he gets deducted from his paycheck each week *or* how much he pays in taxes (broken down into a weekly amount). Although he claims he earns $750 per week, after he pays his tax bill, he's only left with $373.50. Are you with me so far? Now let's look at how Jack spends that money:

EXAMPLE 5.5: JACK'S WEEKLY EXPENSES

8. WEEKLY EXPENSES

a)	Rent or Mortgage (PIT)	$ 127.00	l)	Life Insurance	$ 0.00
b)	Homeowners/Tenant Insurance	$ 0.00	m)	Medical Insurance	$ 0.00
c)	Maintenance and Repair	$ 0.00	n)	Uninsured Medicals	$ 14.00
d)	Heat	$ 27.00	o)	Incidentals and Toiletries	$ 10.00
e)	Electricity and/or Gas	$ 23.00	p)	Motor Vehicle Expenses	$ 65.00
f)	Telephone	$ 24.00	q)	Motor Vehicle Payment	$ 117.00
g)	Water/Sewer	$ 0.00	r)	Child Care	$ 0.00
h)	Food	$ 75.00	s)	Other (explain	$
i)	House Supplies	$ 5.00		Cable TV	$ 18.00
j)	Laundry and Cleaning	$ 7.00			$
k)	Clothing	$ 5.00			
			e) Total Weekly Expenses (a through s)		$ 522.00

Wait a minute! If Jack only has $373.50 left in his paycheck (or self-employment check) after he pays his taxes, then how is he managing to pay $522.00 per week for his rent, utilities, food and cable television? He's spending $148.50 more per week than he earns! But we're not done yet. Jack also claims he's paying outstanding liabilities.

EXAMPLE 5.6: JACK'S LIABILITIES

11. LIABILITIES (Do not list expenses shown in item 8 above)

	Creditor	Nature of Debt	Date Incurred	Amount Due	Weekly Payment
a)	Big Bank Card	Credit Card	2011	$7,000	$55.00
b)	City Smitty Card	Credit Card	2010	$3,000	$22.00
c)	Car Loan Central	Car Loan	2008	$17,500	$75.00
d)	Bob Rayme	Personal Loan	2012	$5,000	$100.00
	e) Total Liabilities			$32,500	$252.00

So not only is it costing Jack $522.00 per week simply to live and eat, but he claims to be paying another $252.00 per week on top of that to pay down some debts he owes. $522 + $252 = $774. That's more money than Jack claims to be taking home *before* he pays any taxes! Pretty fishy, don't you think? Maybe you should point that discrepancy out to the judge?

If I were Jack's attorney, I'd get out my violin and play a sad song about how poor Jack has been living beyond his means, racking up his credit card bills and borrowing money to meet his basic living expenses because he has to pay *you* (you evil witch). I'd complain about how, even though Jack is *supposed* to be paying those weekly liabilities listed on his financial statement, not only has he been unable to do so, but he's actually been racking up those expenses even *higher*. Poor Jack. The judge will probably be gushing sympathy for poor Jack who can't pay his bills by the time Jack's attorney is done.

If you were a wise woodland creature and diligently gathered the Acorns documents in Chapter Three, you'll show up to court with all of your credit card and bank statements neatly organized into a three-ring binder so you can readily access the information you need. The moment you are handed a financial statement with an amount you know to be far below what Jack earns (usually 5 minutes before your court hearing), whip out that 3-ring binder, flip to the last credit card statement you have for each account Jack has listed (the ones Jack is claiming he's racking up because he can't afford to survive), and *look* at how much the balance on those debts has increased since the date you separated. Perhaps Jack is telling the truth? Perhaps that *is* all he earns and he *is* living off of his credit cards.

If the liabilities balance hasn't increased all that much, Jack is probably lying. And because you, clever woodland creature, brought in your neatly organized three-ring binder and can produce recent credit card bills on those debts, the judge is probably going to believe *you.* Not Jack's lawyer!

Here's another suspicious item on Jack's financial statement:

EXAMPLE 5.7: JACK'S FISHY PERSONAL LOAN

11.	LIABILITIES (Do not list expenses shown in item 8 above)				
	Creditor	Nature of Debt	Date Incurred	Amount Due	Weekly Payment
a)	Big Bank Card	Credit Card	2011	$7,000	$55.00
b)	City Smitty Card	Credit Card	2010	$3,000	$22.00
c)	Car Loan Central	Car Loan	2008	$17,500	$75.00
d)	Bob Rayme	Personal Loan	2012	$5,000	$100.00
	e) Total Liabilities			$32,500	$252.00

Why does Jack suddenly owe his brother Bob $5,000? Jack's attorney is going to claim Jack *borrowed* the money he's using to live off of (that suspicious amount that's beyond his means) from his brother. And the judge will probably go for it. Unless...

EXAMPLE 5.8: JACK'S LEGAL FEES

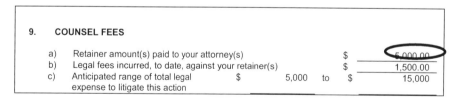

9.	COUNSEL FEES		
a)	Retainer amount(s) paid to your attorney(s)	$	5,000.00
b)	Legal fees incurred, to date, against your retainer(s)	$	1,500.00
c)	Anticipated range of total legal expense to litigate this action $ 5,000 to $		15,000

... it just so happens you know Jack borrowed that money from his brother to retain his attorney. By all means ... if it's in the financial statement, point this out. How did Jack cough up legal fees for the attorney standing there arguing with you today? Don't get me wrong ... the judge is *happy* Jack borrowed $5,000 to hire an attorney rather than stand there and argue his case alone. But Jack is claiming he borrowed that money to live off of because he isn't earning enough money to pay *you.* Not because he needed to cough up a retainer to hire his lawyer.

Now usually b.s. in a financial statement, by itself, will not be enough to sway a judge (unless it's pretty  egregious). Which is lucky for you, because *you* are probably the person living far beyond your means right now, borrowing money from relatives, not paying your debts, and racking up charges on your credit card because *you* still have to take care of the kids and pay the mortgage while Jack is shirking his duty to pay child support. But if you can add a few more feathers to the scale of distrust, you may be able to sway the judge in your favor. How do you do that?

If you both managed to pay your bills consistently while you were still together despite your expenses exceeding *both* of your available income (the income Jack is claiming now that you are separating), it will add weight to your claims. But don't expect the judge to go poring through your old invoices and bills on his own (not even your neatly organized 3-ring-binder). Judges are very busy people. They don't have time to rifle through your old bills. If you want the judge to look, you're going to have to put it into a format he can easily digest. If you happen to use Quicken or Microsoft money, it's as easy as going into your software and clicking on 'reports.'

EXAMPLE 5.9: JANE'S QUICKEN INCOME/EXPENSE REPORT

EXPENSES:	Jan	Feb	Mar	Apr	May	Jun	July	Aug	Sep	Oct	Nov	Dec	Total
Mortgage PIT	$1,546	$1,546	$1,546	$1,546	$1,546	$1,546	$1,546	$1,546	$1,546	$1,546	$1,546	$1,546	$18,552
Homeowners Insurance	$100	$100	$100	$100	$100	$100	$100	$100	$100	$100	$100	$100	$100
Home Repair	$0	$0	$0	$0	$1,250	$0	$65	$0	$0	$121	$0	$0	$0
Colonial Gas	$600	$600	$400	$400	$300	$100	$80	$80	$100	$300	$400	$600	$3,960
NSTAR	$140	$140	$120	$100	$90	$80	$100	$150	$80	$90	$100	$180	$1,370
Cellular One (H & W)	$160	$160	$160	$160	$160	$160	$160	$160	$160	$160	$160	$160	$1,920
Comcast Triple Play Cable/Internet/Telephone	$127	$127	4127	$127	$127	$127	$127	$127	$127	$127	$127	$127	$1,524
Septic Service	$0	$0	$0	$0	$0	$0	$0	$380	$0	$0	$0	$0	$380
Groceries	$650	$600	$625	$500	$650	$625	$700	$650	$625	$600	$825	$775	$7,825
House Supplies	$200	$100	$200	$100	$200	$100	$200	$100	$200	$100	$200	$100	$1,800
Clothing	$50	$50	$50	$50	$50	$200	$50	$50	$700	$300	$50	$200	$1,800
Life Insurance	$200	$200	$200	$200	$200	$200	$200	$200	$200	$200	$200	$200	$2,400
Medical Insurance	$600	$600	$600	$600	$600	$600	$600	$600	$600	$600	$600	$600	$7,200
Dental Insurance	$25	$25	$25	$25	$25	$25	$25	$25	$25	$25	$25	$25	$300
Vision Insurance	$10	$10	$10	$10	$10	$10	$10	$10	$10	$10	$10	$10	$120
Uninsured Medicals	$15	$35	$15	$170	$25	$15	$0	$15	$0	$0	$0	$15	$305
Jack's Car Payment	$500	$500	$500	$500	$500	$500	$500	$500	$500	$500	$500	$500	$6,000
Jane's Car Payment	$500	$500	$500	$500	$500	$500	$500	$500	$500	$500	$500	$500	$6,000
Car Insurance	$180	$180	$180	$180	$180	$180	$180	$180	$180	$180	$180	$180	$2,172
Gas & Maintenance	$550	$500	$575	$500	$475	$500	$575	$800	$500	$550	$500	$725	$6,750
Daycare	$645	$645	$645	$645	$645	$645	$645	$645	$645	$645	$645	$645	$7740
Birthday/Xmas Gifts	$15	$0	$25	$100	$15	$0	$15	$25	$15	$25	$0	$1,250	$1.475
Furniture/TV Purchases	$2,750	$0	$0	$0	$0	$0	$0	$0	$0	$500	$0	$0	$3,250
Total Expenses by Month	**$9,563**	**$6,618**	**$10,603**	**$6,513**	**$7,648**	**$6,213**	**$6,378**	**$6,843**	**$6,813**	**$7,179**	**$6,668**	**$8,438**	**$81,469**
INCOME:													
Jane's Monthly After-Tax Income	$1,505	$1,505	$1,505	$1,505	$1,505	$1,505	$1,505	$1,505	$1,505	$1,505	$1,505	$1,505	$18,060
Expenses minus Jane's wages	**$8,058**	**$5,113**	**$9098**	**$5,008**	**$6,143**	**$4,713**	**$4,873**	**$5,338**	**$5,308**	**$5,674**	**$5,163**	**$6,933**	**$63,409**

This spreadsheet demonstrates the marriage of Jack-n-Jane, Inc. incurred an average living expense of $6,789 per month. Jane only earned enough after-tax wages to cover $1,505 of those expenses. It means the family was getting an additional $5,284 per month ($1,229 per week) from *somewhere*. While they were married, Jack brought home enough money to cover $1,229 per week in living expenses. Now that they're separated and getting a divorce, Jack claims he's only bringing home $373 per week after-taxes ($750 before taxes). The math just doesn't add up. *This* will hopefully get the judge curious enough to start digging. Just because judges are busy doesn't mean they're stupid.

Judges –do– report tax evaders to the IRS. Be very careful you do not admit you knowingly under-reported your joint taxes or were aware your husband was committing tax fraud! Innocent spouse provisions in the tax code only apply –if– you were truly unaware, until now, that you –should–have been claiming more. If your husband handled nearly all of the money, it's understandable you may have been in the dark until now. But be careful what you say!

Opposing counsel will often use the –threat- of the judge dropping a dime to the IRS after their client testifies she just realized her husband was under-claiming his self-employment income all these years to force a lying husband to come clean and file an honest financial statement.

What if you don't use Microsoft Money or Quicken? If you think your husband might lie about his income, either you're going to have to purchase MSMoney/Quicken and go through your old credit card bills, checkbook registers and receipts, or create this spreadsheet manually using pen-and-paper or MSExcel, or take it on the chin financially and let Jack get away with lying through his teeth. With the Acorns you gathered in Chapter Three, you *should* have enough information to do a credible archeological dig.

Now if Jack earns a straight salary from a reputable employer (one that is easily recreated using a W2 form and paystubs) and you don't think he's going to hide money, doing this might be a waste of time. But if Jack is self-employed or has a side-job you've relied upon during the marriage to make ends meet, recreating an accurate financial picture of your past year's living expenses *before* you go into court would be wise.

HIDING MONEY: ACT 2 - SPOTTING FISHY DEDUCTIONS IN A SCHEDULE C

The other place to hide money is legally, in plain sight. If you are self-employed, there are lots of tax deductions the government legally allows you to deduct for income tax computation purposes which are *not* deductible for Child Support and/or Alimony computation purposes. Why might this be? If you are paying $1,000 per month on your mortgage and legally deduct $200 per month of that as a home office, the self-employed spouse is gaining an unfair advantage (at *your* expense) over a wage-earning spouse who doesn't get to deduct part of a mortgage they have to pay anyways. If you run a business out of the home and deduct the car payment, gasoline, maintenance and repairs for your one-and-only car, that is an unfair advantage over the wage-earning spouse. If you depreciate business equipment, that is an unfair advantage over a wage-earning spouse, who has to pay taxes on the money they use to pay for their car and doesn't get to depreciate it. Therefore, if your husband is self-employed, coming to court with his Schedule C in hand and knowledge of places you might get a judge to add income back in can be a great equalizer.

EXAMPLE 5.10: JACK'S 1040 INCOME

Jack claims he only earned $39,000 last year

If you look at Jack's 1040, he claimed he only earned $39,000 last year, which breaks down to $750 per week, the amount Jack listed in the 'Income' section of his court Financial Statement. The burden of proof is upon *you* to show the court should use a different figure. Here's how you do that. When you're self-employed, you need to fill out a document called a Schedule C. If we look at the Schedule C which should be attached to Jack's tax return, we'll see his before-deduction income was a very different number. Jack's gross (before deduction) income was $83,000 per year!

EXAMPLE 5.11: JACK'S SCHEDULE C INCOME

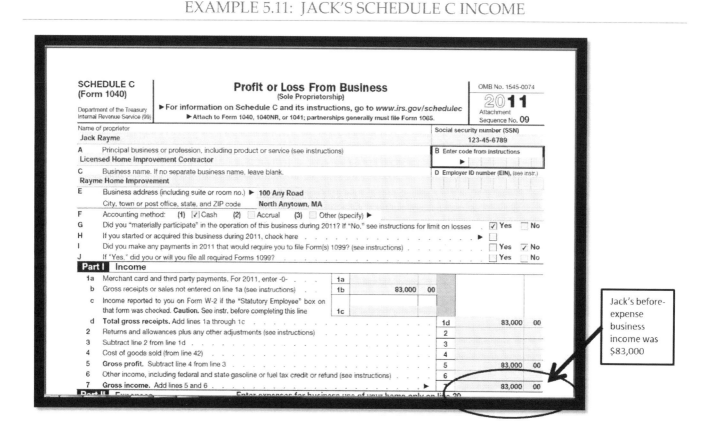

Whoopee! You can collect child support or alimony on $83,000! Right?

Wrong…

When you are in business for yourself, you incur many legitimate expenses which the court will allow Jack to deduct when they figure out how much child support he has to pay you. However, because Jack owns a small business, the tax code favors his taking certain perfectly legal deductions which the judge *might* allow you to add back in for alimony or child support computation purposes. Let's look at the Expenses section of Jack's Schedule C:

EXAMPLE 5.12: JACK'S SCHEDULE C EXPENSES

7	Gross income. Add lines 5 and 6									7	83,000	00
Part II	**Expenses**				Enter expenses for business use of your home only on line 30.							
8	Advertising	8		2,600	00	18	Office expense (see instructions)		18			
9	Car and truck expenses (see instructions)	9		7,000	00	19	Pension and profit-sharing plans		19			
						20	Rent or lease (see instructions):					
10	Commissions and fees	10				a	Vehicles, machinery, and equipment		20a		780	00
11	Contract labor (see instructions)	11		8,500	00	b	Other business property		20b			
12	Depletion	12				21	Repairs and maintenance		21		1,250	00
13	Depreciation and section 179 expense deduction (not included in Part III) (see instructions)	13		6,000	00	22	Supplies (not included in Part III)		22		16,220	00
						23	Taxes and licenses		23		600	00
						24	Travel, meals, and entertainment:					
14	Employee benefit programs (other than on line 19)	14				a	Travel		24a		4,100	00
15	Insurance (other than health)	15		7,200	00	b	Deductible meals and entertainment (see instructions)		24b		700	00
16	Interest:					25	Utilities		25		2,400	00
a	Mortgage (paid to banks, etc.)	16a				26	Wages (less employment credits)		26			
b	Other	16b		700	00	27a	Other expenses (from line 48)		27a			
17	Legal and professional services	17		650	00	b	Reserved for future use		27b			
28	**Total expenses** before expenses for business use of home. Add lines 8 through 27a							▶	28		41,600	00
29	Tentative profit or (loss). Subtract line 28 from line 7								29		41,400	00
30	Expenses for business use of your home. Attach **Form 8829**. Do **not** report such expenses elsewhere								30		2,400	00
31	**Net profit or (loss)**. Subtract line 30 from line 29.											
	• If a profit, enter on both **Form 1040, line 12** (or **Form 1040NR, line 13**) and on **Schedule SE, line 2**. If you entered an amount on line 1c, see instr. Estates and trusts, enter on **Form 1041, line 3**.								31		39,000	00
	• If a loss, you **must** go to line 32.											
32	If you have a loss, check the box that describes your investment in this activity (see instructions).											
	• If you checked 32a, enter the loss on both **Form 1040, line 12**, (or **Form 1040NR, line 13**) and on **Schedule SE, line 2**. If you entered an amount on line 1c, see the instructions for line 31. Estates and trusts, enter on **Form 1041, line 3**.							32a ☐	All investment is at risk.			
								32b ☐	Some investment is not at risk.			
	• If you checked 32b, you **must** attach **Form 6198**. Your loss may be limited.											
	For Paperwork Reduction Act Notice, see your tax return instructions.					Cat. No. 11334P			Schedule C (Form 1040) 2011			

Advertising Expenses (Line 8 - $2,600) are usually not something you can attack and add back into the bottom line for child support/alimony computation purposes. Unless, of course, your husband ran an advertisement which wasn't really for business. Add back in - $0.

Car & Truck Expenses (Line 10 - $7,000) is one common area of attack. Is this the only vehicle Jack owns? Or does he have one vehicle for the home and a second vehicle for business? If the truck Jack is deducting is the only vehicle Jack owns, sometimes you can get the judge to add some or all of that line item back into the bottom line for child support/alimony purposes. Car & Truck Expenses also includes the actual cost of getting back and forth to work. If Jack works from home, allowing him to deduct his travel to get back and forth to his various jobsites when *you* have to pay to get back and forth to work would be unfair. If, on the other hand, Jack had to travel to your state  capital to take a licensing exam or run to Home Depot to buy 2x4's for a job, that would be an allowable business expense. The only way to ferret out which is which is to demand Jack produce his mileage log (which under IRS guidelines he is legally *required* to keep). For purposes of this exercise, we're going to pretend Jack didn't keep his log and has been using the truck to get back and forth to work. Add back in - $7,000.

Contract Labor (Line 11 - $8,500) is the cost to hire somebody else to do work on your behalf. It usually won't be added back in for child support/alimony purposes. Add back in - $0.

Depreciation (Line 13 - $6,000) is another area you can often get expenses added back in. If the items Jack deducted are the vehicle you just attacked above, or some other asset which is used partially for business and partially for the home (for example, your home computer), you may be able to get some or all of that line item added back in. To find out what was depreciated, ask to see the 179 Expense Depreciation worksheet which Jack's accountant should have prepared for each item that is being depreciated. It's a nightmare to sort through because it doesn't itemize, but if you find 'year 1' from when the equipment was brought in service, you can figure out which item is which. For purposes of this exercise, we're going to pretend $3,000 of that depreciation expense is Jack's truck. Add back in - $3,000.

Insurance (Line 15 - $7,200). If the insurance which was purchased was business insurance (for example, as a home improvement contractor, Jack probably has workmen's compensation insurance, a business policy, plus insurance on his business equipment), it is a legitimate deduction. However, if some of that insurance is for the truck Jack uses for both business and home, that portion he is paying for his personal vehicle might be added back in for child support/alimony computation purposes. For purposes of this exercise, we're going to say $1,200 per year of that insurance is Jack's personal truck. Add back in - $1,200.

Other (Line 16b - $700) - whether or not this can be added back in depends upon what the 'other' expense really was. Was it an expense that was pure business? Or was it an expense that, if your husband didn't happen to be self-employed, a normal wage-earning spouse would not be able to deduct off their child support income? For purposes of this example, we'll say it was pure business. Add back in - $0.

Legal and Professional fees (Line 17 - $650). Judges love it when lawyers and accountants get paid. This will almost never be added back in unless part of that fee was incurred to seek *personal* services as well (such as to divorce *you*). Add back in - $0.

Vehicles, Machinery or Equipment (Line 20 - $780). - if the *Rent or Lease* was the cost of Jack to rent a car to use both for both personal use and also for work, a judge might order some or all of that expense to be added back into the bottom line. For purposes of this exercise, we'll pretend that was the cost for Jack to rent a floor nailer, concrete saw, and sheet-rock lifter. Add back in - $0.

Repairs and Maintenance (Line 21 - $1,250) says Jack spent $1,250 to get equipment repaired last year. However, if we examine Jack's business records, we might find some of those repairs were to a piece of equipment (i.e., Jack's personal car) that a judge might add back into the bottom line. For purposes of this exercise, we're going to say $600 of that repair expense was to fix Jack's truck. Add back in - $600.

Supplies (Line 22 - $16,220) is usually legitimate, but not if your spouse is also funneling non-legitimate expenses through the business account. Remember my earlier example of the husband who picked apart his wife's hairdressing business to discredit furniture she'd bought for the home and expensive gifts she'd bought for her parents? The only way to differentiate these expenses is to look at your husband's business records. For the sake of this exercise, we're going to say Jane agrees all of the business expenses are legitimate *except* for $4,400 worth of pressure-treated lumber Jack bought and used to replace the deck on the marital home. Add back in - $4,400.

Taxes/License fees (Line 23 - $600) are most likely all legitimate business expenses. However, if the tax was related to something that was personal, you might be able to get it added back in. For purposes of this exercise, we'll say it was $0.

Travel (Line 24a - $4,100) is the cost to travel, such as to fly to attend a home improvement conference, or to take a bus or train, and other expenses associated with that trip, such as your hotel room. It is other-than-routine expenses. If Jack wrote off the cost of travelling to a conference as a business expense, but

drove there and took the entire family on vacation while there so he could deduct the cost of his hotel room and car, you may be able to get a judge to add *some* of that trip back into the bottom line. Otherwise, it is a legitimate expense. For purposes of this exercise, we're going to say it was legitimate. Add back in - $0.

Meals and Entertainment (Line 24b - $700) is the cost to take a business associate out to lunch. Jack is legally required to keep a record of who he ate lunch with, what they talked about, and to keep the receipt. If you can examine his business records, if you discover he took his new girlfriend (or mother, brother, sister, cousin) to lunch, you can get it added back in. You can also usually get it added back in if Jack has a pattern of buying himself lunch on the company tab every day for no legitimate purpose. Otherwise, it will be a legitimate business expense. For purposes of this exercise, we're going to say Jane examined the records and could find no discrepancy. Add back in - $0.

Utilities (Line 25 - $2,400) – usually utilities are a straightforward business expense. However, since Jack works from home and the utilities he claims are also a portion of the house utilities, especially since most of his work is performed *away* from home, you may be able to get a judge to add some or all of those utilities back in. Based on the facts of Jack's working from home, I would guess the judge might add *all* of it back in - $2,400.

Business Use of Home (Line 30) – you can *usually* get a judge to add this expense back in unless you happen to have an industrial bay attached to your home. Add back in - $2,400.

So after doing all this work, how might Jane compile this information so that it is easily digestible for the judge to look over the figures she is proposing? Another table is in order:

EXAMPLE 5.13: JANE'S PROPOSED SCHEDULE C EXPENSE EXCLUSIONS

Expense Type	Schedule C Amount	Deductions Wife Agrees are Pure Business Expenses	Deductions Wife Proposes Should Count towards Child Support/Alimony
Advertising	$2,600	$2,600	$0
Car & Truck Expenses	$7,000	$0	$7,000
Contract Labor	$8,500	$8,500	$0
Depreciation	$6,000	$3,000	$3,000
Insurance	$7,200	$6,000	$1,200
Other	$700	$700	$0
Legal and Professional Fees	$650	$650	$0
Vehicles, Machinery & Equipment Rental	$780	$780	$0
Repairs	$1,250	$650	$600
Supplies	$16,220	$11,820	$4,400
Taxes/Licenses/Fees	$600	$600	$0
Travel	$4,100	$4,100	$0
Meals	$700	$700	$0
Utilities	$2,400	$0	$2,400
Business Use of Home	$2,400	$0	$2,400
TOTALS	$44,000	$23,000	$21,000

EXAMPLE 5.14: JANE'S PROPOSED CHILD SUPPORT INCOME BASIS FOR JACK

Jack's Pre-tax Gross Income	$83,000
Minus Allowable Expenses	$23,000
Jack's Child support Income	$60,000
÷ 52 (weeks/year)	$1,153.85/week

The amount Jane has to gain by forcing Jack to claim his expenses the same way a non-self-employed person has to claim them is substantial. Under Jack's old claim of $750 per week income, Jane would only get around $187 per week in child support. Under Jack's adjusted income of $1,153 per week, Jane would be entitled to receive around $288 per week child support, an increase of over $100 per week/$5,200 per year. Will the judge 'go' for Jane's proposed adjustments? Who knows. If people could predict with any certainty what judges would do, lawyers wouldn't make so much money.

Some of Jack's legitimate business expenses, such as business use of the home and use of his business pickup truck for personal use, tend to be readily added back in. *Especially* if paired with a 'Financial Statement B.S.' spreadsheet as outlined in the prior section. If the judge sees your family used a lot more income than is being reported to the court, he will usually look for ways to make sure you have enough money to feed your kids and survive.

 *Hiring an attorney to make these arguments in court for you is usually a prudent use of scarce dollars.* The judge is much more likely to listen to an attorney, who is used to articulating such abstract issues, than a layperson. However, YOU should do all the preliminary computations and spreadsheets recommended above, backing up your estimates with clear references (and photocopies) of the Acorns document you are using to back up your claim. Otherwise it will cost thousands of dollars to hire a forensic accountant to do this nasty chore for you!

Note that very little of what Jack deducted from his income was 'fraud' in this second example of 'hiding money.' Questionable … maybe. But with a smooth talking accountant at his back, Jack would probably survive an audit by the IRS. With the exception of the lumber to repair the deck, Jack didn't break any laws. That doesn't mean, however, that he gets to not pay *you* when it comes to alimony or supporting his children! It's unfair that one many collects a wage and pays more child/spousal support, while a second man collects that same amount as self-employment income and through a few fancy accounting tricks gets to pay less. It's not fair. If you point that out to a judge, sometimes you can get them to agree with you (but not always).

The burden is on *you* to convince him!

ON-YOUR-FEET EXERCISE 5-1: CONTESTED HEARING ON CHILD SUPPORT

Magistrate:	I call the case of Jane Doe-Rayme versus Jack Rayme. Please state your names for the record?
Jane Doe-Rayme:	I'm Jane Doe-Rayme.
Jack Rayme:	I am Jack Rayme.
Judge:	I have before me a motion filed by Mr. Rayme to reduce his child support from the $126 per week set by the District Court at a December 9th restraining order hearing. Mr. Rayme, would you explain to the court why I should reduce your child support obligation?
Jack:	The economy is really bad right now. I've found a few odd jobs doing things like repairing a broken step or putting insulation in a friend's attic, but for the last nine weeks I haven't been able to find work.
Judge:	Mrs. Doe, do you care to respond.
Jane Doe-Rayme:	That's not true. Seven or eight times in the past nine weeks I've received calls from customers looking to hire him. One was a friend's sister looking to have him build a 1,500 square foot addition onto their ocean-view cottage. Another was a lady he's worked for before wanting a quote to remodel her kitchen. I've given every single one of those customers his cell phone number.
Judge:	Mr. Rayme, why haven't you taken any of those jobs?
Jack Rayme (getting huffy):	Well, -I- didn't get any of those phone calls. She must have bad mouthed me to them so they didn't want to hire me or given them the wrong number.
Jane Doe-Rayme:	Sir, I may be upset at my husband for his behavior, but I'm not stupid! No jobs, no child support… I had nothing but *good* things to say about his work to them!

Judge:	Mr. Rayme, I find it hard to believe you didn't get a single call. Why aren't you accepting work?
Jack Rayme:	I *have* been looking for work. I just can't find any.
Jane Doe-Rayme: *(Jane holds out the list to the bailiff, who takes it and hands it to the judge).*	Sir, I kept a telephone log of the names and telephone numbers of customers who called looking to hire my husband as well as notes about the kind of work they were looking to have done.
Judge:	Mrs. Doe, is there anything else you'd like to add before we conclude this hearing?
Jane Doe-Rayme: *(Jane holds out the tax returns to the bailiff, who takes them and hands them to the judge)*	Yes, sir. When I went to the restraining order hearing on December 9th, I had no idea child support would be getting set that day. I didn't think to bring financial paperwork to show how much my husband earns. I brought our tax returns from the last three years with me today, including my husband's Schedule C. If you look at his average income for the past three years, you'll see he earned, on average, $50,000 per year.
Judge (to Mr. Doe):	I see here you earned $54,000 in 2009, $49,000 in 2010, and $51,000 in 2011. Is that correct?
Jack Rayme:	Yeah, but that's not true now. The bottom has fallen out of the economy and I can't find work.
Jane Doe-Rayme:	Sir, it's only March. I find it hard to believe the market has gone from $51,000 to zero in three months.
Judge (giving her a stern look):	I'll be the judge of that…
Jane Doe-Rayme: *(looking humble)*	My apologies, sir. If I might point out one other thing on the tax return? My husband has one vehicle, a 2001 Ford F-150 pickup truck, which he fully depreciates as a business expense. He also deducts business use of the home and the garage where he stores his tools. These two amounts totaled $5,000 last year. I'm requesting those two figures be added back into his income when you compute child support.
Judge:	I'll take the matter under advisement. You'll get my decision in the mail.

Analysis: Jane has done a good job of documenting how much her husband *should* be earning. I would guess the judge will average her husband's income for the past 3 years and attribute an additional income of $5,000 for the legitimate write-offs of business use of his truck from home and depreciation for the home office. Although these are legitimate business expenses, a "normal" wage earner would not be allowed to deduct his commute to work or part of his home from his wages. By referring to the last three years of Schedule C tax returns, Jane  demonstrated her husband's base income (before adding depreciation back in) should be around $50,000.

The telephone log of customer inquiries, telephone numbers, and types of work they sought to have done supports Jane's argument that her husband claims that he can't find work are suspect. It also discredits Jack's claim he didn't receive the phone calls. Why would she keep such careful records if she didn't intend to forward them to him?

LEVERAGE THE MIGHT OF YOUR STATE CHILD SUPPORT ENFORCEMENT DIVISION

Always ask the court to order your husband pay child support through your state's Child Support Enforcement Division. Don't give up this option because of "scare stories" to trick foolish woodland creatures into passing up this great equalizer. A few states charge a modest intake fee to process the paperwork in non-welfare cases (the most I've heard of is $25), but in most states, this service is completely free.

The Child Support Enforcement Division can be a hassle to work with. When you first set up a new account, it may delay getting your first child support check as much as six weeks. In some states there may be a modest fee to initially set up your account. It's a huge, mindless *BUREAUCRACY*. If you word something wrong in your court agreement, you may need to go back to court to fix it.

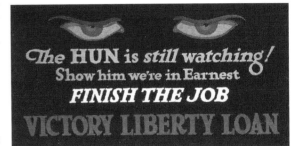

 That being said, use them anyway!!!

The Child Support Enforcement Division's sole purpose for existing is to *help you collect your child support!* They eat deadbeat dads for breakfast and spit their bones upon the courthouse steps for lunch. Their computers talk to every state and federal computer in the country. If your husband gets a driver's license, files a tax return, opens a bank account, or gets an above-the-table job anyplace in the country, they will find him. If he gets more than five thousand dollars behind on his child support, they may garnish his bank accounts and seize his tax refunds. Just for kicks, they might revoke his professional and drivers licenses. Sometimes, they'll even publish his name and amount he owes in the newspaper in a list of "worst deadbeat dads" so all his friends and colleagues know what a loser he is. If he gets even further behind on his child support, they might even prosecute him criminally.

You are a small woodland creature seeking to feed her cute fuzzy young. You need a goon squad such as the Child Support Enforcement Division watching your back!

Do not let your husband con you into thinking the Child Support Enforcement Division is a bad idea!!! Think Rottweiler, Pit bull, Doberman, and Bulldog ... all rolled into one!

To help you streamline the process, here are steps you should take when dealing with your state's Child Support Enforcement Division:

1. GET A COURT ORDER FOR ENFORCEMENT: The Child Support Enforcement Division can't help you collect your child support until you get the court to order it be collected through them. Chapter Thirteen: Temporary Orders explains how to insert an enforcement clause into your motion requesting child support.

2. HAVE THEIR OFFICIAL APPLICATION ALL FILLED OUT AND READY TO GO: Go back to the 50-state list at the beginning of this chapter and hunt around your states Child Support Enforcement Division website until you find their Application for Services. Some let you fill it out online and mail in the supporting paperwork. Others make you fill out a pen-and-paper form. In

either situation, you'll need a copy of your court order for child support and children's birth certificates (plus whatever else they might request). Read what information they ask for and include it or your application won't be processed!

3. MAIL OR HAND-DELIVER YOUR PAPERWORK: As soon as you get your order back from the court with the Child Support Enforcement Division box checked off (or written in), or get back a copy of any stipulation which includes wage assignment, bring or mail your application, supporting documents, and a copy of the court order down to the nearest Child Support Enforcement Division office. Most Massachusetts full-time probate courts have a satellite Child Support Enforcement Division office located right in the courthouse.

Do not rely on the court to forward the child support order to the Child Support Enforcement Division. Both the courthouse staff *and* the Child Support Enforcement Division staff are overworked and understaffed. If you don't include all requested paperwork, it might never catch up with your application and won't get processed. Weeks, often months will go by before you finally get a notice telling you your application has been rejected because you were missing critical paperwork. Play it safe! Do it yourself!

4. FOLLOW UP: Approximately a week after you drop off or mail your application, call, check online if you applied electronically, or go down to their office and ask if your application has been processed. Case managers are egregiously overworked, so calling may give you a voicemail and no return call. If that happens, keep trying or go down to the main office or satellite at the courthouse in person. Always be courteous and appreciative to your case worker, even if they're grumpy and less than helpful. If you worked as hard as *they* do, you'd be grumpy, too.

5. FINANCIALLY PREPARE FOR THE 6 WEEK DELAY: Anticipate a delay of four to six weeks before you get your first check. Your husband is supposed to pay them directly until his employer starts deducting child support from his paycheck, but most don't. If you're a smart woodland creature who took my advice in Chapter Three: Acorns to heart, you'll anticipate this tomfoolery and budget a cushion to pay your bills before you file for divorce. *The delay to get paid is well worth the enforcement power you gain and he still owes you that money.*

6. MORE FOLLOW-UP: Check back with the Child Support Enforcement Division if you still haven't received your first check within 3 weeks of giving them the order to see if your husband is paying into the system. If he hasn't, file a Complaint for Contempt (covered in Chapter Twenty) to get the court to order him to pay it. If your husband has paid but they haven't forwarded a check yet, find out why. The Division forwards money at certain times of the month, so it may be you missed a deadline.

7. CHECK FOR 'HOLDS': If it's been several weeks and you still haven't received any money, ask them to make sure there aren't any 'holds' on your account. Sometimes, a piece of paper is missing or a "hold" incorrectly gets entered into the system which can hold your checks up indefinitely. It's up to you to resolve this as soon as possible.

If, at a later date, you have your court order modified, you should repeat the above seven steps to make sure the new order is entered properly.

An important legal benefit of using the Child Support Enforcement Division is the court is required to give heavy consideration to the amount of child support state agencies records show your husband owes. Without a collection order in place, the burden of proof is on *you* to prove he didn't pay you and

how much he goes. He says he paid you cash. You say he didn't. You're now into a war of credibility.

If, however, you get your child support collected through the Child Support Enforcement Division, the burden of proof shifts to *him* to prove the government agencies records are wrong. No more haggling about whether or not he paid you cash, gave you a check, or the check is in the mail. If the Child Support Enforcement Division says they didn't get it, case closed.

If your husband moves to another state and tries to get *that* court to order retroactive reduction of child support to wipe out his arrearage in *your* state, that new court *has* to honor the records and child support guidelines of the Child Support Enforcement Division and *cannot* just wipe it out. These are protections you risk losing if you don't use the state agency.

Last but not least, if you suspect he's suddenly earning a lot more money, you can go down to the Child Support Enforcement Division office, ask them to help you file for modification, and they will usually prosecute your case for you for a very low fee or free of charge. Massachusetts courts entertain cost of living requests every two or three years *or* if income increases more than 10%. Although the Child Support Enforcement Division is prohibited from telling you how much the state revenue records show your husband now earns, some caseworkers will give you a thumbs up or thumbs down if it means the difference between needing to go on welfare or remaining self-sufficient.

MY HUSBAND WON'T CONTEST CUSTODY IF I AGREE TO WAIVE CHILD SUPPORT

Never bargain away your child's right to be supported!!! The right to be supported by both parents belongs to the child, not you or your husband. Most states have passed laws stating you can *never* sign away your children's right to collect child support (no matter *what* your separation agreement might say). These laws weren't passed because the legislature felt sorry for parents who were stupid enough to sign away their legal rights. They were passed because short-sighted parents usually end up on welfare. Taxpayers don't like it when private divorce decrees increase taxpayer bills.

CHAPTER FIVE SUMMARY

1. All states have formal mathematical formulas called "child support guidelines" which determine how much child support you can expect to collect or pay if you divorce your spouse. Most state guidelines can be computed right on line.

2. These formulas are often inadequate to meet your child's actual needs. You will need to plan for these shortcomings.

3. There are many ways your spouse can hide money, resulting in less child support than you deserve. The burden is on *you* to document his real earning capacity and prove to the judge he should pay more.

4. Many judges are overly-prone to believe self-employed husbands sad tales about not being able to find work. You need to prove *overwhelmingly* your husband is lying.

5. Always ask the court to order your husband to pay the child support through your state's Child Support Enforcement Division. The benefit of having the state keep track of payments, monitor his income, and go after him when he doesn't pay far outweighs the occasional lost check or hassle of dealing with a huge *BUREAUCRACY*.

6. The Child Support Enforcement Division is a single mother's best friend. They'll watch your back and mess up your husband's world if he gets too far behind on his child support payments. Hug a grumpy, overworked Child Support Enforcement Division caseworker today!

CHAPTER 6

ALIMONY

Alimony (also called maintenance or spousal support) is a legal obligation to provide financial support to each other upon separation and/or divorce. Most alimony awards order your spouse to pay for a specified length of time, often based on the length of the marriage, to even out disparities in your incomes. Most courts recognize a wife of a long-term marriage who stayed home to raise children or support her husband's career did not have the opportunity to acquire job skills, seniority, and a cushy retirement account to buffer her finances. Women born prior to the 1960's were *expected* to stay home and be a homemaker and mother. On the other hand, most women today spend at least *some* time in the workforce.

Alimony is meant to be a *temporary* solution to help the lower-earning spouse transition to financial independence. It's not a source of income you should depend upon for the rest of your life. Although courts might allocate some portion of your support entitlement to be child support and another portion to be alimony, the net total cannot exceed the amount the legislature has determined your husband is legally obligated to pay. That's the law.

Your husband needs to eat, too…

It doesn't matter whether divorce leaves you financially destitute. It's up to *you* to calculate your post-divorce budget and take steps to rein in your expenses. Everything you built together during your marriage required joint sacrifices. Now that you're getting divorced, unless you lived very frugally, chances are there's not going to be enough money to maintain your prior lifestyle. Courts don't have a magic wooden gavel to create more wealth than you already have.

THE 1/3 - 1/3 - 1/3 GUESSTIMATE

Alimony laws vary wildly not only from state-to-state, but can also vary county-to-county. This refusal of state legislatures (often due to lobbying by bar associations who make a *killing* out of litigating alimony) to standardize alimony awards nationwide is what gives lawyers a bad name. By one estimate, eighty percent (80%) of all divorce litigation is about how much alimony one spouse should pay to the other. However, if you look at the big picture, despite all the Swiss-cheese exceptions and bad applications of the law, a general nationwide pattern emerges. A conservative 'guesstimate' for financial planning purposes is the 1/3-1/3-1/3 rule-of-thumb. It's a 'safe' formula to use until you can meet with an attorney to give you more accurate numbers:

- 1/3 for the tax man
- 1/3 for support obligations (child support + alimony)
- 1/3 to support *himself*

An example of a 1/3 – 1/3 – 1/3 alimony award our hypothetical litigant, Jane Doe-Rayme might expect if based on the national average is below:

TABLE 6-1: HYPOTHETICAL 1/3 – 1/3 – 1/3 ALIMONY ESTIMATE (NO CHILD SUPPORT)

Jack's gross (before tax) income:	$ 55,016
+ Jane's gross income:	+ $ 22,880
Total marital income =	$ 77,896
Marital income ÷ 3 =	$77,896 ÷ 3 = $ 25,965
Minus Jane's gross income:	-$ 22,880
Alimony to Jane (annually):	$ 3,085

(for initial planning purposes only)

Not a lot of money to live on, is it? That translates into an extra $59 per week. But remember, we're not done yet. Jane has children and estimated in Chapter Five how much child support she might be entitled to receive.

TABLE 6-2: HYPOTHETICAL 1/3 – 1/3 – 1/3 ALIMONY ESTIMATE W/ CHILD SUPPORT

Potential alimony:	$ 3,085
Minus child support:	$16,016
Alimony to Jane (annual):	(-12,931) or $ zero

(for initial planning purposes only)

Oh, well. It looks like Jane will be on her own in most states as far as alimony is concerned. But what happens if you're an older woman? The largest group of women getting divorced right now is women over the age of 50. Let's pretend Jane's children left the nest a few years ago and she now earns $128 per week working part time (16 hours) as a store clerk? Your computations might look a little different:

TABLE 6-3: HYPOTHETICAL 1/3 – 1/3 – 1/3 ALIMONY ESTIMATE

Jack's gross income:	$ 55,016
+ Jane's gross income:	+ $ 6,656
Total marital income =	$ 61,672
Marital income ÷ 3 =	$61,672 ÷ 3 = $ 20,557
Minus Jane's gross income:	-$ 6,656
Alimony to Jane (annual):	$ 13,901

(for initial planning purposes only)

Jane *might* be entitled to receive approximately $1,158 per month (varies) in many states to tide her over until she's able to stand financially on her own two feet. That's not a lot of money. Paired with her earned income of $555 per month from her job as a clerk, she'll only have $1713 per month to meet all her living expenses. As we saw from the financial statement Jane filled out in Chapter Four, her living expenses are nearly twice that amount. *Which is why the emphasis of the first part of this Bootcamp Manual focuses on getting your financial house in order!*

Worse … at some point alimony is going to end….

In many states, alimony is *also* contingent upon *other* factors besides fault, such as the ability to find work or likelihood one partner might inherit a substantial sum of money. The court expects Jane to increase her working hours from 16 per week to 40 per week. After a set period of time she'll be cut off. The court may even order her to start working 40 hours per week right away, only awarding temporary alimony long enough for her to find a full-time job. At the $8 per hour Jane is capable of earning based on her prior work history and experience, the resulting $1,280 per month would exceed Jack's alimony obligation.

Lastly, most states have durational rules-of-thumb about how long the ex-wife can expect to receive alimony. Once again, these vary wildly by state, but a national trend emerges based on the length of the marriage:

- < 10 yrs. = 50% length of marriage
- 10-20 yrs. = slightly more?
- 20 yrs. = longer???

Our hypothetical couple, Jack and Jane, were married 10 years and 2 months *or* 122 months total. How long Jane's entitled to receive alimony (if she meets the financial criteria) would vary, but most likely she could safely count on alimony for 5 years.

- 10 years 2 months –*or*- 122 months ÷2 = 61 months –*or*- 5 years 1 mo.

- *Or until Jack retires, whichever comes first!!!*

So here's a recap of the nationwide trend to help you plan financially until you can consult with an attorney in *your* jurisdiction. This may or may not be the end-result in *your* home state:

1. Many women will qualify for 1/3ʳᵈ of the total marital income as alimony, minus whatever income they are capable of earning on their own;

    ***Must prove fault grounds when asking for alimony:*** Alabama, Connecticut, Georgia, Florida, Kentucky, Louisiana, Maryland, Michigan, Mississippi, Missouri, New Hampshire, New Jersey, New York, North Carolina, North Dakota, Pennsylvania, Rhode Island, South Carolina, South Dakota, Texas, Utah, Virginia, and West Virginia.

   Texas has some of the most unfavorable alimony laws in the country.

2. Child support gets deducted from any alimony you might be entitled to receive. In many cases, child support cancels out potential alimony.

3. Alimony is probably going to end.

   a. Based on half the length of your marriage or slightly longer once you meet certain threshold requirements;

   b. When your husband reaches full Social Security retirement age;

   c. If you get remarried or cohabitate;

   d. If you get a better-paying job ... or the court perceives you are *capable* of getting a better paying job.

Now you understand why I'm so adamant women *plan* before they file for divorce! I urge you to pay for an hour consultation or at least speak to a courthouse lawyer-of-the-day to get a straight answer! Google 'how much alimony can I receive in X-state?' and see what turns up. Unfortunately, this will prove to be a frustrating experience for many of you. Unlike here in Massachusetts, which just adopted formal alimony guidelines, most states lag far behind the times. Finding out this number falls under the 'high priority legal advice' category if it is something you'll depend upon.

TYPES OF ALIMONY

Although definitions vary state-by-state, the American Academy of Matrimonial Lawyers (AAML) proposed Model Guidelines which have been creeping into the statutes of all 50 states. I include AAML terminology in this book because it is the closest I can come to educating you about a nationwide standard so I can use 'hypothetical' examples. AAML proposes breaking alimony into four types: *general term, rehabilitative, reimbursement,* and *transitional.* What type you might be entitled to receive, how much, and how long it will last depends upon what type of marriage you had and how long it lasted. The types of alimony are explained below.

1. GENERAL TERM ALIMONY: this is the 'old fashioned' type of alimony, which presumed one partner in the marriage worked while the other stayed home to rear children and support their husband's career. It presumes the wife is economically dependent upon the husband. *If your income is not substantially lower than his at the time of the divorce, you will not be entitled to receive anything.*

Although the old 'norm' is now quite rare … few families can afford to have both marital partners out of the workforce for an extended period of time, at some point in their lives, most women will take at least *some* time out of their career to rear children. Furthermore, few careers are tolerant to the needs of rearing children. Although many assume women have achieved equal rights, 'equality' usually comes upon the backs of the children (and for those who protest, I am speaking from my own experience). Once you have kids, whether you continue working but go home at 5:00 every day to make supper, work part-time, or stay home with your children, your career prospects and retirement benefits take a 'hit.'

General Term Alimony is computed according to how long your marriage lasted. To help you get your head around what this means, I will use the proposed AAML guidelines, but be aware that *your* state may use a different formula:

   a. 5-years or less: no greater than half the length of your marriage.

      i. Example: You are married for 4 years and 6 months, or 54 months. The court can order General Term Alimony for up to 27 months, or one year and three months. The court recognizes that after more than four years out of the work force, it is going to take you time to brush up on your job skills and find a job to support yourself.

      ii. Example: You are married for one year and make major changes in your work habits to support his career, but then realize you made a big mistake. The court can order General Term Alimony for up to 6 months to give you time to polish your resume and re-enter the work force.

      iii. Example: You get married in the Elvis Chapel in Las Vegas. Three days later, you sober up and file for an annulment. You will get zero alimony because you weren't married long enough that it should have impacted your ability to work.

   b. More than 5-years but less than 10-years: no greater than 60% of the number of months of the marriage. The court understands the longer you are out of work, the more difficult it is to simply re-enter the work force. Old connections you had to the job market are usually long gone, so they give you a bit more time.

      i. Example: You are married for 12 years and 3 months, or 147 months. The court can order general term alimony for 147 x .60 = 88 months or 7 years and 3 months.

   c. More than 10-years but less than 15-years: no greater than 70% of the number of months of the marriage. Once you've been out of the work force for a decade or more, not only have you lost important connections and job references, but the job market itself has usually changed. You will often need to go back to school and start at an entry level someplace, so the legislature has authorized the court to order your husband to provide a safety net for a longer period of time.

    i. Example: You are married 10 years, 1 month, or 121 months. The court can order general term alimony for 121 x .70 = 85 months or 7 years.

d. More than 15-years but less than 20-years: no greater than 80% of the number of months of the marriage.

    i. Example: You are married 19 years and 11 months or 167 months. The court can order general term alimony for 167 x .80 = 134 months or 11 years.

e. Marriages longer than 20 years: the court can order general term alimony for an indefinite length of time for marriages that lasted more than 20 years.

Remember ... these hypothetical examples are based on a nationwide *trend* which has emerged due to states adopting guidelines which have been repeatedly proposed, but not adopted by the American Academy of Matrimonial Lawyers (AAML). I include them to help you familiarize yourself with the rationale behind why one person may get alimony for only a few years (or none at all) while another might get it for the rest of their life. For a clearer picture of how alimony might work in *your* state, make an appointment with a local attorney!

2. REHABILITATIVE ALIMONY: is alimony paid to provide a safety net for you long enough for you to back on your own two feet financially, usually through re-employment; completing a job training program, or the receipt of monies due to you from your former husband (for example, the sale of the former marital home). Under the AAML model, the court would not be authorized to order this type of alimony for longer than 5 years.

Rehabilitative Alimony ends either when you hit the 'end date' specified in your court order or Separation Agreement, if you get remarried or cohabitate with a new partner, or if you die.

3. REIMBURSEMENT ALIMONY: is alimony the court orders to compensate you after a

marriage of not more than 5 years for economic or non-economic contributions you made to the marriage such as working while your husband put himself through medical school to become a doctor or a long training program and apprenticeship to become an electrician. Although *he* may have been economically dependent upon *you* while he was still in school, he is capable of earning much more than you *now*. The legislature finds 'kicking the starter-spouse to the curb' after they worked their fingers to the bone supporting their spouse through school to be repugnant. The court is not authorized to offer this type of alimony for longer than 5 years.

Reimbursement Alimony is the only type of alimony you can receive even if the difference in your incomes would otherwise not entitle you to alimony. This ensures that your newly-minted physician husband can't simply avoid paying you by volunteering for Doctors Without Borders until your divorce is final.

4. TRANSITIONAL ALIMONY: is alimony the court orders after a marriage of not more than 5 years to help you transition to an adjusted lifestyle (i.e., drastically reduced) or move to a new location as a result of a divorce. The maximum length of time a court can order your spouse to pay you Transitional Alimony is 3 years.

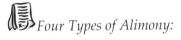*Four Types of Alimony:*

- *General Term – alimony based upon years of marriage;*
- *Rehabilitative – alimony just long enough for you to find a job and start supporting yourself;*
- *Reimbursement – alimony to repay you for putting your husband through grad school and he thanks you by kicking you to the curb;*
- *Transitional – alimony to wean you off a nice lifestyle into a really crappy one.*

ALIMONY INCOME

Although the definition of *alimony income* changes state-by-state, Child Support Guidelines have been in effect in all 50 states for decades. Most judges have grown accustomed to thinking of 'marital income' as being the same thing as 'child support income.' Therefore, you would not be amiss in using the same gross income figure you used in Chapter Five to guesstimate alimony until you can speak to a local attorney to give you a more accurate number.

If the 'income' comes from an asset that was part of your property division (i.e., interest and dividend income from an asset one of you took as part of your property division), it will generally not be considered part of either parties 'income' for the purposes of computing an alimony order. This is to avoid penalizing a spouse who took stock and retirement accounts as their share of the property division.

WHAT IS ALIMONY NEED?

Alimony is only awarded based on economic *need*. In other words, not only must there be a difference in your income, but you must prove you *need* it to maintain as closely as possible the same standard of living you enjoyed during the marriage. *Economic need* is an often-litigated area of alimony law. The Acorns you gathered in Chapter Three and used to fill out your Financial Statement in Chapter Four will be needed to justify to the court you *need* additional money from your ex-husband in the form of alimony to survive. Your husband, on the other hand, will try to reduce his alimony order by claiming you don't *really* need that much money. That's why gathering your old financial statements is so important!

In Chapter Four, Jane Doe claimed she had $637 week worth of general living expenses, $360 week worth of mortgage payments, and $222 week of other debt payments. Her *economic need* would be as follows:

TABLE 6-4: HYPOTHETICAL JANE DOE 'ECONOMIC NEED' COMPUTATION

Jane's annual expenses	$33,124
Mortgage payments	$18,720
Other debt payments	$11,544
Potential economic need	$63,388
Minus Jane's earned income	$22,880
Residual economic need	$40,508

(AAML guidelines - for initial planning purposes only)

Depending on whether Jane resides in a more conservative 1/3-1/3-1/3 type state where she'd only receive a few hundred dollars a month in alimony or a more generous one such as Massachusetts AAML-based formula where she'd receive nearly $1,000 per month, Jane's economic need is going to *far exceed* her own salary and any alimony she might receive. Unfortunately, the court isn't going to give Jane more money simply because she needs it. It's up to *her* to bring her post-divorce living expenses in line with her post-divorce income. We'll look at ways to address this shortfall in Chapter Eight.

Go back over the draft court Financial Statement you created in Chapter Four with a fine tooth comb and make sure you've included all of your expenses. Include oddball expenses that only occur once every few months (or years) such as renewing your driver's license, pumping out your septic tank, or replacing the tires on your car. Alimony need is usually culled from the Expenses section of the court Financial Statement.

CAN I GET BOTH ALIMONY AND CHILD SUPPORT?

Generally you cannot receive alimony and also receive child support. However, if you are entitled to receive more of one type of support than the other, the court will often allocate those amounts as being part alimony and part child support. If you are both moderate income, child support probably cancels out alimony, but at some point you might be entitled to switch from child support to alimony once your kids become emancipated. The following examples are based on Massachusetts durational limits, but should give you a general idea of how alimony and child support are interrelated:

1. EXAMPLE: you were married 12 years. You have two children, ages 12 and 15. Your husband earns $60,000 per year and you earn $15,000 per year. Under the alimony guidelines you would be entitled to receive $15,750 per year for 100 months or 8.4 years. You would have to pay the taxes on that $15,750 or $4,410 per year to Uncle Sam. Under the child support guidelines with other factors thrown in, you are entitled to receive $18,512 in child support, tax-free. The Child Support cancels out alimony, but if your youngest child turns 18 and does not go to college, you would have 2 years left to receive alimony.

2. EXAMPLE: you were married 7 years. You have three children, age 3, 5, and 8. Your husband earns $45,000 per year. You earn $28,000 per year. You would be entitled to receive up to $5,950 per year in alimony for 42 months/3.5 years, for which *you* would pay the taxes. You are entitled to receive $13,832/yr. in child support, for which *he* pays the taxes. Child support 'cancels out' potential alimony. Your right to receive it will expire before your children become emancipated.

TAX IMPLICATIONS OF ALIMONY VS. CHILD SUPPORT

Taxation of alimony rewards remains fairly constant in all 50 states. Sometimes child support cancels out any potential alimony award. Other times, after computing both types of spousal support, the court might order him to pay part of his obligation as child support and part as alimony. And then there are marriages where the children are grown and he'll be ordered to pay pure alimony. How you receive your spousal support (division of marital assets, child support, or alimony) has serious tax implications.

1. THE RECIPIENT PAYS THE TAXES ON ALIMONY: Taxes on alimony must be paid by the recipient (you). For example, if your husband gives you an alimony check for $1,000 per month, at the end of the year, you will owe the federal government a check for taxes on that $12,000 income (for most middle-income taxpayers, that would be the 28% tax bracket or $3,360 you owe Uncle Sam). If you live in a state with a state income tax, you would also owe the state government an additional percentage (here in Massachusetts its 5.3% of that $12,000, or $636). Thus, a $12,000 alimony order is really only worth $8006. Every month, when you receive your alimony check for $1,000, you will need to set $330 of it aside.

TABLE 6-5: HYPOTHETICAL JANE DOE ALIMONY TAX

Alimony to Jane (Mass.)	$10,701
State/Federal taxes ~25%	- $2,675
Post-tax alimony income	$8,026

(AAML guidelines - for initial planning purposes only)

2. **THE PAYOR PAYS TAXES ON CHILD SUPPORT:** Taxes on Child Support must be paid by the non-custodial parent (your husband). Child support is tax-free to *you*. Therefore, if you get $12,000 worth of child support, you get to *keep* $12,000 worth of child support. Let's pretend for a moment Jane Doe's alimony award is classified as child support (below):

TABLE 6-6: HYPOTHETICAL JANE DOE CHILD SUPPORT TAX

Child Support to Jane (Mass.)	$10,701
State/Federal taxes ~25%	- $0
Post-tax child support income	$10,701

(AAML guidelines - for initial planning purposes only)

3. **IF YOU GET PART CHILD SUPPORT AND PART ALIMONY, YOU PAY TAXES ON EACH PORTION ACCORDINGLY.** It is important that your Separation Agreement (covered later) delineate what is alimony, what is child support, and who is to pay the taxes on it. If your agreement states you are to collect child support until your youngest child is emancipated and then, at some point, child support will end and the amount will be classified as alimony, it's important you budget for the taxes you will need to start paying.

TABLE 6-7: HYPOTHETICAL JANE DOE ALIMONY + CHILD SUPPORT TAX

Child Support to Jane (Mass.)	$5,701	
State/Federal taxes ~25%	- $0	-
Child Support after taxes	$5,701	
Alimony to Jane (Mass)		$5,000
State/Federal taxes ~25%		$1,250
Post-tax alimony		$3,750
Post-tax alimony + child support	$5,701 + $3750 = $9,451	(tax loss = $1,250)

(AAML guidelines - for initial planning purposes only)

If your children are not emancipated, classify as much as your spousal support as possible as child support. Child support is worth more than alimony because -your husband- pays the taxes on it! Not you!

CAN –I- BE ORDERED TO PAY MY HUSBAND ALIMONY?

Alimony is meant to be gender-neutral. If your spouse is the one who earns significantly less than you do, it could be *you* who is ordered to pay *him* alimony. Whether or not that happens depends upon the same factors that will decide your property division as outlined in most states divorce statutes, such as length of the marriage, age of the parties, health of the parties, both parties income, employment and employability, including employability through reasonable diligence and additional training, and if necessary, economic and non-economic contribution to the marriage, marital lifestyle, ability of each party to maintain the marital lifestyle, lost economic opportunity as a result of the marriage, and other factors that the court may deem relevant and material.

1. EXAMPLE: your husband worked graveyard shift to be home with your two toddlers during the day while you built a successful career. He turned down several offers to work a daytime position with better career advancement opportunities because child care was too expensive. You *might* be ordered to pay *him* alimony.

2. EXAMPLE: your husband was fired from his job and refused to hunt for a new one. He was emotionally abusive and constantly undermined your self-esteem even though *you* worked hard to build *your* career. Your children were in school most of the time. He also had a drinking problem. Now he is asking for alimony. The court *might* be persuaded to refuse his request *if* you can prove his staying home provided little value to your economic unit.

3. EXAMPLE: your husband fell off a roof from his job as a home improvement contractor and broke his back. He now collects (or recently applied for) Social Security Disability and depends upon you for support. The court will *most likely* order you to pay him alimony.

WHEN DOES ALIMONY 'END?'

Alimony ends whenever your alimony order *says* it ends, when you get remarried, or when you cohabitate with a new partner. If you cohabitate and lose your alimony, but that relationship later breaks up and you *would* have otherwise been still entitled to receive alimony, you can often petition the court to reinstate it. The reinstated order will then end when it normally would have ended. If your former husband remarries, he still has to pay your alimony. It's only when *you* get remarried (or cohabitate) that it ends.

⚑ *The moment you have a new boyfriend spend the night at your house (or word gets out YOU are spending the night at your new boyfriend's house) your husband is going to have you back in court trying to cut off your alimony.*

Most states also end alimony when your husband reaches his natural 'Social Security Full Retirement Age' which is between 66 and 67 years old for most individuals at the moment. Early retirement, even if authorized under a private or government pension program, does not entitle him to end alimony. Only reaching the official 'Social Security Full Retirement Age' in states that recognize this end-date would entitle him to end alimony. It doesn't matter if *he* is old enough to retire, but you are not. Or if he chooses to still work. Once he's old enough to retire, he might not have to pay you anymore. This 'end when retire' trend is having *catastrophic* consequences for women of long-term marriages whose husbands suddenly decide to up and leave them close to retirement. The largest demographic of marriages ending these days is women over the age of 50. If *you* are the one thinking of leaving your husband, please see a financial planner before you take another step!

 *Alimony ends when your husband dies. If he dies, your source of income disappears, so you'd better plan accordingly!*

Alimony Generally Ends:

- *When your divorce decree says it ends;*
- *When you get remarried;*
- *When you live with a new boyfriend;*
- *When your husband reaches full Social Security Retirement Age (~67);*
- *When he dies.*

LIFE INSURANCE AND ALIMONY

Alimony ends if your spouse dies, or if *you* die. To protect against economic insecurity, many divorce decrees require the husband to take out a life insurance policy on his own life for the anticipated amount of alimony he would have to pay until its end. However, in most states, the *cost* of this policy is then deducted from your monthly alimony award.

1. Example: you were married for 30 years and the court ordered alimony of $1,000 per month up until the day your spouse is due to retire, an amount you calculated to be 184 months. You can get the court to order him to take out a life insurance policy worth $184,000 on his own life insurance policy naming *you* as the beneficiary. However, if the premium is $1,000 per year, the judge may reduce your alimony award by that amount.

If you will be dependent upon alimony to fund your lifestyle, it's prudent to take out a life insurance policy on your spouse so you're not left with nothing if he drops dead.

HEALTH/DENTAL INSURANCE AND ALIMONY

The government wants to keep as many people as possible insured. If your husband is ordered to keep you on his existing health insurance plan or purchase a new one for you, the court will generally exclude the cost of that insurance from the amount of alimony he has to pay you, the same as it did for life insurance.

WHAT IF MY FORMER HUSBAND GETS REMARRIED?

If your former spouse gets remarried, his insurance company will kick you off his health insurance plan and you'll need to buy one on your own (or go back to court to get the judge to order him to buy you an individual plan and make *him* pay the difference in cost between the old and new plan). If you have a pre-existing medical condition which makes staying on his plan critical or you gave up other assets in order to remain on his plan, you want to spell this out in your Separation Agreement so you can go back to court and modify things if your husband gets remarried. Most men get remarried within three years after getting divorced (more so than women).

Other than that, not much should change. If he owes you alimony, the fact he chose to get remarried will  not absolve him of his duties to support you even if it is a financial hardship on his new family. If, on the other hand, his new wife is fabulously wealthy, that doesn't help you get a higher alimony award. Income from his new spouse is not used to compute 'available income' for alimony purposes (although there are rare exceptions … consult an attorney).

WHAT IF –I- GET REMARRIED OR GET A NEW BOYFRIEND?

The day you get remarried, alimony will end. However, if you move in with (cohabitate) with a new boyfriend, alimony will most likely *also* end. Your ex-husband *will* drag you into court the moment he catches wind you have a new boyfriend who sometimes spends the night at your house. Therefore, unless you're certain your new boyfriend will marry you and replace the alimony from your first husband, be cautious about who you date and how much time they spend at your house.

Dirty Lawyer Trick: Your ex-husband might hire a private investigator to document how many nights per week your new boyfriend sleeps over your house and then drag you into court to end alimony.

Dirty Lawyer Trick: Your ex-husband's lawyer will drag your new boyfriend into court and ask him, under oath, what belongings he keeps you your house, how much money he gives you towards your living expenses, how many nights he spends there, etc.

Needless to say, even if you 'win' and prove your new boyfriend isn't cohabitating in court, chances are, you're going to 'lose' when your new boyfriend decides you're more trouble than you're worth and dumps you!

CAN I WAIVE ALIMONY IN EXCHANGE FOR AN ASSET?

Some states encourage judges to examine whether there are enough assets in the marriage to 'buy out' the potential alimony award. Other states don't have any such official policy, but it's a common posturing for attorneys to take during settlement negotiations. If your state does not empower the judge to ram a 'buyout' down your spouse's throat, you might still be able to *entice* him to go for it with the promise of 'being rid' of you. One common 'buyout' is to keep the marital home in exchange for 'waiving' alimony.

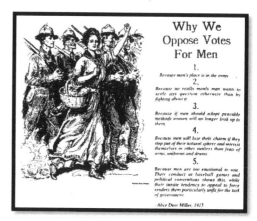

Usually when contemplating a buyout, you agree to take substantially *less* money than what you'd get if you simply waited and took it bit-by-bit each month in exchange for getting that money *now*. This concept is called the *time value of money*. A dollar today, invested in a safe investment vehicle over a period of years, is worth more than a dollar received many years from now. Computing an 'alimony buyout' is easy here in Massachusetts, which has adopted concrete Alimony Guidelines. In other states, you'll have to 'guesstimate' what you might be entitled to receive.

1. EXAMPLE: We'll pretend Jack is 59 years old and will be eligible to retire at age 66. Jane has estimated she is entitled to receive $10,701 per year until Jack retires, or $74,907. Jane doesn't trust Jack not to simply skip town to avoid paying her. Jane would, however, love to get her hands on Jack's $40,000 Merrily-Merrily Retirement stock portfolio. Jane might offer to waive alimony forever, waving the promise of not having to pay *her* and the $30,000 savings, in exchange for that asset.

If you can negotiate an alimony buyout, take the money and run!

Always consult with a certified financial planner when contemplating an alimony buyout … especially if you're inexperienced with handling large sums of money.

EXHIBIT 6-8: SAMPLE CONTESTED HEARING SCRIPT ON ALIMONY

Magistrate:	I am now calling the case of Jane Doe-Rayme versus Jack Rayme. Could you please stand there (pointing to two tables) and state your names for the record?
Jane Doe-Rayme:	I'm Jane Doe-Rayme.
Jack Rayme:	I am Jack Rayme.
Judge:	I understand the both have you have been to see the Family Services Officer and there is still a dispute about whether or not your husband owes you alimony. Mrs. Doe, could you please explain to the court the nature of the dispute?
Jane Doe-Rayme	Sir, if you will refer to my affidavit, I tried to put my thoughts in writing in case I forget to mention anything. During the 12 years we were married, I put my career on hold to help my husband with his business and raise our family. My earning capacity is far below what it should be for someone with my educational background because I've been out of my field for the past dozen years and my training is outdated. Working full time, I earn less than half of my husband's salary.
Judge:	Mr. Rayme, do you care to respond?
Jack Rayme:	It's not *my* fault she doesn't earn as much as me! Nobody *made* her quit her job and hang around the house all day long!
Judge:	Mrs. Doe?
Jane Doe-Rayme:	Sir, that's not true. When we were first married, I was in nursing school pursing a degree as a registered nurse. But then Jayne was born, and there were complications. She had a leg brace and a feeding tube, and none of the daycare centers would take her. I had no choice but to stay home with her. By the time her medical issues began to clear up, Johnnie was born and it no longer made sense to go back to work. Jayne still has dyslexia, and it takes her a long time to do her homework. She needs a lot of help that can't be provided by a full-time working mother.
Judge:	Mr. Rayme, what is your daughter's disability?
Jack Rayme:	Nothing. She's fine. She just doesn't like doing her homework.
Jane Doe-Rayme: *(getting somewhat off track, but making her point)*	That's not true sir. She has been evaluated by the school and has a Special Education Plan. She also had a thorough evaluation from a private special needs school, including a PET scan from a neurologist, and they have confirmed Jayne has special needs. Jayne needs help from a private tutor *and* nightly help completing her homework.
Judge:	Mr. Rayme, do you have anything else left to say?
Jack Rayme:	There's absolutely no reason why my Wife can't get off her behind and earn more money! Most charge nurses I know earn $40,000 per year or more. It's her choice to work private duty instead of getting a job at a hospital.
Jane Doe-Rayme:	Sir, if I may respond. When we first were married, we lived near Big City. We moved to North Anytown after Johnnie was born because there was a lot of work down here for my husband. For the past 9 years, I've helped him run his business by doing the bookkeeping, taking calls from customers, and helping him manage his work schedule. North Anytown is 85 miles from the nearest hospital and nearly 45 miles from any nursing home or other big enterprise that would pay the kind of salary my husband is talking about. Besides, after 12 years of doing nothing but in-home private duty, I'd be hard pressed to get a job at a hospital.
Judge:	I'll take the matter under advisement. You'll get my decision in the mail.

(usually will be part of Temporary Orders hearing)

Analysis: The judge will probably order Jane is entitled to receive alimony. Under an AAML-type guideline, for a 12 year marriage she might be entitled to receive up to 70% of the number of months they were married (approximately 100 months), up to 35% of his gross income. Because Jane is in a field with a good career outlook, at some point she'll be expected to get more profitable work. However, her remote location and children's ties to that location (especially with a child who has a learning disability) greatly hamper he ability to jump in a car and drive 45 miles to the nearest large employer.

Because Jane is already entitled to receive child support, there will likely be no additional income to allocate as alimony.   Since her children will not grow up and become emancipated before her 100 months would end, Jane would be much better off taking whatever income she can allocated as child support, which is taxable to Jack, instead of alimony, which is worth less money due to the tax burden.

THE MASSACHUSETTS ALIMONY REFORM ACT OF 2011

Election Day!

If you happen to live in Massachusetts, where I practice law, your outcome is more predictable. In September of 2011, Massachusetts became the first state in the nation to officially adopt clear-cut guidelines heavily based upon (but not identical to) the AAML Proposed Model Guidelines. Here in Massachusetts, alimony is computed much the way Child Support Guidelines are computed. It is possible to simply download the Alimony Reform Act of 2011, read it, figure out which of the four types of alimony apply in your situation, and compute how much you're entitled to receive. The non-1/3-1/3/1/3 examples used in this chapter were based heavily upon the Massachusetts statute. The Alimony Reform Act of 2011 can be downloaded at:

http://www.malegislature.gov/Bills/187/House/H03617

If you're *not* from Massachusetts, I suggest you write your legislature, complain, and ask them to adopt the AAML proposed guidelines. Why should the taxpayers of your state have to foot the bill to hire extra judges and court staff to litigate alimony? 80% of all divorce cases that go to trial do so because of alimony issues! Think what you could do if you could suddenly eliminate 80% of all money you were paying out for any single item in *your* household expenses?

HIDING MONEY

If you never had children or your children are emancipated, you may have skipped over Chapter Five: Child Support. If your husband is self-employed, worked side-jobs, or you have reason to believe your husband may otherwise be deliberately understating his income so he doesn't have to pay you the full amount of alimony you deserve, I recommend you go back and read Chapter Five. Although the focus of that chapter is on computing child support, in many jurisdictions Child Support Income has become synonymous with Alimony Income. Pay particular attention to all the ways men can hide money … and what you can do to prove it!

CHAPTER 6 SUMMARY

1. In many states, a rough rule of thumb to see if you might get alimony is to add your salary to your husbands, divide by three, and then deduct *your* salary from that amount.

2. Some states have guidelines. Most make you litigate whether or not you'll get alimony. *Not* having guidelines is a stupid waste of taxpayer money. Write your state legislature and complain.

3. States have different types of alimony. The most common types are *general alimony, reimbursement alimony, rehabilitative alimony, and transitional alimony.*

4. You'll generally receive alimony for a set period of time based on the duration of the marriage (i.e., 50% of the number of months).

5. It's not enough to be *entitled* to receive alimony. You must also, using old statements and bills, prove you *need* it.

6. You can't receive more child support and alimony combined than alimony alone.

7. Child support is worth more than alimony because *he* pays the taxes on it.

8. If your spouse earns less than you, you might be ordered to pay *him* alimony.

9. Alimony usually ends when your spouse reaches the full Social Security retirement age.

10. If your spouse pays for life insurance, health or dental insurance, it will generally be deducted from your alimony order.

11. If you get remarried or move in with your boyfriend, alimony will generally end.

12. If you can possibly 'buy out' your future alimony entitlement in exchange for an asset, take the money and run! Speak to a financial planner first so you don't simply squander it.

(This page left intentionally blank)

CHAPTER 7

PROPERTY DIVISION

Once you view your divorce as the dissolution of a financial partnership, figuring out what you're entitled to receive becomes fairly predictable. Generally, if you got it, bought it, earned it, or inherited it during the marriage, you're entitled to half. That's the position you should take (absent exigent circumstances) unless the judge decides otherwise. As explained in Chapter One, courts will rarely deviate any more than 60:40 on a property division.

This doesn't guarantee you'll *get* half if your case goes to trial. Some states are *community property* states which require all property to be divided equally while others are *equitable distribution* states which might order an unequal split. *The legal distinction between community property and equitable division goes beyond the scope of this book.* If there are complex trust issues, a juicy inheritance, or your husband built his highly successful business *before* you were married, the judge *might* be persuaded to exclude certain assets from the marital kitty. Attorneys for the wealthy split hairs because excluding a high-value asset from the marital kitty can mean big bucks for the winner. However, this book is the *Divorce Bootcamp for Low- and Moderate-Income Women.* Therefore, I'm assuming you don't have a trust fund or business worth millions of dollars! If you do, please hire an attorney.

Community Property – everything a husband and wife acquire once they are married is owned equally (fifty-fifty) by both of them, regardless of who provided the money to purchase the asset or whose name the asset is held in.

Equitable Distribution - property acquired during a marriage is jointly owned by both spouses. Equitable distribution does not necessarily mean equal distribution, and ownership does not automatically split fifty-fifty. Rather, the distribution must be fair and just (equitable).

For all the posturing about the differences between states with community property laws and states with equitable distribution, the end result for most divorcing couples (absent an asset which might be declared to be separate property such as an inheritance or property earned prior to marriage) is remarkably similar. For planning purposes, work with the range between a 50:50 split and a 60:40 split until you have a chance to consult with an attorney about any areas which might skew your individual case from the 'norm.' We'll discuss ways to get residual legal questions answered affordably in Chapter Nine.

WHAT IS 'PROPERTY?'

In its simplest definition, *property* means an asset. When most people think of an asset, they think of something tangible such as a house, a car, a stock portfolio or the balance in a bank account. But *property* also includes non-tangible items, such as frequent flyer miles or intellectual property. If an item has value and it belongs to you, it may be considered *property.*

 Real property - real estate, such as a house, land, business property, or a condo.

 Personal property – such as motor vehicles, furniture, household goods, antiques, just about anything you can walk into a store and buy.

 Business property – such as tools of trade, office furniture and equipment, accounts receivable, business 'goodwill,' just about anything a business might consider valuable or include in a tax statement or bank application for a business loan.

 Investments – such as savings accounts, stocks, bonds, IOU's, etc.

 Intellectual property – such as copyrights on written matter, trademarks, patents, or potentially copyrightable/patentable matters.

 Retirement assets – such as the value of vested or unvested pension, 401(k), deferred compensation, IRA, etc.

 Professional or other licenses – such as a taxi cab medallion, a liquor license, a medical license, a law license, a pharmacists license, etc.

 Options to purchase – such as stock options, option to purchase a closely held company, etc.

 Rights to a claim or lawsuit – such as a pending workers compensation claim, pending personal injury lawsuit, pending payment due from insurance, or other pending claim.

Insurance – such as the cash value of life insurance, but also an outstanding claim against insurance on something or someone who was insured.

Interest in a professional practice or closely held business – such as a law firm, real estate agency, auto dealer, construction company, mom & pop business, family business.

Intangible property – such as frequent flyer miles, cash-back rewards, stock options, etc.

Inheritances or gifts – including trusts. In some states, gifts are considered separate property, not subject to division. In others, that house your mother just put in trust for you when she dies becomes something your spouse is entitled to a share of.

This list is by no means exhaustive, but hopefully it will get your mind mulling over whether or not you should add any items to that Acorns List you dutifully gathered in Chapter Three.

WHICH PROPERTY IS SUBJECT TO DIVISION?

Courts tend to break property down into two different types. *Marital property* came into the marital unit during the marriage. As a general rule, if you got it, bought it, or otherwise acquired it during the marriage it is marital property subject to division. *Separate property* sometimes includes property you owned before the marriage or (sometimes) acquired after separation but before you filed for divorce. In some states, you *may* be able to exclude some of your assets from being added into the marital kitty which then gets divided. For example, what if you own a hunting cabin from prior to getting married which you kept in your name *only*, never had a mortgage on it or paid any other major expense out of joint marital funds, and never lived in it with your spouse. Or perhaps you signed a prenuptial agreement? If the parties never *commingled* an asset with the marital estate, a judge *might* be persuaded to exclude it. Most litigation over property division occurs because one party wants a valuable asset declared to be separate property so they don't have to share it.

Marital Property – assets acquired during the marriage

Separate Property – assets acquired outside of the marital relationship, including business assets, gifted assets, and inheritances. State definitions of what constitutes separate property vary widely from state-to-state and can make a *huge* difference in how much money you'll receive.

Commingled – to mix your assets together.

What is commingled? Commingling occurs when you each bring something of value to the marriage, but over time, you use each other's 'stuff' so much you no longer think of it as yours and mine. One good example is when one of you owns a house before you're married, but you both live there, refinance it several times, pay the mortgage on it from joint marital funds, and share the upkeep, maintenance and repair. Depending on how long you were married and how much you commingled your assets, the judge might declare the entire thing is a joint marital asset, none of it is a marital asset, or pick some number in the middle. One common formula for figuring out how much of a formerly separate asset is now joint marital property follows:

Equity ÷ number of years owned x length of marriage = marital property

$$E \div YO \times LOM = MP$$

Back to our hypothetical couple. Jane Doe and Jack Rayme were married for 11 years. They have equity in their home worth $145,850. Let's pretend for a moment that Jack plunked down a 10% down payment for that house three years before they were married. During the marriage, the house was refinanced twice and also a home equity line of credit. *Both* contributed to the mortgage payment from their earnings. Jane co-signed each new mortgage and did all the landscaping and painting, while Jack did the heavier repairs. They added an addition after one of their children was born using joint marital funds. The value shot up during the early 2000's, and then crashed and burned during the 2008 market recession, but the house is still worth about twice what Jack originally paid for it. How will a judge sort out that mess?

$$E \div YO \times LOM = MP$$

or

$$\$145,850 \div 14 \text{ yrs.} = \$10,418 \times 11 \text{yrs.} = \$114,596$$

A judge might determine that $114,596 should be counted as a 'joint marital asset' which then would be divided according to whatever split the rest of the marital estate is divided into (50:50 but never more than 60:40). This isn't the *only* formula a judge might use, but it's a common way to divvy up an asset that started out as separate property and, over time, became shared.

The judge could, of course, declare the entire house is a joint marital asset. The longer you were married, the more likely a judge is to do this. Or he might take that same formula and deduct out Jack's original 10% down payment. But judges don't like having to do a lot of math. Jack deducts out his 10% on the house. You demand he deduct the car Jack took over for you 11 years ago. Jack then says he wants the judge to *also* deduct out some other trivial asset. Yada yada yada… Judges don't like doing math and writing elaborate orders explaining why they chose to exempt this piece of property and not that one. It's too much work! If you stick a fair-looking formula like this in front of them and your reasoning is sound, there's a good chance the judge will go for it.

It's unlikely the judge would exempt the house hypothesized above from the property division completely even though Jack purchased it before the marriage. Jane expended effort and her own funds in keeping and maintaining the house and most of the equity was built up during the marriage. What happens, however, if Jack *hadn't* commingled a piece of property? Let's hypothesize Jack inherited a hunting cabin in the Great North Woods of New Hampshire 15 years ago and, except for writing a check for $2,000 for the property tax bill and buying a couple of bricks of shingles a few years ago to re-shingle the roof on his annual hunting trip, the property was otherwise kept separate? In that case, Jack would have a valid claim the hunting cabin should be kept separate from the marital estate.

This same formula (E ÷ YO x LOM = MP) can be used to divide other commingled assets, such as a 401(k) or other pension plan, a stock portfolio, etc. There are other formulas, of course. If the opposing parties' lawyer or a mediator sticks a proposal with a different formula in front of you, compare how their proposed math fares versus your proposed math. If their figure is within 10% of yours (remember that 50:50 vs. 60:40 number), it may be more prudent to accept their figure rather than go to trial. If the asset in question is valuable, consult first with an attorney.

WHAT ABOUT GIFTED OR INHERITED PROPERTY?

Property that was inherited by or gifted to one party before, during or after the marriage is treated differently state to state. Although *most* states exclude the gifted or inherited property as *separate property*, some states (including Massachusetts) might include the asset as part of the marital estate. Valuable gift and inheritance assets go beyond the scope of this book.

 Consult an attorney if you have inherited or gifted property because you have a lot to lose!!!

THE BURDEN OF PROOF IS ON THE PERSON CLAIMING IT'S SEPARATE PROPERTY

The burden of *proving* something should be treated as separate property is generally on the person claiming its not marital property. Who bears the *burden of proof* is a big deal if your case goes to trial. Think of it as one of those walls you see soldiers climbing over in boot camp. Sure, any reasonably fit soldier can get over the wall, but an unfit one cannot. When somebody has the burden to prove something, it means the court isn't simply going to take their word for it. They need more. Deeds. Bank records. Witness or expert testimony. Something to prove enough marital funds weren't expended when Jack paid the property tax bills or re-shingled the roof to justify Jane laying claim to it.

 Burden of Proof - the obligation of a party to prove his allegations during a trial.

Keep *burden of proof* and *commingling* in mind when you negotiate a property settlement with the evil trapper. To meet a burden of proof, you often have to put on a dog-and-pony show using expert testimony and witnesses, not simply testify you think you should keep it because its' yours. Trials are expensive (we'll discuss this in a few moments). If you truly believe you put enough of your own time and money into a previously-owned asset to lay claim to it, don't let the evil trapper (or his lawyer) browbeat you into giving it up without first consulting an attorney.

INSIDE A JUDGES HEAD - HOW PROPERTY DIVISION HAPPENS IN COURT

There's no set formula about how property is divided, but results are fairly consistent nationwide. Good lawyers try to rub elbows with the judges who decide our cases so we can gain insight into what goes on inside their heads. You can take all the Continuing Legal Education classes in the world, but it's those rare occasions when a group of judges sit down 'off the record' and discuss the latest legal trend that you can gain breathtaking insight into what goes on inside their minds. A highly respected Massachusetts family court judge lauded for consistency and fairness once privileged a group of brother-judges, and those few attorneys who'd happened to brown-bag their lunches that day, with detailed insight into the way he divides assets. His brother-judges all nodded their heads with approval and agreed, despite using less mathematically precise formulas, that their *own* thought processes were remarkably similar. I will pass along this insight even though it is neither a 'rule' nor a 'law,' because this insight has never once served me wrong.

This judge always starts with a presumption of a 50:50 split. He then considers evidence supporting each 'factor' outlined in the state divorce statue. Some common nationwide divorce 'factors' are as follows:

TABLE 7-1: COMMON DIVORCE 'FACTORS'

• Length of the marriage	• Estate (assets)
• Conduct during the marriage	• Liabilities
• Age	• Needs of each party
• Health	• Opportunity for future acquisition of capital or inheritance
• Station of the parties	• Opportunity for future acquisition of income
• Occupation	• Contribution to increasing their respective estates
• Amount and sources of income	• Contribution as homemaker
• Vocational skills	• Needs of the children
• Employability	

As evidence is given, this judge assigns 'points' to each party on a scale of 1-5. For example, if the husband is a saint and the wife drinks and had numerous affairs, under 'conduct during the marriage' he'd award the husband 5 points and the wife a negative five. If both parties are in good health, he'd award each 0 points. If the husband built a successful business, he'd get 5 points under "contribution of the parties," whereas the wife might get 4 points for 'contribution as homemaker.'

This judge then takes the points, averages them, and makes it fit within the maximum 60:40 split (the amount he knows he can deviate from a 50:50 property division without risking being overturned on appeal). If both parties contributed fairly equally to the marriage, they end up with close to a 50:50 split. If one parties' behavior was egregious, that percentage could move the property division towards the 60:40 extreme.

In other words: Start at 50:50. Never more than 60:40. You're usually fighting over a lousy 10%.

This 'points system' is by no means a formula to count on in your divorce, just one *particular* judge's method for coming up with a number. However, despite the use (or lack thereof) of any formal formula, you'd be amazed at how similar most property divisions end up after much costly litigation. For purposes of this book, we're assuming you have no significant inherited assets or separate property. Here's a sample 50:50 property division Jane Doe might negotiate with her husband based on the Financial Statement she shared with us in Chapter Four:

TABLE 7-2: SAMPLE 50:50 PROPERTY DIVISION

Description of Asset	Equity or FMV	Wife	Husband
Equity from sale of marital home	$145,850	$91,990	$53,860
Merrily-Merrily Retirement IRA	$15,000		$15,000
Vanguard IRA	$2,500	$2,500	
Present cash value of Husband's whole-life insurance policy	$1,630		$1,630
Big Bank checking account	$1,500		$1,500
UTMGA savings account	$6,000	$6,000	
Wife's 2004 Dodge Tahoe	$1,000	$1,000	
Husband's 2001 Ford F-150 pickup truck	$12,500		$12,500
Husbands' contractor tools	$17,000		$17,000
Total Assets to be Divided (proposed 50:50 split)	$202,980	$101,490	$101,490

The proposed property division is fairly straightforward. Although Jane keeps some assets (such as her car) and Jack keeps others (such as his tools-of-trade), there is enough cash left over from the sale of the marital home so that each person gets an equal share. Both have enough money to put a down-payment on a modest home of their own and continue their separate lives and they can *agree* to start this process before they even go to court. But what happens if negotiations fail and Jack and Jane decide to hire two attorneys to go to trial, each claiming they contributed more to the marital estate than the other? Here's the carrot Jack's lawyer might dangle in front of him of what the marital estate might look like:

TABLE 7-3: SAMPLE 60:40 PROPERTY DIVISION

Description of Asset	Equity or FMV	Wife 40%	Husband 60%
Equity from sale of marital home	$145,850	$71,692	$74, 158
Merrily-Merrily Retirement IRA	$15,000		$15,000
Vanguard IRA	$2,500	$2,500	
Present cash value of Husband's whole-life insurance policy	$1,630		$1,630
Big Bank checking account	$1,500		$1,500
UTMGA savings account	$6,000	$6,000	
Wife's 2004 Dodge Tahoe	$1,000	$1,000	
Husband's 2001 Ford F-150 pickup truck	$12,500		$12,500
Husbands' contractor tools	$17,000		$17,000
Total Assets to be Divided (60:40 split)	$202,980	$81,192	$121,788

At first glance, it looks like Jack made out like a bandit. He now has $40,000 more than Jane. Whoopee! He won! He won! He showed that little gold digger who was the big dog!

Now here's the rest of the story…

TABLE 7-4: SAMPLE 60:40 PROPERTY DIVISION *AFTER* ATTORNEY FEES

Description of Asset	Equity or FMV	Wife 40%	Husband 60%
Total Assets to be Divided	$202,980	$81,192	$121,788
Attorney Fees ($15,000 each)		-$15,000	-$15,000
Residual Estate		$66,192	$106,788
Loss/profit over a 50:50 split	50:50 - $101,490	($32,298)	+$5,298

Jack didn't win all that much after all … did he? The *real* number when computing your *return on investment* when investing in litigation fees is how much Jack won *over and above* what he would have gotten had he simply settled the case. *Not* how much more he got than Jane. Two years of litigation with assets were tied up in a non-interest-bearing attorney IOLTA account, $15,000 in attorney fees (*if* no custody dispute, which would drive costs even higher), and all Jack got was a measly $5,298.

Jane is the big loser. She gets $32,298 less than she would have gotten if the case had not gone to trial. Jack's $40,000 'win' cost their marital unit (and their children and/or heirs) $30,000, money *no* low- or middle-income couple can afford to simply throw away. If Jack and Jane were thinking like rational human beings, they'd *never* expend money on something which tied them up for two years and only yielded a few thousand dollars.

Unfortunately, it's usually the male of the species who goes off half-cocked without asking tough questions about the return-on-investment for legal fees. Jacks attorney may encourage him to 'fight' paying alimony or child support as if all the legal fees in the world could change what your states' divorce statute says about how the judge must process your divorce. It's the law. Most lawyers will *not* spell out, in dollars and cents, how *bad* of an investment going to trial. If Jack is being a jerk, Jane has several options:

1. Settle the case for a 60:40 split. That way, she's only down $20,298 instead of $32,298. It's unfair … but Jane makes a strategic decision to take her money and run.

2. Keep her attorney on a short leash. Jane might ask her attorney to make minimal efforts to defend the case (i.e., introduce evidence already gathered and help her testify about *her* contribution to the marriage, but forego spending money on depositions, expert witnesses, and other experts). It would likely cost her $5,000 instead of $15,000 and her attorney will make her sign a waiver.

3. Represent *herself* at trial (not recommended, but sometimes you don't have a choice). Jane may or may not end up with better than a 60:40 split, but so long as she's careful to only forward legitimate arguments as to why she deserves 50:50, she's unlikely to do *worse* than 60:40 (barring some weird 'separate property' exclusion). This is what the Fathers' Rights aka Batterers' Rights movement advocates batterers do to jack up the wife's legal fees.

 *Spouses Behaving Badly:* A Fathers' Rights advocate launched a four-day pro-se (self-represented) trial alleging his wife didn't *really* want a divorce because she was suffering from peri-menopause and that, in the alternative, if the judge *did* find the marriage was irretrievably broken, he should get *everything* because she violated the 'marriage contract' of 'til death do you part.' The wife's legal costs were in excess of $25,000. The judge gave the husband a 58:42 split … and then ordered the husband to pay the wife's attorney fees … putting the wife back on 50:50 footing.

Remember earlier I said Jack's attorney is going to dangle the *carrot* of getting more than Jane in the property division? If you remember the facts of our hypothetical case, Jane recently got a restraining order against Jack for beating the dog in front of the kids and implying she was next. Jane also testified Jack drinks heavily. She has traditionally earned 1/3rd of the income in the family, *and* been the primary caretaker of the children. If Jack were my client and I was being honest with him, I'd advise him I anticipate the judge would order a 45:55 split, with 45% to Jane and 55% to Jack (since he earned more), even *if* we were to go to trial. This is what the final property division *might* look like if Jane advises her attorney she only wants to take minimal steps to prosecute the case and minimize her legal fees:

TABLE 7-5: SAMPLE 55:45 PROPERTY DIVISION *AFTER* ATTORNEY FEES

Description of Asset	Equity or FMV	Wife 45%	Husband 55%
Equity from sale of marital home	$145,850	$81,841	$64,009
Merrily-Merrily Retirement IRA	$15,000		$15,000
Vanguard IRA	$2,500	$2,500	
Present cash value of Husband's whole-life insurance policy	$1,630		$1,630
Big Bank checking account	$1,500		$1,500
UTMGA savings account	$6,000	$6,000	
Wife's 2004 Dodge Tahoe	$1,000	$1,000	
Husband's 2001 Ford F-150 pickup truck	$12,500		$12,500
Husbands' contractor tools	$17,000		$17,000
Total Assets to be Divided (55:45 split)	$202,980	$91,341	$111,639
Attorney Fees ($15,000 Jack/$5,000 Jane)		-$5,000	-$15,000
Residual Estate		$86,341	$96,639
Loss/profit over a 50:50 split	50:50 - $101,490	($15,149)	$4,851
Profit/loss over a 60:40 split	60:40 - $81,192/$121,788	$5,149	($25,149)

These numbers are confusing, but what it essentially means is that if Jane understands she's fighting for a portion of 10% and keeps her lawyer on a short leash, while she may lose money over a 50:50 split, if the judge awards a 55:45 split she'll come out $5,149 ahead of taking it on the chin with a 60:40 split. Jack, on the other hand, who's hell-bent on winning, comes out $25,149 dollars *behind* the $40,000 he *thought* he was going to get when he decided to go to trial. In a situation such as this, in addition to everything listed above, Jane might want to do the following:

1. File a Motion to Compel Mediation/Arbitration and get the court to order Jack kicking-and-screaming to a neutral third-party mediator to point this out to him (court-ordered mediation/arbitration is covered in Chapter Nine).

2. Be willing, after much posturing, to *concede* that additional 5% to Jack during mediation to avoid trial completely and save herself the attorney fees. *But —only-after speaking to an attorney about what you have to lose!!!*

Dirty Lawyer Tricks: I had a case where the opposing attorney insisted his client wouldn't give my client more than 20% of the marital property. I filed a motion asking the court to refer the case to mediation and attached the letter from opposing counsel with that 20% offer of settlement. The judge burst out laughing. The case settled.

TABLE 7-6: SAMPLE 55:45 PROPERTY DIVISION *AFTER* MEDIATION

Description of Asset	Equity or FMV	Wife 45%	Husband 55%
Equity from sale of marital home	$145,850	$81,841	$64,009
Merrily-Merrily Retirement IRA	$15,000		$15,000
Vanguard IRA	$2,500	$2,500	
Present cash value of Husband's whole-life insurance policy	$1,630		$1,630
Big Bank checking account	$1,500		$1,500
UTMGA savings account	$6,000	$6,000	
Wife's 2004 Dodge Tahoe	$1,000	$1,000	
Husband's 2001 Ford F-150 pickup truck	$12,500		$12,500
Husbands' contractor tools	$17,000		$17,000
Total Assets to be Divided (55:45 split)	$202,980	$91,341	$111,639
Mediator Fees ($1,000 ÷ 2)		-$500	-$500
Residual Estate		$90,841	$111,139
Loss/profit over a 50:50 split	50:50 - $101,490	($10,649)	$9,649

Because the mediator is a neutral third-party, Jack is more likely to listen. Once Jack's potential *return-on-investment* after going to trial is put into a spreadsheet, *most* men will start to listen. At the very least, Jack will go back to his attorney and start asking pesky questions about how much he's *really* going to gain by spending all this money on World War III.

WHAT IF YOU DON'T OWN A HOME?

In expanding this *Bootcamp Manual* over the years to include the middle-income woman who suddenly finds herself impoverished once the marriage ends, I've added assets the women I originally wrote this book to help might only dream of someday owning. A house. Two cars. A savings account. A little money set aside in a retirement account. I'd like to devote a bit of space to looking at what Jane Doe's property division might look like if she and Jack are part of that 15.1% of all American families who live below the federal poverty line, or, if you are about to become a single mother, the 26.6% who live in poverty.

For purposes of a low-income hypothetical example, we'll pretend Jack and Jane lease a three bedroom apartment which they have no ownership interest in. They *do* each have a motor vehicle, so we'll leave those in, but their retirement accounts will be significantly smaller (if they have one at all). They probably don't have $6,000 cash sitting in a kiddie trust-fund, so I'll make that $60 UTMGA money grandma gave the kids for birthday money. Nor can they likely afford a cash-value life insurance policy. We'll pretend Jack works as a carpenter for somebody else and only has one-third the number of tools to work his trade. Here's what their proposed 50:50 property division might look like:

TABLE 7-7: LOW-INCOME HYPOTHETICAL 50:50 PROPERTY DIVISION

Description of Asset	Equity or FMV	Wife	Husband
Big Bank checking account	$1,500	$1,500	
UTMGA savings account	$60	$60	
Wife's 2004 Dodge Tahoe	$1,000	$1,000	
Husband's 2001 Ford F-150 pickup truck	$12,500		$12,500
Husbands' contractor tools	$6,000		$6,000
Total Assets to be Divided	$21,060	$2,560	$18,500
Proposed 50:50 split ($21,060 ÷ 2)	$10,530	-$10,530	-$10,530
Shortfall Jack Owes Jane		($7,970)	+$7,970

Although Jack and Jane don't have to worry about divvying up a house, they still have a problem. Jack uses his pickup truck and his contractor tools to ply his trade, so the judge will not assign them to Jane (in most jurisdictions it's statutorily forbidden to deny someone the means to work). Nor does she *want* his pickup truck. She has two children to cart around. A pickup truck devours gasoline and is not very kid-friendly. If her apartment costs more than she can afford alone, Jane will *need* that $7,970 shortfall for first, last and security deposit on a new apartment, but all Jack can give her is an IOU.

Dirty Lawyer Trick: many opposing lawyers will try to convince Jane that Jack's tools, and even perhaps his pickup truck, are 'tools of trade' and therefore not subject to being divided as part of the marital estate. *Tools of trade* does NOT mean Jack's business equipment is not part of the marital estate! But rather that the judge won't take Jack's tools away from him and give them to Jane if doing so will prevent Jack from working. Jack is going to have to come up with some other asset to reimburse Jane or give her an IOU. Don't fall for this dirty trick! I get lawyers who try to pull it on *me* from time-to-time, and I'm a family law attorney!

Although it's likely the judge will order Jack to reimburse Jane for the $7,970 shortfall, a judge's gavel is not a magic wand. The judge can't make more money appear into the marital estate than the parties have at the time they file for divorce just because the parties *need* more money. The judge might order Jack to take out a personal loan, but if he's not credit-worthy, the judge doesn't have any power over the bank. Jane will likely going to end up with an IOU with a monthly payment that the judge determines Jack can afford, likely a payment that is quite small, until Jack reimburses her for the extra $7,970 he's getting out of the marital estate.

You can't get blood from a stone...

If you rent, you are (in a way) better off than your lower-middle income peers. Because renters tend to move around more than homeowners, they may find it much less disruptive to simply pull up roots and move to a cheaper apartment. A renter doesn't have to deal with the hassle of hiring a real estate broker, making major repairs or renovations of the house to make it marketable, locating a seller willing to pay a

reasonable price, and then closing (all while dealing with a combative spouse who sabotages every attempt at selling). Time your divorce to the end of a lease, peruse the market months before you file to get an idea of what you can afford, and squirrel away your first, last, and security deposit. Be happy you don't need to engage in elaborate ploys to "buy out" a house. Focus your energies on getting your fair share of the assets and making the evil trapper pay his fair share of the debts (covered in Chapter Eight).

WHAT HAPPENS IF ONE PARTY WISHES TO KEEP THE MARITAL HOME?

The earlier proposals were straightforward because Jack and Jane sold their marital home and used the proceeds to balance out any inequalities that incurred when they divided their other assets. However, if Jane wants to keep the marital home, she'll have a problem:

TABLE 7-8: SAMPLE 50:50 PROPERTY DIVISION (WIFE KEEPS HOUSE)

Description of Asset	Equity or FMV	Wife	Husband
Appraised equity in marital home	$145,850	$145,850	
Merrily-Merrily Retirement IRA	$15,000		$15,000
Vanguard IRA	$2,500		$2,500
Present cash value of Husband's whole-life insurance policy	$1,630		$1,630
Big Bank checking account	$1,500		$1,500
UTMGA savings account	$6,000		$6,000
Wife's 2004 Dodge Tahoe	$1,000	$1,000	
Husband's 2001 Ford F-150 pickup truck	$12,500		$12,500
Husbands' contractor tools	$17,000		$17,000
Total Assets to be Divided	$202,980	$146,850	$56,130
Shortfall Jane Owes Jack		(45,360)	+$45,360

Since most of the couple's nest egg is invested in the marital home, an asset not easily liquidated, Jane has a problem. Jack is entitled to his fair share. His claim on the house doesn't go away simply because Jane wishes to keep it ... not even if they have children. Although the court will bend over backwards to help Jane remain in her home if their children are still dependent on her, the court won't allow Jane to tie up Jack's money indefinitely. Jane has a hard decision to make. Sell the house? Or come up with a strategy to 'buy out' Jacks residual share?

"BUYING OUT" THE MARITAL HOME

Most middle-class families' only major asset is their home. Unless you have little equity and enough other assets to buy out your husbands' share, most small woodland creatures will be forced to sell. I list below several strategies which might help you accomplish a buyout so you can analyze the Acorns gathered in Chapter Three to figure out if a buyout is possible:

1. WAIT UNTIL YOUR KIDS GRADUATE HIGH SCHOOL AND BUY HIM OUT THEN, OR AGREE TO SELL THE HOUSE THEN AND SPLIT THE PROCEEDS: If I were Jack's attorney, I would advise him this was not in his best interests. The downside of waiting includes:

   a. If his name is on the mortgage, he will remain liable if you default on the loan;

   b. That debt will show up on all future credit reports, lowering his credit rating and hampering his ability to borrow money for his *own* future home;

   c. If you're late on the payment, it will ruin *his* credit;

   d. Once he's been out of the house more than three years, he'll lose his capital gains tax exemption and pay taxes on it once you finally sell.

   e. If the market depreciates (as it's doing now) he could lose money.

   f. You could trash the house or undertake a bizarre renovation, diminishing its value.

   g. It could burn down and he finds out after-the-fact you let the insurance lapse.

   h. More often than not, when the time comes to buy out Jack's share of the house or to sell it, Jane will be too broke to buy him out but will refuse to sell without going to court to force the sale because she's attached to the house.

   Jack isn't the only one I'd advise to think twice before coming to such an arrangement. If you recall Jane's Financial Statement from Chapter Four, Jane is a private duty nurse who has a child with learning disabilities. Because she lives in an economically disadvantaged area, she only earns $753 per week from all sources (including child support) and pays $360 of that for the first and second mortgage. If all she had to do was assume the mortgage and keep making payments on it, by cutting her budget to the bone and getting the court to order Jack to assume a larger share of the other debts from the marriage, Jane might make it.

However... with an income so low, Jane will have a hard time qualifying for financing. So long as she lives in an economically depressed area, she will have a hard time earning more. It may serve her better to pull up ties and move someplace where she can get a higher paying job. Jane should shop around with several banks and find out if she qualifies *before* she files for divorce lest she end up launching World War III in a futile attempt to force Jack to swallow a future buyout. If the bank won't go for it, chances are neither will the judge.

2. YOU HAVE ENOUGH MONEY IN OTHER ASSETS (INCLUDING ONES' OFTEN OVERLOOKED) TO BUY OUT YOUR HUSBANDS' SHARE – most marriages accumulate hard assets, such as equity in a house, a car, a stock portfolio, an IRA, and then more soft assets such as furnishings, electronic equipment, tools, collectibles, and personal belongings. In Chapter Three, I urged you to carefully document and value your smaller assets. Our hypothetical divorcing couple has $12,000 worth of contractors tools attributed to Jack. Your husband's hidden assets may be quite different. Perhaps he has a home office with lots of electronic equipment? Or a mini auto-shop in his garage to pimp out classic cars? Or maybe he's set up an entire basement full of antique toy trains, complete with miniature volcanoes and trestle-bridges. Jack will usually attempt to hide or deny the value of his own 'stuff.'

If you are close to a buyout and there are children involved, sometimes you can convince a judge to order your husband to take all the "stuff" (the car, the IRA, the furniture, his power tools) while your share goes towards a buyout of the house. You may still need to come up with additional money to buy out your spouse's share, but 'stuff' can go a long ways towards bridging the gap. However, I don't wish for you to be lulled into an overly optimistic view of what you can accomplish. *Get everything valued and do the math!*

 Dirty Lawyer Trick: your spouse's attorney will try to convince the judge your husband's 'stuff' is too *de minimus* (unimportant) to include in the marital estate. It's up to *you* to document his stuff and get it properly valued so this doesn't happen. If an item is worth more than $1,000 (or can be lumped together into collections worth more than $1,000 such as 'antique key collection' or 'power tools') it is *not* de minimus!

de minimus – too insignificant to care about.

If the stuff is *your* stuff and you don't want to have *your* share of hard assets get decreased because of 'stuff' you no longer care about, go through your house and get rid of everything you don't want to keep *before* you tell your husband you want a divorce. Hold a yard sale and use the proceeds to create your 6- to 12-week financial buffer so you can continue paying the joint marital bills until you get into court for a temporary order. Use any monies *more* than that to pay down your joint marital debt. If stuff is in good condition, donate it to charity and get a donation receipt. If not, throw it away.

3. SWAP A RETIREMENT ACCOUNT FOR THE MARITAL HOME – Judges will often entertain assigning a 'cash value' retirement account such as an IRA, 401(k), or deferred compensation plan to

one spouse so the other can keep the marital home. Your spouse may argue this isn't fair because he can't touch those monies until he retires, and also that a house is taxed differently than a stock portfolio or an IRA. It's always prudent to speak to a financial planner about the tax impact of who gets which asset as most judges *are* receptive to the notion of after-tax value and it could sink your plans.

4. SWAPPING A PENSION FOR THE MARITAL HOME – If your spouse has a traditional pension and you had it valued as recommended in Chapter Three, sometimes you can convince your husband to give you the house in exchange for keeping his pension. If your husband is still young, you will have a hard time convincing him to do this, but if he's nearing retirement age, pointing out you're entitled to half (or whatever the percentage is) of every pension check he gets until the day he dies will often cause him to reconsider. A pension-house swap is a common negotiating chip during mediation. It's an uphill battle convincing a judge to order your husband to keep his pension and give you the house. Your husband may not be able to collect on that valuable pension for many years or may die before he receives its full value. However, I've seen it done when there were children involved and the husband's income was too low to provide his wife and/or children with adequate alimony and/or child support. In some states, judges are *required* to examine whether alimony awards can be met by allocating assets such as a pension. Consult with an attorney.

5. SWAPPING ALIMONY FOR THE MARITAL HOME – If the alimony laws in your state are fairly well-settled, you can often propose waiving (giving up) your right to receive alimony in exchange for being allowed to keep the marital home. To do this, multiply how much alimony you think you'd be entitled to receive per year times the number of years you'd be entitled to receive it, then deduct out how much tax you would likely have to pay on that alimony. Since a dollar now is worth more than a dollar tomorrow, sweeten the pot by adjusting that amount for inflation (the past two decades averages 3% per year).

6. REFINANCE THE HOUSE INTO YOUR OWN NAME AND GIVE YOUR HUSBAND A SECOND MORTGAGE – unlike the scenario where your husband continues to maintain an ownership interest in your house (and micromanages everything you do), an outright buyout will alleviate many concerns his attorney will raise about impact on his credit rating, tax implications, or the risk of holding a stake in a decreasing asset he has no control over. Once again, this is more a tactic to use in mediation, rather than litigation since judges are loathe to order one party to wait to get their money any longer than a few years. –If– you can refinance the house entirely into your own name, your spouse can give you a Quitclaim Deed (in other words, the house will become totally yours) and record a mortgage against the house to secure his interest. If I were your husband's attorney, I'd advise him the following criteria must be met:

   a. You must refinance the house entirely into your own name so that his credit rating is not impacted if you can't meet the payments;

   b. He would give you a Quitclaim Deed, which must then be recorded, releasing him from all future responsibility if something happens (i.e., you get sued after someone slips and falls on your walkway);

c. There must be enough equity if you let the house go into foreclosure that he'll get his money (the bank always gets their money first, second-mortgage holders only get what's left over);

d. You must demonstrate you're *able* to pay the primary mortgage, and also the second mortgage to him, out of your anticipated future income;

e. His mortgage must be secured by both a note, and a formal mortgage filed at the local registry of deeds;

f. His second-mortgage must be payable for a reasonable period of time (i.e., 5 years, not 30 years) and spell out how often the mortgage is paid;

g. He should collect interest at whatever the prevailing rate;

h. I'd want to see verbiage that you agree to maintain the house in good condition so his claim against the property remains a valuable investment;

i. You must agree to provide him with proof of insurance every year so that, if the house burns to the ground, he gets his money

If I were your husband's attorney, I'd advise him to consider any plan which gets him his fair share of the money while being as reasonable as possible to you. If your children are young, I'd remind him a responsible father ensures his offspring grow up in a stable environment, something a financial advisor would have a hard time putting a price tag on. This advice might or might not be in *your* favor if I perceive you can't *afford* to keep your house. If you own a fancy house and would live more securely in a smaller one, I might urge him to reject your offer. If he walks away without enough money to put a down payment on his *own* house, I might advise him to reject your offer. It's up to *you* to come to the negotiating table with a clear, well-thought out plan to buy out your share of the marital home.

Many houses purchased within the last 5 years are worth less than what you owe. Do your homework before you agree to a buyout of the marital home as it may not be in your best interests!!!

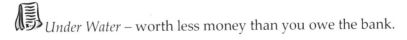 *Under Water* – worth less money than you owe the bank.

THE TAX-MAN COMETH

Always consider the tax implications of whatever asset you choose to keep. Since attorneys are not tax accountants, it would not be appropriate for me to render tax advice. However, here are common middle-class assets which you should red-flag for tax implications when figuring out which assets you wish to keep:

Your home – you can legally exclude up to $250,000 in capital gains, $500,000 per couple, of a house you have lived in for 2 of the past 5 years. All monies over and above that is currently taxed at 15%. If, however, one of you moves out of the marital home, after 3 years the person who moved is going to have to pay taxes on every penny of the sale.

 See IRS Publication 523 - http://www.irs.gov/publications/p523/

 Stocks and bonds (including stock options) – you must pay taxes on whatever proceeds you make upon sale over and above what you paid for a share of stock. How long you hold onto that stock or bond impacts what tax rate you pay. Long-term stocks get taxed at the lower capital gains rate, but short-sale stocks pay at the higher income tax rate.

FANCY PORTRAIT.

 See IRS Publication 550 - http://www.irs.gov/pub/irs-pdf/p550.pdf

Pensions – once you start receiving a pension, or a share of somebody else's pension, you must pay income taxes on it.

 See IRS Publication 575 - http://www.irs.gov/publications/p575/

Retirement accounts – IRA's, 401(k)'s, and deferred compensation plans come with hefty tax penalties if you need to draw from them before you are entitled to retire. Not only do you get whacked with a penalty, but you then must pay income tax on them. If you transfer the asset to your spouse and don't word your Separation Agreement properly so the IRS knows it's part of a court-ordered property division, *you* could end up paying the taxes on that asset while *they* pocket the money. Even if you wait until you retire, most retirement assets come with complicated withdrawal schedules and you still have to pay taxes on them.

 For IRA see IRS Publication 590 - http://www.irs.gov/publications/p590/index.html

For 401(k) see IRS Publication 575 - http://www.irs.gov/publications/p575/

Alimony Lump-Sum Buyout – Alimony is taxable to the recipient because it's considered a future stream of income. A division of marital property is not because you presumably paid the taxes on it when you bought it. When you swap one form of compensation for another, you must be careful how you word your Separation Agreement or the IRS might come after you for additional taxes.

See IRS Publication 504 - http://www.irs.gov/publications/p504/

Although property you already own which the judge assigns you in the divorce is generally not taxable, once you go to *sell* those assets, you may find out they're worth far less than you thought. Seek additional guidance from someone familiar with taxes, such as a financial planner or tax advisor, to figure out the after-tax value of any asset you're contemplating keeping before you agree to a swap.

In Chapter Five: Child Support we discussed two ways men hide income to avoid paying child support and/or alimony. But there are more insidious ways men try to screw you out of what's rightfully yours. This hiding of assets tends to fall into three categories: (1) Hiding money from the IRS; (2) hiding money from creditors; (3) mad money; and (4) hiding money from *you* in anticipation of a future divorce.

If your husband believes you are not aware this money even exists, the temptation is great for him to simply omit it from his financial statement. Although it is a crime to hide assets from the court, the sad truth is that even if you *do* nab him and bring it to the judge's attention, the court is usually all-too-willing to forgive some lame excuse that it was an inadvertent omission. Therefore, your best defense is to pore through your old financial records and, if things don't add up, start asking questions. This is by no means a replacement for a good forensic accountant, but it's one way a small woodland creature can level the playing field with her more affluent peers.

1. HIDING MONEY FROM THE IRS: There are two major ways men hide money from the IRS. The first is to open an offshore bank account and funnel any excess earnings *there* to quietly earn investment income without disclosing it to the IRS. The other is to hide actual, physical cash or other fungible assets that appreciate over time, such as gold, diamonds or out-of-country bearer bonds, in a safe or safety deposit box. This was probably not done initially to screw *you* out of that money, but now that it's hidden, why tell you now?

   a. Does your husband periodically travel out of the country on business? If so, pore through old bank records and investment accounts looking for withdrawals of cash of more than $10,000 shortly before he made those trips.

   b. Look for receipts or cancelled checks made out to pawnbrokers or other vendors of gold or jewelry. If there's receipt for gold or diamonds, chances are there are chunks of gold or loose diamonds in a safe deposit box that have appreciated *far* beyond what he paid for them.

   Spouses Behaving Badly: A client challenged her husband in mediation about gold coins she knew he'd bought earlier in their marriage which had been omitted from his financial statement. The husband pretended to 'come clean' on 20 gold Krugerrands, giving her 10 of them. The wife then did an archeological dig through their bank records and receipt and found another missing 22 purchases of gold coins (42 total). At ~$1,650 per gold coin, that was nearly $70,000 the husband omitted, half of which she was entitled to receive.

   c. Have you ever noticed money transactions on your bank statement to or from an out-of-the-country bank? If the bank is located in a country that is a known tax-haven, such as Andorra, Anguilla, Antigua, Antilles (Netherland), Aruba, the Bahamas, Bahrain, Barbados, Belize, Bermuda, British Virgin Islands, Canary Islands, the Caribbean, Cayman Islands, Channel Isles, Cook Isles, Costa Rica, Cyprus, Dominica, Dubai, Gibraltar, Grenada, Guernsey, Isle of Man, Latvia, Leichenstein, Luxembourg, Malta, Mauritus, Monaco, Nevis, Panama, Saint Kitts, Switzerland, Thailand, Turks-Caicos, United Arab Emirates, Vanuatu (New Hebrides), or West Somoa, you should start asking questions.

Pore through old bank records looking for large cash withdrawals totaling $10,000 or more immediately prior to your husband taking an out-of-country trip. By law, he was supposed to disclose that money to customs. Ask for the customs receipt.

Pore through old bank and investment records looking mysterious deposits from offshore accounts shortly prior to a major investment, such as a major stock purchase or purchase of a piece of real property.

Have you ever received proxy share notices or dividend reinvestment statements for offshore companies which aren't part of your regular investment portfolio (i.e., Ameritrade, mutual fund, 401(k), IRA)? If so, start digging.

2. HIDING MONEY FROM CREDITORS: If your husband works in a line of work where he fears (or *is*) being sued, is nearing retirement age and has begun obsessing about Medicare seizing assets to pay for long-term chronic care, is dodging child support or other wage garnishments from previous malfeasance, or is or has been recently bankrupt, he may have set up an elaborate network of checking, savings and investment accounts under somebody else's name, usually a close friend or sibling.

Spouses Behaving Badly: I once found an $8,000 discrepancy in a purchase of land a divorcing couple had mutually agreed to purchase out of joint marital funds for their daughter three years before they separated. The husband was obsessed with not having their assets seized by Medicare for the wife's long-term care. The wife recalled the husband had come up with the money for the daughter's land after complaining they didn't have enough. Additional digging dug up an undisclosed trust fund worth $2.5 million dollars!

3. MAD MONEY: Mad money is that little bit extra slush fund we all keep to pay for purchases we don't feel like justifying to anybody but ourselves. It's the extra cash you keep stashed in your wallet, the Christmas Club you set up with your bank to set aside money for presents, or that small bank account you keep in your own name just so you don't drop off the planet and cease to exist from a credit standpoint. There's nothing *wrong* with Mad Money accounts so long as you disclose them. In fact, from a financial standing viewpoint, keeping at least *some* autonomy is prudent. You were encouraged to set up your *own* Acorn's slush fund earlier in this book to tide you over in that period of time between when you announce you want a divorce and you can get into court to secure an alimony or child support order. However, what happens if your husband has his *own* secret accounts and doesn't disclose them? In that case, it's up to *you* to document where your husband buried the bones.

Spouses Behaving Badly: A client found an $11,000 cash 'slush fund' in her self-employed husband's business safe. He claimed it was to purchase building supplies. That's all good and well, but he didn't *disclose* it in his financial statement and *she* was entitled to half of it!

You MUST disclose your –own– Mad Money slush fund!

4. HIDING MONEY FROM –YOU- IN ANTICIPATION OF DIVORCE: If your husband is the one who wants a divorce and has had time to plan, he's also had time to funnel money out of the marital account that you weren't aware he might have been doing it. Often, the timing of this big drain on your marital finances will coincide with the beginning of an extramarital affair. Not only is he squandering money to see the other woman, but he's also setting money aside so he doesn't have to share it with you once he kicks you to the curb. We're not talking the modest setting aside of money for anticipated legal fees, establishing credit, or paying bills while your divorce is winding its way through the courts, but the movement of fairly substantial sums of money to get it out of your hands. In addition to the tricks outlined above, here are a few more dirty tricks:

a. *Loaning Money to Family and Friends:* This may be repetitive small amounts, a few hundred dollars here, a few thousand dollars there, or one large sum. It doesn't matter if his brother was broke, homeless, and his kids were hungry. If it adds up to a lot of money and you didn't consent to it, he was probably trying to hide it from you. You are entitled to half of the eventual repayment.

Spouses Behaving Badly: A client found a series of cancelled checks written to two of her husband's brothers and sister all written in the year before he announced he wanted a divorce totaling $55,000. She also found more cancelled checks written to two close friends totaling $35,000. The husband claimed they were gifts. The wife demanded those loans be added back into the marital kitty.

b. *Questionable 'Business Investments':* If you find a large chunk of money written off to a business you have no recollection doing business with, ask questions. Especially if that business is owned by a friend. That loan is an 'account receivable' and you are entitled to half of it when it is repaid.

Spouses Behaving Badly: A client found two suspicious large checks written to businesses she had no recollection of doing business with totaling $23,000. She got them added back into the marital kitty as accounts receivable.

c. *Purchases of Real Property in His or a Family Member's Name:* Go online to the Registry of Deeds not only in your *own* county and/or state, but also the same counties and/or states any close personal friends or relatives may live in and see if any of them recently purchased real estate or land. If you know your sister-in-law is broke, but suddenly she owns a piece of land in the woods, ask questions.

This is by no means an exhaustive list of ways to funnel assets out of the marital estate. However, the first step any good attorney or forensic accountant will take to see if there is any validity to your claims you think there should be more money in the marriage will be to pore through your old bank records and look for red flags, at a cost of $85 to $300 per hour. Save yourself a wad of cash and arm yourself to not get the wool pulled over your eyes. *Nobody* knows your personal bank accounts the way you do. If you see something suspicious, circle it on your bank statement, stick a post-it note on it, and start asking questions. Judge's might overlook one omission if the amount is not too great, but if you can document a pattern of suspicious financial activity, even if you actually can't *find* where your husband hid all the bones, sometimes the judge will try to reimburse you some other way, such as a larger share of the property division or increased alimony.

WHICH ASSETS SHOULD I ASK FOR?

Before you file for divorce, come up with a rough idea of which assets you hope to keep and which assets you plan on giving away. If you did the Acorns exercises in Chapter Three, you should have a good idea how much your 'stuff' is worth. Take all the valuations you gathered in Chapter Three and plug those numbers into an Excel spreadsheet.

To make good decisions, break things down into four categories. Appreciating assets, depreciating assets, stable-value assets, and high-maintenance assets. Go down your spreadsheet and assign each item a letter … (A↑), (D↓), (S=) and (HM!). You want to keep as many Appreciating (A↑) and Stable-Value (S=) assets as possible, while jettisoning Depreciating (D↓) and High-Maintenance (HM!) assets.

1. APPRECIATING ASSET - (A↑) – an asset which can generally be relied upon to increase in value over time. The most common appreciating asset people think of is real estate, although at the current time some locations are still falling in value. Stocks, bonds, or other assets might also be appreciating assets. Market factors, tax liability, and the speed with which you need to liquidate an asset in an emergency can alter their desirability.

2. DEPRECIATING ASSET – (D↓) – something you bought which will be worth very little or nothing in a few years. Examples of depreciating assets are cars, television sets, home electronics, clothing, and *most* other personal property. Most people grossly overestimate the value their "stuff" will fetch on the open market if they were forced to liquidate it suddenly due to a divorce. If your husband refuses to pay the mortgage and you are forced to have an emergency yard sale, you are not going to *get* the $15,000 insurance value for that antique Persian wool carpet you bought 6 years ago. I generally consider antiques to be a *depreciating asset*.

3. STABLE-VALUE ASSET – (S=) - these are items whose relative value doesn't change much over time. Usually, these are older items which make your life more comfortable, but if you had to suddenly replace them, it would cost you far more money than to just keep the old ones. You don't need Lenox china to eat off of … you just need plates. You don't need a brand-new SUV … you just need a reliable car big enough to fit your family into that gets you to work.

Spouses Behaving Badly: As much as the now-lawyer in me snivels over how much *money* my former husband walked away with, the item I missed the most was my ancient avocado-green Kenmore washing machine with the vice-grips to turn the knob. I washed my laundry by hand for two years because I couldn't afford a new one.

4. HIGH-MAINTENANCE ASSET – (HM!) - A high-maintenance asset is one which costs you a great deal of money to maintain. One example is a car that guzzles gasoline. With fuel costs rising, the sooner you can foist a gas guzzler off on somebody else the better. Another is an asset that carries hefty tax penalties or onerous terms to access your assets. Other potentially high-maintenance assets include cars, appliances, time shares, or electronics equipment which costs a great deal of money to perform routine maintenance. If you have a foreign-made car or a 'lemon',

you know exactly what I'm talking about. If you're on a first-name basis with the Maytag repair guy or your local television repairman, get rid of it!

🐿 *This would include any asset which might carry a high tax burden for you.*

Property division is, in many ways, a game of liars' poker. As a pleasurable side-diversion, I write fiction. Every book begins and ends with a scene of God and the devil playing chess. To get a property division which works for *you*, you need to be omniscient and always think 12 steps ahead of your spouse. Anticipate which assets will increase in value over time, which will go down, which will help you get by until you can afford to buy better stuff, and which will become a downright pain in the butt to keep.

Don't hang onto something simply because you *like* it. Once you financially recover (usually a few years), you can always buy bright, shiny *new* stuff that's far better than the old stuff you got rid of along with the evil trapper. However, if you take things that don't serve your long-term interests and let the evil trapper walk away with the *real* assets from your marriage, it will be an anchor around your neck for many years to come.

🐿 *I recommend all of my clients see a financial planner when figuring out what assets they should ask for in their divorce. If my client is low-income, I send them to the library with a recommended list of reading.*

It's now time to rough out, given what you have learned so far, what property you might wish to keep or give away. A sample blank form with some common items to job your memory is included below to get you started. Since everybody's assets are different, I suggest you create your own spreadsheet in Excel or fold a piece of lined paper into four columns and start roughing out what you might use as a start to open negotiations with your husband either over your kitchen table, via a mediator, or through your attorney.

TABLE 7-9: *YOUR* PROPOSED 'DREAM' ASSET DIVISION

Description of Asset	Equity or FMV	Wife Keeps	Husband Keeps
Equity in marital home	$	$	$
Husbands' bank account	$	$	$
Wife's bank account	$	$	$
Husbands' IRA/401(k)	$	$	$
Wife's IRA/401(k)	$	$	$
Husbands' car	$	$	$
Wife's car	$	$	$
Husbands' personal property	$	$	$
Wife's personal property	$	$	$
Other	$	$	$
Total Assets	$	$	$
Divide 50:50	$	$	$
Excess/shortfall owed?	$	$	$

Note: Hawaii has its own Property/Debt Division Worksheet available online at:
http://www.courts.state.hi.us/docs/docs1/PDC_First_Circuit_Property_Division_Chart_Instructions.pdf

CHAPTER 7 SUMMARY

1. Most property accumulated during the marriage is considered either marital or community property.

2. Many states, but not all, exclude gifts and inheritances from the marital kitty as separate property. Consult with an attorney as a large asset being classified (or excluded) as separate property can ruin your escape plans.

3. Absent extreme circumstances, most divorces in this country will end up with the court dividing the couple's assets somewhere in the range between 50:50 and 60:40.

4. Before you announce you want a divorce, work out several different proposals for dividing the assets and come up with an allocation which will work for you financially.

5. Figure out the potential tax burden before agreeing to take an asset as your share of the marital estate. It may be worth far less money than you think.

6. Pore through your old financial records looking for suspicious financial activity.

7. Property division is a game of liar's poker. Figure out what you want in advance and emotionally prepare to let go of things you know you can't afford to keep so you don't get railroaded into taking less than what you deserve.

8. Try to keep appreciating and stable value assets.

9. Try to slough off depreciating and high maintenance assets onto your husband.

10. It's only stuff… You can always buy *new* stuff!

CHAPTER 8

MARITAL DEBT

Neither a borrower nor a lender be;
For loan oft loses both itself and friend,
And borrowing dulls the edge of husbandry.
This above all: to thine own self be true,
And it must follow, as the night the day,
Thou canst not then be false to any man.

Hamlet - William Shakespeare

All marriages accumulate debt. Mortgages. Car loans. Student loans. In this day and age of easy-access credit cards, zero-money-down cars, rampant unemployment and under-water mortgages, it's even common for couples to have nothing to divide *except* debt. Although laws regarding how marital debts are treated vary from state-to-state, like all other aspects of family law, a common nationwide picture appears.

1. If you keep an asset with a *secured debt* against it (i.e., the item itself guarantees payment of the debt), you are generally responsible for paying that debt;

    a. If you keep the house, *you* pay the mortgage;

    b. If you keep a car, *you* pay the car loan;

TABLE 8-1 – JACK AND JANE'S SECURED DEBT ALLOCATION WORKSHEET

Creditor	Nature of Debt	Total Amount Due (before interest)	Weekly Payment	Amount to be paid by Wife	Amount to be paid by Husband
Big Mortgage	Mortgage	$200,000	$300	$300	$0
Little Bank	Home Equity Loan	$29,150	$60	$60	$0
Car Loan Central	Car loan – H's truck	$17,500	$75	$0	$75
Total Weekly Payments				$360	$75

2. Debts incurred during the marriage are generally considered to be 'community' or 'joint marital' debts, absent evidence to the contrary;

   a. Most states presume *either* spouse may act unilaterally to incur a debt which binds the marital estate;

   b. The burden of proving a debt *isn't* marital debt generally falls upon the person claiming the debt should be held separate and assigned to the other party. If you recall our explanation from Chapter Seven, overcoming a burden of proof in court is like being a soldier at boot camp climbing a tall wall. Only fit evidence can get over the wall.

   Spouses Behaving Badly: – a client's husband incurred over $5,000 to have hair transplant surgery after announcing he was having an affair. The court held the husband was responsible for his *own* hair transplants.

   Spouses Behaving Badly: – a wife incurred a $10,000 undergoing breast augmentation surgery six months *before* the couple had separated. The court ruled the debt was joint marital debt, delicately implying the husband had been given ample opportunity to enjoy the use of said implants.

   Spouses Behaving Badly: – a wife discovered over $1,000 in charges to a phone-sex service. The court held the husband responsible for reimbursing the wife, citing the phone-sex charges were not consensual. The court did, however, comment that had the debt been ordinary long-distance charges, it would have ruled the bill was a joint marital debt.

   Spouses Behaving Badly: – a husband bought a brand new pickup truck after filing for divorce for zero money down. At the time of trial, the vehicle was worth less money than he owed on it. The court ruled the truck was *not* joint marital debt.

   Just because a debt is solely in your name doesn't mean he doesn't have to help pay!

c. Student loans are an often a hotly contested area of marital debt. Once again, generalities occur:

    i. If the student loan was incurred during the marriage so one spouse could obtain a better education, courts look at whether or not the marital unit benefitted from the education received.

    ii. If the student loan was incurred *prior* to the marriage and is still payable at the time of divorce, courts may or may not decide to allocate it as marital debt (much depends upon the length of the marriage and income that degree brought into the marriage).

    iii. If the student loan was incurred by the parties on behalf of a child, it will nearly always be allocated as joint marital debt.

    iv. If the student loan was incurred *after* the parties separated, it will nearly always be allocated to the spouse who incurred it.

    v. If the student loans were to get an advanced degree, then the day you're handed your diploma you kick your spouse who supported you through college to the curb, *you* will be assigned that debt.

d. Credit card debt is generally assumed to be joint marital debt no matter *who* is the cardholder. It doesn't matter if the wife charged gas, groceries, clothing and household supplies and the husband was unhappy about the wife spending the money. If you can produce a reasonable explanation of *why* you spent that money (i.e., 'little Johnnie needed new clothes for school) the court will generally rule it's joint marital debt.

    i. If you use a card specifically for business, the court will likely consider that debt to be separate debt;

    ii. If you charge something which might offend the sensibilities of *Mrs. Reasonably Prudent Person*, the judge might rule it's separate debt;

    Spouses Behaving Badly: combing through a husband's credit card and bank records, dozens of charges to Victoria's Secret caught my attention. My client was a heavyset, wheelchair bound woman suffering from Multiple Sclerosis. The court ruled the credit card debt was the husband's sole responsibility.

    iii. Evil trappers have this silly notion that if it isn't a power tool, it wasn't beneficial to the marriage. Be prepared to defend each and every charge on your last year or so of credit card bills.

e. Medical and dental debts will generally be allocated according to when they were occurred.

    i. If occurred during the marriage, they're generally considered joint marital debt;

    ii. If incurred *before* a short-term marriage, they're usually considered separate debt;

iii. If incurred after the parties separate, but before they file for divorce and/or obtain their final decree, courts differ on how they're treated.

iv. If incurred on behalf of the parties' children, the debt will nearly always be considered joint marital debt.

f. If you borrowed money from family or friends, expect to show evidence there really *was* a loan and it was not a gift.

Spouses Behaving Badly: a husband whose family had given the couple $15,000 as a wedding present for a down payment on a house testified on the husband's behalf the money had been a loan. The husband was unable to produce any documentation signed by the wife indicating the money had been anything other than a gift. The court rejected the husband's claim the wife should reimburse his family for half the down payment.

Many times a small woodland creature will borrow from family to hire an attorney. Put something in writing, get it notarized, and leave a clear paper trail from money borrowed to attorney. Although it's unlikely the court will order your attorney fees to be joint marital debt, if your husband took cash from joint marital bank accounts while *you* were forced to take out a loan, a judge might be persuaded to include it as a joint marital debt to level the playing field.

Low- and moderate-income women are often forced to borrow money to meet their living expenses while their divorce is winding its way through the courts. Write a formal agreement and get it notarized!

3. Debts incurred on behalf of a party's business will generally be assigned to whichever party assumes control of that business;

4. If a debt has already been paid, the court generally doesn't want to hear about it. What's in the past is in the past. Do you *really* want to pay your attorneys $300 per hour to argue about some old cell phone bill?

MARITAL DEBTS ARE *NOT* ALWAYS DIVIDED 50:50

Earlier we learned the court starts with a presumption of a 50:50 property division and rarely exceeds a 60:40 split. Marital debt, however, is sometimes treated differently. If there is a significant disparity in your income, a judge *might* be convinced to divide repayment of the marital debt according to ability to pay, not 50:50.

For example, if the wife earns $30,000 per year in combined earned income and child support, while the husband earns $50,000 per year, the court will still likely order whichever spouse takes control of the house to pay the mortgage and whoever takes a car to pay the car loan. However, forcing the poorer spouse to pay 50% of the other marital debts is unfair. When you incurred those debts, you assumed you would pay them off in proportion to how much you contributed to the marital income. A 50:50 split means the poorer spouse pays a larger share of their income for old debts, while the richer spouse is better off because they pay proportionately less.

Judges can often be convinced to divide marital debt according to proportion of the marital income, not 50:50. In the hypothetical above, a court might be persuaded to order the husband to pay 2/3rds of the debt and wife 1/3rds until paid in full. Or … he might order the husband to assume some debts and the wife to assume others, along lines that come out to a 1/3 – 2/3 split. For Jack and Jane, an debt division might look as follows:

TABLE 8-2 – JACK AND JANE'S 2/3 – 1/3 UNSECURED DEBT DIVISION

Creditor	Nature of Debt	Amount Due	Total Weekly Payment	Husband to Pay	H's weekly payment	Wife to Pay	W's weekly payment
Big Bank Card	Credit Card	$7,000	55.00	2/3rd	$36.85	1/3rd	$18.15
City Smitty Card	Credit Card	$3,000	$22.00	2/3rd	$14.74	1/3rd	$7.26
Dr. Orthodontist	Sons braces	$4,500	$11.00	2/3rd	$7.37	1/3rd	$3.63
Nurses University	Wife's student loan	$2,000	$24.00	* $0	* $0	* 100%	* $24.00
XYZ HVAC Repair	Loan	$5,000	$10.00	2/3rd	$6.70	1/3rd	$3.30
Learn'M College	Daughters' Student Loan	$15,000	$25.00	2/3rd	$16.75	1/3rd	$8.25
Total Debt Payments		$38,500	$147		$82.41		$64.59

*Jane has been attributed 100% of her student loan to get an advanced nursing degree. For purposes of this exercise, we'll pretend Jane strategically chose to pay 100% of her own student loan debt to facilitate a settlement because student loans are often a sore topic.

For our hypothetical couple, Jack earns $55,000 per year, while Jane only earns $22,880. However, Jack also pays Jane $16,000 per year in child support. If in our example that $16,000 was alimony, not child support, the court would most likely deduct that $16,000 off of Jack's income, add it onto Jane's, and declare their incomes are similar enough that the marital debt should *also* be divided 50:50.

But what happens when that money is child support, not income? Jack only has himself to take care of, while Jane needs that money to feed and house Jack's kids. How courts treat Jane's child support income differs from state to state. In some states, the court will treat that $16,000 in child support as ordinary income and still order a 50:50 split. In other jurisdictions (including Massachusetts), the court understands Jane can't simply work extra hours to pay off the Mastercard *because* she's obligated to care for his children. For planning purposes, assume a 50:50 split on that portion you estimate would be tagged as joint marital debt until an attorney in your local jurisdiction tells you otherwise, but you *may* be entitled to a more favorable debt division.

 If you have a lot of debt, consulting with an attorney in the early planning stages makes sense.

ANOMALY SPOTTING WHEN LISTING LIABILITIES

The courts financial statement asks for a lot of information which, if you aren't watchful, might accidentally be counted twice … or *not* counted at all! Attorneys, judges, and court personnel are never as familiar with your debt as *you* are. There are certain assumptions we make which, if you aren't careful, could mean you mistakenly get less than your fair share. The next section is designed to help you ferret out where misunderstandings commonly occur so you can guard against them.

If you examine Jane's financial statement (Table 8-3), you'll see she has $127 listed in her Weekly Expenses section under 'Rent or Mortgage (PIT)'.

TABLE 8-3 –JANE DOE'S MORTGAGE PAYMENT

8. WEEKLY EXPENSES

a)	Rent or Mortgage (PIT)	$ 127.00	l)	Life Insurance	$ 0.00
b)	Homeowners/Tenant Insurance	$ 0.00	m)	Medical Insurance	$ 0.00
c)	Maintenance and Repair	$ 0.00	n)	Uninsured Medicals	$ 14.00
d)	Heat	$ 27.00	o)	Incidentals and Toiletries	$ 10.00
e)	Electricity and/or Gas	$ 23.00	p)	Motor Vehicle Expenses	$ 65.00
f)	Telephone	$ 24.00	q)	Motor Vehicle Payment	$ 117.00
g)	Water/Sewer	$ 0.00	r)	Child Care	$ 115.00
h)	Food	$ 75.00	s)	Other (explain	$
i)	House Supplies	$ 5.00		Cable TV	$ 18.00
j)	Laundry and Cleaning	$ 7.00			$
k)	Clothing	$ 5.00			
			e) Total Weekly Expenses (a through s)		$ 637.00

Most lawyers (and judges) will transpose the information from your Financial Statement to a spreadsheet which spells everything out in one place. Someone who is unfamiliar with Jane's finances might assume the $127 listed in under 'Weekly Expenses' is the same number listed under 'Liabilities' where Jane lists $300 per week payable to Big Mortgage Company (Table 8-4) and $60 per week to Little Bank. Are these the same amount? Or aren't they?

TABLE 8-4 – JACK AND JANE'S MORTGAGE PAYMENT

ADDENDUM A TO WIFE'S FINANCIAL STATEMENT

		Creditor	Nature of Debt	Date Incurred	Amount Due	Weekly Payment
a)		Big Mortgage	Mortgage	2001	200,000.00	300
b)	Little Bank	Home Equity Loan	2006	29,150.00	60
c)	Big Bank Card	Credit Card	Ongoing	$7,000	55
d)	City Smitty Card	Credit Card	Ongoing	$3,000	$22
	Dr. Orthodontist	Sons braces	2012	$4,500	$11
	Nurses University	Wife's student loan	2000	$2,000	$24.00
	XYZ HVAC repair	Loan to replace boiler	2011	$5,000	$10.00
	Learn'M Tutors	Daughters out-standing tutoring bill	2011	$15,000	$25.00
	Car Loan Central	Car loan – H's truck	2008	17,500	75.00
e) Total Liabilities			*(transferred from Addendum A)*		$283,150	$582

Jane didn't want to list her mortgage payment twice, so she only listed the leftover $127 for mandatory PMI insurance and bank-collected property taxes, not the mortgage payment itself, under expenses. The judge, however, will look at this financial statement and assume $127 per week is all it costs her to live in her home, not the $542 combined total per week it costs her for her mortgage, principal, interest, property taxes, and mandatory homeowner insurance collected by her bank. Remember my earlier warning that judges don't like to do math? If Jane wishes to receive alimony (which is based on financial need) and isn't absolutely clear when she lists her liabilities and expenses, she could be hurting herself. Therefore, even though it essentially may mean her mortgage gets counted in two separate places, she should follow the directions for the form literally and list the mortgage payment every place she is prompted to ask for it.

If an attorney is handling this paperwork, don't assume they can read your mind! It's up to *you*, the person most familiar with your own finances, to ask questions, clarify, and make sure debts are counted properly when dividing your marital debt.

Judges don't like to do math!!! When answering a question about expenses, the judge will usually only *look* at the section about weekly expenses. When answering a question about debt, the judge will usually only *look* at section listing debt.

Equally important is making sure every debt that *belongs* with an asset is properly credited with that asset. If you look at Table 8-3, Jane lists a $117 per week car payment as an expense.

TABLE 8-5 –JANE DOE'S CAR PAYMENT

8. WEEKLY EXPENSES

a) Rent or Mortgage (PIT)	$ 127.00	l) Life Insurance	$ 0.00
b) Homeowners/Tenant Insurance	$ 0.00	m) Medical Insurance	$ 0.00
c) Maintenance and Repair	$ 0.00	n) Uninsured Medicals	$ 14.00
d) Heat	$ 27.00	o) Incidentals and Toiletries	$ 10.00
e) Electricity and/or Gas	$ 23.00	p) Motor Vehicle Expenses	$ 65.00
f) Telephone	$ 24.00	q) Motor Vehicle Payment	$ 117.00
g) Water/Sewer	$ 0.00	r) Child Care	$ 115.00
h) Food	$ 75.00	s) Other (explain	$
i) House Supplies	$ 5.00	Cable TV	$ 18.00
j) Laundry and Cleaning	$ 7.00		$
k) Clothing	$ 5.00		
		e) Total Weekly Expenses (a through s)	$ 637.00

Nowhere, however, did she list *her own* car payment in Table 8-4 – Liabilities. She listed Jack's car payment, but not her own. She must be careful to list *all* debts so she doesn't lose credit for debts she *has* assumed. If she is going for alimony, documenting her living expenses will become significant, including her car payment.

TABLE 8-6 –JANE'S MISSING CAR LOAN

ADDENDUM A TO WIFE'S FINANCIAL STATEMENT

	Creditor	Nature of Debt	Date Incurred	Amount Due	Weekly Payment
a)	Big Mortgage	Mortgage	2001	200,000.00	300
b)	Little Bank	Home Equity Loan	2006	29,150.00	60
c)	Big Bank Card	Credit Card	Ongoing	$7,000	55
d)	City Smitty Card	Credit Card	Ongoing	$3,000	$22
	Dr. Orthodontist	Sons braces	2012	$4,500	$11
	Nurses University	Wife's student loan	2000	$2,000	$24.00
	XYZ HVAC repair	Loan to replace boiler	2011	$5,000	$10.00
	Learn'M Tutors	Daughters out-standing tutoring bill	2011	$15,000	$25.00
	Car Loan Central	Car loan – H's truck	2008	17,500	75.00
	Total Liabilities	*(transferred from Addendum A)*		$283,150	$582

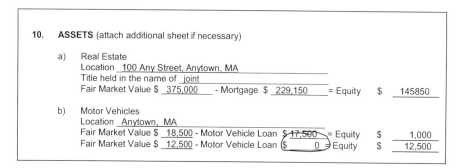

Jack's car loan is listed on Jane's financial statement, but not Jane's?

Let's pretend for a moment that you are Jack and that Jane's car loan happens to be titled in *your* name. In that case, you want to make sure everyone understands that if Jane will be taking that car, *she* will be making the car payment on it from now on. Not you. If you look back at Table 8-6 – Jane's Missing Car Loan, you'll see she listed the $17,500 debt listed for Jack's truck (presumably because both of their names are on it). If you look at Table 8-7 – Assets, you'll see that same $17,500 for Jack's truck is listed there, but Jane's $117 per week car payment is once again *not* listed. What's up with that? You'll need to question it and change the information so it's consistent.

Jane probably did not list the car loan on the car she drives because it's not titled in her name and *she* is not the one paying it. However, it is a joint marital debt and she *will* be responsible for assuming that loan if she wants to keep that car. Therefore, both parties must make sure the court understands Jane drives a car with a loan against it titled in Jack's name. Jane so she her expenses get counted properly for the computation of alimony. Jack so that he is not left saddled with a loan for a car he no longer owns.

TABLE 8-7 – JACK AND JANE'S ASSETS

10. **ASSETS** (attach additional sheet if necessary)

    a)   Real Estate
        Location _100 Any Street, Anytown, MA_
        Title held in the name of _joint_
        Fair Market Value $ _375,000_ - Mortgage $ _229,150_ = Equity $ _145850_

    b)   Motor Vehicles
        Location _Anytown, MA_
        Fair Market Value $ _18,500_ - Motor Vehicle Loan $ 17,500 = Equity $ _1,000_
        Fair Market Value $ _12,500_ - Motor Vehicle Loan $ 0 = Equity $ _12,500_

The last item I'd like to point out is the mortgage payment itself. If you look back at Table 8-7 – Assets, you'll see Jane listed the mortgage of $229,150 when computing the equity in her house. But if you look back at Table 8-6 – Addendum to Liabilities, she has it listed again as the first and second mortgage. In this case, Jane has listed the information the way the court asked, even though the same expense has essentially been listed twice. In some states, they break out the difference between rent and a mortgage payment so judges aren't guessing about whether or not items are being counted twice. In my state, they just lump it all together. Always fill out the form literally!

There's nothing insidious about the anomalies pointed out above. Court forms are confusing and people *always* make these kinds of errors. I point them out because, if you don't understand the places an attorney or judge might misinterpret your financial data, you're less likely to correct him if he doesn't understand what you're trying to say. It's *your* financial statement. If *you* don't understand it, how will a judge?

CAN I OFFER TO PAY OFF A DEBT TO KEEP AN ASSET?

The court views marital property and debts as part of the same 'marital kitty' they will need to divide. Many of your assets were originally funded by debt, whether a mortgage to buy your house or the refrigerator you charged on your Sears card. Even if the court agrees to divide your debts in proportion to your income rather than along the same lines as your marital property, you can sometimes offer to assume the other parties' debt in order to keep some other asset. Remember my analogy of God and the devil sacrificing chess pieces to outwit one another? Sometimes, you can unequally swap off an asset for a debt, or vice versa, if that would better serve your purposes.

Let's pretend Jane wants to keep the house, but even after scrimping for money, inventorying every single screwdriver and wrench, handing asset she owns to Jack, and even getting a 1/3 – 2/3 debt allocation, her mortgage company refuses to refinance her house for enough additional money to buy out Jack's $45,000 share? She's so close! She's computed her budget and *knows* she can live, at least for a few years, with a much higher debt-to-income ratio than a traditional lender would allow. What is Jane to do?

FROM TABLE 7-8: SAMPLE 50:50 PROPERTY DIVISION (WIFE KEEPS HOUSE)

Description of Asset	Equity or FMV	Wife	Husband
Total Assets to be Divided	$202,980	$146,850	$56,130
Shortfall Jane Owes Jack		(45,360)	+$45,360

What if Jane offered to assume some or all of the unsecured marital debt? Although there is only $38,500 in unsecured debt available to offset the $45,360 she owes Jack for his share of the mortgage, only $24,455 which is attributable to Jack.

FROM TABLE 8-6 – JACK AND JANE'S 2/3 – 1/3 UNSECURED DEBT DIVISION

Creditor	Nature of Debt	Amount Due	Total Weekly Payment	Husband to Pay	H's weekly payment	Wife to Pay	W's weekly payment
Total Debt Payments		$38,500	$147		$82.41		$64.59

There are two arguments Jane might use to persuade Jack (or the judge) to go for this. The first is factor is if Jack is a decent guy, he might not want Jane to pull up roots and relocate with his children someplace where she can earn a decent living as a nurse. Once that house is sold, she has little incentive to stay in an area where she has no prospect of earning enough money to survive. Increased distance usually means decreased access for visitation.

The second argument is that nearly all of these debts are either high-interest credit card debt, or debt which is not dischargeable in bankruptcy should you run into financial trouble. Although the present cash balance appears lower than the balance owed to buy out Jack's share of the marital home, high interest rates and credit cards fees are going to sap vitality from Jack's fresh start. Perhaps Jack would like to just put the whole situation behind him and start over?

Before Jane gets excited about her brilliant idea, she should examine her anticipated post-divorce budget and see if she can really *afford* this strategy.

TABLE 8-7 – JANE'S PROJECTED WEEKLY LIVING EXPENSES/DEBT PAYMENT WORKSHEET

Description	Debit	Credit
Gross Earned Income	$445.00	
Less Income Taxes	95.67	
Net Earned Income	349.33	
Child Support	308.00	
Total Income	657.33	
Mortgage Payments		$360.00
Car Payment		$127.00
Routine Living Expenses		$520.00
Unsecured Debt Repayments		$147.00
Total Expenses		1154.00
Unallocated Cash (I – E = U)	(497.67)	

Okay ... that's not going to work. That's more than twice as much money as Jane anticipates earning from all sources. Now what?

Before you move onto the next phase of divorce planning ... finding an attorney, you need to compute your *own* interplay between your future anticipated income and expenses and come up with a rough idea of what property you can afford to keep. Take time now to use the information you have learned over the course of the past eight chapters to do just that.

A sample projected weekly living expenses worksheet follows as a guide for you to use the knowledge you've gained so far to estimate your own viability as a single woman. Take a bit of time to give yourself the gift of counting your acorns and figuring out what your post-divorce finances might look like:

TABLE 8-8 – *YOUR* PROJECTED WEEKLY LIVING EXPENSES/DEBT PAYMENT WORKSHEET

Description	Debit (+)	Credit (-)
Gross Earned Income	$	
Less Taxes		$
Net Earned Income	$	
Anticipated Child Support	$	
Anticipated Alimony	$	
Other Income	$	
Total Income	$	
Mortgage Payments		$
Car Payments		$
Routine Living Expenses including non-mortgage rent (from Financial Statement)		$
Unsecured Debt Repayments (from Financial Statement)		$
Other Expenses not covered elsewhere		$
Total Expenses		$
Unallocated Cash or Shortfall (I – E = U)	$	$

THE JUDGE'S GAVEL IS NOT A MAGIC WAND

How'd you do?

If you're like Jane, you have the same problem *most* small woodland creatures have when trying to extricate themselves from a bad marriage. Do your post-divorce living expenses exceed your anticipated post-divorce income? If so, you're not alone. It's time to come up with a Plan B. If you're not being abused or facing some ticking time bomb which could undermine your legal rights, you'll want to take a bit of time to cure this imbalance in your ability to provide a living for yourself. It's either fix it now, or circumstances will fix this imbalance *for* you in a way which will likely prove unpleasant.

The judge's gavel is not a magic wand. As badly as he might feel for you when you break down in tears and cry, the judge cannot create more money in your marital estate than existed when you filed for divorce, nor can he make your debts go away. Even if he orders your spouse to assume certain debts, it does not absolve *you* of the responsibility to make sure those bills get paid. You are divorcing your husband, not Citibank.

🚩 *The judge has no power to alter contracts you signed with outside parties.* If your husband defaults, *you* will be left holding the bag. Therefore, you need to come up with a plan!

Your sorry financial state is not the judge's problem. It's not your lawyers' problem. It's *your* problem. But there *are* ways to crawl out of the hole. Let's start looking at ways to deal with it?

Because you took the initiative to educate yourself and did your Bootcamp exercises, you are one smart woodland creature. Smart woodland creatures deal with reality, not illusion. There are two time-honored routes to get out of the situation you're in:

1. Take a job training class; certificate program or college course which will improve your ability to earn a higher salary;

2. Cut your budget to the bone.

I live in an academically-rich area of the country where there's a college on every street corner, so I don't wish to make presumptions about locations where you can't simply hop in the car and drive 20 minutes to attend night school. I shall therefore list the most likely places to increase your earning capacity in the order you're most likely to find retraining for low cost or free:

1. Ask your employer if they offer any in-house training which would increase your value to them as an employee;

2. Contact your local high-school or technical high-school and find out if they offer any low-cost adult education training programs;

3. Contact your local unemployment office (even if currently employed) and find out if they know of any career retraining programs in your area;

4. Look online for your local Small Business Administration and sign up for any low-cost classes they have listed (often $5 to $20 per class);

5. Search for a woman's service agency in your area who may be able to refer you to a career counselor or mentorship program;

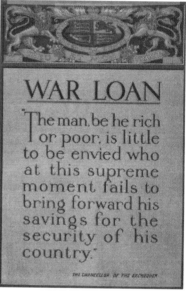

6. Check out the night class offerings at the nearest colleges in your area. Find out if they have an adult re-entry program. If they do, they can help you set career goals and figure out what kind of credentials you need to get to get a higher paying job.

7. Educate *yourself!* My grandfather was not a man of letters, but he was the most pragmatic, knowledgeable man I ever met. The moment he sat down to relax, he had a book in his hand borrowed from the local library.

There's a wealth of information out there for anyone motivated to educate themselves and create a plan. If you've run your numbers, snipped and trimmed everything you can think of, and *still* can't make it work, you'll need a long-term plan which includes both increasing your income and reducing debt as part of your divorce strategy. The stress you face every day as you grit your teeth and cut back on your expenses *now* is a lot less than the stress you'll be facing if you have to choose between groceries and the mortgage payment once you cut the evil trapper loose.

Yes … that may mean you need to have to grit your teeth and stay with the evil trapper until you've gathered enough additional acorns to leave him…

Use reverse "as you wish" thinking when dealing with the Evil Trapper until you're ready to strike out on your own. In the movie "The Princess Bride," Buttercup realizes that every time she torments the farm boy Wesley and he says "as you wish," what he's *really* saying is "I love you." Now flip that statement on its head! The best advice I ever got was how to say "F--- you" without the other person knowing it. People who know me well crack up laughing whenever they see me become really, really nice to a difficult person. If the evil trapper is mean, be nice. If he's stubborn, be helpful. If he's grouchy, be chipper and happy. The nastier he gets, the nicer you should act. My eldest daughter couldn't contain her laughter when we went through Russian customs and I profusely thanked the grumpy officials and complimented them on their dedication to their job. If you know anything about former Soviet-bloc nations, you know dealing with their civil servants makes getting an audit from the IRS seem pleasant in comparison.

When the evil trapper goes blah blah blah blah, smile and say 'yes, dear, as you wish...' As soon as you've finished doing the *both* of you the enormous favor of digging yourself out of the financial hole, it's bye-bye Evil Trapper. Smile ☺

VOLUNTARY DOWNSHIFTING IN PREPARATION FOR A DIVORCE

Many clients have shy away from financial planning because they view it as an austere fad *die*-it. If you're like *me,* you grew up with some naggy old tightwad forever harping on you to never spend money. Ugh! No wonder women avoid financial planning like the plague! Whose voice is still robbing *you* of the desire to take control of your financial destiny? A parent? A relative? The evil trapper? Smash that tired old broken record and start over!

Financial planning is a tool to plant a seed and help it grow into a mighty oak. If you cut your expenses *and* reduce your debt *and* put money aside to survive life's inevitable ups and downs, you *will* be able to survive without your controlling spouse. The 'zen' way to cope with voluntarily lowering your standard of living far below your current means is to view each act of self-determination as an act of passive aggression. Although I do these things to save money because I am inordinately cheap (hence my nickname 'The Cheap Yankee' which was pegged by friends long before I ever wrote books about it), here are a few Cheap Yankee strategies adapted to give yourself a needed mental boost while you're quietly squirreling acorns away to ditch the evil trapper:

Every time you flip off a light switch to save on electricity, use your middle finger and picture you're giving your soon to be ex 'the bird' (I do this picturing oil-producing terrorist nation sponsors as the recipient).

Every time you cook tuna noodle casserole for supper so you can skim off the grocery bill, chuckle "heh-heh-heh" and enjoy that modest supper with the gusto of filet mignon.

"OF COURSE I CAN!"

I'm patriotic as can be—
And ration points won't worry me!"

Every time you shop at a thrift shop then starch and iron your kids 'new' clothing so nobody knows it's used, hum "money makes the world go around" and complement yourself on how clever you are for beating the system (my kids don't know what it's like to *not* have designer clothing which passed through somebody else's washing machine a few times before landing in their closet).

Whenever you write a check with a few extra dollars paid down on that credit card bill or put extra cash into your savings account, sing "ding dong the witch is dead!"

Your spouse will be thrilled if you announce "we're going on a money diet." Since most men think every purchase that is not a power tool is frivolous, he'll be quite happy when you stop buying "frills" like underwear for your children. He probably cares less if *you* drive an 12-year-old clunker held together with coat hangers and duct tape so long as *he* gets to cruise around in his brand new Dodge Ram, so announcing you want to trade in your 110% financed gas-guzzling SUV for an inexpensive 5-year old Consumer Reports best-buy will elicit little more than a yawn.

Turn the thermostat down to 60 degrees and tell him you're doing your part to reduce global warming and end your family's dependence upon Middle Eastern oil. If you cut your kids' ballet lessons and enroll them in Girl Scouts, cite research which states you're harming your children by over-scheduling their time. If you need to get rid of your negatively-financed new car, complain about how much you hate being payment-poor and have a magazine article photocopied from Consumer Reports.

The Zen Master avoids conflict and confrontation by quietly changing their behavior without discussion or argument. Always be prepared with a logical, well-thought-out reason for changing your behavior. If he disagrees, don't argue. Just say "yes, dear, as you wish…" and quietly continue doing exactly what you're doing … becoming financially independent so you can stand on your own two feet. The evil trapper won't suspect a thing.

CREDIT COUNSELING, SHORT-SALES, AND BANKRUPTCY

What if you're doing everything you can to cut your expenses, but a debt such as an under-water mortgage, under-water car, unpaid medical bills, or other expense makes it impossible for you to crawl out of the financial hole even if you were to work two jobs and cut your budget to the bone for a hundred years?

I'm a big advocate of financial responsibility. Read everything you can about financial planning and frugal living and *live it!* However, -if- after cutting your budget to the bone and using the savings to pay down your debts you estimate you're still going to be paying the same high-interest credit cards longer than a 5-year period, you need help.

If *credit card* debt is your major problem, a credit counseling agency may be able to help you negotiate more favorable terms. *But be aware that most credit counseling agencies have a less than stellar record of serving their clients.* High upfront costs, high fees, and unfavorable payment dates may actually put you in *worse* shape than you started in. These agencies get money from the creditors to make you pay as much as possible, not necessarily to serve you. However, the Department of Justice has compiled a list of agencies they found to be reputable and have up-to-the-minute information about what to look for when hiring one of these agencies:

The Drunkards Cloak.

http://www.justice.gov/ust/eo/bapcpa/ccde/cc_approved.htm

What if the problem resides entirely with a particular asset or debt, such as a medical bill or under-water mortgage? I can't tell you how many women I offend when I look at their financial statements and tell them their best strategy is to negotiate a short sale on their house or file for bankruptcy. I'm a fan of financial responsibility, but when a couple pays a brokers fee to *their* broker, a mortgage origination fee to *their* banker, an appraisal fee to *their* appraiser, and then an attorney fee for what they thought was *their* attorney to handle the closing, I have no problem advising clients to tell the 1% who crashed our economy to shove it and hand back the keys. Although both short-sale and bankruptcy will negatively impact your credit for many years to come, it's better than slitting your throat financially while Wall Street sips champagne and laughs.

A bankruptcy attorney can help you decide which option works best in *your* situation. Although some realtors can handle short sales, only a call from a bankruptcy attorney will make most other creditors stand up and take you seriously. There are two kinds of bankruptcy. Chapter 7 is when you want to hand back the keys to your house, your car, and other debts and get a fresh start. Certain debts, such as student loans, can't be discharged, but other debts can. You'll walk away from a Chapter 7 bankruptcy with a few assets and very little debt.

The second kind of bankruptcy, Chapter 11, can help you keep your house and force creditors who won't negotiate with you for repayment terms you can afford to accept them. The bankruptcy court will make you pay as much as you feasibly can for approximately five years, and then the rest will just go away. This is a gross oversimplification of bankruptcy law, but if it sounds like this might be your only way to survive, consult with a bankruptcy attorney as to your rights. Filing for joint bankruptcy is something you want to do *before* you file for divorce because, otherwise, your spouse will be hauling you back into court to modify your separation agreement.

WHICH STRATEGIES SHOULD I USE?

In writing this Boot Camp, I've listed many strategies small woodland creatures can use to build up their store of acorns to weather the upcoming storm. Some may seem contradictory (pay off the car loan vs. trading in the car for a cheaper used car with a small loan on it, for example). In fact, I've suggested so many strategies you may be perplexed about how to implement them. Relax! It's unlikely every strategy will be appropriate for every woman who reads this book.

You are the most knowledgeable person about your individual financial situation. Only *you* know how your children are going to react when you announce you're dropping the $1,500 baseball clinic next summer in favor of Cub Scouts, or cut HBO package from your cable bill, or when you throw their grade-destroying, useless cell phones into the trash where they belong. With the exception of the "big offenders" (cell phones, car payments, too many activities for the kids), the rest of suggestions in this book are just that, suggestions. Take what works for you and leave the rest.

Here are some resources to educate yourself about voluntary simplicity, anti-consumerism, frugal lifestyle and similar movements:

- *The Cheap Yankee Guide to Financial Triage: How to Survive a Financial Emergency,* by Anna Merrill (2011)

- *The Cheap Yankee Guide to Radical Frugality,* by Anna Merrill (2009)

- *The Complete Tightwad Gazette,* by Amy Dacyczyn (1998)

- *Frugal Living for Dummies,* by Deborah Taylor-Hough (2003)

- *America's Cheapest Family Gets You Right on the Money: Your Guide to Living Better, Spending Less, and Cashing in on Your Dreams,* by Steve Economides and Annette Economides (2007)

- *Your Money or Your Life,* by Joe Dominguez and Vicki Robin (1999)

- visit the frugal living website http://frugalliving.about.com (fun and free)

- visit the dollar stretcher community http://community.stretcher.com/forums (other people like *you* trying to stretch their money)

- visit the anti-consumerist website www.verdant.net (a bit radical, but their information is backed up by credible sources). A real eye-opener!

TOUGH LOVE FROM THE AUTHOR

If my tone sounds harsh, it's not because I'm speaking from a high horse. When I divorced my first husband, he left me tens of thousands of dollars in credit card debt because I didn't realize he was obligated to help me pay it back. At 18% interest, a child to raise, and a low-wage job (I wasn't a lawyer back then), I teetered at the edge of bankruptcy until I got my expenses under control and paid it off. Since then, I live as close to debt-free as possible. *-If only-* someone had pulled me aside and told me what I was facing! I would have taken a year, grit my teeth, and paid down that debt while I was still married to him. My life would have been *so* much easier!

Education is learning from the mistakes of others.

Experience is the process of learning through trial-and-error mistakes.

Please learn from my *experience* and take the time to figure out how you're going to manage your post-divorce finances before you tell your husband you want a divorce.

1. Marital debt is treated much like marital property, only sometimes you can get the court to divide it in accordance with your ability to pay, not just 50:50.

2. If you take an asset which secures a debt, such as a mortgage or car payment, that debt usually goes with the asset.

3. Some debts might be ruled 'separate' and one party will be solely responsible for paying them.

4. Make sure you don't double-count … or omit … debts from your financial spreadsheet.

5. Many small woodland creatures need to delay divorce until they get their financial house in order.

6. Most Americans live far beyond their means. Become a Cheap Yankee!

7. If there's no other way to climb out of the hole, credit counseling, short-sales, and bankruptcy are ways to make a fresh start.

(This page left deliberately blank)

CHAPTER 9

PIECING TOGETHER LEGAL SERVICES ON A 'REAL' PERSON'S BUDGET

If you are resolutely determined to make a lawyer of yourself,
The thing is more than half done already.

Abraham Lincoln--November 5, 1855, Letter to Isham Reavis

In an ideal world, *everybody* would be able to afford the services of a good, full-service attorney who would be their superhero, stepping between the small woodland creature and the evil trapper at every step of the war, sword raised, to act as their shield. Unfortunately, that level of service comes with a hefty price tag. If you don't have that kind of money, what are you supposed to do?

We'll start in order of what your state bar association views to be the 'right' answer, hire a lawyer. It's my hope at some point during your journey you'll find your way into a local attorney's office, financial statement already prepared, acorns neatly organized into a 3-ring binder. We're not *all* blood-sucking predators! In this chapter, we'll discuss what to look for in an attorney, how to vet their credentials, and things attorneys look for in *you* as a client when they're figuring how much to ask for a retainer. We'll also look at ways to force your husband to loan you money from your anticipated share of the marital estate if the money is all in his name.

We'll then discuss Legal Services and Legal Aid. Unfortunately, only the poorest of the poor can get a free attorney. But even if you don't qualify, they're an important resource to find referrals to other legal resources in your area.

From there we'll discuss mediation, its benefits and pitfalls. If done properly, mediation can help you and your spouse amicably hash out the terms of your divorce settlement and get all the necessary paperwork drafted for a reasonable fee. We'll also discuss programs your local courthouse may have put in place to help people like you navigate the system, such as court-ordered mediation, arbitration, and self-help programs.

If you've tried the approved 'traditional' and 'alternative dispute resolution' channels and determined you can't afford them, this is where this book differs from other resources. Throughout this book I've tried to get you into the habit of referring back to your *own* courts website or other free sources of information so you'd become familiar with using them. We'll discuss places you might line up low-cost or free legal consultations, how to navigate your state-court website, how to navigate your courts law library (either bricks-and-mortar or online), how to use Continuing Legal Education manuals, and where to find support within your community for the insanity known as divorce.

DO I REALLY NEED AN ATTORNEY?

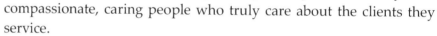

It's rare to see a case that wouldn't benefit from both parties having ethical, responsible attorneys willing to negotiate a settlement and explain the implications to each decision to their clients. Although I've met what I consider to be a few bad apples (a scorched earth attorney has no place in family court), the overwhelming majority of my peers have earned nothing but my respect. Our opinions may differ and we may end up litigating one issue or another to death, but generally family law attorneys are

compassionate, caring people who truly care about the clients they service.

That being said, I'm assuming the reason you were drawn to this Bootcamp manual is you're afraid you can't afford the retainer. Or, perhaps you heard that by doing the Bootcamp exercises outlined earlier and referring to later sections of this book as a guide, you can better position yourself for divorce and save money off your legal bill? Hopefully this chapter will help you get the most bang for your buck.

HOW TO FIND AN ATTORNEY

The best way to find a divorce attorney is to ask recently divorced friends who *they* used. Divorce is never a pleasant process, but here are some questions to help you rate their recommendation:

1. Did their attorney help them obtain the fairest possible outcome given the limitations of the law?

2. Did the attorney return all phone calls within 24 hours (or 1 business day if over a weekend or holiday)?

3. Did they understand invoices sent to them by the attorney and understand where their money went?

4. Did they feel the number of hours the attorney billed them was fair, keeping in mind the amount of time the attorney had to put into the case.

5. If outside experts were hired (guardian ad litem, special master, expert witnesses such as accountants, valuation experts, etc.), did the attorney explain to them how much it would cost and what they hoped to gain by hiring the expert?

6. Did the attorney explain, in language they could understand, the purpose of the many hearings and types of paperwork involved in their case?

7. Do they feel the attorney worked well with the opposing spouses' attorney?

8. Do they feel the attorney made every effort to be *fair* to their ex-spouse, all the while never losing site of the fact they were there to zealously represent *them*.

9. Do they feel the attorney was knowledgeable about family law?

10. Are they happy (or as happy as can be possible given the circumstances) with their case?

If your friends can't recommend an attorney, interview attorneys who volunteer for pro bono (free) and low-cost legal clinics in your area. If you're a small woodland creature, you want an attorney who cares about access to justice for the lower end of the socioeconomic scale. Small 'boutique' attorneys (specialists who keep their practices deliberately small and narrowly-focused) often teach seminars or do pro bono work through agencies who serve low-income litigants to find clients they'd enjoy representing. Lastly, attorneys who volunteer their time to help low- and moderate-income people tend to keep better touch with *real* peoples' issues, not just the uber-wealthy.

If all else fails, there's the internet or yellow pages. You are searching for a '*divorce*' or '*family law*' attorney. Internet sites that include helpful legal blogs and links to free information (such as FindLaw.com or LawGuru.com) usually have lists of attorneys who advertise with them (click the 'find an attorney in your area' button).

If child custody is a major concern (covered in Chapter Fourteen) you may also want to contact your local Public Defenders office and ask if they can recommend attorneys in your area who take both Department of Child and Family Service cases and also private custody dispute cases. *Do not tell them your woes!* Just call and ask who takes those kinds of cases. Most public defenders offices are comprised of full-time staff attorneys (who you will not be able to hire), and then a roster of private attorneys who take their overflow cases. An experienced public defender has ins and outs with people such as guardians-ad-litem, court investigators, child therapists and your state child and family services agency that most private attorneys will not have.

Boutique attorneys (attorneys who focus on only one or two areas of law) rarely advertise in the yellow pages. Big ads cost tens of thousands of dollars per year and the return on investment is very low. If you *do* go hunting in the yellow pages, look for attorneys with one or two-line listings alphabetically, small ½" to 1" long ads right in the text, or what they call 1/8th page ads. These are attorneys who keep their costs low so they can pick and choose their cases. Otherwise ... that beautiful full page advertisement is coming out of *your* budget!

One hint about the yellow pages. They're alphabetical, which means the guy fortuitous enough to have a last name beginning with the letter 'A' gets more calls and can charge more. Start someplace near the bottom and work your way backwards!

SETTING UP YOUR FIRST APPOINTMENT

If you got a referral to an attorney through a program such as your local courthouse Lawyer-of-the-Day program or a women's service agency, whoever is scheduled to serve that day is who you'll get.

If you found the attorney through a friend or advertisement, you'll need to call and schedule an appointment. It's rare (unless you call a solo-practitioner) to speak to the actual attorney the first time you call. Usually a secretary or paralegal will ask general questions about your name, your husband's name, and how many children you have. They may mail/email an introduction packet. If the attorney happens to be free at that moment, they may speak to you, but usually they'll call back (if they provide free consults over the telephone) or wait for you to arrive at your scheduled appointment.

Find out if the attorney provides free initial consultations. Many attorneys screen potential clients through their pro bono (free) work via an agency, will meet with you anywhere from the first 10 minutes to 30 minutes for free, or will provide a free telephone conversation. Always be clear about how long the 'free' consultation is so you know when you're starting to run over. There's nothing worse than chatting off an attorney's ear about things not particularly relevant to your divorce, thinking it's free, and then getting a bill for time that ran over your free consult. If you're going to pay for services, make it count!

If this is your first time ever working with an attorney, I suggest you interview at least three of them to get a feel for how each attorney might handle your case.

PREPARING FOR YOUR FIRST APPOINTMENT

The attorney's office may mail or email you a client intake packet, or ask you to arrive a half hour early to fill it out. Having done the preparatory exercises recommended in the prior eight chapters, much of this paperwork will seem very familiar!

Always carefully fill out every piece of information they mail/email to you, even if it's information you consolidated into your beautiful, neatly-indexed 'acorns' three-ring binder. Attorneys get used to quickly digesting information in a particular format. Photocopy an extra copy of the court's financial statement you filled out in Chapter Four to hand to the attorney to keep for his records as *all* family law attorneys are familiar with that document. Here's a mathematical formula you can always count on:

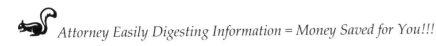 *Attorney Easily Digesting Information = Money Saved for You!!!*

If you have missing information from your Acorns checklist, gather and neatly index it into your Acorns binder along with the other information. You shouldn't hand your prospective attorney your binder unless you decide to retain them since it probably cost you $40 to photocopy all those pages, but be prepared to flip to the relevant invoice, bill or statement as you speak to them. Think of your appointment as an open-book examination. You can bring all the answers you want with you to the examination, but you only have a set period of time to access that information and use it to write out the correct answers on the test. If you fail … you get a bigger lawyer bill. Once again:

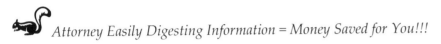 *Attorney Easily Digesting Information = Money Saved for You!!!*

To make the most of your interview, prepare a bulleted list of questions. If you'll be referring to a document in your Acorns binder, note exactly where that piece of paper is so you can flip to it. Put sticky-notes with an arrow pointing to the information you question. Brevity and good organization are the small woodland creature's equalizer when procuring expensive legal advice. Since three times is the charm, be sure to always remember:

 *Attorney Easily Digesting Information = Money Saved for You!!!*

HAVE REALISTIC EXPECTATIONS ABOUT WHAT AN ATTORNEY CAN DO

Attorneys base their retainer on two things: (1) how long it takes to prosecute the issues in your case; and (2) how difficult they think you're going to be to work with as a client. If they perceive you need a lot of hand-holding or might contest issues even when advised it's not in your best interests, they'll add

thousands of dollars onto the up-front retainer. This isn't because they're out to rake you over the coals. If you keep calling their office over trivial matters or make them contest things you've been advised you have little chance of winning, it takes time away from their *other* clients. Time = money. The more *time* they think your case will need, the higher the retainer. It's simple economics.

If you work as a sales clerk and a customer comes into the store three minutes before closing, you're not going to stay after-hours unless your employer *pays* you to work extra. Especially if it's the same customer coming into your store night after night. Nobody likes working for free. Keeping that in mind, here's some generalized advice about how *not* to get pegged by your attorney as one of *those* clients:

$ *Ka-ching!!!* DO NOT argue if your attorney has a different opinion about your likelihood of success on an issue than what was outlined in this book. This book is a general overview of the law, not the gospel. When you argue at your initial interview, your attorney will assume you'll argue in *every* meeting, prolonging the amount of time he'll need to spend explaining things to you. Resolving arguments adds time to your case.

$ *Ka-ching!!!* You repeat the words 'but how am I supposed to live on so little money' more than three times. The first time you say it, you're informing them economic need is an issue. The second time, you're voicing trepidation. The third time ... the attorney groans and realizes you don't have a grip on your finances and are looking to *him* to solve problems better resolved by a financial advisor. Your budget woes are not your attorney's problem.

$ *Ka-ching!!!* You go on and on about all the mean, rotten things the Evil Trapper has said about you, emotional abuse, or how lousy that makes you feel. Your attorney is not your therapist.

$ *Ka-ching!!!* Your attorney advises you it would be tactically wise to stall (delay) for some event to happen (a deadline to pass, a DSS investigation to finish, a certain amount of time for something to become established as a pattern) and you wail 'but I want an attorney who will fight for me!'

$ *Ka-ching!!!* You go on and on about how people are out to get you. Although being paranoid doesn't mean it's not true (believe me, sometimes it *is* true!), perseverating about this during an initial meeting will make the attorney question your sanity.

$ *Ka-ching!!!* If the attorney is one you spoke with previously over the phone or at a free legal clinic, if they suggested self-help 'homework' and you didn't do it...

$ *Ka-ching!!!* When you speak of other attorneys, therapists, financial planners, or other professionals you've used in the past, don't say the evil magic words, 'I should probably sue them for malpractice.' Chances are, it won't even *be* ka-ching. The attorney will say he isn't suited for your case and never return your phone calls.

There are many other things you might say which could nudge that retainer up, but those are the biggest offenders. Bar associations warn attorneys to watch for red flags when screening potential clients. Unsophisticated clients who don't understand lawyers are meant to *guide* you through the process, not be your personal guardian angels, are usually the clients who badmouth you in the community, file complaints with the state bar association, or sue you for malpractice.

If they're truly a lousy lawyer, this might be warranted. But more often than not, the failure is because *you* don't understand a lawyer can only help you procure your fair share under the law. They are not your therapist. They are not your financial planner. They cannot get you a bigger share of money you do not have. Nor can they make your old mistakes (such as alcoholism or a criminal record which might impact child custody) disappear.

When you meet with your attorney, show him you understand his *role* in your life is a limited one. Show him that although you are a small woodland creature, you have a wealthy CEO's understanding of what a lawyer can do for you. The lawyer is a hired gun. It's up to *you* to aim it. Show him you're a self-starter who has all their ducks in order and won't take up an inordinate amount of his time. You'll likely be rewarded with a lower retainer.

INTERVIEWING YOUR PROSPECTIVE ATTORNEY

When you meet with your attorney for the first time, there are certain things you should look for:

1. DOES THIS ATTORNEY APPEAR TO BE KNOWLEDGEABLE ABOUT FAMILY LAW? They should know significantly more than what I've outlined in this *Bootcamp* manual and be able to answer questions related to things that were touched upon here, but which you were warned might vary from state to state, off the cuff. On the other hand, if you're asking about one of the issues you were warned were 'complicated,' don't be surprised if your attorney requests time to look into it.

2. DOES THE ATTORNEY READILY ADMIT THE LIMITS OF HIS EXPERTISE? A good attorney only has time to specialize in 2-3 practice areas. Within those practice areas, they should have a good grasp of the law. Once you get beyond those practice areas, they're relying on imperfect information. Just because an attorney hesitates about an issue doesn't mean she isn't capable of quickly coming up to speed, but be wary of attorneys who 'don't know what they don't know.' Some areas of law, such as family law and criminal law have totally different standards of proof, rules of procedure, and are frequently even heard in different buildings.

Dirty Lawyer Tricks: I once represented a father where the state took custody away from *both* parents due to continued domestic violence. The wife would call the police, have him arrested, then return to him. The police finally had DCF intervene. I practiced under a judge affectionately nicknamed Lock-em-Up who had zero tolerance for kids witnessing abuse. I represented the father, whom I advised to request a three-month continuance to attend an anger management program. It would be three months out of the house, but the judge would let the

kids return home to the mother right away and the father to return home after completing the program. The mother, on the other hand, hired a well-known criminal attorney to have her testify she had lied about being abused. I warned them this strategy was a loser. The issue under review *wasn't* the criminal case, where whether or not the mother had lied when she'd called the police mattered. This was juvenile court. The issue was whether the mother's denial about the father's abuse was placing the kids at risk. The wife's attorney strutted around the courtroom like Perry Mason, spewing reasonable doubt about the mother having lied... and *proved* the state's case which was the mother's denial put the children at risk. Judge Lock-em-Up ordered the kids to stay in foster care.

3. PERSONALITY IS IMPORTANT. This person is going to be your sword and shield for the next 1-2 years. Make sure your personalities mesh. Some attorneys are very soft-spoken and attentive to details when mediating your case ... but they may not be up to the task of litigation should your case go to trial. Others are aggressive and blunt ... sometimes to the point of hindering negotiations ... but will gleefully skewer the Evil Trapper in court. Neither personality type is 'wrong.' What matters is whether *you* can work with this attorney as you navigate your divorce. In England, they divide lawyers into solicitors and barristers so you know at the outset what you are getting. Here ... you should try to figure out which type they are during your first interview.

4. WHAT CREDENTIALS DOES THE ATTORNEY HAVE (besides a law degree) to handle your case? Ask whether they've attended any Continuing Legal Education (CLE) classes about family law in the past 3 years or how they keep up with the latest developments in family law. Most attorneys attend at least one 8-hour CLE class per year in their practice area.

5. DOES THE ATTORNEY HAVE A WORKING RELATIONSHIP WITH OTHER PROFESSIONALS WHO MIGHT BE OF ASSISTANCE IN YOUR PARTICULAR CASE? For

example, if you expect to receive retirement assets as part of your divorce settlement, a financial planner? If you anticipate a custody dispute, has the attorney worked with guardians-ad-litem, court investigators, and psychological expert witnesses before? If your husband is hiding money and you can afford it, do they work with a private investigator? A forensic accountant? On-staff is not as important for a small woodland creature as a prior working relationship and/or familiarity with unique issues.

6. DOES THE ATTORNEY PERFORM ANY PRO BONO OR SLIDING-FEE-SCALE WORK related to family law? Or do they devote their time to an organization devoted to lobbying for legislative fixes for some of the more common problems in family law? Be wary of attorneys who don't devote any time at all to help ordinary people access justice.

What you should *not* be swayed by are a big office with an army of professional staff, mahogany paneling, or a 60-foot long conference table with a panoramic view of some beautiful site. I'm not bashing the big-boys … they serve an important function … but you're looking for help navigating your divorce. Not launching an anti-trust suit against Microsoft or petitioning the World Trade Organization to penalize a competitor for dumping trade goods in violation of the GATT. If you're a mid- to upper-middle class woman who's accumulated some red-flag issues, a *midsized* law firm with several lawyers, paralegals and an accountant on their staff might be a prudent investment of your money, but a small woodland creature will get lost at a big-boy law firm.

Small woodland creatures with few assets to divide and no lurking issues such as a trust, complex business valuation or custody dispute are usually better served by a solo-practitioner or small firm (less than 3 attorneys) as they usually have more freedom over their billing practices. Once you go to a large or mid-sized law firm, they've got large overhead and strict policies over how they must bill their time. This isn't meant to knock on the big boys … sometimes you need a bigger gun. It's just that most small woodland creatures don't *need* all that ammunition.

If you shoot a Tweety-bird with a bazooka, the result will be a bloody, unrecognizable mess!

GETTING YOUR SPOUSE TO LOAN YOU MONEY TO HIRE AN ATTORNEY

So you interview attorneys, find one you like, and now you're wondering how you're going to *pay* for their services when all the money is in your husband's name. If your research revealed he has enough money squirreled away, you might be able to get your prospective attorney to go into court and get them to order something called a 'Motion for Attorney Fees Pending Litigation.'

A Motion for Fees is a *loan* from *your* anticipated share of the marital estate to pay your attorney. You'll still be responsible for paying your own legal fees at the end of the day. Any fees fronted to you will come out of your eventual share of the marital assets. Courts would much rather you have an attorney than go it alone, so if you can show your husband has money stashed away in a bank account, IRA, CD, or even enough equity in the marital home to take out a home equity loan, you can frequently get a judge to order him to cough some of it up.

A sample Massachusetts Motion for Attorney Fees Pendente Lite follows. Usually the attorney you selected will file this motion *for* you. However, if you have interviewed several attorneys, gotten price quotes, but none of them is willing to go to court, sometimes you can file this motion on your own, get it granted, and *then* hire the attorney.

Most states have some version of this motion available right online at their official family court website. Because I am from Massachusetts, I will give an example of a Massachusetts form, but the base information the judge will usually be looking for in all states is similar.

EXAMPLE 9-1: SAMPLE MOTION FOR ATTORNEY FEES PENDENTE LITE

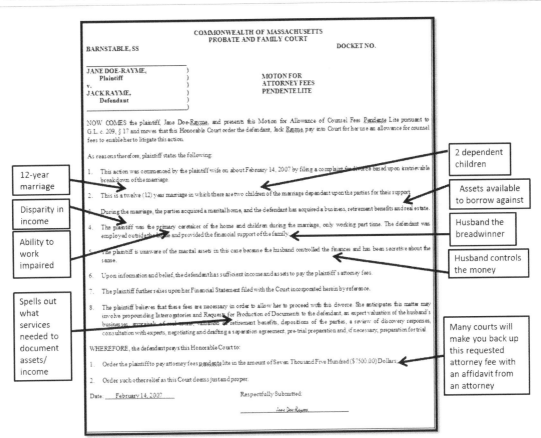

KEEP YOUR ATTORNEY ON A SHORT LEASH!!!

Most people wouldn't dream of letting their Rottweiler out to roam around the neighborhood. People who get Rottweiler's do so because they want to send a message they're not someone to be trifled with. Say 'sit' and a good dog sits and wags its tail. Say 'heel' and the dog trots obediently at your side. If someone comes up to you in a threatening manner, the dog will growl. Say 'sic em!' and he'll rip the face off of anybody who's messing with you. But if you simply let your Rottweiler off the leash and let him roam unsupervised, he's going to rummage through your neighbors trash cans and leave garbage strewn on their front yard. He's going to pee on every bush, dig holes in flower beds, chase cats up trees, bark at your neighbor's kids and scare the crap out of them. He may even bite somebody for no reason. You wouldn't *dream* of giving an aggressive dog like that free rein, would you?

So why on earth do people think they can treat their lawyers any differently?

People don't hire lawyers because they want somebody to wag their tail and give them nice puppy-dog eyes (although having your feared Rottweiler put their slobbery head down upon your lap *is* satisfying). People hire lawyers because they need a big nasty dog to stand between them and whoever they're afraid of and get them to back off. Lawyers are natural predators. After the judge, we're the highest beasts on the food chain in that body of water called court. We like to hunt. We enjoy the sport. There's nothing more satisfying than setting up the opposing prey … um … party for a fall and then moving in for the kill. Lucky you … you get to *pay* us to do what we love best. Blood sport!

Many of us are *so* aggressive that the only way we can function in the *real* world when we're not litigating cases is to take up an extreme sport such as base jumping, hang gliding, or martial arts. I study Urban Goju karate and keep a pair of Okinawan sais above my desk. I've had occasions I've showed up at court even *more* black and blue from sparring than a client I was helping to get a restraining order. It was … fun.

Remember this when you decide how much authority you're going to give your attorney as far as incurring legal fees is concerned. In Section III we cover tools the attorney has in their toolbox to help you get a favorable outcome. If you leave it up to your attorney, he'll throw every single tool in the toolbox at the Evil Trapper, whether needed or not, just to be certain you'll win. Lawyers *like* winning. That's why we became lawyers. But if money is a concern, you'll need to calculate your potential *Return on Investment* before you authorize your lawyer to wield a weapon on your behalf. Section III will hopefully educate you about what questions to ask before deciding to use a tool.

It's good practice to write verbiage into your Retainer Agreement that your attorney will consult with you before incurring any legal fees likely to drive your legal bill above that of your quoted retainer. Don't micromanage your case! Five hundred phone calls to your attorney to ask about costs will drive your legal bill up! That's what Section III of this book is for! But don't just let your attorney off the leash and let him run wild, either. If you do, you're going to be wandering through the street in your pajamas with a trash bag and a shovel, picking up garbage, scooping up dog turds, and apologizing to angry neighbors. Keep your attorney on a short leash … or it's *you* who might get bitten. Woof!

MEDIATION/ARBITRATION/COLLABORATIVE LAW

Mediation and arbitration are forms of Alternative Dispute Resolution (ADR) which have arisen to help divorcing couples amicably negotiate the terms of their divorce, hopefully out-of-court, but sometimes in conjunction with court action. I have two things to say about ADR: (1) when it works, it is a beautiful thing; and (2) mediation attempted prior to actually filing for divorce often fails.

Does this mean you shouldn't give mediation a try? Of course not! It's my sincere hope that you *will* find your way into the mediators office before filing for divorce. But before you go, be aware of warning signs mediation might not be a good fit:

1. Your spouse has physically abused you in the past;

2. Your spouse has always been able to emotionally intimidate you into letting him have his way;

3. You suspect your spouse is being less than forthright about his finances;

    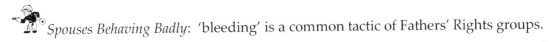*Spouses Behaving Badly*: while one client was mediating in good faith, his wife emptied out the bank accounts and forged his name on a bill-of-sale for his car.

4. Alcohol or drug abuse is an issue;

5. Your spouse is a neglectful or abusive parent to your children;

6. You can't disagree with your spouse without saying something hurtful;

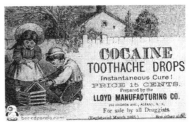

7. One of you views mediation as an opportunity to drag out the divorce and increase your costs.

    Spouses Behaving Badly: 'bleeding' is a common tactic of Fathers' Rights groups.

Although the following issues won't rule out mediation (and may in fact be especially well suited to it), a lack of understanding by one of the parties may cause mediation to fail if:

1. You (or your spouse) don't understand the underlying financial issues in your case;

2. One of you is against the divorce and wishes to reconcile;

3. There are lurking tax-evasion issues which could get you in hot water with the IRS;

My personal reservation with *some* mediation models (such as Collaborative Law) is it's a combination of traditional legal representation combined with quasi-marital therapy for the wealthy. It does *not* save money over traditional litigation. What it *does* do is give the parties a safe forum to vent and come up with creative agreements that work better than what the court might propose, especially if there are minor children involved. If you are wealthy and can afford a 'collaborative law' divorce, it is *definitely* the way to go. But if you're a small woodland creature, mediation may not be the cure-all you're hoping for.

Screen your suitability to enter mediation before actually agreeing to enter into it. In some states, even if you're living apart, the clock will keep ticking for deadlines such as alimony. If you live in a state that has a 'set' term-limit for reaching certain thresholds (such as 10 years for alimony), while you're negotiating in good faith to end your marriage, a deadline could pass or something could happen to harm your case. Mediation should be something you try for a few sessions and then go promptly to court if it fails. Do not drag it out for months on end if it appears to not be working.

Most mediators will be wary of your working with a private attorney while mediation is in process. There is a good reason for this. Some attorneys view the mediator as having stolen money out of their pocket. Attorneys antagonistic to mediation may sabotage your attempts to negotiate a settlement. On the other hand, there are many issues that will come up that you should consult with an outside attorney before agreeing. Ask whether your attorney is willing to work with a mediator, and the mediator with a

private attorney (or at least tolerate your consulting with one out-of-session during the mediation process). If your attorney happens to be on friendly terms with your spouse's attorney, the two may be able to help you reach settlement out of court as well as any mediator. But if your attorney is opposed to mediation in general, find out why. Is it because your case has a red flag? Or is it because they're hoping to extract as many legal fees as they can out of you? Figure out which scenario fits.

🚩 *Be careful that while you're attempting mediation in good faith, that your spouse isn't liquidating assets and hiding the proceeds.* Until you file for your divorce and get the court-ordered protection of an automatic stay, you're vulnerable.

📃 *Automatic Stay* – an automatic injunction that prevents two parties in a legal dispute from taking any action which would upset the financial status quo.

🚩 THE MEDIATOR IS NOT 'YOUR' ATTORNEY

Many couples assume the reason they can save money with a mediator is because they are paying for one attorney (if the mediator happens to be one … sometimes they are therapists or similar social services professionals). Even if your mediator happens to be an attorney, you need to understand they are not *your* attorney. A mediator is bound by the rules of ethics to do no harm. Since they represent both clients, they cannot say or do anything which would materially harm the other party.

In English, this means if your mediator suspects the Evil Trapper is lying through his teeth, he can't come right out and say, "I think the Evil Trapper is a lying piece of dirt" or he could lose his license. The mediator may try to warn you by saying something like, "why don't you go show this financial statement to your own attorney and ask them what they think of X." It's the mediators way of tipping you off he thinks something is fishy. Does this mean your husband is lying? Perhaps not. The mediator may simply be trying to get someone else to point out a course of action is not in your financial best interests because you're not listening to him when *he* points it out.

Once you're done mediating an agreement, the mediator should send *both* of you to your own, separate attorneys to read through what he had drafted and explain it to you before you sign. This is good business practice. If there's one place you should spend money for legal fees, it's to have your own attorney read through and explain the convoluted Separation Agreement so you understand what the heck you are signing.

COURT-ORDERED MEDIATION/ARBITRATION/ADR

Most states now have a process to order the parties into mediation with someone specially trained and certified by the state to handle court-connected mediation cases. Court-connected mediation (or Alternative Dispute Resolution/ADR) generally offers their services on a sliding-fee scale (in other words, if you're dirt poor, it won't cost much). If the parties are unable to reach an agreement after attending in good faith, the court does not have the power to *make* them mediate their case without their day in court (i.e., attendance is mandatory, but reaching an agreement is voluntary).

The nice thing about court-connected mediation is you can have your cake and eat it too if liquidation of assets is a problem. Because you've filed for divorce, the court's automatic stay holds the threat of jail over your spouse's head if he liquidates marital assets, but then you get to attempt mediation. Court-referred mediation holds the greatest promise of helping an average person negotiate an agreement for a reasonable sum of money. Although court-referred mediation has been on the books in most jurisdictions for many years now, private attorneys have been slow to embrace it and judges apprehensive to order it unless one party is unrepresented and *asks* for it.

What's the difference between a regular divorce mediator and a mediator certified to accept court-connected cases? In some states, anybody can claim they're a mediator whether experienced or not, but those certified to accept court-appointments are certified through a state program for 'court connected' mediators.

In addition to court-connected mediation services, your jurisdiction may also have a non-profit mediation program that will enable you to leverage mediation without paying the full market rate of a private mediator, usually on a sliding scale fee. To find out what's available in *your* jurisdiction, check out your local court website or pay your local courthouse a visit.

LEGAL SERVICES/ LEGAL AID

Once upon a time, people who couldn't afford an attorney would go to Legal Services and get one for free or a sliding fee they could afford. Due to budget cuts, Legal Services now runs in "triage" mode. Triage is a combat medical term where only the most life-threatening cases get helped. Marital problems are non-critical problems (i.e., you get helped last).

Legal Services handles elder-abuse and eviction cases, murderers on death row who might be innocent, and then only after all these people are helped will they ever consider handling a divorce case. Since there are always far more people in crisis than Legal Services has the funding to help, they rarely get around to helping small woodland creatures unless you show up with your jaw wired shut from a beating. They're not oblivious to your dilemma. Rather … there are only 168 hours in a week and your average Legal Services attorney is already working 170 of them.

You can, however, often find somebody in the office to answer questions, help you fill out forms, and refer you to other programs in your area. Legal Services is usually listed in the telephone book. Call them *first* to get referrals to more obscure agencies in your area which can be hard to find if you don't know who they already are (and who knows, they just might be having a slow week and agree to take your case).

Even if you don't qualify for free legal services, it doesn't mean they aren't worried about your well-being. Legal Services attorneys are often post free self-help legal information (forms, brochures, even entire self-help books) online or provide links to other sites so a motivated litigant can help themselves. Legal services are either set up statewide, or county by county. To find them, type into your internet browser:

" (Your State)   Legal Services"

" (Your State)   Legal Services"

" (Neighboring County)   Legal Services"

Look around and see what they have, including legal services agencies that might serve a different region within your same state. Since the law is usually created at the state-level, so long as the Legal Services agency serves a county or region is within the same state as the one where you will be getting your divorce, the information is good.

COURTHOUSE 'LAWYER-OF-THE-DAY' PROGRAMS

Many bar associations pool their resources to staff a volunteer 'lawyer of the day' at your local courthouse. The lawyer of the day is just that … philanthropic local attorneys take turns manning a Q&A booth to answer quick questions for free. The lawyers don't get paid, but they can answer quick questions about your divorce in the brief time allotted (usually 5-10 minutes). Volunteer attorneys may not be family law specialists, but they are a great resource in a pinch.

THE COURT'S FAMILY SERVICES DEPARTMENT AND SELF-HELP CLINICS

Most family courts have personnel assigned to help couples more narrowly define the issues which will be brought before the judge. In some courthouses this person will be a magistrate who writes down what the issues are and may give suggestions about how he's seen the judge rule in similar cases. Other courthouses may have trained mediators who can help couples reach agreements. Some even assign court investigators to conduct limited investigations, such as whether there's any basis to a custody allegation.

Some jurisdictions have adopted a hybrid model … with mandatory court-connected arbitration in place (a sister to mediation) for all contested issues *before* you're allowed to get in to see a judge.

Arbitrators/conciliators may have quasi-judicial decision-making authority on routine matters (such as setting child support) similar to a having a magistrate decide small-claims-court cases under $1,000 or decide cases contesting traffic tickets (a most *sensible* use of scarce taxpayer dollars!). Find out what's available in *your* jurisdiction as part of your Bootcamp information-gathering process.

Other jurisdictions are experimenting with self-help legal clinics where pro-se litigants can fill out forms online, attend self-help classes with an instructor, or leverage a variety of other court-connected self-help legal services. If your local courthouse sponsors such a program, I strongly urge you to take advantage of it! Even if there is a fee involved!

Although the family services department is not a judge, they can be helpful in leveling the playing field in situations where one party has a lawyer and the other doesn't, or where one party is overbearing and bringing improper influence upon the other party to settle. *However, they are not your own private attorney.* Family courts are as under-funded as legal services and can only give perfunctory attention to your case, so don't expect them to hold your hand through a 5-hour conciliation session. I've seen excellent outcomes from some family conciliation sessions, but I've also seen outcomes which were truly appalling.

Do your Bootcamp exercises before you walk into the Family Service Officers office!!!

NON-PROFIT LEGAL CLINICS AND HOW-TO CLASSES

Many agencies sponsor programs which can help you get a quick overview of the law and get answers to questions. For example, I offer a four-hour *Divorce Bootcamp Seminar* for non-profit agencies where I address a group of women summarizing information contained in the first nine chapters of this *Bootcamp* manual. A sister-attorney offers a two-hour class on how to fill out the courts' forms. Another sister-attorney offers a one-hour class on how to gather the financial information outlined in the Acorns chapter, but covers more in-depth the financial issues which plague the upper end of the economic sphere. We refer clients to each other's classes and urge them to attend as many as they can. Furthermore, we all offer half-hour legal clinics from time-to-time at the sponsoring agency offices.

Why do private attorneys develop these types of classes and then work with non-profit agencies to host them? Three reasons:

1. Someday we are all going to die. When we get to that pearly gate, we need something good to say quickly to Saint Peter before he hits the *All Lawyers Go to Hell* button;

2. It's a good way to drum up good will in the community. Although the low-income woman who attends your class might not be able to afford your services, chances are she has a friend who someday *will.*

3. A lot of lawyers went to law school because we want to *help* people, but we just can't help them all. A class is a good way to offer information to a lot of people in a short period of time without becoming embroiled in somebody else's legal troubles.

I do a lot of pro bono work for an IOLTA-funded non-profit agency that provides a place for attorneys to host informational classes and do all the work to bring people who need to learn together with lawyers who are willing to teach. They give women someplace to go to ask questions, gain referrals to other community services, join a divorce support group, undergo career counseling, find a mentor, and learn budget and job skills. It's a potent little package built up around the notion of women-helping-women and self-help.

I wish *all* jurisdictions had such a well-rounded program. But even if your jurisdiction doesn't, chances are there is an agency in *your* jurisdiction which offers at least *some* of these services. Legal Services, as cut-to-the-bone as they are, should be able to tell you who to call if you earn too much money to qualify for free legal services but not enough to hire a full-service attorney. Most non-profit organizations charge a sliding scale fee or will ask you for a free-will donation to cover their overhead, but they rarely turn anyone away. If you can afford to give, please do. If you're broke, remember that your time is also a valuable gift. Once you get back on your feet, offer to volunteer.

DO-IT-YOURSELF BOOKS AND DOCUMENT PREPARATION SERVICES

If you can reach a *fair* agreement with your spouse, do-it-yourself books and document preparation services are a good way to draft paperwork you need to file your divorce. However, be aware that, these days, many of the standard forms these services offer to fill out *for* you can be downloaded from your state's court website for free (filling them out and the law behind them is a different story). Although using boilerplates from a website or book is an excellent tool when you and your spouse are hammering out your proposed agreement, hire a licensed *attorney* draft your Separation Agreement (also called "ghost writing").

Do not make the mistake of copying a generic separation agreement out of a 'do it yourself' book (not even this book!) and then signing it without first having an attorney review it!!! You could end up signing something which will hurt you or incur draconian financial penalties. If worded improperly, the IRS might even tax you on the transfer of assets you already own! If you have $300 left on earth, the Separation Agreement is the place to sit down with a licensed attorney and ask questions!

Be wary of document preparation services which offer to memorialize an agreement you reached on your own. If you are not an attorney and did not know the law before, how are you supposed to know what is fair? And how will you know if your spouse included all divisible assets and accurately valued them when you bring your hand-written scribbles to them to memorialize in dozens of pages of legal mumbo-jumbo? Many so-called document preparation services *are not* attorneys and they *do not* know the intricacies of the law. They will write exactly what your husband tells them to write, whether it's fair or not.

Document preparation services are a good resource to dig up samples of less routine forms and provide instructions on how to fill them out, but are not a replacement for an attorney. Always consult with a –real-attorney after filling out a form, even if only a 5-minute consult with a courthouse lawyer of the day.

Every year, I get calls from people who used document preparation services that didn't address serious issues or were grossly unfair. There are many fine attorneys out there willing to *ghost write* your Separation Agreement for a reasonable fee. As part of their preparation, they'll advise you of the best course of action and warn you of potential problems.

Ghost Write – when an attorney dispenses legal advice and helps you draft paperwork, but doesn't represent you in court.

Commercial document preparation services may be prudent is if you need a specialized portion of many Separation Agreements known as a Qualified Domestic Relations Order (QDRO) or Qualified Pension Order (QPO) to help you divide a retirement asset. Because there are only a finite number of pension management companies nationwide and these services deal with them on a regular basis, firms that special in drafting QDRO agreements can often provide a faster, more economical service on that aspect of your divorce than a private attorney.

YOUR OWN STATE COURTS WEBSITE

Visit your state court website and see what materials they have for you to educate *yourself*. Teaching you how to help yourself piece together legal services at a reasonable rate is what this book is all about. I'm providing links to all official state court websites nationwide that I'm aware of. Many state court systems provide not just forms, but helpful brochures or refer you to programs low-income people can leverage to obtain their divorce. Why pay for something you can get for free? The whole point of this book is *not* to spend money unless absolutely necessary!

At the time of publication of this book, state family courts are being flooded by laypeople such as yourself handling some or all of their own divorces because they can't afford to hire a full-service attorney. In some cases, your state legislature may have woken up and smelled the coffee. Enough voters wrote to them and complained they wanted more access to the courts and your legislature may have funded the development of an organized official state-court portal or program to get forms. It's as simple as doing an internet search:

"_____(Your State)_____" Divorce Forms

"_____(Your State)_____" Family Court Forms

As you can see from the sample, by typing the search terms 'X-State Family Court Forms' I pulled up an entire page of helpful court forms for my home state.

In other states, greedy bar associations hell bent on maintaining their function as a gatekeeper of legal services may still be lobbying your elected officials to act against the interests of the public. However, this doesn't mean you can't get forms. It just means you'll have to hunt around the internet for a county court website where an enterprising Clerk Magistrate or Legal Services organization posted divorce forms online so pro se (self-represented) litigants stop coming into their office and begging them for help.

"_____(Your County)_____" Family Court Forms

"_____(Your County)_____" Divorce Forms

Our state posts lots of forms online, but our local county Court Magistrate has built a nice user-friendly website which is much more attractive and pleasant to navigate with practical information such as how much the filing fee will be conspicuously posted. Perhaps yours has too? Why not find out? You're only a mouse-click away from finding out the inside scoop at *your* local county courthouse and it won't cost you any money!

Divorces are handled at a *county* level, but it is your *state* which sets the rules which determine which forms you'll need to use to file for your own divorce. Therefore, with a few exceptions for minor procedural issues, the forms posted on one counties website will be the same forms you use in a different county *so long as it is within the same state.* If your state does not list the forms and neither does your county, there's a pretty good chance at least *some* of the forms are listed on some other county website within your state. Therefore, if you can't find the information you need, type in a search request for neighboring counties as well.

"_____(Neighboring County)_____" Family Court Forms

"_____(Neighboring County)_____" Divorce Forms

Now why bother mucking around in a neighboring counties website? Because, as former Secretary of Defense Donald Rumsfeld once said, 'there are also unknown unknowns -- the ones we don't know we don't know … it is the latter category that tend to be the difficult ones." As a small woodland creature, your post-divorce survival may hinge on some arcane tidbit of legal information that you *don't know you don't know.* That's why lawyers make so much money … finding out all this information takes a huge investment of time and money outside of what we can bill for your case. But if the issue is something which has frequently tripped up laypeople coming into the courthouse for justice, at some point some ambitious court clerk, magistrate, or lawyer may have jotted down an article about the topic so the next poor slob stumbling blindly through their courthouse wouldn't make the same mistake. This book started out as a loose-leaf notebook with hundreds of such articles! If I pull up the website of tiny, distant Hampshire County, look what I find:

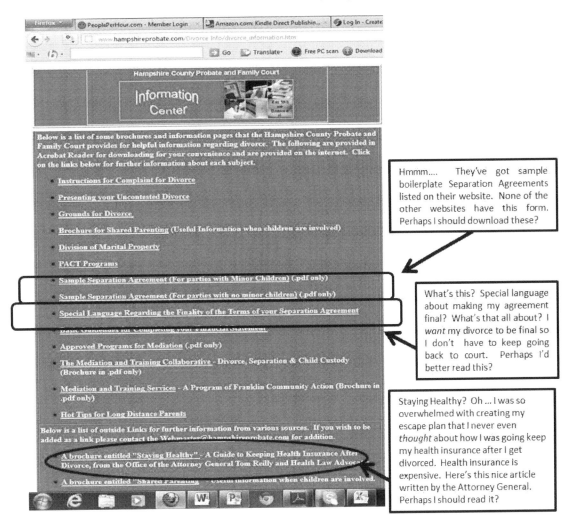

Big-city lawyers used to scoff at the idea of tiny Hampshire County being at the cutting edge of courthouses nationwide. The county is poor, rural, poorly educated, and one of the most underfunded in the state. What they *did* have, however, was enterprising staff and flexible judges willing to help the poor indigent litigants they saw coming through their courtroom getting slammed. They remembered their job is to serve the taxpayers who pay their salaries, not line the pockets of the legal profession. Most legal reforms and cutting-edge pilot programs which have happened in *my* home state of Massachusetts have originated from this tiny little backwater courthouse. Online self-help forms and brochures. How-to classes. Court-connected mediation pilot programs. Limited Representation (which allows a lawyer to go to court one time instead of being obligated to take on your entire case so they don't have to charge a huge retainer). Perhaps *you* have such a little gem somewhere in *your* state? You won't know until you look.

Official state and county court websites usually end in .gov or .us. If the court website doesn't have them, sometimes your local Legal Services agency or Association of Law Librarians will have them listed on *their* website. Failing that, www.divorce-forms.com is one national site clients have used to get the forms they need, although there are many others. These form services are usually reasonably priced and convenient if you happen to live in a state that is still in the dark ages about self-help.

This following list is provided for informational purposes only:

TABLE 9-1: 50-STATE LISTING OF FREE SELF-HELP DIVORCE WEBSITES

State	Official Court Self-Help Websites
Alabama	http://eforms.alacourt.gov/ http://www.alabamalegalhelp.org/issues/families-and-children/divorce
Alaska	http://courts.alaska.gov/forms.htm http://courts.alaska.gov/selfhelp.htm
Arizona	http://azcourts.gov/selfservicecenter/SelfServiceForms.aspx
Arkansas	http://www.arlegalservices.org/node/31 *Arkansas Legal Services
California	http://www.courts.ca.gov/selfhelp.htm
Colorado	http://www.courts.state.co.us/Forms/Index.cfm
Connecticut	http://www.jud.ct.gov/publications/fm179.pdf http://www.jud.ct.gov/publications/fm180.pdf *very helpful 60-page 'do it yourself in CT' guide and forms
Delaware	http://courts.delaware.gov/Help
D.C.	http://www.dccourts.gov/dccourts/superior/family/selfhelp.jsp
Florida	http://www.flcourts.org/gen_public/family/forms_rules/
Georgia	http://www.georgiacourts.org/aoc/selfhelp/forms.html
Hawaii	http://www.courts.state.hi.us/self-help/divorce/divorce.html
Idaho	http://www.courtselfhelp.idaho.gov
Illinois	http://www.law.siu.edu/selfhelp *Southern Illinois University School of Law http://www.dupageco.org/CourtClerk/3198/
Indiana	http://www.in.gov/judiciary/selfservice
Iowa	http://www.iowacourtsonline.org/Court_Rules_and_Forms/Family_Law_Forms *No Minor children only
Kansas	http://www.kansasjudicialcouncil.org/DivorceForms.shtml
Kentucky	http://kyjustice.org/onlinedivorce *No Minor children only
Louisiana	http://www.lawhelp.org/LA/StateSubTopics.cfm/County/%20/City/%20/demoMode/%3D%201/Language/1/State/LA/TextOnly/N/ZipCode/%20/LoggedIn/0/iTopicID/619/sTopicImage/familyjuvenile.gif/bAllState/0 *official court website unhelpful. LawHelp.org website http://www.edivorcepapers.com/louisiana-divorce-forms-and-papers.html *unofficial website. Helpful, but may be out of date.
Maine	http://www.courts.state.me.us/fees_forms/forms/index.shtml#fm
Maryland	http://mdcourts.gov/faq.html#divorce http://www.dhr.maryland.gov/mcw/pdf/lrmd0328.pdf (helpful guide)
Massachusetts	http://www.mass.gov/courts/courtsandjudges/courts/probateandfamilycourt/selfhelp.html http://www.mass.gov/courts/courtsandjudges/courts/probateandfamilycourt/forms.html http://www.lawlib.state.ma.us/subject/forms/index.html#divorce
Michigan	http://courts.michigan.gov/scao/courtforms/domesticrelations/drindex.htm#foc http://courts.michigan.gov/scao/selfhelp/family/divorce.htm *Michigan not have official divorce forms, but you can obtain financial and child support forms online http://www.midivorceonline.com/startnow.asp *a commercial, for-pay document preparation service that has self-help divorce forms available for a reasonable fee
Minnesota	http://www.mncourts.gov/selfhelp/?page=310
Mississippi	http://www.edivorcepapers.com/mississippi-divorce-forms-and-papers.html

	*Not an official court website
Missouri	http://www.courts.mo.gov/page.jsp?id=38346 http://www.selfrepresent.mo.gov/file.jsp?id=31147
Montana	http://courts.mt.gov/library/topic/default.mcpx
Nebraska	http://www.supremecourt.ne.gov/self-help/families.html
Nevada	http://lawlibrary.nevadajudiciary.us/forms/standardizeddivorceforms.php
New Hampshire	http://www.courts.state.nh.us/fdpp/forms/index.htm
New Jersey	http://www.judiciary.state.nj.us/prose
New Mexico	http://www.nmcourts.gov/cgi/prose_lib
New York	http://www.nycourts.gov/divorce/forms.shtml
North Carolina	http://www.nccourts.org/Courts/CRS/Policies/LocalRules/
North Dakota	http://www.ndcourts.gov/court/forms/
Ohio	http://www.drcourt.org/ *Butler county
Oklahoma	http://www.tulsacountydistrictcourt.org/family_court.html *Tulsa county
Oregon	http://courts.oregon.gov/OJD/OSCA/cpsd/courtimprovement/familylaw/FL_Divorce.page?
Pennsylvania	http://www.courts.phila.gov/common-pleas/family/dr/ *Philadelphia county
Rhode Island	http://www.courts.ri.gov/PublicResources/forms/Family%20Court%20Forms/Forms/AllItems.aspx *Currently does not have all forms online. Need to go to courthouse to get 'divorce packet.'
South Carolina	http://www.judicial.state.sc.us/forms/searchType.cfm
South Dakota	http://ujs.sd.gov/forms/default.aspx
Tennessee	http://www.tncourts.gov/help-center/court-approved-divorce-forms
Texas	http://www.txcourts.gov/pubs/pubs-home.asp *has links to forms in both English and Spanish
Utah	http://www.utcourts.gov/ocap/utah/divorce/ *has links to free legal clinics and places to get forms
Vermont	http://www.vermontjudiciary.org/masterpages/Court-Forms-Family.aspx *Includes 'civil union' forms
Virginia	http://www.courts.state.va.us/forms/home.html *has links to mediation
Washington state	http://www.courts.wa.gov/forms/?fa=forms.contribute&formid=13
West Virginia	http://www.courtswv.gov/lower-courts/family-forms/index-family-forms.html *includes mediation forms
Wisconsin	http://www.wicourts.gov/ecourts/prose.htm
Wyoming	http://www.courts.state.wy.us/DandCS.aspx

*Sites with an asterisk are either limited or not official government entity

USE THE SAME LEGAL RESOURCES YOUR LAWYER DOES

What happens when your *attorney* has a legal question, you might ask yourself? Do we *really* walk around with all that arcane legal knowledge stored in our brains? Although attorneys *do* tend to be walking encyclopedias, lawyers buy special trade publications which give us a starting point to research issues we're unfamiliar with. These publications are written by judges and lawyers to help other lawyers, but if you feel capable of wading through scholarly topics, these may be useful:

- *MCLE Family Law Practice Manual and Forms* – www.mcle.org (Massachusetts specific/helpful in other New England states).
- *Property Division in Divorce Proceedings: A Fifty State Guide* – www.aspenpublishers.com
- *Value of Pensions in Divorce* – www.aspenpublishers.com
- *Valuing Specific Assets in Divorce* – www.aspenpublishers.com
- *Determination of Income in Child Support* – www.jamespublishing.com
- http://store.westlaw.com – (go to 'Practice Area' dropdown menu and then 'Family Law') – Westlaw carries specialty practice manuals for all 50 states.

Trade publications are usually too expensive for a casual layperson to justify purchasing. I spend thousands of dollars each year keeping my personal law library up to date. If you need that much knowledge, it would be wiser to hire an attorney. However, sometimes you need to look up an arcane issue which isn't covered elsewhere. These books give an overview of the law (much as this book has done only they're written in 'legal-ize' so nobody but another lawyer can understand). However, what these books give you that this book *does not* is a listing of all the legal cases the authors relied upon when they wrote their summary.

In other words, whilst both trade publications and this book can only give you a general overview of the law, a case law citation referring to a legal precedent specifically covering your legal issue is a bullet your lawyer can use to shoot the evil trapper right between the eyes and stop him dead in his tracks. If you've got a specific legal problem, figure out which trade publication may have the answer to your question and dig up a copy of it. Most counties have a law library for judicial reference, usually some musty corner of a basement, which are open to the public for reference purposes only. You can read the trade publication and photocopy scholarly articles out of them, but not take the books home. Or perhaps there's a law school library near your house?

To find your local state law library, type the following search parameters into your internet browser:

"____(Your State)____ law libraries"

"____(Your County)____ law libraries"

Why are case law citations important? Remember earlier when we learned 'the law' is really a holey old block of Swiss cheese? A case law citation is shorthand code lawyers use in legal pleadings to refer to a legal case some judge decided way-back-when that carved an exception into the block of cheese called a 'precedent.' Judges don't have to follow trade publications when deciding the fate of your case any more than they follow what I've written in this book. Legal precedents, on the other hand, are the law. Judges *must* follow legal precedents or your case could be overturned on appeal.

Legal Precedent – a legal case establishing a principle or rule that a court or other judicial body adopts when deciding later cases with similar issues or facts. Most legal cases are about as interesting to read through as quadratic equations, which is why lawyers buy expensive trade manuals to compile, organize and summarize them instead.

Case Law Citation – a shorthand code lawyers use when referring to legal precedents. For example, the citation *International Shoe v. State of Washington*, 326 U.S. 310 (1945) tells us that in 1945, the U.S. Supreme Court (U.S.) created a legal precedent about when somebody can be hauled into a distant state to be sued. If you say 'International Shoe' to most lawyers, they'll nod their head and exclaim, 'Aha! Minimum contacts!'

Once you find a case law citation referring to a precedent which may cover your situation, digging up a copy of the actual legal decision written by the judge who set the precedent in the first place is usually easy. Simply type the name of the case into your internet browser and chances are you'll pull up the actual legal decision that judge wrote back when he decided the case. Legal decisions aren't easy to decipher, but if you have the temperament to read through them, it can be empowering.

In addition to trade manuals, there are other websites which might have helpful information:

- *Your local Continuing Legal Education website:* Type "__(your state)__ Continuing Legal Education" into your web browser an hunt around for what resources they have available. These agencies have state-specific books written by lawyers for other lawyers, but sometimes they post scholarly articles about cutting-edge legal trends that are occurring right now within your state.

- *Your local Bar Association website:* Type ""__(your state/county)__ Bar Association" into your web browser and hunt around for what resources they have available. Most bar associations will charge you to access their stuff, but some publish newsletters and provide additional content about cutting-edge legal topics for free.

A little knowledge is a dangerous thing!!! Remember that case law citation I quoted earlier? *International Shoe v. State of Washington* was decided in 1945. Since that date, there have been more than 15,000 legal decisions citing that case, either upholding it or carving out some even *more* arcane exception to what that case meant. If it was that easy, lawyers wouldn't make so much money, which is why we buy trade manuals. Trade manuals are updated every few years to bring lawyers up to date on the latest potholes in the road.

INTERMISSION

Whew!!! Is your head spinning from information overload? Do yourself a favor. Before you move into Section II (uncontested divorces), give yourself the gift of a lower-stress, moderate-cost divorce that won't leave you financially destitute while you lick your wounds. If your husband hasn't already filed for divorce and you don't have a red flag issue screaming at you to move, now, do the preparatory exercises. Gather the information recommended in Chapter 3 and neatly index it until you can pull up any given document in less than a minute. Take the steps I recommend to begin disentangling your finances from your soon-to-be ex and start building credit in your own name. If you still have hope you might be able to reconcile, drag your husband to marriage counseling.

Prepare the Financial Statement in Chapters 4 and use it to compare your likely post-divorce budget. Set enough money aside to maintain your living expenses for the 6-12 weeks it may take your lawyer to get your case into court and get your husband to start paying his fair share. If you will be dependent upon child support or alimony, re-read Chapters 5 and 6, compute how much you might be entitled to receive, and be honest with yourself if you suspect your husband may be a snake and try to screw you. An ounce of prevention now, while you can still get your hands on financial records or document your husband's *real* earnings, is worth an army of attorneys and forensic accountants from the best downtown law firm of your state.

Take the time to rough out three or four different scenarios for property and debt division and figure out *now*, while the decision is still in *your* hands and not some opposing attorney or judge, what assets you want to hold, which would be wise to dispose of now while the Evil Trapper is still on the hook to eat any losses, and how you're going to pay down any debt you may be left holding.

If you've read through the book this far, you are one smart woodland creature. Most women are woefully unprepared for what their post-divorce life will look like. Studies show that women experiencing divorce face roughly a 30 percent decline in the standard of living they enjoyed while married. If you are low- or moderate-income, the reduction in your standard of living will be even *more* devastating if the Evil Trapper decides to play games.

The Challenge of the Mountains

When you *are* ready to move on, do as much of your own legwork as you possibly can. Always be mindful that every single thing your attorney does on your behalf is going to cost you money. Lots of money! If it's something you can't handle on your own, its money well spent. But much of what drives up legal bills has very little to do with that core activity most lawyers are paid to figure out … comparing legal statutes and case law to what, in their experience, the judge sitting in your district is likely to do when faced with *your* unique situation.

In Section II, we'll learn how you and your husband might sit down, either across the kitchen table or at a mediator's office, and use what you have learned to hammer out your own divorce.

In Section III, this book covers material most other self-help legal guides skimp on. What happens if you have to file a contested divorce and don't have enough money to hire a full-service attorney? We'll walk by Jane Doe's side as she navigates the legal system and see steps she can take to solve common problems. Although by no means meant to be an exhaustive resource on the topic, hopefully it will show you that between hiring a full-service attorney and having no legal representation at all lay a myriad number of shades of gray. By skimming through the 'toolbox' and educating yourself about what's to come, you won't panic when that 37-page discovery motion or a summons arrives in the mail. You'll recall it was covered in this book, flip to the appropriate page, and see whether it is to be expected.

TABLE 9-1: ACTIVITIES TO SAVE MONEY ON YOUR LEGAL BILL

Step	Attorney does	Layperson does	Cost Savings
Gather documents in Chapter 3 *before* you see an attorney	Called "discovery" (Chapter 15). Costs $300 to $10,000+	Free	$300 - $10,000
Put the documents in order arranged by type of item, account number, and date in 3-ring binders (versus handing him a stack of paperwork)	Attorney usually has his paralegal organize this for him before reading it. Will charge you $25 - $85 per hour.	Free plus cost of a 3-ring binder (around $2.99)	$100 - $850
Make 3 photocopies, neatly arranged as described above (original for you, one for attorney, one for opposing attorney)	Attorney has his secretary or paralegal stand at the photocopier to do this. Will charge you $25 - $85 per hour *plus* an average of 25 cents per page.	Your time is free. You can make copies at an office supply store such as Staples for 10 cents per page.	$150 - $750
Fill out your own Financial Statement (Chapter 4) and bring it with you to your first attorney visit.	It will take 10 minutes to elicit the information in this document (versus glancing over it) at a cost of $150 - $300 per hour. Your attorney must then type it up and verify the information against your Chapter 3 binder, but having a draft already filled out saves time and money.	Free	$50
Compute your own *estimated* Child Support Guidelines (Chapter 5)	Once you fill out your financial statement, the first question most clients want to know is "how much will I get?" By knowing this number in advance, you save 20 minutes to an hour of your attorneys' time to explain it and compute a rough guideline at a cost of $150 - $300 per hour.	Free.	$50 - $300
Fill out Child Support Enforcement Division intake packet in advance of your first court date (Chapter 5)	Many courthouses make you hand in the judge's order before allowing you to leave. Filling out this form while your attorney waits will cost 45 minutes of your attorney's time.	Free.	$110 - $225
Understanding the basics about what your attorney is talking about.	Every time you call and/or ask your attorney a DFQ it costs you. A 10-minute phone call costs $25 - $50. An explanation about a common topic such as "what is this long scary preamble to my spouses Request for Documents?" will cost you at least ½ hour of your attorney's time. Even if you only talk to the secretary, most attorneys will bill you for wasting the secretary's time.	Negligible (if you look the scary forms up in the upcoming chapters of this Bootcamp manual before you call your lawyer).	DFQ's add $500 to $1,500 to an average legal bill.
Understanding your attorney is not your therapist	Your attorney charges you to call and gripe about your evil ex-spouse even if there is nothing	Griping is what friends are for. Mail a generic "thank you for	Calling to gripe adds $300+ to the average legal bill. I once had

	they can do about it as you are taking valuable time away from their other clients.	being a friend" card after dumping an earful ($1.59 card plus a 45 cent stamp).	a client rack up $6,000 worth of "griping calls."
Having all of the paperwork related to your divorce neatly organized so you can easily refer to it whenever you speak to your attorney.	Hunting for lost paperwork and not being organized when your attorney calls with a question easily eats up 2 hours of legal fees.	Cost of a 3-ring binder (around $2.99)	$300 - $600
Making a concise list of questions to ask your attorney whenever you call or meet with them.	Babbling off point easily consumes another 2-3 hours of your attorney's time over the course of an average case.	Steno notebooks only cost around $1.59.	$300 - $900
Documenting your spouse's real income and real joint marital assets before he "goes underground" and absconds with the money.	So sad, too bad, if you don't do your homework, you're going to lose out on tens of thousands of dollars in income and assets you would otherwise be entitled to receive and no attorney will be able to undo all the damage you caused by not being prepared.	Free. I once "found" $3 million dollars a clients' husband hid.	The *average* client spends $5,000 chasing an extra $50/wk. worth of child support from a self-employed spouse.
If you suspect your spouse is hiding income or assets, go through your Arcorn binder, circle and note suspicious anomalies, and flag them with a post-it note.	Attorney will hire a special expert witness called a 'forensic accountant' to do this.	Free	Costs anywhere from $5,000 to $50,000.

CHAPTER NINE SUMMARY

1. Hire the best legal representation you can afford;

2. Ask your friends who *they* used in their divorce. Failing that, search out attorneys who volunteer time at local women's services agencies. They will usually be more sensitive to the budget realities of the lower end of the income spectrum;

3. Neatly arrange Acorns paperwork and prepare the documents suggested earlier in this book (financial statement, rough draft child support estimate, etc.) to bring to your first appointment.

4. Fill out *all* paperwork the attorney may send you in advance. Even if redundant.

5. The mediator is not 'your' lawyer. He serves two masters. Keep that in mind!

6. Learn to navigate your local court website, law library, or other places you can dig up the same legal resources your lawyer does.

7. Keep your attorney on a short leash! Always ask what the potential return on investment is for any strategy.

SECTION II

NEGOTIATED (UNCONTESTED) DIVORCES

(This page left intentionally blank)

CHAPTER 10

UNCONTESTED DIVORCES

*"Ultimate excellence lies not in winning every battle,
But in defeating the enemy without ever fighting."*

Sun Tzu: The Art of War

Divorces can be obtained in one of two ways. Either you and your spouse sit down and *agree* what your post-divorce life will look like (an uncontested divorce). Or one spouse drags the other kicking and screaming to the courthouse because one (or both) of you have unrealistic expectations (a contested divorce). Although some states divide these two classes of divorces even further into sub-categories such as Simple Divorce, No-Fault Divorce, Fault Divorce, Summary Divorce, etc., all that *really* matters is the following: are you walking into court with a signed Separation Agreement ready for the judge to rubber-stamp? Or is the judge going to actually have to *listen* to you two argue about issues related to your case?

An *uncontested (negotiated) divorce* is when you and your spouse sit down and negotiate who will get custody of your children, how your assets will be divided and debts paid, and other issues such as child support, alimony, taxes, health insurance, etc. It can either be done by hiring separate attorneys and asking *them* to draft something up, via mediation, or over your kitchen table with a packet of fill-in-the-blank forms.

A *contested divorce* is when you file for divorce yourself, have the sheriff serve a summons onto your soon-to-be ex-spouse, and force them to go to court whether or not they want a divorce. Many women will file a *contested* divorce to force their spouse to the negotiation table, but later convert it to an uncontested one once an agreement is reached.

A *Separation Agreement* (aka property or marital settlement agreement) is a written contract between two divorcing spouses dividing your property and debts, spelling out your rights, and settling issues such as alimony, child support, custody, visitation, tax issues and insurance. Requirements vary from state-to-state (Separation Agreements are covered in more detail in Chapter 11: Separation Agreements).

After doing the preparatory exercises in Section One, you'll hopefully know enough to approach your spouse with well thought-out and coherent demands. If you have a firm grasp of your legal rights, you'll be able to swap and trade assets (or issues) without letting hurt feelings or anger cloud your judgment. Treat your spouse fairly, and hope he is willing to do the same.

Failing that, at least you can say you tried the high road *first* before moving onto Section III and declaring all-out war!

If you and your spouse agree you both want a divorce, but are unable to hammer out a Separation Agreement, you will need to file a contested divorce and ask the court to resolve the remaining issues. Contested divorces are covered in more detail in Chapters 12-20. To be considered *uncontested*, you must reach full agreement on all issues which lie between you and memorialize those arrangements in a Separation Agreement (Chapter 11).

NEGOTIATED (UNCONTESTED) DIVORCES ... PRO AND CON

ADVANTAGES (PRO):

* Negotiated divorces are less stressful and costly than traditional, litigated divorces;

* The court filing fees are usually less;

* Your day in court should be a breeze. In some states you may not need to appear at all;

* In states without a mandatory separation period, you may be able to file your paperwork and have your divorce decree in hand within a matter of weeks;

* In states with a mandatory separation period, the uncontested Separation Agreement you draft and sign is an enforceable contract between you and your spouse until the day you file, protecting your legal rights;

* Negotiation can be done out-of-court with the help of a trained mediator, a collaborative law team, or informally over your kitchen table with two cooperative spouses. It can also be done out-of-court between two attorneys who assist their clients pre-filing to draft or ghost-write a proposal.

* You can include terms in your Separation Agreement that a court would not otherwise order.

- You are more likely to remain on marginally civil terms with your former spouse (important if children are involved).

DISADVANTAGES (CON):

 If your spouse is stubborn or unreasonable, you may end up negotiating away a lot more than you would through a traditional litigation process simply to reach agreement;

 *If your spouse is domineering, he may terrorize you into signing away important legal rights* no judge would otherwise agree to;

Spouses Behaving Badly: a client's husband threatened that if she didn't secretly sign a second mortgage on the marital house granting an additional $10,000 not listed on the Separation Agreement to his mother, he would take her children and move back to Portugal, which has a history of ignoring U.S. custody agreements. No judge would have ever allowed such a thing!

 Many pre-court mediations fail to reach agreement. Most husbands ask to enter mediation in the hope the mediator will 'talk some sense' into the wife and absolve them of their obligation to divide marital assets and income fairly. The moment they learn the mediator isn't simply going to dictate their world-view, the husband no longer wants to play ball.

 While you are negotiating out-of-court in good faith without the benefit of an Automatic Restraining Order, your spouse may be liquidating your assets and hiding money;

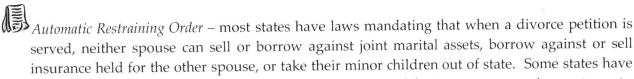 *Automatic Restraining Order* – most states have laws mandating that when a divorce petition is served, neither spouse can sell or borrow against joint marital assets, borrow against or sell insurance held for the other spouse, or take their minor children out of state. Some states have additional provisions against changing beneficiaries on life insurance or retirement assets. These orders remain in effect until your final judgment is signed by the court or an interim order is entered stating otherwise.

 Without the protection of the Automatic Restraining Order, you will not be able to hold him criminally responsible. You may be able to recover those assets later if you diligently documented your Acorns, but it will be very costly. If you fear your spouse may do this, don't attempt to negotiate your divorce until *after* you file a contested divorce. You can always file a motion to convert it into an uncontested one after you reach an agreement.

 A lot of protective verbiage found in Separation Agreements drafted by two opposing attorneys in a litigated divorce has a way of getting cut out of mediated agreements. In high conflict cases, both attorneys may recommend spelling out exact criteria for commonly post-divorce contested items such as visitation, selling the former marital home, or the repayment of debts. These tightly worded criteria have a way of being omitted from mediated agreements because the process assumes continued cooperation.

 The Separation Agreement you both sign has the force of law unless the judge at your final hearing rules it was patently unreasonable. If you don't understand what you are signing, you could sign away important legal rights.

 Judges tend not to examine the fairness of a pre-negotiated divorce the way they would if your case was before them over several contested hearings, only look for glaring inconsistencies. If the judge rules your Agreement is fair and grants your divorce, but you later discover you made a grave error in judgment, you *will* be bound to it and you *will not* be able to go back and fix it (with very few exceptions).

If you have diligently done your Bootcamp exercises and prepared for the worst by gathering all the paperwork, doing all the prep work, and following all of the steps outlined in the previous chapter, you should be in a good position to at least *try* to negotiate your own divorce before you resort to court action. However, if any red flags listed above give you pause, speak to an attorney in your jurisdiction about whether or not this would be wise.

BEFORE YOU BREAK THE BAD NEWS

If you are to have any hope at all of obtaining your divorce without becoming embroiled in costly litigation, you must come to the negotiating table from a position of strength and fairness. You must know in advance what aspects of your property division (or child custody) you are willing to bargain away versus which items are non-negotiable. You must already have a firm grasp on the possible range of outcomes a family court judge would order in *your* cases so you neither negotiate away more than is fair, or end up litigating your case anyways because your demands are unreasonable. And most importantly at all, you must come at your spouse from a position of emotional strength and clear-headedness so that hurt feelings don't sabotage your efforts. That means you should have *already* done the following before you break the news:

- *Do your Bootcamp Exercises first!!!* Be ready to freeze your joint marital bank/credit accounts and quickly go to court to file a contested divorce if your attempt at negotiation fails!

    Spouses Behaving Badly: In my own failed first marriage, my ex-husband tried to stab me with a screwdriver. I was *not* prepared to survive post-divorce and had absolutely *no* idea what my legal rights were. Don't do this!!! Why do you think I took the time after going back to school to become a lawyer to write this book?

- *Be certain this is what you want.* Many litigants come to me because they are deeply unhappy with their marriage, but aren't certain they want to divorce their spouse. Do your soul-searching *before* you tell your spouse you want a divorce or you may end up having the decision made *for* you.

❖ *Individual therapy is a wonderful thing!* A trained therapist can help you sort out the source of your misery and come up with a clear plan of action.

Spouses Behaving Badly: My greatest regret in my first marriage was dropping out of college due to castigation from my first husband. The therapist helped me see I shouldn't tolerate a man who had dropped out of high school in the 9ᵗʰ grade calling me 'stupid' all the time.

❖ *Marriage counseling can help you save your marriage if it isn't beyond hope … or break the news to your spouse if it is.* A good marriage counselor can usually tell when therapy isn't going to work and provide a safe forum for you to tell your husband that you're throwing in the towel.

Spouses Behaving Badly: After telling my first husband that I was miserable because I wanted to finish college and he wouldn't let me, we tried marriage counseling. After a long diatribe about how a woman's place was in the home, the therapist suggested I attend individual therapy to teach me how to stick up for myself. Unfortunately, the entire process leapfrogged into crisis mode when I actually *did* begin to stick up for myself and my former husband tried to stab me with a screwdriver, but I'm glad we tried. It made me feel much less guilty when my spouse later accused me of 'throwing away' our bad marriage.

❖ *Read books on this subject.* Can't afford therapy or not sure whether it would be worth your investment in time? There are many wonderful books written by therapists that can help you get clear on what you want. You *may* even be able to borrow them for free from your local library. Although not an endorsement, the following are books clients reported they found useful (in alphabetical order):

- *Contemplating Divorce: A Step-by-Step Guide to Deciding Whether to Stay or Go,* by Susan Gadoua (2008)

- *How to Know If It's Time to Go: A 10-Step Reality Test for your Marriage,* by Dr. Lawrence Birnbach and Dr. Beverly Hyman (2010)

- *Should I Stay or Go? How Controlled Separation (CS) Can Save Your Marriage,* by Lee Raffel (1999)

    Do not attempt a controlled separation without first getting a formal written Temporary Separation Agreement in place or you could jeopardize your legal rights! How you conduct your affairs during a controlled separation has a way of becoming permanent, especially when it comes to matters of child custody. Most trial separations end in divorce, but they can be less messy from a legal standpoint because the couple has already begun to financially extricate themselves from one another and emotionally come to grips with their separate lives.

A sample Temporary Separation Agreement is given later in this chapter, Example 10-4.

- *Should I Stay or Should I Go? A Guide to Knowing if Your Relationship Can – and Should – Be Saved*, by Lundy Bancroft and JAC Patrissi (2011)

- *Too Good to Leave, Too Bad to Stay: A Step-by-Step Guide to Help You Decide Whether to Stay In or Get Out of Your Relationship*, by Mira Kirshenbaum (1997)

- *Make an appointment with a financial planner and/or your company Benefits Administrator.* Once you get divorced, you're on your own as far as retirement is concerned. Most states cut off alimony when your husband retires and many women discover they *aren't* eligible to take advantage of their former husband's higher social security payment schedule for a variety of reasons. You probably accumulated far fewer retirement benefits than your husband because you either stayed out of the work force to rear children, or took lower-paying jobs that could accommodate your children's schedule. The largest group of divorcing women I'm seeing at the moment is women over the age of 50. Their prospects for survival once alimony ends are *grim.*

- *Have your safety plan in place … just in case!* This would be a good time to review Chapter Two and make sure you are prepared to do whatever is necessary if things go to hell in a hand basket when you tell your spouse you want a divorce.

- *Be prepared to move quickly into your separate life.* Your spouse may react to your request for a divorce, or even to enter marriage counseling, by filing for divorce. If that happens, you may be summonsed into court for a Temporary Orders Hearing within a matter of days or weeks. What will happen if you suddenly end up with a court order to vacate your house? Or if you are ordered to pay your living expenses with nothing but your own income and whatever income you may be entitled to receive from child support or alimony? Are you ready to survive?

PUT TOGETHER A PROPOSED SEPARATION AGREEMENT PACKAGE

During your first visit to a mediator's office, they will bill $150 to $300 per hour to explain the divorce process and tell you what financial forms you need to gather so they can guide you through the mediation process. During your second mediation session, they will examine both of your financial statements, put the numbers into a spreadsheet, and explain everything you *never* wanted to know about things like property division, marital debt, child custody and support, alimony, and other issues. When your spouse chokes on that information, the mediator will suggest your husband go consult with an independent, third-party attorney as to his rights. You usually won't get around to negotiating who should get what asset (or debt) until the third mediation session.

Didn't you just *already* do all that work? Why not save yourself (and your spouse) *two* unnecessary sessions with the mediator and *weeks* of angry posturing where you threaten each other back and forth about the unknown while waiting to see a mediator by using everything you've learned in this Bootcamp manual to skip the first two steps?

If you did your Bootcamp exercises, you probably have everything you need to generate a Proposed Separation Agreement. Review the sample Separation Agreement in Chapter Eleven before you break the news to your spouse. Either consult with a private attorney to help you ghost write a first draft proposal, or visit your state-court website or any other local self-help resource that has sample agreements appropriate for *your* home state. As soon as you break the news to your spouse that you want a divorce, hand him your proposal and tell him to go see an attorney.

If there is one place I would say is your top priority to spend scarce dollars on a flesh-and-blood attorney, it would be getting professional help to draft and finalize your Separation Agreement. This document will dictate how you live the rest of your post-divorce life.

Be sure the words DRAFT PROPOSAL are conspicuous on the header of every single page. It will reinforce your husband's perception that you are willing to negotiate.

In this package, you should include the following:

- Your *Draft Proposed Separation Agreement*;

- A three-ring binder with a copy of all your financial information neatly organized and indexed for his records (or for *him* to take to his attorney). Remember you were told to do this in Chapter Three: Acorns? This is why. You have just saved the *both* of you several hundred dollars;

- A copy of your *own* fully filled-out financial statement;

- A blank financial statement for *him* to fill out;

- A copy of your state's child support guidelines (if applicable);

- A copy of whatever child support computation sheet you used to come up with a number (if applicable);

- A copy of your state's alimony laws;

- A copy of whatever worksheet/estimate you used to compute alimony;

- A copy of whatever spreadsheet you used to rough out a proposed division of your marital property and debts;

- A written list of places where *he* might obtain free legal help (often a courthouse lawyer-of-the-day program). Make it clear to him this is just a *first* proposal and you will not discuss the matter with him any further until he speaks to an attorney.

- A copy of *A Judge's Guide to Divorce: Uncommon Advice from the Bench,* by Judge Roderick Duncan (2007), list price $24.99 ($15 on Amazon). After, of course, reading it *yourself!* It's an easily read general overview of divorce written by a judge disgusted with unnecessary divorce litigation. Judge

Duncan dispenses advice to men such as 'don't fight alimony' and 'keep your divorce out of divorce court at all costs.'

Gather this information into a nice, well-organized little box. As soon as you're done dropping the bomb, hand it to him. Getting divorced is a bit like jumping off a cliff, not knowing if your parachute will work. Your husband's fear of the unknown and ignorance of the law will cause him to give you more grief than true unreasonableness. If you stick a draft Separation Agreement under his nose and order him to go speak to an attorney, most husbands will either tweak a few items and sign it, or agree to go to mediation to iron out the sticking points. The secret to this strategy working is that the agreement you propose must be *fair*.

80% of divorce litigation in this country could be avoided if *both* parties had realistic expectations. Give yourself the gift of assisting your husband's steep learning curve. Otherwise, be prepared to spend the next two years watching him impale *himself* upon his own stupidity, a journey *you* will be forced to make at his side at *your* expense as you get needlessly dragged into court to litigate issues which are probably clear-cut and pre-ordained.

PROTECT YOUR CREDIT RATING

Throughout this book, you've been urged to extricate your finances from those of your soon-to-be ex-husband and establish credit in your own name. If you are one of the hapless 29% of women who got blindsided by your *husband* being the one to announce he wants a divorce, you may have skipped ahead to this section from Chapter One. Either way, it's time to finish erecting a shield between yourself and your husband's poor spending decisions. I will lead you through the steps you should take a day or two *before* you tell your husband you want a divorce, or as soon as possible after *he* tells you he wants one (or you are forced to take out a restraining order to protect yourself from abuse):

1. Call any credit cards you hold in which your husband is either a joint-cardholder or an authorized user and ask them to revoke his authorization to use that card

    a. Fold or draw lines onto an ordinary sheet of lined paper to divide it into eight columns. Title them as follows:

EXAMPLE 10-1: SAMPLE CREDIT CARD CANCELLATION WORKSHEET

Credit Card Name	Account Number	Customer Service Number	Date Called	Person Spoke To	Case #	Notes:	Follow-up Letter
Big Bank Mastercard	109-876-543-210	(800) 999-9999	1/15/11	Dave	210987	Jack an authorized user. They are closing the account and migrating charges to a *new* account in my name only. Said I should get new card in the mail within 7 days.	1/16/11
City-Smitty Visa	123-456-789-012	(800) 444-4444	1/15/11	Sue	567921	Card in both my name and Jack's. They said they can't close the account without Jack's permission, but would note on the account I had called.	1/16/12

b. Grab every credit card and credit card statement you can find and jot down the credit card name, account number, and customer service number off the back of the card or statement.

c. Starting at the top, go down the list and start making phone calls.

d. *Jointly Held Accounts:* these are accounts which *both* you and your husband applied for together as husband and wife. You are jointly and severally liable to pay these cards, which means if one person doesn't pay, the credit card company will come after the other person for payment.

   i. Ask for a 'hard close' on jointly held credit cards that are held in both you and your spouse's name. You want to structure the account so that you will continue paying the bills as you originally agreed when you signed up for that credit card, but so that *neither* party can continue to make charges to that account.

   ii. Some credit card companies will bust your chops about needing your husband's permission to close a joint account. Be very clear that you are no longer authorizing new charges and are cutting up your credit card;

   iii. You will still need to pay these bills;

      1. Most credit card companies record all calls that come through their call centers (if you later have problems with them claiming you didn't request your name off the account);

      2. If you have utilities, car payments, or other invoices automatically billed to this credit card, you will need to contact them and give them a new credit card number or start writing a check;

      3. As soon as you are done; send a 'hard close' follow-up letter (example follows):

EXAMPLE 10-2: SAMPLE 'HARD CLOSE' REQUEST FOLLOW-UP LETTER

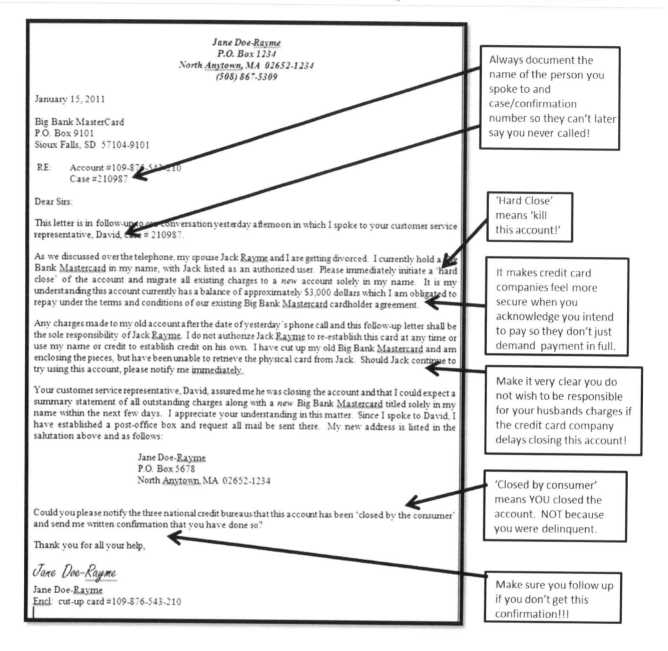

Jane Doe-Rayme
P.O. Box 1234
North Anytown, MA 02652-1234
(508) 867-5309

January 15, 2011

Big Bank MasterCard
P.O. Box 9101
Sioux Falls, SD 57104-9101

RE: Account #109-876-543-210
        Case #210987

Dear Sirs:

This letter is in follow-up to our conversation yesterday afternoon in which I spoke to your customer service representative, David, case # 210987.

As we discussed over the telephone, my spouse Jack Rayme and I are getting divorced. I currently hold a Big Bank Mastercard in my name, with Jack listed as an authorized user. Please immediately initiate a 'hard close' of the account and migrate all existing charges to a *new* account solely in my name. It is my understanding this account currently has a balance of approximately $3,000 dollars which I am obligated to repay under the terms and conditions of our existing Big Bank Mastercard cardholder agreement.

Any charges made to my old account after the date of yesterday's phone call and this follow-up letter shall be the sole responsibility of Jack Rayme. I do not authorize Jack Rayme to re-establish this card at any time or use my name or credit to establish credit on his own. I have cut up my old Big Bank Mastercard and am enclosing the pieces, but have been unable to retrieve the physical card from Jack. Should Jack continue to try using this account, please notify me immediately.

Your customer service representative, David, assured me he was closing the account and that I could expect a summary statement of all outstanding charges along with a *new* Big Bank Mastercard titled solely in my name within the next few days. I appreciate your understanding in this matter. Since I spoke to David, I have established a post-office box and request all mail be sent there. My new address is listed in the salutation above and as follows:

                Jane Doe-Rayme
                P.O. Box 5678
                North Anytown, MA 02652-1234

Could you please notify the three national credit bureaus that this account has been 'closed by the consumer' and send me written confirmation that you have done so?

Thank you for all your help,

Jane Doe-Rayme

Jane Doe-Rayme
Encl: cut-up card #109-876-543-210

> Always document the name of the person you spoke to and case/confirmation number so they can't later say you never called!

> 'Hard Close' means 'kill this account!'

> It makes credit card companies feel more secure when you acknowledge you intend to pay so they don't just demand payment in full.

> Make it very clear you do not wish to be responsible for your husbands charges if the credit card company delays closing this account!

> 'Closed by consumer' means YOU closed the account. NOT because you were delinquent.

> Make sure you follow up if you don't get this confirmation!!!

iv. *Authorized User Accounts* – these are accounts held in your name only, but which you have asked the credit card company to allow your husband to use your account to make charges. *You* are responsible for paying the bill on these cards, not your husband.

1. Ask the credit card company to remove your husband's name as an authorized user and roll your existing balance into an entirely *new* account the way they would if you reported your card lost or stolen.

2. You will still need to pay these bills as before;

3. If you have utilities, car payments, or other invoices automatically billed to your credit card, you will need to contact them and give them your new credit card number;

4. As soon as you are done; send a 'follow-up letter (sample 'rollover' request follows):

EXAMPLE 10-3: SAMPLE 'ROLLOVER' REQUEST FOLLOW-UP LETTER

Jane Doe-Rayme
P.O. Box 1234
North Anytown, MA 02652-1234
(508) 867-5309

January 16, 2011

City-Smitty Visa
P.O. Box 5678
Sioux Falls, SD 57104-1234

RE: Account #123-456-789-012
       Case #567921

Dear Sirs:

This letter is in follow-up to our conversation yesterday afternoon in which I spoke to your customer service representative, Sue, case # 567921.

As we discussed over the telephone, my spouse Jack Rayme and I are getting divorced. We currently hold a card with City-Smitty Visa in both of our names. Your customer service representative, Sue, assured me she would immediately close my existing account, the same way you would for a lost or stolen credit card, and shift my balance into an entirely new account for which Jack is no longer an authorized user. It is my understanding this account currently has a balance of approximately $3,000 dollars which I understand I remain obligated to repay under the terms and conditions of our existing City-Smitty Visa cardholder agreement.

> Rolling it over into a new account ensures nobody accidentally lets your husband use your card.

Any charges made to the old account after the date of yesterday's phone call and this follow-up letter shall be the sole responsibility of Jack Rayme. I do not authorize Jack Rayme use this card at any time or use my name to establish credit on his own. I have cut up my old City-Smitty card and am enclosing the pieces. Should Jack continue to try using this account, please notify me immediately.

> This is YOUR account. The moment you notify them you don't wish your husband to use it, they MUST remove his name!

Your customer service representative, Sue, assured me I could expect a summary statement of all outstanding charges and a new credit card in the mail within the next week or so. I appreciate your understanding in this matter. Since I spoke to Sue, I have established a post-office box and request all mail be sent there. My new address is listed in the salutation above and as follows:

Jane Doe-Rayme
P.O. Box 5678
North Anytown, MA 02652-1234

Could you please notify the three national credit bureaus that the former authorized user account has been 'closed by the consumer' and send me written confirmation that you have done so?

> Protect your credit rating! Make sure this was done!

Thank you for all your help,

Jane Doe-Rayme

Jane Doe-Rayme
Encl: cut-up card 123-456-789-012

Make sure you leave yourself at least –one– credit card to use until you have a chance to obtain a new one entirely in your own name!

8. Remove your name from any other joint marital bank or credit card account for which you could be held jointly and severally liable to repay if your husband makes charges against the account (or writes bad checks).

   a. If you use a joint marital checking account to pay your joint marital bills (such as your mortgage) and your husband has always been financially responsible, you may want to hold off on taking your name off that account. Otherwise, paying bills while your divorce winds its way through the courts could become unwieldy.

   b. If you get direct deposit, contact your employer or other paying agency and request they start depositing your money into your sole checking account;

   c. From now on, deposit all of your own funds into your *own* account;

   d. Always pay your share of the joint marital bills by *check,* not cash! If possible, pay your share directly and give your husband a receipt.

   e. If you have to give your husband money and trust him to pay a joint marital bill while your divorce is winding its way through the courts, always follow up and make sure he actually *paid* it.

      Spouses Behaving Badly: A client came into one of my free legal clinics seeking protection from being evicted from her apartment. She'd been giving her husband money for her share of the apartment and utilities, but instead of paying the bills, he squandered it. The landlord started eviction proceedings once they fell three months behind. Unfortunately, the landlord was inflexible. Her credit rating was poor and the landlord refused to let her establish a new lease in her own name even though she had enough money to catch up on the rent. She was evicted.

9. Hunting down potential credit landmines is a bit like killing cockroaches. You need to make sure you kill *all* of the filthy little buggers or you'll keep finding roaches eating your food (income). Therefore, a few weeks after you've called all of your credit card companies and requested your accounts be rolled over or closed, it's wise to run your credit report. You can do this for *free* without subscribing to one of those bogus credit monitoring agencies *once per year* by writing to the following address:

Annual Credit Report Service
P.O. Box 105281
Atlanta, GA 30348-5281
(877) 322-8228
www.annualcreditreport.com

You'll need to provide your name, current address, social security number and date of birth. They *may* ask you to sign and mail back a waiver or provide additional identification if your current address or some other piece of information does not match up with the information they have on file. If you've *already* ordered your free credit report *once* this year, you will need to contact the three major credit reporting bureaus directly and pay their fee to order copies of your credit reports from *each* of them. Do not skimp on this step! It could cost you dearly!

Equifax
P.O. Box 740241
Atlanta, GA 30374
800-685-1111 (general)
800-525-6285 (fraud)
www.equifax.com

Experian
P.O. Box 2002
Allen, TX 75013
888-397-3742
(general and fraud)
www.experian.com.

TransUnion
P.O. Box 2000
Chester, PA 19022
800-888-4213 (general)
800-680-7289 (fraud)
www.transunion.com.

BREAKING THE BAD NEWS TO YOUR SPOUSE

Giving people bad news is always unpleasant, especially if your spouse is unaware how deeply unhappy you are with the marriage. How you break the news will become etched in his memory for the rest of his life. To him, it will become one of those life-altering events such as the day Pearl Harbor was bombed, John F. Kennedy was shot, the space shuttle Challenger blew up, or the World Trade Center attacks. It is important to be compassionate, but firm when you tell your spouse you want a divorce.

The surgeon cuts… A quick slice with a very sharp blade heals faster than a jagged tear caused by repeated injuries. Give your husband the mercy of a clean break. Don't mess around with his heart by wanting him one moment and not the next or go to him every time you need him to bail you out because you didn't plan for some contingency! He *will* make your life a living hell if you string him along with false hope.

Have a mediation session already set up approximately two weeks after you break the bad news.

Try to find a quiet time when there are no other people around. Send your children off to a babysitter for the night (or weekend) if at all possible or do it after they've gone to bed.   You probably want to do this on a weeknight when he has to go to work the next morning, rather than on the weekend, so you're not in each other's face with no escape.

If you fear physical abuse, do not break the news alone! Have adult witnesses nearby to intervene if you need help! Or better yet! File a contested divorce (Chapter 12) and have him served when you are away from the house for a few 'cooling off' days with your children and/or pets! Most incidents of domestic violence occur shortly after the woman announces she wishes to leave her abuser.

Plan a few days away. Even if you *don't* fear physical abuse, now might be a good time to take your kids and/or pets and visit Great Aunt Bertha until your husband has a chance to review your Proposed Separation Agreement with an attorney. Otherwise, he's going to be following you around harping *'is there someone else?'* or *'how could you just throw our marriage away?'* or making unrealistic threats about *'leaving you penniless and taking everything.'*

Repeat after me ... your spouse is going to throw all kinds of verbal garbage at you in the coming weeks. Practice repeating the following phrases in the mirror using an unemotional, completely flat face and monotone voice until they become so deeply ingrained you mumble them in your sleep:

- "I told you we couldn't discuss this until *after* you spoke to an attorney."

- "What does your attorney say?"

- "That isn't what that judge in that book I gave you said. Perhaps you should make another appointment and go speak to your attorney again?"

- "Really? Your attorney said that? Wow! Well then I guess you need to re-read that book by that judge I gave you and go speak to your attorney *again*."

- "I don't care what you attorney says. I know a judge is going to give me more."

- "I can't discuss this now. We'll talk about it in our next mediation session."

- Shake your hand three times as though shaking water off of your hands and with a flat, emotionless voice say ...

What if you've decided you're miserable enough to get divorced if things don't change, but are willing to give marriage counseling one last try? Create a written list of milestones you wish to accomplish in marital therapy when you give your husband your ultimatum (along with your Proposed Separation Agreement and supporting paperwork) and have an appointment already set up within the next few days. Your list-of-demands may be a formal list culled from your individual therapist and/or a self-help book or simply a list of things which are making your life miserable. Write it out and give him a copy, saying 'these things *must* change.' If your husband truly wishes to save your marriage, you are giving him concrete goals (men are clueless ... you need to spell it out). By simultaneously handing him your Proposed Separation Agreement and supporting paperwork, not only are you showing you are serious, but you're also spelling out what he stands to lose if he doesn't shape up. If he doesn't wish to change, you gave him the *option* to fix the problem and he declined.

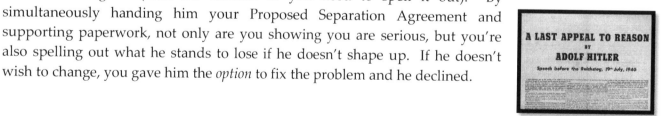

WHO WILL STAY IN THE MARITAL HOME?

Whether you own your home or rent, having both parties remain in the marital home while your marriage falls down around your ears is rarely wise. *Especially* if one spouse wants out of the marriage while the other is hoping to save it. All of the issues which caused you to become unhappy enough about your marriage to seek a divorce are going to *escalate* the moment you start wading into the hurtful territory of who will get what.

 Watch *'The War of the Roses'* starring Michael Douglas, Kathleen Turner and Danny DeVito (1989) to see a slapstick comic-tragic example of this phenomenon.

A temporary move may seem a better solution, but if you haven't documented your assets, you move out without taking your children, you don't set up a stable living environment for your minor children to move into, or you haven't taken other steps recommended in this book to preserve your legal rights, you could discover assets disappear, or that what you *thought* were temporary actions on your part become permanent court orders.

Temporary actions have a way of becoming Temporary Orders, and Temporary Orders usually become PERMANENT divorce decrees.

It's helpful to know during negotiations which way a judge might lean if you were to file for divorce and asked a judge to decide. The following generalities are not 'law' but rather factors many judges will consider if asked to make this decision *for* you:

- Whoever is the primary caretaker of any minor children will usually be granted temporary use of the home until the rest of the property division issues can be sorted out. Even if the house is in only one person's name;

  Never move out of the house and leave your children behind or you will lose custody of them.

- If one spouse has a disability which would make it difficult to relocate, they will usually get preference until a final decision can be made;

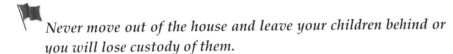

- If the house is only in one person's name and there are not issues such as minor children or disability, the spouse whose name the house is *not* in may be asked to leave;

- Whichever spouse can *afford* to remain in the home and keep paying the mortgage will usually get priority.

- If neither spouse has priority, abuse or inappropriate behavior in front of minor children is not an issue, and neither spouse can afford their own place, you may need to remain together in the same house until you can better disentangle your finances or your divorce becomes final.

I once had a client with a complex life estate issue impairing title to the marital home. She had no choice but to live in an in-law apartment on the same property until the issue resolved (they had to wait for the beneficiary to die before they gained clear title to the land the marital house was built upon). Neither spouse could afford to leave and there weren't enough assets for a buyout. They agreed to stay, living side-by-side, until grannie kicked the bucket. The judge can't divide property you don't quite own yet!

Never use an Abuse Prevention Order to get your pesky soon-to-be ex-spouse out of the house unless you really –are- being abused!

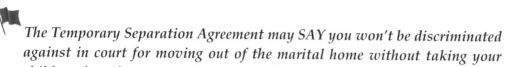

If you decide having one of you move out of the house while you attempt mediation and/or negotiation is the best course of action, it is wise to sign a Temporary Separation Agreement until you can come to a more final arrangement so you don't jeopardize your legal rights. A Sample Temporary Separation Agreement follows:

The Temporary Separation Agreement may SAY you won't be discriminated against in court for moving out of the marital home without taking your children, but if you are not exceptionally diligent about performing your day-to-day parental duties and taking care of the children at least 50% of the time, that is likely what will happen anyways! Especially if your divorce case languishes for months or years in court while you duke out a property division. We discuss the concept of 'primary caretaker' in Chapter Fourteen: Child Custody and Custody Disputes.

EXAMPLE 10-4: SAMPLE TEMPORARY SEPARATION AGREEMENT

TEMPORARY SEPARATION AGREEMENT

This TEMPORARY AGREEMENT is signed between __Jane Doe-Rayme__ and __Jack Rayme__ this __13ᵗʰ__ day of __February__ , 20 _12_ ;

1. It is our intent to separate at this time until a divorce agreement can either be mediated, or obtained through court;

2. Both parties agree that this TEMPORARY AGREEMENT shall apply to both parties;

3. Jack Rayme agrees to move out of the marital home;

4. Both parties agree that Jack's property rights and/or his rights related to child custody or other issues which may be divided in mediation or in court will not be compromised by this move;

5. Both parties agree that Jane's property rights and/or her rights related to child custody or other issues which may be decided in mediation or in court will not be compromised by her assuming temporary control of the marital home;

6. In lieu of child support, Jack shall continue to pay the mortgage principal, interest, taxes and insurance on the marital home in the amount of $1,527 per month until a final dissolution can be reached;

7. Jack shall also pay to Jane alimony in the amount of $133 per month;

8. Jack shall make the car and auto insurance payments on his own truck;

9. Jane shall be responsible for paying all utilities on the marital home;

10. Jack shall be responsible for paying his own rent and living expenses;

11. All other bills shall be divided equally as they come due until a final dissolution can be reached;

12. Both parties agree that neither shall incur debt in the name of the other without first consulting the other. If a debt is disputed, it shall be the sole responsibility of the debtor unless a court declares otherwise;

13. Both parties agree that Jack will have overnight visitation with the children from 6:00 p.m. on Friday night until 7:00 p.m. Sunday night. Both parties agree that Jack shall also be entitled to attend the children's school and sporting events, have access to the children's school and medical records, and take the children for additional visits with reasonable notice to Jane.

14. Both parties agree that Jane shall keep and take care of Scruffy, the family dog.

Neither of us gives up our right to ask for a different arrangement, financial or otherwise, from the court should mediation fail, nor do we intend this to be a permanent arrangement.

Signed:

Jane Doe-Rayme   Jack Rayme

_____   _____
Jane Doe-Rayme   Jack Rayme

WHAT COURTHOUSE HAS JURISDICTION TO GRANT MY DIVORCE?

Jurisdiction refers to the court's ability to hear a case. If a court does not have jurisdiction over your case, it is not allowed to grant your divorce. Jurisdiction is controlled by state, federal, and case law. Although rules vary from state-to-state, there are general overarching trends:

- If you both still live in the same county where you once lived together as husband and wife, you will file there;

- If *one* of you still lives in the same county where you both once lived together as husband and wife, you will file there;

- If *neither* of you still lives in the same county where you both lived together as husband and wife, but one or both of you still lives in the same state, you will file in the courthouse nearest that in-state spouses new address. There may be a time requirement involved to establish residency in the new in-state county in some states;

- If *neither* of you live in either the same county or same state, you may be able to file for divorce in whichever state one of you has lived long enough to establish residency, but you *may* need to go to your *spouse's* new state to get property division/alimony issues resolved if he contests it.

Dirty Lawyer Trick: If one or both of you has moved out of the original jurisdiction where you formerly lived together as husband and wife, *two* courts may have possibly gained the authority to decide your case. In such a situation, attorneys should scrutinize the laws in both jurisdictions, including trends towards property division, alimony, child support, child custody issues, and the division of debt, and file whichever place can get their client the better deal! Whoever files first … wins. Whoopee!!!

Forum Shopping: When an attorney cherry picks a courthouse to file a lawsuit based on which jurisdictions policies or laws can get their client the most money.

Clients Behaving Badly: A client whose husband moved out of state attempted divorce mediation. The husband sought half of property the wife's mother had technically gifted to her, but retained a life estate (she could neither live in it, sell it, or take a mortgage against it until the mother died), which in Massachusetts is considered a joint marital asset subject to division. Upon examining the laws of the state the husband had relocated to, we learned gifted property is *excluded* as Separate Property. The wife filed her divorce in the husband's *new* state before he could file here, denying him a share of her parent's property.

Clients Behaving Badly: A father obtained a 50:50 shared physical custody agreement and zero child support in another state. The mother later moved a few miles over a state line (after obtaining permission from the original court) to the one county in Massachusetts where the opinion of the judge most likely to sit on her case at the time was 'shared physical custody doesn't work.' The mother sued for modification and regained sole physical custody and child support.

Smart Woodland Creature Tip: When faced with two potential jurisdictions where you can file your divorce (even within the same state), always consult attorneys in *both* jurisdictions before hiring one to find out who can get you the better deal.

If you have any questions about which courthouse can hear your case, consult with an attorney or call the Family Court clerk and ask. Make sure you are filing in the right county or you may get all the way to your final divorce hearing and discover, to your dismay, that the judge does not have the authority to grant your divorce!

WHAT PAPERWORK MUST I FILE TO GET AN UNCONTESTED DIVORCE?

For ten chapters now we've talked about preparing for your divorce. Now it's time to do it. If you work with a mediator or an attorney, they will draft this paperwork for you. If you choose to work with a commercial document preparation service, they should be able to advise you which forms you need in *your* home state to file. If you decide to fill out your *own* paperwork, then you're going to have to scrounge up your own forms.

Paperwork requirements vary from state-to-state. Your best source of information about what paperwork *your* local state court requires is your local court clerk or court website (refer to chart in Chapter Nine). Unfortunately, not all states have a handy 'you need these forms' checklist. There's nothing worse than taking a morning out of work to drive to the courthouse and being turned away because you forgot some obscure form. To help you know what to look for when digging through your state court website, here are some common forms most states require you to file along with your uncontested divorce:

- A Joint Petition for an uncontested or summary divorce (using whatever form your court requires);

- A certified (state) copy of your marriage certificate. You'll need one with an official embossed (raised) state seal. Town, county or church-issued abstracts or older, un-embossed copies will usually not be accepted. You can get a certified copy of your marriage certificate directly from the state Registry of Vital Statistics in the state where you were married or order them online for around $35 (internet search terms " __X-state__ Registry of Vital Statistics");

- A notarized Affidavit of Irretrievable Breakdown of the Marriage or similar document swearing you have been living apart (even if only in separate bedrooms) for X-amount of time and believe your marriage to be irretrievably broken;

- A notarized Separation Agreement (see Chapter 11: Separation Agreements);

- An affidavit disclosing any court proceedings which might be occurring in a different court for custody of your children so the judge doesn't issue conflicting court orders (i.e., if you live in a state which decides child custody in a separate court from property issues, or if you obtained a restraining order against your husband in criminal court which dictates custody of the children, or if a state agency is currently overseeing the care of your children, etc.);

- Your Financial Statement with attached copies of all W-2's from the previous year (see Chapter Four) printed out on whatever colored paper *your* state requires;

- Your spouse's Financial Statement with copies of all W-2's from previous year;

- A completed Child Support Guidelines Worksheet, if applicable (see Chapter Five to obtain instructions on how to locate and fill out your state's form);

- A Parenting Plan spelling out who your children (if unemancipated) will live with, who will have primary legal custody, who shall be primarily responsible for what task, and when the non-custodial parent will have visitation. If you agree to shared physical custody, you will need to spell out how those tasks will be divided. This Parenting Plan is often written into the Separation Agreement as an Exhibit. Child Custody and its affiliated issues are covered more extensively in Chapter 15: Custody Disputes;

- A certificate stating *both* parents have completed your states required Parent Education Program (if applicable);

- A statistical form most courts use to notify your state Registry of Vital Statistics that you are no longer married (some states still do this –for- you);

- Any QDRO (qualified domestic relations order) or Pension Division Order forms that may be necessary to convey ownership of any retirement assets, if applicable. You will need to contact your pension or 401(k) administrator to get a form they will accept as forms vary widely and submit them to the court;

- A form requesting you be assigned a date for an uncontested divorce hearing;

- The filing fee (many states require a bank check or money order);

- A cover letter to the Clerk of Court (if you choose to mail it in).

- There may be other forms your state requires to grant you a divorce. See your court website.

The following sample forms are listed to familiarize you with the general anatomy of a court form. Since I am licensed in Massachusetts, I will be using that state's forms as an example, but if you print out your *own* state's forms from your state court website, you'll see they look for the same recurring information. Pay special attention to the notes at the side of each form as these are pieces of information which can trip a layperson up when filling out their own forms!

EXAMPLE 10-5: SAMPLE JOINT PETITION FOR DIVORCE

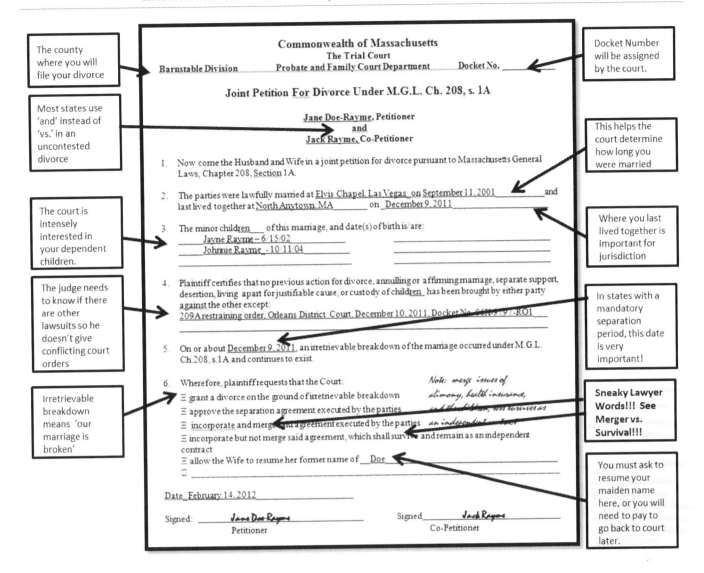

The county where you will file your divorce

Most states use 'and' instead of 'vs.' in an uncontested divorce

The court is intensely interested in your dependent children.

The judge needs to know if there are other lawsuits so he doesn't give conflicting court orders

Irretrievable breakdown means 'our marriage is broken'

Docket Number will be assigned by the court.

This helps the court determine how long you were married

Where you last lived together is important for jurisdiction

In states with a mandatory separation period, this date is very important!

Sneaky Lawyer Words!!! See Merger vs. Survival!!!

You must ask to resume your maiden name here, or you will need to pay to go back to court later.

Commonwealth of Massachusetts
The Trial Court
Barnstable Division   Probate and Family Court Department   Docket No. _____

Joint Petition For Divorce Under M.G.L. Ch. 208, s. 1A

Jane Doe-Rayme, Petitioner
and
Jack Rayme, Co-Petitioner

1. Now come the Husband and Wife in a joint petition for divorce pursuant to Massachusetts General Laws, Chapter 208, Section 1A.

2. The parties were lawfully married at Elvis Chapel, Las Vegas, on September 11, 2001 _____ and last lived together at North Anytown, MA _____ on December 9, 2011 _____

3. The minor children ____ of this marriage, and date(s) of birth is/are:
   Jayne Rayme – 6/15/02 _____
   Johnnie Rayme, - 10/11/04 _____

4. Plaintiff certifies that no previous action for divorce, annulling or affirming marriage, separate support, desertion, living apart for justifiable cause, or custody of children has been brought by either party against the other except:
   209A restraining order, Orleans District Court, December 10, 2011, Docket No. 06R9797-RO1

5. On or about December 9, 2011, an irretrievable breakdown of the marriage occurred under M.G.L. Ch.208, s.1A and continues to exist.

6. Wherefore, plaintiff requests that the Court:
   ☰ grant a divorce on the ground of irretrievable breakdown
   ☰ approve the separation agreement executed by the parties
   ☰ incorporate and merge said agreement executed by the parties
   ☰ incorporate but not merge said agreement, which shall survive and remain as an independent contract
   ☰ allow the Wife to resume her former name of __ Doe _____
   ☐ _____

   Note: merge issues of alimony, health insurance, ... an independent contract

Date February 14, 2012 _____

Signed: _Jane Doe-Rayme_   Signed _Jack Rayme_
        Petitioner   Co-Petitioner

SNEAKY LAWYER WORDS: MERGER AND SURVIVAL

If you look at the notation boxes alongside Example 10-5: Joint Petition for Divorce, you'll notice one of them warns you about one set of check-off boxes which ask whether you wish for your divorce to be the following:

   ⫿ incorporate and merge said agreement executed by the parties
   ⫿ incorporate but not merge said agreement, which shall survive and remain as an independent contract

These innocuous looking boxes (which probably mean absolutely nothing to you) can mean the difference between whether you or your spouse can go back to court in the future to modify things. Sometimes *want* an ironclad agreement which can never be changed, other times you might want the ability to go back into court and seek a modification if circumstances change. Often, you might want things ironclad in respects to some issues (such as the property division), but open to change in other areas (such as child support and future alimony). Your first encounter with sneaky "legal mumbo-jumbo" that you could potentially hang yourself with are two innocuous sounding boxes in section six of the Joint Petition for Divorce:

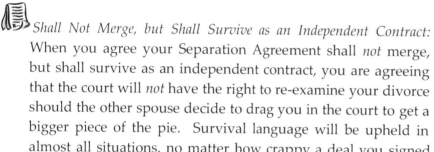*Incorporate and Merge:* When you incorporate and merge the Separation Agreement with your divorce, it means you are giving the court continuing power to look at your Separation Agreement should either party need to come to court in the future for a material change of circumstances. Merger is statutorily *required* in most states as far as child support and certain health insurance issues because you do not have the right to sign away legal rights that will leave the taxpayers holding the bag to support a disabled spouse or minor children, but not other areas such as property division, where the judge earnestly hopes he'll never see you again.

Shall Not Merge, but Shall Survive as an Independent Contract: When you agree your Separation Agreement shall *not* merge, but shall survive as an independent contract, you are agreeing that the court will *not* have the right to re-examine your divorce should the other spouse decide to drag you in the court to get a bigger piece of the pie. Survival language will be upheld in almost all situations, no matter how crappy a deal you signed off on, except for a few statutorily created exceptions.

Merger may be *desirable* in some situations, such as if you may be entitled to alimony but that alimony will be cancelled out by the child support your husband is obligated to pay you, but not others, such as your property division. Merger may also be desirable if access to health insurance is a major concern (such as when one party is disabled). Merger is generally not favored in regards to the property division. You do not want your spouse to be able to keep dragging you back into court and seek a bigger piece of the marital pie after you've started to move on with your life, especially if things start looking up in life due to your own frugal spending habits and hard work, while your husband is a spendthrift. However, there are some rare situations (such as an expected inheritance) where you may desire this.

When I have a situation that I want some parts to merge, and other parts to survive, I usually check off both boxes and hand-write the words "except for issues related to the children and alimony" next to the two boxes (see Example 10-5) *in addition* to writing this language into the Separation Agreement. It's messy looking, but it makes your intentions very clear from the outset if you ever have to go back into court.

'OFFICIAL' AND 'UNOFFICIAL' MARRIAGE CERTIFICATES

Whenever you get married or divorced, it creates a major change in your rights for things such as obtaining credit, transferring property, buying a house, paying taxes, or collecting Social Security or other benefits. Therefore, courts only accept copies of your marriage certificate which have been *certified* by your *state*. Not your church. Not town hall or your county seat. Not some other entity which issues beautiful certificates of marriage suitable for framing. It's easier to keep track of the current Keeper of the Records for 50 states versus the 25,000 towns and 300,000 churches nationwide.

Pro-se litigants get turned away from the courthouse with great regularity because what they *thought* was an acceptable marriage certificate wasn't. To save you from making such an error, there are several examples to help you figure out if what you have will work. An example of an official certified copy of a marriage certificate follows:

EXAMPLE 10-6: SAMPLE 'OFFICIAL' MARRIAGE CERTIFICATE

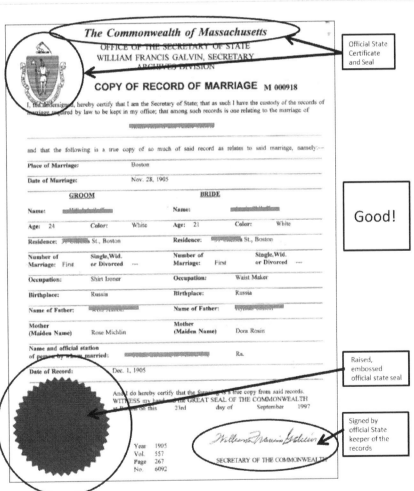

EXAMPLE 10-7: SAMPLE 'UNACCEPTABLE' CHURCH-ISSUED MARRIAGE CERTIFICATE

As lovely as that beautiful, scrolled, calligraphy-laden marriage certificate is that your local priest, rabbi, minister or imam gave you the day you got married, the court can't accept it. With more than 300,000 churches in the USA, busy court clerks have no way to verify your marriage certificate is authentic:

NO GOOD!
You may be married before god, but not the state!

EXAMPLE 10-8: SAMPLE 'UNACCEPTABLE' TOWN-ISSUED MARRIAGE CERTIFICATE

You'd think a true-copy-attest from your local town clerk or county registrar would suffice? Once upon a time, it did. Unfortunately, ever since September 11th 2001, states have become paranoid about verifying any document which could later be used to establish credit, obtain a driver's license, get a passport, and then steal an airplane to fly into a skyscraper. With over 25,000 named 'places' nationwide, town clerk certified abstracts of local marriage records are no longer accepted in most courts.

NO GOOD!
It's not that they don't trust the town or county clerk, just that, well, they don't trust the town or county clerk!

EXAMPLE 10-8: SAMPLE AFFIDAVIT OF IRRETRIEVABLE BREAKDOWN

Although the requirements of this form vary from state to state, they all look for basically the same information. You must swear you have both chosen to end your marriage because it is irretrievably broken. Massachusetts doesn't make you include the date you separated in this affidavit, but many states do so they can verify you have met their mandatory separation period.

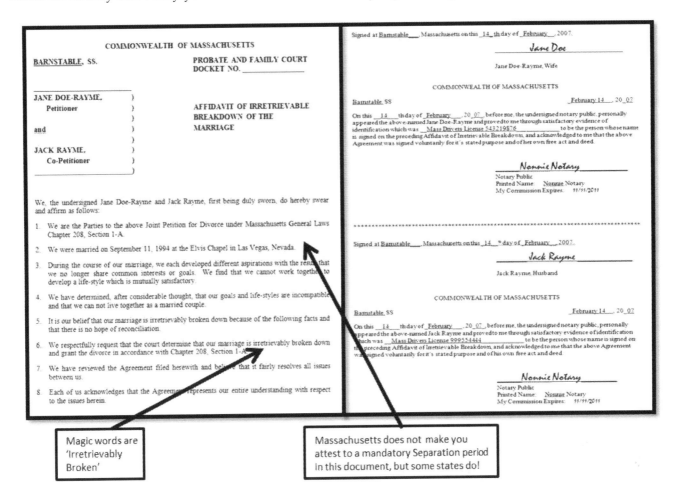

Magic words are 'Irretrievably Broken'

Massachusetts does not make you attest to a mandatory Separation period in this document, but some states do!

EXAMPLE 10-9: SAMPLE FORM DISCLOSING OTHER COURT PROCEEDINGS THAT MAY INVOLVE YOUR CHILDREN (OR SOMETIMES YOURSELVES)

The following form is state-specific to Massachusetts, where I practice, but no matter *where* you live, your family court judge wants to make sure no court order *he* issues conflicts with a court order some *other* judge has already issued. This helps avoid the all-too-common situation where the wife gets a restraining order against the husband in district or criminal court which says 'no contact,' and then weeks or months later the couple files for a divorce, emotions cool down, the couple reaches a formal agreement in family court allowing the husband visitation with the kids, and then the police see him in the driveway picking up the kids and arrest him. Which court order takes precedent?

The other all-too-common situation is the police, after witnessing Jane get abused, call and involve the state Division of Children and Families (DCF, DSS, DCYF, etc.) and *they* initiate a court action to force

Mom to leave Dad. Although your 'other court action disclosure' form will probably not look anything like this form, the *information* they're seeking (listed on the side-bar) *will* be asked in some form or other. Look for a form asking for this information, because your local court most likely has one!

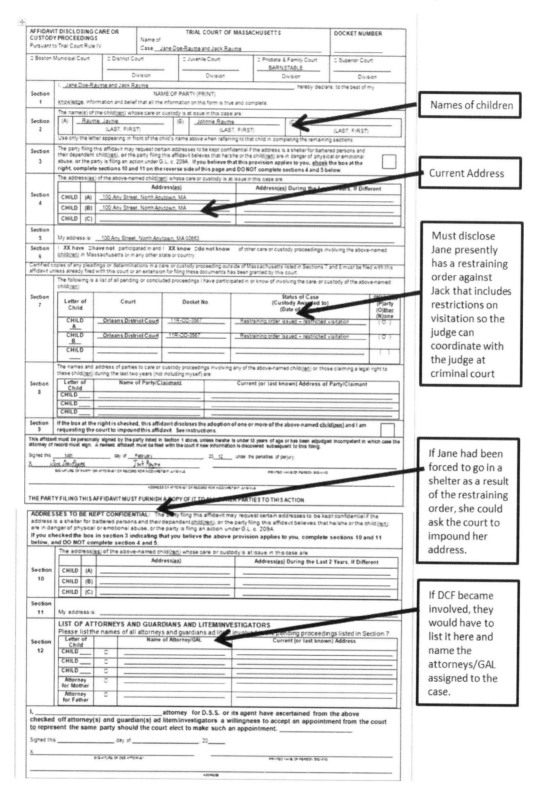

Names of children

Current Address

Must disclose Jane presently has a restraining order against Jack that includes restrictions on visitation so the judge can coordinate with the judge at criminal court

If Jane had been forced to go in a shelter as a result of the restraining order, she could ask the court to impound her address.

If DCF became involved, they would have to list it here and name the attorneys/GAL assigned to the case.

EXAMPLE 10-10: REGISTRY OF VITAL STATISTICS CHANGE FORM

The government likes to keep track of things such as who got married, who got divorced, how many kids you have, and whether or not your dog is licensed, spayed, or neutered. It's not out of curiosity, but because every step of the way, there's some way for the tax collector to dig their greedy little claws into you to increase your taxes or tear away some nice tax deduction.

Courts *used* to take care of reporting this pesky information *for* you, but thanks to budget cuts, most states now have *you* fill out your *own* darned statistical form. After all, *you* know your date of birth and mother's maiden name better than any clerk rifling through a folder full of legal forms.

A sample form follows. In Massachusetts, you're supposed to print this out onto canary yellow paper so the clerk can easily pull it out of the file. Your state's form will probably look slightly different, but it will ask essentially the same information. FYI: In Alabama, you're not allowed to fold the form to fit in an envelope so you can mail it!

EXAMPLE 10-11: MILITARY AFFIDAVIT

To initiate a divorce, the defendant can be served by having the Sheriff serve a copy of the Complaint in-hand, or by the plaintiff publishing a notice in the local newspaper. If you are serving in Afghanistan, obviously you're not going to read a newspaper ad that you've been summoned to court. To prevent this, all active members of the armed services are afforded extra protection. The purpose of this form is to put the court on notice extra measures may be required to notify one party a lawsuit has been initiated.

Now wait a minute? But this is a joint petition! My husband signed the divorce paperwork!

Nobody ever said court procedures made sense. If they did, lawyers wouldn't make so much money.

If your spouse serves in the military, you will have to fill this out. Just do it. It makes the clerk happy when you don't argue with them about stupid procedures rammed down their throat by the federal government. The worst that will happen is you fill it out and then they don't need it. This form is nearly identical in all fifty states. A sample military affidavit follows:

EXAMPLE 10-12: REQUEST FOR A FINAL HEARING

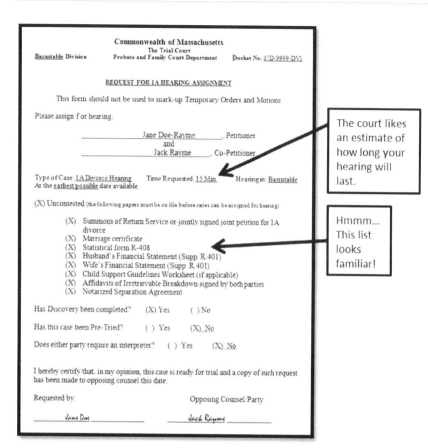

If you simply mail your Joint Petition for Divorce into the courthouse along with your filing fee, you may wait a very long time (sometimes years) before the clerk gets around to realizing you want a final hearing scheduled. This is because lawyers mail lots of paperwork to the clerk to simply place in the case file which doesn't need a hearing, and also because there are certain documents which *must* be submitted by law before the judge can grant your divorce. A final hearing form is a signal to the clerk to check your case file to make sure it's complete so they can schedule a date.

Dirty Lawyer Trick: 'Putting a case to sleep' is when a lawyer deliberately postpones a hearing without requesting a new date and then floods the opposing party with irrelevant paperwork in the hopes they won't notice their case just dropped out of the court's tracking system. If you don't specifically ask for a hearing date, it may take years before one of the courts internal audits picks up on your case languishing in the system.

The burden is upon *you* to make sure the paperwork you file actually gets a hearing date! Depending upon the backlog at your local courthouse, it generally takes between 3 weeks and 6 months to get a hearing. A sample hearing request form follows, but your court may have its own form:

EXAMPLE 10-13: COVER LETTER TO THE CLERK

It's always good practice to include a cover letter to the Clerk of Court spelling out exactly what it is you are asking them to do and what paperwork you are including in your mailing. If you are requesting a hearing date, most clerks will avoid dates you are not available (within reason) if you ask at the outset. If you need for them to mail back copies of anything (such as a hearing confirmation notice) it's good practice to include a self-addressed, self-stamped envelope. Making things easier for the Clerk is the same as making things easier for your lawyer. 'Easy' means it costs you less money, fewer delays and fewer mistakes.

A sample cover letter follows.

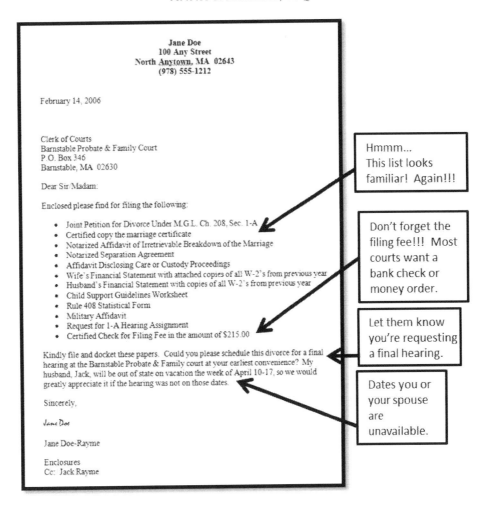

Jane Doe
100 Any Street
North Anytown, MA 02643
(978) 555-1212

February 14, 2006

Clerk of Courts
Barnstable Probate & Family Court
P.O. Box 346
Barnstable, MA 02630

Dear Sir/Madam:

Enclosed please find for filing the following:

- Joint Petition for Divorce Under M.G.L. Ch. 208, Sec. 1-A
- Certified copy the marriage certificate
- Notarized Affidavit of Irretrievable Breakdown of the Marriage
- Notarized Separation Agreement
- Affidavit Disclosing Care or Custody Proceedings
- Wife's Financial Statement with attached copies of all W-2's from previous year
- Husband's Financial Statement with copies of all W-2's from previous year
- Child Support Guidelines Worksheet
- Rule 408 Statistical Form
- Military Affidavit
- Request for 1-A Hearing Assignment
- Certified Check for Filing Fee in the amount of $215.00

Kindly file and docket these papers. Could you please schedule this divorce for a final hearing at the Barnstable Probate & Family court at your earliest convenience? My husband, Jack, will be out of state on vacation the week of April 10-17, so we would greatly appreciate it if the hearing was not on those dates.

Sincerely,

Jane Doe

Jane Doe-Rayme

Enclosures
Cc: Jack Rayme

Hmmm... This list looks familiar! Again!!!

Don't forget the filing fee!!! Most courts want a bank check or money order.

Let them know you're requesting a final hearing.

Dates you or your spouse are unavailable.

THE FINAL HEARING ON AN UNCONTESTED DIVORCE

Compared to the angst of deciding to get divorced, gathering the paperwork, figuring out who should get what, notifying your husband (or *being* notified) of the bad news, hammering out a Separation Agreement, and mailing in the paperwork, the actual divorce hearing in an uncontested divorce will be dull by comparison.

Depending upon the laws in your state, in approximately 90-120 days, your divorce will become final. If you are one of the lucky couples who were on good enough terms to work things out for yourself, congratulations!!! You just saved yourself a bloody fortune in legal fees.

ON-YOUR-FEET EXERCISE 10-1: TYPICAL UNCONTESTED DIVORCE HEARING

Magistrate:	I now call the case of Jane Doe-Rayme and Jack Rayme. Do you both swear the testimony you are about to give is the truth, the whole truth, and nothing but the truth, so help you god?
Jane and Jack:	We do.
Judge:	I see we're here today for a final hearing on a divorce. Is that correct?
Jane and Jack:	Yes.
Judge (flipping through paperwork)	I have before me a Separation Agreement. It says that you shall both joint legal custody of the minor children, with primary physical custody to remain with the mother. Is that correct?
Both:	Yes.
Judge:	And that Jack will pay Jane $180 per week in child support. I don't see a child support guidelines worksheet amongst these papers. How did you come up with this figure?
Jane:	Sir, I went online and computed the amount on the state child support guidelines website.
Judge:	Yes … very good. And I see you requested that child support be collected via wage assignment through the state Child Support Enforcement Division?
Both:	Yes.
Judge:	And I see here that you've submitted a parenting plan to determine visitation?
Both:	Yes.
Judge (shuffles papers some more)	I see here, Sir, that it states in this Separation Agreement you shall have sole ownership of JR Construction Company, but nowhere on your financial statement is this company listed. Could you please explain why it's omitted?
Jack:	If you look on my financial statement under 'other,' you'll see I've got $17,000 listed in tools. That's the business, sir. The tools. The business doesn't earn money unless I work.
Judge:	Are you satisfied with this explanation, Ma'am?
Jane:	Yes, sir. I made him go through every drill bit and wrench and put a value on it.
Judge:	[*laughs*] Very well. And I see here that Jane will continue to provide health insurance coverage for the family?
Both:	Yes, sir.
Judge:	And Jane agrees to waive her right to receive future alimony?
Both:	Yes, Sir.
Judge:	And I see here that you wish this Separation Agreement to survive and become an independent contract as to issues of property division and debt, but would like to leave the agreement open to future review of this court as to issues of child support, the children, and health insurance. Is that correct?
Both:	Yes.
Judge:	Have you both had the opportunity to read this agreement in full?
Both:	Yes, sir.
Judge:	Do you both understand this agreement fully?
Both:	Yes.
Judge:	Have you both had the opportunity to seek out independent legal counsel?
Both:	Yes, sir.
Judge:	Do you both agree this agreement is a fair and equitable division of all your marital property and marital affairs?
Both:	Yes, Sir.
Judge:	Have you signed this agreement freely, voluntarily, and of your own free will?
Both:	Yes, Sir.
Judge	I hereby find this Separation Agreement to be a fair and equitable division of all marital affairs. Now … do you both agree that your marriage is irrevocably broken, and cannot be repaired?
Both:	Yes.
Judge:	And that you wish to separate, and go your separate ways, as individuals?
Both:	Yes.
Judge:	I hereby find that this marriage is irretrievably broken and am granting the divorce. You'll get the final decree in the mail when the divorce becomes final in 120 days. May god bless you and good luck.

1. An out-of-court agreement to get divorced is called an *uncontested divorce.* If you can reach a fair agreement with your spouse out-of-court, you will save much emotional grief and a fortune in legal fees;

2. If you weren't diligent about documenting your real income and assets, or your spouse is domineering, you may end up losing or signing away a lot more than you would get in court. The burden is upon *you* to assert your legal rights;

3. Judges tend to rubber-stamp whatever you sign, so be careful!

4. If there is only one place in your entire divorce you hire an attorney for help, getting help drafting and revising your Separation Agreement as you go through negotiations is the place you want to spend the money;

5. You should make your last-ditch effort at marriage counseling (if you so choose) *before* you announce you want a divorce (unless you are hoping the shock will force your recalcitrant spouse to change);

6. Protect your credit rating by cancelling or rolling over all credit cards so your spouse can't use them. Close joint bank accounts and start using your own credit cards and bank accounts;

7. Be compassionate when you tell your husband you want a divorce, but also be firm. A single cut of a very sharp knife heals faster than repeated, jagged cuts. No matter what you do, he's going to remember this day, and whether or not you treated him harshly or took advantage of his attempts to reconcile for your own gain, for the rest of his life;

8. If one of you moves out of the house or you attempt a trial separation, sign a Temporary Separation Agreement stating you don't intend this to be a permanent establishment of the way things should be in your divorce agreement;

9. There's lots of paperwork required to file. Check out your state website to find out exactly what you need for *your* home state;

10. Watch out for sneaky lawyer words such as Merger and Survival!!! They can hang you!

11. The Separation Agreement we've kept referring to throughout this chapter is covered in Chapter Eleven: Separation Agreements

12. Your final hearing will be almost anticlimactic.

13. Rent a copy of *The First Wives Club* and invite your friends over for a quite night with the girls.

(This page left intentionally blank)

CHAPTER 11

SEPARATION AGREEMENTS

Before the court can grant your divorce, you must agree upon a plan to divide your assets, pay your bills, and ensure ongoing obligations (such as alimony, child support, or health insurance) are paid in an orderly manner. In other words, the court wants to make sure that you don't keep coming back to court to resolve every minor dispute. The Separation Agreement is a legally binding a contract between you and your spouse about how you will conduct your affairs once your divorce is final so the state doesn't become obligated to micromanage your life.

Separation Agreements vary. Assumptions which are valid in some states (such as the right for a custodial parent to continue to receive child support while their child goes to college) are not true in other states. There is no single "model" separation agreement for all 50 states, or even for any single state or jurisdiction. In fact, state courts are *so* dodgy about encouraging laypeople to write their own Separation Agreements that very few of them even post model agreements online. This often isn't because the language, itself, is unclear. To a layperson reading a typical Separation Agreement, especially the streamlined ones posted on court websites of those few states that *do* post model agreements online, the document often appears to be a deceptively simple list of 'thou shalt' and 'thou shalt not's.' No … what makes these documents dangerous for a layperson is the fact this is a legally binding contract you signed memorializing an entire body of law that you, as a layperson, at best only vaguely grasp.

If there is one place in your entire divorce you should beg, borrow, barter or steal to scrape together a few hundred dollars to consult with an attorney, drafting your Separation Agreement is the place!!! This document is a legally binding contract which carries the force of law once a judge accepts it. It will dictate what legal rights you have (or lose) for the rest of your unmarried life. Once a judge accepts it, you can almost *never* go back to court to change it!

In the folk tale *The Devil and Daniel Webster,* the devil tempts a down-on-his-luck farmer with seven years of prosperity if only he will sign a simple contract. The farmer signs and gets his seven years of good luck, but has second thoughts when the devil shows up demanding repayment. He recruits Daniel Webster to argue for a reprieve, arguing the contract is unconscionable. That argument goes nowhere and the devil prepares to seize the farmer's soul. Luckily for the farmer, Daniel Webster is able to appeal to the jury's sense of decency and they find for the farmer.

The devil has learned from his mistakes. Thanks to legal doctrines about sanctity of contract dating back to the middle ages, unlike the demon jury in the Daniel Webster myth, there *will not* be a jury to sway with tales of decency and hardship. You *will* be held to whatever Separation Agreement you sign, whether you understood it or not, whether your spouse lied to you about hiding assets or not, or whether it is conscionable or not!

That being said, when you are a small woodland creature with few resources to hire an attorney, sometimes you just don't have a choice. If you have no choice but to draft your own or your soon-to-be ex-husband shoves an inch-thick packet of paperwork under your nose and says 'here, sign this,' what are you supposed to do? Sign like Daniel Webster's farmer and sell your soul? Or go to trial pro-se and get thrown to the wolves? Either way, if you don't have a rudimentary understanding of what all that legal mumbo-jumbo says, you're screwed.

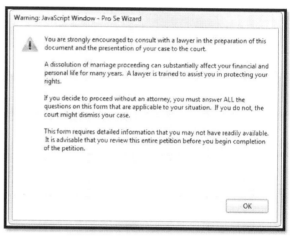

This Bootcamp manual will try to strike a balance between walking you through the elements common to most Separation Agreements, giving a general overview and outlining some of the more egregious pitfalls they can pose for the unwary, and educating you about how to better work with an attorney to get a more finely tailored final agreement. The information in this book is by no means exhaustive.

SEPARATION AGREEMENT CHECKLIST

You must memorialize a great deal of information in your Separation Agreement. It's easy to lose track of small details and forget them. Even if you use an attorney, they'll be juggling numerous other details and could forget to include something in your final draft. Once you sign it, you're stuck with it. Therefore, its good practice to make a checklist and verify everything is included in your final draft. If you end up negotiating a different agreement than you initially proposed, cross update your checklist as you go. Here's a sample checklist to get you thinking:

EXHIBIT 11-1: SAMPLE SEPARATION AGREEMENT CHECKLIST

Topic	Sample Question	Sample Answer
Merge or survive?	Will this agreement merge with the divorce, or survive as a separate contract?	All issues shall survive as a separate contract, except for issues related to the children, which shall merge with and become part of the divorce.
Child custody	Who is getting custody of the kids?	Wife
	Do you expect the custodial parent to remain in the state?	Yes
	Do you want to be notified if the other parent takes the children out of state? How?	Yes. Two weeks' notice if leaving the state for more than 24 hours or going more than 100 miles away from Massachusetts.
	How will you contact the children when they are with the other parent?	Dad must provide the address and phone number where the children will be staying at all times.
Visitation	When will the children be with each parent?	With dad every other weekend from 5:00 p.m. Friday until 7:00 p.m. Sunday.
	Who will get the children during which holiday?	Mom gets mothers' day. Dad gets fathers' day. Mom gets Christmas. Dad gets Thanksgiving.
	Which school vacation weeks will the children spend with the other parent?	Dad gets February vacation week and two weeks every summer.
	Who will pay the babysitter when the child is with each parent?	Each parent shall be responsible for the cost of child care when the child is scheduled to be with them.
Child Support	Who will pay what?	Dad will pay $250 per week child support.
	Will the DOR collect it for you?	Collection will be via wage assignment through the DOR.
	Will the other parent be expected to pay part of the child's school fees or activities?	Dad will pay 50% of all school fees, such as bus fees, field trip fees, etc. Dad will contribute 50% of the children's extracurricular activities, up to $500 per year.
Education	Who will pay for college?	The parties shall pay according to their respective incomes at the time.
	Will income from new spouses be considered when computing who shall pay what?	No.
Other Child matters	Do children have any special needs, such as tutoring or counseling?	No.
Alimony	Is the Wife eligible to receive alimony?	The husband shall pay the wife $350 per week alimony.
	Will child support be deducted from the alimony?	The husband's alimony allotment will be reduced by the amount of child support.
	Who is going to pay the taxes on the alimony?	Those portions of the alimony order above the child support order shall be taxable to the Wife.
	When does alimony end?	Alimony shall cease upon remarriage of the Wife or 5.5 years, whichever occurs first.
Health insurance	Who is going to provide health insurance for the kids?	The Husband.
	Who is going to provide health insurance for the Wife?	The husband.
	Who is going to provide health insurance for the husband?	The husband.
	Will any adjustments be made in payments to the other party due to health insurance premiums?	50% of the cost of the family plan will be deducted from the husband's child support obligation.
	Who is going to pay for unreimbursed medical expenses and co-pays?	The couple will divide all unreimbursed medical expenses and co-pays 50:50.

	What happens if the kids need glasses or dental work?	50% of the cost of the family dental plan will be deducted from the husband's child support obligation. Glasses and eye exams 50:50 Unreimbursed dental work 50:50
	What happens if the kids need braces?	Braces – parties will consult with each other as to best plan and cost prior to hiring an orthodontist, split costs 50:50.
	Who is responsible to pay the other parents unreimbursed medical bills?	Each party shall be responsible for their own unreimbursed medical, dental and other bills.
	What happens if a better, cheaper medical plan becomes available?	The parties shall consult with each other from time to time as to cost/benefit of any given plan and may request modification.
	When will health insurance terminate for the kids?	Upon graduation from high school or college, whichever is later.
Property Division	Who is going to keep the house?	The Wife.
	Who is going to pay the mortgage on the house?	The Wife.
	Are there any outstanding debts on the house which need to be settled?	The husband shall pay the home equity line of credit he took out on the house to buy his truck until paid in full.
	Are there going to be any reimbursements for down payments or unrecorded loans on any asset?	The husband shall reimburse the wife's parents 50% of the loan he took from them last year to hire a criminal attorney to defend himself against a drunk driving accident.
	Who will keep which car and pay the loans on them?	The wife will keep her 2004 Chevy Tahoe and pay all car loans and costs associated with it. The Husband shall keep his pickup truck and pay all costs associated with it (no loans).
	Any jewelry?	The wife shall give the Husband the engagement ring, wedding band, and diamond earrings.
	Stocks/bonds/investments?	The husband shall keep his 500 shares of Dell computer stock. The Husband shall sign over 30 shares of Berkshire Hathaway stock to the Wife.
	Retirement plans?	The husband shall draft a QDRO assigning 50% of the current value of his 401(k) plan to the Wife.
	Pensions?	The Wife shall draft a QPO granting the husband an 8/22nd share of her Mass State Teachers' Pension when she becomes eligible to receive said pension.
	Other motor vehicles?	The husband shall keep his Harley Davidson motorcycle and pay all loans and expenses associated with it. The husband shall keep the 20 foot travel trailer and pay all loans and expenses associated with it.
	Collectibles?	The Husband shall keep his baseball card collection.
	Other assets?	The husband shall keep his tools, except for a toolbox with a complete set of basic tools (hammer, wrench, screwdriver, etc.)
Liabilities	Who is going to pay the mortgage?	The Wife.
	Who is going to pay the car/vehicle loans?	Whoever keeps a vehicle pays the loan on it.
	Who is going to pay the Wife's student loans?	The Wife.
	Who is going to pay the credit card bills?	The Wife shall pay her Capital One visa. The husband will pay his Citibank card. All other credit cards will be paid in proportion to the couples income, with the husband paying 2/3rds (67%) and the wife paying 1/3rd (33%).
	Any other loans?	The husband shall reimburse the wife's parents

		$10,000 he borrowed for his business.
Tax issues	How will last years' tax refund or liability (if still outstanding) be divided?	50:50
	Will the parties file together, or separately this year?	Separately.
	Who will claim the children as dependents?	The Wife shall claim Johnnie and the husband shall claim Janie.
	Any outstanding tax debt?	The husband shall be solely responsible for paying any and all taxes related to his business.
Legal fees	Who is going to pay for the lawyer/mediator?.	Each party shall be responsible for paying their own legal bill.
Life insurance	What happens if the person responsible for paying child support or alimony dies?	Include a life insurance benefit in the Separation Agreement.

Make allowances for your friend Murphy. Even if you pay an attorney $150,000 to draft you a 2,000 page Agreement detailing how many sheets of toilet paper little Johnnie or Susie is entitled to use while visiting the other parent's house, Murphy's Law dictates you'll forget something. The ultimate responsibility for ensuring everything you need ends up clearly spelled out rests with *you*. If you something has been omitted or a requested change gets overlooked, *you* will be stuck with the consequences. Not your lawyer! Refer back to your checklist and make sure you read the final agreement, in full. Resist pressure to sign agreements modified at the courthouse without thoroughly reading and understanding it. The judge will ask "did you read this agreement and fully understand it" before he grants you your divorce, so make sure you do!

Once an agreement has been accepted by the court and your divorce granted, it will take the second coming of Christ to get a judge to reverse it. If you don't understand what it means, don't sign it!!!

SCROUNGING UP A SAMPLE SEPARATION AGREEMENT

Think of your Separation Agreement as the car you will use to journey into your new life. Although it would be nice to ride in a classy Lexus, all most people need is a reliable car that won't keep breaking down and leaving you stranded on the side of the road. If, on the other hand, you anticipate travelling through hostile territory, with the evil trapper lobbing grenades at every turn, you're going to want a two-inch thick Sherman tank of a Separation Agreement spelling out every contingency so you can force him to tow the mark.

The Honda Fit of Separation Agreements is whatever model boilerplate your local family court has posted on your state-court website or, failing that, has made available in their Clerk's office or courthouse law library for pro-se litigants who walk in the door and *ask*. Like the Honda Fit, your courts boilerplate is a no-frills subcompact that will often leave you wishing for a car with more room, but it is basically reliable and will get you where you are going. Before we begin building your new car, I suggest you look on your *own* state family court website to see if there is a boilerplate available to refer to as you follow along.

If your state doesn't have its own model Separation Agreement posted online, download a 'scratch copy' from a neighboring state to use as a first rough draft. Once you feel you've covered all your bases, take it (along with your financial statement and proposed property division worksheet) to a local attorney to help you iron out the bugs. It will save you money over having the attorney start completely from scratch and the result will be superior to what you would likely be able to draft on your own.

Most states with Model Separation Agreements have *two* versions: one for couples with no children and the other for couples who *do* have minor children still dependent upon them for support. Some also have restrictions about the dollar value of your marital estate. A few states even have interactive fill-in-the-blank boilerplates or copies available in a word .doc so you can download and modify it as needed.

Type the search terms: "___X-state___ family court divorce forms separation agreement" into your internet browser and see what pops up.

Always search *first* for an official court-posted model agreement (your Honda Fit) before resorting to one of the commercial document preparation services. The Honda Fit, as tiny and bare-bones as it is, is a reliable car. Some of the commercially prepared documents winging around the internet right now are *not*. If you *do* end up resorting to a for-pay commercial service, I recommend you search for models prepared by an attorney-run document preparation service unique to *your* home state. Avoid nationwide sites that claim they'll help you fill in the blanks for a low fee unless that fee includes at least a one-hour consultation with a flesh-and-blood attorney! Think about it … do you *really* want some unlicensed, minimum-wage worker from a call center in India spelling out the road map for you future life as a single woman? No? Didn't think so…

EXHIBIT 11-2: STATES WITH MODEL SEPARATION/DISSOLUTION/CONSENT DECREES AVAILABLE ONLINE (AS OF 2012)

Arizona	http://www.superiorcourt.maricopa.gov/SuperiorCourt/Self-ServiceCenter/Forms/FamilyCourt/fc_dr7.asp
California	http://www.courts.ca.gov/1035.htm *California has a series of interactive fill-in-the-blank forms that add up to a complete agreement
Colorado	http://www.courts.state.co.us/Forms/Forms_List.cfm?Form_Type_ID=14 *Colorado has a lovely interactive fill-in-the-blank form
Connecticut	http://www.jud.ct.gov/webforms/forms/fm172.pdf
Florida	http://www.flcourts.org/gen_public/family/forms_rules/ *Three different marital settlement agreements available
Georgia	http://www.lawhelp.org/documents/clusters/GA/271/English/Divorcechild.shtml *Two different settlement agreements
Illinois	http://www.dupageco.org/CourtClerk/3198/ *scroll down to 'Marital Settlement Agreement for Joint Dissolution of Marriage
Massachusetts	http://www.lawlib.state.ma.us/subject/forms/index.html#divorce
Missouri	http://www.selfrepresent.mo.gov/file.jsp?id=31147
Montana	http://courts.mt.gov/library/forms/end_marriage/dis_wc.mcpx *Click on 'decree' with/without children
Nevada	http://www.washoecourts.com/index.cfm?page=familyForms *click on one of three 'conversion' forms
New Hampshire	http://www.courts.state.nh.us/forms/nhjb-2071-fs.pdf
Oregon	http://courts.oregon.gov/OJD/OSCA/cpsd/courtimprovement/familylaw/flpacket1.page?#B *click on 'packet' applicable for your case
Washington	http://www.courts.wa.gov/forms/?fa=forms.contribute&formID=13 *click on Decree of Dissolution (DCD)/Legal Separation (DCLGSP)/Concerning the Validity of the Marriage (DCINMG)
Wisconsin	http://www.wicourts.gov/forms1/circuit/ccform.jsp?FormName=&FormNumber=&beg_date=&end_date=&StatuteCite=&Category=12&SubCat=All *click on appropriate 'Marital Settlement Agreement'

Getting divorced is a bit like embarking on an exciting journey. Where do you hope to go? Will the terrain be rough? Or will there be a nice, paved highway bring you there? Is the territory you'll be travelling through peaceful and orderly? Or will there be highwaymen setting up roadblocks and stealing your supplies every step of the way? Do you need a tank that will guard you against every mortar and provide lots of ammunition to blast the evil trapper out of the sky? Or will a well-maintained subcompact get you there? Your post-divorce agreement has certain functional components necessary to make the vehicle move.

The most important part of the car is the drive train (the preamble). The engine, transmission, gears and tires make your car move forward. Assets are the body of your car. You may have enough to build a sleek outer shell, complete with air conditioning, satellite radio and a moon roof. Or you may have no more than a crude seat bolted to the chassis while you bump along hanging on for dear life.

To move forward, your car needs fuel. You need to map out where the gas stations are for your future income stream, whether that be solely your own future income or include periodic refills from child support or alimony. The most important thing you need to ensure is the *predictability* of future gas. If you've ever driven through the Mojave Desert and encountered one of those 'next gas 300 miles' signs, you understand the importance of predicting when you'll encounter the next gas station. Boilerplates addressing future income, child support, and alimony map out where the gas stations are so you don't run out of gas.

Debt is the sugar some nasty bastard dumped into your gas tank. It will gum up your engine and make it seize. If you've got sugar in your gas tank, you need to come up with a formal written Debt plan to filter it out before your engine drops out of your car and leaves you stranded at the side of the road.

If your children will be making this journey with you, you need to make sure you have enough seats in your car to carry them (custody boilerplates and parenting plans), seat belts to keep them safe (agreements dividing their future medical or other expenses), and map out where all the bathroom breaks are (visitation).

The law is the road upon which you will be forced to travel. In many instances the law will try to make your journey smooth, but it will demand tolls (taxes). Exhibits spelling out how old tax liability and future tax deductions or obligations prevent your car from getting pulled over and ticketed.

Then there are the highwaymen looking to run your car off the road and leave you laying in a ditch. Health insurance. Life insurance. Other kinds of insurance (or assurances) should spell out how you will deal with the not-quite-unforeseen.

A well-crafted Separation Agreement should contain the following elements (use this as a checklist as you weigh which model agreement *you* will use):

1. The Preamble (the drive train):

   a. Identification of the Parties
   b. Statement of Basic Facts
   c. Statement of Purpose
   d. Reference to your state divorce statute
   e. Divorce court docket number
   f. Warranty of full disclosure
   g. Warranty of free will
   h. Warranty of opportunity to consult with legal counsel
   i. Separate lives
   j. Waiver of estate clause
   k. Waiver of liability clause
   l. Final authority clause
   m. Reference to attached exhibits
   n. Merger or survival clause
   o. Strict performance clause
   p. Invalidity clause
   q. Breach clause
   r. Indemnification clause
   s. Choice of law clause
   t. Choice of forum clause
   u. Verbiage stating how the agreement will be handled in relation to the divorce
   v. Confession of judgment clause
   w. Mediation clauses
   x. Notarized signature

2. Exhibits (the gas, road map, insurance and tolls):

   a. Custody and Visitation
   b. Child Support
   c. Alimony
   d. Education of the Children
   e. Health Related Insurance and Expenses
   f. Division of Assets and Retirement Funds
   g. Payment of Marital Debts
   h. Income Taxes
   i. Legal Fees and Expenses
   j. Life Insurance

We will now pick apart two different kinds of Separation Agreements, one a sample boilerplate posted by a local family law court as a guide for pro-se litigants, the other drafted by an attorney, and examine them to see if they have all the elements necessary to get you from point A to point B. There's nothing worse than *thinking* you have an iron-clad agreement, only to discover after it's too late to go back and make changes. If you would like a 'scratch copy' for your own purposes, the complete attorney-drafted Separation Agreement (minus the circles and arrows) can be found at the end of this chapter.

⚑ ***The following Samples are just that … samples!*** Please do not copy something out of a book you do not understand. They are broken down to teach you how to critically pick proposed verbiage apart.

THE PREAMBLE

The drive train of your new car is the preamble. Although preambles vary and references to state statutes differ from state to state, they usually contain elements which are designed to help the reader gain an understanding of where the party is coming from and where they are hoping to end up by drafting the agreement. Common elements are as follows:

Identification of the Parties – the parties who will be bound by the agreement must be specifically identified by name, address, and occasionally date of birth or other specific information.

Statement of Basic Facts – most separation agreements list when and where the parties were married, how many children were born of the marriage, the place and date where they last lived together as husband and wife (important for jurisdiction), and some sentence to the effect that the parties have chosen to separation. In a custom-drafted Agreement, your attorney may also add a brief explanatory blurb just after the statement of basic facts to explain an unusual extenuating circumstance (i.e., having lived apart for many years) which may cause the parties to deviate from a "typical" property division.

> *This is not the place to include recriminations such as "we're getting divorced because he cheated on me."* (Save that for the Complaint for Divorce if he refuses to settle).

Statement of Purpose – a statement about what the parties wish to accomplish by writing the agreement, such as settling property rights, child support, alimony, or other issues. Usually contains verbiage about this agreement is meant to be *binding.*

Since all of this legal terminology is meaningless without a real-life example, here is what these three items would look like in a court-model boilerplate Separation Agreement:

Image: Queen Elisabeth II Serving in the Motor Pool During WWII
(Yes ... the Queen of England knows how to fix her own car)

EXHIBIT 11-P-1:   SAMPLE COURT-MODEL PREAMBLE

COMMONWEALTH of MASSACHUSETTS
The Trial Court
Probate and Family Court Department

Barnstable, ss.

Docket No. ___06D-0000-DV1___

_____Jane Doe-Rayme_____   Plaintiff/Petitioner

_____Jack Rayme_____   Defendant/Petitioner

SEPARATION AGREEMENT APPLICABLE TO ALL DIVORCES

AGREEMENT made between _____Jack Rayme_____
(Name of Husband)
of ___55 Easy Street, Anytown, MA 02345___
(Street Address)   (City/Town, State. Zip)
(referred to as the Husband), and _____Jane Rayme_____
(Name of Wife)
of ___100 Any Street, North Anytown, MA 06345___
(Street Address)   (City/Town, State. Zip)
(referred to as the Wife.)

> *Identification:* The parties bound by this agreement must be clearly identified.

The Husband and Wife were married in _____Las Vegas, Nevada_____
(City/Town & State)
on 9 /11/ 1994 and last lived together as Husband and Wife at 100 Any Street,
(Date of Marriage)   (Street Address)
North Anytown, MA 06345   on _11_ / _9_ / _2007_
(City/Town, State)   (Date of Separation)

> *Statement of Basic Facts:* when married, when separated. Helps judge watch for property rights based on length of marriage.

    No children were born of this marriage.
    None of the children born of this marriage are under the age of eighteen years or are dependent on the parties for support.
  X   The following dependent child[ren] was/were born of this marriage
      (list names and dates of birth on the following page):

> This section warns the judge to be on the lookout for child support, custody, visitation, other issues.

1) _Janie Rayme_ date of birth ___/___/___
2) _Johnnie Rayme_ date of birth ___/___/___
3) _____ date of birth ___/___/___
4) _____ date of birth ___/___/___

This Separation Agreement is made in order to settle and determine:

a) the property and support rights of the husband and wife; and
b) the care, custody, support, maintenance and education of the minor and/or dependent child[ren] of this marriage (attach Schedule A); and
c) all other rights and obligations arising from the marital relationship.

In consideration of the mutual promises contained in this Separation Agreement, the Husband and Wife agree that:

> *Statement of Purpose:* Remember the farmer signing a contract with the devil? This language is BINDING!!!

The court's model boilerplate is a perfectly functional Separation Agreement. What could trip up you, as a layperson, is just how truly binding the phrase 'this separation agreement is made in order to settle…" This agreement *is* binding!

Now we will go through an attorney-drafted agreement paragraph by paragraph, first explaining what it is, and then I'll give an example. Because the court's sample (if your state has one) is always the best starting place, we will use *that* as a model and then compare a paragraph drafted by an attorney. A complete (uncut) copy of the attorney-drafted version can be found at the end of the chapter.

EXHIBIT 11-P-2: SAMPLE ATTORNEY-DRAFTED PREAMBLE

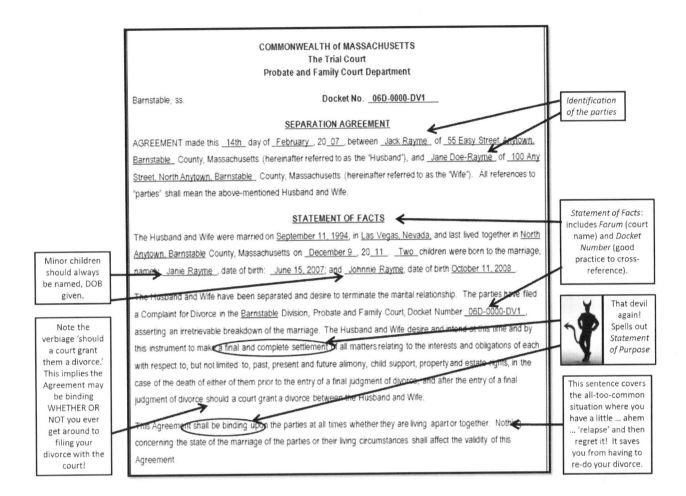

The attorney-drafted Separation Agreement does a slightly better job of spelling out that this agreement is meant to make 'a final and complete settlement.' It adds the verbiage 'this agreement shall be binding.' Hopefully the stronger wording will clue you to ask questions.

A former wife took pity upon her ex-husband when he lost his job and became homeless, allowing him to move back into the former marital (now her) home in exchange for a $100 per week rent for a room in the basement. Weeks turned into months and he refused to leave, especially as they had a few amorous encounters during the early portion of that period of time. When she initiated eviction proceedings to have him removed, the former husband retaliated by cross-filing in family court, claiming he'd added new value to the former marital estate by paying rent and making a few repairs around the house, and also claiming he wanted custody of the kids. The action was eventually dismissed and he was evicted, but not after several evidentiary hearings and hefty legal fees.

BOOTCAMP EXHIBIT 11-P-3: SAMPLE COURT-MODEL PREAMBLE (CONT'D)

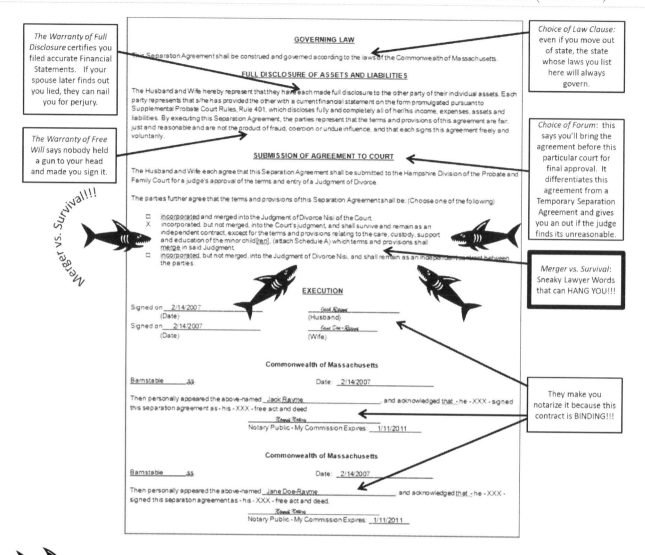

In case you didn't take the hint, the little sharks swimming around the sneaky lawyer words 'merger' and 'survival' are supposed to clue you to go ask an attorney which situation is right for *your* individual divorce!

Merger or survival clause – a statement about whether this agreement will be merged with the divorce, survive as a separate contract, or have some portions survive and others merge.

For a refresher on 'merger' versus 'survival,' go back and re-read "Sneaky Lawyer Words' in Chapter Ten.

Moving on with our dissection of verbiage you're likely to encounter when you start drafting *your* Separation Agreement, here are more sneaky lawyer words you need to know:

Governing Law or Choice of Law clause – most Separation Agreements spell out which states' law must be used for resolving disputes which arise in the future about interpreting the agreement. This is because statutes and case law differ from state to state. This may not sound like a problem if you both live in the same state the day you get divorced, but if one or both of you later move to different states, your Separation Agreement could take on meanings neither of you ever anticipated. Choice of law clauses usually specify the laws of the state where you obtained your divorce will govern future disputes. Outside of the divorce context, be observant of choice of law clauses in your business contracts (such as credit cards) as businesses usually designate a state that has laws very friendly to their side of the story and very hostile to the consumers rights (such as credit card companies in South Dakota, corporate headquarters in Delaware, etc.)

Choice of Forum clause – forum refers to which courthouse your case can be heard. The chosen forum is usually the courthouse where you file your divorce. If you both stay in the same county after you divorce, this will not be an issue. However, if one party later moves across the state (or out of state completely), another courthouse may gain jurisdiction. Do you really want to get summonsed to a court in Pittsfield (or Hawaii) when you got your divorce on Cape Cod? The courts sample boilerplate doesn't contain this clause, but it is wise to include in order to limit the ability of the other party to inconvenience you and gain an advantage by moving far away from you (or any witnesses). Outside of the divorce context, be observant of choice of forum clauses in your business contracts (such as plane tickets or rental car agreements) as businesses usually designate a state that is very inconvenient or expensive to get to and has laws hostile to consumers rights.

Warranty of full disclosure –the parties must each swear they have honestly and truthfully disclosed all assets, liabilities, and any other items which might affect the other party's rights or the courts' decision. If you later find out your husband lied about his finances, it gives you a chance to drag him back to court for a full accounting (but no guarantee).

Warranty of free will – both parties must assure the judge they have fully and fairly negotiated the agreement based on all available facts, that they ultimately feel the agreement they reached is fair (or as fair as hurt feelings and property division laws allow), just and reasonable, and that nobody held a gun to their head to force them to sign it. Even after writing this into your Separation Agreement, most judges are going to make you swear this again, in person, before granting your divorce just to be sure.

EXHIBIT 11-P-4: SAMPLE ATTORNEY-DRAFTED PREAMBLE (CONT'D)

Warranty of Full Disclosure: if you later find out your husband lied to you about hiding money, this gives you a CHANCE to go back to court (but no guarantee)

Warranty of Understanding: so you can't later come back and claim you didn't understand what you signed!

Warranty of OPPORTUNITY to see a lawyer: If you choose NOT to, it's all on your head!

Warranty of Sole Agreement: this is so you can't come back later and say there was some additional contract (remember the guy that made his wife sign a $10,000 out-of-court mortgage as a condition to avoid a custody dispute? This was how she invalidated it).

Warranty of Full Disclosure: The parties represent and acknowledge that each has fully described his or her assets and liabilities to the other party to the best of his or her knowledge and ability as set forth on the financial statements of each filed herewith and incorporated by reference herein. Each party is fully cognizant of his or her rights, and each executes this Agreement based upon his or her personal knowledge and the representations of the other party which each believes to be a true, complete and accurate reflection of the other party's current financial status and circumstances. It is agreed and understood by the parties that they have been afforded the opportunity for full discovery and any and all pertinent data with regard to the assets, liabilities, income and expenses of the other.

Warranty of Understanding: The Husband and Wife declare and acknowledge that each of them understands the position, circumstances, financial resources, income, expenses, liabilities and prospects of the other based upon and in reliance on the aforesaid financial statements of each party and based upon the discovery which each has conducted, and that each of them understands the terms, provisions and conditions of the within Agreement, and believes its terms, provisions and conditions to be fair and to be reasonable.

Warranty of Opportunity to Consult with Legal Counsel: The parties further state that they have negotiated the terms of this Agreement, that each has had the opportunity for independent legal advice by counsel of his or her own choosing and that, after consultation with his or her respective attorney and after being advised fully and fairly as to all facts and circumstances herein set forth, and after having read this Agreement line by line, each freely and fully accepts the terms, conditions and provisions hereof and enters into this Agreement voluntarily and without any coercion whatsoever.

Warranty of Sole Agreement Between the Parties: The parties further acknowledge and declare that this Agreement contains the entire agreement between the parties hereto and that there are no agreements, promises, terms, conditions or understandings and no representations or inducements leading to the execution hereof, express or implied, other than those herein set forth (except for those documents or exhibits expressly annexed and incorporated by reference), and that no oral statement or prior written matter extrinsic to the four corners of this Agreement not expressly annexed and incorporated by reference shall have any force or effect.

'opportunity for full discovery' means you had the CHANCE to make your husband cough up all those Acorns I told you to gather in Chapter One and either did, or foolishly chose not to! If you try to come back later claiming he lied, you will have a higher burden of proof to obtain NEW discovery.

'independent legal counsel' means somebody BESIDES the mediator. You should EACH speak to a different non-partisan attorney!

'incorporated by reference' means there are additional pieces of paper attached, stapled, or that otherwise belong with this Agreement. If it's not specifically listed, the court considers it to NOT be part of the Agreement.

'Four Corners' is a legal doctrine stretching back to the middle ages that prevents somebody from coming back after you signed claiming there were additional terms.

Warranty of opportunity to consult with legal counsel – this is not always contained in court boilerplates, nor all attorney-drafted boilerplates, but often both parties will attest they had an opportunity to read the agreement and consult with an attorney before signing it. *Opportunity to consult* and *opportunity to read* are not the same thing as *actually did consult or read.* If you choose to copy some boilerplate agreement, not read it thoroughly, don't understand it, and then sign it, this paragraph prevents you from going back to court to say "I didn't read it" or "I didn't hire a lawyer." Most judges will ask you this question, whether or not it is written into the Agreement, the day of your divorce hearing because they don't want to be bothered with you coming back into court at a later to change things.

EXHIBIT 11-P-5: SAMPLE ATTORNEY-DRAFTED PREAMBLE (CONT'D)

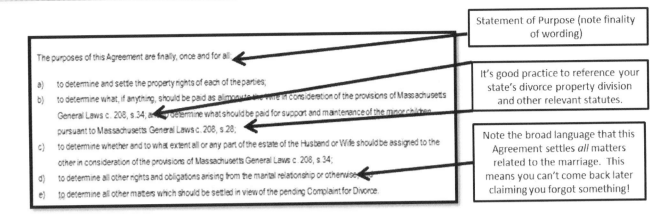

The purposes of this Agreement are finally, once and for all:

a) to determine and settle the property rights of each of the parties;

b) to determine what, if anything, should be paid as alimony to the wife in consideration of the provisions of Massachusetts General Laws c. 208, s.34, and to determine what should be paid for support and maintenance of the minor children pursuant to Massachusetts General Laws c. 208, s 28;

c) to determine whether and to what extent all or any part of the estate of the Husband or Wife should be assigned to the other in consideration of the provisions of Massachusetts General Laws c. 208, s 34;

d) to determine all other rights and obligations arising from the marital relationship or otherwise;

e) to determine all other matters which should be settled in view of the pending Complaint for Divorce.

Statement of Purpose (note finality of wording)

It's good practice to reference your state's divorce property division and other relevant statutes.

Note the broad language that this Agreement settles *all* matters related to the marriage. This means you can't come back later claiming you forgot something!

An attorney-drafted Separation Agreement should have a Statement of Purpose the same as a court-boilerplate might have. This is to differentiate it from another contract such as a Pre-Nuptial Agreement or the Lease on your car. This might sound obvious, but I've had cases where a husband looking to bail on a marriage in the near future conned the wife into signing an agreement waiving her rights to major pieces of marital property in exchange for some trivial favor, such as borrowing money against the house to start a business loan or to use marital funds to fly and visit a sick family member. A poorly drafted Statement of Purpose might open the door for your spouse to negate certain portions of your Separation Agreement (although most judges will ask you questions about your understanding of what you sign which will shut that door). A Statement of Purpose is useful in those situations where you sign a Separation Agreement but don't get into court until months (or years) later (common in states with long timeframes to live apart before granting your divorce).

Note that this particular attorney-drafted boilerplate references the state divorce property division statute and also the state child support statute. Not listing these will not make your agreement invalid as the court will usually err on the side of enforcing a valid contract, but it's good practice.

EXHIBIT 11-P-6: SAMPLE ATTORNEY-DRAFTED PREAMBLE (CONT'D)

NOW, THEREFORE, in consideration of the mutual promises, agreements and covenants hereinafter contained, the Husband and Wife mutually agree as follows:

1. <u>Covenant to Live Apart</u> - From the date hereof, the Husband and Wife may continue to live separate and apart from one another for the rest of their lives, and each shall be free from interference, authority or control, direct or indirect, by the other as fully as if sole and unmarried.

2. <u>Covenant of Non-Interference</u> - Neither the Husband nor the Wife shall molest the other, nor shall the Husband or Wife compel or attempt to compel the other to cohabit with him or her, nor shall the Husband or Wife commence any legal, equitable or other action or proceeding for the restitution of conjugal rights. The Husband and Wife to not intend that this clause shall be criminally enforceable.

3. <u>Covenant to Waive Claims to the Other Parties Estate:</u>

   A) The Husband and Wife each hereby waives any right at law or in equity to elect to take against any last will made by the other, including all rights of dower or of curtsey, and each hereby waives, renounces and relinquishes unto each other, their respective heirs, executors, administrators and assigns forever, all and any interest of any kind or character which either may now have or may hereafter acquire in or to any real or personal property of the other and whether now owned or hereafter acquired by either, except as expressly provided by the terms of this Agreement.

   B) The Husband and Wife shall have the right to dispose of his or her property by will, or otherwise, in such manner as each may in his or her uncontrolled discretion deem proper, and neither one will claim any interest in the estate of the other, except to enforce any obligation imposed by this Agreement.

4. <u>Covenant to Release All Claims and Legal Actions Against the Other</u> - The Husband and Wife hereby mutually release and forever discharge each other from any and all actions, suits, debts, claims, demands and obligations whatsoever, both at law and in equity, which either of them has ever had, now has, or may hereafter have against the other, upon or by reason of any matter, cause or thing up to the date of this Agreement, whether arising from the marital relationship or otherwise, including, but not limited to, claims against each other's property, it being the intention of the parties that henceforth there shall exist as between them only such rights and obligations as are specifically provided for in this Agreement and in any judgment entered on the Complaint for Divorce;

5. <u>Covenants Against New Liabilities:</u>

   A) The Wife warrants, represents that, other than as specifically set forth in this Agreement, she will not hereafter contract or incur any debt, charge or liability whatsoever for which the Husband, his legal representatives, or his property or estate, will or may become liable, and that as of the date of this Agreement there are no outstanding bills incurred by her (except for those expressly listed and agreed upon in this Agreement) which are the obligation of the Husband. .

   B) The Husband warrants, represents and agrees that he will not hereafter contract or incur any debt, charge or liability whatsoever for which the Wife, her legal representatives, or her property or estate will or may become liable, and that at the time of the Agreement there are no outstanding bills incurred by him (except for those expressly listed and agreed upon in this Agreement) which are the obligation of the Wife.

> Here's a leftover from English common law ... this means he can't sue you to make you have sex with him!

> This prevents your spouse from contesting your will if you later die.

> This prevents your spouse from suing you in a different court to get a better outcome than he got in divorce court.

> This means you can't go wracking up credit card charges in each other's name.

Separate lives aka Covenant to Live Apart – separation agreements usually state that the couple agrees, from this day forward, to live separate and apart from each other. There is often language about not incurring debts in the other parties name and not attempting to restrain the other person in any way from going about their new life.

Waiver of estate clause – the courts simplified Agreement does not contain this verbiage, but most attorney-drafted Separation Agreements will spell it out that any claims you may have against your spouses' estate are being settled in this document. For example, you can choose to agree to waive some of your rights and keep other rights (such as to waive your right to your husbands' estate *except* for being named beneficiary of an outstanding pension or life insurance policy) if this is what you both want to do. However, this does *not* prevent your spouse from collecting on any asset, retirement plan, or will you may have forgotten to change. If you want to prevent him from getting your money after the divorce, you still need to tie up loose ends by changing beneficiaries and heirs. This clause only prevents him from claiming there was some *additional* right arising out of the defunct marriage should you later kick the bucket. I have had clients die, then have their children contact me for copies of the Separation Agreement to prevent the other parent from contesting the well and stealing their inheritance. Case law on estate issues is fairly settled, but why leave it to chance?

Waiver of liability clause – the court agreement does not contain this verbiage, but most attorney drafted agreements have some blurb stating you each agree to not hold the other spouse responsible or liable for any debts which you may incur in the future and/or which you may have already occurred in the period of time between when you separated and signed the agreement.

EXHIBIT 11-P-7: SAMPLE ATTORNEY-DRAFTED PREAMBLE (CONT'D)

6. Covenant of Indemnification:

A) The Wife further covenants at all times to hold the Husband free, harmless and indemnified from and against all debts, charges or liabilities previously contracted or incurred by her in breach of the provisions of this paragraph, and from any and all attorneys' fees, costs and expenses incurred by the Husband as a result of any such breach.

B) The Husband further covenants at all times to hold the Wife free, harmless and indemnified from and against all debts, charges or liabilities previously contracted or incurred by him in breach of the provisions of this paragraph, and from any and all attorneys' fees, costs and expenses incurred by the Wife as a result of any breach.

7. Procedure in the Event of Breach: Any breach of any term or terms of the within Agreement shall give either party the right to take immediate action, either at law or in equity, concerning such breach. If either the Husband or the Wife shall commit a breach of any of the provisions of this Agreement and legal action, required to enforce such provisions, shall be instituted by the other, the Court may make a determination or allocation as to the payment of reasonable attorneys' fees incurred in instituting and prosecuting such action, by the party in breach.

8. Additional Terms. The parties agree:

(1) to accept the provisions made for each and every undertaking as set forth in this agreement in full satisfaction and discharge of all claims, past, present and future, which each may have upon the other and which in any way arise out of the marital relationship;

(2) to waive any claim to property division, alimony or support for each, other than as provided in this Agreement;

(3) not to seek the entry of an order or judgment which differs in any way from the terms of this Agreement; and

(4) to indemnify and hold harmless the other from any amount he or she is ordered or required to make, in excess of the actual payments or division of property he or she is required to make pursuant to this Agreement.

> The most commonly litigated breach is one party doesn't pay a bill they promised to pay and the creditor goes after the other spouse.

> This is more verbiage reinforcing the Statement of Purpose. It seeks to convey the FINALITY of this Agreement.

Indemnification clause – the courts sample boilerplate does not contain this language. However, most attorney-drafted Separation Agreements state that if one party's creditors come after the former spouse to pay debts the other party agreed to pay, the spouse who chased the breach will have to reimburse the blameless spouse for any consequences of that breach, including the cost of hiring a lawyer to defend yourself against the creditors. This does **not** protect you from having to pay for a credit card bill or mortgage payment originally co-signed in both your names. Family court does not have the right to nullify third-party contracts and you will still be held liable (only a bankruptcy court has the power to declare otherwise). However, this gives you the right to drag your former spouse back to family court to be reimbursed (a more friendly forum for these situations) instead of having to sue him like any other ordinary businessperson in district court.

Breach clause – most attorney drafted agreements spell out what happens if one party fails to live up to their end of the bargain and the other party has to drag them back to court. Breach clauses usually spell out that the person causing the breach has to pay the other persons reasonable court costs and attorney fees. "Reasonable" does not mean whatever it may cost you to win, only what most attorneys would charge to handle a similar case, so keep a close watch on how much your attorney wracks up in legal fees and don't assume your spouse will be ordered to pay 100% if you don't pay attention to your legal bill getting out of hand.

Final authority clause – attorney drafted agreements will usually contain a statement that the Separation Agreement will be the final authority on all matters between you. What this means is that, if you go to court for your final hearing and the court accepts the agreement and grants your divorce, one spouse cannot come back at a later date and claim there was some "secret" or "verbal" agreement between you which can be enforced. If you need to have something agreed to, you'd better put it in writing in the Agreement or it will be gone because, even without this clause, getting a judge to enforce a "secret" agreement you were too sneaky to disclose in the first place is a tough sell. Note: sometimes state statutes (such as laws allowing for modification of child support if your financial situation changes substantially) can override a final authority clause.

Verbiage stating how the agreement will be handled in relation to the divorce –most couples negotiated and sign their Separation Agreements days, weeks, months, or sometimes even years before they actually get around to going to court for their final hearing. Language outlining how the Agreement is to be submitted to and handled by the court makes these agreements enforceable for the period of time between when it is signed and the day you get to court. Attorneys usually specify the Agreement goes into effect the day it is signed (not submitted) unless otherwise rejected by the judge. This is because court dates can take months to obtain, but also because many couples separate, hammer out an agreement, sign it, and go about their lives without actually filing their divorce until years later.

EXHIBIT 11-P-8: SAMPLE ATTORNEY-DRAFTED PREAMBLE (CONT'D)

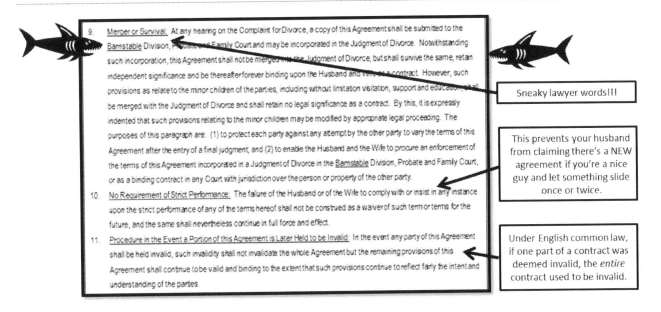

9. **Merger or Survival:** At any hearing on the Complaint for Divorce, a copy of this Agreement shall be submitted to the Barnstable Division, Probate and Family Court and may be incorporated in the Judgment of Divorce. Notwithstanding such incorporation, this Agreement shall not be merged with the Judgment of Divorce, but shall survive the same, retain independent significance and be thereafter forever binding upon the Husband and Wife as a contract. However, such provisions as relate to the minor children of the parties, including without limitation visitation, support and education, shall be merged with the Judgment of Divorce and shall retain no legal significance as a contract. By this, it is expressly indented that such provisions relating to the minor children may be modified by appropriate legal proceeding. The purposes of this paragraph are: (1) to protect each party against any attempt by the other party to vary the terms of this Agreement after the entry of a final judgment; and (2) to enable the Husband and the Wife to procure an enforcement of the terms of this Agreement incorporated in a Judgment of Divorce in the Barnstable Division, Probate and Family Court, or as a binding contract in any Court with jurisdiction over the person or property of the other party.

10. **No Requirement of Strict Performance:** The failure of the Husband or of the Wife to comply with or insist in any instance upon the strict performance of any of the terms hereof shall not be construed as a waiver of such term or terms for the future, and the same shall nevertheless continue in full force and effect.

11. **Procedure in the Event a Portion of this Agreement is Later Held to be Invalid:** In the event any party of this Agreement shall be held invalid, such invalidity shall not invalidate the whole Agreement but the remaining provisions of this Agreement shall continue to be valid and binding to the extent that such provisions continue to reflect fairly the intent and understanding of the parties.

Callout boxes:

Sneaky lawyer words!!!

This prevents your husband from claiming there's a NEW agreement if you're a nice guy and let something slide once or twice.

Under English common law, if one part of a contract was deemed invalid, the *entire* contract used to be invalid.

Strict performance clause – most attorney drafted agreements contain language stating the parties are not required to "strictly perform" the separation contract. In general contract law, it is held that if you fail to go to court right away to enforce a business contract every time the other party fails to live up to their end of the bargain, it is the behavior you *allowed*, not what is actually written into the contract, which becomes the new standard of what that contract means. For example, if you are in the habit of paying your homeowners insurance a few weeks after the due date every year and the insurance company doesn't immediately cancel the policy, then one year your house burns down during that 2-week period when the policy has lapsed but you haven't paid the premium yet, the insurance company may have to accept your policy renewal payment and cover the claim. What this case law does is punish you for being a nice, patient person and giving the other person a break. Obviously, when dealing with ordinary people who are dealing with a former spouse, they're not going to have the heart (or the money) to cough up a retainer and head back to court for every single nit-picky breach of contract. In order to empower the court to overlook your reticence to drag your slacker spouse back to court, you *should* include this clause in your Separation Agreement or you may find your overdue alimony gets treated like a homeowners' insurance contract.

Invalidity clause – most attorney-drafted agreements contain a clause stating that if any part of your Separation Agreement is later found to be invalid, it will not cause any other part of the agreement to become invalid. In general contract law, if the law changes about one portion of a business contract, a court could be forced to declare the *entire* contract is null and void. For example, husbands used to have wives sign contracts stating the amount of child support agreed upon in the Separation Agreement could never be modified. This sounded good on the date of divorce, but over time the husband's income would increase, while inflation would erode the value of child support so much it often became almost meaningless. This resulted in many families being forced onto welfare while their former spouses lived luxurious lives. The state responded by passing a law stating child support could not be ceded by private contract. Under traditional contract law, such a change of statute would render your *entire* Separation Agreement null and void and you would have to renegotiate everything all over again!

EXHIBIT 11-P-8: SAMPLE ATTORNEY-DRAFTED PREAMBLE (CONT'D)

12. Choice of State Law. This Agreement shall be construed and governed according to the Laws of the Commonwealth of Massachusetts.

> Even if you move to a different state, this means any modifications you try to make in the future will use this state's laws.

13. Choice of Forum. so long as either party resides in Barnstable County, Massachusetts, the Barnstable County Probate & Family Court shall be the designated forum for all matters.

> You can't later move to a different county and file for modification *there* to get a better deal.

14. Attachments, Addendums and Exhibits. There are annexed hereto and incorporated by reference herein Exhibits A through J. Both Husband and Wife agree to be bound by, and to perform and carry out all the terms of said Exhibits to the same extent as if each was fully set forth in the text of this Agreement.

- A) Exhibit A – Custody and Visitation
- B) Exhibit B – Child Support
- C) Exhibit C – Alimony
- D) Exhibit D – Education
- E) Exhibit E – Health Related Insurance and Expenses
- F) Exhibit F – Division of Assets and Retirement Funds
- G) Exhibit G – Payment of Marital Debts
- H) Exhibit H – Income Taxes
- I) Exhibit I – Legal Fees and Expenses
- J) Exhibit J – Life Insurance

> Always list *everything* you attach to your Separation Agreement or it may be barred later.

15. This Agreement shall not be altered or modified except by an instrument signed and acknowledged by the Husband and Wife and executed before a notary public.

> This mandates a certain level of formality for future agreements so you don't get hoodwinked.

Signed at Barnstable, Massachusetts on this ___14___ day of __February__, 2007. Executed in several counterparts.

Signed on __2/14/2007__   *Jack Rayme*
(Date)   (Husband)

Commonwealth of Massachusetts

Barnstable ___ss___   Date: __2/14/2007__

Then personally appeared the above-named __Jack Rayme__, and acknowledged that - he - XXX - signed this separation agreement as - his - XXX - free act and deed.

____*Nonnie Notary*____
Notary Public- My Commission Expires: __1/11/2011__

> Notarization prevents fraud and also imparts a sense of formality and intent to any agreement.

Signed on __2/14/2007__   *Jane Doe - Rayme*
(Date)   (Wife)
Commonwealth of Massachusetts

Barnstable ___ss___   Date: __2/14/2007__

Then personally appeared the above-named __Jane Doe-Rayme__, and acknowledged that - he - XXX - signed this separation agreement as - his - XXX - free act and deed.

____*Nonnie Notary*____
Notary Public- My Commission Expires: __1/11/2011__

Reference to attached exhibits – if you adopt the common practice of breaking down each separate topic of your agreement into exhibits (such as child custody, alimony, division of assets, etc.), you should note how many exhibits are attached in the main body of the Separation Agreement. Otherwise, your spouse could attempt to come back at some date in the future and claim everything after the notarized signature page has been fabricated. Believe it or not, there is actually case law interpreting the meaning of the staple holes used to attach exhibits or additional pages to a legal agreement). I know of one divorce case where the husband requested to view the main divorce file at the courthouse (a public document), stole evidence out of the case file, then went back to court for modification arguing the exhibits never existed. Cover your backside!!! Always list your attachments.

Notarized signature – you must both sign and date the form in front of a Notary Public, and have that notary affirm your signatures with an embossed seal. Notarization implies a level of formality and seriousness to an agreement. Since September 11, 2001, notaries have gotten a lot pickier about notarizing legal documents without several forms of identification, so be sure you bring plenty with you to the notary's office.

Mediation clauses – some agreements specify the parties will first attempt to mediate future disputes before going back to court. Courts usually *will* enforce a mediation clause unless there is a good reason (such as physical abuse) why they should not, so be careful about agreeing to meet with mediator and giving him binding authority over your case unless you already know you trust that mediator and can also afford his fees. Otherwise, you may find yourself with a large bill and no satisfaction.

EXHIBIT A: BOILERPLATES RELATING TO CUSTODY, VISITATION, AND RELATED MATTERS

The issue of what will happen to your children (if unemancipated) is the single most important item you will address in your divorce. Even if you agree which parent the children will reside with, no area is fraught with more ongoing conflict as the common life decisions you will make from this day forward regarding the care and well-being of your children. Long after the assets are divided and debts paid, disagreements about your children will be a thorn in your side until the day your youngest child graduates from college. A well-crafted Separation Agreement can help you weather those disputes without having to run back to court.

What changes might occur between now and the day you watch your youngest child step onto the stage in their cap and gown? Will you stay in the same house, the same town, the same state? Will you remarry? Have more children? What school will your child attend? Public or private? If one parent wants to send the child to private school the other objects (or can't afford it), who will pay?

Who will get the children for Christmas, Thanksgiving, school vacation week? Who will have the child on their birthday? Mother's day? Father's day? Are you going to want the same holiday schedule every year, or would you rather take turns with major holidays? Do you feel comfortable with your spouse travelling out of state with your children? Out of the country? To nearby states, but not distant ones? What will happen if you wish to take your child on vacation the same week your spouse has their regular visitation?

What will happen if little Johnnie starts having trouble in school, or Susie contracts a terrible illness? Should your spouse be involved in every decision, or just the major ones? How much access should your spouse have to your child's school records? Medical records? Records of private talks with a therapist if they need counseling?

What will happen if *you* think it's important for your child to be involved in as many enrichment activities as possible, but your spouse believes children need time for unstructured play? Who will pay for activities?

If one spouse is angry at the other for divorcing them, they may use ongoing child custody issues to punish you. Abusive men, in particular, have banded together into so-called 'father's rights' groups to teach one another how to misuse child custody issues to control a former (for more information, read Chapter Two). However, I have also seen living proof of the adage 'hell hath no wrath like a woman scorned.' Your spouse is going to want reassurances that *you* won't misuse your children as a way to get back at *him*. A well-crafted agreement can nip problems in the bud.

   Be careful about just checking off boxes on a court's sample agreement!!! It's easy to check off a box such as 'sole' or 'shared' legal custody without understanding what rights you are giving up (or obligations you are taking on).

Exhibit 11-A-1 (the Massachusetts boilerplate) prompts litigants to discuss areas of frequent future disagreement in advance. Hundreds of families go to court every single day to argue about stupid things such as what happens if Father's Day falls on the mothers designated weekend. Discuss it *now* or you'll find you get a less-than-friendly attitude from the judge.

EXHIBIT 11-A-1: SAMPLE COURT "SCHEDULE A – CHILD RELATED MATTERS"

SCHEDULE A - CHILD RELATED MATTERS

LEGAL CUSTODY (which parent(s) make(s) major decisions for the child[ren], for example, health care, religion, education, etc.)

- [X] The parties shall have shared legal custody of the minor child[ren].
- [ ] The Father shall have sole legal custody of the minor child[ren].
- [ ] The Mother shall have sole legal custody of the minor child[ren].
- [ ] _____ shall have legal custody of the minor child[ren].
  (Name of Third Party)

Shared legal custody is the norm absent abuse.

PHYSICAL CUSTODY (where the child[ren] live(s) and which parent makes the day-today decisions regarding the child[ren]).

- [ ] The Father shall have sole physical custody of the minor child[ren].
- [X] The Mother shall have sole physical custody of the minor child[ren].
- [ ] The parties shall have shared physical custody of the minor child[ren] of the parties in accordance with the following schedule: _____
  _____
  _____

- [ ] The parties shall have split physical custody as follows:
  The Mother will have physical custody of _____
  AND
  The Father will have physical custody of _____
- [ ] _____ shall have physical custody of _____
  (Name of Third Party)
  _____

Physical custody – who the child lives with most of the time.

PARENTING SCHEDULE

The Father shall have the right and opportunity to spend time with the child:
- [X] at all reasonable times upon ___*72 hours*___ advance notice
- [ ] upon the following days and times _____
  _____
  _____
  _____

24- to 72-hour notice is the norm

The Mother shall have the right and opportunity to spend time with the child:
- [ ] at all reasonable times upon advance notice
- [ ] on the following days and times: _____

- [X] school holidays shall be shared as follows: *Whoever is scheduled to have the children that day shall have them that holiday unless agreed otherwise.*

- [X] summer vacation shall be as follows: *Dad may take the kids for two one - consecutive weeks every summer from Friday afternoon until the following Sunday after supper.*

- [X] the child[ren]'s birthdays shall be shared as follows: *Mom shall have the children on their birthday, but shall agree upon a day either before or after that day to allow for the father to have his own special celebration with the child.*

- [X] the parties' birthdays shall be shared as follows: *The parties will consult each other and agree upon a time for the children to spend special time with whichever parent has a birthday*

- [X] Mother's Day and Father's Day shall be shared as follows: *the mother shall have the children on Mother's Day and the Father shall have the children on Father's Day.*

- [X] transportation will be provided by: *the father.*

- [ ] the parties will meet to exchange the child[ren] at: _____
  _____

- [ ] any additional provisions: _____

Better to spell it out now rather than go back to court later.

Transportation is usually provided by the person who is taking the children for visitation.

Now here is an attorney-drafted version which has the same custody arrangement (shared legal custody, sole physical custody to Mom). Note that most attorney drafted boilerplates don't spell out the holidays the way the Massachusetts court version does. Couples who divorce amicably usually want this flexibility. However, if your spouse is unreliable or controlling, that may be a mistake. If you feel the need, ask *your* attorney to spell things out for you! If your husband won't agree to things *now,* he *certainly* won't agree to it later! There is a *reason* the version the judges cooked up has birthdays and holidays spelled out!!!

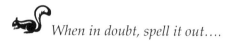 *When in doubt, spell it out….*

EXHIBIT 11-A-2: SAMPLE ATTORNEY-DRAFTED "STANDARD" AGREEMENT WHERE MOM GETS PHYSICAL CUSTODY, MOM & DAD SHARE LEGAL CUSTODY

EXHIBIT A
CUSTODY AND VISITATION

CUSTODY

1. The Husband and Wife shall have joint legal custody of the minor children, <u>Johnnie Rayme and Janie Rayme</u> and shall consult with each other regarding all major, non-ordinary life decisions related to the children.

2. The Wife shall have sole physical custody and the children shall reside with her, except as outlined in the "visitation" section below. She will be responsible for making ordinary day-to-day life decisions regarding the care of the children.

PARENTING PLAN

3. Neither the Husband nor the Wife shall attempt, or condone any attempt, to estrange the children from the other parent or to impede the respect or affection of the children for the other parent, but on the contrary, shall at all times encourage and foster in the children respect and affection for both parents.

4. The parties shall consult in an effort to reach mutual agreement concerning major life matters and decisions, not part of the daily routine of the children, which affect their emotional, psychological, educational, social or physical well-being, including without limitation extraordinary medical, dental and psychological treatment; religious upbringing; educational choices and alternatives, including schools to be attended; whether the children shall attend summer camp, and if so, where and for how long; age appropriateness of social activities and personal pursuits; and, participation in inherently dangerous or hazardous activities. The parties shall attempt to adopt a harmonious policy calculated to promote the welfare and best interests of the children.

5. In the event that the parties, after conferring, are unable to agree upon major life matters and decisions regarding the children, and furthermore, are unable to determine an appropriate schedule for visitation, the parties shall confer with <u>Molly Mediator</u>, or his/her designee, who will act as mediator with respect to any and all disputes over the children. The determination of the mediator shall be binding upon the parties, unless a party determines that on his or her reasonable belief such would not be in the best interest of the children. In such instances, the issue shall be determined by the Justice of the <u>Barnstable</u> Division, Probate and Family Court Department. The fees and costs of the mediator shall be shared equally by both parties, unless the mediator determines otherwise.

6. Each party shall have the right to consult, and have direct access, without further permission of the other parent, to review medical and dental records of the children, consult with experts providing services to the children and with

any educational institution which the children are attending, and to act as custodial parent in order to give authorization for the provision of emergency medical treatment for the children.

7. Each party shall have the authority and responsibility for decisions concerning daily living needs, care and activities of the children when the children are with him or her, all with the context of the provisions set forth in paragraph 4 of this Exhibit A. In the event of any serious illness or accident of a child, the parent with whom the child is then staying will notify the other parent as soon as possible.

VISITATION

8. The Husband may have reasonable visitation with the children in Massachusetts at all times and on a schedule to be agreed upon with the Wife;

9. The parties shall share vacation and holiday time with the children on a flexible basis on a schedule to be agreed upon by the parties, taking into account the desires and schedules of the children.

10. Each party may have the children with him or her during a portion of the summer for uninterrupted vacation time to be agreed upon by the parties.

11. Other than as set forth hereinabove, the children shall reside with the Wife.

12. Each party shall have the right to remove the minor children temporarily from the Commonwealth for the sole purpose of vacationing and/or attending family functions with the minor child. Locations and telephone numbers shall be provided to the other parent in advance of any such travel.

The next example (Exhibit 11-A-3) is a shared physical custody agreement. In this hypothesis, the parents agree to each take the children for one week on a rotating basis and modify a boilerplate to suit their needs. Other shared custody agreements might be drawn up by using a calendar and dividing 50:50 who gets which days.

If your spouse tries to "sell" you a shared physical custody agreement and he has not traditionally been a 50:50 caretaker, refuse. He is probably only doing this to get out of paying child support and will slack off the minute the ink is dry on the agreement, leaving you with all the childrearing duties and no money to do it with. What the following boilerplate does is saddle you with all of the responsibility and expense of being a parent, takes away your right to make even the most routine decisions without your spouse controlling you!!!

Shared Physical Custody ... very bad!

Exhibit 11-A-3: Sample Shared Physical Custody (50:50) Agreement

EXHIBIT A
CUSTODY AND VISITATION

1. The Husband and Wife shall equally share full legal and physical custody of the minor children, Jane Rayme and Johnnie Rayme.

2. Due to the shared physical custody arrangement and the similarity of income between the households, the child support guidelines shall not apply and neither party shall be obligated to pay child support to the other.

3. The Mother shall maintain health insurance for the benefit of the minor children. The Father shall reimburse the mother 50% of all health insurance costs.

4. Both parties shall be reimbursing the other 50% of all uninsured medical, dental, vision, psychiatric and other co-pays within 30 days of a written request (with receipt) from the other parent.

5. Both parties shall consult with the other parent and reach agreement before incurring any extraordinary non-emergency expenses, such as orthodontic care, in order to allow the parties to seek the most cost-effective treatment provider, change insurance plans to one with more appropriate coverage, or set money aside in an employer-sponsored Flexible Spending Account. (keeping in mind that such planning may incur delays as great as the end of the next enrollment period). Neither parent shall unreasonably withhold agreement regarding treatment.

6. Each party shall be responsible for child care on their scheduled day and times with the children. Should one parent pre-pay the cost of said child care (for example, tuition at a preschool), the other shall reimburse them their portion of said tuition as soon as incurred and due.

VISITATION PLAN

7. The Husband shall have the children on even weeks from Friday afternoon immediately following school until the following Friday immediately before school. If the Husband's week should fall upon a school vacation week or holiday, then the exchange will take place at 12:00 noon or another mutually agreeable time;

8. The Wife shall have the children on odd weeks from Friday afternoon immediately following school until the following Friday immediately before school. If the Wife's week should fall upon a school vacation week or holiday, then the exchange will take place at 12:00 noon or another mutually agreeable time.

9. Each parent is responsible for providing the appropriate supervision and bearing the cost of any additional child care which may be necessary during their scheduled week.

10. The parties shall share vacation and holidays with the children on a flexible basis on a schedule to be agreed upon by the parties, taking into account the desires and schedules of the children.

11. Each party may have the children with him or her during a portion of the summer for uninterrupted vacation time to be agreed upon by the parties.

12. Each party shall have the right to remove the minor children temporarily form the Commonwealth for the sole purpose of vacationing and/or attending family functions with the minor child. Locations and telephone numbers shall be provided to the other parent in advance of any such travel.

In this example, child support has been waived, but sometimes a court will order at least some child support to equal out the standard of living in both homes.

Most states expect whichever parent has health insurance to cover the kids and will either tweak child support, or have the other parent pay half

The parties are expected to cooperate on unusual expenses, such as orthodontics, but can't escape needed care simply by withholding agreement.

Usually you pay for child care needs that occur on your watch.

Always be skeptical about a proposed 50:50 shared physical custody agreement.

EXHIBIT B: CHILD SUPPORT

All states have statutory formulas known as child support guidelines which will usually be the amount you fill in on this form (see Chapter Five: Child Support). Occasionally, courts may vary from the formula. If you agree to Shared Physical Custody (50:50), the court might also deviate from the formula to waive child support completely, waive all child support except for 50% of the cost of providing medical and dental insurance, waive child support but order the daycare bill be divided equally, order an amount of child support sufficient to equalize the standard of living between the two households, or some combination of all these. Judges try to balance fairness in parenting time with the necessity of children not getting shuffled between an affluent and an impoverished household. Occasionally, a court will agree to shared physical custody, but order child support according to the guidelines anyways. This is often done when the judge suspects the Husband obtained a 50:50 custody agreement through threats or coercion and/or suspects the Husband will disappear the moment the ink is dry on the divorce decree.

EXHIBIT 11-B-1: SAMPLE "CHILD SUPPORT" PORTION OF COURT'S "SCHEDULE A - CHILD RELATED MATTERS"

CHILD SUPPORT

Starting on _2_ / _14_ / _2007_ the ___father___ shall pay child support as follows:
     (insert Date)   (Mother / Father)

The sum of $ _250.00_ each and every ___week___
                              (week – two weeks – month)

by Wage Assignment which (choose ONE):

☐   shall be payable directly_____and will be SUSPENDED
                                        (Mother / Father)

                                   OR

X   shall be payable through DOR and implemented IMMEDIATELY

> Always have your state Child Enforcement Division collect your child support *for* you!!!

The parties acknowledge that the child support order which would result from the application of the Child Support Guidelines is $ _250.00_ per week.

☐   The agreed amount of support is different than the Guidelines amount because:
_____
_____
_____

Child support shall terminate:
☐   upon the youngest child having attained the age of eighteen (18) years.
X   Upon the emancipation of the youngest child _____
_____
_____

> In some states child support might continue through college, in others, not.

Child support for a child or children over the age of eighteen who are principally domiciled with one parent and dependent upon the parents for support:
☐   Shall continue at the above rate until_____
☐   Shall increase to $_____ and terminate_____
☐   Shall decrease to $_____ and terminate_____
X   Shall be determined by the Court at that time by filing a Complaint for Modification

Emancipation – the day your child is considered mature enough to provide their *own* upkeep. Depending upon state, may be the day he turns 18 and finishes high school, or the day she finishes her undergraduate education or turns 23, whichever occurs first.

To avoid confusion in case either you or your spouse move to another state, define *emancipation* in your Separation Agreement.

School Fees and Extracurricular Activities – the Child Support Guidelines assume child support covers the cost of extracurricular activities and school fees. Unfortunately, after several decades of 'education reform' parents now find themselves facing all manner of fees thought unthinkable by their parents, including bus fees, parking fees, sports fees, textbook fees, even fees to buy pencils and paper for the class. Most Child Support Guidelines do not adequately adjust for this reality, resulting in an unfair burden on the custodial parent. Therefore, many attorney negotiated agreements include language to address school fees and activities.

Child Care Expenses – this is another area where outdated child support formulae shortchange the custodial parent. The presumption of the court is that child support includes the cost of the custodial parent paying daycare so they can work. Unfortunately, child support is usually inadequate to either meet the children's living expenses or allow the mother to pay daycare so she can work to make up the difference. Either way, the custodial parent gets slammed. Many mothers compensate by working on days their spouse has visitation (such as weekends). To discourage your spouse from becoming too flakey to show up on time (so you can go to work) or blow off their weekend with the kids to take off with their new girlfriend (preventing you from working), it is good practice to spell out that the person scheduled to have the children is responsible for providing daycare.

EXHIBIT 11-B-2: SAMPLE ATTORNEY-DRAFTED CHILD SUPPORT BOILERPLATE

EXHIBIT B
CHILD SUPPORT

1. Commencing on the first day of the month after the execution of this Agreement, and continuing on the first day of each month thereafter for so long as the Wife is receiving alimony under the terms of this Agreement, the Husband shall pay two hundred fifty dollars ($250.00) per week to the Wife as child support, with said payments to be offset by the Husband from the amount of alimony paid to the Wife as set forth in Exhibit C. Upon termination of alimony, the parties shall confer with regard to the issue of further child support, if any, until the emancipation of the children, taking into account the parties' contributions to educational costs as set forth in Exhibit D.

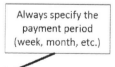

Always specify the payment period (week, month, etc.)

2. Child support shall be collected via wage assignment via the Massachusetts Department of Revenue.

3. As outlined in Exhibit E – Medical Insurance, the Husband shall maintain health insurance through his employer for so long as it is available to him, for the benefit of the children so long as the children are unemancipated, as that term is defined herein (see Exhibit E). Health insurance premiums have been included in computation of the Child Support Guidelines.

> Medical insurance is a big issue!

4. Emancipation with respect to the minor children shall occur or mean to have occurred on the earliest happening of the following:

   a. Obtaining the age of 18 years or graduation from high school, however, no later than obtaining age 20, whichever occurs later, unless the child has plans for future education as a full-time student, as set forth below.

   b. If the child is attending a post-secondary accredited educational training school or a two year or four year accredited college program as a full time student, at age 23 or the completion of such school or college, whichever occurs sooner. The child shall not be deemed emancipated the summer between completion of high school and beginning of said post-secondary training, or for a period of educational travel of up to one year.

   > *Emancipation* should be spelled out according to your local state guidelines, which may vary..

   c. Death or marriage of the child.

   d. Permanent residency away from the residence of the Wife. Residency at boarding school, camp or college is not to be deemed as residence away from the Wife.

   e. Engaging in full-time employment after the age of 18 except that full-time employment during vacation and summer periods shall not be deemed emancipation. Such emancipation shall be deemed to terminate upon cessation by the child for any reason of full-time employment; thereafter, emancipation shall be determined in accordance with other applicable provisions of this paragraph.

   f. A child shall not be deemed to be emancipated if she is disabled and dependent upon the Wife.

5. The Wife shall be entitled to claim the children as dependents for state and federal income tax purposes, and the Husband agrees that he shall not so claim the children, except if the Wife does not derive a tax benefit from such exemptions, in which case the Husband may take the exemptions. In such event the Wife shall sign all such forms necessary for the Husband to claim such dependency exemption. The Wife shall be entitled to claim head of household status for tax purposes, and the parties acknowledge she is entitled to do so.

> Who gets to claim the kids as tax dependents is one of those areas that usually drives couples back to court!!!

6. Husband and Wife agree to divide the cost of all ordinary public school fees, such as school bus rider fees, school-sponsored sports fees, school-sponsored music or instrument fees, classroom and text book fees, school-sponsored "club" fees, and school supplies, evenly (50:50).

> Most states assume the custodial parent pays out of child support unless you spell this out!!!

7. Husband and Wife agree to consult with each other about fees for activities which are not sponsored by or traditionally considered part of a public education, such as private lessons at a location other than the school. The parties agree to split the fees 50:50 for one (1) mutually-agreed upon non-school-sponsored activity and neither party shall unreasonably withhold consent for said activity. Should the children desire to enroll in a second non-school-sponsored activity, the parties shall consult on the matter and, should one party not wish to help pay for said additional activity, there will be no obligation to do so. The Husband's obligation to sponsor non-school-sponsored activities shall be capped at $500 per year.

8. Each parent shall be responsible for providing and/or paying the cost of child care or babysitting on days and at times when the children are scheduled to be with them.

> Spell out cost of child care.

EXHIBIT C: ALIMONY BOILERPLATES

There are two common Alimony scenarios you tend to see memorialized in Separation Agreements. The first occurs when the couple has been married long enough to trigger an alimony review and both parties recognize this. In that situation, the attorneys will usually agree upon a figure which they believe, based on their experience in front of that particular judge, the court would order if the case were to go to trial and craft an agreement based on that consensus. The second occurs when the parties either wish to waive alimony, often because one spouse wishes to trade an asset for the cash value of that alimony payout over time, or because the parties were not married long enough for one spouse to be obligated to the other to pay it.

Exhibit 11-C-1 covers situations you might see in a mid-term marriage where there are un-emancipated children living with the Wife, but she expects to be able to go back to work and support herself on her own once she is no longer tasked with raising the children. In most cases, child support will be deducted from alimony so that the Husband is not paying twice. In other words, you collect the larger of the two amounts, but for tax purposes the Agreement specifies which is alimony and which is child support because the IRS taxes them differently. In the sample exhibit, we presume $475/week in alimony is due to the Wife, but in reality she can only collect $225/week alimony (which she has to pay taxes on) and $250 per week in child support (which her husband has to pay taxes on). Review Chapter Six: Alimony to refresh your memory about common alimony situations.

EXHIBIT 11-C-1: SAMPLE COURT ALIMONY BOILERPLATE

ALIMONY

☐ Each party hereby waives past and present alimony from the other and reserves the matter of future alimony for consideration by the Court

☐ Each party hereby waives past, present, and future alimony from the other.

X The __Husband__ shall pay to the __Wife__ the sum of $ __225.00__
　(Husband/Wife) (Husband/Wife)
each and every week, beginning - __2__ / __14__ / __2007__ , as alimony. Payments of alimony shall end:

　☐ on ____ / ____ / ____
　X when the following event(s) occur(s): __the youngest child becomes emancipated__

> This court version fails to mention anything about a child support offset from alimony (it is implied). Why fight about it? Spell it out!

Generally, alimony automatically ends when the Wife remarries. What is not generally clear is what happens when the Wife cohabitates with a new boyfriend but doesn't get married in order to retain the right to continue to receive alimony. Obviously, your former Husband doesn't want to continue to pay alimony if you are getting help paying the overhead by somebody else. However, in this day of transient relationships, do you really want to give up the security of a steady alimony check for a boyfriend who may or may not eventually marry you? Your husband's attorney will insist you sign an agreement stating alimony ends upon cohabitation, but you should refuse to sign it lest you end up with an ex-husband perpetually following you around with a camera to 'prove' your new boyfriend spends enough time at your house to qualify as a cohabitant.

EXHIBIT 11-C-2: SAMPLE GENERIC ALIMONY OBLIGATION BOILERPLATE

EXHIBIT C

ALIMONY

1. Commencing on the first day of the month after the execution of this Agreement, and continuing on the first day of each month thereafter until the first to occur of the terminating events set forth herein below, the Husband shall pay nine hundred seventy five ($975.00) Dollars per month ($11,690.00 per year) to the Wife as alimony, net of the child support offset of $546.00 per month set forth in paragraph 3 of this Exhibit C.

2. Said payments shall be made in cash and shall terminate on the first to occur of the death of the Wife, the death of the Husband, the remarriage or cohabitation of the Wife, or the Wife's 45th birthday on July 17, 2020.

3. The parties recognize that an additional $546.00 per month in alimony is being offset in satisfaction of the Husband's child support obligations set forth in Exhibit B, paragraph 1 of this agreement.

4. For income tax purposes, only those portions of alimony which are not being offset in satisfaction of the Husband's child support obligation shall be taxable to the Wife, or $225.00 per month.

5. The amount of the alimony payments set forth in this Exhibit C has been determined on the basis of currently prevailing federal and state income tax laws, rules and regulations, with the intention and understanding that all payments made pursuant to the above paragraphs 1 and 2 of this Exhibit C, qualify as alimony payments for income tax purposes, as those terms are defined in Section 71 and any other applicable section of the United States Internal Revenue Code as amended and M.G.L. c.62 as amended, each as in effect as of the date of the execution of this Agreement. Accordingly, such alimony payment shall be deductible to the Husband and taxable to the Wife. In the event of any change of the rules, rulings or regulations of the Internal Revenue Service, or in the event of subsequent statutory amendment, judicial or administrative order or decision contrary to this result, the amount payable pursuant to this provision shall be

This example spells out that although alimony *should* be $975/month, $546 of that is being counted towards the husband's child support obligation.

Alimony usually ends when either party dies, the Wife remarries, or moves in with a boyfriend. Resist signing a "cohabitation" clause, but a judge may order it anyways.

Since our hypothetical couple has only been married 12 years and the Wife probably won't qualify for lifetime alimony, they have compromised by agreeing to end alimony in 6 years, a period equal to half the length of the marriage.

This agreement spells out how much alimony is being offset and counted as child support, and to whom the tax burden of each amount falls to.

This is tax mumbo-jumbo. Very important! The *recipient* usually pays the taxes on alimony received unless agreed otherwise!

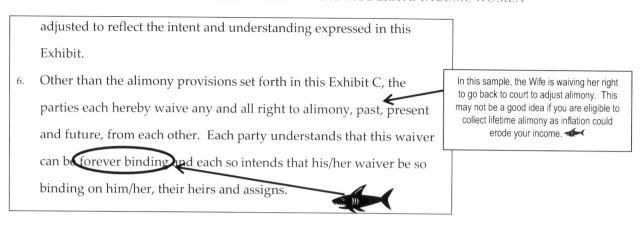

adjusted to reflect the intent and understanding expressed in this Exhibit.

6.   Other than the alimony provisions set forth in this Exhibit C, the parties each hereby waive any and all right to alimony, past, present and future, from each other. Each party understands that this waiver can be forever binding and each so intends that his/her waiver be so binding on him/her, their heirs and assigns.

In this sample, the Wife is waiving her right to go back to court to adjust alimony. This may not be a good idea if you are eligible to collect lifetime alimony as inflation could erode your income.

Exhibit 11-C-3 is a good boilerplate to use if you have not been married long enough to trigger an alimony review, or if you decide to waive alimony in exchange for other assets you desire more than a monthly check.   Just remember, if you waive alimony and state it 'survives as a separate contract,' there is no going back to ask for it later. If you are unsure, don't sign a waiver unless it states it 'merges with the divorce and does *not* survive as a separate contract' and make sure you note that fact a second time in the Preamble of the Agreement. A mutually binding alimony waiver can sometimes *benefit* the former wife if her husband works in an industry (such as construction) where he could later become injured and disabled. It won't block a court from ordering alimony, but they are much less likely to do so than if you didn't include this verbiage at all.

▶ *Separation Agreements MEAN it when they say forever binding!* If there is one place to spend scant financial resources on legal advice, it is your Separation Agreement!!!

EXHIBIT 11-C-3: SAMPLE WAIVED ALIMONY CLAUSE

EXHIBIT C

ALIMONY

1.   The parties each hereby waive any and all right to alimony; past present and future; from each other. Each party understands that this waiver can be forever binding and each so intends that his or her waiver be so binding on him or her, their heirs and assigns.

Once you waive alimony in a clause such as this, it is waived forever with very few exceptions.

2.   The issue of alimony shall not merge with the divorce, but shall survive and retain independent legal significance as a separate contract.

Review "survival clause" in Chapter 10, "sneaky lawyer words."

Exhibit 11-C-4 is good to use in situations where you don't need alimony badly enough to bother with the expense of trial and your spouse is dangling a juicy enough property settlement that you are willing to waive it, but issues with your health mean you would like the option of going back to court if something really terrible happens (such as that vague tingling in your legs turns out to be Multiple Sclerosis). This sample lists a statutory exception to a survival clause and acknowledges there may be other, limited exceptions that could arise in the future. Note that this sample does *not* contain verbiage stating it survives as a separate contract. Although it will still be a very high hurdle to drag your spouse back to court and get a modification, this boilerplate leaves the door open a crack.

EXHIBIT 11-C-4: SAMPLE WAIVED ALIMONY, EXCEPTIONS TO SURVIVAL CLAUSE

EXHIBIT C

ALIMONY

1. Husband and Wife agree and acknowledge that the Wife has had the training, background and experience to provide fully for her own support, not only for the present, but for the future. Accordingly, and in consideration of the terms of this Agreement, the Wife agrees and hereby waives any and all right she may have, past, present and future, to alimony or support under the laws of the Commonwealth of Massachusetts or any other jurisdiction as they are now written.

2. Husband and Wife agree and acknowledge that the Husband has had the training, background and experience to provide fully for his own support, not only for the present, but for the future. Accordingly, and in consideration of the terms of this Agreement, the Husband agrees and hereby waives any and all right he may have, past, present and future, to alimony or support under the laws of the Commonwealth of Massachusetts or any other jurisdiction as they are now written.

3. Husband and Wife acknowledge that despite the afore-stated waivers of alimony, under the laws of the Commonwealth of Massachusetts, under certain circumstances the Court may enter an order of alimony in the future. For example, if either party becomes substantially or totally disabled and is dependent upon the state for support, upon application, the Court may consider the awarding of alimony provisions in this agreement.

This sample points out that the parties *should* theoretically be able to support themselves.

Both parties waive alimony against the other, but notice the absence of a "survival" clause.

This sample lists disability as one possible cause of overturning the waiver and hints there may be other reasons, but undoing this waiver would be a very high hurdle.

EXHIBIT D: BOILERPLATES ADDRESSING THE CHILDREN'S EDUCATION

The threshold question to ask is 'do we reside in a state that obligates divorced parents to provide for their child's college education?' The second question is, if not, do we wish to spell it out anyways? If the answer is 'no,' then this boilerplate can simply be omitted. This section will proceed from here on forward as if either you *are* legally obligated or you *do* wish to spell things out.

If you were to gaze into a crystal ball to see your child's future, you might see your child graduating with a full scholarship to Harvard University. On the other hand, he could thwart your best intentions by dropping out of high school the day he turns sixteen to join a cult. Most likely, your child will struggle through high school with average grades and attend the first decent college which will accept him. With tuition, fees, room and board averaging $30,000 per year, how can you budget for it?

Separation Agreements covering every possible outcome are impossible to draft, especially with spiraling tuition costs and unknown eligibility in the future for financial aid. Tuition varies from several thousand dollars per year to commute to a local community college to six-figure tuition bills to live in the dormitory of an out-of-state ivy-league school. It is even more difficult to predict when you have little control over which school your child chooses to attend.

In states that *do* require both parents to contribute to a child's college education, courts expect both parents to share the cost of college, but they usually temper that situation with reality. What 'reality' means varies from state to state, but a good benchmark is often the in-state tuition rate for a local state university or college within your own home state. Most states that include the cost to live in a dormitory, but some presume your child will live at home and commute. College costs include meals, tuition, fees and books.

If your child is eligible for financial aid, that amount is deducted from the amount parents are expected to pay. Unfortunately, courts have different opinions about whether or not college work studies or federally subsidized student loans constitute "financial aid." If one parent is impoverished, the other parent will be expected to pick up the slack. Tuition is frequently divided in proportion to the parents' income at the time the child goes off to college. If you are *both* indigent, the court may order both parents to pay whatever they can towards tuition, but it would then be up to your child to find a way to finance their own education.

In some states it is possible to still collect child support while your child is away at college. However, many courts will limit your former husbands total obligation (college + child support + any alimony he may owe) to no more than 30%-50% of his income so he has enough money left over to support himself.

Every year, there are several publications which rate the "bang for your buck" that you can get from colleges, both public and private, including Consumer Reports. Start talking to your child early about college expectations so they understand what you (and your spouse) are willing to pay for and what you are not. Research "bang for buck" ratings *with* them and help them make good decisions. Having attended classes at both "prestigious" and "budget" colleges, I can attest the only real difference between the quality of classes was who you rubbed elbows with (Nellie Rockyfellow vs. Joe Schmoe). Don't fill your child's head with notions of a free ride to Harvard, but don't discourage them from going there, either, if they are willing to take out loans to make up the difference of what Mom and Dad can afford.

The Massachusetts sample agreement is silent about future education, relying upon whatever the whim of the legislature and case law is when your child is finally ready to go. This is not a wise choice as getting to college takes much planning and saving. A change in case law or statutory amendment could deep-six your child's lifelong education plans (as well as your finances) at the last moment.

Unlike child support agreements, courts *will* tend to enforce agreements outlining how to pay for college. Exhibit 11-D-1 includes verbiage many attorneys like to include in their draft agreements.

EXHIBIT 11-D-1: SAMPLE BOILERPLATE ADDRESSING THE CHILDREN'S EDUCATION

EXHIBIT D
EDUCATION

1. The Husband and Wife agree that the children should receive the most appropriate educations available to them in light of their developing aptitudes and interests, including education at the college level, and public or private school education, as needed and appropriate. Both parties recognize that the educations of the children will require substantial financial expenditure.

   This is an aspirational statement which leaves the issue of which college the children attend to a future date.

2. The Husband and Wife may utilize funds from any Educational Trusts (such as 529 Plans, Education IRA's, or Education U.S. Savings Bonds) they set up for the benefit of the children to pay for college expenses at any college the children may choose to attend, for up to four years of undergraduate studies.

   Most moderate-income people don't have much money to set aside for their children's education, but occasionally parents may set a bit of money aside in savings bonds or have relatives who set up a 529 Plan on their children's behalf.

3. Any Education Trusts set up by the parents or his or her relatives subsequent to this divorce to fund the children's education shall be applied against that parents' share of the children's educational expenses.

   Noting how trust money shall be applied eliminates fears about being penalized for planning for your children's while your spouse does not.

4. For the purposes of this Exhibit, the term "expenses" shall include tuition, board, room, books, usual and normal student activity fees and any other expenses shall be benchmarked to those normally charged at the University of Massachusetts, Amherst, and a reasonable allowance for transportation to and from such institution.

   This definition of 'expenses' is a good benchmark. Name YOUR state's flagship in-state university.

5. In the event the educational expenses of the un-emancipated children exceed the amounts available in the trusts, the parties shall be responsible for payment of any additional amounts (not to include graduate or professional school), to the extent they are then financially able to do so and in proportion to their then assets and incomes from all sources (not to include income from new spouses).

   It is a good idea to exclude income from new spouses as nothing will cause your new marriage to fall apart faster than having your new husband get ordered to essentially cough up for your snotty teenager who refuses to give him the time of day.

EXHIBIT E: BOILERPLATES DICTATING WHO PROVIDES HEALTH INSURANCE AND PAYS UNINSURED HEALTH-RELATED BILLS

The court wants you to keep yourselves and your children insured. Here are some general presumptions that apply in *most* states:

1. Most states allow you to stay on your spouse's employer-sponsored health insurance even after you get divorced. Guidelines vary from state-to-state. You will need to either split the cost of the policy, or pay the difference between the individual plan and the family plan.

   a. If you already have a plan for yourself and/or your children, but your spouse is not on that plan, the court will usually order you to sign them up. Your spouse usually has to reimburse you 50% of the total plan cost.

2. If you have children, whichever parent has health insurance available to them *must* insure the children for so long as those children remain unemancipated. It does not matter whether you have chosen to remain uninsured up until this point because you cannot afford it. If it is available, the court will probably order you to sign everybody up because, otherwise, the taxpayers foot the bill.

   a. The parent who does not have health insurance will be ordered to pay a percentage of the premiums (usually 50%) and have it adjusted within the child support. This presumption is contained in most Child Support Guidelines (see Chapter Five).

   b. Many child support guidelines presume the custodial parent will pay the first $100 to $250 of all uninsured health expenses and co-pays unless you insist on dividing all unreimbursed medical, dental, and vision expenses 50:50 in your Separation Agreement.

3. If you don't have a plan available to you through work but you live in a state which has an 'insurance pool connector' plan, the court will likely order you to sign yourselves and/or your children up. Your spouse will have to reimburse you 50% of the children's premiums, but you will each be expected to pay for your *own* plan.

4. If you remarry, you will be kicked off of your former spouse's health plan. If your spouse remarries, you will be dropped off of his medical plan. Your children have the right to stay on the plan whether or not one of you remarries.

5. If one of you gets a new job, loses your health benefits, or the other spouse becomes entitled to participate in a more cost-effective medical plan, you can go back to court on a Complaint for Modification to change things. Don't delay doing this or you will be stuck footing any extra expenses! It is best to write this presumption of change into your Separation Agreement.

6. Health insurance *may* include dental and vision insurance plans as well, depending upon what your state considers 'insurance.' Make sure you spell out each type of plan in your Agreement.

   Research your health care needs *before* entering negotiations for your Separation Agreement . The law keeps changing. By the time you read this chapter, it will probably be outdated!

Our first boilerplate relates to coverage for you and your spouse. Our hypothetical couple (Jane and Jack) do not have affordable health coverage available through *either* of their employers. Massachusetts has a state-sponsored 'connector' plan which matches uninsured people with 'affordable' coverage. Jack and Jane will each be responsible for paying their own co-pays and uninsured medical bills. The following boilerplate is usually adequate for young divorcing couples in good health with no children, but it could prove problematic if one spouse is disabled, has medical issues, or if the entire family is covered on an employer-sponsored 'family plan.'

EXHIBIT 11-E-1: SAMPLE COURT "HEALTH INSURANCE FOR THE PARTIES" BOILERPLATE

HEALTH INSURANCE FOR PARTIES

The Wife's health insurance coverage will be provided:

X   by the Wife

☐   by the Husband

☐   by the Husband for so long as it is available to him, and if there is any additional cost to continued coverage for the insurance:

_____

_____

> Each party buys their *own* insurance. Note that this boilerplate does not mention dental, vision, or other health related plans.

The Husband's health insurance coverage will be provided:

X   by the Husband

☐   by the Wife

☐   by the Wife for so long as it is available to her, and if there is any additional cost to continued coverage for the insurance:

_____

_____

> If one of the parties has a family plan available through work, they should check off the third box and write verbiage such as "the Wife will reimburse the husband 50% of the cost of the family plan" or other language appropriate to the situation.

The cost of all reasonable uninsured and unreimbursed medical, dental, hospital, optical, prescription medication and therapeutic counseling services for the Wife shall be paid:

X   by the Wife

☐   _____% by Wife;

☐   _____% by Husband

The cost of all reasonable uninsured and unreimbursed medical, dental, hospital, optical, prescription medication and therapeutic counseling services for the Husband shall be paid:

X   by the Husband

☐   _____% by Wife;

☐   _____% by Husband

> Each adult is generally expected to pay their own uninsured health care related expenses and co-pays.

The part of your Separation Agreement involving health care coverage is an important provision. A guide has been developed by Health Law Advocates (HLA) and the Massachusetts Attorney General's Office to inform divorce litigants of their health insurance rights and options. "Staying Healthy: A Guide to Keeping Health Insurance After Divorce" is available at the Probate Court or on the internet at www.hla-inc.org/public/staying health02.pdf.

> This court boilerplate refers you to a website to learn more information.

If you have children, the Sample court boilerplate covers this information in a completely different section, their 'Schedule A: Child Related Matters.' The court lists it separately because Massachusetts law requires the court to order medical coverage along with the child support order and including it there is the simplest way for the judge to remember. Be wary that *your* state court boilerplate may leave unresolved issues which you will end up fighting about and probably going back to court about later. If you are relying upon a state-court boilerplate, attach an addendum with any terms the boilerplate leaves unresolved.

$ *Ka-ching!!!* If you don't spell out uninsured medical costs, you will need to cough up $1500 to hire a lawyer and run back to court every time your kid scrapes a knee! Spell it out!!!

EXHIBIT 11-E-2: SAMPLE COURT "SCHDEULE A - MEDICAL INSURANCE FOR CHILDREN" BOILERPLATE

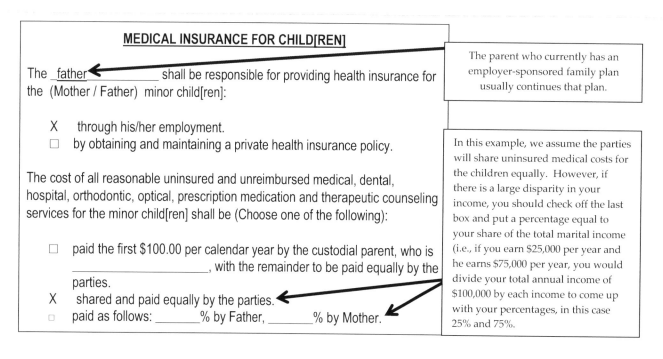

Most attorney drafted health plan agreements fill in many of the gaps left in the courts sample boilerplate. The courts boilerplate does not address what happens when one spouse gets remarried and loses coverage for the other one. Does your spouse still have to provide health insurance for you (or you for him), or is it up to you to now go find your own health plan? If you rely on the court agreement, a judge could decide either way. Why leave it to chance? Even if you enlist the services of a lawyer, ultimately it is up to *you* to make sure your health needs get met. Although the general presumption is that you (an adult) will pay your own unreimbursed medical bills (unless you contract otherwise), things get really dicey when they involve health expenses for your children.

Everybody can agree that if your child gets sick or injured, of course the right thing to do is run to the emergency room and worry about paying the bills later. However, what happens if your child needs braces? Should one parent have the right to unilaterally sign the most expensive orthodontic contract in the nation and bind the other to pay whatever percentage they agreed to? Or should the parents put their heads together and find ways to minimize the expense? What happens if your Husband buys little Susie a $400 pair of prescription designer eyeglasses and she immediately loses them (the third pair this year)? Should you have some say as to whether those glasses get replaced with another pair Ralph Lauren's (at half your expense), or a pair off the $50 rack? An attorney-drafted agreement can fill in some of these unknowns, but be wary that many Bar Association boilerplates aren't much more specific about addressing these pitfalls than the courts boilerplate. When in doubt, spell it out!!!

EXHIBIT 11-E-3: SAMPLE ATTORNEY BOILERPLATE ON HEALTH INSURANCE AND EXPENSES

EXHIBIT E

MEDICAL INSURANCE

1. The Husband shall maintain health, dental, and vision insurance through his employer for so long as it is available to him, for the benefit of the children so long as the children are unemancipated, as that term is defined herein. See Exhibit B, Item 3.

2. The Husband shall maintain health, dental and vision insurance through his employer for so long as it is available to him, for the benefit of the Wife until her death or remarriage, as long as coverage is available for her without additional cost or premium in excess of that which the Husband was required to pay to maintain such coverage for himself and the unemancipated children. If there is an additional cost or premium, the Wife shall reimburse the Husband for said cost as each payment becomes due. In the event the Husband remarries and thereby affects the Wife's eligibility for continued coverage, the Wife shall have the right, pursuant to Massachusetts General Laws chapter 175 and other applicable law, to continue to receive benefits as are available to the Husband by any means then available, including by rider to the existing policy or conversion to an individual policy, which would have benefits reasonably equivalent to those which she would be receiving pursuant to this Exhibit E paragraph 2, had the Husband not remarried.

    > This verbiage spells out what happen if insurance costs increase. Although most employers only offer an option of a single plan or a full-blown family plan, if you only have one child an employer may offer a less expensive 'employee +1' plan. If so, you'll be expected to pay more to stay on his plan.

3. In the event that continued coverage for the Wife subsequent to the remarriage of the Husband results in an additional cost or premium as defined herein and the Wife elects to continue such coverage, then the Wife shall pay the additional cost or premium incurred as a result of her election as each payment comes due. If the Wife elects to continue such coverage, the Husband shall cooperate with her in making the necessary arrangements for, and shall execute any documents necessary to effectuate the continuation of said coverage. In addition to any obligation imposed by applicable law upon the insurer to notify the Wife of cancellation of coverage, the Husband shall notify the Wife within 30 days after becoming aware of any circumstances which would affect her eligibility for, the availability of, or the nature of her continued health insurance coverage.

    > If the insured Husband remarries, you will be kicked off his medical plan. The burden is usually then on *you* to pay for future coverage. However, if you had a long-term marriage, consult with an attorney. You *may* be able to get him to buy you a new plan.

4. Each party shall be responsible for paying his/her own uninsured medical, dental, vision, psychiatric, orthodontic, prescription and hospital expenses.

    > Adults paying their own expenses is the norm.

5. The Husband and Wife shall divide all uninsured medical and psychiatric expenses for the children equally, with either parent being obligated to reimburse the other parent 50% of the bill upon request. To request reimbursement, the payor should provide a photocopy and written request to the other spouse. The

    > In this scenario, the parents agree to split unreimbursed medical expenses 50:50.

    > Spell it out!!! Most contempt cases are because people don't!

payee spouse shall then be obligated to reimburse the payor spouse within 30 days.

6. All uninsured dental and vision expenses of the children shall be divided in proportion to the parties income, with the Husband being obligated to pay two-thirds (67%) of all unreimbursed dental and vision expenses and the Wife being obligated to pay one-third (33%). If one parent pays, the other is obligated to pay their share upon request as outlined in Item 5 above.

> This party agreed to divide children's dental/vision expenses in proportion to their income, or 1/3rd to 2/3rd.

7. The parties agree to consult with one another and attempt to minimize all non-emergency dental and vision expenses by comparing policy coverage, plan limits, providers, the availability of flexible health spending accounts, and less expensive alternatives to all non-emergency proposed treatment. Neither party shall, however, use this Item to unreasonably withhold consent to provide appropriate dental or vision care for the children. The purpose of this Item is to encourage budgeting and planning, not denial of care.

> If you could have saved a significant amount of money had your spouse consulted you before beginning treatment, it *might* give you an opportunity to reduce the portion you are 'on the hook' for.

8. The Husband and Wife may pay their share of all uninsured medical, dental, vision and other health-related expenses of the children from any health care trust funds they may set up (such as flexible spending accounts) to make said payments, with any tax advantages realized by utilizing such trusts flowing to the party who does the planning and saving. Husband and Wife shall share information about anticipated and upcoming expenses and time any proposed non-emergency treatment so that both parties may budget accordingly.

> This avoids penalizing a responsible parent who saves and plans for the children's health needs.

9. If one or all of the children require orthodontic care, the parties shall jointly consult with area orthodontists and review all available dental insurance plans to minimize the cost of providing such care. If, for example, one party has available a slightly more expensive plan which would justify its cost by covering a larger portion of treatment after a reasonable waiting period, the couple may agree to change insurance plans, modify insurance reimbursement to the other spouse, and wait until the new coverage eligibility requirements are met before proceeding with the child's orthodontic regimen. This includes time for one party to leverage tax benefits for an employer-sponsored flexible spending account. All unreimbursed orthodontic expenses shall be divided in proportion to the parties income, with the Husband being obligated to pay two-thirds (67%) of all unreimbursed dental and vision expenses and the Wife being obligated to pay one-third (33%). If one parent pays, the other is obligated to pay their share upon request as outlined in Item 5 above.

> Orthodontic care is rarely an emergency. Waiting a year to plan and save will rarely affect the outcome. Since orthodontic care costs vary widely and different dental plans offer different coverage, mandating the parties to consult and plan avoids the unpleasant surprise of being handed a $7,000 bill.

10. The parties agree that, from time to time, they shall compare all medical, dental, and vision plans which may be available to them through their employers or other sources and discuss what cost, coverage, and co-pay schedules would be most beneficial to them and the minor children. If health, dental, vision or other insurance premiums increase or another plan becomes available at a lower rate or which provides better coverage, the parties may reach a new agreement regarding reimbursement for their share of said costs or file a Complaint for Modification to address this issue in the Barnstable Division of the Probate and Family Court.

> Give yourself the right to go back to court to change plans if something else becomes available. With coverage and premiums changing every year, you want to give yourself flexibility.

Our last example is an unusual one. What happens if the Wife is eligible to receive alimony, but would prefer to take a bigger chunk of the property settlement instead of a monthly check? Simply waiving alimony could put her right to also receive health insurance from her former spouse at risk because, normally, if her spouse remarries, she will get kicked off his plan and has no recourse. This happens a lot when parties are nearing retirement age and the Husband wishes to cash out his pension and take an early retirement, or when an older Wife has been "traded in" for a younger model and the husband is planning on marrying his mistress the moment the ink is dry on the divorce decree. Normally, a former Wife can continue coverage at her own expense on COBRA for 36 months, but COBRA is ridiculously expensive and after 36 months she will find herself uninsured. Spelling out that the Wife is waiving her right to receive alimony, but not other rights that normally accompany that right can help protect her from losing coverage. Exhibit 11-E-4 is one possible agreement parties might reach to address this situation, though not the only one as caselaw interpretations of this right vary wildly.

EXHIBIT 11-E-4: SAMPLE ALIMONY WAIVER-DRIVEN AGREEMENT ABOUT HEALTH INSURANCE

EXHIBIT E
MEDICAL INSURANCE

1. The parties acknowledge that although the Wife is eligible to receive significant lifetime alimony from the Husband, she has chosen to waive that right. However, the parties agree that the Wife has *not* agreed to waive her right to receive medical coverage.

2. The Husband shall maintain his group medical insurance for the benefit of the Wife for so long as she is eligible under the plan and/or the provisions of Massachusetts General Law, Chapter 175, Section 110(1).

3. In the event there is a change of eligibility for said coverage for any reason, the Husband shall give the Wife 60 days' notice in writing and, in that event, if the Wife's continued coverage is available and requires an additional premium, the Wife, at her option, may maintain said coverage so long as she pays one half of the additional premium therefore. In that event, the Husband agrees to pay the other half of the additional premium.

4. If continued coverage is not available, the Wife may, at her option, purchase similar coverage. In that event, the Husband agrees to pay one half of the premium.

5. When the Wife turns 65 and becomes eligible to receive Medicare, the obligation of the Husband to provide half her premiums shall end and the Wife shall assume sole responsibility for providing her own health insurance.

6. Each party shall be responsible for his or her own uninsured health expenses.

This verbiage puts the court on notice that although one right was waived, another right has not been waived. (Caveat – don't say you're taking a bigger piece of the property division in lieu of alimony or the IRS will tax you on it).

Because early retirement and remarriage were imminent in the real-life case and the Wife would not waive alimony without assurances, the Husband agreed to do this.

When you turn 65, most health insurance policies terminate and you are forced to apply for Medicare.

EXHIBIT F: BOILERPLATES ADDRESSING WHICH SPOUSE GETS WHAT ASSET

If you read the earlier chapter about property division, you should now have a pretty good idea about who is entitled to what asset. If you wish to 'buy out the marital home' by trading every other non-real piece of property that isn't nailed down, you may meet resistance from your spouse. Otherwise (once you let go of your emotional attachments), property division is a fairly routine event.

Once you hammer out a rough agreement about who gets what, you need to memorialize that understanding so the court can enforce it. If you have not yet informed your spouse you want a divorce and are hoping to convince him to mediate, handing him a copy of a fair proposed Agreement to bring to his lawyer is a good idea (notice that I don't say *your spouse* will find it reasonable ... they always freak out when they first read it). It probably won't be the final agreement, but once your spouse's attorney informs them your requests are fundamentally reasonable, it usually becomes easier to iron out the remaining issues.

Exhibit 11-F-1 is the courts simplistic property division boilerplate. If you have few assets or debts, this may work for you. Otherwise, you should look elsewhere for a boilerplate. Although the court (and some attorneys) lump assets and debts into one Exhibit or section because they interact with and affect one another, I feel it is better practice to separate the two into separate Exhibits and cross-reference any liens. We will cover Liabilities in the next section.

You may have noticed many caveats about using the courts sample document to divide assets. That is because it fails to deal with many things needed to actually transfer title from one spouse to the other, such as deeds, titles, continuing debt obligations, Qualified Domestic Relations Orders, or verbiage that allows you to avoid paying taxes on the transfer of your own property to yourself. Most of these assets cannot be transferred by simple order of the court without other documentation. Exhibit 11-F-2 is a sample attorney-drafted agreement.

EXHIBIT 11-F-1: SAMPLE COURT BOILERPLATE ADDRESSING ASSETS

PROPERTY DIVISION AND DEBTS

A. Real Estate:

☐ Neither party holds any interest in real estate.

X The parties have already divided their interest in the marital home located at:
100 North Main Street, Anytown, MA _____

_____

☐ The disposition of the parties real estate shall be as follows: _____

_____

_____

> This boilerplate is too simplistic for situations where the marital home will be sold years later. You should look to the attorney drafted example that follows for guidance.

B. Personal Property:

The parties hereby agree that:

X There has been a full and satisfactory division of all other personal property and each party shall hold full right, title and interest in all items of personal property now in his/her possession.

X Husband shall have full right, title and interest in the following items:
His car _____

X Wife shall have full right, title and interest in the following items:
Her car _____

> This clause is laden with unexploded land mines!!! If you don't spell out what you agreed to divide (especially if some of those assets are still in the control of the former spouse) then the court can't rectify the situation if your spouse later digs in and claims you didn't agree to it. When in doubt, spell it out!!!

> This fails to spell out what happens if a vehicle is titled in the other parties name!

C. Pension/Retirement Benefits:

☐ The parties have no retirement or pension benefits to be divided.

X The retirement or pension benefits of the parties shall be divided as follows:
The Wife shall keep her IRA, the Husband shall keep his Merrily-Merrily Retirement 401(k)

D. Stocks/Bonds

X The parties have no interest in stocks or bonds.

☐ The stocks and bonds of the parties shall be divided as follows:

_____

_____

> If you are transferring an IRA, pension or similar retirement account, you *must* file a Qualified Domestic Relations Order (QDRO) or the IRS will come knocking on your door!

E. Bank Accounts:

The parties hereby agree that the:

X Husband shall have full right, title and interest in the following bank accounts:
Sea Man's Bank – Checking Account ending in -2345 (see financial statement)

☐ Wife shall have full right, title and interest in the following bank accounts:
Cape Cod Savings Bank – Checking Account ending in -5678 (see financial statement)

> Identify each bank account … *but* … refer the court to your Financial Statement for the actual account number. Your Separation Agreement is a public document, while your financial statement is kept private.

EXHIBIT 11-F-2: SAMPLE ATTORNEY BOILERPLATE ADDRESSING ASSETS

EXHIBIT F
DIVISION OF ASSETS

1. The conveyances, transfers and payments described in this Exhibit F are not contingent upon any event other than the execution of this Agreement and do not qualify as alimony as that term is defined by applicable sections, including s.71 of the United States Internal Revenue Code, as amended, and M.G.L. c.62, as amended, each as in effect as of the date of the execution of this Agreement, and further it is the parties' intent that these transfers qualify under Section 1041 of the Internal Revenue Code. Therefore, the parties agree that these transfers and payments shall neither be deductible by the Husband nor taxable to the Wife, as income, for federal and state income tax purposes. The Husband and Wife own real estate, personal property, pension and profit sharing plans, securities, investments, and other marital assets. Each party agrees to execute any and all documents necessary to effectuate the terms of this Exhibit F and the transfers, conveyances and payments required by said terms. In exchange for the mutual covenants contained in this Agreement, the parties agree to the following:

> Attorney boilerplates repeat tax mumbo jumbo to ensure the IRS doesn't come knocking on your door demanding you pay taxes on the 'sale' of your own assets to *yourself*!!! Be careful you don't say you are waiving alimony in exchange for a larger share of the assets (although that is what frequently happens) or the IRS can tax you on it!!!

> The parties agree to sign any documents needed to make the transfers such as deeds, titles, QDRO, etc.

MUTUAL WAIVERS

2. Except as otherwise provided by the terms of this Agreement, the Husband expressly waives and relinquishes any and all claim, right, title and interest he may have, whether arising out of the marital relationship of the parties or otherwise, in and to any bank or investment accounts, certificates of deposit, trusts, securities, bonds, shares of stock, IRA, pension or profit sharing plans, business interests of the Wife, inheritances, past, present, or future, causes of action, receivables, uncollected fees, entity or entities or other form of property, either real or personal, held by the Wife individually, or with others, or in any other form for the benefit of the Wife.

3. Except as otherwise provided by the terms of this Agreement, the Wife expressly waives and relinquishes any and all claim, right, title and interest she may have, whether arising out of the marital relationship of the parties or otherwise, in and to any bank or investment accounts, certificates of deposit, trusts, securities, bonds, shares of stock, IRA, pension or profit sharing plans, business interests of the Husband, including without limitation the Husband's inheritances, past, present or future, causes of action, receivables, uncollected fees, entity or entities or other form of property, either real or personal, held by the Husband individually, or with others, or in any other form for the benefit of the Husband.

> If you don't specifically state you have a continuing interest in a piece of property, then you are waiving it. The waiver is listed twice, once for each spouse.

4. Except as otherwise provided by the terms of this Agreement, the Husband and the Wife each release and relinquish any interest in real property or items of personal property of or in the possession of the other. Henceforth, each of the parties shall own, have and enjoy, independently of the other party, all real estate and items of personal property of every kind, nature and description and wherever situated, which are now owned or possessed by him or her, or may be hereafter acquired, with full power in him or her to dispose of the same as fully and effectually in all respects and for all purposes as if he or she were unmarried.

> You may dispose of any property you keep as you see fit without asking permission.

REAL PROPERTY

5. The Husband and Wife own, as tenants by the entirety, the real estate located at 100 Any Street, North Anytown, Barnstable County, Massachusetts (hereinafter the "Anytown" real estate). Simultaneously with the execution of this Agreement, the Husband shall convey by deed to the Wife all of his right, title and interest, whether arising out of the marital relationship or otherwise, in and to the Anytown real estate, subject to any outstanding mortgages or other encumbrances thereon.

> The Husband will sign a Quitclaim deed to record at the Registry of Deeds. A family court order alone is insufficient to convey clear title.

6. From and after the conveyance as aforesaid in paragraph 5, the Wife shall assume all outstanding indebtedness on said North Anytown real estate, and shall pay from her own funds all expenses incurred in connection with that real estate, including, without limitation, mortgage, principal and interest, real estate taxes, repairs and maintenance, homeowners insurance, utilities and all other related expenses. The Wife shall indemnify and hold the Husband harmless from any amounts he is currently obligated to pay or may become obligated to pay in connection with said real estate after the date of this Agreement, including, without limitation, any payments as an obligor on any outstanding debt or any debt thereafter incurred on the real estate. (also, see Exhibit G, Item 3 – Liabilities).

> Spell out who is responsible to pay the mortgage. Cross-reference this debt to the Liabilities exhibit.

7. Within 90 days of the signing of this Agreement, the Husband will refinance said North Anytown property entirely into her own name, removing the Husband's name from said lien.

LUMP-SUM PAYMENT

8. As a division of assets and not as alimony the Wife shall pay to the Husband the sum of forty-five thousand ($45,000.00) Dollars in or within 90 days of the entry of a Judgment of Divorce Nisi, to be transferred to the Husband from a home equity line of credit the Husband will take out when refinancing the North Anytown house. It is expressly intended and agreed that this amount shall not be deductible by the Wife nor taxable to the Husband for income tax purposes.

> More IRS CYA tax mumbo-jumbo!

QUALIFIED DOMESTIC RELATIONS ORDER

9. As a division of assets and not as alimony, the Husband shall transfer to the Wife by Qualified Domestic Relations Order the sum of two thousand five hundred ($2,500.00) Dollars to be transferred from the Husband's Profit Sharing or 401K plan to and individual retirement account of the Wife's choice, said transfer to be made within 30 days of the date of approval of the Qualified Domestic Relations Order. The Husband's attorney shall be responsible for the drafting of the Qualified Domestic Relations Order for review by the Wife's attorney. Other than as set forth in this Agreement, the Wife hereby waives any and all claim to and interest in any pension, profit sharing or retirement plans of the Husband, and shall execute whatever documents are necessary to implement said waiver.

> If you are transferring an IRA, pension or similar retirement account, you *must* file a Qualified Domestic Relations Order (QDRO) or the IRS will come knocking on your door!

10. The Husband shall keep his Merrily-Merrily Retirement 401(k) in the sum of fifteen thousand ($15,000.00) dollars. The Wife hereby releases any and all claim to and interest in any pension, profit sharing or retirement plans of the Husband, and shall execute whatever documents are necessary to implement said waiver.

11. The parties shall execute whatever documents are necessary to implement said QDRO.

PERSONAL PROPERTY

12. The Wife shall own, have and enjoy, independently of any claim or right of the Husband, all personal property in her possession, as well 2004 Dodge Tahoe, the children's bedroom sets, two sets of linens fitting the children's beds, and the small black and white television located in the children's bedroom. The wife shall bear sole responsibility for paying the loan on her car (see Exhibit G, Item 4).

> There is a lien on the Wife's car which she agrees to pay. This cross-references the Liability Exhibit.

13. The Husband shall own, have and enjoy, independently of any claim or right of the Wife, all personal property in his possession, as well as the household furniture, furnishings and contents of the North Anytown real estate (except for the items listed in Item 12 above), together with his personal Big Bank checking account, the UTMGA Totten Trust savings account, his 2001 Ford F-150 pickup truck, his power tools, his business, the utility trailer, the 30 foot Boston Whaler

> While the Husband is keeping the contents of the marital home, it notes there are exceptions in the paragraph above. Always cross-reference!

boat, the cash value of his life insurance policy, and his toy train collection. The Husband's pickup truck is free of all liens.

14. The parties have compiled a list titled "Small Items to be Divided" signed by both parties and dated February 7, 2007. The parties shall give the other party all items on the aforementioned list within 30 days. Said list is hereby incorporated by reference to this Agreement.

> If you have a lot of personal property, attach a separate document. You *must* specifically say you are attaching and incorporating that document by reference or it will be unenforceable!

TRANSFER TIMELINE

15. The parties shall execute all necessary documents to implement the transfer set forth hereinafter within 30 days of the date of the Judgment of Divorce Nisi.

> Spell out a reasonable timeline to tie up any loose ends to prevent stonewalling. 30 days is usually enough time to sign all necessary documents. If you need more time, you can say so.

When you go before the judge for your final decree, he will roughly compute whether the property division you both agreed to seems fair. It is in your interest to make his job as easy as possible, but modern concerns about identity theft make putting that level of detail into your Separation Agreement unwise. To avoid wasting both your time and the judges, attach an Addendum to the pink Financial Statements you and your spouse will submit that day outlining what exactly you did to reach agreement. Exhibit 11-F-3 is one possible way of conveying this information in an easily understood manner. Make sure your math adds up!!!

⚑ ***Do not attach this to your Separation Agreement … staple it to your pink Financial Statement.*** Separation Agreements are a matter of public record. Financial Statements are kept private.

EXHIBIT 11-F-3: SAMPLE PROPERTY DIVISION WORKSHEET

Financial Statement Addendum to Separation Agreement Exhibit F1 – Property Division Worksheet			
Description of Asset	Equity or FMV	Wife	Husband
Equity in marital home (minus liens)	$145,850	$145,850	$0
Husband's Merrily-Merrily Retirement 401(k)	$15,000	$0	$15,000
Wife's Vanguard IRA	$2,500	$0	$2,500
Present cash value of Husband's whole-life insurance policy	$1,630	$0	$1,630
Big Bank checking account	$1,500	$0	$1,500
UTMGA savings account	$6,000	$0	$6,000
Wife's 2004 Dodge Tahoe (minus lien)	$1,000	$1,000	$0
Husband's 2001 Ford F-150 pickup truck	$12,500	$0	$12,500
Other Assets (including husbands power tools, trailer, 4-wheeler, boat, toy train collection, and furniture)	$17,000	$0	$17,000
Total Assets to be Divided (50:50 split)	$202,980 /2 =**$101,490**	$146,850	$56,130
Cash Settlement to Husband (wife will take out a 2nd mortgage)			$45,360
Final Property Division after all Settlements		**$101,490**	**$101,490**

In your Separation Agreement, you agreed to both execute a Qualified Domestic Relations Order (QDRO). However, before you can do that, you need to specifically ask the court (file a separate Motion) to approve that QDRO. A Motion to Approve a QDRO is *not* part of your Agreement. Exhibit 11-F-4 will accomplish this task.

EXHIBIT 11-F-4: SAMPLE MOTION REQUESTING THE COURT APPROVE A QDRO

COMMONWEALTH OF MASSACHUSETTS
PROBATE AND FAMILY COURT

<u>BARNSTABLE</u>, SS.　　　　　　　　　DOCKET NO. <u>07D-9999-DV1</u>

JANE DOE-RAYME,　　　）	
Plaintiff　　　　　　）	**ASSENTED MOTION TO**
）	**APPROVE QUALIFIED** ←
v.　　　　　　　　　　）	**DOMESTIC RELATIONS**
JACK RAYME,　　　　　）	**ORDER**
Co-Petitioner　　　　）	
）	

> This motion is not the QDRO! It is a request that the court approve an attached QDRO!

Now comes the Petitioners in the above-entitled action and hereby move this Honorable Court to approve the proposed Qualified Domestic Relations Order.

As grounds for this Motion the Parties state::

1. The Parties signed a separation agreement which was incorporated into the Judgment of Divorce on February 14, 2007. The Agreement requires assignment of 100% of Jane Doe-Rayme's Vanguard IRA to Jack Rayme by Qualified Domestic Relations Order (QDRO) as of that date.

2. The attached Qualified Domestic Relations Order makes provision for the above assignment as of February 14, 2007.

3. Both parties have had the opportunity to review the proposed order with legal counsel.

> This states the parties had the opportunity to consult with a lawyer. You fail to do so at your own risk!

Wherefore, the Petitioners respectfully request the Court to approve the attached Qualified Domestic Relations Order and incorporate it into the Judgment of Divorce.

Respectfully submitted,

_____Jack Rayme_____　　　　_____Jane Doe_____

Jack Rayme, Co-Petitioner　　　　　　Jane Doe-Rayme, Plaintiff

Dated: February 14, 2007

Exhibit 11-F-5 is one possible example of a Qualified Domestic Relation Order (QDRO).

Smart Woodland Creature Tip: Call the Benefits Administrator of your retirement plan *yourself* and ask them for their boilerplate QDRO. Better yet, have them *email* you a copy so your attorney can just fill in the blanks and save you half an hours legal fees chasing it down and typing it. Most retirement plans have their *own* fill-in-the-blank form. Every company requires different verbiage.

EXHIBIT 11-F-5: SAMPLE QDRO

BARNSTABLE, SS.	**COMMONWEALTH OF MASSACHUSETTS** **PROBATE AND FAMILY COURT**	**DOCKET NO. 07D-9999-DV1**

JANE DOE-RAYME, Plaintiff)))	
v.)	**QUALIFIED DOMESTIC**
JACK RAYME, Co-Petitioner))))	**RELATIONS ORDER**

IT IS HEREBY ORDERED, ADJUDGED AND DECREED that this ORDER shall be incorporated into and shall become an integral part of the Decree of Divorce signed and entered by the court in this case on the 14th day of February, 2007.

The Court, having examined the pleadings and heard the evidence and argument of counsel finds that all legal requirements have been satisfied and that this Court has jurisdiction of all parties and the subject matter of this cause and, the Court further finds that certain interests and rights under a certain 401(k) retirement plan sponsored by Merrily-Merrily Retirement are part of the estate of the parties and should be partitioned and paid out in accordance with this order.

This Order is intended to constitute a qualified domestic relations order (QDRO) as defined in Section 206(d) of the Employee Retirement Income Security Act of 1974, as amended ("ERISA") and Section 414(g) of the Internal Revenue Code of 1986 (Code) and shall be administered and interpreted in conformity with such laws.

The Court further finds and it is further ORDERED AND ADJUDGED as follows:

1.   **Names, Addresses and Social Security Numbers of Parties**

    a.   Jane Doe-Rayme (Alternate Payee), has the following date of birth, Social Security number and current address:
Date of Birth:	June 20, 1967
Social Security number:	000-11-2222
Address:	100 Any Street North Anytown, MA 02367
Relationship to Participant:	Former spouse

    b.   Jack Rayme (Participant) , has the following date of birth, Social Security number and current address:
Date of Birth:	July 25, 1969
Social Security number:	999-88-7777
Address:	55 Easy Street Anytown, MA 02532

2.   **Plan Covered by Order:**

    a.   Name of Plan: Merrily-Merrily Planning 401(k) Retirement Plan

    b.   Plan Administrator: Merrily-Merrily Retirement

    Send all orders and correspondence to: Merrily-Merrily Retirement 555 Commercial Street New York, NY 10000

3.   **Benefit Payable to the Alternate Payee**

    a.   *Assignment of the Marital Portion of the Account Balance.* It is hereby ORDERED that: 100% of the Participant's account balance in the Plan determined as of February 14, 2007 (Assignment Date) be assigned and transferred to a separate account under the Plan for the exclusive benefit of the Alternate Payee (Alternate Payee Separate Account), and adjusted to reflect future earnings, gains and losses. The Participant's account balance under the Plan shall be irrevocably reduced by the percentage as of the Assignment Date.

b. *Contribution Subaccounts:* The amounts assigned to the Alternate Payee Separate Account shall be deemed to consist (where applicable) of a before-tax contributions subaccount, rollover contributions subaccount and employer contributions subaccount (Subaccounts) in the same proportions as such subaccounts with respect to the Participant bear to the Participant's entire account balance in the Plan determined as of the Assignment Date.

c. *Investments:* As soon as reasonably practicable, amounts assigned to the Alternate Payee shall be withdrawn from the Participant's investment funds in the Participant's account on a pro rata basis and invested in a similar manner under the Alternate Payee Separate Account under the plan. The Alternate Payee shall have the ability to change the investment of the amounts transferred to the Alternate Payee Separate Account pursuant to the terms of the plan.

d. *Commencement of Benefit Payments:* If the Alternate Payee so elects, she shall be paid her benefits as soon as administratively feasible following the date this Order is approved as a QDRO by the Plan Administrator, or at the earliest date permitted under the terms of the plan, if later.

e. *Form of Payment:* Benefits will be payable to the Alternate Payee in any form or permissible option otherwise available to participants alternate payees under the terms of the Plan, including, but not limited to a single lump-sum cash payment.

4. **Death of the Alternate Payee.** If the Alternate Payee dies and there is a balance credited to the Alternate Payee's Separate Account, such balance shall be paid in a lump sum amount to the beneficiary designated by the alternate Payee as soon as reasonably practicable after the date of death. If no valid designation of a beneficiary exists at the date of death for the Alternate Payee, the balance shall be paid as provided for in the Plan. No adjustment to the Participant' benefit under the Plan shall be made on account of the death of the Alternate Payee.

5. **Death of the Participant.** The death of the Participant shall have no effect on the Alternate Payee's Separate Account. The Alternate Payee shall not be entitled to any portion of a death benefit payable on account of the death of the Participant unless the Participant has designated the Alternate Payee as a beneficiary with respect to the Participant's benefits.

6. **Tax Consequences.** The Alternate Payee shall be responsible for all taxes applicable to payments made to the Alternate Payee.

7. **Excess Payments.** The Participant shall be designated as a constructive trustee of any benefits assigned to the Alternate payee under this Order which may be paid to or received by the Participant. The Participant, as trustee, shall promptly pay or transmit any such benefits to the Alternate Payee, at the Alternate Payee's last known address.

8. **Retention of Jurisdiction.** It is intended that this order meet all requirements of a Qualified Domestic Relations Order (QDRO) under ERISA and the Code and all applicable regulations issued pursuant to such laws, and the court retains jurisdiction to modify the Order for the purposes of meeting or monitoring its qualification as a Qualified Domestic Relations Order.

9. **Limitations.** This Order shall not be construed to require the Plan, the Plan Administrator, or any Plan fiduciary to:

   a. Make any payment or take action which is inconsistent with any federal law, rule, regulation, or applicable judicial decision;

   b. Provide any type or form of benefit or any option which is not otherwise provided under the terms of the Plan;

   c. Provide total benefits having a greater actuarial value than would have been payable in the absence of this order; and\

   d. Pay benefits to the Alternate Payee that are required to be paid to another alternate payee under another order previously determined to be a qualified domestic relations order.

10. **Additional Provisions.**

   a. A certified copy of this Order shall be sent to the Plan Administrator;

   b. If the terms of this Order and the terms of the Plan conflict, the terms of the Plan shall prevail;

   c. The Plan Administrator shall be entitled to fully rely upon the terms of this Order and shall not be bound by the terms of any other court order or decree which has not been received by the Plan Administrator.

   d. The Alternate Payee shall be responsible for keeping the Plan Administrator informed of the Alternate Payee's address;

   e. The Plan, the Plan Sponsor, the Plan Administrator, and the Plan fiduciaries shall not be responsible for any attorney's fees incurred by the Participant or the Alternate Payee in connection with this order;

   f. The Participant and the Alternate Payee shall hold each of the Plan, the Plan Sponsor, the Plan Administrator, and the Plan fiduciaries harmless from any liabilities (including attorney's fees) incurred in connection with any claims which are asserted because the Plan honors this order.

Signed this _____14th_____ day of _____February_____, 2007.

_____Johnny B. Goode_____

Johnny B. Goode, Justice
Probate & Family Court

EXHIBIT G: BOILERPLATES DICTATING REPAYMENT OF DEBTS

Just as the court wants to see a fair division of marital assets in your divorce, you also need to demonstrate that you have a plan to pay debts incurred during the marriage in an orderly manner. Curiously, the courts sample boilerplate as well as many Bar Association boilerplates do not address the issue of which spouse will pay the credit card bills. An extra credit card payment of $50/month may not seem like a lot of money to a judge or upper-middle-class client who can afford to hire a full-service attorney, but it can make or break or more modest income client.

⚑ *Never take your spouse's word that they will take care of the credit card bills!* Spell it out!!!

Exhibit 11-G-1 is the courts sample boilerplate regarding debt. You will notice that there is precious little detail provided for paying *joint* debts incurred during the marriage. Since many debts are joint debts, simply stating you will pay individual debts listed on your financial statement leaves gaping grey areas to fight about later. Who will pay what percentage of debt? What happens if one party fails to make their payment? What happens if you want to pay off the highest rate credit card first, but your spouse wants to make the minimum payment each month? The paltry 3 lines the court's boilerplate allows for addressing joint marital debt does not give you room to spell this out, nor does it contain important indemnification language to recoup your costs and attorney fees if you end up paying the bill in full.

EXHIBIT 11-G-1: SAMPLE COURT BOILERPLATE ADDRESSING DEBTS

F. Debt:

X   The Husband will be responsible for his individual debts and liabilities as listed on his financial statement dated __2_ / _14_ / _2007___

X   The Wife will be responsible for her individual debts and liabilities as listed on her financial statement dated __2__ / _14_ / _2007__

X   The marital debts of the parties shall be paid as follows:
Each party will pay 50% of each joint debt payment (except for the Wife's Car and the former Marital Home) as it becomes due and payable.

> When you fill out your Financial Statement, you are supposed to note whether a debt belongs to you, your spouse, or is "joint."

Exhibit 11-G-2 provides more detail about who is going to pay which debt. Whoever is assigned an asset (such as a house or car) is generally expected to pay any liens against that property. If a debt is incurred under your name but really should be considered a joint marital debt (such as a credit card bill incurred paying for your joint vacation last year), you must specifically note it in your Agreement or you will be stuck with it. However, due to privacy concerns and identity theft, you want to avoid revealing *so* much information that a identify thief can steal it. You should also address the issue of what happens if one of the parties fails to make their agreed-upon payments and creditors come after the other party for payment. Many couples agree to divide joint marital liabilities 50:50, but if there is a significant disparity in income and those debts were not paid 50:50 during the marriage, occasionally you can get the court to order a different repayment schedule. My preference is to list all debts and liabilities in their own Exhibit and cross-reference any debts that are secured by an asset listed in the Assets section.

EXHIBIT G

DEBTS AND LIABILITIES

1. The parties agree to cancel any joint credit cards.

Note the cross-reference to the Assets exhibit.

2. Except for the "Lump Sum Payment" referred to in Exhibit F, Item 8, of this Agreement, the Wife shall not incur any further debt against the marital home or home equity line of credit until such time as she has refinanced the house completely out of the Husband's name.

3. As outlined in Exhibit F, Item 7, of this Agreement, the Wife hereby assumes and is responsible for paying all mortgages associated with the North Anytown real estate. At the time of the signing of this Agreement, there exists a primary mortgage to Big Bank and a home equity line of credit with Little Bank. The Wife Agrees to refinance the North Anytown property solely into her own name within 90 days of the signing of this agreement at the prevailing mortgage rate. The Wife assumes sole responsibility, indemnifies, and holds the Husband harmless for any breaches caused by her ownership of the North Anytown property.

It is good practice to require the other party to refinance any debt associated with an asset they are taking into their own name so you credit rating is not impaired. Unfortunately, this is not always possible. If the bank says no (or gives you a ridiculous interest rate out of line with prevailing mortgage rates), there's not a lot you can do about it.

4. As outlined in Exhibit F, Item 12 of this Agreement, the Wife shall be sole responsibility for paying the car loan associated with her 2004 Dodge Tahoe. The Wife shall thereafter assume sole responsibility, indemnify, and hold the Husband harmless for any breaches caused by her ownership of the 2004 Dodge Tahoe.

Although it *is* possible to get student loans originating from the parties *own* education declared a joint marital debt, this usually turns into World War III. On the other hand, the court will *readily* declare student loans incurred on behalf of the children to be joint marital debts.

5. The parties agree that the Wife shall bear sole responsibility for paying her student loans.

6. All other joint marital debts, including interest, fees, and penalties, incurred during the marriage shall be paid in proportion to the parties income, with the Husband responsible for paying 2/3rd (67%) of all invoices, and the Wife paying 1/3rd (33%) of all invoices, in accordance with the spreadsheet attached to the parties Financial Statement labeled "Financial Statement Addendum G-1: Unsecured General Liabilities Allocation Worksheet" outlining the transfers taking place. This Addendum is part of and hereby incorporated into this Agreement.

If you attach a Debt Addendum to your Financial Statement, you *must* incorporate it by reference so it becomes part of your Separation Agreement.

7. Except as specifically set forth herein, each Party shall be responsible for all expenses, bills and obligations of themselves and their property. Neither party will incur any debts, charges or liabilities for with the other Party, their legal representative, property or estate will or may become liable, except to enforce or pursuant to the provisions of this Agreement.

Translation: you make a bill, you pay the bill. Don't go around opening bogus accounts in your former spouse's name.

8. Should any violation of this Agreement occur, the Party who caused the violation agrees to hold the other Party harmless and to reimburse them for any and all debts, charges and liabilities contracted or incurred (including attorney's fees, costs and expenses) because of the violation. Should additional interest, penalties, or late fees be assed against any joint marital debt because one party paid their portion on time and the other failed to pay on time, the party who incurred the additional interest, fees and penalties shall make additional payment equal to the amount of excess penalties, interest and fees before the next payment cycle so that the account balance is adjusted *as if* all payments had been made on time.

Spell out what happens if one party doesn't pay a bill or pays late. Why should *you* have to pay 18% interest, $40 late fee and $18 penalty if you sent in your 1/3rd payment on time and your slacker spouse mails it late? Getting the court to order the other party to pay late fees is like pulling teeth, so include this in your agreement.

Due to privacy concerns and the prevalence these days of identity theft, be careful how much information you disclose in those court records which are open to the public. Since your Financial Statement is privileged information, the clerk will remove all financial statements from your docket file whenever a non-party to the case requests to see it. This is why it is important you print out your Financial Statement on whatever color paper as the court requires and not simply give the clerk a white photocopy. Exhibit 11-G-3 is a Sample Addendum you might attach to your Financial Statement detailing what you just memorialized in the debt section of your Separation Agreement.

EXHIBIT 11-G-3: FINANCIAL STATEMENT ADDENDUM G-1: UNSECURED GENERAL LIABILITIES ALLOCATION WORKSHEET

Creditor	Nature of Debt	Amount Due (before interest)	Total Weekly Payment	Husband to Pay	H's weekly payment	Wife to Pay	W's weekly payment
Big Bank Card	Credit Card	$7,000	$55.00	67%	$36.85	33%	$18.15
City Smitty Card	Credit Card	$3,000	$22.00	67%	$14.74	33%	$7.26
Dr. Orthodontist	Sons' braces	$4,500	$11.00	67%	$7.37	33%	$3.63
Nurses University	Wife's student loan	$2,000	$10.00	0%	$0	100%	$24.00
XYZ HVAC Repair	Loan	$5,000	$10.00	67%	$6.70	33%	$3.30
Learn'M College	Daughter's Student Loan (taken out by parents)	$15,000	$25.00	67%	$16.75	33%	$8.25
Total Weekly Unsecured Debt Payments					$82.41		$64.59

EXHIBIT H: TAX AGREEMENTS

Tax issues are easily overlooked. Come April 15th, who gets to claim the kids as dependents, whether or not child support is taxable to the custodial parent, who gets last year's tax refund, who pays the taxes on alimony, and other issues can erupt into a bitter dispute. If you filed 'married filing jointly' during the marriage, you also need to worry about whether one of you made a mistake on your taxes that the other person could be held liable for. This is especially true if one party is self-employed or earns income from a source other than a traditional wage.

The courts sample boilerplate is silent on the issue of what happens if you file for divorce in one year, but your divorce doesn't become final until the next calendar year. Technically, you are supposed to file 'married filing separately' or 'married filing jointly.' If you file jointly to reduce your taxes, the court's agreement does not indemnify you for your spouse's mistakes. The IRS could come after *you*! What happens if you *do* sign your spouse's return, but then he refuses to give you your share of the tax refund? Before you sign anything (even if you aren't at the Separation Agreement stage yet) you should get a stipulation in writing how you are going to divide any tax refunds.

If you have dependent children, the courts sample Agreement (Exhibit 11-H-1) *does* provide room to specify who gets to claim the children as dependents. If you are the custodial parent and your spouse is providing less than 50% of your total household income (including child support), you should resist pressure to check the 'alternate years' box and insist you get to claim them as your own dependents every year as this will affect your tax burden significantly (the judge may disagree with you).

EXHIBIT 11-H-1: SAMPLE COURT BOILERPLATE ADDRESSING TAX DEPENDENTS

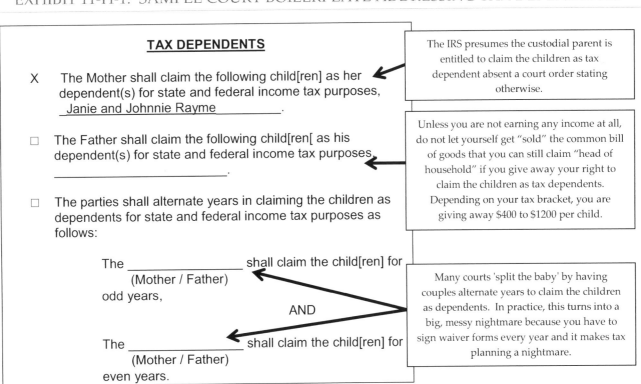

Exhibit 11-H-2 spells out common tax issues much more extensively. Be aware that some attorney-drafted Agreements lump tax dependents in with the child support section. It is good practice to list all tax issues in the tax section and, if you choose to also list child-related tax issues in with the child support section, to verify the language is consistent and cross-referenced between both exhibits.

EXHIBIT 11-H-2: SAMPLE TAX BOILERPLATES

EXHIBIT H
INCOME TAXES

The parties agree to file joint federal and state income tax returns for 2006. The Husband shall be responsible for the preparation of said returns. The Wife may retain and independent accountant to review said tax returns for signature. Any payments or refunds shall be shared by the parties in the same proportion as their incomes.

The parties shall file separate federal and state income tax returns for 2007 and thereafter.

TAX DEPENDENTS

The Mother shall be entitled to claim both children as tax dependents, unless she derives no benefit from said status, in which case she will notify the Father and allow him to claim the children as dependents.

The Mother shall have the exclusive right to claim the children for Head of Household status.

TAX INDEMNIFICATION

The Wife covenants at all times to hold the Husband free, harmless and indemnified from and against all income tax obligations, deficiencies, penalties or interest assessed, which have been or may be incurred in connection with the filing of any joint tax return, state or federal, by them, and which obligation, deficiency, penalty or interest is attributable to the Wife's income, error or omission. Notwithstanding anything to the contrary contained in this Agreement, the Wife further covenants at all times to hold the Husband free, harmless and indemnified from and against all debts, charges or liabilities incurred by her in breach of the provisions of this paragraph, and from any and all attorneys' fees, costs and expenses incurred by the Husband as a result of any such breach.

The Husband covenants at all times to hold the Wife free, harmless and indemnified from and against all income tax obligations, deficiencies, penalties or interest assessed, which have been or may be incurred in connection with the filing of any joint tax return, state or federal, by them, and which obligation, deficiency, penalty or interest is attributable to the Husband's income, error or omission. Notwithstanding anything to the contrary contained in this Agreement, the Husband further covenants at all times to hold the Wife free, harmless and indemnified from and against all debts, charges or liabilities incurred by her in breach of the provisions of this paragraph, and from any and all attorneys' fees, costs and expenses incurred by the Wife as a result of any such breach.

If your spouse is self-employed, you should be cautious about signing a joint tax return.

The couple agrees to split tax refunds, which means whoever gets to the mailbox first can't simply pocket the check.

Once your divorce is final, you must file single.

-If- the custodial parent has no income other than child support, SSDI, or TAFDC, she will receive no benefit from claiming the children.

Head of household status gives you a break in your tax bill, but not enough to offset giving away your deductions. Fight it tooth and nail!

This indemnifies you if one of you made a mistake on a past tax return (the IRS can look back 7 years) and the IRS comes after you for back taxes. Indemnification language allows you to go back to court and force the other party to reimburse you.

EXHIBIT I: ATTORNEY FEE BOILERPLATES

Generally, each person is responsible for paying their own attorney fees. The Legal Fees section of the Separation Agreement will most often contain a simple statement that each person is paying for their own fees and not much else. The sample court agreement is silent on the issue of legal fees.

This can confuse spouses who may have gotten an advance on joint marital assets 'pendent lite' to hire an attorney. *'Pendente lite'* is a loan given to you against your share of the marital estate, not a court order to have your spouse pay your legal fees. However, if your spouse also raided the marital kitty to pay his *own* legal fees, chances are legal fees will be a wash. If, however, the amounts are not similar or your husband agrees to reimburse your attorney for some of your legal fees (often a share of the cost of drafting the Agreement or a QDRO), this is the place to address this issue.

EXHIBIT 11-I-1: LEGAL FEES AND EXPENSES

EXHIBIT I

LEGAL FEES AND EXPENSES

1. Each party shall be responsible for the payment of his or her own attorney's fees, expenses and expert witness fees incurred in the prosecution, negotiation and settlement of the pending divorce litigation between the parties, except for those items listed below.

   If either of you agrees to pay part of the other parties fees, you need to note that here.

2. The parties agree to divide the cost equally to have the Husband's attorney draft a Qualified Domestic Relations Order (QDRO) and take all necessary steps to ensure the Husband's Merrily-Merrily Retirement 401(k) is transferred to the Wife as outlined in Exhibit F, Items 9-11 of this Agreement. The Husband shall provide the Wife with written documentation of said legal fees and the Wife shall reimburse him within 30 days of request.

   Parties often agree to share the cost of mutually incurred legal services, such as paying an independent mediator, appraisal of the marital home, or cost of drafting the Separation Agreement or a QDRO.

Sometimes, there may be an ongoing civil litigation involving one or both parties (such as bankruptcy or a civil suit against your spouse's business where the Plaintiff is seeking to attach your joint marital home). In that case, it is good practice to include language in this section specifying who is going to pay to defend that action, especially if the blameless spouse gets dragged into court. Exhibit 11-I-2 contains verbiage drafted to protect the Wife in an especially convoluted divorce.

EXHIBIT 11-I-2: SAMPLE FOR ONGOING LITIGATION - LEGAL FEES AND EXPENSES

EXHIBIT H
LEGAL FEES AND EXPENSES

There are multiple legal proceedings naming both parties as defendants related to the Husband's business in different courts in addition to this divorce action. Therefore:

> Note *why* this is an unusual case.

1. Each party shall be responsible for the payment of his or her own attorney's fees, expenses and expert witness fees incurred in the prosecution, negotiation and settlement of the pending divorce litigation between the parties.

> Each party will pay their own legal fees connected to the divorce ...
>
> ... *but* ...
>
> ... the Husband will pay to defend both parties in the Bankruptcy.

2. The Husband agrees to pay for all future costs and legal fees connected with the Bankruptcy and related suits, including the cost of collection (including legal fees) should the Wife be forced to front said additional legal fees and seek reimbursement from the Husband.

3. Prior to the parties filing bankruptcy, the Husband had seven (7) civil suits and four (4) judgment liens connected to his business, at least one of which is related to a note the Wife had co-signed, which have been stayed by the U.S. Bankruptcy Court pending resolution to the creditors' claims. If these lawsuits are not discharged as expected by the Bankruptcy Court and litigation moves forward, the Husband agrees to pay all court costs, legal fees, and related costs connected to the litigation and resolution of these disputes, including full indemnification of the Wife should judgment be made against her.

> Give the court some context if your case is convoluted.

4. The Parties hereby attach and incorporate by reference the Chapter 7 Petition filed in September of 2006, included amended schedules.

> If there are other pending court cases, incorporate the pleadings by reference so the court has the power to take them into consideration if you later need to go back to court to get reimbursed for your legal fees.

EXHIBIT J: LIFE INSURANCE BOILERPLATES

What would happen if your former spouse suddenly died? If you are counting on receiving alimony or child support to help pay your post-divorce living expenses, you're in big trouble. Although your children *might* be eligible to receive social security benefits, they can only do so if you earn less money from all sources than the eligibility limits. Worse, the day they turn 18, whether or not they are still in high school or plan on attending college, the federal government kicks them out into the cold. You, on the other hand, may not be entitled to receive a penny since you are no longer married.

Under normal circumstances, reasonably prudent people purchase life insurance to ensure their financial obligations are met. Courts tend to be sympathetic when Wives ask their Husbands to continue an existing life insurance policy or take out a new one, *if affordable*, but your alimony or child support *may* be adjusted downward to reflect the cost of premiums, if any.

There are two ways couples tend to address this problem. The first way is to come up with a figure that you think will get you 'over the hump' if your spouse dies and you get cut off, for example, $250,000. The caveat about this strategy is that, unless you are an investment genius, you should generally ask for an amount sufficient to stick into safe (preferably FDIC insured) savings vehicles and pay the total amount of alimony, child support, and the cash value of intangible factors such as college tuition, health insurance, reimbursements for kid's activities, and other expenses your spouse would otherwise have paid over the years. Once you do your homework and come up with a figure, the following court boilerplates (Exhibit 11-J-1 and Exhibit 11-J-2) are adequate to achieve this purpose.

EXHIBIT 11-J-1: SAMPLE COURT LIFE INSURANCE BOILERPLATE FOR EACH OTHER

LIFE INSURANCE

X   The Husband shall maintain life insurance in the face amount of:
$ _250,000.00_____ , naming __the Wife_____ as the beneficiary, and shall be required to keep the life insurance in effect until __the death or remarriage of the Wife,_____ .

☐   The Wife shall maintain life insurance in the face amount of
$ _____ , naming _____ as the beneficiary, and shall be required to keep the life insurance in effect until _____ .

☐   Neither party shall be required to maintain life insurance for the benefit of the other.

> 'Death or remarriage of the Wife' is when alimony would normally end. You should not state 'when alimony ends' because, technically, alimony also ends when your spouse dies.

> The "neither" box is appropriate when you are ending a short-term marriage with no alimony and no children.

EXHIBIT 11-J-2: SAMPLE COURT LIFE INSURANCE BOILERPLATE FOR THE CHILDREN

LIFE INSURANCE

X   The Father shall maintain life insurance in the face amount of:
$ _250,000.00_____, naming __the Wife_____ as the beneficiary, and
shall be required to keep the life insurance in effect until _the emancipation of the
youngest child_____.

> Write 'emancipation' and not '18' if you live in a state where your child is eligible to receive child support or reimbursement for college costs.

☐   The Mother shall maintain life insurance in the face amount of:
$ _____, naming _____ as the beneficiary, and
shall be required to keep the life insurance in effect until _____.

☐   Neither party shall be required to maintain life insurance for the benefit of the child[ren].

Exhibit 11-A-3 is an attorney-drafted boilerplate which accomplishes the same purpose as the two court examples. However, it adds additional protections for the Wife by requiring the Husband to mail the Wife proof of insurance and payment of the policy on the date of renewal each and every year. This is good practice because the first thing most people allow to lapse when they run into financial difficulty is their life insurance. This version is appropriate for a lump-sum payment.

EXHIBIT 11-J-3: SAMPLE FLAT RATE BOILERPLATE - LIFE INSURANCE

EXHIBIT J
LIFE INSURANCE

1. Until such time as he is no longer obligated to provide alimony and child support pursuant to Exhibit B and C of this Agreement, the Husband shall purchase and maintain at his own expense a $250,000 death benefit naming the Wife and Children as beneficiaries.

> This ties the obligation to purchase life insurance to alimony and child support obligations. Note it also states it is to be at the Husband's own expense.

2. On the date of policy renewal each year, the Husband shall mail the Wife a copy of said policy binder showing the named beneficiary, the amount allocated to that beneficiary, and proof that all premiums have been paid for the upcoming year.

> Insist your spouse send proof of coverage each year as life insurance is typically the first thing people allow to lapse when they run into financial difficulties.

3. Said payments shall satisfy any and all alimony and child support obligations required by the terms of this Agreement.

> The 'satisfy all ... obligations' verbiage means you can't go after his estate if he dies.

Agreeing upon a lump sum policy might be the simplest way to draft a Separation Agreement, but if you have young children or are eligible to receive lifetime alimony and have many years left until the day those obligations end, the policy coverage necessary to cover all those years could be prohibitive. As your Husband gets older, his cost to buy life insurance will go up with each year added to his life while, simultaneously, the amount you have to lose if he dies decreases. To avoid unnecessarily burdening the Husband and prevent the Wife from receiving a windfall if she collects alimony or child support for many years before collecting life insurance, many attorneys will use a stepped life insurance boilerplate. To compute this model, use the following formula (round up to the nearest thousand):

EXHIBIT 11-J-4: SAMPLE STEPPED LIFE INSURANCE OBLIGATION COMPUTATION TO MEET A CHILD SUPPORT OBLIGATION

Duration of child support indebtedness:	
Age of youngest child now:	6 years old
Length of obligation:	To age 23* (anticipated age of emancipation if child goes to college) *Note: If you live in a state with no college child support obligation, you would use the anticipated date of your child's graduation from high school after he turns 18.
Number of years H needs to buy life insurance:	17 years
Amount of obligation now:	
Annual obligation:	$250/wk x 52 wks/yr = ~$13,000/yr
Total obligation over 17 years:	$250,000 +/-
Obligation Table:	
Year 1	$250,000
Year 2 (subtract $13,000)	$237,000
Year 3 (subtract $13,000)	$224,000
And so on … until you reach zero	

EXHIBIT 11-J-5: SAMPLE STEPPED LIFE INSURANCE OBLIGATION COMPUTATION TO MEET AN ALIMONY OBLIGATION (NO CHILDREN SCENARIO)

Duration of alimony indebtedness:	
Length of obligation:	1/2 the length of the marriage. *Note: presumed new Massachusetts Alimony Guidelines. Jane Doe was married to Jack for 11 years.
Number of years H needs to buy life insurance:	5.5 years
Amount of obligation now:	
Annual obligation:	$250/wk x 52 wks/yr = ~$13,000/yr
Total obligation over 5.5 years:	$71,500 +/-
Obligation Table:	
Year 1	$75,500
Year 2 (subtract $13,000)	$58,500
Year 3 (subtract $13,000)	$45,500
And so on … until you reach zero	

Smart Woodland Creature Tip: Oooh! Note how easy it is to compute the cash-value of an alimony obligation! Maybe you could use this *same* method of computation if you would rather receive your cash up front out of the marital estate? Sometimes it behooves you to take the money and run!

Once you compute the life insurance schedule, all you need to do is transfer your computations to your Agreement (Exhibit 11-J-6). My sample boilerplate goes from February 14, 2007 to February of each following year because that is when our hypothetical couple is getting divorced, but you can name any policy period you wish (for example, from the day your spouse purchases the policy until it's next annual renewal date).

Your spouse doesn't necessarily need to purchase a separate life insurance policy to cover you if he already had a good policy (especially if that policy is a whole life policy). All he needs to do is change how much would go to each beneficiary on the date of renewal each year, gradually decreasing the amount that would go to you in the event of his death and increasing the amount that would go to another beneficiary of his choice. Either way, it's prudent to be diligent about enforcing the Agreement to receive a copy of the policy (including proof of payment and how much each beneficiary gets) every year lest he die and leave you without adequate financial resources.

EXHIBIT 11-J-6: SAMPLE FLAT RATE BOILERPLATE - LIFE INSURANCE

EXHIBIT J
LIFE INSURANCE

1. Until such time as he is no longer obligated to provide alimony and child support pursuant to Exhibits C and B of this Agreement, the Husband shall maintain a death benefit for the Wife and Children, naming the Wife as beneficiary, in accordance with the following schedule:

February 14, 2007 through February 13, 2008	$250,000
February 14, 2008 through February 13, 2009	$237,000
February 14, 2009 through February 13, 2010	$224,000
February 14, 2010 through February 13, 2011	$211,000
February 14, 2011 through February 13, 2012	$198,000
February 14, 2012 through February 13, 2013	$185,000
February 14, 2013 through February 13, 2014	$172,000
February 14, 2014 through February 13, 2015	$159,000
February 14, 2015 through February 13, 2016	$146,000
February 14, 2016 through February 13, 2017	$133,000
February 14, 2017 through February 13, 2018	$120,000
February 14, 2018 through February 13, 2019	$103,000
February 14, 2019 through February 13, 2020	$90,000
February 14, 2020 through February 13, 2021	$77,000
February 14, 2021 through February 13, 2022	$64,000
February 14, 2022 through February 13, 2023	$51,000
February 14, 2023 through emancipation	$38,000

2. On the date of policy renewal each year, the Husband shall mail the Wife a copy of said policy binder showing who is the named beneficiary, the amount allocated to that beneficiary, and proof that all premiums have been paid for the upcoming year

3. Said payments shall satisfy any and all alimony and child support obligations required by the terms of this Agreement.

A PRELIMINARY 'SCRATCH-COPY' TO ROUGH OUT A PROPOSED SEPARATION AGREEMENT

If you recall from Chapter 1 of this book, once upon a time, long before I decided to go back to college to get my bachelor's degree and then continue on with graduate school to become an attorney, I had no choice but to handle my own divorce. The day we got to the courthouse, my former spouse handed me an agreement that even -I- realized was so one-sided that I should not sign it. I thought I was clever. I went down into the basement of the courthouse and asked if they had any sample forms. They did, and what we ended up with for a Separation Agreement was a melding of the two proposals.

Boy! Did -I- ever shoot myself in the foot! I had absolutely no idea what I was doing. I avoided *some* land mines, but there were other sneaky atom bombs that came back to haunt me later. I have tried to educate the reader how to spot some of the more egregious pitfalls, but this chapter is by no means comprehensive! There's a *reason* lawyers make so much money!

Please go see an attorney before you sign anything!!! Shooting yourself in the foot really hurts!

That being said, if you are on a budget and hope to negotiate some or all of your divorce agreement, having a boilerplate to refer to can be helpful. Therefore, I am including two 'blank' boilerplates as a scratch copy for you to either begin planning what to ask for, or use as a rough draft while negotiating. The first version is for couples with dependent (unemancipated) children. The second version is for couples who either have no children together, or their children are grown.

EXHIBIT 11-K-1: SAMPLE BLANK BOILERPLATE SEPARATION AGREEMENT -WITH- CHILDREN

The sample begins on the next page so you can photocopy it as necessary, or download it from the Seraphim Press website: www.bootcampmanual.com

STATE of _____
Family Court Department

_____ County, ss.   Docket No. _____

SEPARATION AGREEMENT
(for couples *with* dependent children)

SEPARATION AGREEMENT made this _____ day of _____, 20_____, between:

_____ (Name) the _____ (Husband/Wife) currently residing at _____(Street)_____(Town)_____(County)_____(State)
(hereinafter referred to as the _____(Husband/Wife);

and

_____ (Name) the _____ (Husband/Wife) currently residing at _____(Street)_____(Town)_____(County)_____(State)
(hereinafter referred to as the _____(Husband/Wife).

All references to 'parties' shall mean the above-mentioned Husband and Wife.

STATEMENT OF FACTS

The Husband and Wife were married on _____ (Date), in _____(City) _____(State), and last lived together in _____(Town) _____ (County) _____(State) on _____(Date).

_____ (number of) children were born to the marriage, namely:

Name:_____   Date of Birth: _____

Name:_____   Date of Birth: _____

Name:_____   Date of Birth: _____

Name:_____   Date of Birth: _____

STATEMENT OF PURPOSE

The Husband and Wife have been separated and desire to terminate the marital relationship. The parties have filed a Complaint for Divorce in the _____ Division Family Court, Docket Number _____ asserting an irretrievable breakdown of the marriage. The Husband and Wife desire and intend at this time and by this instrument to make a final and complete settlement of all matters relating to the interests and obligations of each with respect to, but not limited to, past, present and future alimony, child support, property and estate rights, in the case of the death of either of them prior to the entry of a final judgment of divorce, and after the entry of a final judgment of divorce should a court grant a divorce between the Husband and Wife. The above statement of purpose of the within Agreement shall not in any way limit the effect of any of the covenants of the parties contained in or the interpretation of this Agreement.

This Agreement shall be binding upon the parties at all times hereafter whether they are living apart or living together or should they become legally separated or divorced in the future, and nothing concerning the state of the marriage of the parties or their living circumstances shall affect the validity of this Agreement, and the same shall nevertheless continue in full force and effect.

The purposes of this Agreement are finally, once and for all:

a) to determine and settle the property rights of each of the parties;

b) to determine what, if anything, should be paid as alimony to the Wife in consideration of the provisions of _____ (state) General Laws c. _____, s.___; (fill in your state alimony statute) and to determine what should be paid for support and maintenance of the minor children pursuant to _____ (state) General Laws c. _____, s.___ (fill in your state child support guidelines statute);

c) to determine whether and to what extent all or any part of the estate of the Husband or Wife should be assigned to the other in consideration of the provisions of _____ (state) General Laws c. _____, s.___ (fill in your state property division statute);

d) to determine all other rights and obligations arising from the marital relationship or otherwise; and

e) to determine all other matters which should be settled in view of the pending Complaint for Divorce.

GENERAL TERMS

NOW, THEREFORE, in consideration of the mutual promises, agreements and covenants hereinafter contained, the Husband and Wife mutually agree as follows:

1. Covenant to Live Apart - From the date hereof, the Husband and Wife may continue to live separate and apart from one another for the rest of their lives, and each shall be free from interference, authority or control, direct or indirect, by the other as fully as if sole and unmarried.

2. Covenant of Non-Interference - Neither the Husband nor the Wife shall molest the other; nor shall the Husband or Wife compel or attempt to compel the other to cohabit with him or her; nor shall the Husband or Wife commence any legal, equitable or other action or proceeding for the restitution of conjugal rights. The Husband and Wife to not intend that this clause shall be criminally enforceable.

3. Covenant to Waive Claims to the Other Parties Estate:

    A) The Husband and Wife each hereby waives any right at law or in equity to elect to take against any last will made by the other, including all rights of dower or of curtsey, and each hereby waives, renounces and relinquishes unto each other, their respective heirs, executors, administrators and assigns forever, all and any interest of any kind or character which either may now have or may hereafter acquire in or to any real or personal property of the other and whether now owned or hereafter acquired by either, except as expressly provided by the terms of this Agreement.

    B) The Husband and Wife shall have the right to dispose of his or her property by will, or otherwise, in such manner as each may in his or her uncontrolled discretion deem proper, and neither one will claim any interest in the estate of the other, except to enforce any obligation imposed by this Agreement.

4. Covenant to Release All Claims and Legal Actions Against the Other - The Husband and Wife hereby mutually release and forever discharge each other from any and all actions, suits, debts, claims, demands and obligations whatsoever, both at law and in equity, which either of them has ever had, now has, or may hereafter have against the other, upon or by reason of any matter, cause or thing up to the date of this Agreement, whether arising from the marital relationship or otherwise, including, but not limited to, claims against each other's property, it being the intention of the parties that henceforth there shall exist as between them only such rights and obligations as are specifically provided for in this Agreement and in any judgment entered on the Complaint for Divorce;

5. <u>Covenants Against New Liabilities:</u>

A) The Wife warrants, represents that, other than as specifically set forth in this Agreement, she will not hereafter contract or incur any debt, charge or liability whatsoever for which the Husband, his legal representatives, or his property or estate, will or may become liable, and that as of the date of this Agreement there are no outstanding bills incurred by her which are the obligation of the Husband. .

B) The Husband warrants, represents and agrees that he will not hereafter contract or incur any debt, charge or liability whatsoever for which the Wife, her legal representatives, or her property or estate will or may become liable, and that at the time of the Agreement there are no outstanding bills incurred by him which are the obligation of the Wife.

6. <u>Covenant of Indemnification:</u>

A) The Wife further covenants at all times to hold the Husband free, harmless and indemnified from and against all debts, charges or liabilities previously contracted or incurred by her in breach of the provisions of this paragraph, and from any and all attorneys' fees, costs and expenses incurred by the Husband as a result of any such breach.

B) The Husband further covenants at all times to hold the Wife free, harmless and indemnified from and against all debts, charges or liabilities previously contracted or incurred by him in breach of the provisions of this paragraph, and from any and all attorneys' fees, costs and expenses incurred by the Wife as a result of any breach.

7. <u>Procedure in the Event of Breach:</u> Any breach of any term or terms of the within Agreement shall give either party the right to take immediate action, either at law or in equity, concerning such breach. If either the Husband or the Wife shall commit a breach of any of the provisions of this Agreement and legal action, required to enforce such provisions, shall be instituted by the other, the Court may make a determination or allocation as to the payment of reasonable attorneys' fees incurred in instituting and prosecuting such action, by the party in breach.

8. <u>Additional Terms:</u> The parties agree:

A) to accept the provisions made for each and every undertaking as set forth in this agreement in full satisfaction and discharge of all claims, past, present and future, which each may have upon the other and which in any way arise out of the marital relationship;

B) to waive any claim to property division, alimony or support for each, other than as provided in this Agreement;

C) not to seek the entry of an order or judgment which differs in any way from the terms of this Agreement; and

D) to indemnify and hold harmless the other from any amount he or she is ordered or required to make, in excess of the actual payments or division of property he or she is required to make pursuant to this Agreement.

9. <u>Approval by Court:</u> At any hearing on the Complaint for Divorce, a copy of this Agreement shall be submitted to the _____ (County) Division Family Court for a judge's approval of the terms and entry of a Judgment of Divorce.

10. <u>Merger or Survival:</u> The parties further agree that the terms and provisions of this Separation Agreement shall be (choose one of the following):

⬜ Incorporated and merged into the Judgment of Divorce Nisi of the court.

⬜ Incorporated, but not merged, into the Court's judgment, and shall survive and remain as an independent contract, except for the terms and provisions relating to:

⊐ the care, custody, support and education of the minor child[ren], (see Exhibit ___) which terms and provisions shall merge in said Judgment. The parties are aware that neither party may permanently bargain away a child's right to receive the care and support of both parents.

⊐ spousal support/alimony (see Exhibit ____) which terms and provisions shall merge in said Judgment.

⊐ Other _____ (see Exhibit ____).

⊐ Other _____ (see Exhibit ____).

⊐ Incorporated, but not merged, into the Judgment of Divorce Nisi, and shall survive and remain as an independent contract between the parties. The parties understand that once an Agreement which contains a 'survival' clause is accepted by the court, it may almost *never* be amended at a later date except by act of the state legislature. If child support is an issue, checking off this clause is inappropriate.

The purposes of this paragraph are: (1) to protect each party against any attempt by the other party to vary the terms of this Agreement after the entry of a final judgment; and (2) to enable the Husband and the Wife to procure an enforcement of the terms of this Agreement incorporated in a Judgment of Divorce in the _____(county) Division Family Court, or as a binding contract in any Court with jurisdiction over the person or property of the other party.

11. <u>Warranty of Full and Complete Disclosure</u>: The Husband and Wife hereby represent that each has fully described his or her assets and liabilities to the other party to the best of his or her knowledge and ability as set forth on the financial statements of each filed herewith and incorporated by reference herein. Each party is fully cognizant of his or her rights, and each executes this agreement based upon his or her personal knowledge and the representations of the other party which each believes to be a true, complete and accurate reflection of the other party's current financial status and circumstances.

A) <u>Exchange of Financial Data</u>: Each party represents that s/he has provided the other with a current financial statement on the form promulgated pursuant to _____ (name of your state court financial statement), which discloses fully and completely all of her/his income, expenses, assets and liabilities. Both parties Financial Statements shall be filed separately with the court for confidentiality and are hereby incorporated by reference into this Agreement.

B) <u>Fiduciary Duty</u>: The Husband and Wife declare and acknowledge that each of them is relying upon the voluntary true, honest and complete full self-disclosure of the other party as to the assets, liabilities, income and expenses of the other in lieu of litigated discovery and acknowledge that each owes a fiduciary duty to the other to be forthright in their disclosure. It is the intent of this paragraph that the parties shall adopt the policy of 'Mandatory Self-Disclosure' during divorce proceedings prevalent in most states.

C) <u>Understanding of Other's Position</u>: The Husband and Wife declare that each understands the position, circumstances, financial resources, income, expenses, liabilities and prospects of the other based upon and in reliance on the aforesaid financial statements of each party and that each of them understands the terms, provisions and conditions of the within Agreement, and believes its terms, provisions and conditions to be fair and to be reasonable.

12. <u>Warranty of the Opportunity to Consult with Legal Counsel</u>: The parties further state that they have negotiated the terms of the Agreement, and that each has had the opportunity for independent legal advice by counsel of his or her own choosing and that, after consultation with his or her respective attorney and after being advised fully and fairly as to all facts and circumstances herein set forth, and after having read this Agreement line by line, each freely and fully accepts the terms, conditions and provisions hereof and enters into the Agreement voluntarily and without any coercion whatsoever.

13. <u>Warranty of Sole Agreement Between the Parties:</u> The parties further acknowledge and declare this Agreement contains the entire agreement between the parties hereto and that there are no agreements, promises, terms, conditions or understandings and no representations or inducements leading to the execution hereof, express or implied, other than those herein set forth (except for those documents or exhibits expressly annexed and incorporated by reference), and that no oral statement or prior written extrinsic to the four corners of this Agreement not expressly annexed and incorporated by reference shall have any force or effect.

14. <u>Warranty of Free Will:</u> By executing this Separation Agreement, the parties represent that the terms and provisions of this agreement are fair, just and reasonable and are not the product of fraud, coercion or undue influence, and that each signs this agreement freely and voluntarily.

15. <u>No Requirement of Strict Performance:</u> The failure of the Husband or of the Wife to comply with or insist in any instance upon the strict performance of any of the terms hereof shall not be construed as a waiver of such term or terms for the future, and the same shall nevertheless continue in full force and effect.

16. <u>Procedure in the Event a Portion of this Agreement is Later Held to be Invalid:</u> In the event any party of this Agreement shall be held invalid, such invalidity shall not invalidate the whole Agreement but the remaining provisions of this Agreement shall continue to be valid and binding to the extent that such provisions continue to reflect fairly the intent and understanding of the parties.

17. <u>Choice of State Law:</u> This Agreement shall be construed and governed according to the Laws of the State of _____(state).

18. <u>Choice of Forum:</u> so long as either party resides in _____ County, _____(state), the _____ County Family Court shall be the designated forum for all matters.

19. <u>Attachments, Addendums and Exhibits:</u> There are annexed hereto and incorporated by reference herein Exhibits A through J. Both Husband and Wife agree to be bound by, and to perform and carry out all the terms of said Exhibits to the same extent as if each was fully set forth in the text of this Agreement.

   A) <u>Exhibit A</u> – Child Custody and Parenting Schedule
   B) <u>Exhibit B</u> – Child Support and Child-Related Financial Matters
   C) <u>Exhibit C</u> – Alimony
   D) <u>Exhibit D</u> – Children's Education
   E) <u>Exhibit E</u> – Health Related Insurance and Expenses
   F) <u>Exhibit F</u> – Division of Marital Assets and Retirement Funds
   G) <u>Exhibit G</u> – Payment of Marital Debts
   H) <u>Exhibit H</u> – Income Taxes
   I) <u>Exhibit I</u> – Legal Fees and Expenses
   J) <u>Exhibit J</u> – Life Insurance

20. This Agreement shall not be altered or modified except by an instrument signed and acknowledged by the Husband and Wife and executed before a notary public.

Signed at _____(town), _____(state) on this _____ day of _____, 20____.
Executed in several counterparts.

NOTARIZED SIGNATURE PAGE

Signed: _____   _____
                          (Husband)   (Date)

State of _____

_____,ss.   Date: _____

Then personally appeared the above-named _____, and acknowledged that - he /
she - signed this separation agreement as - his / her - free act and deed.

_____

Notary Public - My Commission Expires: _____

****

Signed: _____   _____
                            (Wife)   (Date)

State of _____

_____,ss.   Date: _____

Then personally appeared the above-named _____, and acknowledged that - he /
she - signed this separation agreement as - his / her - free act and deed.

_____

Notary Public - My Commission Expires: _____

EXHIBIT A
CHILD CUSTODY

LEGAL CUSTODY: which parent makes all major, non-ordinary decisions for the children (for example, non-emergency/non-routine health care, religion, education, etc.) shall be as follows:

- ☐ The Mother shall have sole legal custody of the minor child[ren].
- ☐ The Father shall have sole legal custody of the minor child[ren].
- ☐ The parties shall have shared legal custody of the minor child[ren].

PHYSICAL CUSTODY: where the children live and which parent makes the day-today decisions regarding the children shall be as follows:

- ☐ The Father shall have sole physical custody of the minor child[ren].
- ☐ The Mother shall have sole physical custody of the minor child[ren].
- ☐ The parties shall have shared physical custody of the minor child[ren] of the parties in accordance with the following schedule:

_____
_____
_____
_____
_____
_____

- ☐ The parties shall have split physical custody as follows:
  The Mother will have physical custody of _____
                          AND
  The Father will have physical custody of _____

PARENTING SCHEDULE:

The Father shall have the right and opportunity to spend time with the child[ren]:
- ☐ At all reasonable times upon _____ advance notice
- ☐ Upon the following days and times:

_____
_____
_____
_____
_____

The Mother shall have the right and opportunity to spend time with the child[ren]:
- ☐ At all reasonable times upon _____ advance notice
- ☐ Upon the following days and times:

_____
_____
_____
_____
_____

Transportation shall be provided as follows:

- ☐ The Father shall pick up and drop off the children.
- ☐ The Mother shall pick up and drop off the children.
- ☐ The Parties shall meet _____ to exchange the children.

☐ The Parties shall pick up and drop off the children as follows:

_____

_____

_____

_____

Special School Holidays shall be shared as follows:

☐ **Christmas:**

_____

_____

☐ **Thanksgiving:**

_____

_____

☐ **Easter:**

_____

_____

☐ **Hanukah:**

_____

_____

☐ **Fourth of July:**

_____

_____

☐ **Mother's Day:**

_____

_____

☐ **Father's Day:**

_____

_____

☐ **Other Holiday (name):** _____

_____

_____

Regular School Holidays shall be shared as follows:

_____

_____

_____

_____

School Vacation Terms shall be shared as follows:

☐ **Fall/Thanksgiving Break:**

_____

_____

☐ **Christmas Break:**

_____

_____

☐ **February Break:**

_____

_____

☐ **April Break:**

_____

_____

☐ **Other Break (name):**

_____

_____

Summer Vacation shall be shared as follows:

_____

_____

_____

_____

_____

The child[ren]'s birthdays shall be shared as follows:

_____

_____

_____

_____

_____

_____

The parties birthdays shall be shared as follows:

_____

_____

_____

_____

_____

PARENTING PLAN (general provisions):

13. *Positive Parenting* – both parents agree at all times to foster a warm and positive relationship with the other parent, to not speak ill of or engage in any course of action which could undermine the other parent's relationship with the child.

14. *Mutual Consultation:* The parties shall consult in an effort to reach mutual agreement concerning major life matters and decisions, not part of the daily routine of the children, which affect their emotional, psychological, educational, social or physical well-being, including without limitation extraordinary medical, dental and psychological treatment; religious upbringing; educational choices and alternatives, including schools to be attended; whether the children shall attend summer camp, and if so, where and for how long; age appropriateness of social activities and personal pursuits; and, participation in inherently dangerous or hazardous activities. The parties shall attempt to adopt a harmonious policy calculated to promote the welfare and best interests of the children.

15. ***Dispute Resolution for Child-Related Matters****:* In the event that the parties, after conferring, are unable to agree upon major life matters and decisions regarding the children, and furthermore, are unable to determine an appropriate schedule for visitation, the parties shall confer with _____, or his/her designee, who will act as mediator with respect to any and all disputes over the children. The determination of the mediator shall be binding upon the parties, unless a party determines that on his or her reasonable belief such would not be in the best interest of the children. In such instances, the issue shall be determined by the Justice of the _____ (county) Division Family Court Department. The fees and costs of the mediator shall be shared equally by both parties, unless the mediator determines otherwise.

16. ***Right to Access Medical and Dental Records:*** Each party shall have the right to consult, and have direct access, without further permission of the other parent, to review medical and dental records of the children, consult with experts providing services to the children, and to act as custodial parent in order to give authorization for the provision of emergency medical treatment for the children.

17. ***Right to Access Educational Records:*** Each party shall have the right to consult, and have direct access, without further permission of the other parent, to review the educational records of the children, consult with teachers and/or administration at any educational institution which the children are attending, and to attend all school events and parent-teacher conferences.

18. ***Daily Living Needs:*** Each party shall have the authority and responsibility for decisions concerning daily living needs, care and activities of the children when the children are with him or her, all with the context of the provisions set forth in this Exhibit A.

19. ***Notification in the Event of Illness or Accident:*** In the event of any serious illness or accident of a child, the parent with whom the child is then staying will notify the other parent as soon as possible.

20. ***Notification in the Event of Travel Out of State:*** Either parent may travel over a state line with the children for the purposes of day-trips at any time or to visit family. Should the duration of the out-of-state trip be more than _____ hours, the parent travelling with the children shall give to the other parent the name of the person or hotel where they will be staying, the address, and a telephone number where they can be reached.

21. ***Travel Out of the Country:*** Neither parent may travel with the children out of the country without a written, notarized agreement signed by both parents granting permission to travel.

OTHER CHILD CUSTODY-RELATED TERMS NOT COVERED ELSEWHERE: (explain)

_____

_____

_____

_____

_____

_____

_____

EXHIBIT B
CHILD SUPPORT AND CHILD-RELATED FINANCIAL MATTERS

CHILD SUPPORT:

Starting on _____/_____/_____ and payable every:

- ☐ Week
- ☐ Two weeks
- ☐ Bi-monthly on the _____th and _____th of the month
- ☐ Monthly on the _____th of the month

The:

- ☐ Father shall be obligated to pay $_____ child support, under the _____ (state) child support guidelines, to the Mother.
- ☐ Mother shall be obligated to pay $_____ child support, under the _____ (state) child support guidelines, to the Father.
- ☐ Neither party shall be obligated to pay child support at this time. The reasons for such are (explain below):

_____

If the agreed child support amount above deviates from the guidelines by 5% or more, explain the reason(s) here:

_____
_____

The Child Support Guidelines Worksheet is completed, attached, and hereby incorporated by reference to this Agreement.

Child support shall be by via wage assignment which (choose ONE):

- ☐ Shall be payable directly to the _____ (father/mother);
- ☐ Shall be payable through the _____ (state) Child Support Enforcement Division and implemented immediately;

Child support shall terminate (check all that apply):

- ☐ Upon the youngest child having attained the age of eighteen (18) years old and graduates from high school, however, no later than obtaining age 20, whichever occurs later;
- ☐ Upon the youngest child having attained the age of eighteen (18) years old and graduates from high school, unless the child has plans for future education as a full-time student as set forth in Exhibit D - Education;
- ☐ If the child is attending a post-secondary accredited educational training school or a two year or four year accredited college program as a full-time student, at age 23 or the completion of such school or college, whichever occurs sooner. See Exhibit D - Education. The child shall not be deemed emancipated the summer between completion of high school and beginning of said post-secondary training (including full-time work) or work periods during summer break.
- ☐ Until the youngest child becomes emancipated as defined by the current laws of _____ (state);
- ☐ If after the age of 18, until (date) _____

Child support for a child or children over the age of eighteen (18) who are principally domiciled with one parent and dependent upon the parents for support:

- ☐ Shall continue at the above rate until _____
- ☐ Shall increase to $ _____ and terminate_____

☐ Shall decrease to $ _____ and terminate_____

☐ Shall be determined by the Court at that time by filing a Complaint for Modification

CHILDREN'S HEALTH INSURANCE: (Cross-reference with Exhibit E - Health Insurance)

☐ The Mother shall maintain health insurance for the parties' minor child[ren].

☐ The Father shall maintain health insurance for the parties' minor child[ren].

☐ Health insurance is not reasonable in cost and accessible to the child[ren] at this time.

Any uninsured/ unreimbursed medical costs for the minor child[ren] shall be assessed as follows:

☐ Shared equally (50:50) by both parents.

☐ Prorated according to the child support guideline percentages with the Father paying _____% of the cost and the Mother paying _____% of the cost;

☐ Other (explain): _____

The party providing coverage will provide insurance cards to the other party showing coverage.

CHILDREN'S DENTAL INSURANCE: (Cross-reference with Exhibit E - Health Insurance)

☐ The Mother shall maintain dental insurance for the parties' minor child[ren].

☐ The Father shall maintain dental insurance for the parties' minor child[ren].

☐ Dental insurance is not reasonable in cost and accessible to the child[ren] at this time.

Any uninsured/ unreimbursed dental costs for the minor child[ren] shall be assessed as follows:

☐ Shared equally (50:50) by both parents.

☐ Prorated according to the child support guideline percentages with the Father paying _____% of the cost and the Mother paying _____% of the cost;

☐ Other (explain): _____

The party providing coverage will provide insurance cards to the other party showing coverage.

CHILDREN'S VISION INSURANCE: (Cross-reference with Exhibit E - Health Insurance)

☐ The Mother shall maintain vision insurance for the parties' minor child[ren].

☐ The Father shall maintain vision insurance for the parties' minor child[ren].

☐ Vision insurance is not reasonable in cost and accessible to the child[ren] at this time.

Any uninsured/ unreimbursed vision costs for the minor child[ren] shall be assessed as follows:

☐ Shared equally (50:50) by both parents.

☐ Prorated according to the child support guideline percentages with the Father paying _____% of the cost and the Mother paying _____% of the cost;

☐ Other (explain): _____

The party providing coverage will provide insurance cards to the other party showing coverage.

PROCEDURE FOR ORTHODONTAL CARE:

If one or all of the children require orthodontic care, the parties shall jointly consult with area orthodontists and review all available dental insurance plans to minimize the cost of providing such care. If, for example, one party has available a slightly more expensive plan which would justify its cost by covering a larger portion of treatment after a reasonable waiting period, the couple may agree to change insurance plans, modify insurance reimbursement to the other spouse, and wait until the new coverage eligibility requirements are met before proceeding with the child's orthodontic regimen. This includes time for one party to leverage tax benefits for an employer-sponsored flexible spending account. All unreimbursed orthodontic expenses shall be divided as follows:

Any uninsured/ unreimbursed orthodontia costs for the minor child[ren] shall be assessed as follows:

- ☐ Shared equally (50:50) by both parents.
- ☐ Prorated according to the child support guideline percentages with the Father paying _____% of the cost and the Mother paying _____% of the cost;
- ☐ Other (explain): _____

The party providing coverage will provide insurance cards to the other party showing coverage.

PROCEDURE FOR UNINSURED/UNREIMBURSED EXPENSES: (Cross-reference with Exhibit E)

As to all uninsured/unreimbursed medical, dental, vision or orthodontia expenses, the party who incurs the expense shall submit a written request for reimbursement to the other party within 30 days and attach copies of all receipts. The other party, within 30 days of receipt, shall submit the applicable reimbursement for that expense, according to the schedule of reimbursement set out in this Exhibit B.

DUTY TO CONSULT ANNUALLY AS TO COVERAGE PLANS: (Cross-reference with Exhibit E)

The parties agree to consult with one another at least once annually about all anticipated medical expenses for the upcoming calendar year and provide information/brochures to the other party about all available options prior to any 'open enrollment' or insurance deadlines and compute the cost/benefit of any changes in said plans. The purpose of this paragraph is to encourage budgeting and planning for the upcoming year.

DUTY TO CONFER ON NON-EMERGENCY OR RECURRING EXPENSES:

The parties agree to consult with one another and attempt to minimize all non-emergency dental and vision expenses by comparing policy coverage, plan limits, providers, the availability of flexible health spending accounts, and less expensive alternatives to all non-emergency proposed treatment. Neither party shall, however, use this Item to unreasonably withhold consent to provide appropriate dental or vision care for the children. The purpose of this Item is to encourage budgeting and planning, not denial of care..

LIFE INSURANCE: (Cross-reference with Exhibit I - Life Insurance)

- ☐ The Mother shall be required to maintain life insurance coverage for the benefit of the parties' minor child(ren) in the amount of $ _____ until the youngest child becomes emancipated.

- ☐ The Father shall be required to maintain life insurance coverage for the benefit of the parties' minor child(ren) in the amount of $ _____ until the youngest child becomes emancipated.

IRS INCOME TAX DEPENDENT DEDUCTION(S): (Cross-reference with Exhibit H - Income Taxes)

- ☐ The Mother shall claim the following child[ren] as her dependent(s) for state and federal income tax purposes, _____.

☐ The Father shall claim the following child[ren] as his dependent(s) for state and federal income tax purposes,

_____.

☐ The parties shall alternate years in claiming the children as dependents for state and federal income tax purposes as follows:

The _____ shall claim the child[ren] for odd years,
    (Mother / Father)

AND

The _____ shall claim the child[ren] for even years.
    (Mother / Father)

☐ The assignment of any tax deductions for the child(ren) shall be as follows (explain):

_____

The other parent will convey any applicable IRS form regarding the income tax deduction.

COST OF ORDINARY PUBLIC SCHOOL FEES:

The cost of ordinary public school fees, such as school bus rider fees, school-sponsored sports fees, school-sponsored music or instrument fees, classroom and text book fees, school-sponsored 'club' fees, and school supplies, shall be split as follows:

☐ Shared equally (50:50) by both parents.
☐ Prorated according to the child support guideline percentages with the Father paying ____% of the cost and the Mother paying ____% of the cost;
☐ Other (explain): _____

COST OF NON-ORDINARY ACTIVITY FEES:

The parties agree to consult with each other about fees for activities which are not sponsored or traditionally considered part of a public education, such as private lessons at a location other than the school.

COST OF CHILD CARE/BABYSITTING:

Each parent shall be responsible for providing and/or paying the cost of child care or babysitting on days and at times when the children are scheduled to be with them.

LIFE INSURANCE: (Choose if applicable)

☐ Life insurance in the amount of $ _____ to secure the above Child Support will be provided by the obligor as outlined in Exhibit J of this Agreement.

OTHER PROVISIONS RELATING TO CHILD SUPPORT: (elaborate)

_____

_____

_____

EXHIBIT C
ALIMONY

ALIMONY OBLIGATION:

The parties agree that alimony shall be as follows (check only one box):

☐ Each party hereby waives past and present spousal support (alimony) from the other and reserves the matter of future alimony for consideration by the Court;

☐ Each party forever waives their right to receive any past, present or future spousal support (alimony) that they may have. The parties understand that once the Court accepts a party's waiver, that party may **never** request maintenance (except as may be overridden by certain acts of the legislature) ;

☐ The Husband agrees to pay the Wife spousal support (alimony) in the amount of $ _____ every:
    ☐ Week;
    ☐ Two weeks;
    ☐ Bi-monthly on the ____th and ____th of the month;
    ☐ Month;
Beginning on _____ (date) ___ and continuing until the termination date specified below:

☐ The Wife agrees to pay the Husband spousal support (alimony) in the amount of $ _____ every:
    ☐ Week;
    ☐ Two weeks;
    ☐ Bi-monthly on the ____th and ____th of the month;
    ☐ Month;
Beginning on _____ (date) ___ and continuing until the termination date specified below:

Said payments shall be made in cash and shall terminate on the first to occur of the death of the Wife, the death of the Husband, or:

☐ The remarriage or cohabitation of the alimony recipient _____ (husband/wife);
☐ The alimony recipient _____ (husband/wife) attaining their _____th birthday;
☐ The alimony payor _____ (husband/wife) reaching their full social security retirement age;
☐ The passage of _____ months;
☐ The passage of _____ years;
☐ Other event (specify): _____

INTERACTION BETWEEN ALIMONY AND CHILD SUPPORT: (Cross-reference with Exhibit B - Child Support)

The parties acknowledge that alimony payments are being offset from Child Support as follows:

☐ Neither party is eligible for alimony -or- alimony has been waived;
☐ The parties recognize that an additional $_____ per _____ (payment period) of alimony is being offset in satisfaction of the _____ (husband's/wife's) child support obligations set forth in Exhibit B of this Agreement;
☐ Alimony shall be payable along with the Child Support through the _____ (state) Child Support Enforcement Division for so long as the aforementioned Child Support obligation exists;

TAX PROVISIONS: (Cross-reference with Exhibit H - Income Taxes)

For income tax purposes, only those portions of alimony which are not being offset in satisfaction of the _____ (husband's/wife's) child support obligation shall be taxable to the recipient _____ (husband/wife), or $_____ per month.

The amount of the alimony payments set forth in this Exhibit C has been determined on the basis of currently prevailing federal and state income tax laws, rules and regulations, with the intention and understanding that all payments made pursuant to the above paragraphs 1 and 2 of this Exhibit C, qualify as alimony payments for income tax purposes, as those terms are defined in Section 71 and any other applicable section of the United States Internal Revenue Code as amended and _____ law chapter _____ as amended, each as in effect as of the date of the execution of this Agreement. Accordingly, such alimony payment shall be deductible to the Alimony Payor _____ (husband/wife) and taxable to the Alimony Recipient _____ (wife/husband). In the event of any change of the rules, rulings or regulations of the Internal Revenue Service, or in the event of subsequent statutory amendment, judicial or administrative order or decision contrary to this result, the amount payable pursuant to this provision shall be adjusted to reflect the intent and understanding expressed in this Exhibit.

TYPE OF ALIMONY:

Explain type of alimony:
- ☐ Temporary
- ☐ Rehabilitative
- ☐ Lump Sum (amount) $_____
- ☐ Permanent/lifetime;
- ☐ Other (name specifics): _____

LIFE INSURANCE: (Choose if applicable) (Cross-reference with Exhibit J - Life Insurance)

☐ Life insurance in the amount of $ _____ to secure the above Spousal Support/Alimony will be provided by the obligor as outlined in Exhibit J of this Agreement.

HEALTH INSURANCE: (Choose if applicable) (Cross-reference with Exhibit E - Health Insurance)

☐ Health insurance will be provided by the obligor as outlined in Exhibit E of this Agreement.

OTHER ALIMONY TERMS NOT COVERED ELSEWHERE: (Outline below):

_____

_____

_____

_____

_____

_____

EXHIBIT D
CHILDREN'S EDUCATION

1. The Husband and Wife agree that the children should receive the most appropriate educations available to them in light of their developing aptitudes and interests, including education at the college level, and public or private school education, as needed and appropriate. Both parties recognize that the educations of the children will require substantial financial expenditure.

2. The Husband and Wife may utilize funds from any Educational Trusts (such as 529 Plans, Education IRA's, or Education U.S. Savings Bonds) they set up for the benefit of the children to pay for college expenses at any college the children may choose to attend, for up to four years of undergraduate studies. Any tax benefits which result from said financial planning shall flow to the party who plans.

3. Any Education Trusts set up by the parents or his or her relatives subsequent to this divorce to fund the children's education shall be applied against that parents' share of the children's educational expenses. Any tax or other benefits shall flow to the party whose family plans.

4. For the purposes of this Exhibit, the term "expenses" shall include tuition, board, room, books, usual and normal student activity fees and any other expenses shall be benchmarked to those normally charged at the _____ (state) university/college at _____ (name flagship state university), and a reasonable allowance for transportation to and from such institution.

5. In the event the educational expenses of the un-emancipated children exceed the amounts available in any trusts, the parties shall be responsible for payment of any additional amounts (not to include graduate or professional school), to the extent they are then financially able to do so and in proportion to their then assets and incomes from all sources (not to include income from new spouses).

6. Other Terms (explain):

    _____

    _____

    _____

    _____

    _____

    _____

    _____

    _____

    _____

    _____

    _____

    _____

EXHIBIT E
HEALTH-RELATED INSURANCE AND EXPENSES

HEALTH INSURANCE FOR THE PARTIES:

The Wife's health insurance coverage will be provided (check all that apply):

☐ by the Wife
☐ by the Husband
☐ by the Husband through his employer for so long as it is available to him, and if there is any additional cost to continued coverage for the insurance:

_____

_____

☐ If the Husband remarries and affects the Wife's eligibility, the Husband shall procure insurance for the Wife's benefit at his own expense under the following terms and conditions (explain):

_____

_____

The Husband's health insurance coverage will be provided (check all that apply):

☐ by the Husband
☐ by the Wife
☐ by the Wife for so long as it is available to her, and if there is any additional cost to continued coverage for the insurance:

_____

_____

☐ If the Wife remarries and affects the Husband's eligibility, the Wife shall procure insurance for the Husband's benefit at her own expense under the following terms and conditions (explain):

_____

_____

OTHER HEALTH-RELATED INSURANCE FOR THE PARTIES:

The Husband shall continue to maintain the following health-related insurances for the benefit of the Wife for so long as it remains available to him (check all that apply):

☐ There is no additional health-related insurance available;
☐ Dental
☐ Vision
☐ Orthodontia
☐ Therapeutic
☐ If there is additional cost involved, it shall be handled as follows (explain):

_____

_____

The Wife shall continue to maintain the following health-related insurances for the benefit of the Husband for so long as it remains available to her (check all that apply):

☐   There is no additional health-related insurance available;
☐   Dental
☐   Vision
☐   Orthodontia
☐   Prescription medication
☐   Therapeutic
☐   Other (name): _____
☐   If there is additional cost involved, it shall be handled as follows (explain):

_____

_____

UNINSURED/UNREIMBURSED HEALTH-RELATED EXPENSES:

The cost of all reasonable uninsured and unreimbursed medical, dental, hospital, optical, prescription medication and therapeutic counseling services for the Wife shall be paid:

☐   by the Wife
☐   _____% by Wife;
☐   _____% by Husband

The cost of all reasonable uninsured and unreimbursed medical, dental, hospital, optical, prescription medication and therapeutic counseling services for the Husband shall be paid:

☐   by the Husband
☐   _____% by Wife;
☐   _____% by Husband

HEALTH INSURANCE FOR THE PARTIES UNEMANCIPATED CHILDREN:

Check all that apply:

☐   The parties have no unemancipated children;
☐   The parties' children are legally emancipated, but still eligible to remain on one parent's health insurance policy until age _____. The parties agree to allow the children to remain on said policy so long as there is no additional cost or expense or to (elaborate):

_____

_____

☐   The parties agree to provide health, dental, vision and orthodontia insurance (as outlined in Exhibit B - Child Support and Child-Related Financial Matters of this Separation Agreement.

IMPACT OF REMARRIAGE UPON ELIGIBILITY:

The parties acknowledge that the eligibility for health and health-related insurance is a significant matter. Should one party contemplate remarriage, the other party will usually be terminated from the Insured's health and health-related insurance plans. Therefore, should the Insured Party contemplate remarriage, the Insured Party shall give the Insurance Dependent a minimum of 60 days' notice to explore other options. Furthermore, the Insured Party shall assist the Insurance Dependent in executing any paperwork necessary to take advantage of any COBRA or other extension plans available to them.

DUTY TO INFORM OF ANY EVENT WHICH WOULD IMPAIR COVERAGE:

The parties acknowledge that the eligibility for health and health-related insurance is a significant matter. In addition to any obligation imposed by applicable law upon the insurer to notify the Insured Party of cancellation of coverage, the Insured Party shall notify the Insurance Dependent within 30 days after becoming aware of any circumstances which would affect his or her eligibility for, the availability of, or the nature of his or her continued health, dental, vision, or other health-related insurance coverage.

Should one party contemplate remarriage, the other party will usually be terminated from the Insured's health and health-related insurance plans. Therefore, should the Insured Party contemplate remarriage, the duty of the Insured Party to give the Insurance Dependent notice shall increase to a minimum of 60 days' notice.

The Insurance Dependent shall have the right, pursuant to any applicable law, to continue to receive benefits as are available to the Insured Party by any means then available, including by rider to the existing policy or conversion to an individual policy, which would have benefits reasonably equivalent to those which they would be otherwise receiving pursuant to this Exhibit E. If the Insurance Dependent elects to continue such coverage, the Insured Party shall cooperate in making the necessary arrangements for, and shall execute any documents necessary to effectuate the continuation of said coverage.

DUTY TO CONSULT:

If one party is providing health-related insurance for the other, the parties agree that from time to time or at minimum once per year prior to any open-enrollment period, that they shall compare all medical, dental, vision and other health-related plans which may be available to them through their employers or other sources and discuss what cost, coverage, and co-pay schedules would be most beneficial to them and the minor children. If health, dental, vision or other insurance premiums increase or another plan becomes available at a lower rate or which provides better coverage, the parties may reach a new agreement regarding reimbursement for their share of said costs, or file a Complaint for Modification to address this issue in the _____ (county) Division of the Court.

HEALTH TRUST CARE FUNDS:

The Husband and Wife may pay their share of all uninsured medical, dental, vision and other health-related expenses (if any) from any health care trust funds they may set up (such as flexible spending accounts) to make said payments, with any tax advantages realized by utilizing such trusts flowing to the party who does the planning and saving.

OTHER INSURANCE -RELATED TERMS NOT COVERED ELSEWHERE: (explain)

_____

_____

_____

_____

_____

_____

_____

_____

_____

_____

_____

EXHIBIT F
DIVISION OF MARITAL ASSETS AND RETIREMENT FUNDS

The Husband and Wife own real estate, personal property, pension and profit sharing plans, securities, investments, and other marital assets. Each party agrees to execute any and all documents necessary to effectuate the terms of this Exhibit F and the transfers, conveyances and payments required by said terms. The parties individual Financial Statements containing sensitive information such as account numbers and exact fair market values are to be filed concurrently with this Agreement and are hereby merged with it and incorporated by reference. In exchange for the mutual covenants contained in this Agreement, the parties agree to divide their assets (everything they own and that is owed to them) as follows:

REAL ESTATE: (check all that apply)

☐ The parties do not own any real estate.

☐ The parties have already divided their interest in the marital home located at (specify) as follows:

_____

_____

☐ The parties agree to the following terms relating to all real estate owned as follows:

Address of Property	Party who will take ownership and title		Party who will assume all obligations (mortgage, taxes, insurance, etc.)			
	H	W	H	W	Both (indicate %)	
					H ___ %	W ___ %
					H ___ %	W ___ %
					H ___ %	W ___ %
					H ___ %	W ___ %

☐ The parties agree to sell the Real Estate located at (specify) _____. Any proceeds or monies owed following the sale will be divided to the parties as follows:

Husband $_____ or _____ %
 and
Wife $_____ or _____ %

☐ The parties agree to prepare documents (e.g., Quit Claim Deed) to transfer title by _____ date.

☐ The party who will take ownership and title of the property will refinance all existing loans, mortgages, home equity lines of credits or other liens against the property and remove the other spouses name from the debt(s) as follows:
 ☐ Within _____ months from _____ date.
 ☐ By _____ date.

☐ The parties agree to an equity payout as follows:
 ☐ The Husband will pay the Wife $_____ by _____ (date);
 ☐ The Wife will pay the Husband $_____ by _____ (date).

☐ The parties have already transferred title and have notified the lender of the change in ownership per this Agreement

☐ Other (specify):

_____

_____

_____

_____

_____

MOTOR VEHICLES AND/OR RECREATIONAL VEHICLES: (check all that apply)

☐ The parties do not own any motor vehicles and/or recreational vehicles.

☐ The parties have already divided their interest in the following motor and/or recreational vehicles (specify) as follows:

_____

_____

☐ The parties agree to the following terms relating to all real estate owned as follows:

Identify Vehicle & Type				Party who will take ownership and title		Party who will assume all obligations (Loan Payment, Registration, Insurance, etc.)		
Year	Make	Model	VIN#	H	W	H	W	Both (indicate %)
				☐	☐	☐	☐	H ___ % W ___ %
				☐	☐	☐	☐	H ___ % W ___ %
				☐	☐	☐	☐	H ___ % W ___ %
				☐	☐	☐	☐	H ___ % W ___ %
				☐	☐	☐	☐	H ___ % W ___ %
				☐	☐	☐	☐	H ___ % W ___ %

☐ The parties agree to sign over the respective title of each vehicle by _____ date.

☐ The party who will take ownership and title of the vehicles will have the following amount of time to refinance the loan and remove the other spouse from the debt.
    ☐ Will have _____ months from _____ date.
    ☐ Will have until _____ date.

☐ The parties have already transferred title and have notified the lender of the change in ownership per this Agreement

☐ Other (specify):

_____

_____

_____

_____

_____

CASH ON HAND, BANK, CHECKING AND SAVINGS ACCOUNTS: (check all that apply)

☐ The parties do not have any accounts.

☐ The parties agree to the following terms relating to all accounts:

Identify Name of Bank or Financial Institution	Identify Type of Bank Account	Distribution of Each Account		
		H = 100%	W = 100%	Both (indicate %)
		☐	☐	H ___ % W ___ %
		☐	☐	H ___ % W ___ %
		☐	☐	H ___ % W ___ %
		☐	☐	H ___ % W ___ %
		☐	☐	H ___ % W ___ %
		☐	☐	H ___ % W ___ %
		☐	☐	H ___ % W ___ %
		☐	☐	H ___ % W ___ %

☐ The parties agree to divide/transfer the funds by _____ date.

☐ The parties have already divided/transferred the funds per this Agreement

☐ Other (specify):

_____

_____

_____

_____

_____

_____

WHOLE LIFE INSURANCE: (cash value)

☐ The parties do not own life insurance.

☐ The parties have life insurance, but it is term insurance only (i.e., no cash value).

☐ One or both of the parties have a Whole Life (not term) policy that has a surrender cash value and it has been accounted for in the property division as follows (specify):

_____

_____

FURNITURE, HOUSEHOLD GOODS, AND OTHER PERSONAL PROPERTY: (check all that apply)

☐ The parties do not have any assets in this category.

☐ The parties have divided the furniture, household goods, and other personal property and are satisfied with the division.

☐ The parties agree to the following terms relating to all furniture, household goods and other personal property:

Identify Items	H	W	Identify Items	H	W
	☐	☐		☐	☐
	☐	☐		☐	☐
	☐	☐		☐	☐
	☐	☐		☐	☐
	☐	☐		☐	☐
	☐	☐		☐	☐
	☐	☐		☐	☐
	☐	☐		☐	☐
	☐	☐		☐	☐
	☐	☐		☐	☐

☐ The parties are attaching an additional listing of personal items to be divided (above) to this Exhibit F which is part of this Exhibit and hereby incorporated by reference to this Agreement.

☐ Any personal item(s) not listed above is the property of the party currently in possession of the item(s).

☐ Other (specify):

_____

_____

STOCKS, BONDS, MUTUAL FUNDS, SECURITIES & INVESTMENT ACCOUNTS: (check all that apply)

☐ The parties do not have any assets in this category.

☐ The parties agree to the following terms relating to all accounts:

Identify Name of Stock, Bond, Mutual Fund, etc.	Distribution of Funds, Shares, etc.		
	H = 100%	W = 100%	Both (indicate %)
	☐	☐	H ___ % W ___ %
	☐	☐	H ___ % W ___ %
	☐	☐	H ___ % W ___ %
	☐	☐	H ___ % W ___ %
	☐	☐	H ___ % W ___ %
	☐	☐	H ___ % W ___ %

☐ The parties agree to divide/transfer the funds by _____ date.

☐ The parties have already divided/transferred the funds per this Agreement

☐ Other (specify):

_____

_____

PENSION, PROFIT SHARING OR RETIREMENT FUNDS: (check all that apply)

☐ The parties do not have any funds.

☐ The parties agree to the following terms relating to all retirement accounts:

Identify Type of Pension, Profit Sharing or Retirement Fund	Distribution of Funds, Shares, etc. Within the Various Accounts		
	H = 100%	W = 100%	Both (indicate %)
	☐	☐	H ___ % W ___ %
	☐	☐	H ___ % W ___ %
	☐	☐	H ___ % W ___ %
	☐	☐	H ___ % W ___ %
	☐	☐	H ___ % W ___ %
	☐	☐	H ___ % W ___ %

☐ The parties agree to divide/transfer the funds by _____ date.

☐ The parties have already divided/transferred the funds per this Agreement

☐ Other (specify):

_____

_____

QUALIFIED DOMESTIC RELATIONS ORDER (QDRO) RELATING TO ABOVE-NAMED PENSION, PROFIT-SHARING OR RETIREMENT FUNDS:

The ☐ husband ☐ wife is responsible for preparing and submitting a Qualified Domestic Relations Order (QDRO) by contacting their fund provider or an attorney by _____ date.

The cost to prepare the QDRO will be paid as follows: ☐ husband _____% ☐ wife _____%

Note: A QDRO is necessary in order for the division of the retirement plan to be completed. Without a QDRO, plans will not be divided regardless of the parties' agreement identified within this form.

☐ Other (specify):

_____

_____

MISCELLANEOUS ASSETS NOT LISTED ELSEWHERE:

The parties do hereby divide any remaining assets not specifically listed elsewhere in this Exhibit F, including items identified in the parties' sworn Financial Statements filed with the court today under 'other' or 'miscellaneous' categories, considered to be 'separate property,' or otherwise not listed as follows:

☐ The parties do not have any assets in this category.

☐ The parties have already divided all of the miscellaneous assets not listed elsewhere in this Exhibit F and are satisfied with the division.

☐ The parties agree to the following terms relating to all miscellaneous assets listed below:

Identify Items	H	W	Identify Items	H	W
	☐	☐		☐	☐
	☐	☐		☐	☐
	☐	☐		☐	☐
	☐	☐		☐	☐
	☐	☐		☐	☐
	☐	☐		☐	☐
	☐	☐		☐	☐
	☐	☐		☐	☐
	☐	☐		☐	☐
	☐	☐		☐	☐

☐ The parties are attaching an additional listing of personal items to be divided (above) to this Exhibit F which is part of this Exhibit and hereby incorporated by reference to this Agreement.

☐ Any miscellaneous asset(s) not listed above is the property of the party currently in possession of the item(s).

☐ Other (specify): _____

_____

TAX TREATMENT OF THE DIVISION OF MARITAL PROPERTY:

The conveyances, transfers and payments described in this Exhibit F are not contingent upon any event other than the execution of this Agreement and do not qualify as alimony as that term is defined by applicable sections, including s.71 of the United States Internal Revenue Code, as amended, and _____ state law, section ____, as amended, each as in effect as of the date of the execution of this Agreement, and further it is the parties' intent that these transfers qualify under Section 1041 of the Internal Revenue Code. Therefore, the parties agree that these transfers and payments shall neither be deductible by the Husband nor taxable to the Wife, as income, for federal and state income tax purposes.

MUTUAL WAIVERS:

16. Except as otherwise provided by the terms of this Agreement, the Husband expressly waives and relinquishes any and all claim, right, title and interest he may have, whether arising out of the marital relationship of the parties or otherwise, in and to any bank or investment accounts, certificates of deposit, trusts, securities, bonds, shares of stock, IRA, pension or profit sharing plans, business interests of the Wife, inheritances, past, present, or future, causes of action, receivables, uncollected fees, entity or entities or other form of property, either real or personal,

held by the Wife individually, or with others, or in any other form for the benefit of the Wife.

17. Except as otherwise provided by the terms of this Agreement, the Wife expressly waives and relinquishes any and all claim, right, title and interest she may have, whether arising out of the marital relationship of the parties or otherwise, in and to any bank or investment accounts, certificates of deposit, trusts, securities, bonds, shares of stock, IRA, pension or profit sharing plans, business interests of the Husband, including without limitation the Husband's inheritances, past, present or future, causes of action, receivables, uncollected fees, entity or entities or other form of property, either real or personal, held by the Husband individually, or with others, or in any other form for the benefit of the Husband.

18. Except as otherwise provided by the terms of this Agreement, the Husband and the Wife each release and relinquish any interest in real property or items of personal property of or in the possession of the other. Henceforth, each of the parties shall own, have and enjoy, independently of the other party, all real estate and items of personal property of every kind, nature and description and wherever situated, which are now owned or possessed by him or her, or may be hereafter acquired, with full power in him or her to dispose of the same as fully and effectually in all respects and for all purposes as if he or she were unmarried.

EXECUTION OF DOCUMENTS:

Each party agrees to execute any and all documents necessary to effectuate the terms of this Exhibit F and the transfers, conveyances and payments required by said terms.

OTHER PROPERTY-DIVISION RELATED TERMS NOT COVERED ELSEWHERE: (explain)

_____

_____

_____

_____

_____

_____

_____

_____

_____

_____

_____

_____

EXHIBIT G
PAYMENT OF MARITAL DEBTS

The Husband and Wife agree to an orderly repayment of all marital debt. The parties hereby refer to their Financial Statements filed with the court today and do hereby incorporate by reference those debts listed as follows:

REPAYMENT OF DEBTS: (check all that apply)

☐ The parties do not have any debt.

☐ The parties agree to the following terms relating to all debt (including interest, penalty and fees) and the party responsible for that debt will indemnify and hold the other party harmless.

Identify Name of Creditor	Date of Balance	Balance	Party Responsible for Future Payments		
			H = 100%	W = 100%	Both (indicate %)
		$	☐	☐	H ___ % W ___ %
			☐	☐	H ___ % W ___ %
			☐	☐	H ___ % W ___ %
			☐	☐	H ___ % W ___ %
			☐	☐	H ___ % W ___ %
			☐	☐	H ___ % W ___ %
			☐	☐	H ___ % W ___ %
			☐	☐	H ___ % W ___ %
			☐	☐	H ___ % W ___ %
			☐	☐	H ___ % W ___ %
			☐	☐	H ___ % W ___ %
			☐	☐	H ___ % W ___ %
			☐	☐	H ___ % W ___ %
			☐	☐	H ___ % W ___ %
			☐	☐	H ___ % W ___ %
Total debt to be assumed by the Husband	$		H ____ %		
Total debt to be assumed by the Wife	$		W ____ %		

☐ The parties do hereby attach a Debt Addendum listing additional debts and do hereby incorporate said former list to this Exhibit G by reference..

☐ The parties agree to cancel any joint credit cards.

☐ The parties agree to repay any mortgages or liens associated with any real estate they take title to as outlined in Exhibit F.

☐ The parties agree to repay any liens associated with any motor vehicle or recreational vehicle they take possession of as outlined in Exhibit F.

☐ Other (specify):

_____
_____
_____
_____
_____
_____
_____
_____
_____
_____

FUTURE DEBT:

Except as specifically set forth herein, each Party shall be responsible for all expenses, bills and obligations of themselves and their property. Neither party will incur any debts, charges or liabilities for with the other Party, their legal representative, property or estate will or may become liable, except to enforce or pursuant to the provisions of this Agreement.

LATE PAYMENT OR BREACH OF ONE OF THE PARTIES:

Should any violation of this Agreement occur, the Party who caused the violation agrees to hold the other Party harmless and to reimburse them for any and all debts, charges and liabilities contracted or incurred (including attorney's fees, costs and expenses) because of the violation. Should additional interest, penalties, or late fees be assed against any joint marital debt because one party paid their portion on time and the other failed to pay on time, the party who incurred the additional interest, fees and penalties shall make additional payment equal to the amount of excess penalties, interest and fees before the next payment cycle so that the account balance is adjusted *as if* all payments had been made on time.

OTHER DEBT-RELATED TERMS NOT COVERED ELSEWHERE: (explain)

_____
_____
_____
_____
_____
_____
_____

EXHIBIT H
INCOME TAXES

CURRENT AND PAST YEARS TAX RETURNS:

☐ The parties agree to file the following type of federal and state income tax returns for the tax year(s) _____ (specify current and past tax years):
- ☐ joint
- ☐ separate
- ☐ married filing separately

☐ State and Federal refunds and/or money owed will be allocated as follows:
- ☐ Husband: _____%
- ☐ Wife: _____%

The following party shall be responsible for the preparation of said returns. Either party may retain and independent accountant at their own expense to review said tax returns for signature.

- ☐ Husband
- ☐ Wife
- ☐ Husband and Wife shall share the cost of tax preparation equally.
- ☐ Husband and Wife shall share the cost of tax preparation services as follows:
  - ☐ Husband: _____%
  - ☐ Wife: _____%
- ☐ Other (specify): _____

FUTURE YEARS TAX RETURNS:

The parties shall file separate federal and state income tax returns for _____ and thereafter.

TAX DEPENDENTS

The parties agree to claim any dependent children as specified in Exhibit B - Child Support and Child-Related Financial Matters of this Separation Agreement.

TAX TREATMENT OF SPOUSAL SUPPORT/ALIMONY:

As outlined in Exhibit C - Spousal Support/Alimony, only those portions of alimony which are not being offset in satisfaction of the Payor's child support obligation shall be taxable to the Recipient.

The amount of the alimony payments set forth in this Exhibit H has been determined on the basis of currently prevailing federal and state income tax laws, rules and regulations, with the intention and understanding that all payments made pursuant to the above paragraphs 1 and 2 of this Exhibit H, qualify as alimony payments for income tax purposes, as those terms are defined in Section 71 and any other applicable section of the United States Internal Revenue Code as amended and _____ law chapter _____ as amended, each as in effect as of the date of the execution of this Agreement. Accordingly, such alimony payment shall be deductible to the Alimony Payor _____ (husband/wife) and taxable to the Alimony Recipient _____ (wife/husband). In the event of any change of the rules, rulings or regulations of the Internal Revenue Service, or in the event of subsequent statutory amendment, judicial or administrative order or decision contrary to this result, the amount payable pursuant to this provision shall be adjusted to reflect the intent and understanding expressed in this Exhibit.

TAX INDEMNIFICATION:

The Wife covenants at all times to hold the Husband free, harmless and indemnified from and against all income tax obligations, deficiencies, penalties or interest assessed, which have been or may be incurred in connection with the filing of any joint tax return, state or federal, by them, and which obligation, deficiency, penalty or interest is attributable to the Wife's income, error or omission. Notwithstanding anything to the contrary contained in this Agreement, the Wife further covenants at all times to hold the Husband free, harmless and indemnified from and against all debts, charges or liabilities incurred by her in breach of the provisions of this paragraph, and from any and all attorneys' fees, costs and expenses incurred by the Husband as a result of any such breach.

The Husband covenants at all times to hold the Wife free, harmless and indemnified from and against all income tax obligations, deficiencies, penalties or interest assessed, which have been or may be incurred in connection with the filing of any joint tax return, state or federal, by them, and which obligation, deficiency, penalty or interest is attributable to the Husband's income, error or omission. Notwithstanding anything to the contrary contained in this Agreement, the Husband further covenants at all times to hold the Wife free, harmless and indemnified from and against all debts, charges or liabilities incurred by her in breach of the provisions of this paragraph, and from any and all attorneys' fees, costs and expenses incurred by the Wife as a result of any such breach.

OTHER TAX-RELATED TERMS NOT COVERED ELSEWHERE: (explain)

_____

_____

_____

_____

_____

_____

_____

_____

_____

_____

_____

EXHIBIT I
LEGAL FEES AND EXPENSES

LEGAL FEES RELATED TO THE DIVORCE:

- ☐ The Husband shall pay all court costs and legal fees (including mediation) for both parties;

- ☐ The Wife shall pay all court costs and legal fees (including mediation) for both parties;

- ☐ The parties shall divide the cost of all court costs and legal fees (including mediation) for both parties equally (50:50);

- ☐ The parties shall divide the cost of all court costs and legal fees (including mediation) as follows:

  - ☐ Husband shall pay _____%

  - ☐ Wife shall pay _____%

- ☐ Each party shall be responsible for the payment of his or her own attorney's fees, expenses and expert witness fees incurred in the prosecution, negotiation and settlement of the pending divorce litigation between the parties.

- ☐ Each party shall be responsible for the payment of his or her own attorney's fees, expenses and expert witness fees incurred in the prosecution, negotiation and settlement of the pending divorce litigation between the parties, except for those items listed below (specify):

  _____

  _____

LEGAL FEES RELATED TO ANY QUALIFIED DOMESTIC RELATIONS ORDERS (QDRO):

The parties agree to pay for the cost of any Qualified Domestic Relations Orders (QDRO's) in accordance with the specifications outlined in Exhibit F - Division of Marital Assets and Retirement Funds of this Separation Agreement. If one party pays, the other shall reimburse them within 30 days.

OTHER MATTERS: (specify)

_____

_____

_____

_____

_____

_____

_____

EXHIBIT J
LIFE INSURANCE

LIFE INSURANCE: (cross-reference to Child Support Exhibit B and Alimony Exhibit C)

☐ The Husband shall maintain life insurance in the face amount of $ _____, naming _____ as the beneficiary, and shall be required to keep the life insurance in effect until _____.

☐ The Wife shall maintain life insurance in the face amount of $ _____, naming _____ as the beneficiary, and shall be required to keep the life insurance in effect until _____.

☐ The _____ (husband/wife) shall maintain life insurance in the face amount and time schedule listed below, naming _____ as the beneficiary.

Post-Divorce Year	Dates of Policy Coverage		Amount of Coverage
		to	$
		to	
		to	
		to	
		to	
		to	
		to	
		to	
		to	
		to	
		to	
		to	
		to	
		to	
		to	
		to	
		to	
		to	

☐ Neither party shall be required to maintain life insurance for the benefit of the other.

Said payments shall satisfy any and all alimony and child support obligations required by the terms of this Agreement

PROOF OF COVERAGE:

On the date of policy renewal each year, the Insured Party shall mail the Other Party a copy of said policy binder showing who is the named beneficiary, the amount allocated to that beneficiary, and proof that all premiums have been paid for the upcoming year.

EXHIBIT 11-K-2: SAMPLE BLANK BOILERPLATE SEPARATION AGREEMENT -*WITHOUT-*DEPENDENT CHILDREN

The sample boilerplate is for couples who either have no children, or their children have reached the age of 'legal emancipation' as define' as defined in your home state. It begins on the next page so that you can photocopy it as necessary, or download it from the Seraphim Press website:

www.bootcampmanual.com

STATE of _____

Family Court Department

_____ County, ss.   **Docket No.** _____

SEPARATION AGREEMENT

(for couples without dependent children)

SEPARATION AGREEMENT made this _____ day of _____, 20_____, between:

_____ (Name) the _____(Husband/Wife) currently residing at
_____(Street)_____(Town)_____(County)_____(State)
(hereinafter referred to as the _____(Husband/Wife);

and

_____ (Name) the _____(Husband/Wife) currently residing at
_____(Street)_____(Town)_____(County)_____(State)
(hereinafter referred to as the _____(Husband/Wife).

All references to 'parties' shall mean the above-mentioned Husband and Wife.

STATEMENT OF FACTS

The Husband and Wife were married on _____ (Date), in _____(City)
_____(State), and last lived together in _____(Town) _____ (County)
_____(State) on _____(Date).

Check one:

☐ The parties have no children together.

☐ The parties have children, but they are legally emancipated according to _____ state laws.

STATEMENT OF PURPOSE

The Husband and Wife have been separated and desire to terminate the marital relationship. The parties have filed a Complaint for Divorce in the _____ Division Family Court, Docket Number _____ asserting an irretrievable breakdown of the marriage. The Husband and Wife desire and intend at this time and by this instrument to make a final and complete settlement of all matters relating to the interests and obligations of each with respect to, but not limited to, past, present and future alimony, property and estate rights, in the case of the death of either of them prior to the entry of a final judgment of divorce, and after the entry of a final judgment of divorce should a court grant a divorce between the Husband and Wife. The above statement of purpose of the within Agreement shall not in any way limit the effect of any of the covenants of the parties contained in or the interpretation of this Agreement.

This Agreement shall be binding upon the parties at all times hereafter whether they are living apart or living together or should they become legally separated or divorced in the future, and nothing concerning the state of the marriage of the parties or their living circumstances shall affect the validity of this Agreement, and the same shall nevertheless continue in full force and effect.

The purposes of this Agreement are finally, once and for all:

f) to determine and settle the property rights of each of the parties;

g) to determine what, if anything, should be paid as alimony to the Wife in consideration of the provisions of _____ (state) General Laws c. ____, s.___; (fill in your state alimony statute);

h) to determine whether and to what extent all or any part of the estate of the Husband or Wife should be assigned to the other in consideration of the provisions of _____ (state) General Laws c. ____, s.___ (fill in your state property division statute);

i) to determine all other rights and obligations arising from the marital relationship or otherwise; and

j) to determine all other matters which should be settled in view of the pending Complaint for Divorce.

GENERAL TERMS

NOW, THEREFORE, in consideration of the mutual promises, agreements and covenants hereinafter contained, the Husband and Wife mutually agree as follows:

21. <u>Covenant to Live Apart</u> - From the date hereof, the Husband and Wife may continue to live separate and apart from one another for the rest of their lives, and each shall be free from interference, authority or control, direct or indirect, by the other as fully as if sole and unmarried.

22. <u>Covenant of Non-Interference</u> - Neither the Husband nor the Wife shall molest the other; nor shall the Husband or Wife compel or attempt to compel the other to cohabit with him or her; nor shall the Husband or Wife commence any legal, equitable or other action or proceeding for the restitution of conjugal rights. The Husband and Wife to not intend that this clause shall be criminally enforceable.

23. <u>Covenant to Waive Claims to the Other Parties Estate:</u>

A) The Husband and Wife each hereby waives any right at law or in equity to elect to take against any last will made by the other, including all rights of dower or of curtsey, and each hereby waives, renounces and relinquishes unto each other, their respective heirs, executors, administrators and assigns forever, all and any interest of any kind or character which either may now have or may hereafter acquire in or to any real or personal property of the other and whether now owned or hereafter acquired by either, except as expressly provided by the terms of this Agreement.

B) The Husband and Wife shall have the right to dispose of his or her property by will, or otherwise, in such manner as each may in his or her uncontrolled discretion deem proper, and neither one will claim any interest in the estate of the other, except to enforce any obligation imposed by this Agreement.

24. <u>Covenant to Release All Claims and Legal Actions Against the Other</u> - The Husband and Wife hereby mutually release and forever discharge each other from any and all actions, suits, debts, claims, demands and obligations whatsoever, both at law and in equity, which either of them has ever had, now has, or may hereafter have against the other, upon or by reason of any matter, cause or thing up to the date of this Agreement, whether arising from the marital relationship or otherwise, including, but not limited to, claims against each other's property, it being the intention of the parties that henceforth there shall exist as between them only such rights and obligations as are specifically provided for in this Agreement and in any judgment entered on the Complaint for Divorce;

25. <u>Covenants Against New Liabilities:</u>

A) The Wife warrants, represents that, other than as specifically set forth in this Agreement, she will not hereafter contract or incur any debt, charge or liability whatsoever for which the Husband, his legal representatives, or his property or estate, will or may become liable, and that as of the date of this

Agreement there are no outstanding bills incurred by her which are the obligation of the Husband. .

B) The Husband warrants, represents and agrees that he will not hereafter contract or incur any debt, charge or liability whatsoever for which the Wife, her legal representatives, or her property or estate will or may become liable, and that at the time of the Agreement there are no outstanding bills incurred by him which are the obligation of the Wife.

26. Covenant of Indemnification:

A) The Wife further covenants at all times to hold the Husband free, harmless and indemnified from and against all debts, charges or liabilities previously contracted or incurred by her in breach of the provisions of this paragraph, and from any and all attorneys' fees, costs and expenses incurred by the Husband as a result of any such breach.

B) The Husband further covenants at all times to hold the Wife free, harmless and indemnified from and against all debts, charges or liabilities previously contracted or incurred by him in breach of the provisions of this paragraph, and from any and all attorneys' fees, costs and expenses incurred by the Wife as a result of any breach.

27. Procedure in the Event of Breach: Any breach of any term or terms of the within Agreement shall give either party the right to take immediate action, either at law or in equity, concerning such breach. If either the Husband or the Wife shall commit a breach of any of the provisions of this Agreement and legal action, required to enforce such provisions, shall be instituted by the other, the Court may make a determination or allocation as to the payment of reasonable attorneys' fees incurred in instituting and prosecuting such action, by the party in breach.

28. Additional Terms: The parties agree:

A) to accept the provisions made for each and every undertaking as set forth in this agreement in full satisfaction and discharge of all claims, past, present and future, which each may have upon the other and which in any way arise out of the marital relationship;

B) to waive any claim to property division, alimony or support for each, other than as provided in this Agreement;

C) not to seek the entry of an order or judgment which differs in any way from the terms of this Agreement; and

D) to indemnify and hold harmless the other from any amount he or she is ordered or required to make, in excess of the actual payments or division of property he or she is required to make pursuant to this Agreement.

29. Approval by Court: At any hearing on the Complaint for Divorce, a copy of this Agreement shall be submitted to the _____ (County) Division Family Court for a judge's approval of the terms and entry of a Judgment of Divorce.

30. Merger or Survival: The parties further agree that the terms and provisions of this Separation Agreement shall be (choose one of the following):

    ☐ Incorporated and merged into the Judgment of Divorce Nisi of the court.

    ☐ Incorporated, but not merged, into the Court's judgment, and shall survive and remain as an independent contract, except for the terms and provisions relating to:

        ☐ spousal support/alimony (see Exhibit ___) which terms shall merge in said Judgment.
        ☐ Other _____ (see Exhibit ____).
        ☐ Other _____ (see Exhibit ____).

⊓ Incorporated, but not merged, into the Judgment of Divorce Nisi, and shall survive and remain as an independent contract between the parties. The parties understand that once an Agreement which contains a 'survival' clause is accepted by the court, it may almost *never* be amended at a later date except by act of the state legislature. If child support is an issue, checking off this clause is inappropriate.

The purposes of this paragraph are: (1) to protect each party against any attempt by the other party to vary the terms of this Agreement after the entry of a final judgment; and (2) to enable the Husband and the Wife to procure an enforcement of the terms of this Agreement incorporated in a Judgment of Divorce in the _____(county) Division Family Court, or as a binding contract in any Court with jurisdiction over the person or property of the other party.

31. Warranty of Full and Complete Disclosure: The Husband and Wife hereby represent that each has fully described his or her assets and liabilities to the other party to the best of his or her knowledge and ability as set forth on the financial statements of each filed herewith and incorporated by reference herein. Each party is fully cognizant of his or her rights, and each executes this agreement based upon his or her personal knowledge and the representations of the other party which each believes to be a true, complete and accurate reflection of the other party's current financial status and circumstances.

   A) Exchange of Financial Data: Each party represents that s/he has provided the other with a current financial statement on the form promulgated pursuant to _____ (name of your state court financial statement), which discloses fully and completely all of her/his income, expenses, assets and liabilities. Both parties Financial Statements shall be filed separately with the court for confidentiality and are hereby incorporated by reference into this Agreement.

   B) Fiduciary Duty: The Husband and Wife declare and acknowledge that each of them is relying upon the voluntary true, honest and complete full self-disclosure of the other party as to the assets, liabilities, income and expenses of the other in lieu of litigated discovery and acknowledge that each owes a fiduciary duty to the other to be forthright in their disclosure. It is the intent of this paragraph that the parties shall adopt the policy of 'Mandatory Self-Disclosure' during divorce proceedings prevalent in most states.

   C) Understanding of Other's Position: The Husband and Wife declare that each understands the position, circumstances, financial resources, income, expenses, liabilities and prospects of the other based upon and in reliance on the aforesaid financial statements of each party and that each of them understands the terms, provisions and conditions of the within Agreement, and believes its terms, provisions and conditions to be fair and to be reasonable.

32. Warranty of the Opportunity to Consult with Legal Counsel: The parties further state that they have negotiated the terms of the Agreement, and that each has had the opportunity for independent legal advice by counsel of his or her own choosing and that, after consultation with his or her respective attorney and after being advised fully and fairly as to all facts and circumstances herein set forth, and after having read this Agreement line by line, each freely and fully accepts the terms, conditions and provisions hereof and enters into the Agreement voluntarily and without any coercion whatsoever.

33. Warranty of Sole Agreement Between the Parties: The parties further acknowledge and declare this Agreement contains the entire agreement between the parties hereto and that there are no agreements, promises, terms, conditions or understandings and no representations or inducements leading to the execution hereof, express or implied, other than those herein set forth (except for those documents or exhibits expressly annexed and incorporated by reference), and that no oral statement or prior written extrinsic to the four corners of this Agreement not expressly annexed and incorporated by reference shall have any force or effect.

34. Warranty of Free Will: By executing this Separation Agreement, the parties represent that the terms and provisions of this agreement are fair, just and reasonable and are not the product of fraud, coercion or undue influence, and that each signs this agreement freely and voluntarily.

35. No Requirement of Strict Performance: The failure of the Husband or of the Wife to comply with or insist in any instance upon the strict performance of any of the terms hereof shall not be construed as a waiver of such term or

terms for the future, and the same shall nevertheless continue in full force and effect.

36. <u>Procedure in the Event a Portion of this Agreement is Later Held to be Invalid:</u> In the event any party of this Agreement shall be held invalid, such invalidity shall not invalidate the whole Agreement but the remaining provisions of this Agreement shall continue to be valid and binding to the extent that such provisions continue to reflect fairly the intent and understanding of the parties.

37. <u>Choice of State Law:</u> This Agreement shall be construed and governed according to the Laws of the State of _____(state).

38. <u>Choice of Forum:</u> so long as either party resides in _____ County, _____(state), the _____ County Family Court shall be the designated forum for all matters.

39. <u>Attachments, Addendums and Exhibits:</u> There are annexed hereto and incorporated by reference herein Exhibits A through J. Both Husband and Wife agree to be bound by, and to perform and carry out all the terms of said Exhibits to the same extent as if each was fully set forth in the text of this Agreement.

   A) <u>Exhibit A</u> – Alimony
   B) <u>Exhibit B</u> – Health Related Insurance and Expenses
   C) <u>Exhibit C</u> – Division of Marital Assets and Retirement Funds
   D) <u>Exhibit D</u> – Payment of Marital Debts
   E) <u>Exhibit E</u> – Income Taxes
   F) <u>Exhibit F</u> – Legal Fees and Expenses
   G) <u>Exhibit G</u> – Life Insurance

40. This Agreement shall not be altered or modified except by an instrument signed and acknowledged by the Husband and Wife and executed before a notary public.

Signed at _____(town), _____(state) on this _____ day of _____, 20____.
Executed in several counterparts.

Signed: _____   _____
                       (Husband)   (Date)

Signed: _____   _____
(Husband)   (Date)

State of _____

_____,ss.   Date: _____

Then personally appeared the above-named _____, and acknowledged that - he / she - signed this separation agreement as - his / her - free act and deed.

_____

Notary Public - My Commission Expires: _____

****

Signed: _____   _____
(Wife)   (Date)

State of _____

_____,ss.   Date: _____

Then personally appeared the above-named _____, and acknowledged that - he / she - signed this separation agreement as - his / her - free act and deed.

_____

Notary Public - My Commission Expires: _____

EXHIBIT A
ALIMONY

ALIMONY OBLIGATION:

The parties agree that alimony shall be as follows (check only one box):

☐ Each party hereby waives past and present spousal support (alimony) from the other and reserves the matter of future alimony for consideration by the Court;

☐ Each party forever waives their right to receive any past, present or future spousal support (alimony) that they may have. The parties understand that once the Court accepts a party's waiver, that party may **never** request maintenance (except as may be overridden by certain acts of the legislature) ;

☐ The Husband agrees to pay the Wife spousal support (alimony) in the amount of $ _____ every:
   ☐ Week;
   ☐ Two weeks;
   ☐ Bi-monthly on the ____th and ____th of the month;
   ☐ Month;
   Beginning on _____ (date) ___ and continuing until the termination date specified below:

☐ The Wife agrees to pay the Husband spousal support (alimony) in the amount of $ _____ every:
   ☐ Week;
   ☐ Two weeks;
   ☐ Bi-monthly on the ____th and ____th of the month;
   ☐ Month;
   Beginning on _____ (date) ___ and continuing until the termination date specified below:

Said payments shall be made in cash and shall terminate on the first to occur of the death of the Wife, the death of the Husband, or:

☐ The remarriage or cohabitation of the alimony recipient _____ (husband/wife);
☐ The alimony recipient _____ (husband/wife) attaining their _____th birthday;
☐ The alimony payor _____ (husband/wife) reaching their full social security retirement age;
☐ The passage of _____ months;
☐ The passage of _____ years;
☐ Other event (specify): _____

TAX PROVISIONS: (Cross-reference with Exhibit E - Income Taxes)

For income tax purposes, alimony shall be taxable to the recipient _____ (husband/wife), or $_____ per month.

The amount of the alimony payments set forth in this Exhibit A has been determined on the basis of currently prevailing federal and state income tax laws, rules and regulations, with the intention and understanding that all payments made pursuant to the above paragraphs 1 and 2 of this Exhibit A, qualify as alimony payments for income tax purposes, as those terms are defined in Section 71 and any other applicable section of the United States Internal Revenue Code as amended and _____ law chapter _____ as amended, each as in effect as of the date of the execution of this Agreement. Accordingly, such alimony payment shall be deductible to the Alimony Payor _____ (husband/wife) and taxable to the Alimony Recipient _____ (wife/husband). In the event of any change of the rules, rulings or regulations of the Internal Revenue Service, or in the event of subsequent statutory amendment, judicial or administrative order or decision contrary to this result, the amount payable pursuant to this provision shall be adjusted to reflect the intent and understanding expressed in this Exhibit.

TYPE OF ALIMONY:

Explain type of alimony:
- ☐ Temporary
- ☐ Rehabilitative
- ☐ Lump Sum (amount) $_____
- ☐ Permanent/lifetime;
- ☐ Other (name specifics): _____

LIFE INSURANCE: (Choose if applicable) (Cross-reference with Exhibit G - Life Insurance)

☐ Life insurance in the amount of $ _____ to secure the above Spousal Support/Alimony will be provided by the obligor as outlined in Exhibit G of this Agreement.

HEALTH INSURANCE: (Choose if applicable) (Cross-reference with Exhibit B - Health Insurance)

☐ Health insurance will be provided by the obligor as outlined in Exhibit B of this Agreement.

OTHER ALIMONY TERMS NOT COVERED ELSEWHERE: (Outline below):

_____

_____

_____

_____

_____

_____

_____

_____

_____

_____

_____

_____

_____

_____

_____

_____

_____

EXHIBIT B
HEALTH-RELATED INSURANCE AND EXPENSES

HEALTH INSURANCE FOR THE PARTIES:

The Wife's health insurance coverage will be provided (check all that apply):

- ☐ by the Wife
- ☐ by the Husband
- ☐ by the Husband through his employer for so long as it is available to him, and if there is any additional cost to continued coverage for the insurance:

_____

_____

- ☐ If the Husband remarries and affects the Wife's eligibility, the Husband shall procure insurance for the Wife's benefit at his own expense under the following terms and conditions (explain):

_____

_____

The Husband's health insurance coverage will be provided (check all that apply):

- ☐ by the Husband
- ☐ by the Wife
- ☐ by the Wife for so long as it is available to her, and if there is any additional cost to continued coverage for the insurance:

_____

_____

- ☐ If the Wife remarries and affects the Husband's eligibility, the Wife shall procure insurance for the Husband's benefit at her own expense under the following terms and conditions (explain):

_____

_____

OTHER HEALTH-RELATED INSURANCE FOR THE PARTIES:

The Husband shall continue to maintain the following health-related insurances for the benefit of the Wife for so long as it remains available to him (check all that apply):

- ☐ There is no additional health-related insurance available;
- ☐ Dental
- ☐ Vision
- ☐ Orthodontia
- ☐ Therapeutic
- ☐ If there is additional cost involved, it shall be handled as follows (explain):

_____

_____

The Wife shall continue to maintain the following health-related insurances for the benefit of the Husband for so long as it remains available to her (check all that apply):

- ☐ There is no additional health-related insurance available;
- ☐ Dental
- ☐ Vision
- ☐ Orthodontia
- ☐ Prescription medication
- ☐ Therapeutic
- ☐ Other (name): _____
- ☐ If there is additional cost involved, it shall be handled as follows (explain):

_____

_____

UNINSURED/UNREIMBURSED HEALTH-RELATED EXPENSES:

The cost of all reasonable uninsured and unreimbursed medical, dental, hospital, optical, prescription medication and therapeutic counseling services for the Wife shall be paid:

- ☐ by the Wife
- ☐ _____% by Wife;
- ☐ _____% by Husband

The cost of all reasonable uninsured and unreimbursed medical, dental, hospital, optical, prescription medication and therapeutic counseling services for the Husband shall be paid:

- ☐ by the Husband
- ☐ _____% by Wife;
- ☐ _____% by Husband

HEALTH INSURANCE FOR THE PARTIES ELIGIBLE BUT OTHERWISE-EMANCIPATED CHILDREN:

Check all that apply:

- ☐ The parties have no children;
- ☐ The parties' children are legally emancipated, but still eligible to remain on one parent's health insurance policy until age _____. The parties agree to allow the children to remain on said policy so long as there is no additional cost or expense or to (elaborate):

_____

_____

- ☐ The parties agree to provide health, dental, vision and orthodontia insurance for the emancipated but eligible children for so long as it is still available to them at no additional cost..

IMPACT OF REMARRIAGE UPON ELIGIBILITY:

The parties acknowledge that the eligibility for health and health-related insurance is a significant matter. Should one party contemplate remarriage, the other party will usually be terminated from the Insured's health and health-related insurance plans. Therefore, should the Insured Party contemplate remarriage, the Insured Party shall give the Insurance Dependent a minimum of 60 days' notice to explore other options. Furthermore, the Insured Party shall assist the Insurance Dependent in executing any paperwork necessary to take advantage of any COBRA or other extension plans available to them.

DUTY TO INFORM OF ANY EVENT WHICH WOULD IMPAIR COVERAGE:

The parties acknowledge that the eligibility for health and health-related insurance is a significant matter. In addition to any obligation imposed by applicable law upon the insurer to notify the Insured Party of cancellation of coverage, the Insured Party shall notify the Insurance Dependent within 30 days after becoming aware of any circumstances which would affect his or her eligibility for, the availability of, or the nature of his or her continued health, dental, vision, or other health-related insurance coverage.

Should one party contemplate remarriage, the other party will usually be terminated from the Insured's health and health-related insurance plans. Therefore, should the Insured Party contemplate remarriage, the duty of the Insured Party to give the Insurance Dependent notice shall increase to a minimum of 60 days' notice.

The Insurance Dependent shall have the right, pursuant to any applicable law, to continue to receive benefits as are available to the Insured Party by any means then available, including by rider to the existing policy or conversion to an individual policy, which would have benefits reasonably equivalent to those which they would be otherwise receiving pursuant to this Exhibit E. If the Insurance Dependent elects to continue such coverage, the Insured Party shall cooperate in making the necessary arrangements for, and shall execute any documents necessary to effectuate the continuation of said coverage.

DUTY TO CONSULT:

If one party is providing health-related insurance for the other, the parties agree that from time to time or at minimum once per year prior to any open-enrollment period, that they shall compare all medical, dental, vision and other health-related plans which may be available to them through their employers or other sources and discuss what cost, coverage, and co-pay schedules would be most beneficial to them and the minor children. If health, dental, vision or other insurance premiums increase or another plan becomes available at a lower rate or which provides better coverage, the parties may reach a new agreement regarding reimbursement for their share of said costs, or file a Complaint for Modification to address this issue in the _____ (county) Division of the Court.

HEALTH TRUST CARE FUNDS:

The Husband and Wife may pay their share of all uninsured medical, dental, vision and other health-related expenses (if any) from any health care trust funds they may set up (such as flexible spending accounts) to make said payments, with any tax advantages realized by utilizing such trusts flowing to the party who does the planning and saving.

OTHER INSURANCE -RELATED TERMS NOT COVERED ELSEWHERE: (explain)

_____

_____

_____

_____

_____

_____

_____

_____

_____

_____

_____

_____

EXHIBIT C
DIVISION OF MARITAL ASSETS AND RETIREMENT FUNDS

The Husband and Wife own real estate, personal property, pension and profit sharing plans, securities, investments, and other marital assets. Each party agrees to execute any and all documents necessary to effectuate the terms of this Exhibit F and the transfers, conveyances and payments required by said terms. The parties individual Financial Statements containing sensitive information such as account numbers and exact fair market values are to be filed concurrently with this Agreement and are hereby merged with it and incorporated by reference. In exchange for the mutual covenants contained in this Agreement, the parties agree to divide their assets (everything they own and that is owed to them) as follows:

REAL ESTATE: (check all that apply)

☐ The parties do not own any real estate.

☐ The parties have already divided their interest in the marital home located at (specify) as follows:
_____
_____

☐ The parties agree to the following terms relating to all real estate owned as follows:

Address of Property	Party who will take ownership and title		Party who will assume all obligations (mortgage, taxes, insurance, etc.)			
	H	W	H	W	Both (indicate %)	
	☐	☐	☐	☐	H ___ %	W ___ %
	☐	☐	☐	☐	H ___ %	W ___ %
	☐	☐	☐	☐	H ___ %	W ___ %
	☐	☐	☐	☐	H ___ %	W ___ %

☐ The parties agree to sell the Real Estate located at (specify) _____. Any proceeds or monies owed following the sale will be divided to the parties as follows:

        Husband $_____ or _____ %
               and
        Wife $_____ or _____ %

☐ The parties agree to prepare documents (e.g., Quit Claim Deed) to transfer title by _____ date.

☐ The party who will take ownership and title of the property will refinance all existing loans, mortgages, home equity lines of credits or other liens against the property and remove the other spouses name from the debt(s) as follows:
    ☐ Within _____ months from _____ date.
    ☐ By _____ date.

☐ The parties agree to an equity payout as follows:
    ☐ The Husband will pay the Wife $_____ by _____ (date);
    ☐ The Wife will pay the Husband $_____ by _____ (date).

☐ The parties have already transferred title and have notified the lender of the change in ownership per this Agreement

☐ Other (specify):

_____

_____

_____

_____

_____

MOTOR VEHICLES AND/OR RECREATIONAL VEHICLES: (check all that apply)

☐ The parties do not own any motor vehicles and/or recreational vehicles.

☐ The parties have already divided their interest in the following motor and/or recreational vehicles (specify) as follows:

_____

_____

☐ The parties agree to the following terms relating to all real estate owned as follows:

Identify Vehicle & Type				Party who will take ownership and title		Party who will assume all obligations (Loan Payment, Registration, Insurance, etc.)		
Year	Make	Model	VIN#	H	W	H	W	Both (indicate %)
				☐	☐	☐	☐	H ___ % W ___ %
				☐	☐	☐	☐	H ___ % W ___ %
				☐	☐	☐	☐	H ___ % W ___ %
				☐	☐	☐	☐	H ___ % W ___ %
				☐	☐	☐	☐	H ___ % W ___ %
				☐	☐	☐	☐	H ___ % W ___ %

☐ The parties agree to sign over the respective title of each vehicle by _____ date.

☐ The party who will take ownership and title of the vehicles will have the following amount of time to refinance the loan and remove the other spouse from the debt.
    ☐ Will have _____ months from _____ date.
    ☐ Will have until _____ date.

☐ The parties have already transferred title and have notified the lender of the change in ownership per this Agreement

☐ Other (specify):

_____

_____

_____

_____

_____

CASH ON HAND, BANK, CHECKING AND SAVINGS ACCOUNTS: (check all that apply)

☐ The parties do not have any accounts.

☐ The parties agree to the following terms relating to all accounts:

Identify Name of Bank or Financial Institution	Identify Type of Bank Account	Distribution of Each Account		
		H = 100%	W = 100%	Both (indicate %)
		☐	☐	H ___ % W ___ %
		☐	☐	H ___ % W ___ %
		☐	☐	H ___ % W ___ %
		☐	☐	H ___ % W ___ %
		☐	☐	H ___ % W ___ %
		☐	☐	H ___ % W ___ %
		☐	☐	H ___ % W ___ %
		☐	☐	H ___ % W ___ %

☐ The parties agree to divide/transfer the funds by _____ date.

☐ The parties have already divided/transferred the funds per this Agreement

☐ Other (specify):

_____

_____

_____

_____

_____

WHOLE LIFE INSURANCE: (cash value)

☐ The parties do not own life insurance.

☐ The parties have life insurance, but it is term insurance only (i.e., no cash value).

☐ One or both of the parties have a Whole Life (not term) policy that has a surrender cash value and it has been accounted for in the property division as follows (specify):

_____

_____

FURNITURE, HOUSEHOLD GOODS, AND OTHER PERSONAL PROPERTY: (check all that apply)

☐ The parties do not have any assets in this category.

☐ The parties have divided the furniture, household goods, and other personal property and are satisfied with the division.

☐ The parties agree to the following terms relating to all furniture, household goods and other personal property:

Identify Items	H	W	Identify Items	H	W
	☐	☐		☐	☐
	☐	☐		☐	☐
	☐	☐		☐	☐
	☐	☐		☐	☐
	☐	☐		☐	☐
	☐	☐		☐	☐
	☐	☐		☐	☐
	☐	☐		☐	☐
	☐	☐		☐	☐
	☐	☐		☐	☐

☐ The parties are attaching an additional listing of personal items to be divided (above) to this Exhibit F which is part of this Exhibit and hereby incorporated by reference to this Agreement.

☐ Any personal item(s) not listed above is the property of the party currently in possession of the item(s).

☐ Other (specify):

_____

_____

STOCKS, BONDS, MUTUAL FUNDS, SECURITIES & INVESTMENT ACCOUNTS: (check all that apply)

☐ The parties do not have any assets in this category.

☐ The parties agree to the following terms relating to all accounts:

Identify Name of Stock, Bond, Mutual Fund, etc.	Distribution of Funds, Shares, etc.		
	H = 100%	W = 100%	Both (indicate %)
	☐	☐	H ___ % W ___ %
	☐	☐	H ___ % W ___ %
	☐	☐	H ___ % W ___ %
	☐	☐	H ___ % W ___ %
	☐	☐	H ___ % W ___ %
	☐	☐	H ___ % W ___ %

☐ The parties agree to divide/transfer the funds by _____ date.

☐ The parties have already divided/transferred the funds per this Agreement

☐ Other (specify):

_____

_____

PENSION, PROFIT SHARING OR RETIREMENT FUNDS: (check all that apply)

☐ The parties do not have any funds.

☐ The parties agree to the following terms relating to all retirement accounts:

Identify Type of Pension, Profit Sharing or Retirement Fund	Distribution of Funds, Shares, etc. Within the Various Accounts		
	H = 100%	W = 100%	Both (indicate %)
	☐	☐	H ___ % W ___ %
	☐	☐	H ___ % W ___ %
	☐	☐	H ___ % W ___ %
	☐	☐	H ___ % W ___ %
	☐	☐	H ___ % W ___ %
	☐	☐	H ___ % W ___ %

☐ The parties agree to divide/transfer the funds by _____ date.

☐ The parties have already divided/transferred the funds per this Agreement

☐ Other (specify):

_____

_____

QUALIFIED DOMESTIC RELATIONS ORDER (QDRO) RELATING TO ABOVE-NAMED PENSION, PROFIT-SHARING OR RETIREMENT FUNDS:

The ☐ husband ☐ wife is responsible for preparing and submitting a Qualified Domestic Relations Order (QDRO) by contacting their fund provider or an attorney by _____ date.

The cost to prepare the QDRO will be paid as follows: ☐ husband _____% ☐ wife _____%

Note: A QDRO is necessary in order for the division of the retirement plan to be completed. Without a QDRO, plans will not be divided regardless of the parties' agreement identified within this form.

☐ Other (specify):

_____

_____

MISCELLANEOUS ASSETS NOT LISTED ELSEWHERE:

The parties do hereby divide any remaining assets not specifically listed elsewhere in this Exhibit F, including items identified in the parties' sworn Financial Statements filed with the court today under 'other' or 'miscellaneous' categories, considered to be 'separate property,' or otherwise not listed as follows:

☐ The parties do not have any assets in this category.

☐ The parties have already divided all of the miscellaneous assets not listed elsewhere in this Exhibit F and are satisfied with the division.

☐ The parties agree to the following terms relating to all miscellaneous assets listed below:

Identify Items	H	W	Identify Items	H	W
	☐	☐		☐	☐
	☐	☐		☐	☐
	☐	☐		☐	☐
	☐	☐		☐	☐
	☐	☐		☐	☐
	☐	☐		☐	☐
	☐	☐		☐	☐
	☐	☐		☐	☐
	☐	☐		☐	☐
	☐	☐		☐	☐

☐ The parties are attaching an additional listing of personal items to be divided (above) to this Exhibit F which is part of this Exhibit and hereby incorporated by reference to this Agreement.

☐ Any miscellaneous asset(s) not listed above is the property of the party currently in possession of the item(s).

☐ Other (specify): _____

_____

_____

TAX TREATMENT OF THE DIVISION OF MARITAL PROPERTY:

The conveyances, transfers and payments described in this Exhibit C are not contingent upon any event other than the execution of this Agreement and do not qualify as alimony as that term is defined by applicable sections, including s.71 of the United States Internal Revenue Code, as amended, and _____ state law, section ___, as amended, each as in effect as of the date of the execution of this Agreement, and further it is the parties' intent that these transfers qualify under Section 1041 of the Internal Revenue Code. Therefore, the parties agree that these transfers and payments shall neither be deductible by the Husband nor taxable to the Wife, as income, for federal and state income tax purposes.

MUTUAL WAIVERS:

19. Except as otherwise provided by the terms of this Agreement, the Husband expressly waives and relinquishes any and all claim, right, title and interest he may have, whether arising out of the marital relationship of the parties or otherwise, in and to any bank or investment accounts, certificates of deposit, trusts, securities, bonds, shares of stock, IRA, pension or profit sharing plans, business interests of the Wife, inheritances, past, present, or future, causes of action, receivables, uncollected fees, entity or entities or other form of property, either real or personal,

held by the Wife individually, or with others, or in any other form for the benefit of the Wife.

20. Except as otherwise provided by the terms of this Agreement, the Wife expressly waives and relinquishes any and all claim, right, title and interest she may have, whether arising out of the marital relationship of the parties or otherwise, in and to any bank or investment accounts, certificates of deposit, trusts, securities, bonds, shares of stock, IRA, pension or profit sharing plans, business interests of the Husband, including without limitation the Husband's inheritances, past, present or future, causes of action, receivables, uncollected fees, entity or entities or other form of property, either real or personal, held by the Husband individually, or with others, or in any other form for the benefit of the Husband.

21. Except as otherwise provided by the terms of this Agreement, the Husband and the Wife each release and relinquish any interest in real property or items of personal property of or in the possession of the other. Henceforth, each of the parties shall own, have and enjoy, independently of the other party, all real estate and items of personal property of every kind, nature and description and wherever situated, which are now owned or possessed by him or her, or may be hereafter acquired, with full power in him or her to dispose of the same as fully and effectually in all respects and for all purposes as if he or she were unmarried.

EXECUTION OF DOCUMENTS:

Each party agrees to execute any and all documents necessary to effectuate the terms of this Exhibit F and the transfers, conveyances and payments required by said terms.

OTHER PROPERTY-DIVISION RELATED TERMS NOT COVERED ELSEWHERE: (explain)

_____

_____

_____

_____

_____

_____

_____

_____

_____

_____

_____

_____

_____

EXHIBIT D
PAYMENT OF MARITAL DEBTS

The Husband and Wife agree to an orderly repayment of all marital debt. The parties hereby refer to their Financial Statements filed with the court today and do hereby incorporate by reference those debts listed as follows:

REPAYMENT OF DEBTS: (check all that apply)

☐ The parties do not have any debt.

☐ The parties agree to the following terms relating to all debt (including interest, penalty and fees) and the party responsible for that debt will indemnify and hold the other party harmless.

Identify Name of Creditor	Date of Balance	Balance	Party Responsible for Future Payments		
			H = 100%	W = 100%	Both (indicate %)
		$	☐	☐	H ___ % W ___ %
			☐	☐	H ___ % W ___ %
			☐	☐	H ___ % W ___ %
			☐	☐	H ___ % W ___ %
			☐	☐	H ___ % W ___ %
			☐	☐	H ___ % W ___ %
			☐	☐	H ___ % W ___ %
			☐	☐	H ___ % W ___ %
			☐	☐	H ___ % W ___ %
			☐	☐	H ___ % W ___ %
			☐	☐	H ___ % W ___ %
			☐	☐	H ___ % W ___ %
			☐	☐	H ___ % W ___ %
			☐	☐	H ___ % W ___ %
			☐	☐	H ___ % W ___ %
Total debt to be assumed by the Husband	$		H _____ %		
Total debt to be assumed by the Wife	$		W _____ %		

☐ The parties do hereby attach a Debt Addendum listing additional debts and do hereby incorporate said former list to this Exhibit D by reference..

☐ The parties agree to cancel any joint credit cards.

☐ The parties agree to repay any mortgages or liens associated with any real estate they take title to as outlined in Exhibit C - Assets.

☐ The parties agree to repay any liens associated with any motor vehicle or recreational vehicle they take possession of as outlined in Exhibit C - Assets.

☐ Other (specify):

_____
_____
_____
_____
_____
_____
_____
_____
_____
_____
_____
_____

FUTURE DEBT:

Except as specifically set forth herein, each Party shall be responsible for all expenses, bills and obligations of themselves and their property. Neither party will incur any debts, charges or liabilities for with the other Party, their legal representative, property or estate will or may become liable, except to enforce or pursuant to the provisions of this Agreement.

LATE PAYMENT OR BREACH OF ONE OF THE PARTIES:

Should any violation of this Agreement occur, the Party who caused the violation agrees to hold the other Party harmless and to reimburse them for any and all debts, charges and liabilities contracted or incurred (including attorney's fees, costs and expenses) because of the violation. Should additional interest, penalties, or late fees be assed against any joint marital debt because one party paid their portion on time and the other failed to pay on time, the party who incurred the additional interest, fees and penalties shall make additional payment equal to the amount of excess penalties, interest and fees before the next payment cycle so that the account balance is adjusted _as if_ all payments had been made on time.

OTHER DEBT-RELATED TERMS NOT COVERED ELSEWHERE: (explain)

_____
_____
_____
_____
_____
_____
_____

EXHIBIT E
INCOME TAXES

CURRENT AND PAST YEARS TAX RETURNS:

☐ The parties agree to file the following type of federal and state income tax returns for the tax year(s) _____ (specify current and past tax years):
- ☐ joint
- ☐ separate
- ☐ married filing separately

☐ State and Federal refunds and/or money owed will be allocated as follows:
- ☐ Husband: _____%
- ☐ Wife: _____%

The following party shall be responsible for the preparation of said returns. Either party may retain and independent accountant at their own expense to review said tax returns for signature.

- ☐ Husband
- ☐ Wife
- ☐ Husband and Wife shall share the cost of tax preparation equally.
- ☐ Husband and Wife shall share the cost of tax preparation services as follows:
  - ☐ Husband: _____%
  - ☐ Wife: _____%
- ☐ Other (specify): _____

FUTURE YEARS TAX RETURNS:

The parties shall file separate federal and state income tax returns for _____ and thereafter.

TAX TREATMENT OF SPOUSAL SUPPORT/ALIMONY:

As outlined in Exhibit A - Spousal Support/Alimony, only those portions of alimony which are not being offset in satisfaction of the Payor's child support obligation shall be taxable to the Recipient.

The amount of the alimony payments set forth in Exhibit E has been determined on the basis of currently prevailing federal and state income tax laws, rules and regulations, with the intention and understanding that all payments made pursuant to the above paragraphs 1 and 2 of this Exhibit E, qualify as alimony payments for income tax purposes, as those terms are defined in Section 71 and any other applicable section of the United States Internal Revenue Code as amended and _____ law section _____ as amended, each as in effect as of the date of the execution of this Agreement. Accordingly, such alimony payment shall be deductible to the Alimony Payor _____ (husband/wife) and taxable to the Alimony Recipient _____ (wife/husband). In the event of any change of the rules, rulings or regulations of the Internal Revenue Service, or in the event of subsequent statutory amendment, judicial or administrative order or decision contrary to this result, the amount payable pursuant to this provision shall be adjusted to reflect the intent and understanding expressed in this Exhibit.

TAX INDEMNIFICATION:

The Wife covenants at all times to hold the Husband free, harmless and indemnified from and against all income tax obligations, deficiencies, penalties or interest assessed, which have been or may be incurred in connection with the filing of any joint tax return, state or federal, by them, and which obligation, deficiency, penalty or interest is attributable to the Wife's income, error or omission. Notwithstanding anything to the contrary contained in this Agreement, the Wife further covenants at all times to hold the Husband free, harmless and indemnified from and against all debts, charges or liabilities incurred by her in breach of the provisions of this paragraph, and from any and all attorneys' fees, costs and expenses incurred by the Husband as a result of any such breach.

The Husband covenants at all times to hold the Wife free, harmless and indemnified from and against all income tax obligations, deficiencies, penalties or interest assessed, which have been or may be incurred in connection with the filing of any joint tax return, state or federal, by them, and which obligation, deficiency, penalty or interest is attributable to the Husband's income, error or omission. Notwithstanding anything to the contrary contained in this Agreement, the Husband further covenants at all times to hold the Wife free, harmless and indemnified from and against all debts, charges or liabilities incurred by her in breach of the provisions of this paragraph, and from any and all attorneys' fees, costs and expenses incurred by the Wife as a result of any such breach.

OTHER TAX-RELATED TERMS NOT COVERED ELSEWHERE: (explain)

_____

_____

_____

_____

_____

_____

_____

_____

_____

_____

_____

_____

EXHIBIT F
LEGAL FEES AND EXPENSES

LEGAL FEES RELATED TO THE DIVORCE:

- ☐ The Husband shall pay all court costs and legal fees (including mediation) for both parties;

- ☐ The Wife shall pay all court costs and legal fees (including mediation) for both parties;

- ☐ The parties shall divide the cost of all court costs and legal fees (including mediation) for both parties equally (50:50);

- ☐ The parties shall divide the cost of all court costs and legal fees (including mediation) as follows:

  - ☐ Husband shall pay _____%

  - ☐ Wife shall pay _____%

- ☐ Each party shall be responsible for the payment of his or her own attorney's fees, expenses and expert witness fees incurred in the prosecution, negotiation and settlement of the pending divorce litigation between the parties.

- ☐ Each party shall be responsible for the payment of his or her own attorney's fees, expenses and expert witness fees incurred in the prosecution, negotiation and settlement of the pending divorce litigation between the parties, except for those items listed below (specify):

  _____

  _____

LEGAL FEES RELATED TO ANY QUALIFIED DOMESTIC RELATIONS ORDERS (QDRO):

The parties agree to pay for the cost of any Qualified Domestic Relations Orders (QDRO's) in accordance with the specifications outlined in Exhibit F - Division of Marital Assets and Retirement Funds of this Separation Agreement. If one party pays, the other shall reimburse them within 30 days.

OTHER MATTERS: (specify)

_____

_____

_____

_____

_____

_____

_____

EXHIBIT G
LIFE INSURANCE

LIFE INSURANCE: (cross-reference to Child Support Exhibit B and Alimony Exhibit C)

☐ The Husband shall maintain life insurance in the face amount of $ _____, naming _____ as the beneficiary, and shall be required to keep the life insurance in effect until _____.

☐ The Wife shall maintain life insurance in the face amount of $ _____, naming _____ as the beneficiary, and shall be required to keep the life insurance in effect until _____.

☐ The _____ (husband/wife) shall maintain life insurance in the face amount and time schedule listed below, naming _____ as the beneficiary.

Post-Divorce Year	Dates of Policy Coverage		Amount of Coverage
		to	$
		to	
		to	
		to	
		to	
		to	
		to	
		to	
		to	
		to	
		to	
		to	
		to	
		to	
		to	
		to	
		to	
		to	

☐ Neither party shall be required to maintain life insurance for the benefit of the other.

Said payments shall satisfy any and all alimony obligations required by the terms of this Agreement

PROOF OF COVERAGE:

On the date of policy renewal each year, the Insured Party shall mail the Other Party a copy of said policy binder showing who is the named beneficiary, the amount allocated to that beneficiary, and proof that all premiums have been paid for the upcoming year.

CHAPTER 11 SUMMARY

1. Separation Agreements set the framework for how you will live after the divorce. They memorialize terms you and your spouse agree to when you separate and are a legally binding contract. ***Once an agreement is accepted by the court, it is very difficult to go back and change it.*** Be sure you understand what you are signing.

2. It is best to hire an attorney to draft your agreement for you. If there is any one aspect of your divorce that justifies the expense of hiring professional help, it is this document. If you plan on handling your own divorce, many attorneys will help you review your paperwork and "ghost write" an agreement for you for a very reasonable price.

3. Always explicitly name and incorporate by reference any documents or agreements you are attaching or using as part of your agreement or they will be barred from evidence.

4. Be wary of sneaky lawyer words such as merge, survive, confess judgment, choice of law, etc.

5. Most agreements break each area of your divorce down into exhibits. If you refer to something in one area (such as child support) that affects or mirrors another area, make sure the language does not conflict. It is good practice to cross-reference things that affect more than one area.

6. Separation Agreements are public documents that anybody can read. Do not explicitly list private information such as social security or account numbers in the agreement, but rather refer to an addendum which is attached to your pink financial statement. Otherwise, you could have your identity stolen.

7. Use a checklist to make sure everything you want in your agreement actually *gets* in your agreement.

8. Before signing an agreement, take a few days to re-read it several times, have it looked over by your attorney, and ask another layperson who you trust (such as a parent or friend) to read it and make sure they understand it the same way you do. Don't get annoyed if you spouse does the same thing.

9. Hire a specialist to handle your QDRO for you. Even many attorneys won't touch these.

10. When in doubt, spell it out!

11. Never, never, never sign an agreement hastily drafted in the hallways of the courthouse moments before a temporary orders hearing!!! If you have not had several days to look it over and think about it, do not sign it no matter *who* pressures you to get it over with (not even the judge). If you refuse to sign and the case is assigned for trial, you can always sign it and settle the case later without trial, but you won't be allowed to go back and get a new agreement if you signed it and were wrong.

SECTION III

JANE DOE LAUNCHES

WORLD WAR III

(A hypothetical case)

Section III is a hypothetical divorce case where a low- to moderate-income woman, Jane Doe, finds herself in the all-too-common situation where she makes too much money to qualify for free legal services, but does not have enough money to hire a full-service attorney. This section is a fictitious story about one woman's journey through the legal system in the state where I practice law, Massachusetts. Although *your* home state may vary somewhat, the steps outlined here are a general overview of steps usually taken in *all* divorce cases in all 50 states.

Use this section as follows:

1. *Skim* through the chapters to familiarize yourself with the content, especially as it relates to things such as deadlines, obtaining documents, child custody disputes, and the various hearings you will attend. However, this material is complex. *Do not* expect to read through it and understand it all.
   a. It's either skim through it yourself, or pay your attorney $300 to explain this to you.
   b. Think of this step as looking for the *skeleton* of a legal case. You just want an idea of where the bones are so you can come back and fill things in later.
2. If a specific issue catches your eye, go back and read that section in depth.
3. As your divorce winds its way through the court, refer back to this book *before* you call your attorney to give yourself a general overview of what is considered 'routine' versus more troublesome issues. Many things which make no sense when you skim through will suddenly become clear.
   a. You will better comprehend what your attorney tells you if you have a bare-bones knowledge of what *should* happen in your case first.
4. When an official looking piece of paper arrives in the mail, use this section as a resource to look things up *before* calling your attorney.
   a. This book is not a *replacement* for calling your attorney!!! It's a resource to help you understand the big picture.
   b. By understanding which paperwork and processes are 'boilerplate,' your overall level of stress and pain should diminish and your divorce will proceed more smoothly.

My hope is that by learning what legal tools are available to solve common problems, you won't wrack up an hour's legal fee learning the basics every time you need your attorney to answer a 10-minute question. This section is to help you speak to your attorney like the CEO of a well-run corporation who seeks advice from a more knowledgeable colleague, not a small woodland creature throwing themselves at the mercy of an expert to 'save' them.

This information is not presented to encourage you to run out and handle your own divorce, but rather to educate you about what steps usually happen to get from point A to point B in case you run out of money and need to triage your legal dollars.

CHAPTER 12

CONTESTED DIVORCES

In an ideal world, after you did your Bootcamp preparation exercises, you would be able to sit down with your Husband at your kitchen table or mediators office and rationally come to an agreement about how you are going to divvy up all the goodies and responsibilities you have accumulated during your marriage.

Unfortunately, this isn't a perfect world.

Although 80% of all divorce cases eventually settle, most start out as a contested divorce. Some women file because their spouses refuse to discuss the matter and they need a judge to coerce dialogue. Other women know their spouses well enough to know that the evil trapper will abscond with the marital assets and burn the financial records the moment they catch wind of a divorce. The court's 'automatic restraining order' may not prevent the evil trapper from playing games, but at least it makes it a criminal offense to do so. Lastly, many women will first attempt to hammer out an agreement with their spouse, but will be forced to resort to court to have a judge decide issues which remain unresolved. Out of all contested divorces, the overwhelming majority will be filed under the state's "no fault" divorce statute. "No fault" simply means "we choose to go our separate ways."

In this chapter, you fill out the minimum paperwork you need to get the ball rolling. **Do not file this paperwork yet!!!** There are also motions and documents you should *probably* fill out covered in subsequent chapters outlined on the following page.

SHOULD I FILE AN AT-FAULT DIVORCE?

Many women feel they are selling themselves short if they do not file on fault grounds. However, fault divorces are complicated, expensive, messy, acrimonious, and carry a lot more risk than no-fault divorces. As we learned earlier, the court really does not want to hear either of you complain about what a rotten lug the other person is, so unless there is a legitimate reason for filing an at-fault divorce, you will probably not get anything except an annoyed judge if you file a "fault" divorce. However, sometimes an at-fault divorce is prudent. In most states, *if* you can prove fault, the day the judge says you are divorced, you are *immediately* divorced (i.e., no mandatory 90- or 120-day waiting period for your divorce to become final). Here are a few examples:

- You live in a state with a long 'live apart' period before you can file a no-fault divorce;
- You are dying and would rather rot in hell then die married to the evil trapper;
- You live in one of the states where inherited or gifted property becomes part of the marital estate and your wealthy parents are about to kick the bucket;
- In some states, you must prove fault to become eligible for alimony;
- Other reasons which may be unique to *your* situation or *your* home state.

Fault divorces *require* a full-blown trial. If you don't prove a sufficient burden of fault, the case with be dismissed without obtaining your divorce. They tend to be more acrimonious, messy, and you must air your dirty laundry for the public eye. Unless your husband put you in the hospital and you can show up in court with your jaw still wired shut (in which case the judge would grant you custody of your kids and a divorce on the spot), you should *probably* file a no fault divorce. There are ways to take advantage of the simplicity of the no fault divorce while still letting the court know of especially egregious conduct your husband may have committed.

Spouses Behaving Badly: An abused wife worded her no fault divorce complaint *'on such-and-such a day an irretrievable breakdown of the marriage occurred when the Defendant came home drunk, slugged me in the face, knocked me down, broke my glasses, pulled a bookcase down on top of me and then kicked me.'* She filed under the no-fault statute because she could not afford a protracted trial, but the judge took one look at her bruises and promptly awarded her sole custody of the kids and a hefty alimony award.

Consult an attorney if you feel there are sufficient fault grounds and circumstances to justify going the at-fault route. There are some situations it could be beneficial.

Once you file your divorce, your assets will be frozen and you will be forbidden to remove any belongings from your home, safety deposit box, or any other location. Either your husband will childishly refuse to help you pay the bills, or he will empty out the bank accounts, the house, and even take away any assets in his name (such as the car *you* use), leaving you stranded. These are steps you should take in the days, weeks, and months before you file to better position yourself for the upcoming war.

Before retreating into your castle for a long siege, lay in an adequate store of rations so the enemy does not starve you out!

TABLE 12-1 - COUNTDOWN TO FILING DAY CHECKLIST

Date Completed	When	Action
	6 months or more before you file	Cut the number of your children's activities to one each. Start transitioning yourself and your children to low cost/high value activities NOW such as family trips to the library, town recreation department sponsored activities, scouting or nature walks so your husband doesn't use the old activities as a custody bribe.
	6 months or more before you file	Ditch the family cell phone contract!!! Start weaning your kids off the thing attached to their ear NOW so their father doesn't use it as a bribe to get custody.
	6 months or more before you file	Save (3) months living expenses into a secret bank account to sustain you in the period of time between when you file your divorce, get a court hearing, and then get your first child support or alimony check (you must disclose this once you file … it only stays secret until you file).
	6 months or more before you file	Open a credit card in your own name, use it once a month to start building credit, and have the bill sent to your secret P.O. Box.
	6 months or more before you file	Consult with an attorney (or several) to discuss your situation and possible outcomes and their retainer requirements. Start saving money to hire them, or at minimum to hire somebody to draft your separation agreement for you.
	3 months or more before you file	Finish collecting and organizing your acorns. Make three copies. Store one at your "safety burrow," keep the other for your husband and your attorney.
	3 months or more before you file	Appraise your house. Document and appraise everything else you own. Finish your appraisal notebook.
	3 months or more before you file	Finalize your post-divorce budget, proposed property division, and survival plan.
	3 months or more before you file	If you plan on buying out the marital home, contact several banks and find out if they will "pre-approve" you to refinance the mortgage or take out a home equity line of credit based on your anticipated post-divorce income to buy out your husband's share.

	3 months or more before you file	Unload your 100% financed gas-guzzling SUV for a decent, Consumer Reports Best Buy 5-year-old used car.
	3 months or more before you file	If you have a will, change it so that your spouse can't gain control of any potential assets you leave to your minor children if you die (he can contest it until your divorce is final, but change it now anyways).
	6 weeks before you file	If you have not already retained an attorney and can afford to do so, now is the time.
	2 weeks before you file	Draft your divorce paperwork, including motions and proposed separation agreement. Obtain a certified check to pay the court's filing fee and summons. Call the Sheriff's office to find out exactly how much it will cost to have your husband served and get a bank check or money order for that amount.
	2 weeks before you file	Pre-pay your utility bills for last and this month out of your joint marital income. Pre-pay your mortgage as well. Your spouse will refuse to pay his share of the utilities and mortgage up until the day you file and the court usually considers such expenses to be too minor to bother arguing about. You will spend more money dragging him into court three times to make him pay, so just assume he won't and *you* pay it.
	2 weeks before you file	Get a finalized mortgage pre-approval commitment from a bank (if applicable).
	2 weeks before you file	Compile an easy-to-use list of credit card numbers, 800 customer service numbers, and other debts you plan on canceling when you file for divorce.
	2 weeks before you file	If you are planning on staying in your house, call the telephone company and ask them to put a 1-900 phone call block, collect phone call block, and caller ID on your telephone line (to prevent expensive games your husband can play alone or in cahoots with your kids)
	2 weeks before you file	Call your life insurance company and remove your husband as a beneficiary under the policy. If you choose to name your children as beneficiaries, specify that the funds are to be paid in trust for your children and name a trusted relative or friend as the trustee.
	2 weeks before you file	If you have an IRA or 401(k) plan, call the benefits administrator and change beneficiaries to someone other than your husband.
	7 days before you file	Move those items you plan on keeping in your Proposed Separation Agreement out of your safe deposit box and into to your new secret box. *You must disclose and account for the value of those items to the court.* It's a good idea to photograph the items in the box and keep a list.
	1 day before you file	Call every credit card and charge account which has your husband listed as a joint debtor or authorized user and cancel them.
	1 day before you file	Move any funds you plan on keeping in your Proposed Separation Agreement out of their respective bank accounts. You must disclose and account for the value of these funds to the court.

CONTESTED DIVORCE CHECKLIST

The court is very strict about submitting certain documents before they will hear your case. Although the court may sometimes allow you to wait a few weeks to fill out some of the documents, this is not good practice. In fact, the best way for a pro se litigant to get their divorce rolling is to file and have the Sheriff serve a whole menu of documents upon their spouse at the same time so that your spouse has these documents to hand their attorney (if they hire one). If you don't, some documents will cause delay in getting hearing dates and the failure to promptly request other documents will severely inhibit your ability to strategize and get a fair property division.

Although the exact rules and timelines vary somewhat from state-to-state, thanks to the Federal Rules of Civil Procedure (a nationwide boilerplate which every state has adopted with only a few local tweaks), the following paperwork and deadlines should have some correlation in *your* state. Most states usually require *some* version of the following forms to be filed (or served) along with your contested divorce:

TABLE 12-2: FORMS THAT START YOUR DIVORCE

Date Filed	Document Name	When to File It	Reference Chapter
	Complaint for Divorce	Mandatory	12
	Certified copy of your marriage certificate (state copy, embossed seal)	Mandatory	n/a
	Motion to Delay Filing of Certified Copy of Marriage Certificate	Optional - if you need to file in a hurry and cannot find your marriage certificate	12
	Your Financial statement	Mandatory	4
	Affidavit Disclosing Other Custody Proceedings Involving Your Minor Children	Mandatory	10
	Filing Fee	Mandatory – can waive if indigent	n/a
	Summons fee	Mandatory – can waive if indigent	n/a
	Affidavit of Indigency	Optional – file if you cannot afford the filing and summons fees	12
	Service on Sheriff's Summons	This form will get mailed back to you after the Sheriff serves your husband a copy of the divorce paperwork. It *must* be forwarded to the court	12

The following forms are forms I *recommend* you have served *at the same time* as your other divorce paperwork if your state requires it:

TABLE 12-3: FORMS FILED WITH OR SHORTLY AFTER FILING FOR DIVORCE

Date Filed	Document Name	When to File It	Reference Chapter
	Registry of Vital Statistics change-form	Mandatory – best to file with divorce paperwork as it can delay your case	10
	Military Affidavit	Mandatory if your husband doesn't "Answer" the Complaint. Best to file with divorce paperwork as it can delay your case.	10
	Motion for Temporary Orders	Optional, but strongly recommended. Gets you temporary child support and other protections while the divorce is winding its way through the courts.	13
	Affidavit in Support of Temporary Orders	Optional. Part of Temporary Orders.	13
	Motion to Appoint a Family Services Investigation or Guardian ad Litem (GAL) (if applicable)	Optional. File with divorce paperwork if you are positive there will be a custody dispute or if you have serious reservations about unsupervised visitation. Can file at any time during the divorce if new issues arise regarding your children.	14
	Affidavit in Support of Motion to Appoint a Family Services Investigation or GAL (if applicable)	Optional. Part of Guardian ad Litem (GAL) motion.	14
	Request for Defendants Financial Statement	Optional. Spouse is supposed to give you his financial statement before the Temporary Orders hearing within 10 days of service of process (so you get an inkling about whether or not he's going to lie about his income), but usually won't unless coerced.	15
	Request for any Mandatory Self-Disclosure financial documents	Optional. In most states your spouse is supposed to give you a copy of his financial records within 45 days of being served with divorce papers, but most won't until coerced.	15

If you are fairly confident that once you compel your spouse to the negotiating table, you will be able to work out a reasonable property division and there are not many *other* issues to dispute, I recommend you have the Sheriff hand him a first draft of the following or mail it to him shortly thereafter:

TABLE 12-4: FORMS A SMART WOODLAND CREATURE PREPARES IN ADVANCE

Date Filed	Document Name	When to File It	Reference Chapter
	Proposed Separation Agreement	Mandatory at time of final hearing. Optional earlier in the divorce process if you think your spouse will be amenable to settling many of the issues.	11

These are documents that *you* owe your *husband* shortly after you file for divorce. If you were a good little woodland creature and did all your Chapter Three "acorns" exercises, you will already have copies of everything neatly photocopied, arranged by date, stapled and paper clipped together as appropriate, and separated by account number with colored pieces of paper.

TABLE 12-5: DOCUMENTS YOU -MUST- FILE ON TIME

When Due	Document Name	Why you Need It	What will happen if you don't send it
Have the Sheriff serve with the initial divorce documents Date Sent:_____	Financial Statement (see Chapter 4)	You must disclose the state of your finances, *including* bank accounts and credit cards you have kept secret until now, to your husband the same as he must disclose his finances to you. If you moved assets which he might "disappear" into safe new accounts while the divorce is pending, this is your opportunity to let him know the money has been moved, not liquidated.	The court will not hold a hearing to give you child support until you file this. You could be fined by the court and forced to pay your spouse's attorney fees if you refuse to give this to him.
Within 45 days of the filing of the divorce. Best done ASAP after he is served Date Sent:_____	Mandatory Self-Disclosure Documents (the exact same documents *you* are going to request from *him*)	In nearly *all* states, you both must provide each other with full copies of these documents.	If you omit something and it materially affects the property division, the court could find you guilty of criminal fraud.

The following documents are *owed* to you by your spouse shortly after you file for divorce. If you don't get them within the timeline, you must be diligent about sending him a reminder letter.

TABLE 12-6: FORMS YOUR SPOUSE IS SUPPOSED TO GET BACK TO YOU

When Due	Document Name	Why you Need It	What to do if you don't get it
Usually within 10 days after he is served by the Sheriff Due:_____	Financial Statement	You need to know if he is going to lie about his income at the Temporary Orders hearing so you can be prepared with documents to prove he is lying. If you do not know in advance that he is going to lie, you could end up with a lot less child support than you are owed.	Send him a request and blank financial statement along with the Sheriff's documents. If you don't get it on the 10th day, send him a demand letter and a second blank financial statement and complain like mad to the judge at the Temporary Orders hearing if he then lies about his income and does not file it. You can also have a disinterested witness serve him with a notarized subpoena demanding the underlying documents be brought to the temporary orders hearing (covered in Chapter 15 - Discovery)
20 days after he is served by the Sheriff Due:_____	"Answer" to the Complaint to Divorce	This lets you know if your husband is going to do anything weird, such as counterclaim for custody. If he does not file within If you don't file a "Motion for Temporary Orders" and a hearing date, the court will frequently not schedule a hearing on its own for many months.	Do nothing. If he doesn't "Answer" within a reasonable period of time after the deadline passes, this is taken by the court to essentially mean "everything the plaintiff said is true."
45 days after he is served by the Sheriff Due:_____	Mandatory Self-Disclosure (financial) Documents	By law, you both must provide each other with full copies of these documents.	If he omits something, you will lose your share of it. Make sure he discloses all assets you may be entitled to a share of. If you get the paperwork back from him and suspect he is omitting something material, you can send a more specific "Request for the Production of Documents" to get it.

To manage all of this paperwork, you need to organize it into a Docket File. Get a large 3-ring binder and a set of 5 tab dividers and divide it into the following sections. A list of possible documents appropriate for each section are:

TABLE 12-7: SAMPLE DOCKET FILE ORGANIZATION CHART

Motions and Pleadings	Discovery Requests	Financial Statements	Correspondence with OP/Atty	Miscellaneous
Complaint & supporting documents	Request for Financial Statement	Financial Statements	Letters to your husband	Anything that you don't know where else to file it.
Husband's "Answer"	Request for Documents	Documents supporting your financial affairs (i.e., your 'Acorns')	Letters to his attorney	
Motion for Temporary Orders	Requests for Admissions			
Motions to Compel	Interrogatories			
GAL Report	Your husband's Discovery requests of you			
Request for Pre-Trial Conference				
Pre-Trial Order				
Anything requesting or requiring a hearing				

Don't stick anything into your Docket File that you would not want to accidentally fall out onto the floor of the courthouse and have your husband (or his attorney) see!

It is good practice to place a "document control sheet" at the beginning of each section and log each piece of paper as you put it into your notebook as your case file will very quickly develop a life of its own and it will become impossible to find anything. A good attorney knows how to quickly put their hands on every slip of paper within their control. A sample Document Control Sheet format follows:

EXHIBIT 12-1 - SAMPLE DOCKET FILE DOCUMENT CONTROL SHEET

MOTIONS AND PLEADINGS			
Document Date	Document Description	Originator	Disposition
2/14/07	Plaintiff's Motion for Temporary Orders	Wife	Granted 4/1/07
3/14/07	Defendant's Opposition to Temp Orders	Husband	Denied 4/1/07
5/1/07	Plaintiff's Request for GAL Investigation	Wife	Granted 6/3/07
6/17/07	Plaintiff's Motion to Compel Discovery	Wife	Granted 6/29/07

Your Docket File Document Control sheet is your friend. It can be something you make up on your computer, such as the sample above, or simply a sheet of lined notebook paper folded into four sections or with lines drawn down the page. What matters is that you place each new sheet of paper chronologically in the appropriate section of your docket file binder and mark down what that piece of paper was on your Document Control Sheet. Nothing communicates to the opposing attorney not to play you for a fool than being organized.

HOW TO FILL OUT THE COMPLAINT FOR DIVORCE

The first document you must fill out is the Complaint for Divorce. Since I am licensed in Massachusetts, we will use Massachusetts forms, but the information courts gather is similar from state to state. The Complaint is usually self-explanatory. If you are the one filing for divorce, you will be the Plaintiff and your spouse the Defendant. You can refer back to Chapter Nine to get an idea of where to dig *your* official state form up.

*If you print out this form on your printer or a photocopy, you **must** use the exact quality and color paper your state specifies or the court will reject it.* Read your state guidelines carefully.

A few states still do not have an official 'Complaint for Divorce' form, in which case you will need to research and make up your own. Have all paperwork sent to your secure P.O. Box and check it frequently.

Spouses Behaving Badly: I've had clients complain their ex-spouse was stealing mail out of their mailbox and digging through their trash for 'evidence.' I once even had an ex-husband try to introduce stolen mail, trash, and even underwear stolen off the laundry line as 'evidence' at hearings.

EXHIBIT 12-2 - SAMPLE COMPLAINT FOR DIVORCE

Commonwealth of Massachusetts
The Trial Court

Barnstable Division   **Probate and Family Court Department**   Docket No. _____

Complaint For Divorce

_____ Jane Doe-Rayme _____ , Plaintiff

v.

_____ Jack Rayme _____ , Defendant

1. Plaintiff, who resides at __100 Any Street, North Anytown, MA 02652__
     (Street and No.)   (City or Town)   (County)   (State)   (Zip)
was lawfully married to the defendant who now resides at __55 Easy Street__
                                                           (Street and No.)

__Anytown, Barnstable County, MA 02743__
(City or Town)   (County)   (State)   (Zip)

> Where you last lived together as husband and wife is usually critical for conferring jurisdiction.

2. The parties were married at __Elvis Chapel, Las Vegas__ on __September 11, 1994__ and last lived together at __100 Any Street, North Anytown, MA__ on __December 10, 2006__

3. The minor children __of this marriage, and date(s) of birth is/are:
     Janie Rayme – 6/15/95
     Johnnie Rayme - 10/11/98

4. Plaintiff certifies that no previous action for divorce, annulling or affirming marriage, separate support, desertion, living apart for justifiable cause, or custody of child __ren__ has been brought by either party against the other except:
     __209A restraining order hearing, Orleans District Court, December 10, 2006__

> You must disclose parallel court actions.

5. On or about __December 10, 2006__, the defendant __came home drunk, beat the dog nearly to death in front of the minor children, and threatened he would do the same to me.__

> If you are filing no-fault but have fault grounds, this is a good place to drop the judge a hint!

6. Wherefore, plaintiff requests that the Court:
     Ξ grant a divorce for __irretrievable breakdown of the marriage__
     Ξ prohibit defendant from imposing any restraint on plaintiff's personal liberty
     Ξ grant xxx/her custody of the above-named child__ren__
     Ξ order a suitable amount for support of the plaintiff and said minor child__ren__
     Ξ order conveyance of the real estate located at __100 Any Street, North Anytown, MA__
     standing in the name of __jointly husband and wife__
     as recorded with __Barnstable__
     Registry of Deeds, Book __999__ Page __1022__
     Ξ allow plaintiff to resume her former name of __Doe__

> No-fault grounds.

> If you want to resume your maiden name, ask here. It's a pain in the neck to go back and ask to change it later!

Date __January 10, 2007__

Signature of Attorney or Plaintiff if pro se:

Address: __100 Any Street__
           __AnyTown, USA 02652__

Sign the bottom of the form and write the words "pro se" next to your signature. "Pro se" loosely translates into "for myself" or acting as your own attorney.

⚑ *There are still a few ridiculously out-of-date states that do not have a standardized form.* In that case, you will need to obtain a copy of a manufactured one and replicate it.

WHERE DO I FILE?

Jurisdiction is a *critical* issue. You usually file your divorce in the Family Court located in the county where you last resided with your husband (unless *neither* one of you now lives there). If *you* moved out of the house and into a different county, you will need to go back to your original home county to file for divorce. If *he* moved out, you can file in your home county and he will have to come back there to tie up loose ends. If you have *both* since moved out of that county, then you will most likely need to chase after him to get your divorce.

Jurisdictional issues CANNOT be waived. Ask an attorney, lawyer of the day, or the clerk at your courthouse when you file to make sure you are in the right place. Otherwise, your divorce will be invalid.

WHAT IF I NEED TO FILE IN A HURRY AND DON'T HAVE A CERTIFIED COPY OF MY MARRIAGE CERTIFICATE ON-HAND?

Ever since the terrorist attacks on September 11, 2001, the government has become careful about what documents can be used in any legal proceeding. Where it was once permissible in some jurisdictions to submit a photocopy or town clerk abstract of your marriage certificate, you must now provide an original, state-certified copy of your marriage certificate containing a *raised, embossed seal* and issued by the state Registry of Vital Statistics. The court will not allow you to get a divorce without it.

Generally, it is best if you take the time to get an "official" copy of your marriage certificate *before* you file for divorce. In some situations, however, you have no choice. If you just landed in a battered women's shelter because your spouse beat you to a bloody pulp, obviously you don't have time to wait two weeks for the official certificate to come in the mail. Or, if a person you mistakenly confided in has 'spilled the beans' and you suspect your husband is shredding his financial records and emptying out the bank accounts, waiting would probably be a bad thing. Or, if your spouse has kidnapped your children, you don't have time to play namby-pamby with the paperwork. There are larger issues at hand. In dire situations such as these, there is a way to get around filing the marriage certificate when you file your divorce and file it later.

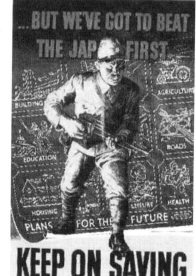

A sample "Motion for Late Filing of Marriage Certificate" follows:

EXHIBIT 12-3: SAMPLE MOTION FOR LATE FILING OF MARRIAGE CERTIFICATE

COMMONWEALTH OF MASSACHUSETTS

BARNSTABLE, SS.

PROBATE AND FAMILY COURT
DOCKET NO.

JANE DOE-RAYME,   )
   Plaintiff   )
)
v.   )
JACK RAYME,   )
   Defendant   )
)

MOTION FOR LATE
FILING OF MARRIAGE
CERTIFICATE

NOW COMES the plaintiff, Jane Doe-Rayme, and respectfully requests that this court grant her ex-parte permission to file a certified copy of her marriage certificate at a later date. As grounds for such, the plaintiff states as follows:

1. She and the defendant were married on September 11, 1996 in Las Vegas, Nevada;
2. She just learned the original notarized marriage certificate given to her at the time of marriage is unacceptable to this court (copy attached) because it does not have a raised seal;
3. It will take a reasonable period of time to obtain a suitable copy from Nevada;
4. The wife and minor children are separated from the husband at this time and in dire need of temporary protective orders.

Date: February 14, 2007

Respectfully submitted,

Jane Doe
Jane Doe-Rayme, Plaintiff, pro se

CERTIFICATE OF SERVICE

I, Jane Doe-Rayme, the Plaintiff in the above-captioned case, did serve a copy of this Plaintiff's Motion for Late Filing of Marriage Certificate upon the Plaintiff, Jack Rayme, on February 14, 2007 via the following method (check method):

   X   sheriff's service
   o   in hand
   o   mailing via USPS first class mail, postage prepaid

Signed under the pains and penalties of perjury of law this 14 th day of February, 2007.

Jane Doe
Jane Doe-Rayme, Plaintiff

WHAT IF I CAN'T AFFORD THE COURT'S FILING FEE?

Although getting a free lawyer to handle your divorce for you is *not* a Constitutional right, having access to the courts to actually *file* for your divorce *is*. If you live below poverty level, or you have some income, but not enough to meet your basic living expenses (such as your mortgage or rent, food, heat, and medical bills), sometimes you can ask the court to waive the filing fee.

Bring a finalized copy of your Financial Statement to the courthouse and ask them for an "Affidavit of Indigency." If the court finds you indigent, they will waive the filing and sometimes also the sheriff's service-of-process fees. They may also charge you a reduced rate for any court-mandated parent education classes, arbitration/conciliation, or other mandatory programs. It will usually take the court a week to process the request and mail it back to you. Don't be ashamed to ask for a waiver if you need it!

You *must* attach a copy of your Financial Statement to this affidavit!

A sample "Affidavit of Indigency" follows. *Your* state's form will look a bit different, but gather essentially the same information.

In the sample, our hypothetical wife, Jane Doe-Rayme cannot come up with the filing fee because her husband responded to her getting a restraining order by refusing to pay any of the bills or mortgage payment. He has also stopped paying child support. Although Jane would normally be able to pay, her husband's behavior has put her in the hole and she must choose between keeping a roof over her kids head and filing for help. The court will most likely decide to waive the filing fee.

EXHIBIT 12-4: SAMPLE AFFIDAVIT OF INDIGENCY

THE AUTOMATIC RESTRAINING ORDER

When you file the complaint, you will get a copy of a piece of paper informing you both that an "Automatic Restraining Order" on all of your money and assets went into effect the moment you filed for divorce. This means neither of you can sell or remove assets from the marital home or take money out of your bank accounts except for money used for the ordinary bills you normally pay (such as your mortgage and your electric bill). It is a crime to move or liquidate money or assets once you have filed the Complaint for Divorce!!!

This is why the boot camp has so much emphasis on preparation!!! Once you file, everything becomes frozen.

The purpose of this Automatic Restraining Order is to prevent either of you from emptying out the bank accounts and absconding with joint marital funds. That might not prevent your husband from doing that anyways, but if he does *after* you file for divorce, he can be found in contempt of court and jailed, whereas if he does it *before* you file, good luck chasing him down!

There are exceptions for things such as paying the mortgage or other routine bills, making your ordinary and usual payroll deductions into any flexible spending accounts, employee stock purchase plans, or retirement savings accounts. You may also make routine repairs on your house or car. You may not, however, file for divorce and then start moving large sums of money around without first gaining the permission of the court *or* coming to a signed stipulation with your husband.

Automatic Restraining Order: Prohibits the parties from liquidating joint marital assets without first gaining the permission of the court.

THE SHERIFF'S SUMMONS

When you go to the courthouse to file your divorce, you must generally pay to *purchase* a divorce summons (usually around $5-$10). You do not need to have this paper to go to the courthouse and file, but rather it is something you get at the courthouse *when* you file and you must immediately take it to the Deputy Sheriff's office (along with a complete copy of all paperwork you have filed with your divorce) to serve upon your husband. The Automatic Restraining Order doesn't kick in until your husband has been served, in-hand, by the Sheriff or certain other limited statutorily approved people.

Notice of divorce proceedings must generally be served *in hand*, not simply mailed or left at the front door. Therefore, unless you want to wait for weeks for the Sheriff to catch up with your husband, information about where your husband can be found will get him served as soon as possible. The Sheriff typically works 9-5, Monday through Friday, the same as everybody else. If your husband is typically working during those hours and is not at home, the Sheriff won't be able to hand him the paperwork and state those ominous words "you've been served." Therefore, try to find out where your husband will be during the day.

Your divorce does not officially "begin" until the Sheriff personally puts the divorce paperwork into your husband's hands and utter the words 'you've been served.' If you tip your husband off the paperwork is coming, he will frequently try to "avoid" service by dodging the Sheriff!!!

Spouses Behaving Badly: I once had a husband dodge service by the Sheriff for *weeks*. He even went so far as to lie and say he wasn't himself. I finally paid a pretty young Russian exchange college student to flirt with him. When he told her his name, she served him in-hand with the divorce summons and told him in heavily accented English 'you've been served.' It was an exciting experience for her in American justice!

Write a note to the Sheriff explaining where you think your husband would most likely be found at certain times of day. List those addresses, the telephone numbers (if you have them), and the times you think your husband will be there. Frequently, the Sheriff will call (not identifying who he is or why he is calling), ask for the person, and then show up a few minutes later. I tend to favor the husband's place of employment as most men are married to their jobs and can always be found there. If your husband has a job which varies (such as different job sites), discreetly try to inquire where he expects to be working that week so you have good information to give the Sheriff.

You must mail the original summons with the Sheriff's signature on it back to the courthouse or your divorce will be dismissed.

Some Sheriff's offices are in the habit of mailing the original summons back to the courthouse themselves and mailing the plaintiff a copy. If you receive a photocopy, assume that is what the Sheriff did, but it is still a good policy to mail a photocopy of the photocopy back to the courthouse just in case things got lost in the shuffle.

CHAPTER TWELVE SUMMARY

1. A "contested" divorce is any divorce which has unresolved property or custody issues which you and your husband can't agree on. If you both agree you want to get divorced, but have been unable to create a full Separation Agreement on all issues, you will have to file a "contested" divorce.

2. Make sure you have your acorns and a survival plan in-hand *before* you file. There are many steps you can take to better position yourself financially in the months and days before you actually file.

3. There are lots of documents that will be passed back and forth once you file. Learn what they are, when to use them, and keep them well organized in a 3-ring binder so you can put your hands on them at a moment's notice.

4. If you cannot afford the court's filing fee, you can file a special request asking them to waive it.

5. In God we trust, but the Sheriff only takes cash...

CHAPTER 13

TEMPORARY ORDERS

When you file your divorce, there is an important motion you should file *at the same time* called a 'Motion for Temporary Orders.' This motion requests the court hold a hearing shortly after you serve your spouse with divorce papers to determine things that will help you maintain the status quo. This hearing determines who will remain in the marital home, where the children (or pets) will live, how much child support and/or alimony you are entitled to receive, who can use which motor vehicle, and who will pay which bills. It is your first opportunity to introduce the judge to your case.

Warning!!! Things decided at the Temporary Orders hearing have a way of becoming permanent!

Ask the court to schedule a Temporary Orders hearing when you file your Divorce. Pick a date two weeks after you think the sheriff will be able to serve him (it usually takes the sheriff at least a week) but you may not be able to get in for four or five weeks. You *must* include a copy of this motion with the Complaint for Divorce when you have the Sheriff serve him or it will cause delay.

These motions (and subsequent hearings) vary in what they contain, but sample motion and supporting affidavit follows to give you an idea of what to ask for and how to ask for it. Remember, this first hearing is about *maintaining the status quo* so your house does not go into foreclosure, your cars do not get repossessed, bill collectors don't (hopefully) begin pounding upon your door, and your spouse does not do something vindictive such as cancel your health insurance. It is to ensure your children have a stable place to live, do not go hungry and have access to both parents. This hearing is *not* about litigating your entire divorce case right out of the starting gate.

A sample Motion for Temporary Orders based upon our hypothetical Jane Doe litigant's case follows:

EXHIBIT 13-1: SAMPLE MOTION FOR TEMPORARY ORDERS

COMMONWEALTH OF MASSACHUSETTS

BARNSTABLE, SS.

PROBATE AND FAMILY COURT
DOCKET NO.

JANE DOE-RAYME,
    Plaintiff)
)
v.)
)
JACK RAYME,)
    Defendant)
)

PLAINTIFF'S MOTON FOR
TEMPORARY ORDERS

NOW COMES the plaintiff, Jane Doe-Rayme, and respectfully moves for a temporary order of support and maintenance pursuant to G.L. c. 208, § 17 and states as reasons therefore the following:

1. The plaintiff has filed a Complaint for Divorce pursuant to G.L. c. 208, § 1B.

2. The parties were married on September 11, 1994, have been married for twelve (12) years. There are two (2) minor children of the marriage: Jayne, date of birth June 15, 1995; and Johnnie Rayme, date of birth October 11, 1998.

3. The plaintiff is currently unaware of the parties' marital assets and liabilities in that, upon information and belief, the defendant, Jack Rayme, has managed the family finances and incurred significant debt.

4. Throughout the marriage, the plaintiff has been the primary caretaker of the children and the home. The defendant has been the primary financial provider and remains so for the family.

5. Although the plaintiff is now a Registered Nurse, she has limited income and job experience beyond raising a family because, until the last year, she has only worked outside the home part-time since the birth of the first child and has devoted herself to the rearing of the children, to homemaking and to the full-time advancement of the husband's career and business.

6. The plaintiff continues to reside in the former marital home with the children. The Wife's property maintenance and household expenses alone require substantial support and maintenance.

7. In addition to the necessities of food, shelter, clothing, medical attention and education, the following requirements exist:

    a. Both children must be placed in full-time after school child care and school vacation summer camp so that the mother can work. Until the parties separated, the Wife worked overnight shifts so that her husband was home in case of emergency while the children slept and took school vacations off. Now, however, the Wife is incurring significant child care bills for after-school care and has no way to pay the cost of summer child care for both children as that will exceed her income.

    b. The oldest child, Jayne, suffers from dyslexia and previously required intensive private diagnosis and tutoring (there is an outstanding bill of $15,000 which she have been paying on a payment plan of $25 per week). She *currently* requires ongoing private tutoring at a cost of $65 per week to help her succeed in public school.

    c. Both children have been in therapy since witnessing their father beat their dog nearly to death on December 9, 2006 (the incident prompting the current restraining order);

    d. The North Anytown School Department requires that parents pay a $250 per child fee in order to allow the children to ride the school bus, for a total of $500.

    e. The younger child, Johnnie, is in cub scouts and has been earning citizenship merit badges and planning for the past year to travel with his Troup on a trip to Washington, DC, during this upcoming February school vacation week. Both his father and I had previously promised him he could go on this trip and signed the Troup's committal slip. The trip will cost $375, which I cannot afford. If the Father does not pay, Johnnie will not be able to go.

The courts top priority is always your minor children.

This is legal mumbo-jumbo for 'I don't know *what* we have.'

Primary caretaker factors to get custody are covered in Chapter 14 - Child Custody

Jane explains *why* she needs child support and/or alimony

Jane educates the judge about unique facts about her case.

f. The younger son, Johnnie, has braces. There is currently $4,500 outstanding to the orthodontist to finish treatment.

8. The defendant's income is substantial and enables him to readily provide ample, significant income for the needs of the plaintiff and the children at the marital home.

WHEREFORE, the plaintiff, Jane Doe-Rayme, respectfully requests the following:

1. Temporary shared legal custody of the children and physical custody of the children to be with the plaintiff;

2. Temporary child support based upon the respective Financial Statements of the parties filed with the Court;

3. Temporary alimony based upon the respective Financial Statements of the parties filed with the Court;

4. That said payments be collected through the Massachusetts Department of Revenue;

5. Payment by the defendant of any reasonable medical, dental, optical and pharmaceutical bills not covered by insurance in proportion to the parties income;

6. Maintenance of medical, dental, and vision insurance by the defendant for the family;

7. Maintenance of outstanding life insurance on the defendant's life for the benefit of the plaintiff;

8. Since it was the violent acts of the father that necessitated therapy, 100% reimbursement for all uninsured therapist bills and co-pays for the children;

9. That the two school bus transportation fees be divided according to the couple's income;

10. That Jayne's ongoing special needs tutoring bill be divided according to the couple's income.

11. That the husband be ordered to pay the weekly payment on the outstanding $15,000 tutoring bill in proportion to the couple's income.

12. That the Husband be ordered to pay $375 for Johnnie's cub scout trip;

13. That the Husband be ordered to pay all of the liabilities listed on Section 11 of the court's financial statement in proportion to the couple's income.

14. All other orders which are meet and just.

As grounds therefore, the plaintiff further relies upon her Financial Statement filed with the Court and incorporated herein by reference.

Date: ___February 14, 2007___

Respectfully Submitted:

___*Jane Doe-Rayme*___

Be sure you ask for the right kind of custody for your situation:

-Sole physical and legal (sometimes granted in case of physical abuse/drug addiction)

-Shared legal/sole physical (the norm in most cases)

-Shared physical and legal (50:50 custody)

Always collect child support (and if possible alimony) through your state's Child Support Enforcement Division!!

The government *wants* you to keep your existing health insurance so the taxpayers don't get stuck paying the bill.

These requests are more unusual. The judge may grant them, or he may rule Jack is already paying enough through child support/alimony.

Jane asks that Jack pay *all* of the debts. It is unlikely he will be ordered to pay 100%.

The court can only give you what you *ask* for. The *All Other Orders* verbiage gives the judge a way to add things if something unexpected comes up at the hearing.

🚩 *Some states require you to file motions on very specific paper with numbered lines upon it or they will reject your paperwork.* You can either buy this lined paper at a stationary supply store, or if you have a newer version of Microsoft Word, when you open a new document, go into [New Document] + [Forms] + [Legal Forms] and see if they have a free boilerplate with the correct number of lines for you to use.

🚩 *If you fear your husband might contest custody, read Chapter 14 - Child Custody before you file this motion.*

At the end of this motion, you *must also* attach a "certificate of service" swearing you gave the other side a copy of everything you filed with the court, and also a "notice of hearing" informing your spouse of the court date. As soon as you get the date from the clerk, write this date into that "Notice of Hearing." If you do not write the date in the form, then your motion is not valid.

A sample Certificate of Service and Notice of Hearing follows:

EXHIBIT 13-2: SAMPLE CERTIFICATE OF SERVICE AND NOTICE OF HEARING

COMMONWEALTH OF MASSACHUSETTS

BARNSTABLE, SS.

**PROBATE AND FAMILY COURT
DOCKET NO.**

JANE DOE-RAYME,
    Plaintiff)
)
v.)
)
JACK RAYME,)
    Defendant)

**NOTICE OF HEARING FOR
TEMPORARY ORDERS**

NOTICE OF HEARING

The following matters have been scheduled for hearing at ___9:00___ A.M. on ___April 1st___ _____, 2005 at the Barnstable County Probate and Family Court.

> You must state **what** (type of hearing), **when** (time and date) and **where** (name of courthouse).

    1.   Motion for Temporary Orders

Respectfully submitted,
Jane Doe-Rayme,

Date: ___February 14, 2007___   *Jane Doe-Rayme*

> You must list every single document you served or the other side might ask the judge to exclude it.

CERTIFICATE OF SERVICE

I, Jane Doe-Rayme, hereby certify that a copy of the attached Motion for Temporary Orders, Affidavit in Support of Temporary Orders, and Notice of Hearing were served upon Jack Rayme in the following manner:

    X   sheriff's service
    o   in hand
    o   mailing via USPS first class mail, postage prepaid

> Each state has very specific rules about how much time must pass between when you give the other side a copy and when the hearing can be held. If the sheriff hands him something, you know when he got it. If it was mailed, the court requires more time.

Signed under the pains and penalties of perjury of law this __14_th day of February, 2007.

Signed: *Jane Doe-Rayme*

If you experience a *dire* emergency (such as your spouse putting your children at risk of harm or a your house about to be auctioned in foreclosure), sometimes you can get the court to grant an emergency hearing. If you feel you have such an emergency, contact an attorney for guidance.

SUPPORTING AFFIDAVITS

Normally, when a motion comes before the court to be heard, the attorneys will stand up, argue the case, elicit testimony, and be able to cite case law to support their side of the story off the top of their heads. You are not a lawyer. You have probably never been to court before, and once you do get there, you will be too tongue-tied to get evidence in front of the judge in order to enable him to give you the help you are asking for. Having a checklist helps, but you may ramble off on a tangent and forget what you really needed to say. If you forget something, you may not be allowed to go back later to fix the problem. Worse, what the judge decides in the Motion for Temporary Orders often becomes the final situation for child custody, child support, and alimony even after you go to trial. How, then, does a pro se litigant ensure they give the judge all of the information he needs?

The smart woodland creature will attach an affidavit to every motion they file. That way, the judge will read your affidavit when he reads your motion. Getting the chance to make your position known *first*, before your husband stands up and tries to discredit you, confers an enormous advantage. If you have additional supporting affidavits from witnesses or items such as copies of invoices, medical records, or police reports (review Chapter Two - Safety Planning), include those as well. The worst that can happen is your husband will object to it and the judge will rule it cannot be introduced … *after* he has already read it!

Affidavits should address each point you wish to make in your motion. In the sample Affidavit which follows, our heroine, Jane Doe, gives the judge a little piece of information and background for each request. Her main areas are as follows:

1. Custody of the children. Jane points out that she is the primary caretaker of the children and lists many of the mundane, day-to-day tasks she does to accomplish this.

2. Alimony background. Normally a registered nurse earns more money than Jane. Jane explains to the judge that she has only worked part-time and worked graveyard shifts through an in-home private nursing service so she could be home to take care of the children. She also points out that she passed up decent paying jobs to move to remote North Anytown to further her husband's career.

3. Although Jane knows the court will order visitation, she makes it clear the children do not want it. She also outlines specific incidents, such as the alcohol and abuse, to support this fact.

4. She points out that her husband is refusing to pay any bills and is currently three weeks behind on the child support ordered at the Restraining Order hearing;

5. Her children have specific needs, such as school bus fees, orthodontists, ongoing tutoring for one child's learning disability, therapy bills, and the son's upcoming trip to Washington, which need to be paid for. It is unlikely the judge will grant her every request, but it does not hurt to ask.

Although her husband will try to discredit each claim in court, Jane has gotten the information before the judge before Jack even begins to speak. Furthermore, it would be a good idea for Jane to staple copies of major outstanding documents she may need to refer to (such as police reports) right to her affidavit, and staple the entire thing to her original motion.

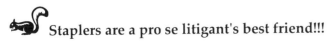 **Staplers are a pro se litigant's best friend!!!**

EXHIBIT 13-3: SAMPLE AFFIDAVIT IN SUPPORT OF TEMPORARY ORDERS

COMMONWEALTH OF MASSACHUSETTS

BARNSTABLE, SS.

PROBATE AND FAMILY COURT
DOCKET NO.

JANE DOE-RAYME,)
    Plaintiff)
v.)
JACK RAYME,)
    Defendant)
)

PLAINTIFF'S AFFIDAVIT
IN SUPPORT OF
TEMPORARY ORDERS

Now comes the plaintiff, <u>Jane Doe-Rayme</u>, and hereby does swear and affirm the following statements;

1. I have been married to my husband for 12 years;

2. We have two children born of the marriage, Jayne, age 10, and Johnnie, age 8;

3. During the course of the marriage, I have been the primary caretaker of the children. Every morning I either awaken and/or come home from my overnight shift as a private duty nurse at approximately 7:20 a.m., get the children up, get them dressed, serve them breakfast, make their lunches, and see them off to the school bus at approximately 8:35 a.m.. If I worked the previous night, I get my sleep while the children are at school. If there are any meetings or parent-teacher conferences, I am the one to attend. Three days per week, I pick the children up at school at approximately 3:10 p.m. and drive them to the tutor, cub scouts, or their therapist's office. The other two days I greet the children at the school bus at approximately 3:45 p.m. Once the children are home, I discuss how their day went at school, help them with their homework, and prepare supper. Once they have eaten, I help them brush their teeth, get into their pajamas, read them a bedtime story, and tuck them in.

4. For the past three years, my husband has tended to go out after work with his friends for a drink and miss supper. On many occasions, he does not come home until it is time for me to go to work. Twice, he was so late that I was late for work.

5. Although I completed my nursing degree in 1999, I have only worked overnight shifts as an in-home, private duty nurse because my primary focus was on taking care of my husband and raising my children. Until this past year, I rarely worked more than two nights per week. Because of our remote location far from any hospital or nursing home and due to my lack of seniority, my earning capacity is limited.

6. When I first completed my nursing degree, we lived within commuting distance of Big City and there were many large hospitals willing to hire me to work for them. We moved to North Anytown, which is nearly 85 miles from the nearest hospital and 45 miles from the nearest nursing home, to further my husband's home improvement business.

7. For the past three years, my husband has become dissatisfied, angry, and combative. He has engaged in an increasing pattern of physical threats, emotional abuse, and alcohol. On several occasions, his anger became physical. Examples include the time he punched a hole in the wall or bent my finger back so far I needed to seek medical attention for a sprained finger. Many of these incidents occurred in the presence of the children. On more than one occasion, I was frightened enough to lock myself in a room. On December 9, 2006, my husband came home in a drunken rage, started yelling so badly it woke the children up and caused the dog to urinate on the floor in terror. He then proceeded to beat the dog in the children's presence so badly that he nearly killed it. When I threatened to call the police, he threatened to kill the dog. I called the police, got a restraining order, and that restraining order was made permanent a week later in Orleans District Court.

8. The children have stated, both to me and their therapist that they are afraid of their father and do not wish to see him.

9. Ever since the restraining order hearing, my husband has refused to pay a single bill. He is also three (3) weeks behind on his child support. We are currently two months behind on our mortgage and the bank has sent us a notice of intent to foreclose if I do not pay up in full by the end of the month. On January 11th, we ran out of oil, spent 3 days without heat, and the Cape Cod Times Needy Fund had to help me fill the oil tank. All of our utilities are past-due, my car payment is past due, my student loans are past due, and our homeowners insurance is coming up for renewal at the end of the month. I cannot pay these bills on my income alone, even with the amount of child support ordered by the District Court at the restraining order hearing. We have never had to live like this before.

10. The children were so distraught about seeing their father nearly kill the dog and then witness the police arrest him that their pediatrician recommended they see a therapist. Therapy for the children costs $85 per week per child, for a total of $170 per week. Although our health insurance has picked up all but a $15 co-pay for each child up until now, the insurance company has

informed me we are reaching the end of our allotted benefits and will have to begin paying 100% of the bill beginning in March. The therapist recommends that treatment continue. I cannot afford to pay this bill.

11. Every year, payable in two installments due in September and January, we must pay $500 for the two children to ride the school bus to their public school. As we live 7 miles from the school, they cannot walk. I have been unable to pay the January installment of $250, and do not know how I will pay it from now on.

12. We are currently three months behind on Johnnie's orthodontist bill. The orthodontist is refusing to make any further adjustment to Johnnie's braces until this account is made current.

13. For over a year now, Johnnie's cub scout troop has been learning about civic responsibility, volunteering at the town hall, police department, and public works department, earning citizenship merit badges, and earning money selling first aid kits and magazines to travel to Washington, DC. His father and I signed the contract to send him there last November and owe $375 to his troop. I cannot afford to pay this bill. If his father does not pay, Johnnie will be the only member of his troop who does not go.

Signed under the pains and penalties of perjury of law this __14th__ day of __February__, 20_07_.

_____Jane Doe-Rayme_____

WHAT DO I DO IF MY SPOUSE FILES FIRST?

Being the aggressor confers an immediate advantage. Not only do you get to speak first, but it puts the person who is *defending* a lawsuit or motion into the position where they are merely refuting the other party's allegations, not making allegations of their own. Like any athlete, lawyers are trained to pick up the ball wherever it may land and make an end run around the opposition to the other end of the field, but the person who ad-libs is always at a disadvantage. *Especially* if you don't *have* an attorney!

There *is* a way to level the playing field if your *spouse* files the divorce and/or a motion first. Attorneys will sometimes file a counter-motion called an 'Opposition' which refutes every claim the other side made, or they will file their *own* Counter-Claim (in this case Temporary Orders) and attach their *own* Affidavit and supporting documents. An Opposition or Counter-Claim seeks to do essentially the same thing ... put your *own* facts in front of the judge before either party opens their mouth. You must *still* attach your own affidavit and supporting documents!

When you file an Opposition or Counter-Claim, you must follow the same notice and service of process standards as the original Motion. However, because by the time you receive your husband's motion in the mail you may not have the statutory 7- or 10-days needed to otherwise hold a hearing, you should file your motion as quickly as possible and ask the judge to grant a *Short Order of Notice* on your counter-claim so that both motions can be heard at the same time. Sometimes you would file these as separate motions, sometimes you can get away with lumping it into one. My personal preference is to include all related matters in the same motion, but some states prefer you file three separate motions, an Opposition, a Counter-Claim for Temporary Orders, and a Motion for Short Order of Notice.

A sample *Defendant Wife's Opposition, Counter-Claim for Temporary Orders and Short Order of Notice* follows:

EXHIBIT 13-4: SAMPLE COUNTER-CLAIM FOR TEMPORARY ORDERS

COMMONWEALTH OF MASSACHUSETTS

BARNSTABLE, SS.

PROBATE AND FAMILY COURT
DOCKET NO.

JANE DOE-RAYME,)
    Plaintiff)
v.)
JACK RAYME,)
    Defendant)
)

DEFENDANT WIFE'S COUNTER-
CLAIM FOR TEMPORARY ORDERS
AND
SHORT ORDER OF NOTICE

NOW COMES the defendant, Jane Doe-Rayme, and hereby does oppose her Husband's Motion for Temporary Orders and does hereby move for her *own* counter-claim for a temporary order of support and maintenance pursuant to G.L. c. 208, § 17 and states as reasons therefore the following:

1. The plaintiff Husband filed a Complaint for Divorce pursuant to G.L. c. 208, § 1B.

2. The parties were married on September 11, 1994, have been married for twelve (12) years. There are two (2) minor children of the marriage: Jayne, date of birth June 15, 1995; and Johnnie Rayme, date of birth October 11, 1998.

3. The defendant Wife is currently unaware of the parties' marital assets and liabilities in that, upon information and belief, the plaintiff Husband, Jack Rayme, has managed the family finances and incurred significant debt.

4. Throughout the marriage, the defendant Wife has been the primary caretaker of the children and the home. The plaintiff Husband has been the primary financial provider and remains so for the family.

5. The plaintiff Husband is alleging that he should not be ordered to pay spousal support or child support because the defendant Wife is a licensed registered nurse. Although the defendant is a Registered Nurse, she has limited income and job experience beyond raising a family because, until the last year, she has only worked outside the home part-time since the birth of the first child and has devoted herself to the rearing of the children, to homemaking and to the full-time advancement of the husband's career and business.

6. The defendant Wife continues to reside in the former marital home with the children. Her property maintenance and household expenses alone require substantial support and maintenance.

7. In addition to the necessities of food, shelter, clothing, medical attention and education, the following requirements exist:

   a. Both children must be placed in full-time after school child care and school vacation summer camp so that the mother can work. Until the parties separated, the Wife worked overnight shifts so that her husband was home in case of emergency while the children slept and took school vacations off. Now, however, the Wife is incurring significant child care bills for after-school care and has no way to pay the cost of summer child care for both children as that will exceed her income.

   b. The oldest child, Jayne, suffers from dyslexia and previously required intensive private diagnosis and tutoring (there is an outstanding bill of $15,000 which she have been paying on a payment plan of $25 per week). She *currently* requires ongoing private tutoring at a cost of $65 per week to help her succeed in public school.

   c. Both children have been in therapy since witnessing their father beat their dog nearly to death on December 9, 2006 (the incident prompting the current restraining order);

   d. The North Anytown School Department requires that parents pay a $250 per child fee in order to allow the children to ride the school bus, for a total of $500.

   e. The younger child, Johnnie, is in cub scouts and has been earning citizenship merit badges

Notice that Jane is essentially restating what she would have asserted anyways, only in this hypothetical we pretend Jack was the one who filed the divorce first. Often a first-filing husband will ask for full custody. Jane must be prepared to assert in her Supporting Affidavit that *she* was the primary caretaker.

We're pretending Jack's Motion for Temporary Orders is asking he be excused from paying support, claiming Jane is a career woman who is voluntarily choosing to earn less than her full earning capacity. Jane sets the record straight and should elaborate even more in her supporting affidavit.

Once again, Jane educates the judge about unique facts about her case.

and planning for the past year to travel with his Troup on a trip to Washington, DC, during this upcoming February school vacation week. Both his father and I had previously promised him he could go on this trip and signed the Troup's committal slip. The trip will cost $375, which I cannot afford. If the Father does not pay, Johnnie will not be able to go.

    f.   The younger son, Johnnie, has braces. There is currently $4,500 outstanding to the orthodontist to finish treatment.

8. The defendant's income is substantial and enables him to readily provide ample, significant income for the needs of the plaintiff and the children at the marital home.

WHEREFORE, the plaintiff, Jane Doe-Rayme, respectfully requests the following:

1. Temporary shared legal custody of the children and physical custody of the children to be with the plaintiff;

> Be sure you ask for the right kind of custody!

2. Temporary child support based upon the respective Financial Statements of the parties filed with the Court;

3. Temporary alimony based upon the respective Financial Statements of the parties filed with the Court;

4. That said payments be collected through the Massachusetts Department of Revenue;

5. Payment by the defendant of any reasonable medical, dental, optical and pharmaceutical bills not covered by insurance in proportion to the parties income;

6. Maintenance of medical, dental, and vision insurance by the defendant for the family;

7. Maintenance of outstanding life insurance on the defendant's life for the benefit of the plaintiff;

8. Since it was the violent acts of the father that necessitated therapy, 100% reimbursement for all uninsured therapist bills and co-pays for the children;

> Jane still asks for all the things she would have asked for had she filed first

9. That the two school bus transportation fees be divided according to the couple's income;

10. That Jayne's ongoing special needs tutoring bill be divided according to the couple's income.

11. That the husband be ordered to pay the weekly payment on the outstanding $15,000 tutoring bill in proportion to the couple's income.

12. That the Husband be ordered to pay $375 for Johnnie's cub scout trip;

13. That the Husband be ordered to pay all of the liabilities listed on Section 11 of the court's financial statement in proportion to the couple's income.

14. That the court waive the normal notice requirements for this motion. As cause for such, the Wife asserts the issue of Temporary Orders, filed first by the plaintiff Husband, is already scheduled for a hearing today, no harm will be caused to the Husband by hearing the Wife's request for temporary orders at the same time, and that holding the hearings concurrently would serve the interests of judicial economy. The Wife does hereby assert she both mailed a copy of this notice to the husband on February 7th, 5-days-notice, and also has served him a copy of this Counter-Claim for Temporary Orders in-hand this morning at the courthouse.

> Jane explains *why* it would serve the courts interests to hear *her* motion at the same time as Jack's.

14. All other orders which are meet and just.

As grounds therefore, the plaintiff further relies upon her Financial Statement filed with the Court and incorporated herein by reference.

Date: ___February 14, 2007___

Respectfully Submitted:

_____*Jane Doe-Rayme*_____

HOW TO DRESS AND ACT IN COURT

How you dress affects the court's estimate of your credibility. Here are some general guidelines:

1. Always dress in a formal, respectful manner. Do not dress casually, but do not over-dress either. Think 'church on Sunday' or 'job interview.' Avoid fashion extremes at all cost!!!

2. If you have a "traditional" styled dress or pants suit in a neutral, solid color, wear it. Navy blue, black, brown, taupe and beige are excellent colors. Another good choice is usually a simple, plain, below-the-kneecap skirt or dress slacks with a "twin set" cardigan and shell.

3. Wear sensible closed-toe shoes with a modest heel. No platforms, flashy colors, or "cockroach killers." Court is not the place to wear your Manolo Blanec's!

4. Do not dress 'sexy!' Sexy = bimbo/gold digger. This is the one time in your life you *want* to take fashion advice from your grandmother!

    Spouse's Behaving Badly: The wife of a husband I once represented showed up at court in a mini-skirt and five-inch heels. The judge ordered her to go home and change.

5. If you are one of those wonderful, artsy people who displays their creativity to the world through their hair, tone it down! Bleach blonde = gold digger in the eyes of most judges, dyed jet-black or blue highlights = emotionally disturbed, bright red = hussy or tantrum-prone. Have your hair cut in a neat, conservative, mainstream style. Neatly braided ethnic hair with simple beading is fine, but dreadlocks will make the court think you are a reefer addict (especially if you are white). African-American woman can usually get away with wearing a simple turban to tame their hair, but other women are expected to go hatless. Avoid stiff up do's! Pay a visit to your hairdresser, ask them to help you "dress the part" and go with a solid, neutral color that complements your skin tone. Blondes may have more fun, but dark-blondes and brunettes win more legal battles.

6. Avoid expensive jewelry which lead the judge to believe you have more money than you really have.

7. Avoid things which display a religious affiliation. If you *must* wear a religious symbol, wear it under your blouse. If you're pagan and proud of it, remember that the tri-fold goddess hides her face behind the sun for three days every month and so should you!

    Spouse's Behaving Badly: Against my advice, a client once wore her crystals and silver pentacle on top of her all-black outfit. The husband started screaming: "Look, she's a witch!!! She worships the devil and is making the kids worship the devil. She's wearing the devil's symbol right there on her chest!!!"

8. Stand straight. Don't slouch. Keep calm. Speak only when asked to speak and always wait your turn to contradict your no-good lying husband. *Never* interrupt or talk back to the judge!

    Spouse's Behaving Badly: The judge once ordered the mother and sister of an opposing party, who had accompanied him to court that day, out of his courtroom because they kept rolling their eyes every time my client spoke.

IF AVAILABLE, USE YOUR COURT'S FAMILY SERVICES DEPARTMENT

Due to the explosion of self-represented people, many courthouses have developed a range of services designed to identify and narrow the issues brought before the judge. Courts are funded by the legislature, the legislature listens to their constituents, and very few constituents know or care about what happens at their local courthouse until the day *they* get hauled into court. Therefore, nearly every courthouse in the nation suffers from an appalling lack of resources (including judges) to handle the enormous number of cases brought before them each year. Lawyers learn to work together outside of court to narrow non-essential issues. However, if you are representing yourself, how will you know what to do the day you go to court for your first hearing?

Ask the clerk if *your* courthouse has a Mediation, Arbitration, Family Services or Probation department. *Most* courthouses have someone assigned to this function, although the scope and breadth of their services varies. Some simply make sure you have filled out all the necessary documents, others ask questions to figure out which issues need to go before the judge. Some explain a synopsis of the law regarding a contested issue, while others are full-fledged mediators who will try to help you resolve issues and reach agreement before you even go into the courtroom. Some are not in the courthouse at all, but offered via a local Legal Services agency or pilot program.

If your local courthouse has a fairly well evolved family services department, they may be able to dispel any unrealistic notions you and your spouse have about what the court can and cannot do and help you reach a full or partial agreement. The family services officer can even help you both draft a stipulation (agreement) resolving as many issues as possible before you both get called before the judge. If one party is represented and the other is not, or if it becomes glaringly apparent that one person is exerting undue influence upon the other, the family services officer will frequently go out of their way to ensure the other person has their say.

Family services officers are wonderful resources. However, *they are not judges*!!! Therefore, if you have done your research and feel very strongly that the solution they suggest is not in your best interests, *don't agree to it!!!* If you lay out all of your evidence to the judge, you may get a different outcome.

Lastly, even if your family services or probation officer's task was to do little more than make sure you had filled out all the right forms or they were grumpy or unhelpful, thank them for trying to help. They are some of the most dedicated, overworked and underpaid public servants and have one of the most thankless jobs on the planet. You will most likely end up before this person many times before your divorce becomes final, so always show your appreciation!

A hypothetical Family Services screening session script for Jane Doe follows. I am using the issue of visitation for the children in this sample script, but Family Services is just as likely to help you examine any other issue that has to do with your case (such as who should pay the mortgage or have use of the car) as who should get custody and visitation of the children. What you should take away from this script is the role of 'gatekeeper' the Family Services department has to make sure the parties have all of their paperwork turned in, identify the issues, and help resolve them if possible.

EXHIBIT 13-5: SAMPLE FAMILY SERVICES SESSION

Family Services Officer (FSO):	Good day, Mr. & Mrs. Rayme. I am Franny Dogood of the Family Services Department. I would like to tell you what will happen here today. I will ask you questions, and the person asked will have an opportunity to answer without the other person interrupting. Then, I will ask the other person if they disagree and *that* person will have a chance to speak without interruption. Do you both understand this? Good. Now, before we start, I'd like to ask you both some background questions. Mr. Rayme, what is your social security number?
Jack Rayme:	123-45-6789
FSO (writing it down)	Thank you. Your financial statement says you are self-employed. Did you bring your Schedule C from last year? I don't see it here?
Jack Rayme:	No.
Jane Doe-Rayme (hands documents)	I have a copy of the last three years tax returns right here.
FSO:	Thank you. Mrs. Doe, I've read your Motion for Temporary Orders and supporting affidavit. Mr. Rayme, do you have any objection to any of the items Mrs. Doe is requesting?
Jack Rayme:	Yes. I don't think she should get the kids. I haven't seen them since the restraining order .
FSO:	Mrs. Doe, do you have any objections to Mr. Rayme seeing his children?
Jane Doe-Rayme:	Yes. Before the restraining order he had been drinking heavily and on several occasions became violent. The last straw was when he beat the dog nearly to death in front of the kids. I got a restraining order and the kids are in therapy because of it. The therapist thinks forcing the kids to see their father might harm them.
Jack Rayme:	I don't care what that silly psychobabble idiot says about my kids. They're *my* kids, and I want to see them!
FSO:	Mrs. Doe, is there anything Mr. Rayme could do to make you feel more comfortable about visiting the children?
Jane Doe-Rayme:	The therapist made some suggestions. If Jack goes to an anger management program and has his mother watch the kids at *her* house for a couple of hours every week, it would ease the children back into seeing their father.
Jack Rayme:	The batterers program costs $900. I don't have $900 to throw away on some idiot telling me not to hit my wife. I didn't hit my wife. I hit the dog!
FSO:	Let me explain what I usually see happen in these situations. Mrs. Doe, absent physical abuse, the court will usually order at least *some* visitation. I'm not sure the judge would tell your husband he can't see his children. More likely he will order Mr. Rayme to go to an anger management program, attend the mandatory parent-education class, and have limited supervised visitation with a friend or relative until he can demonstrate he has completed the program. If Mr. Rayme were to agree to all of these things, would you be willing to let him see his children?

Jane Doe-Rayme:	*If* there was some way to make sure he doesn't take the kids from his mother's house, I'd agree to it. I want which states he's not allowed to drink in front of the kids or be with them while he's drunk.
Jack Rayme:	If *I* can't drink in front of the kids, *she* can't drink in front of the kids!
FSO:	Mrs. Doe, do you have any problems with not drinking in front of your children?
Jane Doe-Rayme:	I almost never drink. I'm perfectly willing to not do something I'm already not doing.
FSO:	Mr. Rayme, if it is the only way the court will allow you to see your children, would you be willing to complete a 6-week anger management program and take the court's mandatory parent education class? The six-week program only costs $350, and the parent education class lasts two evenings for $50.
Jack Rayme:	Well, for $350, I think I could afford the anger management class.
FSO:	Are you both in agreement that Mr. Rayme's mother is a suitable supervisor for visitation until Mr. Rayme finishes the classes?
Both:	Yes.
FSO:	How long would you like the visits to last?
Jane Doe-Rayme:	How about every other Saturday from noon until 2:00 at his mother's house?
Jack Rayme (interrupting):	That's not long enough! I want to take them for the entire weekend, every other weekend, like my brother Bob does!
FSO (holding up her hand in a "stop" motion):	How about Mr. Rayme sees the kids for supervised visitation every other weekend for two hours until he completes the anger management and parent education classes, and then after that he can have them for unsupervised visitation every other weekend?
Jane Doe-Rayme:	I have no objection to that.
Jack Rayme (grudgingly):	Well, if it's the only way I can see my kids…
FSO:	Fine. Let's write all of this into a stipulation so you can bring it before the judge.

Once the Family Services officer helps you reach an agreement (even if it is only on *some* of the issues), they will usually help you write up an agreement, called a Stipulation. Notice the similarities between the Stipulation which follows, and the language that was laid out in the sample Separation Agreements in Chapter Eleven. Like a Separation Agreement, you will need to bring any agreement Family Services helps you draft before the judge for approval. Notice how the Stipulation lays out almost word for word what the parties just agreed to in the previous script.

Stipulation - an agreement between the parties that concerns business before a court and is designed to simplify or shorten litigation and save costs.

A sample Family Services drafted partial Stipulation follows:

EXHIBIT 13-6: SAMPLE FAMILY SERVICES STIPULATION

COMMONWEALTH OF MASSACHUSETTS

BARNSTABLE, SS.

PROBATE AND FAMILY COURT
DOCKET NO. <u>07D-9999-DV1</u>

JANE DOE-RAYME,)
    Plaintiff)
v.)
JACK RAYME,)
    Defendant)
)

PARTIAL STIPULATION OF
THE PARTIES REGARDING
VISITATION

We, Jane Doe-Rayme and Jack Rayme, do hereby agree and stipulate to the following:

1. Both parents shall attend the court's mandatory Parent Education Program and file a certificate of completion with each other and this court.

2. Jack Rayme shall attend a minimum 6-week long anger management program and forward a copy of it to his wife and this court.

3. Until Mr. Rayme completes the parent education and anger management courses, he may have supervised visitation with the children every other Saturday from 12:00 noon until 2:00 p.m. at either his mother's or sister's house. As there is currently a 209A restraining order in effect, the details of visitation shall be arranged through Mr. Rayme's sister and mother.

4. Once Mr. Rayme has completed his parent education and anger management classes, he may begin unsupervised visitation with his children every other weekend from Friday afternoon immediately after school until Monday morning immediately before school.

5. If a scheduled visitation day falls on a school holiday, all pick-ups and drop offs shall be in the Anytown police station parking lot.

6. That portion of the 209A restraining order relating to visitation with the children shall be amended to reflect this stipulation.

7. Both parties agree not to consume alcoholic beverages in front of the children, or to be under the influence of alcoholic beverages while the children are in their care.

Agreed to this <u>1st</u> day of <u>April</u>, 20 <u>07</u>.

Wife:<u>   Jane Doe-Rayme   </u>   Wife:<u>   Jack Rayme   </u>

Witness: <u>   Franny Do-Good, FSO   </u>

If we return to our hypothetical self-represented couple, you may recall that Jane (or Jack) asked for things in their Motion for Temporary Orders which are not listed in the above stipulation. What about alimony? Or child support? Or who is going to live in the home? Who is going to make sure bill collectors don't come in and seize everything the parties own while they are distracted fighting *each other* instead of focusing on the nitty-gritty of paying the bills. For the sake of our hypothetical couple, let's pretend they bring the partial Stipulation in before the judge, but have been unable to reach an agreement on the other issues. A sample Temporary Orders hearing before the judge follows:

EXHIBIT 13-7: A SAMPLE TEMPORARY ORDERS HEARING

Magistrate:	Calling the matter of Doe-Rayme versus Rayme, Docket number 07D-9999-DV1
(both parties go up to the tables located in front of the judge's bench)	Raise your right hands. Do you solemnly swear that the testimony you are about to give is the truth, the whole truth, and nothing but the truth, so help you god?
Both parties:	I do.
Magistrate or Judge:	Could you please introduce yourself to the court?
Wife:	I'm Jane Doe-Rayme, the Plaintiff
Husband:	I'm Jack Rayme, the Defendant
Judge:	I have read your motion for temporary orders, Mrs. Doe, and understand that you've both been in to see the family services officer, is that correct?
Both:	Yes, your honor.
Judge:	According to the stipulation you both signed with the help of the family services officer, you both agree that the children should continue to reside in the home with you, is that correct?
Both parties:	Yes
Judge:	And that Mr. Doe is going to visit the children at his mothers or sisters house until he has had the opportunity to complete an anger management class?
Both:	Yes.
Judge:	And that after completing those classes, Mr. Doe will be allowed to take the children for visitation every weekend after school on Friday until before school on Monday?
Judge:	And that since Mrs. Doe will be residing in the house, that she will be responsible for paying all utilities for that house from this day forward?
Both:	Yes.
Judge:	And this stipulation also states that Mrs. Doe will have sole use of the 2004 Chevy Tahoe and assume all car payments on that car, correct?
Both:	Yes, sir.
Judge:	Have you both read this agreement fully and understand it completely?
Both:	Yes.
Judge:	Have you both entered into this agreement freely, voluntarily, and of your own free will?
Both:	Yes.
Judge:	Now, according to the family service officer's notations, you were not successful in reaching an agreement regarding child support and payment of the liabilities, especially the mortgage. What is the problem here, Mr. Rayme?
Husband:	I can't afford to both pay the mortgage, my car payment, the credit card bills, and pay child support, especially if I'm not living there.
Judge:	According to the child support guidelines which have been set by the legislature, Mr. Rayme, do you understand that you are obligated to pay $126 per week in child support to your wife and that I am only allowed to

	vary from that amount for very good reason?
Husband:	The family services officer explained that to me.
Judge:	Let me look at your financial statements. It states here the mortgage on your house is $1200 per month, correct?
Both:	Yes.
Judge:	And that you are paying $585 for your truck payment and insurance?
Husband:	Yes.
Judge:	And that you are paying a total of $225 per week in credit card debt, correct?
Husband:	Yes, but I can't afford that much. Besides, she's the one who ran up most of the charges?
Judge:	Mrs. Doe, is that true?
Wife:	Not exactly. Since I am the one who purchases most of the things we need for the family and we always use credit cards to pay for them, that is correct. However, most of the things I purchased were school clothes for the children and groceries for all of us to eat.
Judge:	Mrs. Doe, if you're staying in the house, then why can't you pay the mortgage?
Wife:	If you look at my financial statement, you'll see that my total earnings for the month are less than the mortgage payment, never mind the credit card bills. On top of that, I pay $115 per week in child care so I can go to work, so there's little left over. Even with $126 per week in child support, there's no way I can pay that mortgage and keep food on the table. I'm willing to pay as much as I can, but with two children, I just can't go out and get a second job to meet that payment.
Judge:	I also understand that up until now, Mr. Doe, you've been earning around $50,000 per year and your wife earns about $23,000 per year? Is that correct?
Husband:	Yes.
Judge:	I'll take the matter under advisement and give you my decision within a few days.
Both:	Thank you, sir.

Not that the first thing the judge does is reiterate the terms of the partial Stipulation the parties just drafted and ask them if they understand what they are signing. The purposes of this are two-fold. If you recall from Chapter 11 - Separation Agreements, the attorney-drafted agreement had a 'Warranty of Understanding' which made the parties swear they understood what they are signing. That is because the judge does not want to approve something you don't understand because if he does, you'll be right back in court. The second reason is purely pragmatic. The judge is an extremely busy, overworked person and wants to memorialize what you *do* agree upon so you don't do something stupid, like be unreasonable about things you *should* agree on to force your spouse to capitulate on something you genuinely *don't* agree upon. Hardball might work in business, but judges have little time for games.

The judge then gets down to the business of deciding issues the party genuinely could *not* reach an agreement on. Note that the judge explained how little discretion he had when it came to matters of child support. The judge then asked questions about the remaining areas of dispute before saying he would take the matter under advisement.

Taking the Matter Under Advisement: The judge wants to read the briefs, look over the evidence, and deliberate before rendering judgment. Often the judge may delay giving his decision until the parties leave the courthouse because he wants to avoid creating a scene (common if he perceives one or both of the parties may be too emotionally overwrought).

A sample Temporary Order and Sample Order for Support and Health Care Coverage follow. Note that while the first part (Exhibit 13-8) addresses the unique issues raised in the party's individual case, the second part (Exhibit 13-9) is a stock boilerplate form. More and more states are using boilerplate forms similar to this (although your state form will likely look a little bit different) to streamline the administration of justice.

EXHIBIT 13-8: SAMPLE TEMPORARY ORDER

COMMONWEALTH OF MASSACHUSETTS
THE TRIAL COURT
THE PROBATE AND FAMILY COURT DEPARTMENT

__BARNSTABLE__   Division   Docket No. 07D-9999-DV1

Jane Doe-Rayme Plaintiff
v.
Jack Rayme Defendant

TEMPORARY ORDERS

After hearing, including a review of the parties' respective financial statements, the Court finds the following:

1. The Stipulation of the Parties regarding visitation is hereby adopted as an order of this court.

2. The Stipulation of the Parties regarding use of and payments on of the parties' respective vehicles is hereby adopted as an order of this court.

3. The parties shall pay all outstanding liabilities listed in Section 11 of the financial statement in proportion to their respective incomes, with the Husband ordered to pay 2/3rds (67%) of all bills, and the Wife ordered to pay $1/3^{rd}$ (33%) of all bills, until said bills are paid in full.

4. The Wife and children shall exclusive use of the marital home. The Husband shall contribute $350 per month towards the mortgage payment, with the Wife paying the remainder, until a final disposition can be had.

5. The attached Order for Support & Health Care Coverage is incorporated by reference and part of this order.

Date: __April 1, 2006__   _____Judy Trudy_____
                                   Trudy Judy, Justice

EXHIBIT 13-9: SAMPLE 'FORM' ORDER FOR SUPPORT & HEALTH CARE COVERAGE

COMMONWEALTH OF MASSACHUSETTS
THE TRIAL COURT
THE PROBATE AND FAMILY COURT DEPARTMENT

BARNSTABLE Division   Docket No. 07D-9999-DV1

ORDER FOR SUPPORT & HEALTH CARE COVERAGE

_____Jane Doe-Rayme Plaintiff   v.   _____Jack Rayme_____ Defendant

CHILD, SPOUSAL AND MEDICAL SUPPORT

Ξ The plaintiff – defendant (obligor) is ordered to provide support payments in the sum of $125.00 _____

    Ξ weekly   ◉ bi-weekly   ☐ monthly

    $_____ shall be considered current child support and $_____ current spousal support

    $_____ shall be applied against arrears of:

    $_____ for child support and $_____ for spousal support

    Should health care coverage for the dependent child(ren) – and spouse – not be provided for any period for which it is ordered, the amount of child support order for that period is increased to $__300.00___ per week.

Ξ The first payment is due on __April 4, 2007__ and the obligation to pay current child support ends on the
    ☐ 18th   ◉ 21st   Ξ 23rd   birthday of the child – youngest child, unless otherwise ordered by the Court

PAYMENT INFORMATION

Ξ All child support payments shall be made by income assignment through the Department of Revenue (DOR).

☐ The obligor shall make child support payments to DOR at P.O. Box 55144, Boston, MA 02205-5144 until the employer begins making deductions. The obligor will be credited only for payments made to the DOR.

☐ Pursuant to a written agreement of the parties or a find of the court, attached hereto, the income assignment in this order is suspended and payment shall be made by the obligor directly to the custodial parent (oblige). If enforced by DOR, the income assignment shall take effect immediately when a total arrearage amounting to the support owing for a 14 day period has accrued, or, in the case of a monthly order, 14 days after a payment is missed or, after one half of the monthly support owing is missed. The income assignment provision shall take effect immediately upon the request of either the obligor or oblige.

All child support payments shall be made by income assignment through the Department of Revenue (DOR).

HEALTH CARE COVERAGE PROVISIONS

Ξ The plaintiff-defendant is ordered to provide health care coverage for the dependent childr(ren) – and spouse as follows:

    ☐ Maintain current health care coverage
    ☐ Immediately. Notify DOR when health care coverage is in effect.
    ☐ If and when it becomes available at reasonable cost. Notify DOR when health care coverage is available.

☐ The obligation to provide health insurance ends on _____

PAST DUE SUPPORT/COSTS

☐ The plaintiff – defendant owes the following in past due – support / costs – and shall pay $_____
    Ξ weekly   ◉ bi-weekly   ☐ monthly   until the past due – support / costs – are paid in full

    ➢ Child support arrears: $_____
    ➢ Retroactive child support: $_____
    ➢ Spousal support arrears: $_____
    ➢ Costs of paternity testing: $_____
    ➢ Other: _____ $_____

    The plaintiff – defendant shall pay $_____ toward the past due amount on or before _____, 20___.

_____   _____Judy Trudy_____
DATE   Justice of the Probate and Family Court

CHAPTER THIRTEEN SUMMARY

1. Temporary orders are designed to help you and your husband maintain the status quo while your divorce is winding its way down the court, such as custody, visitation, spousal support, and who will pay the bills.

2. Although the relief is meant to be temporary in nature, be aware that what the judge orders at the Temporary Orders hearing will be the status quo during the divorce and may very well become permanent.

3. File your Motion for Temporary Orders and supporting Affidavit the day you file your divorce if at all possible. Be sure to schedule a hearing date and write that date down on the attached "Notice of Hearing" or your motion won't be heard by the judge. Have it served along with your divorce paperwork.

4. Dress appropriately for court.

5. Utilize the court's Family Services/Probation/Arbitration department before you go into your Temporary Orders hearing to narrow or reach agreement on as many issues as possible.

6. Prepare a list of "talking points" for your temporary orders hearing similar to that recommended in Chapter Two, but put those points into the affidavit you file along with your motion in case you get tongue-tied.

There's work to be done and a war to be won... NOW!

SEE YOUR U. S. EMPLOYMENT SERVICE
WAR MANPOWER COMMISSION

7. Maintain a calm demeanor while in front of the judge.

8. When the hearing is done, the judge should issue Temporary Orders addressing each of the issues you requested in your motion. If you were unable to reach a full agreement, these orders will usually come a few days later in the mail. Until the court orders otherwise, this is your new reality.

(This page left deliberately blank)

CHAPTER 14

CHILD CUSTODY

The standard in most states for determining who gets custody of the children is the "best interests of the child" standard. You should not assume that simply because you are the mother, that you will automatically get custody of your children. On the other hand, the courts are aware that many fathers choose to spend their time pursuing their careers, dumping the majority of the child-rearing responsibilities onto the mother. Everything that could happen during a full-blown custody dispute is too large to cover in a book for laypeople, especially as most fathers (at least initially until they get the child support bill or need some idle threat to terrorize their ex-wife into making economic concessions) are more than happy to foist the child-rearing expenses and responsibilities off onto somebody else. The purpose of this chapter is to educate you about issues which could put getting custody at risk, how to ask the court do an independent evaluation of what is best for your children, and how to move out of state with your children if you want to move closer to your support network.

TYPES OF CUSTODY

Although there are many flavors of custody for minor children, there are really only two sub-types. Who the children live with and who has the right to call the shots. When you get divorced, most courts examine who does what for the child, and then awards *physical custody* to the parent who has been the primary caretaker during the marriage, but *shared legal custody* to both parents so that either one may step up to the plate or monitor the children's well-being.

📑 *Sole physical custody* - the child shall reside with and be under the supervision of one parent, subject to the power of the court to order visitation.

📑 *Joint legal custody* - both parents share the ability to have access to educational, health, and other records, and have equal decision-making status where the welfare of the child is concerned

📑 *Shared physical custody* - actual lodging and care of the child is shared according to a court-ordered custody schedule (also known as a *parenting plan* or *parenting schedule*).

There is a third custody arrangement popularized by the batterer's rights movement called *shared physical custody*. **Ninety-nine percent of the time, a father will seek shared physical custody simply to avoid paying child support.** If somebody tries to convince you to agree to such an arrangement and your husband has not traditionally been a 50:50 caretaker, fight like hell to avoid it. Unfortunately, in some states, the batterer's rights movement has cajoled their legislature to make shared physical custody the norm. I handle numerous cases each year between embittered parents who use the flip-flop between households as a power struggle to perpetrate their anger at the other spouse. The children become pawns between two warring parents. The case usually ends up back in court several times per year to fight about stupid things that could be avoided if one parent simply had control over the day-to-day parenting decisions. Only in *one* situation have I seen a shared physical custody arrangement truly work. Shuffling a child between two disparate households is extremely destructive!

WHO IS THE PRIMARY CARETAKER OF THE CHILDREN?

There are certain things the court generally considers when deciding who should get physical custody of the minor children. If your children are older than age 13, the court tends to give heavy weight to their preferences so long as there's not some other factor (such as abuse or neglect) to overrule them. However, in children younger than age 13, the court will examine which parent performs what childrearing task on a day-to-day basis to determine who the primary caretaker is.

📑 *Primary caretaker* - the parent who has the greatest responsibility for the daily care and rearing of a child.

Raising children is not glamorous. For all the benefits a wealthy spouse can bestow upon their child, the single most valuable gift you can give your child is the gift of your time. If you spend *time* with a child doing mundane things with them on a day to day basis, that time is much more valuable to their growth and development than spending a weekend carting them around to see the Wiggles. Paying for private school, horseback riding lessons, charm school, and every toy known to mankind is less valuable than simply providing quiet organization and structure to their lives so they can go about the busy work of growing. If you have been the parent to do most of the things outlined Exhibit 14-1, in the last paragraph, you probably have little to worry about in a custody dispute. Absent your husband being able to prove you have a history of abusing or neglecting your children, or that you have a serious drug, alcohol, or mental health issue, most judges will grant physical custody to the parent who has been doing all the heavy lifting for the past few years.

EXHIBIT 14-1: SOME PRIMARY CARETAKER CRITERIA

- Who gets the children out of bed in the morning and helps them get dressed?
- Who makes them breakfast?
- Who makes their lunch for school and gets them off to the school bus or daycare?
- Which parent is the one to usually take a day out of work when a child is home sick?
- Who goes to the principal or guidance counselor's office if your child has a problem?
- Who attends parent-teacher conferences?
- Does either parent volunteer at the child's school or coach their sports team?
- Who brings the child to the doctors' office, the dentist, or the orthodontist?
- Who runs them around to soccer practice, little league, karate or ballet?
- Who is there to greet the child when they get home from school every day (and do you have to cut your work hours short to do it)?
- Helps them with their homework?
- Helps them with special projects?
- Who cooks them supper every night?
- Who give the children their baths?
- Who helps the children put on their pajamas, brush their teeth, reads them a bedtime story, and tucks them in?
- Who purchases the children's clothing and launders it for them?

If all things come out equal, there is still enough of a hint of the old "tender year's doctrine" standard in many judges that the casting feather will fall in favor of the mother. However, you cannot depend upon this outdated bias. If the judge in *your* courthouse has been going home at 5:00 p.m., cooking supper for his brood the past dozen years or so, and delaying writing his legal decisions until *after* he tucks the kiddies into bed, he may think absolutely nothing of awarding custody to another father. The burden is upon *you* to lay out why you should be awarded physical custody of your children.

CUSTODY DEFECTS

If you know your spouse will contest custody, you need to speak to an attorney right away! Often men will contest custody to extract financial concessions or in an attempt to avoid paying child support. If you have been the primary caretaker and don't suffer from some defect that could cause the judge to rule against you, much of the time the men are simply blowing hot air. However, *do not remain willfully blind to defects which could cause you to lose your children!*

How can you repair a serious flaw in your background? There are certain common categories of challenges to your retaining custody which can be addressed different ways. These are not the *only* reasons you could lose custody, but they are the most common. They are as follows:

1. One or more children are very attached to your husband and have a clear preference for him;

2. Your husband cares for the children at least (or close to) 50% of the time;

3. You presently have or recently sought treatment for a drug or alcohol addiction;

4. You presently have or recently sought mental health counseling for a serious mental illness.

5. DSS has supported allegations at some time in the past that *you* physically abused or neglected your children;

6. You have a criminal record;

7. You suffer from a physical disability (such as M.S., cancer, fibromyalgia, etc.) which inhibits your ability to physically care for or emotionally nurture your children;

8. You are having an affair.

We will cover each topic in its own subheading which follows:

If you suffer from one or more of the "serious defects" outlined below, you could lose custody of your children. *Hire a lawyer!* **Without one, you don't stand a chance!** An experienced family law practitioner who has extensive experience working with the GAL's in your district can sometimes flip a bad situation into a good one when you would otherwise fail.

DEFECT #1 –YOUR CHILD HAS A CLEAR PREFERENCE FOR YOUR HUSBAND

If at least one of your children is older than age 13 and has a clear stated preference for your husband, that child's preferences could result in the court awarding custody of *all* of your children to their father.

The scenario usually goes like this. Your husband spends a lot of time with the kids doing fun things like coaching their soccer team. At least one child is always a "daddy's girl" or "daddy's little man" and will more closely relate to your spouse. If that child is over the age of 13 and the oldest, the GAL will usually speak to them first and deem the younger children too young to interview effectively. That child, who is at precisely the age when they think they want freedom from structure and lots of expensive "toys" such as iPods and an X-Box, will easily be bribed into saying they want to live with their father. Even if the younger children are interviewed and express a preference for their mother or no preference at all, the GAL will frequently adopt the wishes of the most articulate child and the judge will be loath to split the children up. Therefore, the father could get custody.

How do you repair this defect before you go to court? The first thing you must ask yourself is, if this guy is really this great with the kids, do you really want to dump his rear-end without giving marriage counseling one last try? Or would it be nice to foist off the burden of childrearing to *him*, give him 25% of your income every week to do the job, simplify your life, go back to college, and pursue that rewarding career you've been lamenting all these years? If the answer is no (many times, the "soccer dad" routine is really just an act), then the burden is upon *you* to quietly wrest control of your children's affections from him without tipping him off there's a divorce in the wind. *Once you have filed for divorce, it is too late to fix anything.*

Do you tend to be critical of one or more of your children? Do you have unrealistic expectations that make them feel like you do not accept them? Do you use harsh words or a raised voice with them? Are you always in too much of a hurry attending to your job, the house work, your friends, your own interests, and the other children to make that child feel valued?

For a primer on "how to drive your kids away," I recommend you rent the first two seasons of "The Gilmore Girls" and take note of the relationships between the heroine Lorelei Gilmore (the daughter), her stern mother (the grandmother), and Lorelei's daughter Rory (the granddaughter). The grandmother is always critical of Lorelei and making her feel bad, whereas Lorelei is always accepting of Rory no matter what the problem. The grandmother doesn't have a clue about Lorelei, but Lorelei knows every detail of Rory's life and is very active in even the most mundane activities. Ironically, because the grandmother had little contact with the granddaughter until recently, she is much more accepting of Rory.

Stop being the stern mother and start being the more accepting one. This doesn't mean you can't set ground rules or boundaries for your children (that is what a parent *does*, after all), it just means you need to spend six months to a year rehabilitating your relationship with the distant child lest you lose custody of the entire bunch.

DEFECT #2 – YOUR HUSBAND CARES FOR YOUR CHILDREN 50% OF THE TIME

If your husband has been an active participant in the day-to-day activities of childrearing, you have a problem. Your husband is a prime candidate for either getting custody of your children, or for getting a 50:50 shared physical custody agreement (leaving you with no child support to actually raise them).

70%

The minimum percentage of time you need to be the primary caretaker!

Once again, you need to ask yourself the question "do you really want to dump his rear-end without giving marriage counseling one last try?" Guys that share the child rearing duties are hard to find. Don't kid yourself!!! If this guy is for real, you may be better off dragging him to a marriage counselor to make things bearable and heading back to college for your emotional satisfaction until the kids are grown. If the answer is "no, if I have to stay with him one more day I'm going to slit my wrists," then you need to correct the 50:50 problem, and continue to correct that problem for at least *two years* before you ever dream of filing for divorce.

The court looks to what you have been doing over the last three years, so there had better be a clear pattern of you being the primary custodian for longer than half that amount of time. How, you may ask, am I going to wrest control of my children's care from this guy without tipping him off I'm up to something? The answer is "very slowly."

It is a natural tendency of human nature, when freed from a task, to not ask questions. If you gradually start spending more time with your children, pleasantly offering to pick up or drop off the kids at structured activities, volunteering to be the one to sit in the bleachers in the icy cold during their hockey practice, never complaining about being the one to stay home when they're sick, volunteering to bring the child to doctor's or dentist appointments, making your presence extremely visible at their school, and getting up extra early every day to cook everyone breakfast, your husband will probably get busy doing other things and not notice that his childrearing contribution has dropped to less than 30%. You're going to end up doing all these things *anyways* after you file for divorce, so you might as well start doing them right now. So long as you do it gradually, without complaint, and never mention the fact he isn't pulling his weight, it will escape his notice. *Then* you can file for divorce.

DEFECT #3 - DRUG OR ALCOHOL ADDICTION

What do you do if your spouse threatens to tell the judge you're a drunk or a drug addict? The first question you must *honestly* answer to yourself is this:

"-*Am*- I a drunk or a drug addict?"

No denial here, now. Small woodland creatures don't have the luxury of denial. Have the day-to-day worries of being trapped in a bad marriage caused you to retreat a little too far into the bottle? Do you go running for the shelter of your "mothers little helper" to make all the cares go away from your busy stressful day? Have you ever used illegal drugs? The second question you must ask yourself is:

"Have I been clean and sober for longer than three years?"

How the court will view your problem depends how far in the past it happened and what you did about it. If you got in a minor drunk-driving fender-bender in your early 20's, sought treatment, and have been clean and sober for the last 10 years, the court isn't going to pay a lot of heed to the mistakes of your youth. On the other hand, if the evil trapper alleges you're downing a fifth of Jack Daniels every night (or popping pills) before bedtime and neglecting the children, the court will research whether there's any truth to his allegations. A recent example of this in the news is pop star Brittney Spears losing her two children to former spouse Kevin Federline. The judge gave her ample opportunity to get her life together and keep her kids, but Brittney kept screwing up and skipped one of her court-ordered drug tests. Once you flunk a court-ordered "piss test," it's game over. You lose … probably forever.

I see a lot of former addicts who get caught up in the "self-help lingo" and wear their recovery on their sleeve like a badge of honor. This isn't a good idea in court. Be proud of your hard-won sobriety … but keep it to yourself unless specifically asked. On the other hand, your AA or NA sponsor can be your best witness if your husband tries to claim you are *still* a drunk and your sponsor testifies that you attend weekly meetings and have been clean and sober for more than two years. If you don't have at least a two-year sobriety record and a sponsor to back you up, then you need to proceed to get one and earn it or you risk losing custody of your children.

Be sure you have at least a two-year sobriety record before you file for divorce. The court will still weigh your prior addiction on the negative side of the scale, but they will usually go back to weighing which parent is the regular caretaker of the children and be less concerned about what you did two years ago.

DEFECT #4 - MENTAL ILLNESS

Mental illness is viewed a bit differently than other defects such as alcoholism or neglect. The court is barred from taking custody away from you based solely on a physical or mental ailment. That being said, the judge will frequently turn around and take custody away from you on some other, more tenuous ground. You have to remember that, when dealing with the other parent, the court's job is to weigh which parent is better equipped to do the day-to-day job of child-rearing. If you are suffering from a mental ailment, they think you may be too focused on your own problems to worry about how your children are faring.

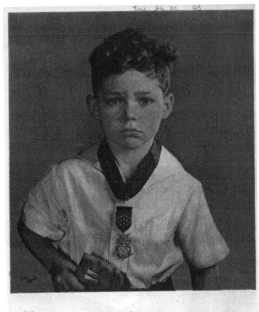

He knows why this Christmas all of us should GIVE WAR BONDS

How are you going to address this problem? Just like any other skeleton which may be hiding in your closet, the court is really only interested in what has been going on for the last 3 years. If you sought counseling after your mother died a few years ago and took Prozac for a couple of months to help you adjust to the loss, with no problems since, the judge isn't going to want to hear too much about it. He'll go back to more important factors such as who has been doing most of the day-to-day childrearing chores for the past three years. On the other hand, if 4 times in the past 5 years your response to life changes has been to become depressed, you have a problem. The judge will want to know your coping mechanisms are up to snuff and that your kids aren't getting used as a crutch for your own mental stability before handing custody of your children to you. *You do not get to keep custody of your children just because you "need" them.*

What if your husband threatens to tell the judge you are crazy, but you're not? Your best bet is to ask one or two of your closest family members and friends, "be honest with me, is there any kernel of truth to his claims?" In court, your husband is going to twist minor quirks and character flaws into a major so-called "mental illness." Work with your friends to eliminate quirky behavior and put a bit of time between the "new you" and the day you file for divorce.

What if you're in counseling right now? First of all, all communications between you and your therapist are privileged information and can't be used by your spouse in open court. He can recite the existence of such counseling, and he can even request the court appoint a special master to look into the matter or that you undergo a mental evaluation. However, the intimate details of your conversations with your counselor are nobody's business and you can block any attempt for him to subpoena either your therapist or your records into court. Second of all, why are you there? Are you there because you've had an acute psychotic break and need help dealing with the hallucinations? Or are you there because you realized your life was meaningless, sought growth counseling to help you find new purpose, and it was through that counseling that you decided to ditch your husband's sorry rear end? The court won't blink an eye over growth therapy relating to failed marriages, but they *will* delve quite deeply into more serious mental health issues and weigh them heavily against you if your husband can demonstrate he is the more stable parent.

🦨 If you are presently or have in the past suffered from a serious mental illness, put at least 2 years of stability (or better yet, 3 or more years) between the day you file for divorce and the day you last had a negative episode that your husband may be able to use against you in court.

DEFECT #5 – DCF HAS FOUND YOU GUILTY OF NEGLECT OR ABUSE

I have represented numerous Care & Protection cases pitting parents against DCF and know the scoop. In some neighborhoods, the "vindictive 51A" is as common as taking out the trash. Your kids sneer at the nerdy kid next door, his mother calls DCF and files an anonymous child abuse or neglect report. You forget to take the trash out to the curb, a different neighbor files one. You call the cops on a neighbor after they keep you awake fighting with their wife all night, they get even by filing one. You look at somebody's "man" the wrong way and the jealous harlot files one. The slumlord landlord wants to evict you so he can get a Section 8 tenant in at twice the rent, so he files one. Somebody in your building has a

51A filed against *them,* and they don't know who did it, so they figure it was *you* and file a 51A right back at you. By the time you get a better job and move to a decent neighborhood where people have better things to do than fill bogus allegations all day long, DCF has been to your house many times they cited you for abuse or neglect simply because they figure you must be doing *something* wrong to be getting so many 51A reports filed against you.

Or, on the other hand, perhaps you *could* work towards being a better parent?

In either situation, if there is no emergency necessitating you jump ship in a hurry from an abusive spouse, you need to treat DCF involvement in your life like any other defect which stands in the way of you getting custody of your kids. *At least the past two years must be free of DCF involvement before you file for divorce.*

One thing you want to point out to the judge is that you were married to your husband at that time and he was equally at fault. If DCF responded because the teacher reported bruises on your child and you were the only person they interviewed, you could point out that you cooperated to cover for your husband and *he* was the one who put them there.

The single most common source of supported child abuse and neglect allegation reports is people calling because they are concerned you are being abused in the presence of your children (which is very harmful to them) and won't leave your spouse. In that case, get the social worker involved and ask them to help you get emotional support and services while you file for divorce. Even if your case has been closed a long time or the social worker tells you they're too busy to help you do anything (unfortunately common), when the inevitable telephone call comes from the GAL or court investigator, the case worker will remember you and remember that you chose to take their advice and leave. The "new improved" opinion of the social worker will carry a lot more weight in a GAL report than 50 affidavits from your biased family and friends.

If you had issues in the past and got help, make sure you have lots of current support people (such as doctors, teachers, school coaches, etc.) willing to tell the court what a wonderful mother you are now and make darned sure you are clearly the primary caretaker. The court is more worried about what you are doing right now than what you've done in the past.

Or, as Janet Jackson sings, "what have you done for me lately?"

DEFECT #6 – YOU HAVE A CRIMINAL RECORD

What if you are afraid that your spouse is going to drag your criminal record into the mix to get an upper hand in a custody dispute? How many crimes did you commit? How long ago were they? Were you found guilty, not guilty, or did you plead sufficient facts? Were these crimes against the person (violent crimes), or crimes against property? Felonies or misdemeanors? Were there any mitigating factors involved which would make the judge lenient on you?

If you have a long history of becoming violent and physically striking out at others, you're screwed. The only way a judge is going to hand custody of your kids to you is if your husband has an even *longer* rap-sheet than you do.

On the other hand, if your "crimes" consist of shoplifting a handbag from Macy's several years ago, the court will weigh the criminal act against your moral fitness to be a parent, but will probably go right back to weighing the primary caretaker factors to determine who should retain custody of the children. If your role as a caretaker overwhelms a few traffic tickets and a shoplifting charge, you may still walk away with custody of your children.

As with any other defect, time plays a part in the judge's determination. Under the rules of evidence, the court is normally barred from using prior bad acts when determining an issue. However, child custody is one of the rare exceptions to that rule, so it's probably going to come in. Try to put at least two years between the bad act and the day you file for divorce and, in the meantime, make darned sure everyone you know (*especially* disinterested parties such as your kids teacher) thinks you're the better parent.

DEFECT #7 – YOU SUFFER FROM A PHYSICAL DISABILITY

There is nothing more heartbreaking than watching the court take custody away from a parent who adores their children because that person is physically disabled.

By "disabled," I don't refer to the unfortunate tendency of people with alcoholism, drug addiction, or mental illness to label themselves with the "disabled" label in order to collect Social Security Disability Insurance (SSDI). If you suffer from a drug or alcohol addiction, or from a mental illness, refer back to the previous captions to address your dilemma.

I have represented clients with Multiple Sclerosis (MS), traumatic brain injuries, crippling rheumatoid arthritis, strokes, paralysis, chronic Lyme disease, severe sciatica, broken backs, cancer, and fibromyalgia. In each situation, the client had an uphill battle convincing a judge that they were capable of physically caring for their children and retaining custody.

I once sat in the back of the courtroom for a hearing where a beautiful young woman with a chronic disease hobbled into court with a cane to expand the scope of a restraining order related to her children. She burst into tears when the judge told her she had to travel 150 miles to a different county to do that. "I'm too sick…" the poor woman cried. Being told she had to cram her aching body into a car and drive four hours (against the advice of her doctor) to shield her children from the man she had moved away from was the last straw in a long series of unfortunate events for this poor woman. A few months later, I was blessed to have this same woman walk into one of my free legal clinics for help on this same issue. Although she still had to drive 150 miles, I was able to explain to the woman how to get protection without having her disability used against her.

If you suffer from a physical disability, the court is not supposed to use that as a basis for denying you custody of your children. They will, but they're not supposed to. What the court *may* consider is, with your disability, how capable are you of taking care of the day-to-day needs of your children versus your non-disabled husband? See? We're back to those mundane day-to-day tasks once more. If chronic disease, a herniated disk, or the after-effects from chemotherapy make you too sick to take care of certain less important daily tasks (such as cleaning the house), work with your insurance company and state agencies to get referrals to services that will help you fill in those gaps. In the pecking order of the court kingdom, having the patience to sit for 3 hours and help your children do their homework every night counts for more than who physically sweeps the kitchen floor. If your children have school and other activities, no matter how bad the pain is that day, be there every single day for your kids, be patient, be kind, and people will notice.

Dirty Lawyer Trick: on several occasions, I have been able to turn the existence of a physical disability into a "plus" for my client. If you have a medical condition which prevents you from working, but otherwise doesn't inhibit your ability to rear your children, you can spin the angle of "thanks to the disability check, I am free to focus on nothing but enjoying my children."

DEFECT #8 – YOU ARE HAVING AN AFFAIR

What if the reason you want to leave your husband is because you've found someone else and want to be free to pursue that relationship? First of all, if either one of you is having an affair, the court generally doesn't want to hear about it unless you have been funneling money out of the marriage to your new boyfriend or you are asking for alimony. Second of all, the court has a presumption that you are a big girl and mature enough to not have your children around somebody who would harm them.

That being said, *nothing* screws up a custody dispute more than mom's new boyfriend…

The kids will hate you for leaving their father, and they will hate the new guy even more for "breaking up the marriage." Your husband will hate you for ditching him for somebody else, and he will make you pay for it. Oh, boy, will he make you pay for it!!!

Your husband and your children will conspire behind your back to do terrible things to your new boyfriend, and your husband will convince your children that every moment you spend away from them *with* this new boyfriend is abuse or neglect. In fact, your husband will use your children's anger at shoving this new boyfriend in their faces to convince them things are so terrible at your house that they must immediately tell the Guardian Ad Litem they want to move in with their father.

Your husband will have you followed, photograph this guy coming and going from your house, and show up at his work to threaten him and get him fired. He will have a cop friend do a criminal background check on this guy, dig up skeletons, file 50 motions to "prove" you are an unfit mother for having this guy around his kids, and generally make your life a living hell. The boyfriend, upset you don't have your "mess" cleaned up, will finally get sick of it and dump you.

If you want a divorce, do yourself a favor and wait until *after* your divorce is final before dating again. If you have your eye on somebody and they think anything of you, they will be willing to wait a few months while you disentangle yourself from a bad marriage and respect you a lot more for not "cheating" on your current husband.

If you want a divorce because you are having an affair and your spouse does not know about it, you need to put an *immediate* stop it right now.

I WANT TO HIRE A LAWYER TO HANDLE MY CUSTODY DISPUTE, BUT WHO?

There are two types of custody disputes, minor and serious. Minor disputes tend to revolve around issues such as how much visitation the other parent should have or routine adjustments to court-ordered child support. Routine matters are relatively clear-cut and predictable. Custody disputes become "serious," or less predictable, when you have one of the major custody flaws described earlier in this chapter.

"Vindictive" custody disputes by a man seeking to gain an upper hand in the property division or avoid paying child support by using the children as pawns often fall into the "serious" category (whether or not you suffer from one of the major custody flaws) because the husband often has no qualms about manufacturing false evidence, committing perjury, intimidating witnesses, withholding child support in order to "starve" the custodial mother into submission, or simply repeatedly dragging the mother into court so many times that the resulting legal fees and/or loss of wages causes the very instability the father is claiming exists in the first place.

In the "sample" GAL motion contained in this chapter, our hypothetical wife, Jane Doe, requests a GAL be appointed to determine visitation in a case where she knows the husband Jack won't get custody due to a restraining order, but Jane is not comfortable just handing the kids over to him every weekend for the typical visitation schedule as the children are afraid of him. This custody matter would be considered "minor" or "routine" because Jane has *clearly* been the primary caretaker for the children's entire life, she does not suffer from any of the "defects" outlined earlier in this chapter, and she knows Jack doesn't stand a snowballs chance in hell of winning custody from her.

Where do you find a lawyer who knows the "system" in your district? If money is no option, you could hire a specialist out of a large law firm with an army of in-house investigators to dig up enough dirt to discredit your husband. Many men who launch vindictive custody disputes with little hope of winning will sometimes win custody this way because they spend their wives into the ground and harass the poor woman with nonstop paperwork requests, intrusions into her life, unnecessary medical and psychological evaluations (which she must pay half of), and harass her family, friends, coworkers, babysitters, and physicians so badly that nobody wants anything to do with her or her children.

Ask prospective attorneys whether or not they have ever handled DCF (social services) cases. Because they have either worked in the past with the state juvenile protection system, or do so now, they may have unique insights into working with local therapists, court investigators, guardians ad litem, school systems, physicians, and other specialists that a regular family law attorney may lack.

HOW MUCH SHOULD I TELL MY KIDS ABOUT THE DIVORCE?

How much should you involve your children in the day to day struggles of your divorce? Children need to be shielded from adult problems. Avoid making your child your "confidant" or badmouthing the other parent when you are angry at them (no matter how justifiably) and shield them from your unmitigated feelings of anger, betrayal, or sadness. Help your children understand that the divorce is

ANNA T. MERRILL, ESQ.

not their fault and Mommy will make everything turn out all right. You will learn more about what is appropriate or inappropriate to discuss with your child in the courts mandatory Parent Education Class.

Unfortunately, one thing the psychological experts *won't* tell you is that if you shield your children *too* much from some of the *effects* of your divorce, you may find yourself playing the "bad guy" and incurring much resentment which you do not deserve. For example, if you make excuses for your spouse's bad behavior (such as when he blows off a scheduled visitation), your children will hate *you* because they are stuck home with *you* and somehow it must be *your* fault. If you can't pay a promised expense (such as your child's sports fee) because your spouse didn't pay his child support on time, the kids will hate *you*, not your spouse. When these things happen, do *not* go into a 40 minute rant about what a lout daddy is (lest you be accused of fostering Parental Alienation Syndrome), but on the other hand you should not take the fall for your spouse's bad behavior.

If daddy *legitimately* needs to reschedule visitation (such as a relative died) and gives you a reasonable amount of notice (as soon as he learns of the funeral), make every effort to help your child understand the cancelled visit is due to an event beyond daddy's control. If daddy calls to reschedule for a *questionable* reason (such as he has to work the weekend), explain daddy can't visit because he has to work, but make no excuses for him. Let the child draw his own inferences and encourage him to discuss with his father why daddy feels work is more important.

If daddy blows off visitation with little or no notice, don't make any excuses at all. Explain that you don't know *why* daddy never showed up (or called an hour beforehand to cancel), but you think it's unfair and the child should discuss the matter with the father the next time he sees him. If the child asks more questions, flatly tell him "you need to talk to your father about it" as many times as he asks and drop the subject. After you've repeated those words in a monotone for the 17th time, your child will get the hint that you don't approve of your spouse's behavior without having to actually state the words.

 Be careful when you speak about your husband in front of the children that you do not cross that fine line between being honest and bad-mouthing him. Do not thwart your husband's visitation!!! There is a generally bogus 'syndrome' first postulated by a psychologist named Richard Gardner called Parental Alienation Syndrome which, in a nutshell, states that if your kids don't like their father it must be *your* fault. The Father's Rights movement has latched onto this 'syndrome' and has been making great headway with it in the courts and psychological community.

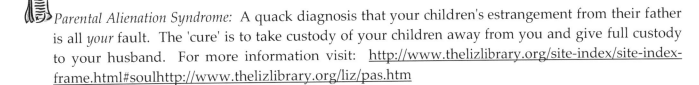 *Parental Alienation Syndrome:* A quack diagnosis that your children's estrangement from their father is all *your* fault. The 'cure' is to take custody of your children away from you and give full custody to your husband. For more information visit: http://www.thelizlibrary.org/site-index/site-index-frame.html#soulhttp://www.thelizlibrary.org/liz/pas.htm

The line between being simply being honest that your situation has changed and recruiting your children to side against your husband as a salve for hurt feelings or financial difficulties is a razor-fine one. *Never* burden your children with the ugliness of your full financial situation! Children need to understand that adults have budgets, adults need to live within those budgets, and sometimes you simply can't afford to do something you would really like to do. On the other hand, it is perfectly acceptable to say 'we can't afford that $3,000 summer basketball clinic anymore.' In other words, although your child *doesn't* need to know that you're running $1,100 per month in the red financially and are worried the bank is going to foreclose on your home, they *do* need to see you model financial responsibility (including using the word "no" frequently and often). If you follow the advice outlined earlier in this Bootcamp, hopefully you cut down the kid's activities and your budget to a manageable amount *before* you filed for divorce.

POST-DIVORCE DATING AND CHILDREN

An issue of much contention is when one parent (either you or your spouse) begins to date (either during or after the divorce is final) and your new partner starts spending time with you and the children. Never let your children know you are dating while your divorce is pending!!! They will hate you!!! Once your divorce is final, it's okay to slowly introduce the idea that Mom is going out on a date and let them briefly meet the guy when he picks you up, but prolong the "dating" period as long as possible (I'm talking months here) to give your children time to adjust to the idea.

Children tend to have unrealistic notions about their parents getting back together, It's best to give them plenty of time to adjust. If you and your new partner become intimate, you need to jump through elaborate hoops (such as arranging for them to sleep over a relative's house) and not let your children know until the relationship becomes serious (by serious, I'm talking the guy has proposed to you). Gradually, after many months have passed, it would be appropriate to arrange for your new "friend" to treat the entire family to a PG rated movie, baseball game, museum trip, or other family oriented activity lasting approximately 2 hours one day per week *out of your house* for another several months. Once at least six months have passed of this gradual acclimation to the idea you've met somebody new, include casual dinners (with him going home afterwards) or watching videos or sports games on the television a few more days per week.

Take it slow!!! If this guy isn't serious enough to marry you, don't subject your kids to their own heartbreak when the relationship suddenly tanks and he leaves!!!

WHO GETS CUSTODY OF THE CHILDREN IS USUALLY DECIDED FIRST

Most states now *bifurcate* (split apart) the child custody decision from the rest of the property division. If you have minor children and do not have an attorney, you will often be sent to the Family Services or court-connected mediation to settle the issue. Some states include a 'custody evaluation' by a court psychologist as part of this process.

Once 'temporary' custody is awarded, it is nearly impossible to undo. Be prepared at all times to prove why *you* are the better parent. Never assume custody will be granted to you just because you are the mother.

PARENT EDUCATION CLASSES

In most states the legislature requires parents to complete an approved parent education class before they will grant your divorce. The purpose of this class is to ensure parents are aware they need to work together to raise the children and not use the children as a go-between to perpetrate a "war" between the parents. If you bad-mouth your spouse in front of your children, your children internalize a lot of that anxiety and feel that they, too, must be "bad" like their other parent. The class usually lasts two evenings, or around four hours of class time total. If you are indigent, you may be able to get the court to reduce your fee for attending this class. As the location and times for these classes changes regularly, you will need to request a listing from your local courthouse when you file your divorce or go online to your state's website to find the latest offerings.

PARENTING PLANS

As part of getting your Separation Agreement approved by the court, you will need to lay out a Parenting Plan outlining which parent has the children when, who makes the major and minor life decisions, and how you will resolve disputes. The sample boilerplates in Chapter 11 cover this requirement. If you both would wish to have shared physical custody, the court may make you write an entirely separate parenting plan outlining your plans in more depth. For example, I've seen plans that state when bedtime will be until a certain age, what the punishment is for not completing homework, how many activities the child will participate in and which parent will oversee it, and many other details. If you would like more detail than you have room to write in your Separation Agreement, you could always write a separate Parenting Plan, attach it to your separation agreement as an addendum to the exhibit, and reference it in your main Child Custody section.

WHAT DO I DO IF MY HUSBAND CONTESTS CUSTODY AND I WANT SOMEBODY TO LOOK INTO IT (GUARDIANS AD LITEM)?

Oftentimes, your child's therapist, school teacher, guidance counselor, doctor, DSS case worker, or sports coach may firmly believe that your child belongs with *you* and not your husband, but they will be extremely reluctant to get involved or give you an affidavit which might tick off your husband if things go the other way. If money were no option, you could have your lawyer subpoena them to a deposition, ask lots of questions designed to elicit that preference on the record, and then subpoena them into trial where you would then put that information before the court. Since you are reading this book, I am assuming you don't have the money to do all that.

The most effective means to get the court to talk to these people is request the judge appoint a special investigator called a Guardian ad Litem (GAL) to look into the matter and recommend a suitable custody arrangement. GAL bills tend to run from $1000 to $7000 and are often divided 50:50 or in proportion to your income. Your local courthouse may have an internal investigation department already set up to screen the more routine cases, in which case you would ask to be included. If your case has a lot of issues, you will likely be assigned (and billed for) a full-blown GAL, but otherwise the in-house investigation usually does the job.

Guardian ad Litem (GAL) - a person appointed by the court to investigate specialized matters and make recommendations regarding complex issues such as which parent should get custody of the children. This person is usually an attorney, but sometimes they might be social workers, psychologists, or somebody else who has experience in dealing with the matter which is being investigated. Sometimes also called a CASA or 'court appointed special advocate.'

The GAL is supposed to go through specialized training to learn how to interview the parents and people involved in the child's life and spot issues which are relevant to the courts decision-making process. GAL's vary in their investigations, but a full investigation should include the following:

1. A criminal records/restraining order check of both parties;

2. A review of DCF records for any past abuse allegations;

3. An interview of each parent;

4. An interview of each child. If a child is very young, sometimes that child will not be interviewed;

5. A medical records review of each child;

6. A school records review of each child;

7. An interview or telephone conversation with professionals connected with the child's life, such as teachers, therapists, daycare providers, social workers, police personnel, doctors, dentists, etc.

8. Interviews or telephone conversations with additional witnesses each parent wishes the GAL to speak to. Common witnesses include witnesses to domestic violence or neglect perpetrated against the child, but might also include character witnesses such as neighbors who are allied with one parent.

If a GAL needs to be appointed, the court will choose one from their approved list and give that person your name. In a few days, the GAL will send an introductory letter requesting that you forward them a brief statement about all the issues in the case and a list of witnesses you would like for them to interview. They will also ask you both to submit a retainer to cover their anticipated fee. If your husband does not pay his fair share, you can go back to court to compel him to pay. The fee alone may cause him to change his tune and drop the custody dispute.

Over the next few weeks or months, the GAL will interview you, your husband, your children (not always), and contact many (but not all) of the people on both of your lists. If they feel a psychological or parental fitness evaluation is necessary, they will request that you submit to that as well.

Always have neutral, third-party proof of any allegations you may be asking the GAL to investigate lest your husband's claim you are 'alienating' the children gains traction!!!

A sample "Motion to Appoint a Guardian ad Litem" follows:

EXHIBIT 14-2: MOTION TO APPOINT A GUARDIAN AD LITEM (GAL)

COMMONWEALTH OF MASSACHUSETTS

BARNSTABLE, SS.

PROBATE AND FAMILY COURT
DOCKET NO. 07D-9999-DV1

JANE DOE-RAYME,)
    Plaintiff)
)
v.)
)
JACK RAYME,)
    Defendant)
)

PLAINTIFF'S MOTON FOR A
GUARDIAN AD LITEM

> Your state citations will be different

Now comes the plaintiff, Jane Doe-Rayme, and hereby moves that the Court appoint a family services officer to do a limited investigation of the custody issues in this case. If the family services investigates the situation and does not have a clear recommendation regarding custody, then the Plaintiff hereby requests that this court then appoint a Guardian Ad Litem to investigate and report pursuant to G.L. c. 215, § 56A and gives as reasons the following:

1. That there is pending before this Court a Complaint for Divorce and motion to establish orders for the care and custody of the minor children of the marriage.

2. On or about December 9, 2006, the Defendant did abuse the Wife in front of her minor children, necessitating that the Wife obtain a 209A restraining order from the Orleans District Court.

3. On or about February 14, 2007, the plaintiff filed his Complaint for Divorce.

4. On or about February 14, 2007, the plaintiff filed a Motion for Temporary Orders seeking custody and supervised visitation of the two minor children, Jayne, date of birth June 15, 1995; and Johnnie, date of birth October 11, 1998.

5. The plaintiff believes that the defendant has a serious alcohol problem and the children are not safe without supervised visitation.

6. The parties are unable to agree as to the care, visitation issues and maintenance of the minor children, and that the issues in relation thereto are likely to be submitted to the Court for final resolution under G.L. c. 208, § 37.

7. That it is in the best interests of the minor children that a guardian ad litem be appointed to investigate and report to the Court.

WHEREFORE, the plaintiff moves that this Court appoint a Guardian Ad Litem to investigate and report pursuant to G.L. c. 215, § 56A.

Plaintiff further moves that this Court appoint a Guardian Ad Litem to mandate either or both of the parties to submit to mental examinations if the Guardian Ad Litem determines same to be necessary in order to fully investigate, report and provide recommendations to the Court on the aforesaid issues.

Plaintiff further moves that this Court order both parties to execute whatever releases are necessary in order to allow the Guardian Ad Litem to communicate with and examine the records of psychiatrists, therapists or other mental health professionals seen by the parties, either jointly or individually if the guardian ad litem determines such communication or review is necessary in order to fully investigate, report and provide recommendations to the Court on the aforementioned issues.

Plaintiff further requests that the Commonwealth pay the costs for the guardian ad litem, as more fully supported by her Financial Statement filed with the Court. In the alternative, should the court not be able to pay the costs, the Plaintiff requests that the parties be ordered to pay the GAL fee in proportion to their respective incomes and ability to pay.

Plaintiff further requests that each party's counsel be entitled to a copy of the report of the guardian ad litem with instructions not to release the report to the parties.

Date: ___February 14, 2007___

Respectfully Submitted:
        ___Jane Doe-Rayme___

Usually, the GAL may ask to speak to your therapist. You do not have to sign the broad, unlimited waiver the GAL will mail you to sign in order to speak to your therapist, but it is usually appropriate to sign a *limited* waiver allowing your therapist to confirm as they could construe your refusal to allow them to speak to the therapist at all negatively. It is good practice to mail them *your* limited waiver when you mail your initial witness list and fees and mail a second copy to your therapist so that the GAL understands you are being helpful in signing a limited waiver and not simply holding back to hide something. Discuss what specific information you are giving your therapist permission to talk with the GAL about beforehand so they know what is on and off-limits.

⚑ *Do not give your therapist the discretion to "give their impressions about your fitness to function as a custodial parent" if you think they may have something bad to say about you.*

A sample limited waiver of privilege follows:

EXHIBIT 14-3: LIMITED WAIVER OF PRIVILEGE

Limited Waiver of Privilege

I, <u>Jane Doe-Rayme</u>, do hereby give Glenda Goodrich, GAL, permission to contact my therapist, Wendy Whatailsya, M.S.W., and confirm the following information:

1. That I am a patient of hers;
2. That I have a diagnosis of dysthymia related to being physically abused over a period of many years by my husband;
3. That I am currently undergoing a course of treatment;
4. That I have attended all scheduled appointments;
5. That I am making progress
6. Any observations Ms. Whatailsya may have made about my ability to function as a custodial parent.

Signed this __5__ th day of __April__, 20_07_ : _____ Jane Doe-Rayme _____

Once the GAL has completed their investigation (it's supposed to only take six weeks, but frequently takes months), they will mail you a notice informing you they have completed their investigation and submitted a copy of it to the court. If you forgot to request that a copy of the GAL report be forwarded to you, you will have to drive to the courthouse to read it and will not be allowed to photocopy it. The clerk's office may schedule something called a "status conference" once the GAL report has been submitted to see where you and your husband are on custody. Either that, or you will be expected to alter your position accordingly in light of that report when you go to the Pre-Trial Conference.

If your case actually goes to trial, you will need to list the GAL as an "expert witness" on your Pre-Trial Memorandum and subpoena them into testify at the trial. Their report is helpful for preliminary hearings and will probably carry the day at trial, but to get it into evidence at trial, you need to have the person who wrote it present to testify.

▌ *Never relinquish temporary custody without the court ordering a full-blown GAL investigation and giving you a review date once the GAL report is ready.* Even if you are later able to prove your husband was lying through his teeth at trial, the court will weigh heavily the stability with one parent, adjustment to school, and attachment to new friends your children will have experienced while your custody dispute dragged on for months or years and will be extremely reluctant to switch custody.

WHAT IF I NEED TO MOVE OUT OF STATE WITH MY CHILD?

The law prohibits you from moving out of state with your children without express permission of the other parent or the court. However, generally if you have sole physical custody, most states allow you to move within a reasonable geographic area *within* the state (usually less than 50 miles). For example, if you live in County X and want to move next door to County Y to be closer to your parents so your whole income isn't going to childcare, you usually have every right to do so. You may, however, have to accept a reduction in child support to compensate your husband for the extra commuting he will need to travel to see them.

Don't Let That Shadow Touch Them
Buy WAR BONDS

▌ **This does not apply if you have a shared physical custody agreement (i.e., the children live with each parent 50:50).** Moving may jeopardize custody!

If you want to move *out* of state completely, it can open a can of worms. You must have a good and sincere reason for wishing to move. It is not a good idea to plan this if your husband is contesting custody and there is currently a GAL investigation pending (it could cost you custody). Examples of good and sincere reasons are an excellent job offer or moving closer to your family support network.

Be warned that there has been a nationwide shift away from the "clear advantage to the mother" standard to a "clear advantage to the *child*" standard when analyzing whether or not to let you haul up roots and move out of state. Be prepared to demonstrate how much more the new environment is going to benefit your kids versus staying put with their father, familiar friends, teachers, grandparents, and other relatives. As the difficulty in gaining permission varies widely from state-by-state, consult with an attorney to gauge how much trouble you'll have getting permission to move. Massachusetts is fairly liberal, but some states, such as Texas, have rules which make it almost impossible to relocate.

If you have gotten your divorce and it is final, you will have to file an entirely new Complaint for Modification asking permission to move. It's a whole new case and the mechanics are not covered in this Bootcamp Manual, but the mechanism for getting permission is otherwise similar. If you anticipate a bitter custody dispute in your divorce, you may want to consider a "two step" process whereby you first get custody and a divorce, establish a clear pattern of primary custodian, allow your husband to do "that thing" men typically do with their children after the divorce (start showing up less and less once the divorce is final), keep very careful records about his visitation track record, and *then* go back to court a year or two later to "get the hell out of Dodge."

A sample Motion to Remove Minor Children from the State and subsequent Sample Hearing follows:

EXHIBIT 14-4: SAMPLE MOTION TO REMOVE MINOR CHILDREN FROM THE STATE

COMMONWEALTH OF MASSACHUSETTS

BARNSTABLE, SS.
PROBATE AND FAMILY COURT
DOCKET NO. <u>07D-9999-DV1</u>

JANE DOE-RAYME,   )
    Plaintiff   )   MOTON TO REMOVE MINOR
v.   )   CHILDREN FROM THE
JACK RAYME,   )   COMMONWEALTH
    Defendant   )
)

NOW COMES Jane Doe-Rayme, Plaintiff in the above-entitled action, and hereby moves this Honorable Court that she be awarded sole legal custody of the minor children of the parties, Jayne and Johnnie, and further that she be authorized to remove the minor child from the Commonwealth to reside with her in Alaska.

1. In support of said Motion, Plaintiff states that both Jayne and Johnnie have indicated on numerous occasions to the Court investigator and to other parties their desire to reside with the Plaintiff.

2. That because of the hostility and conflict that Defendant has exhibited toward the Plaintiff, it is not suitable for the Plaintiff to continue her job in Massachusetts.

3. That the Plaintiff's parents have retired to Juneau, Alaska, and have offered to watch the children free of charge while the Plaintiff works. The children have missed their grandparents terribly since they moved to Juneau two years ago and have clearly expressed they would like to live closer to grandma and grandpa.

4. That housing is much less expensive in Juneau, Alaska, than here on Cape Cod, that a large modern home has come up for sale two doors down from the Plaintiff's parents' house, and said house is well within the plaintiff's financial means. Currently, the Plaintiff does not receive enough income and child support to meet her mortgage payment and there are no significantly cheaper houses to be found within 100 miles of here.

5. That the Juneau public school system has higher nationwide test ratings than the Anytown School District. Furthermore, the Juneau public school system would provide Jayne with a tutor to assist with her learning disability (dyslexia) free of charge, a cost the Plaintiff is currently paying out of pocket.

6. That the Plaintiff has an opportunity to relocate as a head nurse at Kinnicook Hospital, Juneau, Alaska and that, furthermore, Kinnicook Hospital is willing to educate and train the Plaintiff free of charge to become a licensed General Practitioner Nurse. Those opportunities would enable her to provide better for herself and her children.

WHEREFORE, the Plaintiff requests that pending a hearing on the within Complaint for Divorce:

1. Temporary custody of the minor children, Jayne and Johnnie, be awarded to the Plaintiff.

2. That she be authorized to remove herself from the Commonwealth with the minor child to take a position at Kinnicook Hospital and to reside in Alaska.

3. That she and the children be granted such other and further relief as is appropriate in the circumstances.

Date: <u>June 15, 2007</u>   Respectfully Submitted:

                              <u>Jane Doe-Rayme</u>

EXHIBIT 14-5: SAMPLE CONTESTED CHILD CUSTODY HEARING

(Magistrate hands the papers to the judge):	I call the matter of Jane Doe-Rayme versus Jack Rayme, Docket number 07D-9999-DV1. Do you both solemnly swear to tell the truth, the whole truth, and nothing but the truth, so help you God?
Jane and Jack:	I do.
Judge:	We have before us today a Motion for the Plaintiff to move to Alaska, is that correct?
Jane (nods yes):	That's correct, sir?
Judge:	Alaska, that's pretty far away. Why do you want to move to Alaska?
Jane:	Sir, two years ago my parents retired to the Juneau Bay region to pursue their love of whales. My father is a retired oceanographer out of the Woods Hole Oceanographic Institute, and my mother is an artist. Before they moved, my father used to pick the kids up after school one day per week and take them out to help him gather specimens on the beach. (smiling) There's nothing kids like better than picking up crabs and bugs and sticking them into little buckets for scientific study, and he would pay them $1 apiece for all their hard work to buy an ice cream afterwards…
Jack:	That's not true. The kids never told me anything about going to the beach.
Jane:	Sir, if I may finish? (waits for judge to nod) I have here an affidavit from my father, and another one from his former research partner, Randy Researcher of the Woods Hole Oceanographic Institute, stating that as part of their duties they were required to take soil, water, and animal specimens from 3 local beaches every week and that the children frequently accompanied them on these trips as "junior researchers." (Jane holds out the two affidavits until the bailiff takes them and gives them to the judge.
Jack:	They didn't tell me about it…
Jane:	If you would also turn to page 7 of the Court Investigator's report, you will also see that the children mentioned missing their grandparents and wanting to move to Alaska to "chase whales with grandpa and grandpa" when he interviewed them.
Judge:	Mr. Rayme, what do you have to say about your children moving to Alaska?
Jack:	It's cold in Alaska … and it's too far away. How am I supposed to see my children if they're all the way on the other side of the country? I don't want my children moving to Alaska!
Jane:	At the moment, Sir, my husband is only allowed to see the children two hours every other week for supervised visitation at his mothers or sisters house because there is a restraining order in effect. This court gave him the chance to get unrestricted visitation as soon as he completed an anger management program and the parent education class, but in three months he has not done so. To my knowledge, he hasn't even *started* either of these classes yet.
Jack:	I can't afford it. How am I supposed to take the classes if I can't afford it?
Jane:	Furthermore, Jack's *sister* has refused to supervise visitation anymore because on two occasions she picked up the children and then my husband "blew off" his visits

	at her house. The children were devastated! Out of 7 possible visits since the last hearing, he has missed two of them.
Jack:	My car broke down.
Jane:	And then to make matters worse, Jack has violated the restraining order three times by calling the house when he wasn't supposed to, picking through my trash every week for "evidence," and showing up at my work and threatening to kill my boss. He's being prosecuted for violating the restraining order.
Jack:	I only wanted to find out if she's… (shuts up)
Jane:	My boss has threatened to fire me if Jack shows up one more time, and one of my private duty patients has requested the agency find another nurse because Jack spoke to their daughter at the post office and told them I was crazy. I can't support the kids if he keeps interfering with my work! If I move to Juneau, on the other hand, not only would I have a better paying job, but they are so desperate for nursing help that they're willing to send me to school to become a General Nurse Practitioner. A GNP can do a lot of things that a doctor can do. I have here an offer of employment from the director of Kinnicook Hospital. (Jane offers the letter to the judge)
Judge (to Jack):	Do you have anything else to say?
Jack:	What about Jayne's reading problem? She made a stink about needing money at the last hearing because of Jayne's reading problem. Who's going to teach Jayne to read properly?
Jane:	Sir, I have here a letter from the principal of the Juneau Middle School, which Jayne will be starting this September. He said he has reviewed the copy of Janyne's Anytown school records, including her special education records, and he believes they can accommodate her dyslexia. If you look at paragraph two of his letter, you will see he specifically mentions they have a tutor in-house who will work with Jayne two days per week free of charge (hands letter to bailiff, who gives it to the judge).
Jack:	If they're moving to Alaska, I don't want to have to pay child support!
Jane:	One last thing, sir. I have here a photograph of my parents taken from their dock on Juneau Bay. The house I am proposing buying is across the street and not directly on the water, but this is the place where I will be raising my children. (Jane hands the judge a photograph taken last summer of her children standing with two smiling people at the end of a dock. A pod of killer whales is clearly visible in the background).
Judge:	I will take the matter under advisement and you will get my decision in the mail.

An analysis of this hypothetical case follows:

Will Jane Doe be allowed to pack up her kids and move to Alaska? Who knows? Alaska is pretty far away, and most people have an image of it as a cold, wild state. If she were moving to the next state over and had good reasons for moving, permission might be guaranteed. However, Jane has made a very good case for moving. She ended up paying for a GAL report, but the GAL documented a lot of things that are helpful to her case, such as the children stating they miss their grandparents and want to move to Alaska to "chase whales with grandpa and grandpa" when he interviewed them.

In our hypothetical case, Jack has foolishly violated the restraining order a few times and is now being prosecuted for it. He has also failed to follow through on his court-ordered anger management program and parent education class. Worse, he has blown off two of the potential seven supervised visits in the last three months without notice and the children were upset by his callousness. Worst of all, Jack has interfered with Jane's ability to work by threatening her boss and convincing one of Jane's private pay patients to fire her, making her request to move to Kinnicook Hospital much more compelling. Jack has

stated if they move he doesn't want to pay child support. It is doubtful he will get off completely, but the judge will most likely reduce the amount he has to pay to offset the cost of travel to Alaska and also by the increase in Jane's pay and decrease in her child care expenses (she has stated her parents will help her babysit the children so she can work).

To avoid a "he said, she said" situation about the children's past involvement with their grandparents, Jane obtained two affidavits outlining a specific, beneficial activity the children used to enjoy every week until the grandparents moved as well as some "we love them, we enjoy them, we want them to move near us" stuff Jane's father likely wrote into his version. Jack may say he had no idea the kids were going to the beach to collect sea worms and bugs every week, but who are you going to believe? Restraining Order Jack? Or two scientists from the Woods Hole Oceanographic Institute?

To address the issue of Jayne's learning disability, Jane has already forwarded the kids school records to the principal of their new school and obtained a letter from the principal specifically stating that there is a tutor available to help Jayne in the school. This would be a drastic improvement over hiring private tutors out of your pocket to address the problem.

Lastly, the photograph is pure genius. It shows happy, smiling children standing with happy grandparents in an idyllic setting. By giving the judge a photograph of the setting the children will be living in, she is helping to alleviate many fears the judge may have about sending the children off to live in an unknown place.

I cannot say for sure how a judge would rule in this case. Jack is a jerk, so a more liberal judge would probably allow it, but a more conservative judge still might not. I have exaggerated the hypothetical facts such to educate the reader about factors which can help or hurt you.

MY SPOUSE TOOK MY KIDS OUT OF STATE AND FILED FOR CUSTODY THERE!

Which state has jurisdiction over a child custody case is ruled by the Uniform Child Custody Jurisdiction and Enforcement Act (UCCJEA). Whether or not your spouse can get custody of your children in another state goes beyond what is covered in this book, but you must act quickly or you may find yourself subject to the other state's custody laws! Get thee to an attorney right away! The U.S. Department of Justice posts an informational bulletin at:

https://www.ncjrs.gov/pdffiles1/ojjdp/189181.pdf

CHAPTER FOURTEEN SUMMARY

1. The court is concerned with the "best interests of the child" when determining who gets custody. The frequently will decide that the parent who spends the most amount of time every day helping the child do ordinary life tasks (such as dressing, eating, homework, and bedtime) should get custody. Do not assume that, just because you are the mother, you will automatically get custody.

2. There are certain defects which could cause you to lose custody. Learn what they are and correct them before you file for divorce. The court is generally more concerned about how much of a model parent you've been for the last three years, not your entire life, so it is possible to overcome many defects through time and hard work.

3. If you anticipate a serious custody dispute, you should hire a lawyer. Serious custody disputes occur when the other parent is very wealthy and can spend you into the ground, or when you suffer from one of the defects outlined in this chapter.

4. You can ask the court to appoint a GAL to investigate what is best for the children. You will usually have to split the cost of the GAL with your husband.

5. If you have sole physical custody, you can move anywhere *within* the state that you desire. If you want to move *out* of state, you will have to get the court's permission. You need to show you have a good and sincere reason for wanting to move, such as a better job and closer proximity to your support network. If the court lets you move, you are probably going to get your child support reduced to offset the cost of your husband traveling to see the kids.

6. Most courts now use the 'clear advantage to the *child'* standard when evaluating whether to let you move away (not clear advantage to *you*).

7. When you go to your custody hearing, bring letters and supporting affidavits from people who will be helpful to your case. If you are moving to get better housing or a new job, bring examples of the housing market and a job offer letter to support that fact. If your husband is interfering with your life, your job, or your ability to parent, bring evidence to court to show the judge your husband has been a bad actor. Bring evidence that shows the judge you have given great thought to ensuring the children's needs (such as housing, child care, and education) are met. Lastly, it is a good idea to bring photographs of your children, happily smiling, with the people and in the places where you are proposing moving to allay the judge's fears about sending the children out into the unknown.

CHAPTER 15

DISCOVERY

The most frequent question I hear from free legal clinic attendees without full-service attorneys is: *How do I get my husband to give me (discover) a copy of (fill in the blank).*" "Discovery" is the process of finding out ("discovering") information that is relevant (important) to your legal case. Digging for information, witnesses, and documents that the opposing party is trying to hide from you is where most self-represented woodland creatures fall flat on their faces. To "do" discovery, it is best to have an attorney. However, if there is a specific piece of information you are trying to get at and you have an idea of where to look, there are a myriad of ways you can compel your husband or recalcitrant witnesses to cough up the information. Thanks to nationwide adoption of the Federal Rules of Civil Procedure, *every* state makes some version of these tools available to you, or your attorney, to ferret out needful information.

HOW TO USE THIS CHAPTER: This chapter is an OVERVIEW of the attorney toolbox. Skim through the sample checklists, forms and motions. When an information request comes from the opposing party, check to see if the request is 'boilerplate.' Familiarize yourself with what the information request is for and then call your attorney to discuss how this may impact your case.

Say, for example, while you were being a good little woodland creature, busily gathering your acorns, you happened upon a $20,000 stock statement you know nothing about. You dutifully photocopy the mystery statement, file for divorce, request your husband's Financial Statement and Mandatory Self-Disclosure materials (if your state *has* mandatory self-disclosure … a few still don't) and, lo' and behold, no mention is made of the secret $20,000 stock account! What's a poor lil'ol woodland creature to do?

Although it might be tempting to wait until trial and "prove" your husband is a liar, this strategy may backfire on you if you can't subpoena the keeper of the records of the stock broker into court the day of the trial to verify your husband has an account with them. It also may not do much good. I've found judges to be appallingly lax about sanctioning husbands who lie on their financial statements. An attorney might be able to pull this off, but it is doubtful a self-represented layperson could do it.

In this case, a more direct route is appropriate. Your husband probably feels safe omitting the information because he thinks you don't know about it. If you send him a "Request for the Production of Documents" which specifically asks for "the last 3 years of statements for Merrily-Merrily Retirement stock account number XYZ-1234567," your husband won't feel so comfortable about lying to the court. If he has an attorney, the attorney will tell him to cough it up or he will 'dump' him as a client because no attorney wants to lose their license to practice law to cover a client's lies.

Another thing you could do is send your husband a "Request for Admission of Facts" and ask a very specific question such as "as of 9/30/06, your Merrily-Merrily Retirement stock account number XYZ-1234567 showed a balance of $20,000." Staple a copy of the stock report to the Request and mail it to him along with your "Request for Admissions."

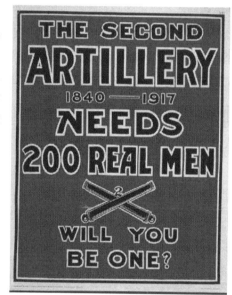

If your husband is being a weasel and continues to deny the existence of the stock account, you can send him an "Interrogatory" asking something direct such as "List, in specific detail, all transactions which have occurred to the Merrily-Merrily Retirement statement, account number XYZ-1234567, dated 9/30/06 (including where the $20,000 value shown on that date) to the present day." You only get 30 interrogatories, so use them wisely!!! They are best saved for things such as finding out what witnesses and expert witnesses he plans to use against you at trial.

If the three traditional methods of discovery (document request, admission, and interrogatory) yield nothing but a stone wall, file a "Motion to Compel Discovery and for Sanctions," stapling a copy of the mystery statement to the back of your motion for the judge. Judges are loathe to babysit discovery disputes, but if you have tried every reasonable method to get the information and the other side is stonewalling you, then the judge will usually issue a specific court order to cough up the information or face contempt sanctions (including jail).

A smart woodland creature knows when a task is beyond their capability and calls in the big guns to do the dirty work. Getting your husband to include missing information where some item may have been mistakenly omitted is within most layperson's means. For example, you produce a stock statement for an old IRA account with only a few thousand dollars in it and your husband slaps himself on the forehead and includes it. On the other hand, self-launching a 'Discovery War' on a spouse who has been deliberately hiding assets for many years (often to hide it from the IRS) is like conducting brain surgery on yourself using a chainsaw.

Normally, if traditional requests failed, an attorney would spend a great deal of your money subpoenaing the keeper of the records of Merrily-Merrily Retirement into an out-of-court hearing called a Deposition and demand they bring all account information with them to explain where the money has gone. Depositions are expensive because they need to be held at a formal location (such as an attorney's conference room) and be recorded by a professional stenographer. For extra effect, your attorney might videotape the session.

If you want to see what a Deposition is, watch the movie "A Civil Action" starring John Travolta. I do not think a small woodland creature would be able to pull off their own deposition, and it would likely backfire into the evil trapper subpoenaing the woodland creature and all her friends to his own deposition. However, I *have* on many occasions been able to get banks and employers to cough up bank and employment records voluntarily *without* attending a deposition by sending them a cover letter to a Deposition Subpoena informing them they can avoid having one of their employees lose an entire day of work to sit in a court hearing if they would simply forward the information with a "keeper of the records affidavit" attached. The company will charge a hefty fee for producing the records for you, but if the amount in question is substantial, it is worth paying $15 per bank statement.

All Discovery *must* be completed before the pre-trial conference held approximately six (6) months after you file your divorce. Therefore, it is *very* important you don't sit on your laurels, but rather start demanding information as soon as you file your divorce and keep on top of your husband (or his lawyer) to give it to you. Some lawyers strategically ignore discovery requests (especially if you are representing yourself) because they think you are too stupid to drag them into court on a "Motion to Compel" if they don't comply. Other lawyers will simply forward the request to the evil trapper and then forget about it if your husband is the one who doesn't comply. If your husband doesn't have a lawyer, he will often "pretend" he doesn't know he was supposed to respond and whine "I can't afford a lawyer" once you drag him into court on a "Motion to Compel."

There are excellent Discovery books with more detailed information published by:

- *MCLE Discovery Practice Manual* (various New England states), www.MCLE.org
- *Guerrilla Discovery*, by Ashley Lipson, James Publishing, www.jamespublishing.com

One note about Discovery courtesy: If you have already been able to gather many of your husband's bank statements or other listed documents from the last three years, when you request them, be a nice little woodland creature and note the exception "all but 1/05, 4/05, 11/05..." in your document request. There's no need to make him pay $15 per bank statement for documents you already have.

DISCOVERY TIMELINE CHECKLIST

These are documents **you** owe your *husband* shortly after you file for divorce. If you were a good little woodland creature and did all your Chapter Three "acorns" exercises, you will already have copies of everything neatly photocopied, arranged by date, stapled and paper clipped together as appropriate, and separated by account number with colored pieces of paper.

EXHIBIT 15-1: DOCUMENTS YOU GENERALLY OWE YOUR HUSBAND AT THE TIME YOU FILE DIVORCE OR WITHIN 45 DAYS

When Due	Document Name	Why you Need It	What will happen if you don't send it
Have the Sheriff serve with the initial divorce documents Date Sent:_____	Financial Statement (see Chapter 4)	You must disclose the state of your finances, *including* bank accounts and credit cards you have kept secret until now, to your husband the same as he must disclose his finances to you. If you moved assets which he might "disappear" into safe new accounts while the divorce is pending, this is your opportunity to let him know the money has been moved, not liquidated.	The court will not hold a hearing to give you child support until you file this. You could be fined and forced to pay your spouse's attorney fees if you refuse to give this to him.
Within 45 days of the filing of the divorce. Best done ASAP after he is served Date Sent:_____	Mandatory Self-Disclosure Documents (if automatic in your state) (the exact same documents you are going to request from *him*)	By law, in *most* states you both must provide each other with full copies of these documents. See your home states rules of procedure.	If you omit something and it materially affects the property division, the court could find you guilty of criminal fraud.

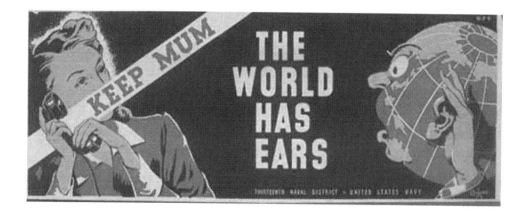

The following documents are *owed* to you by your spouse in states with Mandatory Self-Disclosure laws shortly after you file for divorce (if your state doesn't have these laws, you will need to use the forms that follow to formally request the information. If you don't get them within the timeline, you must be diligent about sending him a reminder letter.

EXHIBIT 15-2: DOCUMENTS YOUR HUSBAND GENERALLY OWES YOU WITHIN 45 DAYS

When Due	Document Name	Why you Need It	What to do if you don't get it
10 days after he is served by the Sheriff Due:_____	Financial Statement	You need to know if he is going to lie about his income at the Temporary Orders hearing so you can be prepared with documents to prove he is lying. If you do not know in advance that he is going to lie, you could end up with a lot less child support than you are owed.	Should send him a request for this and blank financial statement along with the Sheriff's documents. If you don't get it on the 10th day, send him a demand letter and a second blank financial statement and complain like mad to the judge at the Temporary Orders hearing if he then lies about his income and doesn't file it. Also, have a disinterested witness serve him with a notarized subpoena demanding the underlying documents be brought to the temporary orders hearing
20 days after he is served by the Sheriff Due:_____	"Answer" to the Complaint to Divorce	This lets you know if your husband is going to do anything weird, such as counterclaim for custody. If he does not file within If you don't file a "Motion for Temporary Orders" and a hearing date, the court will frequently not schedule a hearing on its own for many months.	Do nothing. If he doesn't "Answer" within a reasonable period of time after the deadline passes, this is taken by the court to essentially mean "everything the plaintiff said is true."
45 days after he is served by the Sheriff Due:_____	Mandatory Self-Disclosure Documents (if automatic in your state)	By law, in *most* states you both must provide each other with full copies of these documents.	If he omits something, you will lose your share of it. Be diligent about making sure he discloses all assets you may be entitled to a share in. If you get the paperwork back from him and suspect he is omitting something material, you can send a more specific "Request for the Production of Documents" to get it.

These are the specialized documents lawyers use to get specific information from your spouse while the divorce is pending:

EXHIBIT 15-3: THE ATTORNEY 'DISCOVERY' TOOLBOX KIT

Date Sent	Date Due	Document Name	What this Does	What to do if you don't get it
		Request for the Production of Documents	This is a request for more detailed documents which may not have been sent with the initial Mandatory Self-Disclosure documents	30 day reminder letter Motion to Compel
		Interrogatories	30 questions designed to elicit information such as "who is the expert witness you are hiring to value your pension?"	30 day reminder letter Motion to Compel
		Expert Interrogatories	30 questions designed to elicit information from an expert witness hired by the other side. Not covered in this manual. You can obtain a sample from your local CLE training manual.	Not covered.
		Request for Admissions	Good for narrowing the "agreed" issues at the pre-trial conference or trial.	30 day reminder letter Motion to Compel
		Deposition Subpoena	A deposition subpoena summons witnesses to a recorded "fishing expedition" mimicking trial where the other side gets to ask lots of questions which they will then use to get hurtful information on you. Very expensive and almost impossible for a layperson to run. Not covered in this manual. You can obtain more information from your local CLE association or West Publishing, James Publishing, Aspen Publishing	Not covered.
		Keeper of the Records Subpoena	Generally, you would subpoena the person holding records (such as a clerk at your husband's bank) to a deposition to get your hands on them. However, because you are pro se and shouldn't be handling a deposition on your own, you can also sometimes subpoena the person holding the records to a court hearing and offer to have them mail the records directly to the courthouse with a "keeper of the records" affidavit.	Criminal sanctions for ignoring a subpoena, but hard to get a court to enforce.

In Chapter Four, you learned how to fill out a financial statement and, along with the divorce paperwork you had the Sheriff serve on your husband, you should have already included a copy of *your* court Financial Statement. To use this list properly, go back to where it says *you* owe your husband your court Financial Statement and write in the date you had him served. Using this list will ensure you don't miss any important deadlines. Note that you must look up your state-specific Rules of Civil Procedure and Supplement Rules of Court to learn the correct statutes and rule numbers to cite.

EXHIBIT 15-4: SAMPLE REQUEST FOR FINANCIAL STATEMENT

COMMONWEALTH OF MASSACHUSETTS
PROBATE AND FAMILY COURT

BARNSTABLE, SS.   **DOCKET NO. 07D-9999-DV1**

JANE DOE-RAYME,)	**REQUEST FOR DEFENDANT'S**
Plaintiff)	**SUPPLEMENTAL RULE 401**
v.)	**FINANCIAL STATEMENT**
JACK RAYME,)	
Co-Petitioner)	
)	

Note: *YOUR* state 'rule number' about financial statements will be different.

NOW COMES the Plaintiff, Jane Doe-Rayme, and hereby requests pursuant to Probate Court Supplemental Rule 401 that the Defendant, Jack Rayme, file with this Court and serve her with a copy of his Probate Court Supplemental Rule 401 Financial Statement within ten (10) days of receipt of this request.

Date: February 14, 2007

Respectfully submitted,

Jane Doe
Jane Doe-Rayme, Plaintiff, pro se

CERTIFICATE OF SERVICE

I, Jane Doe-Rayme, the Plaintiff in the above-captioned case, did serve a copy of this Request for Defendant's Supplemental Rule 401 Financial Statement upon the Plaintiff, Jack Rayme, on February 14, 2007 via the following method (check method):

- X   sheriff's service
- o   in hand
- o   mailing via USPS first class mail, postage prepaid

Signed under the pains and penalties of perjury of law this _14_ th day of February, 2007.

Jane Doe

Jane Doe-Rayme, Plaintiff

EXHIBIT 15-5: SAMPLE REMINDER LETTER – COURT FINANCIAL STATEMENT

Jane Doe-Rayme
100 Any Street
North Anytown, MA 02763

March 2, 2007

Andy Ambulancechaser, Esq.
Stall, Hinder & Delay, PC
500 Commerce Way
30th Floor
Boston, MA 01111

Note: *YOUR* state discovery 'rule numbers' will be different.

Dear Attorney Ambulancechaser:

Along with the divorce paperwork served upon your client, my husband Jack Rayme, by the deputy Sheriff on February 17, 2007, was a Rule 401 Request for Financial Statement and a Rule 410 Mandatory Self-Disclosure Discovery Request. As you are aware, Supplemental Rule 401 *requires* that both parties exchange financial statements within 10 days of the filing of divorce.

More than 13 days have passed since my husband received that discovery request and no financial statement has been forthcoming. You were a copy of *my* financial statement along with the divorce paperwork.

Please be advised that if I am not forwarded the financial statement immediately, I will file a "Motion to Compel Defendant's Rule 401 Financial Statement and Request for Sanctions" seeking any costs associated with my needing to compel this document.

For your convenience, I am enclosing a second copy of my Rule 410 Mandatory Self-Disclosure request served that same day. Those documents are due no later than April 17, 2006.

Sincerely,

Jane Doe-Rayme

Encl: copy of 2/14/07 Rule 401 Request for Financial Statement
          Copy of 2/14/07 Rule 410 Mandatory Self-Disclosure Discovery request

In our "Jane Doe" hypothetical, Jane is concerned that her self-employed husband may try to pull some monkey business at the temporary orders hearing to reduce his child support. Jack is not calling back potential clients interested in hiring him for work and is several weeks behind on the child support ordered by the District Court at her Restraining Order hearing. Jane is also concerned because she knows Jack has a stock account he has been hiding from her and could try to hide other assets. Therefore, Jane has included the threat of filing a Motion to Compel in this letter.

If Jane's husband worked a traditional hourly or salaried 9-5 job at a large corporation and did not have concerns about hidden assets, she should omit the "motion to compel" paragraph and simply mail the otherwise friendly reminder letter. The court will force him to fill out a financial statement at the temporary orders hearing if he has not done so before then.

EXHIBIT 15-6: SAMPLE MOTION TO COMPEL FILING OF FINANCIAL STATEMENT

COMMONWEALTH OF MASSACHUSETTS

BARNSTABLE, SS.

PROBATE AND FAMILY COURT
DOCKET NO. 07D-9999-DV1

JANE DOE-RAYME,)
    Plaintiff)
v.)
JACK RAYME,)
    Co-Petitioner)
)

MOTION TO COMPEL FILING
OF FINANCIAL STATEMENT
AND FOR SANCTIONS

Now comes the Plaintiff, Jane Doe-Rayme, in the above-entitled action and hereby moves this Honorable Court to order the Defendant to file his financial statement in said Court forthwith and to furnish a copy to the Plaintiff.

In support of said Motion, Plaintiff states that she has made demand on two occasions for a copy of Defendant's financial statement in accordance with Rule 401 of the Supplemental Rules of Probate Court and that Defendant has failed to comply with said demands. Plaintiff needs the information requested on said financial statement properly to prepare for court. Plaintiff has requested the financial statement on the following dates:

8.   Rule 401 Request dated February 14, 2007.

9.   Reminder letter with second copy of Rule 401 Request on March 2, 2007

Plaintiff further requests that this Court order the Defendant Jack Rayme to pay costs and attorney fees incurred by Plaintiff in obtaining this order in accordance with Mass.R.Dom.Rel.P. 37.

March 15, 2007

Respectfully submitted,

_____*Jane Doe*_____
Jane Doe-Rayme, Plaintiff, pro se

Note: *YOUR* state discovery 'rule numbers' will be different.

Note: if your husband works a traditional salaried 9-5 job and you know exactly how much he earns, it may not be worth your while to file a Motion to Compel the filing of a Financial Statement. Many lawyers are in the lazy habit of waiting until the day of the Temporary Orders Hearing to hand over their client's financial statement. If you are certain there will be no surprises, you may not want to be bothered losing a day out of work to go to court. If your husband doesn't have a lawyer, the clerk or Family Services Officer will most likely force him to fill one out on the spot. **Bring his most recent paystub and last year's tax return if you take this shortcut!!!**

EXHIBIT 15-7: SAMPLE NOTICE OF HEARING ON A MOTION TO COMPEL FILING OF FINANCIAL STATEMENT

COMMONWEALTH OF MASSACHUSETTS

BARNSTABLE, SS.   PROBATE AND FAMILY COURT
                                                     DOCKET NO.

JANE DOE-RAYME,   )
   Plaintiff   )   NOTICE OF HEARING ON
v.   )   MOTION TO COMPEL
JACK RAYME,   )
   Defendant   )
)

The following matters have been scheduled for hearing at <u>9:00</u> A.M. on <u>April 1st</u>, 2005 at the Barnstable County Probate and Family Court.

   2. Motion for Temporary Orders (previously scheduled)

   3. Motion to Compel Filing of Rule 401 Financial Statement and for Sanctions

> Note: *YOUR* state discovery 'rule numbers' will be different.

Respectfully submitted,
Jane Doe-Rayme,

Date: <u>February 14, 2007</u>   *Jane Doe-Rayme*

CERTIFICATE OF SERVICE

I, <u>Jane Doe-Rayme</u>, hereby certify that a copy of the attached Motion to Compel Filing of Rule 401 Financial Statement and Request for Sanctions, and Notice of Hearing were served upon Jack Rayme in the following manner:

   ○ sheriff's service
   ○ in hand
   X mailing via USPS first class mail, postage prepaid

Signed under the pains and penalties of perjury of law this <u>15</u> th day of <u>March</u>, <u>2007</u>.

Signed: *Jane Doe-Rayme*

EXHIBIT 15-8: SAMPLE REQUEST FOR MANDATORY SELF-DISCLOSURE DOCUMENTS

COMMONWEALTH OF MASSACHUSETTS

BARNSTABLE, SS.

PROBATE AND FAMILY COURT
DOCKET NO. 07D-9999-DV1

> Note: *YOUR* state 'rule number' about mandatory self-disclosure will be different.

JANE DOE-RAYME,
   Plaintiff   )
)
v.   )
JACK RAYME,   )
   Co-Petitioner)
)

REQUEST FOR SUPPLEMENTAL RULE 410 "MANDATORY SELF DISCLOSURE" DOCUMENTS

NOW COMES Jane Doe-Rayme, Plaintiff in the above-entitled action, and requests, pursuant to the provisions of Supplemental Rule 410 of the Rules of the Massachusetts Probate & Family Court (mandatory self-disclosure), that Jack Rayme, Defendant, produce the documents designated herein. These documents are to be delivered to the Plaintiff Jane Doe-Rayme within forty-five days of the date of this Request.

a. Federal and state income tax returns and schedules for the past three (3) years and any non-public, limited partnership and privately held corporate returns for any entity in which either of you has an interest together with all supporting documentation for tax returns, including but not limited to W-2's, 1099's, 1098's, K-1, Schedule C and Schedule E;

b. Statements for the past three (3) years for all bank and investment accounts held in the name of either of you individually and/or jointly, or in the name of a third person for the benefit of either of you or held by either of you for the benefit of your minor child(ren);

c. The four (4) most recent pay stubs from each employer for whom you have worked;

d. Documentation regarding the cost and nature of available health insurance coverage;

e. Statements for the past three (3) years for any securities, stocks, bonds, notes or obligations, certificates of deposit owned or held by either of you or held by either of you for the benefit of your minor child(ren), 401K statements, IRA statements and pension plan statements for all accounts listed on the 401 financial statement;

f. Copies of any loan or mortgage applications made, prepared or submitted by either of you within the last three (3) years prior to the filing of the complaint for divorce; and

g. Copies of any financial statement and/or statement of assets and liabilities prepared by you within the last three (3) years prior to the filing of the complaint for divorce.

Please gather these documents and organize them as outlined above. If you do not have or are unable to provide the document(s) required, you must certify the effort(s) you have made to locate and/or provide the document(s) in a separate written statement.

Date: February 14, 2007

Respectfully submitted,

Jane Doe
Jane Doe-Rayme, Plaintiff, pro se

CERTIFICATE OF SERVICE

I, Jane Doe-Rayme, the Plaintiff in the above-captioned case, did serve a copy of this Request for Supplemental Rule 410 "Mandatory Self-Disclosure" Documents upon the Plaintiff, Jack Rayme, on February 14, 2007 via the following method (check method):

   X   sheriff's service
   o   in hand
   o   mailing via USPS first class mail, postage prepaid

Signed under the pains and penalties of perjury of law this _14_ th day of February, 2007.

Jane Doe

RESPONDING TO YOUR SPOUSE'S REQUEST FOR MANDATORY SELF-DISCLOSURE

As far back as Chapter 3, you were instructed to gather certain documents and prepare an extra copy to give to your husband soon after you filed. You are required to reciprocate and give your husband a copy of the exact same documents you requested from *him*. If you are a diligent little woodland creature, you will promptly hand (or mail) your ex-husband the copy you made of these documents along with a cover letter stating what you are sending.

Do not give your husband the full "valuation notebook" you gathered in Chapter Three as part of your routine Rule 401 or Rule 410 answers unless specifically asked. If he contests it or specifically asks for "the basis of all appraisals" for a specific asset in a later request, you will need to produce it.

A sample "mandatory self-disclosure" cover letter and document list follows:

EXHIBIT 15-9: SAMPLE COVER LETTER FOR JANE DOE SELF-DISCLOSURE DOCUMENTS

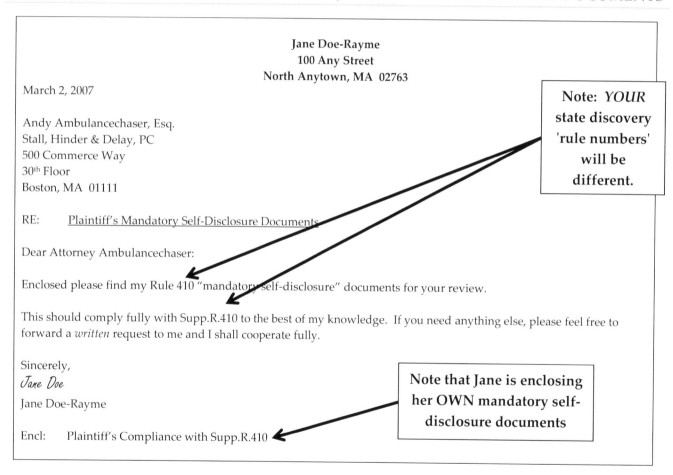

Jane Doe-Rayme
100 Any Street
North Anytown, MA 02763

March 2, 2007

> Note: *YOUR* state discovery 'rule numbers' will be different.

Andy Ambulancechaser, Esq.
Stall, Hinder & Delay, PC
500 Commerce Way
30th Floor
Boston, MA 01111

RE: Plaintiff's Mandatory Self-Disclosure Documents

Dear Attorney Ambulancechaser:

Enclosed please find my Rule 410 "mandatory self-disclosure" documents for your review.

This should comply fully with Supp.R.410 to the best of my knowledge. If you need anything else, please feel free to forward a *written* request to me and I shall cooperate fully.

Sincerely,
Jane Doe
Jane Doe-Rayme

> **Note that Jane is enclosing her OWN mandatory self-disclosure documents**

Encl: Plaintiff's Compliance with Supp.R.410

Note that Jane has stated she wants all requests for information to be sent *in writing*. This avoids the common ploy of the other side attempting to exclude documentation supporting your theory of the case by claiming they asked for certain documents from you and you did not provide them. If they try this to the judge, show him your letter and ask the other side to show you the written request.

EXHIBIT 15-10: SAMPLE MANDATORY SELF-DISCLOSURE COMPLIANCE AFFIDAVIT

COMMONWEALTH OF MASSACHUSETTS
PROBATE AND FAMILY COURT

BARNSTABLE, SS.   DOCKET NO. <u>07D-9999-DV1</u>

JANE DOE-RAYME,   )
    Plaintiff   )   **PLAINTIFF'S COMPLIANCE**
v.   )   **WITH SUPP.R.410 "MANDATORY**
JACK RAYME,   )   **SELF-DISCLOSURE"**
    Co-Petitioner   )
)

> **Note:** *YOUR* state discovery 'rule numbers' will be different.

NOW COMES <u>Jane Doe-Rayme</u>, Plaintiff in the above-entitled action, and hereby furnishes, pursuant to the provisions of Supplemental Rule 410 of the Rules of the Massachusetts Probate & Family Court (mandatory self-disclosure) the documents designated herein.

a. Federal and state income tax returns and schedules for the past three (3) years and any non-public, limited partnership and privately held corporate returns for any entity in which either of you has an interest together with all supporting documentation for tax returns, including but not limited to W-2's, 1099's, 1098's, K-1, Schedule C and Schedule E;

> 1. Enclosed are joint tax returns, including Schedule C's and supporting W-2 and 1099 forms for the tax years the 2005, 2004, and 2003;
> 2. No tax return, either individual or joint, has been filed for 2006;

b. Statements for the past three (3) years for all bank and investment accounts held in the name of either of you individually and/or jointly, or in the name of a third person for the benefit of either of you or held by either of you for the benefit of your minor child(ren);

> 1. Enclosed are joint checking account statements for the past (3) years for Big Bank & Trust;
> 2. Enclosed are saving account statements for the past (3) years for Little Bank
> 3. Enclosed is a photocopy of the Johnnie's UTMGA trust passbook with all entries;
> 4. Enclosed are 9 months of bank statements for the Wife's Stash-M-Bank accounts the entire period this account has been active.

> Notice that Jane included statements for her "acorns stash" bank account. Now that the divorce has been filed, she MUST disclose *ALL* assets.

c. The four (4) most recent pay stubs from each employer for whom you have worked;

> 1. Enclosed are the Wife's last 4 pay stubs from Nurses-R-Us.

d. Documentation regarding the cost and nature of available health insurance coverage;

> 1. The Wife does not provide the health insurance. The Husband has control of these documents.

e. Statements for the past three (3) years for any securities, stocks, bonds, notes or obligations, certificates of deposit owned or held by either of you or held by either of you for the benefit of your minor child(ren), 401K statements, IRA statements and pension plan statements for all accounts listed on the 401 financial statement;

> 1. Enclosed are the last (3) years of statements for the Wife's Vanguard 401(k) plan
> 2. I do not have control of my Husband's Merrily-Merrily Retirement stock account XYZ1234567;

3.   I do not have control of my Husband's IRA account;

f.   Copies of any loan or mortgage applications made, prepared or submitted by either of you within the last three (3) years prior to the filing of the complaint for divorce; and

1.   Enclosed find a copy of my loan application for my 2004 Chevy Tahoe pickup truck;
2.   I do not have control of the loan application for my Husband's pickup truck;
3.   Enclosed is our joint application for a Home Equity Line of Credit at Little Bank;
4.   Our primary mortgage was taken out more than 7 years ago.

g.   Copies of any financial statement and/or statement of assets and liabilities prepared by you within the last three (3) years prior to the filing of the complaint for divorce.

1.   My Rule 401 Financial Statement was forwarded to my husband with the Complaint for Divorce;
2.   I do not recall filling out any other financial statement, except for those included with items f(1) and f(3) above, at any time in the past 3 years.

Signed under the pains and penalties of perjury of law this _21ˢᵗ_ day of February, 2007.

Date: February 21, 2007

Respectfully submitted,

_____*Jane Doe*_____
Jane Doe-Rayme, Plaintiff, pro se

CERTIFICATE OF SERVICE

I, Jane Doe-Rayme, the Plaintiff in the above-captioned case, did serve a copy of this Plaintiff's Compliance with Supplemental Rule 410 "Mandatory Self-Disclosure" and all the therein listed supporting documents upon the Plaintiff, Jack Rayme, on February 14, 2007 via the following method (check method):
- o   sheriff's service
- o   in hand
- X   mailing via USPS first class mail, postage prepaid

Signed under the pains and penalties of perjury of law this _21ˢᵗ_ day of February, 2007.

_____*Jane Doe*_____

> Note that Jane has essentially just rewritten the exact same document request she served upon her husband (or her husband served upon *her*) and used it to show she is disclosing those documents now. This is a good way to answer any request for information (documents, admissions, interrogatories, etc.). If a requested document does not belong to you and is not within your control, state so.

DOCUMENT REQUESTS

Frequently you will get an incomplete response back from your initial Mandatory Self-Disclosure request that your husband has no such documents. This is legitimate if your husband really *has* no such documents. However, if you get a vague response, no response, a complaint that the documents are "too expensive" or "too cumbersome" for your husband to obtain without an offer to provide them for the cost of obtaining them, or a denial they exist, you will need to follow up on it with a more specific Request for the Production of Documents or by filing a Motion to Compel (covered later).

In our Jane Doe hypothetical, Jane stumbled across a $20,000 Merrily-Merrily Retirement stock statement her husband was secretly having mailed to his place of business while she was gathering her acorns and quietly made a photocopy of it before slipping it back into the daily mail without a word. Her husband, Jack, has omitted this account from his financial statement and did not produce information about the account in his Rule 410 Mandatory Self Disclosure materials. Jane has good reason to believe Jack is trying to hide this money from her and the court to get a bigger share. Jane is going to try again by sending Jack a Request for the Production of Documents and specifically request information about the mysterious Merrily-Merrily Retirement account.

State-specific 'rules' about Document Requests should still call this 'Rule 34.' Rule 34 is the Federal Rules of Civil Procedure rule number. All 50 states adopted the F.R.C.P. with minor changes. It is good practice to cite your local *state* rule as well as the federal one.

Dirty Lawyer Tricks: As soon as you mail an information request to your husband's attorney (for documents, admissions, or interrogatories), they usually turn around and send one right back at you! Be careful what you start less you end up in a tit-for-tat battle!

You are responsible for paying your husband's reasonable cost of obtaining any information beyond your state's Mandatory Self-Disclosure documents. If your husband has to pay his bank $15 for each monthly credit card statement you request, and it then costs him another $.25 per page to photocopy it, *you* are going to have to reimburse him for each and every item you request.

Dirty Lawyer Tricks: His attorney will bill you for every penny he can get away with squeezing out of you! The courts idea of 'reasonable' is a lot more money than *you* think is reasonable.

If you do not have a specific reason for wanting a particular piece of information (such as needing old credit card statements to prove your husband charged weekly trips to Cuddle and Bubble to sleep with his mistress *and* this put a financial strain on your family *and* this will help you gain something in the divorce), ask yourself if it is really important. Many of these documents are documents you, the wise woodland creature, *should* have gathered before you filed. Bank and tax records should *always* be scrutinized for buried treasure, but you should have an idea if you really *need* to delve into three years of old water and sewer bills. Look … but be reasonable if you don't really need something.

Do not mail huge, broad requests solely for the sake of intimidation. It usually backfires.

EXHIBIT 15-11: SAMPLE REQUEST FOR THE PRODUCTION OF DOCUMENTS

COMMONWEALTH OF MASSACHUSETTS
PROBATE AND FAMILY COURT

BARNSTABLE, SS.   DOCKET NO. 07D-9999-DV1

JANE DOE-RAYME,   )
    Plaintiff   )   **PLAINTIFF'S REQUEST FOR THE**
v.   )   **PRODUCTION OF DOCUMENTS**
JACK RAYME,   )   **PURSUANT TO FED.R.CIV.PRO 34**
    Co-Petitioner   )   **AND MASS.R.DOM.REL.P 34**
)

In accordance with Rule 34 of the Federal Rules of Civil Procedure and Mass.R.Dom.Rel.P 34, now comes Jane Doe-Rayme, Plaintiff in the above-captioned case, and requests that the Defendant, Jack Rayme produce the following documents set forth in the numbered paragraphs below, materials, memoranda and other tangible evidence for copying and inspection at the offices of your undersigned attorney or mailed to the Plaintiff's home, 100 Any Street, North Anytown, MA 02763, on or before March 30, 2007, at 10 A.M.

DEFINITION OF DOCUMENTS

As used herein, the term "documents" includes any written, recorded or graphic matter however produced or reproduced; draft, rough draft or final; regardless of storage media including paper, recordable tape, celluloid/film, disks, hard drives, electronic mail servers, on-site or offsite cloud server, or any other digitally or other stored media. The term 'document' shall also include the full range of writings described in Rule 1001 of the Federal Rules of Evidence.

All documents requested herein shall be for the period from January 1, 2004 *up to and including the date of production by you of the documents requested herein, unless a different time period is specified.*

DOCUMENTS TO BE PRODUCED

1. All documents in your possession, custody, or under your control, written or created after the date of January 1, 2004 that pertain either directly or indirectly to the divorce that is the subject of this litigation. Please arrange these documents by date.

2. All documents, memoranda (both internal and external), reports, letters, correspondence, or other records or writings (whether paper, electronic, or other media) that mention, concern or discuss any aspect of the divorce or any aspect of the divorce that may be litigated and/or may come into evidence at any time.

3. All documents related to your personal income, including, but not limited to:

    A) All documents relating to your pursuit of any trade or business;

    B) All documents relating to your employment, business and professional status, including wages, salaries, bonuses, stock options, commissions, employment contracts, promotions, pay raises, payroll deductions, other deductions of any kind;

    C) All documents relating to employee stock plans and other benefits or deductions of any kind that are, were or may be paid, available, accepted, rejected, credited, offered or withheld by any individual, agency, department or company, or to which you are, were or may become entitled.

    D) including all documents evidencing all payments made by anyone, including employers and relatives, to you or to others on your behalf, including without limitation, automobile expenses, travel expenses, personal living expenses, club dues or expenses, entertainment expenses, life insurance, bonuses, health, accident and hospital insurance.

4. All federal and state and local income tax returns, including all W-2 forms and other records substantiating said returns, Schedule C's, rental income or other schedules, whether filed by you, individually or jointly, including all estimated income tax returns, local business tax, excise tax, property and local sales/room/other tax statements.

5. All documents relating to your personal expenses, including, but not limited to, household expenses, business expenses deducted from income, all expenses listed on any tax return, financial statement, or expenses listed on the Court Financial Statement. Include any expenses paid by others on your behalf.

6. All documents relating to your current coverage through any medical and dental insurance policies and disability benefits.

7. All documents, including medical records and bills, relating to appointments with physicians, including dates thereof and medical histories concerning your past and present physical condition.

8. All documents relating to all real estate in which you currently have any interest, including, but not limited to, time shares, vacation share interests, and/or real estate which may have been transferred for the benefit for another but which you still retain a life estate, lifetime or term lease, or other interest.

9. All documents relating to any motor or recreational vehicles in which you currently own or have any interest, including, but not limited to, vehicles which may have been transferred for the benefit for another but which you still retain a lease, lien, or other interest.

10. All documents relating to your gross retirement entitlements from your present and all prior employers, including, without limitation, IRA, KEOGH, pension and profit-sharing plans, other retirement plans, stock ownership plans, severance pay plans, excess benefit plans, stock option plans and any and all deferred compensation plans and arrangements, whether or not qualified under Internal Revenue Code Section 401. Such documents shall include, without limitation, the following:

    A) Copies of all statements for all defined contribution plans (such as IRA, 401(k), Keogh, profit-sharing, etc.).

    B) Copies of the plans, plan descriptions, summary plan descriptions, brochures, trust agreements and other documents describing the plans as currently in force.

    C) For each prior employer, all documents, forms and statements regarding your gross retirement entitlements (both defined contribution and defined benefit plans) and when the same are payable.

> **If Jack has a pension (not merely an IRA/401(k)), there are much more specific document requests than this her attorney would need to request to get the pension properly valued.**

11. All documents related to any Tax Deferred Annuity Plan(s) you may have invested in or have an interest in.

12. All documents relating to all life insurance policies currently in force insuring your life, whether whole life, term life, or any other form of life insurance.

13. All documents related to your checking, saving, or other banking accounts held in your name, individually, jointly, in the name of another person for your benefit, held by you for the benefit of your minor children, or as guardian, trustee or in which you had any interest.

14. All documents relating to all accounts in which you had any interest, including credit union shares, savings plans, individual retirement accounts and certificates of deposit.

15. All documents relating to all money market funds, mutual funds, stocks, bonds and securities in which you had any interest, including documents relating to the purchase, sale or transfer of such items and brokers' statements.

    A) *Including Merrily-Merrily Retirement account number XYZ-1234567;*

> **Under the 'investments' related requests, Jane specifically requests the mysterious $20,000 Merrily-Merrily Retirement account which Jack omitted from his financial statement mandatory self-disclosure documents.**

16. All documents relating to your ownership of any personal property valued in excess of $1,000.

    A) *Including purchase receipts, tax depreciation records, insurance lists, and other information regarding all tools and equipment related to your trade;*

    B) *Including all model railroad collections;*

> **Under the 'personal property' related requests, Jane specifically requests information about Jack's 'tools of trade' and also a pricey little hobby collection he insists is worthless, but she thinks might be worth more.**

17. All documents relating to all safe deposit boxes held in your name, individually, jointly or as guardian, trustee or held by another on your behalf, including the locations, numbers and contents.

18. All documents relating to the sale or transfer by you of any personal property valued in excess of $1,000 or more, including 'collections'

which would normally be considered a related group and/or can be grouped together to be worth more than $1,000.

19. All documents relating to any loans, account receivable or debt forgiveness you may have given to any person, business, relative, or other entity.

20. All documents relating to any indebtedness owed by you to anyone, including personal debts, banks, relatives, business associations, partnerships and corporations in which you have any interest, including all loan applications completed by you, whether or not you actually received the loan.

21. All documents relating to any judgments or executions rendered against you in any lawsuits, the nature and type of any lawsuit presently pending against you in any court, all legal cases resolved without litigation, and those currently being negotiated, including, but not limited to, any outstanding workers compensation cases.

22. All documents relating to charitable donations made by you or on your behalf.

23. All documents relating to gifts of any kind made either by, or to you, by or to any individual, firm, trust, partnership, corporation or other entity.

24. All documents relating to all credit cards and charge accounts used by you, or held in your name, individually or jointly.

25. All documents relating to your membership in any clubs, social or religious organizations, including without limitation, all records of initiation fees, dues and donations, whether paid by you or by any other individual or entity on your behalf.

26. All documents, including wills, trusts, and executor and trustee statements, relating to all estates and trusts of which you were or are a beneficiary of any kind.

27. All documents relating to your interest in, and the organization of, all business associations, partnerships and corporations, including financial statements, tax returns, and other documents.

28. All documents containing a list of the names and addresses of all proposed expert witnesses and all written reports rendered to you or your attorney by all proposed expert witnesses or by any other witness who has knowledge of any facts relevant to this action.

29. A copy of your most recent resume or curriculum vitae.

30. All statements evidencing your interest in accumulated airline or frequent flier mileage, or similar benefits.

31. Any other document relevant to the financial estate of the Defendant or the parties which reasonable minds, the court, a tax accountant or financial planner might deem relevant to ascertaining the net worth of the Defendant.

Date: March 30, 2007

Respectfully submitted,

_____Jane Doe_____
Jane Doe-Rayme, Plaintiff, pro se

CERTIFICATE OF SERVICE

I, Jane Doe-Rayme, the Plaintiff in the above-captioned case, did serve a copy of this Request for Production of Documents under Fed.R.Civ.Pro.R.34 and Mass.R.Dom.R.34 upon the Plaintiff, Jack Rayme, on March 30, 2007 via the following method (check method):
- ○ sheriff's service
- ○ in hand
- X   mailing via USPS first class mail, postage prepaid

Signed under the pains and penalties of perjury of law this _30_ th day of _____March, 2007.

_____Jane Doe_____

ANSWERS TO DOCUMENT REQUESTS

To give the reader a sense of the broadest possible sense of the discovery requests possible (and there *will* be discovery requests thrown at you), I have spliced examples of boilerplates together from a variety of sources. Some document requests are deceptively simple. They will consist of paragraphs 1 and 2. Believe it or not, if *you* are the recipient of such a broad request and don't produce a needed document, a clever lawyer will bar your document from evidence at trial. On the other hand, some discovery requests are thirty pages long and list every possible document you might ever think of. This is good for jogging your spouse's memory for documents he may not think are relevant, but if he later produces a document that was not on your very detailed list, you have no grounds to bar it from evidence.

FROM WASTE PAPER TO MUNITIONS OF WAR

I have taken a 'hybrid approach' with the sample, moving from a broad statement, to more detailed requests going in number through classes of common assets most typical court financial statements ask for, and then to even more detailed still requests asking for specific documents Jane Doe suspects her husband is hiding from her. Hopefully it will give you an idea of the range of Document Requests to expect when litigating your divorce.

Not only is Jane looking for information from Jack, but Jack will be looking for the same type of information from *her*. Even though she may have handed Jack her 'acorns' binder, Jack's attorney (if he had one) might be too lazy to go through them all and tailor whatever boilerplate discovery request form he is using to eliminate documents Jane already gave him. Therefore, Jane will receive a Request for the Production of Documents as well which she will formally need to answer.

If you need to do this yourself, don't panic! Let's pretend for a moment it was Jane who got the Request for the Production of Documents above? All Jane needs to do is go through Jack's Document Request, item by item, and answer that she is forwarding the documents now, has already forwarded these documents to Jack with her Acorns binder, that she has no specific knowledge of any documents related to that request number, or that that she thinks such documents may exist, but that they are not in her control. If the document is the subject of *privilege* (a rule that prohibits Jack from seeing it ... such as medical or psychotherapy records) Jane must state *why* she is objecting to it noting the relevant exception listed in the Rules of Evidence.

You must neatly arrange the documents by month and in the order in which the opposing party requested them. For example, if he requests bank statements, credit card bills, and stock funds, you would first organize the bank statements from oldest to newest and neatly paperclip, staple, or put a rubber band around them. Then you would do the same for the credit card statements, then the stock account statements.

You may serve as many Requests for the Production of Documents as you need upon the other side so long as they seek information relevant to your divorce.

An example of an Answer to a Request for Documents follows:

EXHIBIT 15-12: SAMPLE ANSWER TO REQUEST FOR THE PRODUCTION OF DOCUMENTS

COMMONWEALTH OF MASSACHUSETTS
PROBATE AND FAMILY COURT

BARNSTABLE, SS.

DOCKET NO. 07D-9999-DV1

JANE DOE-RAYME,)	
Plaintiff)	**PLAINTIFF'S ANSWER TO DEFENDANT'S**
v.)	**REQUEST FOR THE PRODUCTION OF**
JACK RAYME,)	**DOCUMENTS PURSUANT TO FED.R.CIV.PRO 34**
Co-Petitioner)	
)	

Now comes Jane Doe-Rayme, Plaintiff in the above-captioned case, and hereby answers the Defendant, Jack Rayme 's, document request dated March 14, 2007.

DOCUMENTS PRODUCED:

1. All documents in your possession, custody, or under your control, written or created after the date of January 1, 2004 that pertain either directly or indirectly to the divorce that is the subject of this litigation. Please arrange these documents by date.

   A) Plaintiff previously forwarded all documents she was aware of to the Defendant as part of her compliance with Rule 410 Mandatory Self-Disclosure dated February 21, 2007;

   B) If Plaintiff becomes aware of any additional documents, she will amend this Answer and forward them;

2. All documents, memoranda (both internal and external), reports, letters, correspondence, or other records or writings (whether paper, electronic, or other media) that mention, concern or discuss any aspect of the divorce or any aspect of the divorce that may be litigated and/or may come into evidence at any time.

   A) Plaintiff is unaware of any additional documents beyond Mandatory Self-Disclosure and specific documents listed in this document.

   B) If Plaintiff becomes aware of any additional documents, she will amend this Answer and forward them;

3. All documents related to your personal income:

   A) The Plaintiff's latest paystub is included in this request.

4. All federal and state and local income tax returns, including all W-2 forms and other records substantiating said returns, Schedule C's, rental income or other schedules, whether filed by you, individually or jointly, including all estimated income tax returns, local business tax, excise tax, property and local sales/room/other tax statements.

   A) All past-year tax returns are currently in the possession and control of the Defendant.

5. All documents relating to your personal expenses, including, but not limited to, household expenses, business expenses deducted from income, all expenses listed on any tax return, financial statement, or expenses listed on the Court Financial Statement. Include any expenses paid by others on your behalf.

   A) The Plaintiff previously forwarded electronic printouts for all utility bills and other expenses listed under the 'Expenses' section of the court financial statement for the previous year;

   B) To obtain bills beyond those already obtained, the utility companies have informed the Plaintiff they shall cost between $5 and $15 per statement to obtain. These statements are not within the Plaintiff's control or command. Should the Defendant desire to obtain more than what was already disclosed, please forward a list specifying which statements the Defendant desires, the dates, and a check to cover the cost of obtaining them.

6. All documents relating to your current coverage through any medical and dental insurance policies and disability benefits.

    A) A copy of the Plaintiff's latest health, dental and vision plan is included with this Answer.

7. All documents, including medical records and bills, relating to appointments with physicians, including dates thereof and medical histories concerning your past and present physical condition.

    A) A copy of the outstanding physician bill for the children is enclosed;

    B) Any further details, including dates, is protected by the physician-patient privilege and not subject to disclosure

8. All documents relating to all real estate in which you currently have any interest, including, but not limited to, time shares, vacation share interests, and/or real estate which may have been transferred for the benefit for another but which you still retain a life estate, lifetime or term lease, or other interest.

    A) The only property the Plaintiff has an interest in is the marital home located at 100 Main Street, North Anytown, MA. The Defendant has a copy of the deed already in his control.

9. All documents relating to any motor or recreational vehicles in which you currently own or have any interest, including, but not limited to, vehicles which may have been transferred for the benefit for another but which you still retain a lease, lien, or other interest.

    A) A copy of the title and an Edmunds.com value of the Wife's 2004 Chevy Tahoe is attached.

10. All documents relating to your gross retirement entitlements from your present and all prior employers, including, without limitation, IRA, KEOGH, pension and profit-sharing plans, other retirement plans, stock ownership plans, severance pay plans, excess benefit plans, stock option plans and any and all deferred compensation plans and arrangements, whether or not qualified under Internal Revenue Code Section 401. Such documents shall include, without limitation, the following:

    A) Copies of all statements for all defined contribution plans (such as IRA, 401(k), Keogh, profit-sharing, etc.).

        (1) Plaintiff previously forwarded all documents she was aware of to the Defendant as part of her compliance with Rule 410 Mandatory Self-Disclosure dated February 21, 2007;

    B) Copies of the plans, plan descriptions, summary plan descriptions, brochures, trust agreements and other documents describing the plans as currently in force.

        (1) Plaintiff previously forwarded all documents she was aware of to the Defendant as part of her compliance with Rule 410 Mandatory Self-Disclosure dated February 21, 2007;

    C) For each prior employer, all documents, forms and statements regarding your gross retirement entitlements (both defined contribution and defined benefit plans) and when the same are payable.

        (1) Plaintiff is not the recipient of any defined contribution plans beyond the IRA previously disclosed.

11. All documents related to any Tax Deferred Annuity Plan(s) you may have invested in or have an interest in.

    A) Plaintiff has no Tax Deferred Annuity Plan.

12. All documents relating to all life insurance policies currently in force insuring your life, whether whole life, term life, or any other form of life insurance.

    A) A copy of the Plaintiff's term life policy is enclosed with this Answer.

13. All documents related to your checking, saving, or other banking accounts held in your name, individually, jointly, in the name of another person for your benefit, held by you for the benefit of your minor children, or as guardian, trustee or in which you had any interest.

    A) Plaintiff previously forwarded all documents she was aware of to the Defendant as part of her compliance with Rule 410 Mandatory Self-Disclosure dated February 21, 2007;

14. All documents relating to all accounts in which you had any interest, including credit union shares, savings plans, individual retirement accounts and certificates of deposit.

   A) Plaintiff previously forwarded all documents she was aware of to the Defendant as part of her compliance with Rule 410 Mandatory Self-Disclosure dated February 21, 2007;

15. All documents relating to all money market funds, mutual funds, stocks, bonds and securities in which you had any interest, including documents relating to the purchase, sale or transfer of such items and brokers' statements.

   A) Plaintiff previously forwarded all documents she was aware of to the Defendant as part of her compliance with Rule 410 Mandatory Self-Disclosure dated February 21, 2007;

16. All documents relating to your ownership of any personal property valued in excess of $1,000.

   A) Plaintiff previously forwarded all documents she was aware of to the Defendant as part of her compliance with Rule 410 Mandatory Self-Disclosure dated February 21, 2007;

17. All documents relating to all safe deposit boxes held in your name, individually, jointly or as guardian, trustee or held by another on your behalf, including the locations, numbers and contents.

   A) Plaintiff has a safe deposit box at SeaWard Bank, box number 12345. The contents of this box were listed under the 'other' section of the Financial Statement forwarded with the divorce paperwork.

18. All documents relating to the sale or transfer by you of any personal property valued in excess of $1,000 or more, including 'collections' which would normally be considered a related group and/or can be grouped together to be worth more than $1,000.

   A) The Plaintiff has neither sold nor transferred such property.

19. All documents relating to any loans, account receivable or debt forgiveness you may have given to any person, business, relative, or other entity.

   A) The Plaintiff has no accounts receivable or outstanding loan interests at this time.

20. All documents relating to any indebtedness owed by you to anyone, including personal debts, banks, relatives, business associations, partnerships and corporations in which you have any interest, including all loan applications completed by you, whether or not you actually received the loan.

   A) The Plaintiff has no accounts receivable or outstanding loan interests at this time.

21. All documents relating to any judgments or executions rendered against you in any lawsuits, the nature and type of any lawsuit presently pending against you in any court, all legal cases resolved without litigation, and those currently being negotiated, including, but not limited to, any outstanding workers compensation cases.

   A) The only lawsuit the Plaintiff is a party to at this time is this divorce.

22. All documents relating to charitable donations made by you or on your behalf.

   A) All charitable donations were made on the parties joint tax return, which was forwarded to the Defendant earlier.

23. All documents relating to gifts of any kind made either by, or to you, by or to any individual, firm, trust, partnership, corporation or other entity.

   A) No such gifts were made or received.

24. All documents relating to all credit cards and charge accounts used by you, or held in your name, individually or jointly.

   A) The Plaintiff forwarded a printed summary sheet of all activity on the aforementioned debts with her Mandatory self-disclosure materials for the past year. There is a cost associated of $5 to $15 per statement with going back further than that. Should the Defendant desire additional statements, please state with specificity which statements you want and a check to cover the cost of obtaining them.

25. All documents relating to your membership in any clubs, social or religious organizations, including without limitation, all records of initiation fees, dues and donations, whether paid by you or by any other individual or entity on your behalf.

    A) Membership paperwork for the family YMCA membership is included. Membership expires in two months.

    B) There are no additional memberships.

26. All documents, including wills, trusts, and executor and trustee statements, relating to all estates and trusts of which you were or are a beneficiary of any kind.

    A) The Plaintiff is not aware of being the recipient of any wills.

    B) The Plaintiff is not aware of having any trusts.

27. All documents relating to your interest in, and the organization of, all business associations, partnerships and corporations, including financial statements, tax returns, and other documents.

    A) The Plaintiff does not own a business.

28. All documents containing a list of the names and addresses of all proposed expert witnesses and all written reports rendered to you or your attorney by all proposed expert witnesses or by any other witness who has knowledge of any facts relevant to this action.

    A) As of this time, the wife has no attorney and has hired no expert witnesses.

29. All documents relating to any psychological treatment of the Wife's or children.

    A) This information is protected by the psychotherapist-patient privilege and not subject to disclosure.

> **Jack is trying to get his hands on Jane and Children's therapy records and she is refusing. You must state the nature of the privilege (i.e., psychotherapist-patient) and not simply state the information is privileged. This then puts the burden on Jack to obtain the information through other means, usually via court order. If Jack cannot give a good reason for wanting the information, the court will frequently refuse it. Once Jane gets a request such as this, she should both *speak* to and put *in writing* a request in her and the children's patient files that no information is to be disclosed to any party without a specific court order and informing them that a subpoena alone is not a sufficient court order.**

30. A copy of your most recent resume or curriculum vitae.

    A) A copy of the wife's resume is attached.

27. All statements evidencing your interest in accumulated airline or frequent flier mileage, or similar benefits.

    A) A frequent flyer mile statement is attached. The amount is negligible.

28. Any other document relevant to the financial estate of the Defendant or the parties which reasonable minds, the court, a tax accountant or financial planner might deem relevant to ascertaining the net worth of the Defendant.

    A) The Plaintiff has included or previously forwarded all documents she thought were relevant. Should any additional documents come to her attention, she will forward them promptly.

Date: March 30, 2007

Respectfully submitted,

_____Jane Doe_____
Jane Doe-Rayme, Plaintiff, pro se

REQUESTS FOR ADMISSIONS OF FACT

When you go into hearings, it is helpful if you don't have to "prove" minor points before you start making your case. This is especially important when you need to put certain facts before the judge before he is statutorily allowed to divide your assets. If your husband admits any facts, you can put those admissions in the "uncontested facts" section of your Pre-Trial Memorandum (covered later). Therefore, it is helpful to serve a very general "1+1=2" type of Request for Admissions of Fact on your husband very early on in the proceedings so that you don't have to argue about basic facts every time you go into court. Most of the questions in the sample Request are these type of questions.

🚩 ***Anything you state in any court document, pleading, discovery request, deposition or hearing can and will be used against you in court!!!*** Answer honestly, but don't volunteer any more information than is specifically asked for.

The other use for "Requests for Admissions" is to prove some important aspect of your case that may be being contested. In those situations, your husband (or his attorney) is going to try to weasel their way out of giving you a direct answer, or they will deny the entire admission because you are trying to cram too many facts into one sentence and one word is a tad bit off, thereby rendering your request useless. You can still serve them with a Request, but in those situations, it is more useful to break your question down into its most basic pieces to try to nail down as much of the truth as possible so you have a foundation to build upon at trial.

🐿 *State-specific 'rules' about Requests for Admissions of Fact will likely still call this 'Rule 36' because that is the Federal Rules of Civil Procedure designation number.*

🐿 *When answering an Admission, you either Admit it, Deny it, state you don't have enough information to answer the question, or you can give a qualified answer (in the sample, Jane Doe corrects a mistake in the date of birth of her daughter).*

🐿 *You can serve Requests for Admissions at any time in the proceedings prior to the Pre-Trial Conference or as many times as you feel is necessary. However, since you are hoping to get your divorce as soon as possible and plan on scheduling your Pre-Trial Conference six months from the filing, and it takes a minimum of 30 days to get the information, you'd best serve them consistently and soon!.*

🐿 *You may serve as many Requests for Admission as you need upon the other side so long as they seek information relevant to your divorce.*

Back to our hypothetical divorcing couple, Jack Rayme is in denial about his daughter's learning disability and the need to pay for ongoing tutoring (as well as the outstanding $15,000 special intervention bill). He is also suddenly claiming he can't find work. Lastly, Jane once again tries to ferret out information about Jack Rayme's mysterious $20,000 stock account.

EXHIBIT 15-13: SAMPLE REQUEST FOR ADMISSIONS OF FACT

COMMONWEALTH OF MASSACHUSETTS

PROBATE AND FAMILY COURT

BARNSTABLE, SS.

DOCKET NO. <u>07D-9999-DV1</u>

JANE DOE-RAYME,   )
    Plaintiff   )
    v.   )
JACK RAYME,   )
    Defendant   )
)

REQUEST FOR ADMISSIONS
OF FACT PURSUANT TO
FED.R.CIV.PRO.R. 36
MASS.R.DOM.REL.P. 36

I, <u>Jane Doe-Rayme</u>, Plaintiff in the above-entitled matter, do hereby request that the Defendant <u>Jack Rayme</u> within thirty (30) days after service of this request make the following admissions for purposes of this action only, in accordance with Federal Rule of Civil Procedure Rule 36 and Mass.R.Dom.Rel.P. 36:

1. That the parties were married on <u>September 11, 1994</u> at <u>Las Vegas, Nevada</u>.
2. That the Wife is <u>38</u> years old; and that the Husband is <u>42</u> years old.
3. That there were <u>2</u> children born of this marriage, Jayne, born June 15, 1995, age 11, and Johnnie, born October 11, 1998, age 8.
4. That the Husband owns a home improvement business, <u>Jack-O'-All-Trades.</u>
5. That the Husband had the following annual income during the marriage:
       2005 - $55,463   2004 - $54,982   2003 - $54,931
6. That each party has the following respective educational background:
   a. The Wife has a nursing degree and is a registered nurse;
   b. The Husband has a high school diploma from the Upper Cape Technical High School;
   c. The Husband completed his Home Improvement Contractors license at Cape Cod Tech;
   d. The Husband is currently pursuing a General Contractor's license at Cape Cod Tech;
7. That the Husband enjoys good health.
8. That the daughter, Jayne, has the following health problems:
   a. Jayne has a Special Education Plan at Anytown Middle School;
   b. Jayne has been diagnosed with dyslexia;
   c. That diagnosis was made by Nathan Neurologist, M.D.
   d. Until the third grade, Jayne was unable to read;
   e. Jayne underwent three years of intervention from 2002 until 2003 with Tutors-R-Us;
   f. There is a $15,000 tuition bill outstanding for Tutor's-R-Us.
   g. Jayne needs structured help with her homework after each school day;
   h. Jayne currently sees a tutor one day per week;
9. That the parties lived a middle class lifestyle during the marriage:
10. That the Husband has the following retirement account(s)/plan(s):
    a. Vanguard IRA - $2,000
11. That the Wife was the primary homemaker of the family during the marriage.
12. That the following documents, copies of which are attached hereto, are authentic, genuine and accurate.
    a. Merrily-Merrily Retirement statement dated 9/30/06.

Date: March 30, 2007

Respectfully submitted,
<u>   Jane Doe   </u>
Jane Doe-Rayme, Plaintiff, pro se

CERTIFICATE OF SERVICE

I, <u>Jane Doe-Rayme</u>, the Plaintiff in the above-captioned case, did serve a copy of this Request for Admissions of Fact under Mass.R.Dom.R.36 upon the Plaintiff, <u>Jack Rayme</u>, on <u>March 30</u>, 20<u>07</u> via the following method (check method):

- o   sheriff's service
- o   in hand
- X   mailing via USPS first class mail, postage prepaid

Signed under the pains and penalties of perjury of law this <u>30</u> th day of <u>   March</u>, 20<u>07</u>.
<u>   Jane Doe   </u>

To answer her *husband's* admissions of fact requests of *her*, Jane would follow the format of her Husband's request the way she did to answer his Document Requests earlier. She would go through line by line, and either affirm the question, deny it, or state that she does not know. If a question is so convoluted that you have no idea what they are asking, state such and request in the cover letter that they clarify the question. Read the "privilege" sub-caption later in this chapter before responding to learn what information you should *never* admit to your husband because he is not entitled to know.

EXHIBIT 15-14: SAMPLE ANSWER TO REQUEST FOR ADMISSIONS OF FACT

COMMONWEALTH OF MASSACHUSETTS
PROBATE AND FAMILY COURT

BARNSTABLE, SS.   DOCKET NO. 07D-9999-DV1

JANE DOE-RAYME,   )   PLAINTIFF'S RESPONSE TO
    Plaintiff   )   DEFENDANT'S REQUEST FOR
v.   )   ADMISSIONS OF FACT
JACK RAYME,   )
    Defendant   )

I, Jane Doe-Rayme, Plaintiff in the above-entitled matter, do hereby respond to the Defendant's Request for Admissions of Fact as follows:

1. That the parties were married on September 11, 1994 at Las Vegas, Nevada.
   Admitted.
2. That the Wife is 38 years old; and that the Husband is 42 years old.
   Admitted
3. That there were 2 children born of this marriage, Jayne, born June 15, 1995, age 11, and Johnnie, born October 11, 1997, age 8.
   Admitted that Jayne was born on June 15, 1995
   Johnnie was born on October 11, 1998, not 1997.
4. That the Wife had the following annual income during the marriage, $23,000 in 2005, $22,000 during 2004, and $19,000 in 2003:
       2005 – Admitted
       2004 – the Plaintiff earned $21,982
       2003 – the Plaintiff earned $18,531
5. That the Wife has a nursing degree and is a registered nurse;
   Admitted.
6. That the Wife enjoys good health.
   Admitted
7. That the children have no special health problems or requirements.
   Denied. The eldest child, Jayne, suffers from dyslexia and needs extensive intervention both at school and privately.
8. That the parties lived a middle class lifestyle during the marriage:
   Admitted.
9. That the Husband was the breadwinner during the marriage.
   The Wife does not have sufficient facts to answer this question as written. Although the Husband earns more than twice as much as the Wife, the Wife has helped the Husband's business by receiving telephone calls from customers, scheduling appointments, and managing some of the bookkeeping. The Wife has also always worked part-time as a private duty nurse to contribute to the family unit.

Date: April 14, 2007   Respectfully submitted,
                                        Jane Doe
                                   Jane Doe-Rayme, Plaintiff, pro se

CERTIFICATE OF SERVICE

I, Jane Doe-Rayme, the Plaintiff in the above-captioned case, did serve this Answer to Plaintiff's Request for Admissions of Fact upon the Plaintiff, Jack Rayme, on April 14, 2007 via the following method (check method):
   ○   sheriff's service
   ○   in hand
   X   mailing via USPS first class mail, postage prepaid
Signed under the pains and penalties of perjury of law this _14_ th day of __April, 2007.
                                       Jane Doe

INTERROGATORIES

Interrogatories are useful for ferreting out information your husband may be planning to use against you. No good attorney will ever allow you to fully see what they have up their sleeve, but by serving him with well-drafted interrogatories, you will be able to get a glimpse of what may be coming down the pipe. There is no cost to you to propound interrogatories upon the other side to get information.

> *You are only allowed 30 interrogatory questions total (in some states 25)!* You could send your husband 30 separate requests with one question each, three requests with 10 each, or thirty separate requests of one question each as the need arises, but you only get 30 (including "expert" interrogatories ... covered next).

> *Work with your attorney to help them tailor your thirty interrogatories to ferret out information you were not able to dig up on your own, not simply fire off a 'boilerplate' copied out of a book such as this. Don't waste them!*

Interrogatories are also a good way to ask about things you 'don't know that you don't know.' If your husband is a louse, he will lie on these questions (*as if* he would suddenly let you know he had been having an affair). However, if he denies certain things, sometimes you can use that denial to impeach his credibility on the witness stand. Include questions about cash held, cash transactions, and transfers with or without consideration (gifts). Make the evil trapper commit perjury to hide cash. It is not unusual for the successful cash-hoarding spouse to brag about his or her success after the divorce has been finalized. If he later does, sometimes you can use this perjury to go back and reopen the case to get your fair share.

JUST A GOOD AFTERNOON'S WORK

> Good boilerplate interrogatories have a phrase something like *"these Interrogatories are to be deemed continuing in nature, requiring supplemental answers thereto."*

If you include a request for updating, you can shut down certain ugly surprises your husband may try to spring upon you at trial. For example, if you ask him to disclose the name of any expert he uses to value your assets and he says Billy Blubber, but then at trial he suddenly tries to put Sammy Spader on the witness stand, you can object and get that witness thrown out of the courtroom without testifying.

Sample Interrogatories follow.

> *These are simplified interrogatories to familiarize you with them.* They have been tailored to ask questions about our low- to moderate-income litigant's case. If you have specific or unusual assets or situations in your divorce, there are more highly tailored questions you should be asking.

EXHIBIT 15-15: SAMPLE INTERROGATORIES

COMMONWEALTH OF MASSACHUSETTS
PROBATE AND FAMILY COURT

BARNSTABLE, SS.   DOCKET NO. <u>07D-9999-DV1</u>

JANE DOE-RAYME,   )
     Plaintiff   )
 v.   )
 JACK RAYME,   )
     Defendant   )
)
	PLAINTIFF'S FIRST SET OF
	 INTERROGATORIES TO BE
	 ANSWERED UNDER OATH
	 BY THE DEFENDANT

Pursuant to Rules 26 and 33 of the Federal Rules of Civil Procedure and the Massachusetts Rules of Domestic Relations Procedure and the instructions set forth below, <u>Jane Doe-Rayme</u>, the Plaintiff requires <u>Jack Rayme</u>, the Defendant, to submit written answers to the following Interrogatories, under oath and penalty of perjury, and to serve a copy of said Answers to Interrogatories upon the Plaintiff within thirty (30) days.

I.   INSTRUCTIONS

In answering each Interrogatory, you must ask your agents, attorneys, servants, accountants, banks, brokers, employers, employees, creditors, debtors, trustees and physicians and examine any and all tax returns, schedules and forms, deposit records, contracts, bills and statements, profit and loss statements, notes, memoranda, writings, computer output, correspondence, documents, certificates, policies, applications, ledger books, accounts, and any other records of every type and description which in any way concern the subjects of these Interrogatories. If you are unable to answer with exactness, you are required to answer to the best of your ability.

These Interrogatories are to be deemed continuing in nature, requiring supplemental answers thereto pursuant to Rule 26(e), Federal Rules of Civil Procedure and Massachusetts Rules of Domestic Relations Procedure. If you, your counsel, or anyone representing your interests, learn of any additional person or persons having knowledge relating to the matters into which these Interrogatories inquire, you are requested and directed to furnish the names and addresses of such persons to the undersigned, giving timely notice of additional witnesses to any of the issues involved herein.

II.   DEFINITIONS

As used in these Interrogatories, the terms below are defined as follows:

A.   "You" and "your" refer to <u>Jack Rayme</u>, by or anyone acting on [his/her] behalf.

B.   "Documents" means all documents and all written, recorded or graphic matter of any kind and nature whatsoever, including, without limitation, correspondence, and other communications, however transmitted, personal and business diaries, office and personal memoranda, telephone and other communications, however transmitted, personal and business diaries, office and personal memoranda, telephone and other communication logs and records, bank statements, passbooks and other bank records, insurance policies, insurance premium invoices, police reports, account statements, canceled checks and check stubs, notes, minutes, recordings, data processing reports and forms, physician's, hospital or clinic records, health professionals' records, opinions, analyses, evaluations, pamphlets, books, videotapes and all drafts and non-identical copies of the foregoing.

III.   ANSWERS AS TO WHICH PRIVILEGE OR WORK PRODUCT PROTECTION IS CLAIMED

Interrogatories that you believe that you may refuse to answer on grounds of either privilege or work product protection are to be answered by so declaring and by briefly stating the facts alleged to support such refusal to answer.

IV.   SUPPLEMENTAL ANSWERS

Pursuant to Rule 26(e), Federal Rules of Civil Procedure and Massachusetts Rules of Domestic Relations Procedure, the responses to all Interrogatories which are later found to have been incorrect when made or no longer to be true, are to be deemed continuing in nature so as to require supplemental answers through the time of trial. Such supplemental answer(s) must be furnished within a reasonable time after the occurrence of the event necessitating the supplemental answer(s).

V. INTERROGATORIES

INTERROGATORY NO. 1

Please state your full name, date of birth, social security number, residential address, occupation and business address.

INTERROGATORY NO. 2

If you contend that any of the following is relevant to this divorce action or division of the marital estate, or to the payment of alimony or support, please describe the same in detail, including any witnesses thereto:

    a.   Age;

    b.   Health;

    c.   Station;

    d.   Occupation, vocational skill and employability;

    e.   Amount and sources of income;

    f.   Estate;

    g.   Liabilities and/or needs;

    h.   Opportunity to acquire future capital assets or income;

    i.   Contribution in the acquisition, preservation and/or appreciation in value of the marital estate; and,

    j.   Contribution as a homemaker.

INTERROGATORY NO. 3

Please describe your employment history during the marriage, including:

    A.   The name and address of each employer;
    B.   The dates of employment (from start to finish);
    C.   Your occupation, job title, and type of work you performed;
    D.   Your gross annual income, including bonuses, tips and other compensation, for each of the <u>2004, 2005, 2006, and 2007</u>;

INTERROGATORY NO. 4

Please state whether you presently suffer from any disability, infirmity or condition, whether mental, physical or emotional, which prevents you from seeking or holding full-time employment and, if so, describe the nature of the disability, infirmity or condition in detail, including in your answer the name(s) of the treating physician(s) who diagnosed and who treated each such disability, infirmity or condition.

INTERROGATORY NO. 5

Please describe your educational background including, without limitation, the names of all schools, from and including high school, which you have attended, the dates of your attendance and whether such attendance was full or part-time; diplomas, degrees and/or certifications received; the source of funds used in payment and/or financing of your educational expenses including tuition, books, and review courses; and the source of funds used by you for living and personal expenses during periods of your education.

INTERROGATORY NO. 6

Do you hold, have you held, does or has anyone held on your behalf, since <u>September 11, 1994</u> , any interest in stock, securities, mutual funds, bonds, investment accounts, an interest in any business entity, partnership or limited partnership.

If your response is in the affirmative, list the following:

    a.   Type of interest held; and, if stock, number and type or class of shares held;

    b.   Date acquired;

    c.   Consideration paid, if any;

    d.   Present value and the basis for calculating said value;

e.   Details as to transfer of such interest made by you or on your behalf at any time to any other individual, entity or trust.

INTERROGATORY NO. 7

As to any real estate in which you now have or have had an interest, or in which any interest is or has been held on your behalf, since <u>September 11, 1994</u>, whether individually, jointly, in the entirety or in common, as trustee for any other person, or as beneficiary under any trust, set forth:

a.   Property address;

b.   Date of acquisition and purchase price;

c.   Name(s) in which title was taken;

d.   Source of funds used for any down payment and identification of account on which monies were drawn;

e.   Date of sale and sales price;

f.   Contributions made by you to acquire, preserve, and maintain it;

g.   Present fair market value and your basis for determining said value;

h.   Any mortgage or lien balances encumbering the property and names and addresses of mortgagor or lien holder.

INTERROGATORY NO. 8

Since the date of your marriage, have you have received any gifts, legacies, devises or inheritances with a value in excess of $250, or are you, were or have become in said period a beneficiary of any trust or estate? If so, please state the value, source it was received from, date received, name of donor, value, basis for estimating said value, share you are entitled to receive, date you are entitled to receive, and cost of any fees.

INTERROGATORY NO. 9

Please list all financial accounts in which you and/or your agents and nominees have or had any interest, whether held jointly, individually or by another for your benefit at any time since September 11, 1994. For each account, state:

a.   The name of the account;

b.   The name and address of the institution in which the account is or was held;

c.   The account number;

d.   The current balance and/or present value for each such account; and

e.   The balance in each such account as of January 1, of the current and last four calendar years and the balance of each account as of the date of your answers.

INTERROGATORY NO. 10

Since September 11, 1994 , have you or has anyone on your behalf either individually or jointly maintained any safety deposit boxes, vaults or safes, or other depositories for safekeeping? If so, please state the location and identify each such depository and the identities of other individuals having access to same. Please also list the contents since January 1, 2002 that have been and/or are presently contained therein.

INTERROGATORY NO. 11

Please state all stocks, bonds, bearer bonds, custodial accounts, treasury notes, certificates of deposit or other securities or investments of any type, including without limitation, tax free investments, in which you have a legal or equitable interest, whether held by you jointly, individually or with another, or in trust, or held by another for your benefit at any time since the date of your marriage to the Plaintiff, including:

a.   the name of the security, bond or investment;

b.   the face value or number of shares as applicable;

c.   the CUSIP number of each bond;

d.   the name of the depository or investment account and any account number; and

e.   the maturity date(s) of any certificate of deposit.

INTERROGATORY NO. 12

Please describe in detail the conduct of the Wife which you claim is relevant in this case.

INTERROGATORY NO. 13

Have you engaged in sexual relations with any individual other than your spouse at any time during your marriage to Plaintiff? If so, please state the following:

   a.   Name and address of each such individual;

   b.   Dates and locations of such conduct;

   c.   Any and all financial contributions and payments made by you to each person named and/or from him/her to you or on your behalf, and include all sources from which such funds were derived.

INTERROGATORY NO. 14

Have you made any gifts or loans of, or transferred title to or possession of, real or personal property valued at $100 or more within the past five years? If so, and for each loan, gift, or transfer, please state the date of the event, the nature and value of the gift, loan or transfer, the name, address and relationship to you, if any, of the party to whom such loan, gift or transfer was made. If you are describing a loan, please state the terms of the loan and whether there is a writing evidencing such loan.

INTERROGATORY NO. 15

Please provide the details of each and every admission you have had to a hospital and/or health or mental health care facility since the date of your marriage to the [Plaintiff]/[Defendant] to the present, including in your answer the following:

   (a)   the name(s) of each such hospital and/or health or mental health care facility;

   (b)   the name(s) of each physician who admitted you and/or treated you;

   (c)   the length of each admission;

   (d)   the symptom(s) you were experiencing for which you were admitted in each instance;

   (e)   the diagnosis or diagnoses for each admission; and,

   (f)   the discharge order(s) and prognosis upon discharge from each such hospital and/or health or mental health care facility.

Date: March 30, 2007

Respectfully submitted,

_____Jane Doe_____

Jane Doe-Rayme, Plaintiff, pro se

CERTIFICATE OF SERVICE

I, Jane Doe-Rayme, the Plaintiff in the above-captioned case, did serve a copy of this Plaintiff's First Set of Interrogatories upon the Plaintiff, Jack Rayme, on March 30, 2007 via the following method (check method):

   o   sheriff's service
   o   in hand
   X   mailing via USPS first class mail, postage prepaid

Signed under the pains and penalties of perjury of law this _30_ th day of _March_, 2007.

_____Jane Doe_____

To answer your *husband's* interrogatories requested of *you*, follow the same format outlined to comply with Document Requests. Follow the format of your Husband's request, but state the information you are disclosing (or stating you do not know). If a question is so convoluted that you have no idea what they are asking, state such and request in the cover letter that they clarify the question. Read the "privilege" sub-caption later in this chapter before responding to learn what information you should *never* give to your husband because he is not entitled to receive know.

Privilege - a rule of evidence that allows the holder of the privilege to refuse to provide evidence about a certain subject or to bar such evidence from being disclosed or used in a judicial or other proceeding.

EXHIBIT 15-16: SAMPLE ANSWERS TO INTERROGATORIES

COMMONWEALTH OF MASSACHUSETTS

BARNSTABLE, SS.　　　　　PROBATE AND FAMILY COURT　　　DOCKET NO. <u>07D-9999-DV1</u>

JANE DOE-RAYME,) 　Plaintiff) v.) JACK RAYME,) 　Defendant)	PLAINTIFF'S ANSWERS TO DEFENDANT'S INTERROGATORIES

I, <u>Jane Doe-Rayme</u>, Plaintiff, do hereby submit the following answers to the Defendant's Interrogatories dated March 14, 2007, under oath and under the pains and penalty of perjury:

ANSWER TO INTERROGATORY NO. 1

Please state your full name, date of birth, social security number, residential address, occupation and business address.

> *Jane Doe-Rayme, October 11, 1969, 999-99-9999, 100 Any Street, Anytown MA, nurse, Nurses-R-Us, 100 Commerce Drive, Big City.*

ANSWER TO INTERROGATORY NO. 2

If you contend that any of the following, of or by either of the parties hereto, is relevant to this divorce action or to the disposition or division of the marital estate, or to the payment of alimony or support, please describe the same in detail, including any witnesses thereto:

a. Age;

b. Health;

c. Station;

    d.   Occupation, vocational skill and employability;

At my husband's request, I gave up a lucrative nursing career in Big City to move to North Anytown so he could pursue his home improvement business. There are very limited opportunities in this area and the 10 years out of my field working private duty makes it difficult to obtain a better job at an employer such as a hospital.

    e.   Amount and sources of income;

Jack is working the same as always.

    f.   Estate;

Jack is hiding a $20,000 Merrily-Merrily Retirement stock account from the court.

    g.   Liabilities and/or needs;

The ongoing special needs and learning disability of the eldest child, Jayne, make it impossible for the Wife to return to work full-time or during the day..

    h.   Opportunity to acquire future capital assets or income;

The 10-year sacrifice in moving to North Anytown has permanently impaired the Wife's earning capacity. Ongoing special needs and learning disability of the eldest child, Jayne, make it impossible for the Wife to return to work full-time or during the day for another 7 or 8 years.

    i.   Contribution in the acquisition, preservation and/or appreciation in value of the marital estate; and,

Until 3 years ago, both parties worked equally to acquire and preserve assets. Once Jack started drinking, the burden fell to me to preserve what we had.

    j.   Contribution as a homemaker.

The parties agreed the Wife would put her career on hold and only work part time overnights in order to be home to care for the children. The Wife was and is the primary caretaker of the children.

ANSWER TO INTERROGATORY NO. 3

Please describe your employment history during the marriage, including:

    A.   The name and address of each employer;
        Nurses-R-Us, 111 Business Park Road, NextTown, MA
    B.   The dates of employment (from start to finish);
        September 1997 to present.
    C.   Your occupation, job title, and type of work you performed;
        Private duty nurse, overnight shift
    D.   Your gross annual income, including bonuses, tips and other compensation, for each of the <u>2004, 2005, 2006, and 2007</u>;
        Three year average is $21,000 per year.

ANSWER TO INTERROGATORY NO. 4

Please state whether you presently suffer from any disability, infirmity or condition, whether mental, physical or emotional, which prevents you from seeking or holding full-time employment and, if so, describe the nature of the disability, infirmity or condition in detail, including in your answer the name(s) of the treating physician(s) who diagnosed and who treated each such disability, infirmity or condition.

    None known at this time.

ANSWER TO INTERROGATORY NO. 5

Please describe your educational background including, without limitation, the names of all schools, from and including high school, which you have attended, the dates of your attendance and whether such attendance was full or part-time; diplomas, degrees and/or certifications received; the source of funds used in payment and/or financing of your educational expenses including tuition, books, and review courses; and the source of funds used by you for living and personal expenses during periods of your education.

Suburb High School 1984-1987, Big City Nursing School BS 1988-1994, parents paid first two years, last two years were via student loan, self-pay.

ANSWER TO INTERROGATORY NO. 6

Do you hold, have you held, does or has anyone held on your behalf, since <u>September 11, 1994</u>, any interest in stock, securities, mutual funds, bonds, investment accounts, an interest in any business entity, partnership or limited partnership.

If your response is in the affirmative, list the following:

a. Type of interest held; and, if stock, number and type or class of shares held;

b. Date acquired;

c. Consideration paid, if any;

d. Present value and the basis for calculating said value;

e. Details as to transfer of such interest made by you or on your behalf at any time to any other individual, entity or trust.

Marital share in this divorce of my husband's business, "Jack O All Trades."

ANSWER TO INTERROGATORY NO. 7

As to any real estate in which you now have or have had an interest, or in which any interest is or has been held on your behalf, since <u>September 11, 1994</u>, whether individually, jointly, in the entirety or in common, as trustee for any other person, or as beneficiary under any trust, set forth:

a. Property address;

b. Date of acquisition and purchase price;

c. Name(s) in which title was taken;

d. Source of funds used for any down payment and identification of account on which monies were drawn;

e. Date of sale and sales price;

f. Contributions made by you to acquire, preserve, and maintain it;

g. Present fair market value and your basis for determining said value;

h. Any mortgage or lien balances encumbering the property and names and addresses of mortgagor or lien holder.

The only real property I own is owned jointly with my husband, the Defendant. The down payment was from $10,000 I saved before married and a $10,000 gift from my parents. Jack earned more so contributed more towards the mortgage payment. He repaired the roof in 1999. I did extensive landscaping and interior remodeling such as painting, new trim, and refinishing the hardwood floors. A copy of the current Realty-Smealty brokers appraisal is included for valuation.

ANSWER TO INTERROGATORY NO. 8

Since the date of your marriage, have you have received any gifts, legacies, devises or inheritances with a value in excess of $250, or are you, were or have become in said period a beneficiary of any trust or estate? If so, please state the value, source it was received from, date received, name of donor, value, basis for estimating said value, share you are entitled to receive, date you are entitled to receive, and cost of any fees.

None.

ANSWER TO INTERROGATORY NO. 9

Please list all financial accounts in which you and/or your agents and nominees have or had any interest, whether held jointly, individually or by another for your benefit at any time since September 11, 1994. For each account, state:

    a.   The name of the account;

    b.   The name and address of the institution in which the account is or was held;

    c.   The account number;

    d.   The current balance and/or present value for each such account; and

    e.   The balance in each such account as of January 1, of the current and last four calendar years and the balance of each account as of the date of your answers.

All accounts are listed in my financial statement already forwarded to you.

ANSWER TO INTERROGATORY NO. 10

Since September 11, 1994 , have you or has anyone on your behalf either individually or jointly maintained any safety deposit boxes, vaults or safes, or other depositories for safekeeping? If so, please state the location and identify each such depository and the identities of other individuals having access to same. Please also list the contents since January 1, 2002 that have been and/or are presently contained therein.

> *Box 2345 at Big Bank, 33 Main Street, Anytown. The box contains no valuables, only photocopies of the deed to the house, my expired term-life insurance policy, and our homeowner's policy.*

ANSWER TO INTERROGATORY NO. 11

Please state all stocks, bonds, bearer bonds, custodial accounts, treasury notes, certificates of deposit or other securities or investments of any type, including without limitation, tax free investments, in which you have a legal or equitable interest, whether held by you jointly, individually or with another, or in trust, or held by another for your benefit at any time since the date of your marriage to the Plaintiff, including:

    a.   the name of the security, bond or investment;

    b.   the face value or number of shares as applicable;

    c.   the CUSIP number of each bond;

    d.   the name of the depository or investment account and any account number; and

    e.   the maturity date(s) of any certificate of deposit.

None.

ANSWER TO INTERROGATORY NO. 12

Please describe in detail the conduct of the Husband which you claim is relevant in this case.

> *The husband drank and physically abused me, as proven in the 209A restraining order hearing.*

ANSWER TO INTERROGATORY NO. 13

Have you engaged in sexual relations with any individual other than your spouse at any time during your marriage to Plaintiff? If so, please state the following:

    a.   Name and address of each such individual;

    b.   Dates and locations of such conduct;

c.   Any and all financial contributions and payments made by you to each person named and/or from him/her to you or on your behalf, and include all sources from which such funds were derived.

No.

ANSWER TO INTERROGATORY NO. 14

Have you made any gifts or loans of, or transferred title to or possession of, real or personal property valued at $100 or more within the past five years? If so, and for each loan, gift, or transfer, please state the date of the event, the nature and value of the gift, loan or transfer, the name, address and relationship to you, if any, of the party to whom such loan, gift or transfer was made. If you are describing a loan, please state the terms of the loan and whether there is a writing evidencing such loan.

We gave my Husband's sister a $500 wedding present in 2005. Other than that, none.

ANSWER TO INTERROGATORY NO. 15

Please provide the details of each and every admission you have had to a hospital and/or health or mental health care facility since the date of your marriage to the [Plaintiff]/[Defendant] to the present, including in your answer the following:

(a)   the name(s) of each such hospital and/or health or mental health care facility;

(b)   the name(s) of each physician who admitted you and/or treated you;

(c)   the length of each admission;

(d)   the symptom(s) you were experiencing for which you were admitted in each instance;

(e)   the diagnosis or diagnoses for each admission; and,

(f)   the discharge order(s) and prognosis upon discharge from each such hospital and/or health or mental health care facility.

The requested information is protected under the physician-patient and/or psychologist-patient privilege

Signed under the pains and penalties of perjury of law this <u>14</u>th day of <u>April, 2007</u>:

Respectfully submitted,

<u>   Jane Doe   </u>
Jane Doe-Rayme, Plaintiff, pro se

CERTIFICATE OF SERVICE

I, <u>Jane Doe-Rayme</u>, the Plaintiff in the above-captioned case, did serve a copy of this Plaintiff's Answers to Defendant's Interrogatories upon the Plaintiff, <u>Jack Rayme</u>, on <u>April 14, 2007</u> via the following method (check method):

o   sheriff's service

o   in hand

X   mailing via USPS first class mail, postage prepaid

Signed under the pains and penalties of perjury of law this <u>14</u>th day of <u>April, 2007</u>.

<u>   Jane Doe   </u>

EXPERT INTERROGATORIES

An "expert" witness is any witness you or your husband plan to call to testify to render an *opinion* about a subject which is beyond the normal expertise of the average person. Because somebody is an expert in their field, their opinion would normally carry more weight than yours or mine. A policeman is an expert about crime, a real estate agent is an expert about the housing market, a doctor is an expert about medical conditions, and a mechanic is an expert about car repairs. Sometimes, a person who doesn't have lots of credentials but who has lots of experience in a given area may also be considered an "expert" witness. To get a good idea of how this may happen, I suggest you rent the movie "My Cousin Vinny" and watch what happens when the protagonist Vinny Gamboni calls his girlfriend Mona Lisa to the stand to testify about automobiles.

For discovery purposes, what matters to *you*, the small woodland creature, is that you need to know whether or not your husband will be calling any expert witnesses to testify on their behalf, who these expert witnesses are, what their credentials are, what they will be testifying about, and what they will be relying upon. Therefore, the smart woodland creature will use at least a few of their precious thirty (30) interrogatories to ask about potential expert witnesses.

A sample Expert Interrogatories follows:

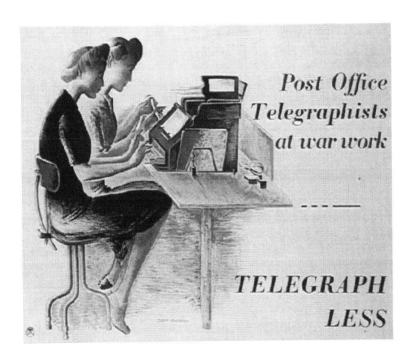

EXHIBIT 15-17: SAMPLE EXPERT INTERROGATORIES

COMMONWEALTH OF MASSACHUSETTS
PROBATE AND FAMILY COURT

BARNSTABLE, SS.   **DOCKET NO. 07D-9999-DV1**

JANE DOE-RAYME,   )
    Plaintiff   )   **EXPERT INTERROGATORIES**
v.   )   **PROPOUNDED BY THE PLAINTIFF**
JACK RAYME,   )   **TO BE ANSWERED UNDER OATH**
    Defendant   )   **BY THE DEFENDANT**
)

Now comes the Plaintiff, Jane Doe-Rayme, and propounds the following Interrogatories to be answered by the Defendant, Jack Rayme. These Interrogatories are to be deemed continuing in nature, requiring supplemental answers thereto to the extent required by Rule 26(e), Federal Rules of Civil Procedure and Massachusetts Rules of Domestic Relations Procedure.

1. With respect to all witnesses whom you will or may call as experts to give opinion testimony in the trial of this matter, state the following:

   (a) Name and address;

   (b) Name and address of his or her employer or the organization with which he or she is associated in any professional capacity;

   (c) The field in which he or she is or may be offered as an expert;

   (d) A summary of his or her qualifications within the field in which he or she is expected to testify;

   (e) The substance of the facts to which he or she is expected to testify;

   (f) The substance of the opinions to which he or she is expected to testify and a summary of the grounds for each opinion; and

   (g) State the dates and addresses of all reports rendered by such experts.

2. With respect to all experts retained or specially employed in anticipation of litigation or preparation for trial in this case, who are not expected to testify, please state the following:

   (a) Name and address;

   (b) Name and address of his or her employer or the organization with which he or she is associated in any professional capacity; and

   (c) State the dates and addresses of all reports rendered by such experts.

Date: March 30, 2007   Respectfully submitted,

                                                _____Jane Doe_____
                                                Jane Doe-Rayme, Plaintiff, pro se

CERTIFICATE OF SERVICE

I, Jane Doe-Rayme, the Plaintiff in the above-captioned case, did serve a copy of this Plaintiff's First Set of Interrogatories upon the Plaintiff, Jack Rayme, on March 30, 2007 via the following method (check method):
- ○ sheriff's service
- ○ in hand
- X mailing via USPS first class mail, postage prepaid

Signed under the pains and penalties of perjury of law this _30_ th day of March, 2007.

                                                _____Jane Doe_____

As with all other discovery requests, if *you* receive an Expert Interrogatory, you would answer it the same way you did all the others. Go through your husband's request, line by line, restate it, and then answer it to the best of your ability.

EXHIBIT 15-18: SAMPLE ANSWERS TO EXPERT INTERROGATORIES

COMMONWEALTH OF MASSACHUSETTS

BARNSTABLE, SS.   **PROBATE AND FAMILY COURT   DOCKET NO. <u>07D-9999-DV1</u>**

JANE DOE-RAYME,   )
    Plaintiff   )
 v.   )
 JACK RAYME,   )
    Defendant   )
)
	PLAINTIFF'S RESPONSE TO DEFENDANT'S EXPERT INTERROGATORIES

Now comes the Plaintiff, <u>Jane Doe-Rayme</u>, and answers the Defendant's Expert Interrogatories under oath as follows:

1. With respect to all witnesses whom you will or may call as experts to give opinion testimony in the trial of this matter, state the following:
   (a) Name and address;
   (b) Name and address of his or her employer or the organization with which he or she is associated in any professional capacity;
   (c) The field in which he or she is or may be offered as an expert;
   (d) A summary of his or her qualifications within the field in which he or she is expected to testify;
   (e) The substance of the facts to which he or she is expected to testify;
   (f) The substance of the opinions to which he or she is expected to testify and a summary of the grounds for each opinion; and
   (g) State the dates and addresses of all reports rendered by such experts.

   The Plaintiff has no expert witnesses at this time; however, if the Husband intends to contend the reality of Jayne's ongoing learning disability, the Wife intends to call personnel from Jayne's school, tutor, and neurologist. The Wife reserves the right to locate an expert and update this answer at any time during the proceedings if she later finds it necessary to hire an expert witness.

2. With respect to all experts retained or specially employed in anticipation of litigation or preparation for trial in this case, who are not expected to testify, please state the following:
   (a) Name and address;
   (b) Name and address of his or her employer or the organization with which he or she is associated in any professional capacity; and
   (c) State the dates and addresses of all reports rendered by such experts.

   None. The Wife reserves the right to retain an expert and update this Answer as necessary at any time during the proceedings..

Date: April 14, 2007   Respectfully submitted,
                                     <u>   Jane Doe   </u>
                                     Jane Doe-Rayme, Plaintiff, pro se

CERTIFICATE OF SERVICE

I, <u>Jane Doe-Rayme</u>, the Plaintiff in the above-captioned case, did serve a copy of this Plaintiff's First Set of Interrogatories upon the Plaintiff, <u>Jack Rayme</u>, on <u>March 30, 2007</u> via the following method (check method):
- o   sheriff's service
- o   in hand
- X   mailing via USPS first class mail, postage prepaid

Signed under the pains and penalties of perjury of law this <u> 14 </u> th day of <u> April, 2007</u>.
                                           <u>   Jane Doe   </u>

DEPOSITIONS

A deposition is an out-of-court hearing, under oath, where one or more of the litigants subpoena's another litigant, a witness, or other person possessing relevant information to the case to testify under oath in a special recorded session. You must give the opposing party notice of the hearing and an opportunity to ask questions of their own. Except in the case of medical or psychological privileges, you are generally required to answer all of the questioning attorneys' questions, no matter how private or embarrassing, no matter how irrelevant the questions may seem, and no matter if the information requested is of a type which would normally be barred by the court at an actual trial or hearing.

Some types of depositions - the Rules are different about how each type of deposition is done:

- *Deposition of a Party Opponent* - when you and your husband depose each other to discover information relevant to the case. Often used to catch the opposing party in lies which can be used to impugn their credibility later at trial.
- *Keeper of the Records Deposition* - when you depose a third party, usually to obtain, explain, and verify the veracity of documents that person, business or government entity may have in their possession.
- *Deposition of an Expert Witness* - when you depose each other's expert witnesses to get an idea of what they may testify about at court. You depose them *before* trial in the hopes you can then dig up information to discredit them.
- *Deposition of a Non-Party Witness* - when you depose the other side's potential witnesses or people related to your case. For example, you depose your husband's brother about the so-called $150,000 'loan' your husband gave him shortly before he filed for divorce against you, and then claimed bankruptcy.

A FEW
CARELESS WORDS
MAY END IN THIS—

Many lives were lost in the last war through careless talk. Be on your guard! Don't discuss movements of ships or troops

Some questioning attorneys use the deposition as an opportunity to threaten or "show" the other side how uncomfortable they are going to make them feel if the case goes to trial. Others will act as if they are your best friend, understanding your side of the case, making fun of their own client, and then "turning" on you once you have foolishly given them your trust. Everything you say at a deposition *will* be used against you in a court of law. Depositions are usually held at an attorney's office and are typically recorded by a special private stenographer who can then listen to and translate the recorded session into a written question and answer script. Sometimes depositions are videotaped. Depositions can last anywhere from several hours to several days.

Depositions are heavy-handed for most low-asset divorce cases because of the cost involved versus the potential benefit. Unlike other types of litigation, you and your spouse know each other intimately. The only word of advice I can give to a small woodland creature who cannot afford an attorney is, if subpoenaed to a deposition, say as little as possible and *do not* volunteer a single piece of information unless directly asked for it. Watch the movie "A Civil Action" to get an idea of what a deposition might be like. Pay special attention to how the deposed factory manager's evasive answers about how the toxic chemicals got into the river, which the protagonist is unable to figure out in time to help his clients at trial, suddenly causes the light bulb to go off in his head at the end of the movie.

COMMONWEALTH OF MASSACHUSETTS
PROBATE AND FAMILY COURT

BARNSTABLE, SS.

DOCKET NO. <u>07D-9999-DV1</u>

JANE DOE-RAYME.)
    Plaintiff,)
)
v.)
)
)
JACK RAYME)
    Defendant.)
)

NOTICE OF DEPOSITION OF PLAINTIFF
JANE DOE-RAYME PURSUANT TO FED.R.CIV.P. 30(b)(6)

To: Jane Doe
        100 Main Street
        North Anytown, MA 02550

PLEASE TAKE NOTICE that on Monday, March 30, 2004, at 9:00 a.m., and continuing from day to day thereafter until completed, at the offices of Rob M. Cheatem, Esq., 666 Elm Street, Nextown, Massachusetts 02666, Defendant Jack Rayme will take the deposition of plaintiff Jane Doe-Rayme. pursuant to Fed.R.Civ.P. and Mass. R. Civ. P. 30(b)(6), before a Notary Public or other officer authorized by law to administer oaths.

    Pursuant to Mass. R. Civ. P. 30(b)(6), Jane Doe-Rayme. is required to testify as to matters known or reasonably available to the divorce.

    Counsel to Jack Rayme will utilize "real time" transcription technology during the course of the deposition. You are invited to attend and to cross-examine.

                JACK RAYME.

                By his attorney,

                _____

                Rob M. Cheatem, Esq. (BBO No. 475650)
                STALL, HINDER & DELAY, LLP
                666 Elm Street
                Nextown, Massachusetts 02666
                (508) 666-9999

Dated: March 13, 2004

Because depositions must be held at a special location, recorded by a special stenographer, and then cost thousands of dollars to transcribe, and also because your husband is probably going to retaliate by deposing you, your family, your boss, and every person you know, I do not recommend small woodland creatures attempt to depose the evil trapper on their own. If your marriage is an abusive one, it may escalate the situation. Always hide behind an attorney when you depose somebody so that your spouse is mad at *them* and not just you. If you get subpoenaed to a deposition, hire an attorney if you can at all afford it. If not, answer questions honestly, but volunteer as little as possible.

If your husband can afford to hire an attorney, an office location, and a stenographer to launch a deposition, chances are he has access to money you should be entitled to share pendente lite for your own legal defense. Even if you were turned down before, file a new Motion for Attorney Fees Pendente Lite along with a Motion to Quash (sample follows) and bring this to the judge's attention.

If you have a Restraining Order against your husband and cannot afford to hire an attorney, you may be able to get a judge to quash (stop) the deposition. File a "Motion to Quash" and simultaneously file a "Motion for Attorney Fees Pendente Lite" requesting that the judge order your husband to loan you enough money to hire an attorney to represent you. Some judges may be bothered enough at the prospect of a batterer having an out-of-court opportunity to intimidate and harass you (especially if there is not much justification for holding a deposition) to either quash (kill) the deposition or order your husband to front the money for an attorney.

A sample "Motion to Quash" follows. This is *not* a typical "boilerplate" motion to quash used by attorneys (who are usually dealing with much more wealthy clients), but rather a desperate attempt by a small woodland creature to bring the inequity of the situation to the judge's attention. Sometimes, even if the judge won't quash it completely, you can get him to limit the scope of the deposition.

EXHIBIT 15-20: SAMPLE MOTION TO QUASH DEPOSITION

COMMONWEALTH OF MASSACHUSETTS

BARNSTABLE, SS.	**PROBATE AND FAMILY COURT**	**DOCKET NO. 07D-9999-DV1**

JANE DOE-RAYME,)
   Plaintiff)
)   **MOTION TO QUASH/**
v.)   **FOR PROTECTIVE ORDER**
JACK RAYME,)
   Defendant)
)

Now comes Jane Doe-Rayme, plaintiff in the above-captioned divorce action, and hereby requests that this Honorable Court quash the deposition subpoena served on her and issue a protective order pursuant to Mass.R.Dom.Rel.P. 26(c).

In support of this request, the Plaintiff states that the Defendant issued a subpoena requiring her to attend a deposition and to bring to the deposition documents described on a Schedule attached to the subpoena, a copy of which is attached hereto as Exhibit A and incorporated here.

There is a 209A restraining order in effect barring the Defendant from contacting the Plaintiff. The Plaintiff does not have an attorney and cannot afford to hire one on her income, whereas the Defendant's financial statement shows he was somehow able to afford to give his attorney a $15,000 retainer to handle his case despite his claims of having no money. The Plaintiff has complied with every document and other discovery request made by the Defendant to date. Plaintiff believes the Defendant is only hosting the prospect of facing her abuser in a deposition without the benefit of court personnel to protect her from physical harm as an attempt to intimidate the Plaintiff into major concessions in the divorce.

The Defendant's attempt to depose the Plaintiff and to require her to bring the demanded documents is harassment, an annoyance, embarrassing, oppressive, and causes undue burden and expense.

WHEREFORE, the Plaintiff, Jane Doe-Rayme, hereby requests that this Honorable Court quash the subpoena and issue a protective order:

1. Quashing the deposition, or, in the alternative; requiring the deposition to be held on court property and supervised by a court officer at the Defendant's expense;
2. That the Defendant be ordered to forward her $11,000 Pendente Lite to hire an attorney to handle her case (the amount requested by two separate attorneys interviewed by the Plaintiff).
3. That the scope of the deposition be limited to financial matters and that matters of the Wife's and Children's privileged communications with their therapists not be inquired into; and
4. That, if the court chooses not to quash the deposition, that it be conducted with no one present except the Husband's attorney and a friend of the Wife (who cannot afford an attorney) to provide moral support.

Date: March 30, 2007   Respectfully submitted,

                                                  _____Jane Doe_____
                                                Jane Doe-Rayme, Plaintiff, pro se

NOTICE OF HEARING

The following "Motion to Quash" has been scheduled for hearing at __9:00__ A.M. on __June 10th__, 2007 at the Barnstable County Probate and Family Court.

Date: __May 14, 2007__   _____Jane Doe-Rayme_____

CERTIFICATE OF SERVICE

I, Jane Doe-Rayme, the Plaintiff in the above-captioned case, did serve a copy of this Motion to Quash and Notice of Hearing upon the Plaintiff, Jack Rayme, on May 14, 2007 via the following method (check method):

- o sheriff's service
- o in hand
- X mailing via USPS first class mail, postage prepaid

Signed under the pains and penalties of perjury of law this _14_ th day of _____ May, 2007.

                                                  _____Jane Doe_____

Sometimes it is not *you* your husband will go after, but the people who are trying to help you get away from him. Most of the time, if he subpoenas them into a deposition or court hearing to force them to give him documents or testify, there is not a lot you can do about it. But sometimes the information your husband seeks is so sensitive that society has deemed it inadmissible. If the information falls into one of the 'sensitive' categories carved out by the legislature, it is said to be privileged.

 *Privileged Information - An exchange of information between two individuals in a confidential relationship.*

Privileged communications exist because society values the privacy or purpose of certain relationships. Privilege is like a band aid. It covers certain communication to protect it from outside influence. Some forms of privilege are common sense, such as medical information divulged to your physician, legal issues divulged to your attorney, or psychological issues divulged to your therapist. If everything you said to your doctor, attorney, or therapist could be aired in open court on a whim, you would never seek help for your medical, legal, or psychological problems, would you? On the other hand, other privileged areas are rather stupid, such as the husband/wife privilege *continuing* to exist *even during a divorce trial* where the divorce may be based upon communications made between the two of you! The most important thing you need to know about privileged information for divorce purposes is that, if your husband is looking to get his hands on it, you may be able to block it.

What is privileged and not privileged is the subject of enormous amounts of case law and confusion. It also varies from state to state. Therefore, if you run up against an area which you think may be privileged, I strongly suggest you obtain a copy of your local bar associations guide to the rules of evidence and read up on the nuances of each privileged area. Generally, privileged areas will be barred unless there is a strong reason to override that privilege and, if so, the court will usually institute certain procedures to shield the information from public scrutiny such as appointing a special GAL to review the information or holding closed hearings when hearing such evidence.

⚑ **If someone else was in the room when the communication occurred, there will usually be no privilege.**

Here are the most well-known classes of privilege:

1. Physician/Patient (including medical records) – all communications made to a physician for the purposes of seeking diagnosis and treatment, including your medical records, have a certain degree of protection.

2. Psychotherapist/patient (including records) – all communications made to a psychiatrist, psychologist, social worker or psychotherapist (the term "therapist" varies in some states) made for the purposes of seeking diagnosis and treatment of a psychological disorder. This includes communications made by your children to *their* therapist!!! A parent *does not* have the untrammeled right to simply access privileged communications between the child and their therapist, although many lawyers and

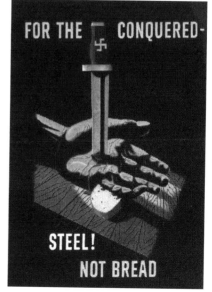

judges have a lot of confusion about this fact.

3. Clergy/communicant - what you communicate in the confessional for the purposes of seeking absolution for your sins is considered privileged.

4. Attorney-Client Privilege – all communications made between you and your lawyer are privileged, whether verbal or written.

5. Husband-Wife Privilege – all communications made between you and your spouse are privileged *except* in the case of restraining order hearing. Therefore, if your husband has been blatantly telling you what a rotten person he is and what terrible things he's done for years, you can't get his statements into evidence *unless* somebody else was in the room and also heard it.

Tell NOBODY— not even HER

CARELESS TALK COSTS LIVES

For more detailed information about privilege and other evidentiary issues, I recommend your hands on a 'Evidentiary Foundations,' by Edward J. Imwinkelried. Used copies can be bought online for as little as $20 with shipping. Although the Rules of Evidence shift slightly from year to year and state to state, even an older version of this book will get you through most evidentiary issues.

If your husband requests privileged information in one of his discovery requests, you must state you cannot disclose that information due to the existence of a privilege and state the privilege (this will be covered later). If he persists and tries to get that information by serving a subpoena to get your medical (or similarly privileged) records or attempts to depose your therapist, for example, you can file a "Motion to Quash" to block them from getting their hands on that information.

A sample "Motion to Quash" follows:

EXHIBIT 15-21: MOTION TO QUASH SUBPOENA - PRIVILEGED INFORMATION

COMMONWEALTH OF MASSACHUSETTS

PROBATE AND FAMILY COURT

BARNSTABLE, SS.   DOCKET NO. <u>07D-9999-DV1</u>

JANE DOE-RAYME,)	
Plaintiff)	**MOTION TO QUASH**
v.)	**SUBPOENA PURSUANT TO**
JACK RAYME,)	**FED.R.CIV.P.45(b) and**
Defendant)	**MASS.R.DOM.REL.P.45(b)**
)	

Now comes Tammy Therapist, M.S.W., a therapist at Outer Cape Therapy Associates, and states that she is a person directed by subpoena to produce copies of all psychological evaluations, notes, correspondence and records and any other documents relative to her consultation and treatment of Jane Doe-Rayme. Said subpoena was served by Defendant's attorney.

Tammy Therapist, M.S.W., moves this Honorable Court to quash said subpoena in accordance with Fed.R.Civ.Pro. 45(b) and Mass.R.Dom.Rel.P. 45(b) for the reason that said information is privileged in accordance with G.L. c. 233, § 20(B) and may not be disclosed to opposing counsel.

Date: July 1, 2007   Respectfully submitted,

                                          <u>   Jane Doe   </u>
                                          Jane Doe-Rayme, Plaintiff, pro se

NOTICE OF HEARING

The following "Motion to Quash Subpoena" has been scheduled for hearing at   <u> 9:00   </u> A.M. on <u> July 8th </u>, 2007 at the Barnstable County Probate and Family Court.

Date: <u> July 1, 2007   </u>   <u>   Jane Doe-Rayme   </u>

CERTIFICATE OF SERVICE

I, <u>Jane Doe-Rayme</u>, the Plaintiff in the above-captioned case, did serve a copy of this Motion to Quash Subpoena and Notice of Hearing upon the Plaintiff, <u>Jack Rayme</u>, on <u>July 1</u>, 20<u>07</u> via the following method (check method):
- o   sheriff's service
- o   in hand
- X   mailing via USPS first class mail, postage prepaid

Signed under the pains and penalties of perjury of law this <u>1st</u> day of <u>   July, 20</u><u>07</u>.

                                            <u>   Jane Doe-Rayme   </u>

WHAT DO I DO IF MY HUSBAND IGNORES MY DISCOVERY REQUESTS?

By now you should have given your husband your *own* court-ordered Financial Statement and Mandatory Self-Disclosure Documents. Hopefully you've been to your Temporary Orders Hearing, gotten *his* Financial Statement. But what happens if you send him your Discovery requests (Mandatory Self-Disclosure, Request for Documents, Admissions, Interrogatories, Expert Interrogatories, etc.) and thirty days pass, and nothing. Now what?

Compelling the other side to produce information can be like pulling teeth. Some of it is laziness on the part of the opposing attorney. Many attorneys are in the bad habit of simply forwarding the request to their client and letting *them* bear the consequences if they don't get it back on time. If *you* aren't diligent about holding the other side's feet to the fire with the threat of sanctions, you will probably never get a response. If your husband is a "deadbeat client" (i.e., they aren't following their own lawyers advice and aren't paying their legal bills in a prompt manner), their lawyer will not chase them to get *your* documents. Other attorneys are simply busy. They forward the requests, they might remember to send their clients a reminder letter when they are due, but they won't keep calling their client at $300 per hour to make excuses for them.

It is up to you to hold your husband's feet to the fire by following through on y our threats of sanctions and force him to cough up information!!!

A third genre of attorneys are what we call "guerrilla fighters." There is actually a trade publication called "Guerrilla Discovery" which lists hundreds of ways to *avoid* giving the other side what they want for the sole purpose of running your opponent into the ground financially. If you are paying your attorney $300 per hour and they have to keep sending, re-sending, filing motions, going to hearings, re-re-sending, reviewing incomplete document requests with slippery, evasive answers, filing more motions, going to more hearings, and re-re-sending more and more specific information requests to pin the sleazy opposing attorney into a corner, you will go broke. These attorneys give lawyers a bad name. I have been on the receiving end of these tactics and, unfortunately, my clients usually end up burning through their retainer before we ever get the requested information.

If you can't afford an attorney, you can still use the exact same methods of forcing your husband to cough up information that your attorney would. Most husbands are simply too lazy to stand in front of the photocopier to give them what you need. If you serve them with a Motion to Compel and for Sanctions, most men will get over their inertia. If your husband is being evasive, you must be diligent about following through on your threat to haul him before the judge. He will quickly learn to behave because he doesn't want to keep paying his lawyer $1000 per hearing day to make excuses.

The court has very detailed rules about how to navigate discovery disputes. What do you do if, as is often the case, 30 days pass (45 if it is your initial Mandatory self-disclosure request), you have given your spouse *your* share of the documents, but nothing happens? Your husband will whine about how expensive or what a nuisance it is to produce these documents, or he will claim he can't get them, or he doesn't have them. Mark the 30th (45th if initial Mandatory Self-Disclosure) day on your calendar (keeping a calendar is very important). On the 31st (46th) day, mail him a reminder letter, one certified mail, the other priority mail with a delivery confirmation, informing him that if he doesn't comply with the request, you will be forced to file a motion in court to make him comply. Mark a reminder for yourself on your calendar another 30 days out. A sample "Reminder Letter" follows:

EXHIBIT 15-22: SAMPLE REMINDER LETTER RE: DISCOVERY REQUESTS

Jane Doe-Rayme
100 Any Street
North Anytown, MA 02763

May 7, 2007

Andy Ambulancechaser, Esq.
Stall, Hinder & Delay, PC
500 Commerce Way
30th Floor
Boston, MA 01111

RE: Plaintiff's Discovery Requests

Dear Attorney Ambulancechaser:

On March 30, 2007, I mailed to your office the following discovery requests:

1. Plaintiff's Request for the Production of Documents
2. Plaintiff's First Set of Interrogatories
3. Plaintiff's Expert Interrogatories
4. Plaintiff's Request for Admissions of Fact

Those discovery requests were due no later than May 3, 2007. I have not received them to this date. Please forward the requested information immediately to avoid the unpleasantness of a Motion to Compel Discovery and Sanctions.

I am enclosing another copy of my information requests for your convenience.

Sincerely,

Jane Doe-Rayme

Encl: copy – 4/1/07 Request for Documents
         Copy – 4/1/07 Interrogatories
         Copy – 4/1/07 Expert Interrogatories
         Copy – 4/1/07 Request for Admissions

Ignore any irate phone calls from him. If he hires an attorney, that attorney may very well think you are stupid and mail you a letter stating that the requested documents are unavailable. What does "unavailable" mean? Well, legally, unavailable is a fairly high hurdle. It means there is no way possible, ever, to get hold of a document because a nuclear bomb blew up the archives –and- the bank computer which held copies of it. It's too darned bad if he has to pay a fee to get it if it's a document listed in the Rule 410 documents. On the other hand, if it is not a Rule 410 document and you are willing to pay the reasonable cost to obtain it, say so (and thus remove the excuse). Therefore, on the 31st day after you mailed the reminder letter, file a "Motion to Compel." For simplicities sake, in the sample motion I have combined all outstanding discovery requests into one "Motion to Compel Discovery." However, if you have a lot of facts you are trying to pin down for trial, it is perfectly acceptable to draft and schedule a separate motion for each outstanding genre of discovery request (documents, admissions, interrogatories, or expert interrogatories) so that you have more room to request sanctions.

EXHIBIT 15-23: SAMPLE COVER LETTER RE: MOTION TO COMPEL DISCOVERY

Jane Doe-Rayme
100 Any Street
North Anytown, MA 02763

June 8, 2007

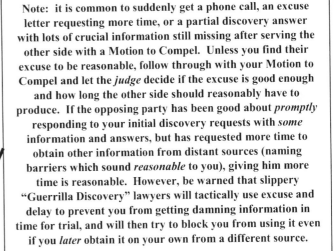

Note: it is common to suddenly get a phone call, an excuse letter requesting more time, or a partial discovery answer with lots of crucial information still missing after serving the other side with a Motion to Compel. Unless you find their excuse to be reasonable, follow through with your Motion to Compel and let the *judge* decide if the excuse is good enough and how long the other side should reasonably have to produce. If the opposing party has been good about *promptly* responding to your initial discovery requests with *some* information and answers, but has requested more time to obtain other information from distant sources (naming barriers which sound *reasonable* to you), giving him more time is reasonable. However, be warned that slippery "Guerrilla Discovery" lawyers will tactically use excuse and delay to prevent you from getting damning information in time for trial, and will then try to block you from using it even if you *later* obtain it on your own from a different source.

Andy Ambulancechaser, Esq.
Stall, Hinder & Delay, PC
500 Commerce Way
30th Floor
Boston, MA 01111

RE: Outstanding Discovery

Dear Attorney Ambulancechaser:

Please find the following motion:

1.   Plaintiff's Motion to Compel Discovery and for Sanctions

The enclosed motion is scheduled for hearing at 9:00 a.m. on June 27, 2007.

Sincerely,

Jane Doe-Rayme

Call the scheduling clerk to schedule your "Motion to Compel Discovery" for a hearing, include a "Notice of Hearing" to each motion you file along with a proof of service affidavit, and mail two copies (one certified mail, one first class with a proof of mailing receipt) to him (or his lawyer if he has one). It is good practice to reference as Exhibits and staple a copy of each outstanding discovery request and all reminder letters to your motion (don't forget to give the clerk a copy of all motions/supporting documents). *The stapler is your friend.* It is okay to mail your motion(s), notice(s) of hearing, affidavit(s) of service, and copies to your husband in one big envelope, just be sure if you break apart your Motions to Compel into separate motions that *each* motion is separately scheduled for the same hearing day with the clerk and a separate notice of hearing/affidavit is included.

99% of the time, the requested documents will appear before the hearing. If that happens, call the clerk and ask them to withdraw your motion without prejudice.

If you have to appear for a discovery dispute hearing, you will need to explain why you find his "can't get it" or his lawyers' unavailability claim is not credible. Except for claims the information is "privileged" (explanation to follow later in a later caption), or that the information does not exist (for example, you serve a boilerplate request for "all insurance policies with a cash value" and your husband honestly writes back "none" because his insurance policy is term life with no cash value), there is rarely a legitimate excuse for failing to cough up the information. Simply explaining that *you* were able to get at least one statement in the series simply by asking the bank for it/going on line/digging through the icky spider closet will usually suffice to get an order to comply or else.

On several occasions, I have had attorneys ignore discovery requests despite several trips to the courthouse on Motions to Compel. Judges tend to take an attorneys word that they "will forward it" and not institute sanctions unless a pattern of evasion becomes blatantly obvious. However, this did not mean you have no recourse. At trial, if the opposing attorney attempts to introduce evidence or pursue a line of questioning based on the foundation of the missing information, remind the judge of the opposing parties non-response to the previous court order (or promise) and ask the judge to exclude that entire line of questioning. Judge's may be loathe to babysit discovery disputes, but they are just as loathe to allow one party to "fight dirty" at trial.

A sample Motion to Compel Discovery and For Sanctions follows:

EXHIBIT 15-24: MOTION TO COMPEL DISCOVERY AND FOR SANCTIONS

COMMONWEALTH OF MASSACHUSETTS

BARNSTABLE, SS. **PROBATE AND FAMILY COURT** **DOCKET NO. <u>07D-9999-DV1</u>**

JANE DOE-RAYME,)
    Plaintiff)
)
v.)
)
JACK RAYME,)
    Defendant)
_____)
	MOTION TO COMPEL
	DISCOVERY
	AND FOR SANCTIONS

NOW COMES Jane Doe-Rayme, Plaintiff, in the above-captioned action, and hereby requests, pursuant to Mass.R.Dom.Rel.P. 26(f) and 37(d) that this Honorable Court order: (1) the Defendant, Jack Rayme, to respond to Plaintiff's First Request for Production of Documents dated April 1, 2007, (the "Document Request"), (2) the Defendant, Jack Rayme, to respond to Plaintiff's First Request for Admissions of Fact dated April 1, 2007, (the "Admissions"), (3) the Defendant, Jack Rayme, to respond to Plaintiff's First Set of Interrogatories dated April 1, 2007, (the "Interrogatories"), (4) the Defendant, Jack Rayme, to respond to Plaintiff's Expert Interrogatories dated April 1, 2007, (the "Expert Interrogatories"), and (5) sanctions for failing to respond to the four above-listed discovery requests as follows:

a. That the Defendant pay Plaintiff's expenses, including attorneys' fees, incurred as a result of his failure and/or refusal to respond to the Plaintiff's above-mentioned four discovery requests;

b. That the Defendant serve a response to and produce all documents and/or information responsive to the Document Request, Admissions, Interrogatories, and Expert Interrogatories on or before July 10, 2007;

c. That Defendant be prohibited from presenting any evidence supporting or opposing the following claims: (1) that the defendant has at least $20,000 in a secret Merrily-Merrily Retirement stock account, and (2) that the Defendant is still working as a licensed Home Improvement Contractor, or from introducing in evidence the following matters: (1) the defendant's secret $20,000 stock account, (2) the Defendant's employment;

d. That the following facts shall be taken as established in the pending divorce action(s): (1) the defendant has $20,000 in a Merrily-Merrily Retirement stock account which is a joint marital asset subject to division; and (2) the defendant is still working full-time as a licensed home improvement contractor;

e. That the following pleading(s) (or the following part(s) of pleading(s)) be stricken: that portion of the Husband's financial statement which willfully omits the existence of a $20,000 Merrily-Merrily Retirement stock account and his income from full-time self-employment as a licensed home improvement contractor;

f. That further proceedings be stayed until the Defendant serves responses to the Document Request, Admissions, Interrogatories, and Expert Interrogatories; and produces all documents requested therein;

g. That the willful failure of the Defendant to respond to the Document Request be treated as a contempt of court.

In support of her requests, the Plaintiff states as follows:

1. On April 1, 2007 the Plaintiff served the Document Request attached hereto as "Exhibit A". Responses to the Document Request were due on or before May 1, 2007. The Defendant has failed to respond to the Document Request that is now nearly two months past due.

2. On April 1, 2007 the Plaintiff served the Requests for Admissions of Fact attached hereto as "Exhibit B". Responses to the Admissions were due on or before May 1, 2007. The Defendant has failed to respond to the Document Request that is now nearly two months past due.

3. On April 1, 2007 the Plaintiff served the First Set of Interrogatories attached hereto as "Exhibit C". Responses to the Interrogatories were due on or before May 1, 2007. The Defendant has failed to respond to the Document Request that is now nearly two months past due.

4. On April 1, 2007 the Plaintiff served the Expert Interrogatories attached hereto as "Exhibit D". Responses to the Expert Interrogatories were due on or before May 1, 2007. The Defendant has failed to respond to the Document Request that is now nearly two months past due.

5. On May 7, 2007 the Plaintiff mailed a "reminder letter" (including another copy of all mentioned discovery

requests) requesting a response to the Plaintiff's discovery requests attached hereto as "Exhibit E". The Defendant has failed to respond to the reminder letter.

6. As a result of the Defendant's willful failure to respond to the Document Request, the Plaintiff has incurred expenses of $81.09. See Affidavit of Plaintiff as to Expenses and Fees, attached hereto as Exhibit F and incorporated herein.

Date: June 27, 2007

Respectfully submitted,

_____Jane Doe_____

Jane Doe-Rayme, Plaintiff, pro se

NOTICE OF HEARING

The following "Motion to Compel Discovery and for Sanctions" has been scheduled for hearing at ___9:00___ A.M. on __July 8th__, 2007 at the Barnstable County Probate and Family Court.

Date: __June 27, 2007__   _____Jane Doe-Rayme_____

CERTIFICATE OF SERVICE

I, Jane Doe-Rayme, the Plaintiff in the above-captioned case, did serve a copy of this Motion to Compel Discovery and for Sanctions, Affidavit of Plaintiff, supporting documents, and Notice of Hearing upon the Plaintiff, Jack Rayme, on June 27, 2007 via the following method (check method):

- o   sheriff's service
- o   in hand
- X   mailing via USPS first class mail, postage prepaid

Signed under the pains and penalties of perjury of law this _27_ th day of __June, 2007.

_____Jane Doe-Rayme_____

Note: when you initially serve the other side with your discovery requests, you do not file a copy with the court. However, if you find it necessary to file a Motion to Compel, you will need to attach a copy of the original documents (including your "certificates of service" and also any correspondence you may have sent in the meantime regarding these requests (such as your 30-day reminder letter). Attaching copies of your postal receipts (such as the cost of postage or certified mail) dated that same day bolsters your credibility.

Note: in our "Jane Doe" hypothetical, Jane has run into two major problems. She has evidence her husband is hiding a $20,000 stock account, and her husband is suddenly claiming he can't find work despite frequent telephone calls to the house from prospective customers looking to hire him. Her original discovery requests had questions aiming at clearing up some of these areas. As one possible sanction, Jane is requesting that the court bar any attempt by the husband at trial to claim he does *not* have a $20,000 stock account and *cannot* find work.

Note: this Motion to Compel lumps together all unanswered discovery requests. If you got some answers, but not others, or if the other side is being evasive, you would modify this sample to accommodate the situation.

EXHIBIT 15-25: AFFIDAVIT IN SUPPORT OF MOTION TO COMPEL DISCOVERY

COMMONWEALTH OF MASSACHUSETTS
PROBATE AND FAMILY COURT

BARNSTABLE, SS.

DOCKET NO. <u>07D-9999-DV1</u>

JANE DOE-RAYME,)
    Plaintiff)
v.)
JACK RAYME,)
    Defendant)
)

AFFIDAVIT IN SUPPORT OF
PLAINTIFF'S MOTION TO COMPEL
DISCOVERY
AND FOR SANCTIONS

The Plaintiff, Jane Doe-Rayme, does hereby swear and affirm the following facts:

1. On April 1, 2007, I served the attached "Request for the Production of Documents," "Request for Admissions of Fact," "Interrogatories," and "Expert Interrogatories" (Exhibits A-D) upon the Defendant, Jack Rayme's, attorney Andy Ambulancechaser, Esq., via USPS first class mail, postage prepaid, with a delivery confirmation, at a cost of $4.60 (receipt attached as Exhibit F). $ 4.60

2. On May 7, 2007, I mailed a "reminder letter" (Exhibit E) to the Defendant's attorney along with a second copy of all above-mentioned discovery requests via both USPS certified mail, return receipt requested *and* also simultaneously via USPS priority mail with a delivery confirmation at a cost of $8.40 (receipt attached as Exhibit G). There was a cost to photocopy two copies of this request and supporting documents plus an additional one for my records at Staples of $2.40 (receipt attached as Exhibit H). $ 10.80

3. On June 8, 2007, I mailed the subject "Motion to Compel the Production of Documents" via both USPS certified mail, return receipt requested *and* also simultaneously via USPS priority mail with a delivery confirmation at a cost of $4.60 (receipt attached as Exhibit I). The original was mailed to the courthouse via regular first class mail at a cost of $1.83 (also Exhibit I). I also incurred photocopying costs of $1.20 to make copies to distribute of these documents (receipt attached as Exhibit J). $ 7.63

4. I cannot afford an attorney to prosecute this action for me, but due to the Defendant's malfeasance, I am losing approximately 4 hours out of work this morning to prosecute this action at a cost to me of $11 per hour x 4 hours = $44, money which I can ill afford to lose. $ 44.00

5. To prosecute this action, I had to drive round-trip from North Anytown to the courthouse, a round trip mileage of 38 miles x .the IRS mileage rate of 37 per mile = $14.06. A "Mapquest.com" mileage tracker is attached as Exhibit K. $ 14.06

TOTAL COST TO PLAINTIFF $81.09

My total costs to date pursuing these documents is $81.09. I hereby request that this honorable court order the Defendant to reimburse me these costs.

Signed under the pains and penalties of perjury of law this <u>27th</u> day of <u>June,</u> 2007.

Date: June 27, 2007

Respectfully submitted,
      Jane Doe
Jane Doe-Rayme, Plaintiff, pro se

Note: Courts tend to forget to address your request for costs and sanctions at these hearings. Be sure to remind the judge to make a ruling on your requests. The judge is unlikely to award costs for Item 1 (cost to mail original discovery requests) and Item 3 (your lost wages), but he *may* decide to award you for the other three items. Include the items you are not sure about as the possibility the court might award your lost wages is an incentive for your husband to "cough up" without a hearing. It is important to convey to the court the true cost of your husband's noncompliance (if you had a lawyer, this motion would cost you $800-$1500).

CHAPTER FIFTEEN SUMMARY

1. Both parties are required to file accurate financial statements with each other and the court within 10 days of the filing of the divorce.

2. Most states require both parties to comply with court "Mandatory Self-Disclosure" within 45 days of the filing of the divorce.

3. If you need more information or want to get an idea of your husband's strategy in the case, there are ways to try to get the information, including document requests, requests for admissions of fact, and interrogatories. You can also depose the other side, but that is difficult and costly for a self-represented person.

4. If your husband avoids, evades, gives incomplete answers, or otherwise tries to ignore your information requests, you can file a Motion to Compel to get the court to order it. You can also sometimes get the court to sanction your husband, either financially or by barring certain categories of evidence at trial.

5. There are certain categories of information which are considered "privileged," i.e., private and not open to public scrutiny. If the other person requests information which you believe is privileged, refuse to give it, state the nature of the privilege, and make the other person go to court to get a court order over-riding the privilege. If your refusal is based on a legitimate privilege, the court will rarely sanction you for refusing to turn the information over without a court order. To learn more about privilege, refer to "evidence" handbooks published by your local state bar or continuing legal education association.

6. If your husband tries to go around your refusal to disclose privileged information by subpoenaing the person or documents directly (either to court or to a deposition), you can file a Motion to Quash to try to get the court to deny your husband the information. If he can't give a very good reason for needing it, the court will often refuse him.

7. To answer your husband's information requests, follow the format of the request he sent you and answer each question honestly line by line. Remember that you are signing under oath and that each admission can and will be used against you in court.

CHAPTER 16

THE PRE-TRIAL CONFERENCE

To prod you and your husband into narrowing the case down to a few contested issues and (hopefully) encourage you to reach an agreement on your own, once you have navigated Discovery, the court will summons you into a Pre-Trial Conference. The purposes of the pre-trial conference is to limit the issues, clarify the parties positions, and search for middle ground for settlement. As a general rule, the Discovery process ends at the pre-trial conference and you will need special permission from the court to gather any new evidence. This is where you must lay your cards on the table and let the other person see what documents, witnesses, and evidence you have to use against them if the case goes to trial.

Nearly 97% of all contested cases are able to draft a Separation Agreement and obtain their divorce the day of the Pre-Trial Conference without the expense or anguish of a trail. Even if you can only narrow down the divorce to a few select issues, oftentimes the Family Services (probation) department will work with you to give you a reality check and help you reach an agreement. If there is only one minor issue which needs to go to trial and it can be settled simply by having you both testify and/or produce a few notarized documents, the judge may hear your evidence on the spot and resolve your case that day.

SCHEDULING THE PRE-TRIAL CONFERENCE

In some states the Pre-Trial Conference is scheduled automatically by the court the day you file your divorce. If that does not happen, when you file your paperwork, count out exactly six (6) months in your calendar and write in huge red letters "file a Request for a Pre-Trial Conference." This is the earliest possible date in most states that you can ask the court to schedule a pre-trial conference.

Request formalities differ from state to state. In Massachusetts, there is a form you fill out, mail one copy to the courthouse, and mail a second copy to your husband (or his attorney). If you still do not have an attorney, you should include in your cover letter to the clerk a request that they schedule an appointment with the family services department shortly before the hearing so you can have the benefit of a probation officer to referee your proposed separation agreement.

🚩 *Most forms will have a list of documents and steps you should have already completed before they will let you ask for a date.* Make sure you have completed those steps or your request will be rejected.

A sample Request for Pre-Trial Conference form follows. Your state-specific form will vary but likely seek the same basic information (length of hearing, contested issues, document checklist):

EXHIBIT 16-1: SAMPLE REQUEST FOR PRE-TRIAL CONFERENCE

Commonwealth of Massachusetts
The Trial Court

Barnstable Division   **Probate and Family Court Department**   **Docket No.** 07D-9999-DV1

REQUEST FOR TRIAL – PRE-TRIAL ASSIGNMENT

This form should not be used to mark-up Temporary Orders and Motions

Please assign for hearing:

Jane Doe-Rayme , Plaintiff

v.

Jack Rayme , Defendant

Type of Case: Divorce   Time Requested: 15 Min.   Hearing in: Barnstable   At the earliest possible date available.

( )   Uncontested

(X)   Contested

( )	Merits
( )	Custody
(X)	Support
(X)	Visitation
(X)	208, s.34
( )	Other

The following papers must be on file before cases can be assigned for hearing:

(X)	Summons or Return of Service
(X)	Marriage Certificate
(X)	Statistical Form R408
(X)	Financial Statement (Supp.R.401)
( )	Affidavits of both parties (1A Divorces)
( )	Notarized Agreement (1A Divorces)

> You have to say how long you think trial will take.

Has Discovery been completed?   (X) Yes ( ) No

Has this case been Pre-Tried?   ( ) Yes (X) No

Does either party require an interpreter?   ( ) Yes (X) No

I hereby certify that, in my opinion, this case is ready for trial and a copy of such request has been made to opposing counsel this date:

Requested by: Opposing Counsel/Party:

Jane Doe   Jack Rayme

A few weeks after you request the pre-trial conference, a Pre Trial Order should arrive from the court informing you of the date the conference has been set, the time, and certain things you must do before that date. It will generally be between 6 weeks and 3 months from the date you mailed in the form Your courts boilerplate form will differ slightly, but they all look for similar information. I recommend you refer to it form as you finish reading this chapter. . A sample Pre-Trial Order form follows:

EXHIBIT 16-2: SAMPLE PRE-TRIAL CONFERENCE ORDER

COMMONWEALTH OF MASSACHUSETTS

BARNSTABLE, SS.   **PROBATE AND FAMILY COURT**   **DOCKET NO. 07D-9999-DV1**

JANE DOE-RAYME,)
    Plaintiff)
 v.)
 JACK RAYME,)
    Defendant)
)
	PRE-TRIAL NOTICE
	 AND
	 STANDING ORDER

The above-entitled action is set for a pre-trial conference before a Justice of the Probate and Family Court on <u>October 15, 2007</u> at Barnstable, MA at <u>9:00 a.m.</u> .

At least one day prior to the pre-trial conference, absent an outstanding restraining order which prohibits contact between the parties, the parties and counsel, if applicable, shall meet and shall confer in person with regard to any unresolved or disputed issues. Failure of parties to hold such a meeting may result in the case being removed from the pre-trial list and/or the imposition of monetary sanctions. Each party/counsel must thereafter exchange and file with the Court at the time of pre-trial conference, a memorandum setting forth the matters noted below:

A. A comprehensive written stipulation of all uncontested facts.

B. A statement of contested issues of fact and law and progress of agreement on such, if any.

C. Certification that all discovery has been completed; if discovery has not been completed, list what remains to be done.

D. Copies of current financial statements and any other pertinent financial data.

E. A list of potential witnesses.

F. A list of all exhibits which party intends to introduce at the trial.

G. Depositions proposed to be used as evidence to be read into the record. Use of depositions at the trial are subject to Mass.R.Dom.Rel.P. 32.

H. Stipulation of current value(s), and cost of all realty and personality in issue. In the event the parties are unable to agree as to the current values, counsel and parties are to submit an opinion of fair market value, either their own or from an appraiser.

I. A realistic time estimate of trial time.

J. It there are issues of alimony and the assignment of property under Chapter 208, section 34, a written offer of proof setting forth the evidence each party intends to produce with respect to each of the factors enumerated under the statute should be filed.

If any party objects to the admissibility of any of the above listed matters, the name of the party objecting and the grounds for objection shall be set forth.

All trial counsel and parties shall attend the pre-trial conference. Failure of counsel to appear at any scheduled pre-trial conference or otherwise to comply with the provisions of this order will result in the imposition of such sanctions as the Court may deem appropriate.

At such pre-trial conferences, the Court will consider the simplification of the issues, the necessity of amendments to the pleadings, the prospects of settlement, or such other matters as may aid in the trial or any other disposition of the action.

At the conclusion of such pre-trial conference, an appropriate order will be entered reflecting the action taken at such conference.

The case may be ordered to immediate trial on the date of the pre-trial if the court determines at the pre-trial that (a) the parties to the action will be the only witnesses; or (b) one party, through a failure to appear at the pre-trial or otherwise, will not present a case: or (c) such commencement of trial is necessary in the judge's discretion to accomplish justice.

If settlement is achieved prior to or at the pre-trial conference, the pre-trial conference time may be utilized for a hearing on an uncontested basis.

Dated this _____ day of _____, 20_____.

_____Johnny B. Wise_____
Johnny B. Wise, First Justice

Remember that YOUR home-state statutory references will vary.

YOUR STATE DIVORCE STATUTE PROPERTY DIVISION FACTORS

When you read through your Pre-Trial Order and try to figure out what information you must provide in your Pre-Trial Memorandum, you will note that item "J" requests "if there are issues of alimony and the assignment of property under your state divorce statute, a written offer of proof setting forth the evidence each party intends to produce with respect to each of the factors enumerated under the statute should be filed."

Your state divorce statute spells out all of the factors a judge should consider when figuring out what piece of property (or custody, or alimony) each person should get in the divorce. When you create your Pre-Trial Memorandum, think of this as you "dear judge" letter (only shorter). The best way to do this is to look at each factor and write a few paragraphs on a piece of scrap paper describing why that factor is important to what you are asking from the judge. Then, go through it, edit out all the personal stuff to make it sound professional, and condense it down to one paragraph per topic. Once you are done, you can transfer all this information to your Pre-Trial Memorandum.

Here are the factors in Massachusetts. Your state may have a few differences, so you should do an internet search to find out exactly what you need to lay out, but the ones outlined will serve you well:

EXHIBIT 16-3: COMMON PROPERTY DIVISION FACTORS

1. Length of marriage.
2. Conduct of the parties during the marriage.
3. Age of the parties.
4. Health of the parties.
5. Station of the parties.
6. Occupation of the parties.
7. Amount and sources of income.
8. Vocational skills.
9. Employability.
10. Estate (assets) of the parties.
11. Liabilities of each of the parties.
12. Needs of each party.
13. Opportunity of each party for future acquisition of capital assets.
14. Opportunity of each party for future acquisition of income.
15. Contribution of each party in the acquisition, preservation or appreciation in value of their respective estates.
16. Contribution of each party as homemaker.
17. Needs of the children.

A LEGAL WRITING EXERCISE: THE "DEAR JUDGE" LETTER

How are you going to introduce all the "factors" the judge needs to know to decide your case to him? Most people only have a fuzzy idea of what they have contributed to their marriage. Fuzzy? If *you* can't articulate what you contributed, then how will you communicate it to the judge when your knees are knocking together and you feel like you're going to faint at court? How will the *judge* figure it out if you, yourself, do not really know? Do yourself an enormous favor and solidify those property division factors inside your own mind *before* you go to court. Not only will it make your Pre-Trial Memorandum

I am about to teach you a better document, but it will make you argue more articulately on your own behalf during mediation, at the family services officers office, in front of the judge, and at trial.

🐿 *Do this writing exercise -especially- if you are working with an attorney.* Nobody knows your own case better than *you* do. Your attorney can skim through your fictitious 'dear judge' letter in a matter of minutes instead of interviewing you over several hours to ferret out these facts. Things may come out you never told them before. Having the factors laid out will save you *at least* an hour's legal fee when they begin drafting your pre-trial memorandum.

Essentially, you *pretend* to write a letter to the judge handling your case, addressing each of the 17 factors listed in the previous Exhibit, explaining why you think you deserve a bigger piece of the marital pie. Think "dear John" meets "Santa Baby." Obviously, you never send this letter, but I find it a wonderfully cathartic exercise for my clients to pour out their hearts and explain their side of the story. Although much of what my clients write about is not relevant to the matters at hand or admissible as evidence, I often find a lot more ammunition to help my client win their case than in the disjointed information they tell me in person and have occasionally copied entire passages from particularly well-written "dear judge" letters into my pre-trial memorandum. A sample 'dear judge' letter follows:

EXHIBIT 16-4: SAMPLE 'DEAR JUDGE' LETTER

Dear Judge:

I am writing to help you understand why I think you should give me the things I am asking for in our divorce and give me lots of alimony.

1. Length of the marriage – Jack and I were married 13 years. We eloped and got married at the Elvis Chapel in Las Vegas, Nevada. The justice of the peace dressed up as Elvis and there was a choir there which sang Elvis tunes.

2. Conduct of the parties during the marriage – when we were first married, Jack appeared to be very charming. He had a lot of debt which he brought to the marriage from a failed business he used to own. I co-signed a loan for his debts and helped him pay them off over the next five years. Jack has always been rather irresponsible, not being where he said he was going to be and forgetting important dates and appointments. This didn't matter so much while I was still working, but after the kids were born, he didn't change his ways and grow up. Jack wasn't very responsible about paying the bills, but he was always very controlling about how I spent money. He has always been a big "tease," calling me names and making fun of me, but around a year after we were married his "teasing" really began to grate on my nerves and he would ignore my pleas for him to stop. I was especially sensitive about the 30 pounds I gained after giving birth to our two kids. I asked him to stop calling me "Shamu" and going "beep, beep, beep" like a dump truck backup beeper every time I would be cleaning the house, but he would ignore me and begin to tease me even harder. Jack has always been a drinker, but around 3 years ago, his company started laying people off and Jack started to drink very heavily. At first, it was just a couple of beers after work with the guys, but over time he began to stay later and later and come home drunk. Towards the end, he rarely came home before 10:00 at night and oftentimes he could barely walk. He began to push me around and say demeaning things to the kids. I put up with his teasing when it was just me, but after Janie started to cry, I stopped putting up with it and would confront him whenever he called the kids names. Last December, things came to a head when he beat the dog nearly to death and I was forced to get a restraining order.

3. Age of the parties – I am 38 years old and Jack is 40.

4. Health of the parties –I have always been in relatively good health. I developed mastitis after the birth of Johnnie, but other than that, I have always been healthy. Jack once fell off a ladder and broke his ankle, but other than that, he is rarely sick.

And so on … and so on …

Do not give this letter to the judge!!! It is for your own internal self-clarification purposes only!

If you look at the sample above, you will notice that Jane Doe has spoken a great deal about all the negative things Jack did during the marriage under "conduct," but she speaks very little about the *good* things *she* did to contribute to the marriage. Remember, to develop a sound case, you must address both the *good* and *bad* things each party did. As an attorney, I would have Jane go back and write some more about the good things she did during the marriage and also have her explain any *bad* things she may have done herself. I would also ask her to state a few *nice* things Jack may have contributed. In this way, Jane could communicate to me a lot more information which might be relevant or rear its ugly head.

Include both good and bad points about yourself and your former spouse in the exercise as it will form the basis of your pre-trial memorandum!!!

MANDATORY MEETING BEFORE THE PRE-TRIAL CONFERENCE:

The sample pre-trial order states: *"At least one day prior to the pre-trial conference, absent an outstanding restraining order which prohibits contact between the parties, the parties and counsel, if applicable, shall meet and shall confer in person with regard to any unresolved or disputed issues. Failure of parties to hold such a meeting may result in the case being removed from the pre-trial list and/or the imposition of monetary sanctions."*

First and foremost, you should notify your husband (and his attorney) that you insist you meet at least one week, not a day, before the pre-trial conference to go over your proposal. You want to have time to think about *his* proposal compared to *your* proposal to increase your chances of compromise. Many attorneys are in the bad habit of putting these mandatory pre-trial conference meetings off until the last moment (or completely), and then expecting you to make decisions on the fly. This might cause no harm when two experienced divorce attorneys discuss things on the fly, but it is an invitation for disaster for an inexperienced pro-se client.

Be cautious about agreeing to anything written in the hallways of the courthouse! Ask your attorney to explain it to you thoroughly or, if you can't afford an attorney, ask to speak to the free courthouse lawyer of the day. You can always come back to court and have it accepted later.

If you have a restraining order in place, do not agree to meet anyplace except in the family services department of the courthouse. Nothing makes your abusive ex-husband behave like the knowledge there is a burly guard with a gun standing just outside the door.

Even without a restraining order in place, if your husband also doesn't have an attorney, when you meet and go over your proposed separation agreement, it is a good idea to have a friend present in the background in case he becomes upset and/or abusive. If your husband has an attorney and you do not, it is a bad idea to meet without a trusted friend present to prevent you from being browbeaten, intimidated, or bamboozled into signing something you shouldn't. That is part of the reason you should request the court automatically schedule you for a family services officer meeting ... family services tends to inform the other side if they are over-reaching.

If you don't have an attorney and meet with your husband at his attorney's office, don't agree to anything on the spot. Listen to their viewpoint, get a copy of their proposal, thank them, and tell them you want to look it over with a friend. Personally, I never meet with pro se's because the judge usually ends up negating any agreement we may have reached, even if reasonable. Request a family services officer meeting the day of your pre-trial conference to review the final proposal if necessary.

The purpose of this meeting before the pre-trial conference is to narrow the issues as much as possible and, hopefully, reach an agreement so you can get your divorce that day. However, do not allow your husband to browbeat you into settling if you feel you need the judge to decide certain issues.

If you won't have an agreement the day you walk into court, you *must* write a pre-trial memorandum explaining what you do and don't agree upon. You must use your state courts format. The easiest way to do this is to simply follow the format used in the Pre Trial Conference Order and answer each question it asks for in the order asked. Since I am licensed in Massachusetts, I will use their form as an example, but the process of 'spoon feeding it back' is similar in most states.

1. **Documents:** If you plan to use your valuation estimates or any other document at trial, you *must* list them in your pre-trial memorandum and give a copy of them to the other side (if you were a good little woodland creature, you gave them within the first 45 days after you filed as part of your Mandatory Self-Disclosure compliance). If you plan to call any witnesses, you *must* state their names and addresses.

    It is a good practice to include at the end of any sub-caption listing evidence the words "the Plaintiff reserves the right to amend her list of _____ with proper notice to the other side." That way, if you find something else you need, you can notify the other side within 30 days of trial and it will still be admissible.

2. **Witnesses and Expert Witnesses:** If you will be calling any witnesses, you must list their names and addresses in the pre-trial memorandum. If you will be calling any *expert* witnesses, such as the Guardian Ad Litem (GAL/CASA) or the real estate broker who valued your home, you must specially list them as *expert* witnesses. An *expert* witness is somebody who is an expert in their field and can render an opinion other than something a common person might know. If you forget to list a witness or expert witness, their testimony could be barred. It is a good policy, if you have an expert witness, to both list them as a regular witness *and* an expert witness (listing them twice).

3. **Objections:** You must state in the pre-trial memorandum any objections you have about any documents, witnesses, or evidence your husband is proposing introducing at trial or you will lose the right to contest it at trial.

    Don't simply say 'I object.' Cite the appropriate evidentiary objection from the Federal and/or State Rules of Evidence. *Evidentiary Foundations,* by Edward J. Imwinkelried can be bought online *used* for as little as $20 with shipping to help you figure out what you may be able to exclude.

4. **Notice of potential immediate trial:** The last item of huge importance in the memorandum is the notice that, if the judge feels there is only one issue to decide and the judge has some time on his hands, he could order you to immediate trial the day of the pre-trial conference. This will generally only happen, however, if there is only one issue left to decide and it can be resolved using the parties' testimony and documents already in evidence. Always go to the pre-trial conference armed with everything you will need to go to trial that day, including potential witnesses on telephone standby to come to court on short notice!

Warning!!! If you do not list a document, witness, objection or other piece of information required by the pre-trial order in your pre-trial memorandum, you will probably be prohibited from introducing that piece of evidence at trial no matter how relevant it is to your case!!!

A sample pre-trial memorandum follows:

EXHIBIT 16-5: SAMPLE PRE-TRIAL MEMORANDUM

COMMONWEALTH OF MASSACHUSETTS

BARNSTABLE, SS.

**PROBATE AND FAMILY COURT
DOCKET NO. 07D-9999-DV1**

JANE DOE-RAYME,)

    Plaintiff)

v.)

JACK RAYME,)

    Defendant)

)

**WIFE'S PRE-TRIAL
MEMORANDUM**

A.   UNCONTESTED FACTS

The Husband and Wife were married on September 11, 1994 at the Elvis Drive-Thru Wedding Chapel in Las Vegas, Nevada and last lived together at 100 Any Street in North Anytown, Barnstable County, Massachusetts on December 9, 2006. Two (2) children were born to the marriage, namely Jayne Rayme, date of birth: October 9, 1998; and Johnnie Rayme, date of birth July 12, 1997.

B.   CONTESTED ISSUES OF FACT AND LAW

The parties have attempted to reach an agreement and tentatively been able to resolve many issues. The latest version of this proposal is attached for review by the court. However, the following issues have not yet been resolved and the proposal not accepted.

    a.   <u>Child Support</u>. The Wife relocated to Alaska this past July and the court ordered a reduced child support obligation for the husband to offset the cost of traveling to see the new children and also to reflect the Wife's improved job prospects. The Husband announced he could no longer find home improvement jobs in July and claims he has not worked since. The Wife has evidence the Husband is working under the table. The Husband also dropped the Wife and children from his health insurance plan in July. The Wife is now providing health insurance for herself and the children and would like her child support adjusted to reflect this fact. The husband is asserting that since he is no longer working and the children live too far away to visit, that he shouldn't have to pay child support at all.

    b.   <u>Tax Deduction for Dependent Children</u>: the Husband is demanding to take one of the children as a tax deduction each year. IRC s.152(e) dictates that the custodial parent gets to take the children as tax deductions. The Husband is not in a high enough income bracket, nor paying a sufficient amount of child support, to justify negotiating otherwise. The Wife is not willing to give away her right to deduct the children. Giving away this deduction will remove another $1200 from her bottom line despite head of household status.

    c.   <u>Visitation</u>: The husband is currently entitled to supervised visits for 2 hours every other weekend at a certified visitation center of his choice in Alaska, or to travel with his mother or sister and have them provide supervision. The Wife's parents are unwilling to supervise visitation in their home. As soon as the husband completes a 6-week anger management program and the court's parent education class, the husband will be entitled to visit with the children one weekend per month either in Alaska, or fly them to his home at his own expense, as well as two weeks every summer. Seven months have passed, but the husband has yet to take the court-ordered class. The husband wishes to compel the Wife to pay for his commuting costs, not pay child support, and to not have to complete either class.

    d.   <u>Wife's Share of Sale of Marital Home</u>: The husband moved back into the marital home when the Wife moved in July. He has not made any payments on the mortgage (despite a court order to pay 2/3rds) and the Wife has had to pick up the full cost to avoid foreclosure. The Wife has located a real estate broker to sell the home, but the Husband is refusing to sign the paperwork or allow potential buyers into the home. Since the Husband has neglected to pay the mortgage on it and the Wife cannot afford to pay two mortgages, the Wife would like the court to order the Husband out of the former marital home to place it on the market. The Husband is demanding that he keep the house and force the Wife to pay the mortgage on it. The Wife is proposing dividing all proceeds 50:50.

e. <u>Merrily-Merrily Retirement brokerage account</u>: The Wife has evidence that the Husband has willfully omitted a $20,000 Merrily-Merrily Retirement brokerage account on his Financial Statement.

f. <u>Alimony</u>: As the Wife's income prospects improved by relocating to Alaska, she no longer desires alimony from the husband. The Husband, however, is now demanding that the Wife pay *him* alimony because he quit his job and refuses to look for work.

g. <u>Attorney's fees</u>: The husband is looking to compel the Wife to pay attorney fees he incurred up through June of 2007, at which time his attorney withdrew from the case and he was unable to hire another. The Wife is unwilling to pay the Husband's attorney fees as she was able, through research and hard work, to represent herself throughout this case and feels the Husband is perfectly capable of doing the same.

C. DISCOVERY

Despite a formal discovery request, a reminder letter, a second reminder letter, and a court order compelling the Husband to produce bank statements for Merrily-Merrily Retirement account number XYZ1234567, the Husband refuses to do so. The Wife was unaware of the account until she accidentally opened the September 30, 2006 statement which showed a balance in the Husband's name of $20,000. The Husband is denying the existence of the account. The Husband's attorney withdrew from the case after the Wife filed a Motion to Compel in June of 2007.

D. FINANCIAL STATEMENTS

Attached. The Wife believes the Husband is deliberately omitting a $20,000 Merrily-Merrily Retirement brokerage account titled in his name from his asset listings.

E. POTENTIAL WITNESSES

Jane M. Doe-Rayme (Wife)

Jack M. Doe-Rayme (Husband)

Betty Broker (licensed real estate broker, Sell-Em Real Estate) – Expert witness

Keeper of the Records, Merrily-Merrily Retirement

The Wife reserves the right to add additional witnesses with proper notice as might prove necessary if the case goes to trial.

F. EXHIBITS LIST

Financial Statements

Statements supporting figures quoted in the Wife's financial statement as needed.

Merrily-Merrily Retirement statements

Checkbook ledgers from Jack Rayme d/b/a Jack-O'-All-Trades.

Husband's financial statements

Tax documents and supporting schedules

Husband's bank records and checkbook ledgers (husband has refused to update since July)

Appraisal of 100 Any Street, North Anytown home

"Valuation Notebook" (handed to Husband at Temporary Orders Hearing on 4/1/07)

The Wife reserves the right to add additional exhibits with proper notice as might prove necessary if the case goes to trial.

G. PROPOSED DEPOSITIONS

The Wife has not conducted any depositions. The Wife reserves the right to depose the Husband and any witnesses and/or experts the Husband proposes. The Wife reserves the right to conduct additional depositions as might prove necessary if the case goes to trial.

H. STIPULATION OF CURRENT VALUES

The Husband is rejecting the Wife's estimates of values on every item they own. The Wife has researched these items and compiled them into a "valuation notebook" which she has provided to the Husband. The Husband is rejecting the Wife's valuations, but has not provided any competing values for the Wife's consideration.

I. TRIAL ESTIMATE

The Wife estimates trial will take half of one day.

J. ALIMONY/PROPERTY ASSIGNMENT

The Husband has voluntarily quit working and is demanding that the Wife pay him alimony. The Wife intends to introduce the following G.L. c.208, s.34 factors:

a. Length of the Marriage: This is a long-term marriage of twelve (12) years.

b. Conduct of the Parties during the Marriage: During the marriage, the parties contributed equally to the marital unit with the Husband being the primary wage earner and managing the finances of the household and the Wife being responsible for managing household chores, caring for her husband, and raising the children. The Wife left a promising nursing career in Big City to relocate with the husband to North Anytown in 1998 and, up until three months ago, worked part-time as a private duty nurse. The Husband started his own home improvement contracting business, Jack-O'-All-Trades. The Wife helped with the Husband's business by receiving telephone calls, describing services to potential clients, booking appointments, and doing the bookkeeping for the business.

Approximately three years ago, the Husband began to go out for drinks after work with co-contractors and friends and not come home until late at night. Over time, his behavior became abusive and the Wife was forced to obtain a 209A restraining order on December 9, 2006. The Wife filed for divorce on February 14, 2007.

Since the couple separated, the husband has refused to complete an anger management program so he could see the children, has violated the restraining order three times, has threatened the Wife's boss and caused her to lose one of her clients, has refused to pay child support, refused to pay the mortgage, refused to pay his court-ordered share of the joint marital debt, and refuses to work.

c. Age of the parties: The Wife is 38 years old. The Husband is 42.

d. Health of the parties: Both Husband and Wife share good health, with neither reporting any significant medical condition.

e. Station of the parties: The parties enjoyed a middle-class lifestyle during their marriage. The Husband took approximately two vacations a year without the family, usually business conferences in desirable vacation spots such as Las Vegas. The Wife visited her parents in Alaska in the summer of 2006 with the children.

f. Occupation of the parties: The Wife is a licensed Registered Nurse. She was primarily a homemaker during the marriage, working with in-home private nursing clients part-time during the overnight shift to help her family make ends meet. In July, she relocated to Juneau, Alaska, to take a position as a nurse there. The Husband is a self-employed licensed home improvement contractor with over 23 years of trade experience. He is currently refusing to work.

g. Amount and sources of income: The Wife earns approximately $32,000 per year at her new nursing job at Kinnicook Hospital in Juneau, Alaska. Up until the husband voluntarily stopped working, he was earning an average of $55,000 per year, after expenses.

h. Vocational Skills: The Husband is a licensed home improvement contractor with extensive experience in the trade. The Wife has a nursing degree and is a Registered Nurse.

i. Employability: The Wife's training as a registered nurse. This provides an adequate ability to find work in most parts of the country, although pay scales vary widely.

The Husband is a licensed home improvement contractor with extensive work experience in the field. There is an enormous demand for home improvement contractors on the Outer Cape, especially from second-home owners and retirees who do not wish to do the work themselves. There is also frequent work over the winter caused by wind during winter storms. The Wife was still receiving 6 or 7 calls a week from prospective clients looking to hire her husband when she moved out of the marital home this past July.

j. Estate (assets) of the parties: During the marriage, the parties had accumulated a home appraised at $465,000, two cars, furnishings, a small pension/IRA, and various other typical personal belongings. The Wife's proposed property division is laid out in the property division exhibit of her Proposed Separation Agreement.

k. Liabilities of Each Party: The parties owe a mortgage on the North Anytown house, two car loans, a $15,000 outstanding student loan incurred on behalf of the minor child to obtain special needs tutoring, an orthodontist bill for the son, the Wife's $2,000 student loan, and the typical credit card bills.

l. Needs of the Parties: The Wife needs the Husband to pay child support based on his real earning capacity, on time, without games or hiding his income, and without having to repeatedly go to court. The parties daughter has dyslexia, a mild learning disability, and has special educational requirements.

m. Opportunity for each party for the future acquisition of capital assets: The Wife is capable of providing for her own needs from now forward. At $32,000 per year, she'll never be wealthy, but the Wife's new employer provides a typical 401(k) retirement plan to help her save for retirement.

The Husband is in extremely high demand for skilled contractor work. He can easily return to work in his profession, either self-employed or for another person. As an experienced contractor, Husband also has the ability to earn "sweat equity" by buying houses and "flipping them."

n. Opportunity of each party for future acquisition of income: As stated in item (i) above, both parties have the opportunity and ability to continue to maintain a middle class lifestyle and save sufficient assets to retire on.

o. Contribution of each party in the acquisition, preservation or appreciation in value of their respective estates: Until the parties separated in December of 2006, the Wife performed all of the childrearing and homemaking duties and also approximately 1/3rd of the couple's income. The Husband worked and contributed 2/3rds of the couple's income. Both parties saved a modest amount of retirement savings. The Husband has also saved a secret Merrily-Merrily Retirement account he is hiding from the court.

p. Contribution of each party as homemaker. The Husband worked full time as a contractor during the day and generally relaxed or played with the children once home from work. The Wife prepared breakfast for the family each morning, cared for the children during the day (the youngest child is now 6 years old and started school last year), got the children off to school, interacted with their teachers, physicians, dentists, coaches, and other personnel important to the children's well-being, attended all parent-teacher conferences, transported the children to sports activities and play dates, made lunch (whether packed or at home) for the children and the Husband, cleaned the house, vacuumed, cleaned, mopped, dusted, washed and folded the laundry, kept the children's rooms clean, and the majority of all the other household functions. At night, the Wife would prepare a nice supper for the children and Husband, clean up afterwards, put the children to bed and read them a bedtime story. The Husband rarely shared the homemaking responsibilities, but he was good about playing sports when not working.

q. Needs of the children: The children initially needed therapy to help them adjust to witnessing their father nearly beat their dog to death and abuse the mother , which showed up largely as depression and poor grades in school. The children are coping very well now that they have moved close to their grandparents and therapy has stopped. Jayne continues to need tutoring in school to cope with her dyslexia, but she has adjusted well to her new school and is getting excellent grades.

Respectfully submitted,

Date: October 15, 2007

_____
Jane Doe
Jane Doe-Rayme, Wife

Remember that YOUR home-state statutory references will vary.

Your pre-trial hearing will be similar to the Temporary Orders hearing in many ways. If one or both of you does not have an attorney, you will probably need to report to the Family Services/Probation Officer. The family services officer will ask you both questions designed to elicit how close you are to settlement. If your court's FSO department hires lawyer/mediators, they may attempt to help you narrow the issues even further before you go in to see the judge.

Once you are done with Family Services, you will go in to see the judge. The judge will look over both of your Pre-Trial Memorandums and any proposed Separation Agreements and see if there is some way he can help you reach an agreement. At the family court level the hearing will frequently be held in open court, but some judges will speak to you both "in chambers."

"In chambers" - an informal session (frequently in the judge's office or 'chamber') where he will feel out what some of the obstacles are to your settling the case and getting your divorce that day and offer informal advice about how courts often interpret such a situation if there is clear precedent.

There has been some discussion lately as to whether it is proper for a judge to speak to litigants "in chambers" and off the record, but I have always found the practice to be helpful. The judge is much more prone to give you much more of an inclination which way he is leaning "in chambers" and save your client a lot of time and money (and let the attorney "save face" if their theory of the case is way out of whack) than when he is "on the record" in open court. Whether "in chambers" or open court, I have often seen judges repeatedly send litigants back out to the hallway or to the Family Services Officer to negotiate the Separation Agreement and encourage them to reach an agreement that day. I know of one judge who regularly keeps litigants there from 8:30 in the morning until 7:00 p.m. at night or later to encourage them to mediate their differences.

In the hypothetical I have used throughout this book, Jane Doe has gained an upper hand through diligence, hard work, and also due to her Husband's dishonesty and stupidity. At this point, Jack is being vindictive and not thinking very rationally. Once Jane got permission to move to Alaska, the direction the case was going became clear and Jack should have settled months ago. Jack Rayme would be very foolish to take this case to trial. Many judges will send Jack and Jane out into the hallway as many times as it takes to make Jack see that. If the case does not settle, it will go to trial. Jane has done a very good job of taking all the steps she needed to win many of the items she has requested.

If Jack and Jane can reach an agreement at the Pre-Trial Conference, they would usually obtain their divorce that day (subject to any mandatory waiting periods). To convert their contested divorce until a uncontested one, most courts will make them file a "Joint Motion to Convert a Contested Divorce to into an Uncontested Divorce." Most states will also make you file an "Affidavit of Irretrievable Breakdown of the Marriage."

A sample "in chambers" session follows, as well as a joint motion to convert the contested divorce into a settled divorce. For a typical final hearing script go to Chapter 19.

EXHIBIT 16-6: SAMPLE "IN CHAMBERS" SESSION AT PRE-TRIAL CONFERENCE

Judge, in chambers:	This case hasn't settled yet? What seems to be the problem?
Jack Rayme:	She took my kids!!! I've been unable to get work ever since my Wife threw me out of the house and now she's gone off to Alaska and left me holding the bag. *I* can't pay those bills!
Jane Doe-Rayme:	If you recall, sir, we were before you in July when I requested to relocate near my parents. At that time, you found the move was appropriate. You significantly reduced the amount of child support to offset the inconvenience travelling to Alaska to see them.
Judge:	Yes, I do recall that now. Let me see … (pulls out the order giving her permission to relocate) … I see … yes, Jack was to move back into the marital home and assume the mortgage on it, but since he said he couldn't afford it, you agreed to continue paying 1/3rd of the mortgage and the rest of the bills until you came up with a more permanent solution. (to Jack) Now's the time, Mr. Rayme. Do you have a permanent solution of how you're going to keep the house?
Jack Rayme:	I want her to pay the mortgage and give me alimony. She can afford it with that new job of hers. Oh, and since I can't see the kids, I don't want to pay child support.
Judge (glancing at a paper):	Mr. Rayme, as I recall, the reason you haven't seen your children is because you haven't completed your 6-week anger management program. Whether or not you get to see them, they're still your children and they still need the love and support of their father.
Jack	I can't afford the batterer's program. I don't see why I'm being punished when I can't afford it. Why can't *she* pay for it?
Judge	Mr. Rayme, you will address this court in a respectful manner or I will find you in contempt of court and let you spend the night up the hill at the House of Correction, is that understood?
Judge:	Let me give you a general idea about the laws governing child support. The amount children receive is set by the legislature. I don't get to deviate from that formula unless I see a very good reason. If you voluntarily quit your job, that is not a good reason. In fact, looking at the new child support guidelines worksheet prepared by the family services office, I see that you dropped your children from your health plan and that your *Wife* is now the one buying health insurance. Therefore, I am going to give her an increase in child support of half of that amount, or $80 more per week. I also see that you are 11 weeks behind on your child support. You have one week to pay the Department of Revenue $1000 of that arrearage or I am going to find you in Contempt and send you to jail. Your Wife is also claiming that are refusing to visit the children by choice. If this case goes to trial and she *proves* that allegation, I *could* decide to take away that $100 per week travel credit to your child support and go purely by the guidelines…
Jack:	Well, if that's the law, then I guess I have no choice…
Judge:	You do have a choice. You can choose to go with this figure the family services officer just worked out minus your $100 per week travel allowance, or you can choose to go to trial and risk getting this figure right here *without* any travel deduction at all.
Jack:	I think I'll agree that I owe $101 dollars in child support.
Judge:	Okay now. I'm going to put a little post-it here in Mrs. Doe's proposed Agreement and you can go out in the hallway and work it out. Are there any other issues outstanding?
Jane:	Sir, Mr. Rayme is refusing to disclose the $20,000 Merrily-Merrily Retirement stock account on his financial statement. I attached a copy of the account to my Pre-Trial Memorandum. In exchange for that stock account, I'm proposing keeping my $2,000 401(k) and having Jack do a QDRO to transfer *his* $15,000 IRA over to my name.
Judge	Is this your stock account? It has your name on it?
Jack:	Oh, I forgot that. Yes.
Judge:	Do you have any problem with Mrs. Doe's proposal.

Jack:	No.
Judge:	I'm going to put another sticky note here for you to deal with that in the hallway. Anything else?
Jane:	The house. Jack moved in back in July, but he's never made a single payment on it. My parents have been helping me swing the mortgage on that house *and* my new home in Alaska. My name is on that account and he's going to ruin my credit! I want to sell the darned thing.
Judge:	Jack, what is the solution you are proposing for that house?
Jack:	I don't want it anymore. There's too many bad memories there. I think I want to sell it.
Judge:	Ok, now we're making some progress. I'm going to send the two of you back to the Family Services Officer and they're going to help you write all this up, and then we'll see where you both are. Oh, one last thing. Mrs. Doe, would it cost you any additional money to add Mr. Rayme to your health insurance plan?
Jane:	No sir. I spoke to the benefits department and they said all they need is a court order for the insurance company to add him onto the plan.
Judge:	I'm going to have the family services officer add the right language while we're here today if you don't mind…
Jane:	Yes, sir. Thank you.

EXHIBIT 16-7: SAMPLE "JOINT MOTION TO CONVERT TO AN UNCONTESTED DIVORCE"

COMMONWEALTH OF MASSACHUSETTS

BARNSTABLE, SS.   PROBATE AND FAMILY COURT
                                   DOCKET NO. 07D-9999-DV1

JANE DOE-RAYME,   )
    Plaintiff   )   JOINT MOTION TO CONVERT
v.   )   1-A DIVORCE INTO UNCONTESTED
JACK RAYME,   )   1-B JOINT PETITION FOR DIVORCE
    Defendant   )
)

Now come the litigants, Jane Doe-Rayme and Jack Rayme, and do hereby jointly petition this Honorable Court to allow them to convert their M.G.L. Ch.208, s.1-A "Complaint for Divorce" into a s.1-B "Joint Petition for Divorce."

The parties do hereby attach their Affidavit of Irretrievable Breakdown and signed Separation Agreement.

Date:____October 15, 2007____

Signed:__Jane Doe-Rayme_____   Signed:__Jack Rayme_____

Remember that YOUR home-state statutory references will vary.

CHAPTER SIXTEEN SUMMARY

1. The day you get word back from the Sheriff that he has served your husband with the divorce papers, go to your calendar, count out exactly six months to the day, and in big letters write "SCHEDULE PRE-TRIAL CONFERENCE."

2. To get a pre-trial conference date, you must fill out a special form and ask for it. You must have all the papers on the list turned into the court or they won't give you a hearing.

3. The court will schedule a date and send you a notice. Use that notice as a guideline to draft your Pre-Trial Conference Memo.

4. Have a brief paragraph describing each of the G.L.208, s.34 property division factors if your divorce is still contested.

5. If there is no restraining order in effect, you are supposed to meet with the other side two weeks before the hearing to try to hammer out a Separation Agreement. Do not do this if you have a restraining order. Always bring a calm, neutral friend along for moral support. Never sign anything that day, but ask for a copy of the other sides proposal and bring it home to think about it at least two days.

6. The day of the conference, you will likely meet first with the family services officer to see if your case has settled. If it hasn't settled, you'll go in to see the judge. If the judge sees your case should be very close to settling and the issues are clear-cut, he may give you an idea about which way he's leaning and send you back to Family Services to negotiate further.

7. If you *are* able to reach an agreement that day, you will have to file a "Joint Motion to Convert Contested 1-A Divorce to Uncontested 1-B Divorce." You will also have to write up an "Affidavit of Irretrievable Breakdown" similar to the one contained in Chapter 10.

8. If you settle, the judge will usually grant you a divorce on the spot. For an idea of what your final hearing will be like, go to the "uncontested hearing" script in Chapter 19.

CHAPTER 17

PREPARING FOR TRIAL

If your case was not one of the approximately 98% of all divorce cases which settles at the pre-trial conference, you have no choice but to prepare for trial. Trial is an enormous undertaking which is best done by an experienced attorney (even amongst experienced attorneys, it is common to not have that many actual trials under your belt). Most other countries differentiate between legal advisors and trial attorneys (for example, Great Britain has solicitors and barristers). In the rest of the world, you would go to one attorney for advice, then hire a second attorney to work with the first attorney if your case goes to trial (since most cases settle, you would not need to hire a barrister).

In the USA, we do not have this system. Every attorney must know how to do both jobs (even though *some* attorneys avoid trial like the plague while others thrive on the adrenaline of the trial theatre). The rules governing trials are tricky, convoluted, and go far beyond the scope of this Bootcamp manual. Once again, I will reiterate my admonition that if you can find any way to afford it, even if you must borrow money, hire an experienced family law attorney to handle your trial.

If your case is going to trial, you must educate yourself far beyond what I can teach you. From here on in, the strategy of this book is to introduce you to certain topics you probably *don't know you don't know* so you don't get blindsided. Hopefully this will motivate you to either bite the bullet and hire an attorney if you have not done so already, or at least educate yourself so you don't get creamed. This is why we attorneys are here. We are not terrible, evil people who thrive on causing needless litigation. We *want* to take this heavy burden off of your shoulders and protect you from as much of the ugliness as we possibly can. If you have taken the advice in this Bootcamp manual to heart, it is my hope your case is in good enough shape to have an attorney just step in and take over at any point in the game.

Do not let your fear of going to trial intimidate you into settling if your research leads you to believe you have a good chance of winning. If you are working with an attorney, ask them to help you prepare to be the best witness possible. If you are too poor to hire one, you have gotten this far on your own by piecing together self-knowledge with piecemeal advice from attorneys, pro bono clinics, financial advisors and other professionals. If you are extremely motivated and think the case is a slam-dunk, it *is* possible to teach yourself enough information to get your facts before the judge.

WHAT YOU DON"T KNOW YOU DON"T KNOW

"There are three types of knowledge:
There are the things you know,
*There are things you **KNOW** you don't know,*
*And then there are things you **DON'T KNOW** you don't know."*

--Donald Rumsfeld (famous last words before invading Iraq)

The most worrisome thing about launching your own trial is that the judge cannot give you a "free pass" on the rules of evidence and procedure no matter *how* much he sympathizes with your case. If you do not follow the rules, the judge risks having his decision overturned on appeal. If you are working with an attorney, understanding a trial is more like a game of chess than football will help you work more effectively with them to get your evidence onto the court record. If you are too poor to hire an attorney, educate yourself enough to have a rough idea of what the judge needs to consider your evidence. If you listen to what he says when the other side objects very carefully, you may find the judge giving you cues about how to get your facts before him over the objections of the other party. In other words, you need to *know what you don't know.*

These are some of the steps (or thought processes) you need to prepare for trial:

1. Define your *theory of your case;*

2. Define what *facts* you need to *support* your theory of the case (including additional facts you may need);

3. Figure out *who* or *what* is the best vehicle to get that fact before the judge and *when* is the best time to have them testify;

4. Prepare a direct examination *script* to help your witness explain those facts to the judge and/or authenticate other evidence you may need to introduce;

5. Figure out what facts your husband is going to use to try to *undermine* your theory of the case and prove his own theories;

6. Prepare a cross-examination *script* you can use to disprove or discredit your husband's witnesses;

7. Subpoena every witness you need to testify or introduce certain documents;

8. Organize a "trial notebook" for each witness (including yourself) so you can easily access each and every piece of evidence you will be introducing to the court and stay "on track."

9. Prepare your opening and closing statements (covered in the Trial chapter).

10. Sit in on an actual trial at the courthouse to see how it's really done.

11. If you can in any way afford it, *get a lawyer get a lawyer get a lawyer get a lawyer!!!*

WHAT IS MY THEORY OF THE CASE?

Defining a clear theory of your case is important to help you come up with a winning strategy. Most people think they can simply waltz into court, state "I'm leaving him because he is bad and I am good," and it will get them someplace with the judge. Well, it won't! The villain-victim strategy may gain some traction in a few exceptional cases where the husband's conduct is so egregious as to elicit a response of "that's outrageous." However, you have to remember that family court has no jury.

> "Jurors believe … that beneath all the pomp and circumstances of the courtroom … is **the truth**. Jurors want to discover this "truth" and thus … reach a just and fair result."
>
> *The How To Win Trial Manual,* by Judge Ralph Adam Fine

When you walk in the doors of family court, you have to understand that, in a place where thousands of people stroll in and out to whine about what a rotten no-good lout the other person is, your husband probably isn't all that bad. The judge hears dozens of similar cases every single day. In fact, if you go into court and launch into a lengthy diatribe about what a jerk your husband is, if he has any common

sense, he will keep his mouth shut, give the judge a helpless look and a shrug to communicate "see what I've been dealing with all these years," and you may find that *you* are the one the court views as a jerk.

First impressions are important, so if you don't walk in the doors of the courthouse with a well-defined theory of your case, you will be at a disadvantage. Judges make quick decisions about which side they find more credible. Once he has found one side to be more sympathetic than the other side, he will jump through hoops to slant his findings to fit his perceptions.

> "At one of Wisconsin's mandatory judicial-education seminars, a family-law judge explained how he used the statutory child-support criteria in deciding how much to award: "I just pick a number and then apply the criteria to justify it.""
>
> *The How To Win Trial Manual,* by Judge Ralph Adam Fine

Since I am assuming you don't have years and unlimited funds to teach yourself advanced trial tactics, the safest way a self-represented litigant can get a fair outcome is to make a logical argument about why your viewpoint is *more fair and reasonable* than your spouse's and then give the judge the evidence he needs to support your theory of the case. "Good guy … bad guy" may work for high paid trial attorneys, but because you are carrying a lot of emotional baggage, it can blow up in a laypersons face. In other words, focus on who gets custody of the kids, how you are going to support them, who is going to keep which piece of property or pay what debt, and not just right and wrong. Here are some possible theories:

1. If your husband has broken your arm and landed you in the hospital, "abuse" will probably get you custody of your children and give you some leverage in the property division. However, it will usually get you no more than 10%.

2. Subpoenaing his mistress to discuss the two out-of-wedlock children your husband secretly fathered and has been supporting all these years while he was supposedly married to *you* will give you some leverage for alimony and in the property division, but it has little impact on custody, so if that is an issue, it can't be your *only* theory.

3. If child custody is the major issue, focus on a strategy such as "I've been the primary caretaker all these years and he's been off pursuing his career … now all of a sudden he wants 50:50???" Not simply "but I'm the *mother*."

4. If removing the children from the state and moving far away is the issue, focus on how much the *children* (not you) will benefit from living closer to your family support network and your being able to earn enough money to make them very comfortable.

5. If you suffer from one of the "custody flaws" described in Chapter 14, focus on "in the past I've had some problems, but I got help, I am better now, and what really matters is how great of a parent I have been for the last 3 years while he could have cared less."

6. If child support and/or alimony are major issues, focus on the disparity between your post-divorce income and expenses and your spouses. Although your expenses don't matter a whole heck of a lot when computing child support, they *can* be a major factor when computing alimony or deciding which spouse gets what asset. In other words, your theory of your case would focus on "equalizing the standard of living between households" and not "isn't it child abuse if the kids can't go to the mall three times a week and shop at Abercrombie?"

7. If your spouse is self-employed and hiding his income, focus on evidence which indicates there is a discrepancy between how much he has been claiming he earns on his tax returns (or business receipt records) for the past 3 years and the amount of money he is claiming he earns now. Your theory would be "for the past three years, he's been earning X, then all of a sudden, the minute I file for divorce, he claims he's earning Y."

8. If you run the financials during your "acorns" exercises and come to the realization he's been paying cash for everything (or paying household expenses out of the business) and understating his income to the IRS for many years, your theory would focus on "he *says* he's been only earning $50,000 per year on the last three years of tax returns, but if you look at our expenses, he's *really* been earning around $75,000 per year." Your theory would be "this man is a liar."

If you've been signing joint tax returns for these years, the IRS may come pay you a visit!

Focus on *issues* which matter once your divorce is final. If you can't come up with one, unified theory of your case, then break it down into mini-issues (property division, alimony, child support, custody, etc.) and come up with mini-theories for each issue. Once you have defined each mini-issue, you may see a

pattern emerge which will help you come up with a master-theory. If all else fails, a good default theory is "my proposed property division is more fair and reasonable than his proposed settlement."

In our Jane Doe hypothetical, Jane's self-employed home improvement contractor is *claiming* he can't find work to pay child support because of the housing slump, but she has dug up credible evidence that he really *is* working. Jane's theory of the case would be "he either is, or *should* be, capable of earning the same amount of money as he traditionally earned during the marriage."

I recommend you read *The How To Win Trial Manual: Winning Trial Advocacy In A Nutshell*, by Judge Ralph Adam Fine (2005) ISBN 1-57823-209-0, Juris Publishing, www.jurispub.com. Judge Fine's book emphasizes how you can use 'storytelling' and the perception of 'truthfulness' to win your trial.

WHICH FACTS *SUPPORT* (OR DISCREDIT) MY THEORY OF THE CASE?

Once you have defined your theory of the case, it's time to make a list of all the evidence you have, good or bad, which either supports or discredits your theory of the case. Every trail has facts that both support and weaken a party's position, the trick is to account for "bad" facts that hurt you in such a way that the judge finds you to be human, credible, and sympathetic while simultaneously painting your spouses "bad" facts in such a way that the other side appears to be inhuman, dishonest, and

unsympathetic. This is not the time to be dishonest with yourself about facts your spouse will bring up to hurt you!!! If you make a list of all of your facts (good and bad, hurting or helping either party) and reference any evidence which may support or discredit each individual fact, you will then be able to figure out a way to use those facts to help you and hurt the other side's case.

The simplest way to do this is to simply fold a piece of paper into four columns and list everything you can think of that *could* possibly be introduced as evidence at trial by either party. This is complicated to explain, but very easy to demonstrate. Below is a chart created by Jane Doe to help her plan what evidence she plans to introduce. Jane has two main issues at the time of trial: (1) Jack is claiming there is no work (and therefore no income) available to pay child support; (2) Jack is hiding an investment stock account worth $20,000. We will focus on the work issue.

EXAMPLE 17-1: SAMPLE METHOD OF WEIGHING FACTS IN CASE

Issue: Can Jack find Work?			
Argument For	**Argument Against**	**Evidence**	**Best person or document to bring the issue before the court**
Jack had plenty of work until I took out a restraining order		Historical earnings	Last 3 years of Jack's Schedule C's on his tax returns
	There is a housing slump	Jack's testimony 2x in the past	o Articles in newspaper o Complaints by other contractors that there is not as much new construction work as there used to be o Bureau of Labor Statistics and other government agency reports claiming new housing starts are down nationwide.
There are plenty of people looking to hire Jack		Prospective clients frequently call the house asking for Jack	My list of prospective clients, work they are seeking, and their telephone numbers.
	Jack claims he never got the phone calls	His testimony at the July removal hearing	Me. I testified that I was not stupid enough to take food out of my kids' mouths and the judge seemed to be receptive to that. I will need to testify again.
There is plenty of remodeling work available here on Cape Cod		Common knowledge of people seeking to get a contractor to even return their phone calls.	How do I quantify this "common knowledge" to the court? Can I get any of the people who called looking to hire jack to testify on my behalf?
	Jack isn't working		Jack's testimony (credibility)
	Other contractors are having trouble finding work	Jack listed his best friend, Bob Bullcowflap, as an "expert witness" on his pre-trial memorandum	Bob Bullcowflap is Jack's best friend. How can I discredit him?

The "can Jack find work" question is just one sub-component of the many questions Jane will need to answer (or refute) at trial. However, by thinking about all the things she might say to sway the judge *and* all the things she anticipates Jack might say to disprove her, Jane can formulate a strategy of how to structure her argument at trial to convince the judge. Trials are not simply a matter of he-says, she-says. Each party must introduce documents or witnesses to support or refute their theory of the case. Where Jane (and most self-represented) people tend to fall flat is they do not know how much weight the judge will give each piece of potential evidence.

At the July removal hearing, Jane handed the judge a list of potential clients who had called the house looking to hire Jack to work for them. Not only did she get their names and telephone numbers, but she also made notes about the type of projects they were looking to hire him to do. Jack testified that nobody had called him. Jane testified that she had given the prospective clients Jack's cell phone number. Although the judge sitting on the bench that day did not issue an order regarding Jack's credibility, there is a pretty good chance whatever judge is sitting on the bench at trial will find this same evidence credible. However, Jack now knows the court is not going to simply believe him that he isn't getting the phone calls, so he will come to court armed with evidence to support his claim that there is no work available in order to avoid paying child support. Not only does Jane need to figure out what pieces of evidence she must bring to trial to convince the judge, but she must also *anticipate* what additional pieces of evidence Jack will bring to court the day of trial to discredit her.

By listing all of the evidence she can think of that either person could use for or against each issue, Jane can anticipate what Jack might do at trial and take steps to nullify it. Jane's strengths lie in the fact Jack had plenty of work until they filed for divorce and plenty of people seem to want to hire him. Jack's strengths lie in scary stories in the newspapers and issued by government agencies claiming there is less work in his field than there used to be. Jane must anticipate what Jack will try to claim and then introduce her own evidence showing Jack's evidence just doesn't apply in this situation.

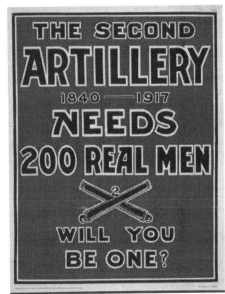

If Jane researches the reports issued by the government agencies, she will discover they are referring to *new housing starts*, not remodeling projects. She needs to point this out at trial. Jack is a *home improvement* contractor, not a *general contractor*. Jane must point out that improving houses, not building them from scratch, is the type of work Jack has always done and the new housing start slump is not affecting him. Jane may also discover (through research) that the depressed market in new housing starts is not affecting her home region (Cape Cod), which has a unique demographic of wealthy second home owners. Jane should introduce her own government reports which show there is a difference.

Jack could subpoena fellow contractors to come into court as "expert witnesses" and report *they* cannot find work, while Jane could hire similar contractors as expert witnesses to come into court and explain they are so swamped, there is no reason for Jack *not* be busy as well. On the pre-trail memorandum, Jack listed his best friend/fellow contractor Bob Bullcowflap as a witness to support his view of the work situation. Jane must discredit Bob Bullcowflap's credibility or show that although *Bob* may not be able to find work (for example, Bob has negative reviews on AngiesList.com), there is no reason *Jack* can't find work. If Jane adds her *own* expert witness to her list, she must immediately notify Jack and the court right away (usually via a letter and an updated pre-trial memorandum) that she is bringing in a new expert witness who was not listed on her pre-trial memorandum or the court will bar her witness.

An excellent trial prep book with a heavy emphasis on discrediting the other side is *Cross Examination: Science & Techniques,* by L.Pozner & R.Dodd. Better yet, if you can catch one of their seminars, they are highly informative and entertaining.

HOW DO I GET MY EVIDENCE BEFORE THE JUDGE?

The rules of evidence are convoluted beyond belief. How many of you watched horrified as the jury let O.J. Simpson walk out of the courtroom after brutally murdering his wife with a "not guilty" verdict. Everybody in America, *except* the jury, knew that O.J. was guilty as hell. Why did he get away with murder? There are several reasons why, but the biggest culprit was the rules of evidence you will have to understand and overcome before the judge is allowed to weigh anything you have to say at trial. The sequestered (locked away) jury let O.J. walk because a lot of the most damning evidence was barred from the jury's ears until *after* they had made their decision and reentered society where things like the

newspapers and televisions told them what chumps they were for making a decision without all the evidence. Up until now, the court has probably been using less stringent "preliminary hearing" rules which allow things like affidavits and copies of written documents to come into evidence in your divorce case. That free ride is now over. It's time to learn the rules of evidence. The "rules" are one of the reasons attorneys earn so much money.

I cannot teach you the rules of evidence. They are complex, lengthy, and many lawyers don't understand them very well. However, what I *can* do is introduce you to the concept of breaking down your evidence into evidentiary *categories* which direct you where to look for more information about the best way to get it before the court. Going back to our Jane Doe hypothetical, Jane should break down her list of evidence created in the last exercise and figure out where to look for direction on how to get it before the judge. She should also note places where she thinks she will need to do more research. She should then go to her local courthouse or law school law library to photocopy relevant sections, or purchase online, the following book (if Jane is in Massachusetts, if she is not, then she should refer to whatever book is published by her state bar training association):

Evidentiary Foundations, by Edward J. Imwinkelried can be bought online *used* for as little as $20 with shipping. Although the Rules of Evidence shift slightly from year to year and state to state, even an older edition of this book will get you through most evidentiary issues.

EXHIBIT 17-2 – SAMPLE EVIDENTIARY ISSUE ANALYSIS

Source of fact	Type of Evidence	How do I get it in?
Last 3 years of tax returns	Document	Need someone (Jack?) to identify his signature
Articles in newspapers	Document	Court does not look favorably on newspaper articles. Jack needs to get reporter who wrote it to testify or person quoted in article. I should object and ask the court to exclude.
Government reports	Document	Government agency. Jack needs a "keeper of the record" certification from the agency who wrote it. Court often will allow even if no certification. Should probably focus on why report doesn't apply to Jack.
My list of prospective clients looking to hire Jack.	Document, me as witness, past recollection recorded.	*I am the real evidence, not the list. I will need to testify that I made this list at the time each call was made.*
Jack's claims he never got the phone calls and he's not working.	Jack is the witness	I need to focus on facts that discredit him. *Note to myself, how can I discredit him?*
There is plenty of remodeling work available here on Cape Cod	*How can I document this?*	I either need government reports or live witnesses to document this. *WHO???*
Bob Bullcowflap – Jack's witness	Bob is an expert witness.	*Bob is Jack's best friend and he's also out of work because he's a really lousy contractor and nobody wants to hire him. I suspect Jack has asked Bob to say he can't find work either. How can I discredit Bob?*

If you are Jane, you are probably in a panic right now about the fact Jack is going to have his best friend testify there is no work. Jane probably is having nightmares about trying to raise her two children with no child support. However, by figuring out what will and will not support her case, Jane has learned some valuable information. She cannot simply hand the judge her list of phone calls and expect she will get the same outcome she got earlier at the July removal hearing. Jane must do more work.

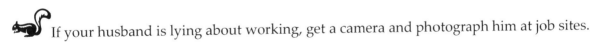 If your husband is lying about working, get a camera and photograph him at job sites.

Does your self-employed husband do any kind of work that requires a license or permit? Check the licensing agency in any towns you suspect he may be working (building inspector, electrical inspector, plumbing inspector, door-to-door salesman, etc.)

In Jane's case, she might go down to the building inspector offices in several towns to ask if Jack has pulled any building permits lately. Although Jane may be barred from introducing the photographs or building permits as *primary* evidence (she did not have them listed on her pre-trial memorandum), there are ways to get such *new* evidence before the court to *impeach* Jack's credibility after he testifies he is not working (to learn more about *impeachment*, read the recommended *Evidentiary Foundations* book).

Most legal guides about introducing evidence have "introduction scripts" to help you get each type of evidence before the court (including objections the other side might make to try to keep it out). Photocopy the appropriate script and paper-clip a copy of it to the front of *each and every piece of evidence* you are planning on introducing. That way, you will know how to proceed if the other side objects or what to argue to the judge so it can come in.

Lastly, since I am recommending an outside book, I have to make 50 disclaimers stating this may not be the best book for you, you should make your own choices, the international space station might fall on your head, etc... Make your own choices.

DIRECT EXAMINATION - THE PROPER WAY TO ASK *YOUR* WITNESS QUESTIONS

Forget everything you thought you knew about asking witnesses questions at trial because most of it is wrong. The judge (if he is any good) isn't going to let you get on a soapbox and grandstand about what *you* think the case is about at trial. I assure you that nearly every lay television show, book, and movie depiction of trial that you may have ever seen or read is *wrong.*

When you call a witness to testify on your behalf and ask them questions to support your theory of the case, it is called "direct examination." There are very strict rules about the proper way to elicit information from your own witness. It is up to the *witness* (not you) to tell their story to the court. You will find most of these rules listed in the *"Evidentiary Foundations"* book recommended earlier.

Witnesses must testify from their own memory or, in certain instances, from things they may have written down but since forgotten. You do not get to lead them around by the nose and ask them questions such as "and then you saw the Defendant hide the knife, right?" If your witness saw your husband hide a knife, they must state it themselves with very little prompting from you. For example:

Q - What did you see?

A - I saw Jack hide a knife.

Q - Where did he hide it?

A - Under the bathroom sink."

Your witness may only testify as to things they *directly* saw, did, or heard. They may *not* testify about things they did *not* personally see, do, or hear. For example, if your witness *saw* your husband hide a knife, he can state "I saw Jack hide a knife under the bathroom sink." He *cannot* state, "Jane told me she saw Jack hide a knife under the bathroom sink." If your witness did not directly see, hear, or do something, that evidence is probably Hearsay and will be excluded. A good way to think of hearsay evidence is this rhyme "If I say that you say, it's hearsay."

To show the court your witness is only testifying about things they personally saw, did, or heard, you must precede your question with "question" words. The direct examination question words are:

EXAMPLE 17-3: DIRECT EXAMINATION QUESTIONS

Who?   **Why?** (be very careful when asking why)

What?   **How?**

When?   **What happened next?**

Where?   **Describe?**

Why be cautious about asking *why*? Why is an open-ended question. It is very hard to control the witnesses answer to such a broad question. Once he starts talking and you realize he has damaged your theory of your case, it can be very difficult to get the judge to order the witness to shut up. For an example of why you have to be careful asking *why*, I suggest you watch the move "A Civil Action" starring John Travolta.

If you are working with an attorney, budget for at least two hours legal fees to rehearse answering whatever list of questions they prepare. Afterwards, photocopy their rough list of questions (it will only be a bulleted list on yellow lined paper at this point and will be tweaked before trial) to bring home and rehearse in front of the mirror. Rehearsal is always money well spent!

In the book *The How to Win Trial Manual*, Judge Ralph Adam Fine lists the following "Three Rules of Direct Examination - Do not ask a question on direct-examination unless:"

1. The [judge] knows the answer before the witness responds; or
2. *You have immediate corroborating material*; or
3. If one or two is not possible, you start at the beginning of the logical train of thought so that the answer rings true.

Until this point, Jane has focused on what *she* would say and what pieces of paper already listed on her pre-trial memorandum she would give to the judge to bolster her testimony. Jane feels her case is a "slam dunk," but she wants to leave Jack no wiggle room for lying. She makes a nice, neat notebook out of the documents listed on her pre-trial memorandum to give the judge.

But Jane's theory of the case is not simply that Jack should pay child support and/or alimony, but that he is also *lying* about how much money he earns. Jane has lost touch of Jack's day-to-day finances since they stopped living together and her evidence of past lies is rather stale. Jack has had *time* to cover his rear-end about past lies by paying cash for building supplies, getting *paid* in cash or cashing his checks at the employers bank so there is no record of a check going through his bank account, and has probably done everything possible to make it look like he is not working. Jack, however, has expenses and like most people, will only keep his head down for so long before getting cocky. Even this late in the game, it would be helpful if Jane could find *new* evidence to prove Jack is *still* lying, also known as impeachment.

Impeach - to cast doubt on and challenge the credibility of a witness.

EXAMPLE 17-4: JANE DOE GATHERS IMPEACHING EVIDENCE

Jane needs more evidence than Jack's past earnings history and her call list to overcome Jack's strategy of having his contractor/best friend testify there is no work. She needs corroborating material to support *her* theory of the case and discredit Jack's.

1. She calls the people on her 'work inquiry' call list and learns Jack actually *did* work for many of them over the last six months. Most are not willing to come to court to testify and a few are angry she called, but one of Jack's customers, Regina Renovator, feels sorry for Jane and is willing to come to court on her behalf. Regina will testify about what work she had done and how much she paid for it if she is subpoenaed.

2. Jane (who is now in Alaska) goes on the internet to find constables in the area and have Regina served with a subpoena. Jane should anticipate that one of the less-helpful homeowners will notify Jack she called looking for information.

3. Jane sees a lawyer at a free legal clinic in Alaska about the problem of finding corroborating evidence about Jack's employment. The out-of-state attorney, although not knowledgeable about Massachusetts law, suggests Jane contact the building departments in surrounding towns and ask if Jack has pulled any building permits lately.

4. Jane tries calling for this information, but the clerks are busy and say she must know the names and street addresses of the houses renovated in order for them to pull the permits. Jane cross-references the last name and first three digits of the people on her "work inquiry" list to isolate what town they are from. She reverse-addresses their telephone numbers on the internet to get the street address.

5. Jane mails a written "freedom of information act" request to the various towns asking if any building permits have been issued in the last 6 months for people at those addresses (keeping in mind the town has 30 days or more to respond). She gets back four building permits for a very modest fee. Jane asked the clerks to include a "keeper of the records" certification certifying that those documents were genuine, which cost her around $2.50 per page, so she does not have to subpoena them into court.

6. Jane is certain Jack has had more work than these permits indicate. She flies back a few days before her trial to do some more sleuthing. The Anytown clerk feels sorry for Jane and allows her to thumb through recent building permit files (no small favor) to see if Jack was listed as any of the contractors. Jane finds seven building permits issued in the past 6 months for various renovation projects, including the addition on Regina Renovators house. Jane gets "keeper of the records" certified copies of the permits (generally, the town clerk will stamp each page with an embossed seal and hand-write "a true copy attest" and sign her name.")

7. Jane then speaks to the assistant building inspector, Billy Buildinginspector, who informs Jane he was the person who inspected three of the seven building sites and that, in his opinion, the cost of the work Jack did on one of the kitchen renovations far exceeds the estimated cost Jack listed in his building permit application. Billy is not too pleased Jack did this as the town collects fees to fund his department based on the scope of the project and he suspects Jack is in the habit of under-reporting his scope of work in order to save money. Billy is willing to come to court if Jane

subpoenas him and pays his mileage, which Jane immediately does.

8. Since Billy Buildinginspector informed her he has heard Jack is currently replacing the siding on a house on Oak Street without first pulling a building permit, Jane grabs her camera and heads over there. She is able to take several photographs of Jack and somebody else nailing siding on the side of a house with a pneumatic hammer.

9. Jane goes to a photo store that offers instant developing and develops her film. One picture in particular shows Jack's face, scaffolding which suggests a major project, and his hands actually nailing the piece of wood on, looks very good. The photo clerk suggests that picture is the best one to blow up. Jane has several photos blown up 8x10 for $12 apiece, but orders the last picture blown up to 20x24 poster size for $58. She will have to come back the day before the trial to pick up the 20x24 picture as it will need to be sent out, but the store attendant assures her it will be here on time.

Now Jane has *new* information proving Jack is a liar which *she can't get into evidence* unless it is offered for impeachment because it is not listed on her pre-trial memorandum and it is so close to trial that she may not be able to convince the judge to let it in!

Jane decides to use a risky, but nasty trick used by DCF attorneys in Care & Protection cases to make no mention of the new evidence in her opening statement, call Jack to the witness stand first, let him lie through his teeth that he can't find work, and then offer her "new" evidence and witnesses for impeachment. Jane plans on then imploring the judge to adopt her view of the case in her "closing statement" (covered in Chapter Eighteen).

 Springing surprises at trial is always risky!

Since Regina Renovator and Billy Building Inspector are Jane's witnesses, she will have to prepare *direct examination* scripts using the who, what, when, where, how, describe, and why questions outlined earlier. Sample direct examination scripts for Billy Buildinginspector follow. You will note that I have broken down each person's testimony into sub-issue sub-scripts (i.e., fact, fact, fact). Remember that these scripts were prepared for a Massachusetts court and may need tweaking to get in the different pieces of evidence if your divorce trial is happening in another state.

 Remember…**Who? What? When? Where? How? Describe?** Be careful when asking **Why?**

EXAMPLE 17-5: FOCUS OF A HYPOTHETICAL DIRECT EXAMINATION SCRIPT

Jane has subpoenaed Billy Buildinginspector into court to do four things:

1. Billy is giving a "double authentication" of the building permits. Because building permits are a Public Document, if Jane wants to introduce the building permits and let the judge draw his own conclusions, the "keeper of the records" certification would probably be adequate.

2. Billy Buildinginspector will testify about three job sites he visited to "sign off" on some of Jack's permits to bolster her claim Jack actually followed through on those jobs. Billy will also state how much Jack claimed he thought each job would cost when he applied for the original building permits as this indicates of Jack's income.

3. While introducing the building permits, Billy will to testify that, in his professional opinion, one of the jobs probably cost a lot more than the estimate stated in the building permit application. Billy believes Jack did this to avoid a higher fee for more extensive work.

4. Billy can identify a house Jack worked at without pulling a building permit which Jane was able to photograph. Jane needs a live witness to identify several 8x10 photographs and one blown up to a 20x24 poster to certify that it accurately depicts the scene at hand. Although Jane could introduce the photograph herself, she feels Billy would be a more powerful witness as he is the one who tipped her off about the work. This also indicates Jack is getting more work than she has been able to document by pulling building permits (an allusion Jane will have to make clear in her closing statement). Just in case, Jane has prepared a mini-backup script to get the photographs in herself as she is the one who took the pictures.

Jane should prepare a 'script' for *each and every witness*, testifying as to each and every fact she needs to make her case. By glancing at the list Jane just made above, she can begin to figure out what who-what-when-where-why-how and describe questions she needs to ask Billy Buildinginspector to get each fact she needs to support her case (and document she needs to introduce) into evidence. Three sample scripts based upon the above hypothetical situation follow:

EXHIBIT 17-6: SAMPLE DIRECT EXAMINATION OF BUILDING INSPECTOR

WITNESS: Billy Buildinginspector	SUBJECT: Authentication … 7 building permits Husband has pulled in Anytown while "not working" *Note: Billy is not on my witness list. Therefore, I can only introduce him after Jack testifies for "impeachment."*	
Question	**Answer sought**	**Exhibit**
Could you please introduce yourself for the record?	I'm Billy Buildinginspector.	
What do you do for work?	I'm the assistant building inspector for the Town of Anytown, Massachusetts	
What are some are your duties as the assistant building inspector?	I spend part of the day in my office reviewing and issuing building permits for the town, and the other part of the day going around to job sites conducting inspections of work that was done.	
Are you familiar with the defendant, Jack Rayme?	Yes. He comes into our office often.	
Has Jack come into your office any time in the last 6 months?	Yes, I believe so.	
Has he pulled any building permits?	Yes.	
I'd like to show you 7 documents labeled Plaintiff's Exhibit A through G. Do you recognize these documents?	Yes.	Refer to Exs. A through G
What are they?	They're building permits issued by the Town of Anytown.	Exs. A-G
Does the town create these building permits in the ordinary course of business?	Yes.	Exs. A-G
Are these records public records?	Yes.	Exs. A-G
Are you the person who issued these permits?	Not all of them. Some of them were issued by our head building inspector.	Exs. A-G
But if you have a copy of a building permit in your file, would it be fair to say that that permit was issued by your department?	Yes.	Exs. A-G
Your honor, I would like to introduce certified copies of 7 building permits labeled as Exhibits A though G. Each of these documents has been certified as authentic by the keeper of the records of Anytown, Celia Townclerk. They have been further certified by Billy Buildinginspector.	(hand permits to bailiff or clerk to give to judge)	Introduce Ex.-A through P-G into evidence

EXHIBIT 17-7: SAMPLE DIRECT EXAMINATION OF BUILDING INSPECTOR (CONT'D)

WITNESS: Billy Buildinginspector	SUBJECT: three permits "signed off" on while Jack was "not working" *Note: Billy is not on my witness list. Therefore, I can only introduce him after Jack testifies for "impeachment."*	
Question	**Answer sought**	**Exhibit**
Mr. Buildinginspector, I would like to draw your attention to plaintiff's exhibit A. What do you recall about this project?	(hand Billy his copy). I inspected this project.	Ex.A
What do you remember about it?	This was a deck added onto a house on South Shore Road.	
How big was the deck?	Pretty big. It was around 12 feet deep and wrapped around two sides of the house.	
Who was the contractor on this project?	Jack Rayme.	
Do you remember who was there when you signed off on the project?	Jack.	
How much did Jack say that project would cost in his building permit application?	$15,000.	
I'd like to draw your attention to plaintiff's exhibit E. What do you recall about this project?	It was a pretty big kitchen renovation. New cabinets, new appliances, a 24 foot carrying beam to support a wall Jack knocked out between two rooms. Several new windows. It was a major project.	Ex.E
How many inspections did you conduct on this project?	Several. Rough wiring inspection. Plumbing inspection. Inspection of the new beam. Occupancy permit signoff.	
Who was the contractor on that project?	Jack.	
How much did Jack say that project would cost on his building application?	$2,000	
Do you find that estimate to be credible?	No. (expect an objection here. Jack may say Billy is now testifying as an expert witness and you did not give notice. State Billy's estimate is not for the truth of the matter, but for impeachment).	
How much, in your experience, would a major kitchen renovation such as this cost?	This was easily a $50,000 kitchen renovation. Easily. If not more.	
Now I'd like to bring your attention to Plaintiff's exhibit G. Do you recall this project?	I inspected this project as well. This was a conversion of a basement into a family room, laundry room, and bathroom.	Ex.G
How much did Jack state this project would cost in his building application?	$22,000.	
Do you find that figure to be credible?	Yea, pretty much. It's a little low for that kind of work, but not outside the realm of what a contractor might charge for that kind of project.	

EXHIBIT 17-8: SAMPLE DIRECT EXAMINATION OF BUILDING INSPECTOR (CONT'D)

WITNESS: Billy Buildinginspector	SUBJECT: photographs	
	Note: Billy is not on my witness list. Therefore, I can only introduce him after Jack testifies for "impeachment."	
Question	**Answer sought**	**Exhibit**
Now, Mr. Buildinginspector, I'd like to bring you back to a conversation we had around a week ago about something you had heard about Jack's work. Do you remember that conversation?	Yes. *(the other side might object about hearsay. Point out you have not asked him to reiterate anything he heard, simply asked him to remember something as a precursor to a question)*	
(place photo)	*(if other side objects, Jane can explain the large picture is simply a "chalk" (a prop) to help the witness testify).*	Silently pace poster-sized Exhibit J on a pedestal in full view of the judge.
I'd like to show you four photographs identified as Plaintiff's Exhibits H, I, J and K. For the record, *I* was the one who took these photographs and I am now certifying they truly and accurately depict the scene I am about to ask the witness to describe and that they have not been altered in any way. Mr. Buildinginspector, do you recognize the scene these photographs depict?	Yes I do. (expect the other side to object both on the grounds the photographs weren't on the evidence list, or that you didn't lay the proper foundation, or that they don't depict the scene) (if you can't get Billy to introduce them, Jane can introduce them herself as she is the one who took the pictures).	Identify Exs. H, I, J, K
What is happening here?	Jack Rayme is illegally putting siding on a customer's house without a pulling a building permit.	Exs. H, I, J, K
Do you know when this happened?	I'm not sure when you took the pictures. I got a complaint from a neighbor about the work sometime last week and told you about it when you were in my office.	Exs. H, I, J, K
Do you know where this work occurred?	Yes. 15 Oak Street.	Exs. H, I, J, K
Do you recognize the people doing the work in this picture?	Yes I do.	Ex. K-A
Who are these people?	Jack Rayme and Bob Bullcowflap	Ex. K-A
Are you sure?	Yes. After you left, I went down to the jobsite and issued a stop-work order until they pulled the required building permit.	
Your honor, I would now like to introduce exhibits H, I, J, and K into evidence. To help you better see, I have taken the liberty of blowing up Exhibit J. I have listed that as Exhibit J-1.	(hand pictures to bailiff or clerk to give to judge).	Introduce Exs. H, I, J and K intro evidence
Mr. Buildinginspector, thank you for coming to court here today to testify.		

Now it is now time for Jack to cross-examine Jane's witness and try to discredit (impeach) him. These are some of the categories one party can use to discredit the other party's witnesses:

- Bias
- Prior inconsistent statement
- Bad character (such as poor reputation in the community or a prior conviction)
- Competency (lack of mental capacity)
- Contradiction

Since Billy Buildinginspector is a town official and testifying about documents and photographs which say it all, the only item Jack may gain traction on is Billy's estimate of how much the kitchen renovation cost. Jack might also ask Billy questions explaining that just because he did a $15,000 deck, after he bought building supplies, he probably didn't *earn* $15,000. Jane then could re-examine Billy (called rehabilitation) and ask him what percentage, in his experience, do the contractors he inspects on a daily basis earn of the projects they do.

Rehabilitate a Witness: the general rule is that you cannot bolster your own witnesses credibility *before* he has been impeached, but you can do so *afterwards*. You can generally only rehabilitate a witness on issues the opposing party has just impeached your witness on.

In other words, if Jack tries to claim Billy never contested the lowball price estimate in his building permit before now, Jane might ask Billy why he never contested it and Billy could claim the town does not have the manpower to verify the price claims on each and every building permit).

WHAT FACTS IS MY HUSBAND LIKELY TO OFFER TO UNDERMINE MY THEORY OF THE CASE AND SUPPORT HIS OWN?

Remember that a trial is about two people's opposing views of the same situation. As much as it would be nice if you could simply put your own witnesses on the witness stand and discredit your husbands, you have to remember that your husband is going to be trying to do the exact same thing to *you*. Earlier you were advised to list not only those things that *supported* your theory of the case, but also to think like your husband and think of all the rotten ways *he* might discredit *your* theory of the case. If you have been lucky enough to work with an attorney until now, chances are the two attorneys would have verbally or via discovery motions 'sparred' over the issues in your case and will know what dirty tricks to anticipate at trial. Experienced attorneys quickly become jaded about the veracity of their own clients and will make you 'fess up about your warts so they can defuse them. When you represent yourself, however, it is all too easy to stay in denial about weaknesses in your own case. *This is a fatal mistake!*

There are two kinds of fatal errors at trial:

1. The other side pulls a fast one (springs a surprise or puts on a witness who is willing to lie, exaggerate, or obfuscate the truth), leaving you unable to respond.

2. Self-inflected gunshot wounds (also known as self-denial).

Back to our hypothetical self-represented woman, Jane suspects Jack listed Bob Bullcowflap as a witness in his pre-trial memorandum because he wants Bobby to lie for him. Jane must be honest with herself if Bob Bullcowflap may have witnessed some bad behavior on *her* part in the past. In this case, she has searched her soul and remains convinced Bobby's only reason for being called to testify is to claim there is no work available in the area where Jack still lives. Jane bases this assumption on the following:

1. Jack and Bobby have been friends since high school and Jack moved to North Anytown so he could start a business with his best friend.

2. A few years after they began to work together, Bobby fell off a ladder and injured his back. Bobby has been classified as totally disabled and now collects SSDI.

3. For the past year or two, Bobby has returned to work "under the table" to meet his living expenses. Bobby is fearful SSDI will find out he sometimes works and revoke his disability payments.

4. Bobby is in too much pain many days to show up for work, and several homeowners have complained about him because he would take their deposit, start the job, and then not show up to complete the work for weeks at a time. Since North Anytown is a small town, most locals know not to hire Bobby unless you have a lot of time on your hands and don't mind waiting with a half-completed construction project for him to feel better and finish the job.

5. Bobby doesn't get called in to do many jobs unless he is working for Jack.

At first glance, Bobby Bullcowflap and Jack are both licensed home improvement contractors who live in work in the same geographic area. Jack is pulling Bobby in to discredit Jane's claim he should be able to find work. However, they are *not* the same. Somehow, Jane must convey to the trial judge that Bobby is not a good "ruler" for judging Jack's ability to find work. She has decided to focus her cross-examination on Bobby's ability to estimate Jack's ability to find work based on his own inability to find work as a disabled person.

ASKING YOUR HUSBAND LEADING QUESTIONS AND CROSS-EXAMINING YOUR HUSBAND'S WITNESSES

You could spend years learning about the nuances of asking questions of the opposing party and his witnesses at your trial and only scratch the surface. The truth is that even amongst attorneys, most are not very experienced with ripping apart the opposing party and the witnesses he tries to put on the stand to bolster his case. If you think you are going to ask a few questions and your husband or his witnesses are going to confess like in the movies, you are dreaming!

The best cross-examination I ever saw was conducted by a DSS attorney in a care and protection case I was handling representing the father. The DSS attorney, a slender, soft-spoken man with the countenance of an accountant, began to ask the mother short yes-or-no questions about details in a stack of police reports issued over the years by various police departments documenting the mother's extensive history of abuse at the hands of the children's father. The mother had hired a very good criminal attorney to "prove" she had faked reports of abuse because she was jealous (DSS had intervened because forcing children to witness spousal abuse is in itself abuse). "Do you recall…" "Do you remember telling officer so-and-so…" There was no grandstanding, no wild gesturing of arms or pounding on the desk or beating of the chest, no raised voices, nothing. Just question and answer, question and answer, question and answer, yes or no, yes or no, yes or no.

If the mother said no, the attorney would point out the mother's signature at the bottom of a written victim statement and ask her again. If she tried to explain or make an excuse about the discrepancy between her earlier written statement and what she was claiming now, the attorney would quietly cut her off and ask the judge to disregard everything the witness had said after his question, order the witness to answer yes or no, and the attorney would ask the exact same question over and over again until the witness answered. If she said she could not give a yes or no answer, he would rephrase the question and ask it again until he got the answer he wanted. I have never seen such a quiet, soft-spoken person totally eviscerate a witness and leave their entrails hanging all over the courtroom.

Cross examination is more of an art than a science. It is too broad of a subject to cover in a "how to" manual for laypeople.

All of this hypothetical posturing is NO SUBSTITUTE for having a qualified attorney represent you! It is my heartfelt hope that, after reading this, if you have not already hired an attorney to handle all of these nasty tasks *for* you, that you will borrow the money to hire one now! The only reason I cover it is because it is like offering sex education in high school. As much as you *wish* students would listen to your abstinence-only advice, the hard truth is that a certain percentage is going to go out and have sex anyways! The best you can do is make sure their ignorance doesn't leave them with a lifelong infectious disease!

The last thing to remember about cross examination (or party opponent questions) is that, to establish or disprove a single fact, you will have to ask dozens of simple yes or no questions to pry a truthful answer out of the witness. This may seem time consuming, but it really is not. If Jane Doe asks her husband, "isn't it true that you're lying through your teeth," he's going to say no. However, if she questions each small tidbit of information leading up to a major fact, even if Jack says no, Jack is not going to look very credible. No matter what Jack says, she will have proved her point.

In the Jane Doe hypothetical, Jane's strategy is to call Jack up to the witness stand to testify *first* (before other witnesses) and let him lie through his teeth about his income, then ask him questions about evidence she has to the contrary, and then call other witnesses/introduce other documents to impugn (impeach) his credibility and prove he is lying. Because Jack is a party opponent, she has the right to ask him leading (cross examination style) questions. However, since Jack has lied on every financial statement he has ever filed with the court and Jane can only get her new evidence in for impeachment (not direct examination), Jane has decided it would be more effective to go through every financial statement and ask Jack if it is true, and then let her other witnesses eviscerate him. *Not every trial would use this technique!!!* This is simply one way I might handle a known liar in a non-jury trial such as the Jane-Jack hypothetical.

FORWARD AMERICA !

If Jane's theory of her case was the fairness of equalizing income between the households for alimony purposes, she would start out first testifying about what her financial needs are and then focus on the *fairness* of having Jack pay more, not focus on discrediting Jack. For more information on trial strategies, read any of the many fine books written by judges and trial attorneys for trial attorneys, but be warned they may be too technical for an average layperson. The script-writing technique would be the same whether you are asking questions of your husband, or a witness your husband puts up on the witness stand to bolster his case.

A sample deliberately direct-examination script of Jack (a party opponent) and a cross-examination script of Jack's friend, Bob Bullcowflap, who Jane anticipates is probably going to claim he can't find work either, follows:

EXHIBIT 17-9: SAMPLE DIRECT EXAMINATION OF PARTY-OPPONENT HUSBAND

(although Jane could use Cross-Examination techniques, she has chosen not to)

WITNESS: Jack Doe-Rayme	SUBJECT: How much Husband is claiming he has been earning for the past year.	
Question	Answer sought	Exhibit
Could you please introduce yourself for the record?	I'm Jack Doe-Rayme, the Defendant in this case.	
Jack, in the financial statement you filed with the court this morning, you stated that you are currently earning around $50 per week, is that correct?	Yes.	Ex.L - today's financial statement
Your honor, I'd like to introduce today's financial statement into evidence as Plaintiff's Exhibit L.	*(Introduce L into evidence)*	Introduce Ex.L into Evidence
When we were here for the pre-trial conference back in October, you also filed a financial statement. Do you remember how much you were earning then?	I can't recall.	Ex.M – financial statement dated 10/15/07
I'd like to show you your financial statement from that date. Is this your signature?	Yes.	Ex.M…
How much did you say you were earning as of October 15th?	I was earning $75 per week doing odd jobs.	Ex.M…
Your honor, I'd like to introduce the Defendant's October 15th financial statement into evidence as Plaintiff's Exhibit M.	*(Introduce M into evidence)*	Introduce Ex.M into evidence
When we were here in July to discuss moving to Alaska, you filled out a financial statement for the court. Do you remember how much you were earning?	About the same, $75 or so…	Ex.N – financial statement dated 7/7/07
Your honor, I'd like to introduce the Defendant's July 7, 2007 financial statement into evidence as Plaintiff's Exhibit N.	*(Introduce N into evidence)*	Ex.N
When we were here for the temporary orders hearing back in March, you filled out a financial statement for the court. How much did you earn?	$50 a week	Ex.O – financial statement dated 3/15/07
Your honor, I'd like to introduce the Defendant's March 15, 2007 financial statement into evidence as Plaintiff's Exhibit O.	*(Introduce O into evidence)*	Ex.O…
Jack, how much have you been earning, on average, every week since we separated?	$50 to $75 per week.	
And is it your position to the court here today that you aren't capable of earning more than $50 to $75 per week?	Yes.	
No further questions on this subject…		

EXHIBIT 17-10: SAMPLE CROSS-EXAMINATION OF HUSBAND'S WITNESS

WITNESS: Bob Bullcowflap	SUBJECT: Cross on Bobby's ability to determine Jack's potential income – Bobby is legally disabled	
Question	Answer sought	Exhibit
Bobby, earlier you testified that, like Jack, you are unable to find work. Is that correct?	Yes.	
How much work have you done in the past year?	Oh, I don't know. A few thousand dollars' worth.	
How much work did you do the year before?	A bit more. Maybe around $20,000.	
What about the year before that?	I can't remember?	
Bobby, you are, in fact, legally disabled, aren't you?	Well, Ummmmm… (evasive answer)	
Your honor, could you please direct the witness to answer the question yes or no?	*Judge: the witness will answer the question.*	
Are you disabled, Bobby?	Yes.	
In fact, 6 years ago, you fell off a ladder and broke your back, didn't you?	Yes.	
And for the past 6 years, you have been in and out of the doctor's office for back pain and cortisone shots, haven't you?	Yes.	
In fact, if you are working, SSDI could revoke your disability payments, couldn't they?	Ummm… Uhhhh.. (evasive answer)	
Your honor, could you please direct the witness to answer the question yes or no?	*Judge: the witness will answer the question.*	
If SSDI catches you working on a job site, could they take away your disability check?	Yes.	
Earlier, we heard the Billy Buildinginspector testify that you were the other person in this photograph. Is this you, Bob?	No.	Ex. K
Is it still your position to this court, under oath, which could be used against you in a hearing by social security, that you are currently working as a licensed home improvement contractor?	No.	
Bobby, do you think it is fair that this court use *your* work experience, as a totally disabled person, as a ruler as to what a healthy person such as Jack could earn?	Yes, or no. (doesn't really matter, Bobby's credibility as an expert witness is toast).	
No further questions.		

SUBPOENAS

A subpoena is a court order that compels somebody to appear in court or to produce documents or records, generally a third-party who is not named on the lawsuit (versus a summons). For example, a party may subpoena bank, telephone, municipal, criminal, business, tax or other records. While there are many different types of records you may need, the steps to subpoena them are usually about the same. In most places, you must visit the court clerk in order to secure an official subpoena form and then serve it according to the requirements of your state court system.

First contact the court clerk and ask what their specific requirements are to subpoena people and/or records; the guidelines vary from state to state. Most courts have an official subpoena form called a subpoena duces tecum. Many states now allow you to go online and download that jurisdiction's form instead of going to the courthouse to pick one up.

Next complete the subpoena form by filling in pertinent details such as the name and address of the person or business who will receive the subpoena, the name and address of the court in which the case will be heard, the case document number, and the date by which the records are needed. The party requesting the subpoena also must list the records she needs, being as specific as possible. You will need to have it notarized either by a notary public or, in some situations, by a justice of the peace. Sometimes you will need the permission of the court and have it signed by *them* as well.

You will then need to have the subpoena served. The requirements for this vary from state to state. In some states, you must serve the opposing party with notice and give them a chance to object before you serve the subpoena on a third party, while in other cases you simply summons them to court or a deposition hearing and the onus is on the other side to run to court and object. Depending upon the rules in your home state, you will then need to have the subpoena served (delivered) in accordance with the laws of your jurisdiction. In some cases, this will mean arranging for the sheriff's department to provide service. In others, a person may pay a constable or professional process server to perform this task. Some laws also allow for subpoenas to be served by any person over 18 years old who is not a party to the case.

There is usually a 'witness fee' involved to pay the person you summons to court for their mileage and time, although the fee is often ridiculously inadequate to compensate them for their time.

In the Contempt hearing exercise in Chapter Twenty, the Wife uses a "keeper of the records" subpoena to produce employment records she obtained from her husband's former employer indicating her husband had just quit, not "lost", his job two weeks ago. In order for the court to accept them, the bookkeeper has to sign a "keeper of the records affidavit" swearing that they are the person who normally keeps these records in the course of business and that these are the records. Most companies will readily do this when served with a keeper of the records subpoena because they do not want their bookkeeper to waste a day in court to simply hand the judge the exact same piece of paper.

A sample subpoena, along with a constable affidavit, follows:

EXHIBIT 17-11: SAMPLE SUBPOENA

Commonwealth of Massachusetts
Subpoena

Barnstable, ss.

To   Billy Buildinginspector
   Anytown Town Hall
   222 Main Street
   Anytown, MA 01763

You are hereby commanded, in the name of the Commonwealth of Massachusetts, to appear before the <u>Probate & Family</u>
Court _____
at __<u>Barnstable Division</u>_ within and for the county of _<u>Barnstable, Massachusetts</u>
_____ on the _<u>20th</u>_ day of _<u>October, 2007</u>_____
at _<u>nine</u>_ o' clock, and from day to day thereafter, until the action hereinafter
named is heard by said Court, to give evidence of what you know relating to an action of
<u>divorce</u> then and there to be heard and tried between __<u>Jane Doe</u>_, Plaintiff and _<u>Jack Rayme</u>__, Defendant and you are
further required to bring with you _____   _____
<u>All Building Permits, including Applications, applied for by Jack Rayme in the last six   (6) months</u>_____
_____

Hereof fail not, as you will answer your default under the pains and penalties in the law
in that behalf made and provided.

Dated at __<u>Anytown, MA</u>_ the __<u>10th</u>__ day of __<u>October</u>___, 20_<u>07</u>_

Notary Public- Justice of the Peace

<u>Nancy Notary</u>
Nancy Notary, Notary Public

RETURN OF SERVICE

I this day summoned the within named _<u>Billy Buildinginspector</u>_
to appear as within directed by delivering to _<u>him</u>_
in hand, —leaving at
abode, to wit: No **Main**_____ *Street,*
in the **Barnstable** *District of said* <u>Barnstable</u>_ *an attested copy of the subpoena together with* _<u>$10.00</u>_ *fees for attendance*
and travel

Service and Travel   *$10.00*

Police Officer, Constable, Deputy Sheriff   *Constable*
Cop.
Pd. Witness
Motor Vehicle

It being necessary I actually used a motor vehicle the distance of <u>21</u>_ *miles in the service of this process.*

Police Officer, **Constable**, Deputy Sheriff

Subscribed and sworn to before me __<u>Charlie Constable</u>____
This   10th   day of   October   , 2007

<u>Nancy Notary</u>___
Nancy Notary, Notary Public

TRIAL NOTEBOOK(S)

Now that you have spent all this time gathering your evidence, creating witness scripts, and figuring out how you are going to get each fact before the judge, it is time to condense all of this information into an easily usable form.

I have found the simplest way is to buy a large 3-ring binder, some of those clear plastic document holders (or pocket holders) to insert each document or photograph into, and a 26-letter set of tabs from A to Z to label what you are planning on calling each piece of evidence. Put your *original* true attested documents here. Make a master list of all of the evidence, calling the first one "exhibit A, exhibit B, exhibit C…" until you have covered all of your exhibits. In large trials, I have introduced hundreds of documents and had to use alphanumeric codes such as DD-Z to include all of them. As you introduce each exhibit over the course of trial and hand it to the judge, this can help you see which pieces the other side may have barred and still need to be introduced (if possible).

The next category will be the testimony (or cross examination) of each witness. Purchase a second 3-ring binder and print out all of the fact "scripts" you created for *each* witness. If that witness will be introducing or authenticating a certain piece of evidence in your master document/evidence binder, make a copy of that evidence to hand to your witness. For example, if you will have Billy Buildinginspector identify seven building inspection applications and permits, you would make a copy of each permit he will be introducing and put a copy of the document immediately following the script-page which references that document. This way, you will always have a copy of the document you are referring to readily at hand and avoid fumbling back and forth between your master court document binder and your witness scripts. If you will be referring to something like a photograph, make a second copy so the judge look at *his* copy while your witness is describing a scene on *their* copy simultaneously. For example, in Jane's trial, she will create the following trial notebooks:

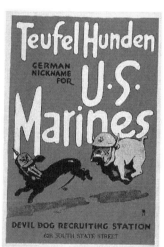

1. Master evidence binder of "originals" to unclip and hand to the judge as he allows her to introduce each item. List every item you have in this binder;

2. Jane's self-direct-examination statement with copies of evidence she will be introducing, including the building permits she scrounged up from other towns and a "backup" self-examination script to introduce the photographs herself if Billy is barred from introducing them.

3. Jack's hostile-party-opponent scripts with copies of evidence she plans on showing the judge (past financial statements);

4. Billy Buildinginspector's scripts with copies of building permit applications and the photographs.

5. Regina Remodelers scripts with copies of cancelled checks and invoices totaling tens of thousands of dollars for the addition Jack built onto her house;

6. Bobby Bullcowflap's cross-examination script with an extra copy of the photographs and any other evidence she intends to use.

Jane should also go through her case files and sort her documents into category folders such as "Admissions" or "other documents." She should create a "master list" of each category folder itemizing what each item contains in case Jack or his witnesses say something that she can refute through an earlier discovery request. It is very frustrating to know you have the answer somewhere, but not be able to put your hands on it, so go through all these documents, organize, and label them in such a way that you can quickly put your hands on it if you must.

There are dozens of other methods of organizing your information so that you can access it when you need it. Many of them are suggested in the various trial strategy books out there in the field published by trial attorneys. Use whatever method of organizing your scripts and evidence feels comfortable.

CHAPTER SEVENTEEN SUMMARY

1. Handling a trial is a lot more difficult than everything you have done thus far in your divorce. It takes an incredible amount of skill to win at trial, and there are many things the layperson doesn't know they don't know. If you can find (or borrow) money, hire an attorney. If not, you will need more resources than this book can give you alone.

2. To figure out how to handle your trial, you must first come up with a clear theory of your case. In an alimony case, your theory might be something like "my expenses are X and his expenses are Y ... it's fair to give me 35% of his income so I can meet my expenses."

3. List every single fact which either supports or does not support your theory of the case. You will need to figure out a way to either introduce it, or discredit it. You need to also figure out what order you are going to introduce your witnesses and evidence in to most effectively make your case.

4. To handle your own trial, you are going to have to learn the rules of evidence.

5. When it is your witness, you must ask who, what, when, where, how, describe, and sometimes why. You cannot ask leading questions. It is best to break down each fact into its own script.

6. Prepare a script for each witness, listing documents or other pieces of evidence you would like for them to introduce and noting any objections you anticipate the other party might make to keep it out.

7. When it is the opposing party *or* one of his witnesses, you can either ask them direct-examination style questions, or you can ask them leading questions.

8. Prepare a cross-examination script for your husband and each of his witnesses focusing on things you think they may be there to testify about.

9. If you want witnesses to appear, you must subpoena them or they will probably not show up. Nobody wants to waste a day in court.

10. Compile your trial scripts and evidence into "trial notebooks" so you can easily put your hands on it at trial.

CHAPTER 18

TRIAL

It's here! The big day you have been waiting for (or dreading). Now what?

It would be impossible to convey to you, the lay reader, all of the skills you need to know to successfully win your case. You were introduced to many fine resources in the previous chapters written by people far more experienced and knowledgeable about the subject than I am. If you wish to launch your own trial, I hope you read and/or buy their books.

However, I wrote this book because I was tired of seeing people who could not afford to hire a full-service attorney get denied a fair trial. Part of the decision about whether or not to hire attorney entails knowing the nature of the beast which you are facing. Therefore, I will outline specific little cameos to give you the general feel of how a trial might unfold (versus what you might have seen on the television) so you can be physically and emotionally prepared. This section is *not* included to lull you into a false sense of security that you can handle your own trial!

⚑ *Your best chance of 'winning' at trial is to hire a full-service attorney!*

The court will make you follow a pattern which should be familiar by now. First you may need to check in with the Probation/Family Services Department and wait to be seen by a family services officer. They will ask if you have agreed upon anything since the pre-trial conference. If you have narrowed down the number of issues or settled the case, they will help you draw up a stipulation. Many cases which have not settled before trial often reach agreement in the eleventh hour because an obstinate party finally hired a lawyer, got a reality check, and decided trial was not in their best interests. Perhaps *you* are the one who decided it isn't worth the hassle or cost.

If you still have not reached an agreement, the family services officer will send you into the courtroom to wait for your turn and hand your case file to the clerk. Once called, the judge may ask you questions about what issues you are asking him to decide (based upon your pre-trial memorandum and usually the family services officer report). He will then give you permission to begin your opening arguments

The Plaintiff (person who filed the complaint) usually speaks first. It is customary to give a brief Opening Statement explaining to the court what the major issues of your case are (your theory of the case) and alluding to facts you intend to introduce at trial to support that theory. If, in a case such as our hypothetical Jane Doe divorce trial, proving the other side to be a liar is a major component in your trial, you will omit references to the other person being a liar and simply make a statement that you believe the evidence will show your husband is capable of earning more money. A sample Opening Statement for Jane Doe-Rayme follows. The Defendant will similarly make their opening statement.

⚑ *If your husband has an attorney and you do not, the court will sometimes subconsciously favor the attorney* and ask them to have them go first whether or not they are the Plaintiff. *Do not let this happen!!!*

If you are the Plaintiff, politely, but firmly, remind the judge that it is your right to be allowed to go first. It is your right, and it is rare the judge (once his error is pointed out) will choose otherwise. If you are the Defendant, you will give *your* opening statement second and should focus on refuting Jack's claims. In Jane Doe's hypothetical case, since she wishes to prove Jack is a liar, she may decide to call *Jack* as her first witness, let him lie under oath, and then call her own witness to discredit him.

The Plaintiff then gets to call their witnesses and examine them (ask them questions) directly. Jack may object to evidence Jane is trying to introduce, so Jane should photocopy her script and attach a copy of each evidentiary foundation (i.e., the page out of your state Rules of Evidence book) with the directions on what she needs to do to get the judge to accept it. Once Jane finishes asking her witnesses questions, Jack will have an opportunity to cross-examine them to challenge their credibility. Since they are Jane's witnesses, Jack is limited to asking them questions which are relevant to issues Jane had them testify about.

Jane decided to read a written statement she prepared in lieu of her testimony (she has no lawyer to ask her questions) following the general chronology her attorney would use if she had one and introduce documents to the court at the appropriate time using modified versions of the scripts suggested by her practical evidence book. Although Jane's statement will not be directed by an attorney, Jane followed a similar fact-fact-fact pattern and created a trial notebook for herself similar to what she prepared for her witnesses. Jane has made a strategic decision in her particular case to call Jack first, the building inspector second, the home remodel lady third, and then she will speak. This is the reverse of how many trials are conducted, but she thinks it makes more sense to prove Jack a liar immediately after he lies since child support is the biggest remaining issue in this case and that, once proven, it will sway the judge to find her more credible about other issues such as the mysterious $20,000 Merrily-Merrily Retirement stock account. A sample self-script follows.

Jack will then have an opportunity to speak. He will similarly make statements which will have to serve as his testimony (or if he has hired an attorney, his attorney will conduct a direct examination of him). If he is introducing his own documents, he will do so. If Jane has learned enough about the rules of evidence to believe Jack is making a statement which is impermissible, she should object. For example, if Jack starts to say "my sister told me that Jane told *her* blah blah blah...", Jane would object and state it is heresay (Jack's sister is the proper party to testify, not Jack). If Jack tries to introduce evidence which was not listed on the pre-trial memorandum and is not being introduced to impeach her, she should object and request it not be allowed. There are many more ways to keep evidence out at trial which Jane can learn about through her evidence book, but those are the two most common areas. Jane knows that Jack is having his best friend Bobby testify and *thinks* he will be testifying about the lack of work. Jane has already prepared her cross-examination script and would then go through it if that is what happens. If that is not what happens, Jane will have to adjust her strategy accordingly.

Once they are both done introducing witnesses and evidence, it is time to make their closing arguments. In our Jane Doe hypothetical, both major issues focus around Jack's tendency to hide income and assets from the court, so she would state such. She would then list through pieces of evidence she thinks support her theory of the case. Then Jack will do the same thing.

The judge will usually state he is going to think things over and send you his decision in the mail.

EXHIBIT 18-1: JANE'S OPENING STATEMENT

Your honor, we're here today because my husband and I cannot agree on two major issues, how much money he *earns* or *should be earning*, and how much money he *has*.

I intend to introduce the following evidence to help this court make its decision. For the three years prior to filing for divorce, Jack made a good income. All of a sudden, the moment I file for divorce, Jack claims he can't find work. I believe the court will agree with me that Jack either *is*, or *should be,* capable of earning a lot more money than he has listed on his financial statement to help support his children.

I also intend to introduce evidence that, shortly before we separated, Jack had $20,000 worth of stock in a secret Merrily-Merrily Retirement account which he has never disclosed. I believe the court will agree with me that the $20,000 stock account is a joint marital asset subject to division in this divorce.

The last issues we have are who will claim the children as tax dependents and who will provide health insurance. My position on these issues is clearly stated on my pre-trial memorandum. I believe the court will have enough information after this trial to make a fair and equitable decision regarding those remaining issues.

I am not an attorney and not very familiar with the rules of evidence, although I have made some effort to learn enough to not slow down the court. Therefore, I would greatly appreciate it if your honor would state the basis of any objection it intends to uphold so I can refer to my notes and try to give you what you are looking for.

Thank you.

Jane's opening statement is short and sweet. She lets the judge know what issues she will be focusing on at trial and gives a hint of things to come. However, since one of Jane's major strategies is to discredit

Jack after he lies (again), she keeps her hints subtle. She hints that Jack–should be- earning a lot more money. Since the secret stock account has been disputed from the beginning, Jane could give a few more hints if she so chose. However, since she already has several "aces" up her sleeve as to Jack's hidden income, she has chosen to not bore the judge with a long list of things she will introduce to prove the existence of the stock account.

Jane reminds the court there are a few other issues which have not been resolved (tax deductions, health insurance, etc.). Since her position has not changed since the pre-trial hearing and the questions are really matters of judicial discretion (and also because she does not have the funds to hire a CPA to argue about her taxes), she is choosing to leave it up to the judge.

Although Jack is still griping about the kids moving, he is not contesting custody and has not taken the basic step of completing anger management in order to see his kids. Therefore, Jane plans on only responding to anything Jack raises on this issue if necessary. We are assuming the marital home has either sold by now, or is on the market to keep this chapter a manageable size.

EXHIBIT 18-2: JACK'S OPENING STATEMENT

Your honor, I am having a hard time finding work. I don't know why Jane keeps insisting I should be earning more money, but the 'housing bust' is all over the news. Nobody is building houses right now! And nobody wants to hire me since Jane bad-mouthed me to everyone in town.

Jane also keeps going on about some secret stock account. There *is* no secret stock account. First she files a bogus restraining order on me, and then she says I am earning money when I'm not. Then she takes my kids and hauls them all the way across the country to Alaska. Alaska!!! My poor kids are freezing in Alaska and I can't see them.

Jane is making me pay money I don't have, sold my house out from under me, took my kids, and now she wants to claim them on her taxes. I want the court to fix this and let me see my kids. Oh, and if I have to pay child support then I want to claim them on my tax return as dependents!

Since Jack is being portrayed as not having an attorney, he is making the kind of speech you might see an uninformed self-represented person make. He is angry about how things have gone so far, but he doesn't really understand that the court will not revisit it's decision to let the kids move out of state or make him attend anger management before seeing them in an unsupervised setting, nor will the court vacate the restraining order or magically buy back the house that was sold after Jack stopped paying the mortgage. It *could* revisit these issues had Jack listed them as contested on his Pre-Trial Memorandum, but since Jack did not do so, Jan can bar him from arguing about these issues.

The only issues the court will likely address is Jack's earning capacity so it can determine how much child support he should pay (adjusted for the distance he must travel) and the issue Jane raised about the secret stock account. The court will make a decision on a tax exemption and health insurance after it makes a decision on the other issues, but the judge will decide what he feels is fair at the end of the trial.

EXHIBIT 18-3: JANE'S TESTIMONY ABOUT JACK'S EARNING CAPACITY

WITNESS: Jane Doe	SUBJECT: Jack's earning capacity	
Question	**Answer sought**	**Exhibit**
I'm the plaintiff, Jane Doe. Since I don't have an attorney, I will introduce evidence I feel the court needs to make an informed decision and explain them as best I can.		
I would like to introduce Exhibits P, Q, and R. These are the last three years of joint tax returns. I would like to point out that Jack earned between Fifty and fifty-five thousand dollars each year.	Give Exhibits P, Q, and R to the judge	Introduce Exs. P, Q, R
Next is a list of telephone calls I received from people looking to hire Jack to do work on their houses between the day I was forced to file a restraining order last December until I moved in August of this past year.	Jack objects. The Judge asks on what basis and Jack says Jane is lying. The judge asks Jane to "lay the proper foundation." "Lay the proper foundation" is code-talk for "you skipped a step … look it up in your evidence book and I'll probably let it in"	Introduce Ex. S
This is a list I made of telephone calls I received at the house between December of 2006 and August of 2007. I am attesting now that this is the actual list I made, it has in no way been altered or changed, and I am swearing under oath that the list represents my recollection of telephone calls I actually received when I wrote it down.	The judge decides the list can come into evidence. Jane adds two things. She swears the list is genuine (not altered or changed) and it represents her recollection of facts recorded at the time she wrote it down (Past recollection recorded).	Ex.S
I swear I gave each and every one of the potential customers on this list Jack's cell phone number.		Ex. S
Earlier, Jack testified there was no work available to him and introduced a government report about new housing starts being down in the USA. I would like to now introduce a different study by the Massachusetts Department of Housing and Urban Development which states that, although *new* housing starts are down, the *renovation* market is as robust as ever.	Jack objects and says the report is a fake. Jane points out the embossed seal and keeper of the records certification the secretary at HUD stamped on the report (Jane contacted them for a true copy attest after finding a copy of the report on the internet) and explains it is a public record. The judge allows it.	Ex. T
Your honor, lastly I would like to give you copies of four *more* building permit applications taken out by Jack in the towns of South Shore and Harbor Village in the last 6 months for projects he listed as totaling around $85,000. These are all public records and all have a keeper of the records certification attached.	Jack objects and states they weren't listed on the witness list. Jane explains they are not being offered for the truth of the matter, but are being offered for impeachment of Jack's earlier claims he is not working. The judge allows it.	Ex. U, V, W, X

Jack's original attorney suddenly withdrew after Jack refused to disclose the Merrily-Merrily Retirement stock account after Jane's discovery requests last spring (we don't know why he withdrew, just that he suddenly did, but the timing is interesting). No attorney would take on Jack as a client unless he agreed to "come clean" about the stock account. Here is Jane educating the judge about that information:

EXHIBIT 18-4: JANE'S TESTIMONY ABOUT JACK'S SECRET STOCK ACCOUNT

WITNESS: Jane Doe	SUBJECT: Merrily Retirement stock account	
Question	**Answer sought**	**Exhibit**
Now, your honor, I'd like to talk about marital assets. Although the court ordered the marital home to be sold and all of our personal property has already been divided, there still remains one outstanding asset which has yet to be dealt with. I would like to introduce now a copy of the 3rd Quarter 2006 statement for a Merrily-Merrily Retirement Stock Account number XYZ-1234567 received in the mail at Jack's post office box in October of 2006.	Jack objects, says not relevant. Jane explains is a basis for testimony she is about to give and asks the judge to accept the statement de bene (depending). The judge allows it.	Ex. U
Your honor, I know nothing about this stock account. Jack has refused to disclose any information about it and his lawyer quit when I sent him a discovery request. If you recall, we were in on a Motion to Compel in May. The court ruled it would bar Jack from introducing or denying the existence of this account at trial if he did not comply with the discovery request. You can clearly see on this statement Jack's name and the last four digits of his social security number. It is my belief that Jack is trying to hide this $20,000 from the court to avoid having you divide it.	Jack does not think to have the judge make a ruling on the "de bene" ruling (a common mistake), so therefore it comes in. Jane also points out she had come in on a Motion to Compel earlier and Jack still didn't comply, although she never came back a second time after Jack still refused to comply for a "firm" order barring the objection. Because of Jack's failure to disclose, the judge may decide it's going to come in anyways. Otherwise, Jane had better have the keeper of the records of Merrily-Merrily Retirement waiting in the aisle to swear it is genuine or it could be barred.	Ex. U
Thank you sir, I have nothing else to give you. I am ready to answer any questions you may have.	Jack cross-examines Jane, asking questions that have nothing to do with anything she has just introduced. Jane states "objection … relevance?" after the more ridiculous statements. The judge will grow tired of Jack's ranting and start to uphold Jane's objections after around 20 minutes.	

Jane's witnesses and things she wrote in her pre-trial memorandum, hinted at in her opening statement, and will state more clearly in her closing argument have done most of the work of making her case for her. Although she is not an attorney, she has done a good job of making her case.

Jack will now testify, introducing his own view of the situation. Because he is pro se, the judge may give him a lot more leeway than he would give an attorney, but at some point (usually around noon) the judge will start looking at his watch and peeking under the case folder at the takeout menu for the sub shop down the street. Judges are human just like the rest of us, so please don't bore them!

EXHIBIT 18-5: JANE'S CLOSING ARGUMENT

Your honor, the two main issues here today are does Jack have enough income to support his children, and is the $20,000 Merrily-Merrily Retirement stock account a joint marital asset subject to division. I would answer that both questions should be answered yes.

Although Jack claims he is only capable of earning around $50 to $75 per week, we learned from Billy Buildinginspector that Jack pulled 7 building permits in that town in the last 6 months. Furthermore, we learned that Jack probably grossly understated the cost of a major kitchen renovation in one of the cases by around $50,000. Although Billy conceded that not every penny of the cost of a home renovation is pure profit, he stated that in his opinion, around 75% of the cost of every project is labor.

We also learned that one of those 7 projects, Regina Renovators house, was a 1200 square foot, two-story addition costing nearly $100,000. Regina had copies of cancelled checks written to Jack, as well as invoices he gave to her showing that $73,000 of that cost was labor.

Anytown isn't the only town Jack did work in. I was able to dig up four additional building permit applications pulled by Jack in South Shore and Harbor Village totaling another $85,000.

Lastly, a picture is worth a thousand words. I photographed Jack doing the siding on a house on Oak Street just a few days ago, and then the Assistant Building Inspector testified he went over and cited him for working without pulling a building permit.

Jack claims he never received any of the telephone calls from the list I gave him, but if you check the names of the people who Jack pulled building permits for and my list, you will see that 9 of the 11 people he pulled building permits for are on my list. Not only is Jack working, but he's got hundreds of thousands of dollars of gross income going through his business this year. Now, I'm not an accountant and I don't know how much profit Jack will have after taxes, but I think the court would agree that Jack is *most certainly* not out of work.

Lastly, there's the matter of the $20,000 Merrily-Merrily Retirement stock account Jack claims doesn't exist. You have a statement issued shortly before the divorce in your hands, and Jack has refused to account for where that money has gone. In light of Jack's honesty in testifying about his lack of income, I invite the court to draw its own conclusions as to whether that stock account exists and is subject to division in this divorce. Thank you.

Besides being a genuinely funny movie, *My Cousin Vinny* is a highly accurate depiction of what happens when a layperson (or in Vinny Gamboni's case, someone with a bit of legal knowledge) attempts to handle their own case. Give yourself the gift of watching the movie through the eyes of an attorney and try to see how many of the following questions you can answer. Although the case covers a *criminal* case, the rules of procedure and many of the errors make are the same errors pro se divorce litigants make. Watch it! This movie will teach you more about what *not* to do at trial than a dozen self-help legal books!

EXHIBIT 18-6: *MY COUSIN VINNY* FUN TRIAL-PREP EXERCISE

QUESTIONS FOR *'MY COUSIN VINNY'*

1. How many cases had Vinny Gambini handled before he took on his cousins murder trial?
2. Was Vinny being honest when he told the judge he'd been practicing for 16 years?
3. How did the judge say he viewed formality and procedure in his court?
4. What book did the judge give Vinny before he left his office the first time?
5. What did the judge tell Vinny he expected him to know before he came into his courtroom?
6. What did the judge say was an insult to both himself and the court?
7. What did the judge say Vinny had better wear the next time he came to court?
8. At the arraignment, did the judge want to hear Vinny give an explanation as to what had happened to the defendants?
9. What sanctions did the judge threaten Vinny with if he said the wrong thing next time?
10. What were the stakes for his client's if Vinny didn't do a good job defending them?
11. As he left the prison the first time, when did Vinny tell Mona Lisa he was going to learn the rules of procedure?
12. Do they teach this in law school?
13. What two ways do lawyers usually learn procedure?
14. At the grand jury investigation, what did the prosecutor state to the court after he showed the witness Mrs. Riley a photograph of the defendants car?
15. How did Vinny end up becoming a lawyer?
16. Why did Vinny go hunting with the prosecutor?
17. Was going hunting a necessary step to get information? What did the prosecutor do as soon as Vinny asked?
18. Do you *have* to let the other side know what evidence you plan on introducing at trial?
19. What is it called when you let the other side know the evidence in your case?
20. Name three things the rules of "disclosure" mandate you let the other side do?
21. Is the prosecution in a murder trial allowed any surprises?
22. At the trial, what happened when Vinny talked back to the judge?
23. Name three things the prosecutor said the evidence was going to show in his opening statement.
24. Why did the prosecutor object to Mona Lisa testifying about cars at trial?
25. What did Vinny do to prove Mona Lisa was an "expert witness?"
26. Are you willing to learn about all these procedural things before you handle your *own* legal case?

CHAPTER EIGHTEEN SUMMARY

1. Each party usually opens their trial with a brief opening statement. The opening statement is designed to frame the issues and hint at what kinds of evidence you might be introducing to support your theory of the case. Think of it as a tiny gourmet appetizer.

2. The Plaintiff generally gets to call their witnesses first, and then the Defendant goes second.

3. After you have your witnesses testify, the opposing party has the right to cross examine them (ask them questions) to discredit them.

4. If the other side objects to a witness statement or piece of evidence and the judge upholds an objection, ask him to state the basis so you can try to get the evidence in some other way. Frequently, the object or statement itself isn't objectionable, but rather the way you are trying to get it in.

5. When you are both done, you both have the right to make a closing argument. A good closing argument reiterates the issues you are asking the court to decide, and then lists off some of the major pieces of evidence you introduced at trial to support your theory of the case.

6. *Caveat:* the sample "trial" in this manual is deceptively short and simple. It included only to impress upon you the idea that handling your own trial requires an enormous amount of knowledge, preparation, and skill which is probably beyond your current abilities. True trial skills go far beyond the scope of this Bootcamp manual. I strongly recommend you either hire an attorney or, failing that, read the resources listed throughout this manual so you are better prepared to go it alone.

(This page left intentionally blank)

CHAPTER 19

FINAL DISPENSATION

There are generally two ways to get divorced. In Section II of this manual, we covered uncontested divorces. In Section III, we looked at what might happen if you have to file in court, but pointed to the reality that 80% of all divorce cases end up settling before going to actual trial (usually at the pre-trial hearing). We will look at what your final communication of divorce will be in both situations.

FINAL DISPENSATION FOR A SETTLED DIVORCE

If you are able to reach an agreement, either in advance of the pre-trial conference or that day with the help of the family services officer, your actual divorce will be almost anti-climactic. After all these months of research, preparation, posturing, and forcing your spouse to comply kicking and screaming with your information requests, the hearing will be dull by comparison.

A typical uncontested divorce hearing goes like this:

1. You will be sworn in under oath and asked to state your names for the record;

2. The judge (who will have glanced through the agreement to make sure it sounds fair) will ask you if you both agree an irretrievable breakdown of your marriage has occurred;

3. The judge will then ask you if you have both read the signed separation agreement, had the *opportunity* to consult with counsel, and understand the items outlined in the agreement.

4. Sometimes, the judge will go through the different exhibits in the separation agreement to make sure you really understand what you signed.

5. The judge will then ask you each if you signed the agreement freely, voluntarily, and without coercion;

6. The judge will then state you are now divorced.

7. Congratulations!!! In a few weeks you will receive a "Judgment of Divorce Nisi" in the mail which will tell you how many days it takes for your divorce to become final (generally 90 to 120 days).

After everything you just did to get divorced, isn't this final hearing almost a slap in the face? It is not unusual for couples who reach an agreement at the last moment to give each other a hug, exchanges promises of mutual cooperation and support, and walk out of the courthouse hand-in-hand.

The cooperation usually ends the moment they get in the car and drive away. But it's a pleasant surprise when it happens…

EXHIBIT 19-1: SAMPLE JUDGMENT OF UNCONTESTED DIVORCE NISI

COMMONWEALTH OF MASSACHUSETTS

BARNSTABLE, SS.   **PROBATE AND FAMILY COURT   DOCKET NO. <u>07D-9999-DV1</u>**

JANE DOE-RAYME, Plaintiff

v.

JACK RAYME,   **Defendant**

<u>JUDGMENT OF DIVORCE NISI UNDER M.G.L. Ch.208, s.1-A</u>

All persons interested having been notified in accordance with the law, and after hearing, it is adjudged *nisi* that a divorce from the bond of matrimony be granted for the parties for the cause of irretrievable breakdown as provided by Chapter 208, section 1(a), and that upon and after the expiration of ninety (90) days from the entry of this judgment, it shall become and be absolute unless, upon the application of any person within such period, the Court shall otherwise order. It is further ordered the parties shall comply with an Agreement filed October 15, 2007, the terms of which are filed, incorporated and not merged in this Judgment, but shall nevertheless survive and have independent legal significance, except for issues related to the couple's minor children, which shall merge with the divorce and not survive as an independent contract. The Court finds that said Agreement is fair and reasonable for the parties in the circumstances of this case.

October 15, 2007

_____Johnny B. Good, III_____
Johnny B. Good, III
Justice of the Probate and Family Court

FINAL DISPOSITION FOR A CONTESTED DIVORCE AFTER TRIAL

So, you've prepped, planned, and sweated your way through your trial. Now what? You wait. It is very rare that the judge will render any decision on the spot after a trial other than the fact he is granting your divorce. Judges are diligent people. They will frequently go back to their offices and look up a few legal precedents to cite when they issue their written order. The other thing Judges want to avoid like the bubonic plague is to make some comment about which way they're leaning after a lengthy trial and have one of the parties start going postal all over the courtroom. Therefore, the judge will usually tell you, "I'll consider the evidence you gave here today and issue my findings in a few days."

Most litigants can live with this. What they *can't* live with is walking out of the courthouse after all that stress without a piece of paper in their hand saying they're divorced. The little magical piece of paper (the one that will allow you to get your icky ex-husbands last name off of your driver's license and all the other documents that won't let change without a court order) won't arrive in the mail for a few weeks. When it comes, it is likely that *neither* party is going to like what the judge ordered. If in doubt, judges tend to "split the baby in half."

A sample "Judgment of Divorce Nisi" under my home state's 'at fault' divorce statute follows:

EXHIBIT 19-2: SAMPLE JUDGMENT OF CONTESTED DIVORCE NISI

COMMONWEALTH OF MASSACHUSETTS

BARNSTABLE, SS.   PROBATE AND FAMILY COURT   DOCKET NO. 07D-9999-DV1

JANE DOE-RAYME, Plaintiff
v.
JACK RAYME, Defendant

JUDGMENT OF DIVORCE NISI UNDER M.G.L. Ch.208, s.1-B

All persons interested having been notified in accordance with the law, and after hearing it is adjudged *nisi* that a divorce from the bond of matrimony be granted the said Plaintiff (hereinafter "Wife") against the said Defendant (hereinafter "Husband"), for the cause of irretrievable breakdown as provided by Chapter 208, section 1(b), and that upon and after the expiration of ninety (90) days from the entry of this judgment, it shall become and be absolute unless, upon the application of any person within such period, the Court shall otherwise order. It is further ordered as follows:

The parties are bound by their partial agreement dated October 15, 2007 which shall be incorporated but not merged into the judgment of divorce *nisi,* but notwithstanding said incorporation, said agreement shall survive and have independent legal significance, *except for* those provisions relating to the children of the parties, which said provision shall be incorporated and merged and shall *not* have independent legal significance.

The Court finds said Agreement to be fair and reasonable and not the product of fraud or coercion.

Regarding the issues of child support and tax dependency exemptions, which issues the parties agreed would be determined by the Court, it is ordered as follows:

The Husband shall pay child support to the Wife in the amount of $101.00 per week. I hereby find the husband has the ability to pay this amount. The Wife shall claim the parties daughter, Jayne, as a dependent for income tax purposes and the Husband shall claim the parties' son, Johnnie, as a dependent for income tax purposes. When only child is able to be claimed, the parties shall alternate claiming that child on a year-to-year basis, with the Husband claiming the child in the first year. However, the Husband's right to claim either of the children is dependent upon the Husband being completely up to date with his child support obligation (meaning zero arrears) as of December 31 in the year he seeks to claim. The records of the Department of Revenue shall be definitive proof as to whether or not there was an arrearage.

The Wife shall add the Husband to her family insurance plan for so long as such a plan is available to her at a reasonable cost, or until either party remarries. The Husband shall reimburse her one-half of the cost of the family plan, with said premiums being already computed into the $101 per week child support order in the preceding paragraph. If an event occurs which will affect coverage for the Husband, the Wife shall give the Husband notice as soon as possible.

The Wife may resume her former name of Jane Doe.

October 15, 2007   _____Johnny B. Good, III_____
                                          Johnny B. Good, III
                                          Justice of the Probate and Family Court

APPEALS – WHAT CAN I DO IF I THINK THE JUDGE WAS WRONG?

What do you do if you get your final order from the judge, and you disagree with it? Generally, you are stuck with what the judge decided to give you. If you forgot to lay the groundwork to get a piece of evidence into the record or the judge shut down one of your witnesses because of some obscure rule of evidentiary procedure, it is probably too bad. Judges have broad, discretionary powers to decide your case and you usually have little recourse against it.

What do you do, however, if you research the issue and realize the judge *clearly* made a mistake? In that case, you must move very quickly to preserve your right to appeal. This book is not going to teach you how to appeal the case, only that you have a right to do so.

🚩 *Most states only give you between ten (10) and thirty (30) days from the date on the bottom of your "Judgment of Divorce Nisi" to file a "Notice of Appeal" with the clerk at the court which issued your judgment.* In some states, that time is even *less!* So if you want to appeal it, you'd better be quick!

Mistakes which *might* allow you to flip a bad decision on appeal are as follows:

- the Findings of Fact are inconsistent with the evidence;

- the judgment entered is inconsistent with the findings of fact;

- the judge exhibits prejudice on the record;

- the judgment appears to be beyond the scope of decency and reason or is beyond the authority of the court;

- the judge has failed to perform his or her statutory responsibility to consider all factors under your state's property division statute requiring evidence of specific factual considerations by the court;

- the judge has failed to find an ability of the defendant to pay an arrearage in a contempt proceeding yet orders him or her to jail;

- the litigant is denied constitutional rights at the commencement of or during the course of the litigation;

- the court delegates judicial responsibility without authority of statute or rule;

- the application of the law is clearly erroneous; or

- there has been judicial abuse of discretion

It is nearly impossible for a layperson to successfully negotiate an appeal. Where the standard in your divorce trial was "preponderance of the evidence" (51% right), the standard to prove the judge made a mistake will be more like the criminal court's "beyond a reasonable doubt" (99.9% right) standard. Worse, if your case has no legal basis other than the fact you are merely unhappy, you could be slapped with the other side's legal. Therefore, if you truly believe the judge made a huge mistake at your trial, preserve your right to appeal the case by going down to the clerk's office to file a "Notice of Appeal," serve a copy on the other side (there is not penalty if you then decide not to follow through), and then get your fanny to the nearest attorney's office to retain them to handle your appeal *for* you.

CHAPTER NINETEEN SUMMARY

1. In an uncontested (jointly filed) divorce, the judge will usually say he is granting the divorce that day. Within 30 days your divorce paper will come in the mail. It usually takes between 90-120 days (depending upon your individual state law) to become final.

   a. This timeline does not include any mandatory 'separation periods' your state may require before filing for divorce.

2. If your divorce starts out contested, but you reach an agreement at any time prior to trial, you can convert your divorce to an uncontested one. It will then be treated the same as a jointly filed one.

3. In a contested divorce, the judge will usually take the case *under advisement* and render a decision sometime within the next few weeks. If you filed an at-fault divorce, the judge *will* usually say he is granting the divorce that day, but you will need to wait for the rest of your terms.

4. If you think the judge made an egregious error, you can appeal it. The timeline for appeal is *very* short. If you don't appeal quick, you will lose that right forever!

5. It is very difficult to turn something over on appeal, but sometimes it happens.

CHAPTER 20

CONTEMPT

Failing to follow a court order is known as contempt. If the court ordered your husband to do something, such as pay child support, pay "x" percent of the mortgage, keep you and your children on his health insurance, give you back your car, whatever, and he doesn't do it, there is a special procedure for getting the matter back before the judge. The court will hold a special contempt hearing and, if they feel he is doing this deliberately, they will order him to comply or face jail time. They usually give him a few weeks to comply the first time through, but if you need to bring him back more than once within a short period of time, they sometimes will just throw him in jail.

The first question you must ask yourself is whether or not your original divorce is still pending. If you have not yet gone to trial (or your final hearing if you settle), you would file a "Motion for Contempt Review," schedule a date with the clerk, and mail a copy of the motion and notice of the hearing to your husband the same as any other motion.

If the judge has already granted your divorce and it has become final, you will need to re-open your case. You must file a Complaint for Contempt, have the Sheriff serve it along with a Contempt Summons to your husband's last known address, and go to court on the date the clerk tells you to go for your hearing. If the Child Support Enforcement Division is collecting your child support for you and the issue the contempt revolves around is child support, you should mail *them* a copy of the complaint as well. It is good practice to staple a copy of the original order to the Complaint.

Some states have a grey area between the date the court grants your divorce, and when it becomes final. In that situation, you may be able to get away with simply filing a Motion for Contempt, or the court may make you file an entirely new Complaint for Contempt. The only way to find out is to ask an attorney or call the courthouse and ask the clerk.

When you file a Complaint for Contempt, you must use whatever forms and grade of paper your local courthouse requires. Most states have this information online, or you can visit your local family court and request blank forms from the clerk. How far past-due your state considers egregious enough to come to court varies, so you will need to research it online, speak to an attorney, or ask the local clerk. You need to fill out a fresh financial statement every time you go to court. Many states do not charge you for filing a Complaint for Contempt, but the Sheriff will *definitely* charge you for serving it. Jane Doe's sample 'Complaint for Contempt' follows.

In most states, unlike your original Divorce summons, a Complaint for Contempt does not need to be served in hand, but can simple be served at your former spouse's home. Unless it is a dire emergency (such as your house is about to be foreclosed upon), you will likely get a court date approximately 6 weeks in the future ordering your husband to appear and explain why he hasn't done what he was ordered to do. The court generally schedules it 6 weeks out hoping the deadbeat will cough up the money (or comply) and you can drop the case. However, if he hasn't paid by then, you will need to appear in court.

I use Child Support as the example in this chapter, but Contempt can be filed for *any* term of your Separation Agreement that your former husband fails to honor. Child Support, Alimony, and the payment of bills are the most common reasons people need to go back to court.

If your husband is more than $5,000 behind on his child support and you are having it withheld by the Child Support Enforcement division (this dollar amount may vary from state to state), you may be able to ask *them* to go to court with you to help you collect it. Many state Child Support Enforcement Division departments will do this for you free of charge or at a greatly reduced rate. If you now live in a different state than the one you lived in while still married, you can even get the Child Support Enforcement Division to work with this Division in another state so that you don't have to travel across the country to collect your child support.

Last, you have the contempt hearing. The usual excuse is that they can't afford to (fill in the blank) pay the child support, pay the mortgage, blah blah blah. Sometimes your husband will deliberately quit his job to get a lower child support or alimony. If that happens, be sure to ask the court to order him to do a job search through probation. If the court genuinely feels they need to adjust the existing order, they will, but usually they know the excuses are just excuses and threaten the deadbeat with a suspended jail term if they don't pay up within a few weeks.

The sample script at the end of the chapter introduces you to what we attorneys call "the three-O'clock speech." Essentially, the second or third time you drag your ex-husband into court to pay his bills, the judge will give them until the end of the day to cough up the money or they send them to jail.

One last note ... if you *can* afford to retain an attorney for this matter, many courts will award your husband to reimburse you for the *reasonable* court costs and attorney fees to have a lawyer prosecute the matter on your behalf. Unfortunately, most courts will *not* reimburse *you* for your time lost out of work chasing your ex-husband for your money. However, they *can* reimburse you any filing fees, private processor fees or the Sheriff, photocopying fees, or similar fees your attorney would bill you for as part as their bill.

EXHIBIT 20-1: COMPLAINT FOR CIVIL CONTEMPT

Commonwealth of Massachusetts
The Trial Court
Barnstable Division   **Probate and Family Court Department**   **Docket No. 07D-9999-DV1**

Complaint For Civil Contempt

_____ Jane Doe _____, Plaintiff

v.

_____ Jack Rayme _____, Defendant

1. Plaintiff, who resides at _17 Whale Watch Point, Juneau, Alaska 99999_
   (Street and No.)   (City or Town)   (County)   (State)   (Zip)
   is the former spouse of the defendant who now resides at ___2 Skid Row___
   (Street and No.)

   Anytown, MA 02673
   (City or Town)   (County)   (State)   (Zip)

2. By judgment – order – of the court dated __October 15, 2007__, the defendant was ordered:
   Ξ to increase child support for minor children to $101.00 per week via income assignment through the DOR beginning in and for the week of and ending October 15, 2007 and every week thereafter
   ⊐ to grant plaintiff visitation rights with _____
   ⊐ not to impose any restraint on the personal liberty of plaintiff
   ⊐ to pay health insurance premiums for the plaintiff and/or minor child(ren)
   ⊐ to pay reasonable medical and dental expenses
   ⊐ _____

3. Defendant has not obeyed that judgment – order – and
   Ξ is in arrears of court-ordered support payments
   Ξ there now remains due and unpaid to plaintiff the sum of $909.00 plus such further amounts as may accrue to the date of hearing
   ⊐ plaintiff has been denied visitation rights on
   Ξ has violated the order by not paying child support

4. Wherefore, plaintiff requests that defendant be required to appear before this court to show cause why said defendant should not be adjudged in contempt of Court and for such other relief as to said Court may deem just.

Date:_January 11, 2008_   Name: _Jane Doe_
                            Address: _17 Whale Watch Point_
                            Juneau, Alaska 99999
                            Tel. No. _(999) 867-5309_

EXHIBIT 20-2: PLAINTIFF'S MOTION FOR ATTORNEY'S FEES AND COSTS

COMMONWEALTH OF MASSACHUSETTS

BARNSTABLE, SS.   **PROBATE AND FAMILY COURT**   **DOCKET NO. 07D-9999-DV1**

JANE DOE-RAYME, Plaintiff)) v.)) **JACK RAYME,** Defendant)	**PLAINTIFF'S MOTION FOR ATTORNEY'S FEES AND COSTS**

Now comes the Plaintiff, JANE DOE-RAYME, in the above entitled and enumerated matter, and moves this Honorable Court to order the Defendant, JACK RAYME, pursuant to the provisions of MGL c.215, s.34A, to pay reasonable attorney's fees and costs incurred in the initiation, attempted resolution and prosecution of Plaintiff's Complaint for Contempt.

In support of this said Motion, the Plaintiff's attorney, Jack B. Quick, Esq., attaches hereto and incorporates herein her Affidavit.

WHEREFORE, the Plaintiff prays that this Honorable Court order the Defendant to pay to the Plaintiff's attorney, , P.O. Box 990, East Anytown, MA, 02345, the sum of Six Hundred Thirty-Seven Dollars and Fifty Cents ($637.50) as attorney's fees and ($54.45) in costs.

JANE DOE-RAYME,
By her attorney,

_____
Jack B. Quick, Esq.
P.O. Box 990
East Anytown, MA 02345
(508) 867-5309   BBO# 123456

Date: January 11, 2008

COMMONWEALTH OF MASSACHUSETTS
PROBATE AND FAMILY COURT   **DOCKET NO. 07D-9999-DV1**

BARNSTABLE, SS.

JANE DOE-RAYME, Plaintiff))) v.)) JACK RAYME,) Defendant)	AFFIDAVIT OF JACK B. QUICK IN SUPPORT OF PLAINTIFF'S MOTION FOR ATTORNEY'S FEES AND COSTS

I, Jack B. Quick, being duly sworn, depose and state the following:

1. I am Jack B. Quick, an attorney duly admitted to the practice of law within the Commonwealth of Massachusetts;
2. My law practice is devoted primarily to Family Law;
3. My hourly rate is ONE HUNDRED FIFTY DOLLARS ($150.00) per hour. This rate is consistent with that charged by other, similarly situated, attorneys practicing within Barnstable County.
4. In the matter of the Doe-Rayme v. Rayme, Barnstable Probate Court, Docket No. 07D-9999-DV1 Complaint for Contempt, I have expended the following time:

Client consultation	.50
Preparation of Complaint for Contempt & Motion, drafting various letters to the client, Probate Court and Deputy Sheriff's Office (arranging for service of process)	1.00
Anticipated travel time	.75
Anticipated appearance at Barnstable Probate Court	2.00
Total time: 4.25 hours	
Total Attorney Fees (x $150/hr):	**637.50**
Postage - 5 stamps x .41	2.05
Photocopies – 20 pp. x .10	2.00
Total Attorney Costs:	**4.05**
Deputy Sheriff's Civil Process to North Anytown	50.40
Sheriff's Costs:	**50.40**
Total Costs and Fees:	691.95

Signed under the penalties of perjury of law this 11th day of January, 2008.

_____
Jack B. Quick, Esq.

EXHIBIT 20-4: CONTEMPT NOTICE OF HEARING AND AFFIDAVIT OF SERVICE

COMMONWEALTH OF MASSACHUSETTS
BARNSTABLE, SS.   **PROBATE AND FAMILY COURT**   **DOCKET NO. 07D-9999-DV1**

JANE DOE-RAYME,) **Plaintiff**)) **v.**)) **JACK RAYME,**) **Defendant**))	**NOTICE OF HEARING AND** **AFFIDAVIT OF SERVICE**

This Motion for Attorney's Fees and Costs has been scheduled to be heard at <u>8:30 a.m.</u> on <u>February 2</u>, 2008 at <u>Barnstable Probate and Family Court</u> in Barnstable, Massachusetts at the same time as the Complaint for Contempt already filed.

Date: January 11, 2008

_____
Jack B. Quick, Esq.

AFFIDAVIT OF SERVICE

I, Jack B. Quick, Esq., hereby certify that a copy of the attached Motion for Attorney's Fees and Costs along with a Notice of Hearing and Affidavit of Costs were served upon JACK RAYME via Sheriff's Process Service simultaneously with a Complaint for Contempt.

A second copy has been forwarded to Mr. Rayme's attorney via USPS first class mail, postage prepaid, at:

Steve S. Slither, Esq.
10 Main Street
P.O. Box 666
Nextown, MA 02666

Signed this 11th day of January, 2008.

_____
Jack B. Quick, Esq.

Date: _____

EXHIBIT 20-5: CONTEMPT HEARING SAMPLE SCRIPT

Judge:	It says here, Mr. Rayme, that you are 9 weeks behind on your child support. Is that correct?
Jack:	Uhhh … I just mailed a payment to the DOR last week.
Judge (to magistrate):	Is that true. Has the DOR received a payment from Mr. Rayme?
Magistrate (to judge):	The DOR shows no record of a recent payment from Mr. Rayme.
Judge:	Do you have a receipt for the payment you sent?
Jack:	Uhhhh …. I didn't make a copy.
Judge (to magistrate):	How much is the DOR showing for an arrearage for Mr. Rayme?
Magistrate (to judge):	$909 as of last Friday.
Judge:	Mr. Rayme, how much did you send the DOR last week?
Jack:	Uhhhh … $200
Judge:	So why haven't you paid the other $700 the past 9 weeks?
Husband:	Uhhhh … I lost my job.
Judge (to Jane):	Is that true?
Jane:	Your honor, my husband was working for ABC Contractors. I spoke to the foreman last week and he said my husband simply stopped showing up for work a few weeks ago and that they had no choice but to fire him.
Judge:	Do you have any proof of that?
Jane:	As a matter of fact, yes. I served a subpoena on the company and their bookkeeper gave me a copy of his employment records with a clear notation that he was fired two weeks ago for not showing up at work.
Judge:	Mr. Rayme, I hereby find you in contempt of court. I am going to give you a 2-week jail term, which I will suspend for two weeks in order to give you a chance to come up with the past due child support. You must also pay your *current* child support. I am scheduling this matter for review in two weeks. If you have not paid by then, Mr. Rayme, the bailiff is going to take you into custody at that time. Do you understand this order?
Jack:	Uhhh…. Uhhhh…. Yea.
Judge:	I am also ordering you to pay Ms. Doe's court costs and legal fees for this hearing. Ms. Doe, I regret that I cannot reimburse you for your personal time lost out of work. Had you been able to afford to hire an attorney, I *could* have awarded you a reasonable amount of attorney fees.
Jack:	Yes, Sir. I understand.
Judge:	I *can*, however, reimburse you for the cost of the filing fee, having the Sheriff serve your husband, and these photocopying and other incidental costs you were able to document here in your affidavit. Mr. Rayme, I am ordering you to reimburse your former wife $54.45. You are very lucky your wife brought you into court yourself or you would be paying a lot more.
Jack:	Yes, Sir.
Judge:	Ms. Doe, if at the end of two weeks your husband has paid the back due child support to you, you do not need to appear.
Jane:	Thank you, sir.
Judge (to magistrate):	Schedule a review date for Monday, February 9th.

EXHIBIT 20-6: SECOND CONTEMPT HEARING SAMPLE SCRIPT (AKA 'THE THREE O'CLOCK SPEECH)

Judge:	I see you are both back before the court for review. Ms. Doe, has Mr. Rayme paid you your child support yet?
Jane:	No, Sir.
Judge (to magistrate):	Has the DOR received a payment from Mr. Rayme?
Magistrate (to judge):	The DOR *still* shows no record of a recent payment from Mr. Rayme.
Judge (to magistrate):	How much is the DOR showing for an arrearage?
Magistrate (to judge):	$1250 as of last Friday.
Judge (to Jack):	Mr. Rayme, I hereby find you in contempt of court and immediately revoke the suspension of your two week incarceration. Bailiff? If you please?
Bailiff:	Yes, your Honor.
Judge:	I want you to escort Mr. Rayme to the telephone to make a few telephone calls. If he has not come up with the $1250 he owes to Ms. Doe by 3:00 p.m. this afternoon, I want you to take him into custody and escort him up the hill to the Barnstable County House of Correction to serve his two week sentence.
Bailiff:	Yes, Sir.
Jack:	Sir! I'll come up with the money somehow, sir!
Judge:	See that you do. These are your own children you are failing to support, Mr. Rayme. The court has no patience when little human beings go hungry.
Jack:	Yes, Sir.
Judge:	Ms. Doe, I am going to schedule this matter for review in one week.
Jane:	Thank you, sir.

CHAPTER 21

CONCLUSION

I hope you found the information and materials contained in this manual to be helpful. If you *do* proceed with getting divorced, the advice "preparation" sections will hopefully enable you to escape the skinners knife and spring the trap without resorting to gnawing off your own leg.

After years of doing low-asset cases and pro bono work, it breaks my heart to repeatedly tell women who did *not* do this prep work or wandered into an attorney's office with no idea what the process entails that they shot themselves in the foot. When I look at the assets/debt the court divided in these "second look" cases, I see a huge gap between the couple's pre-divorce lifestyle and number of liabilities versus the claimed value of the assets. If the Wife and kids are living in poverty, it makes my blood boil!!! Unfortunately, it is too late for me to do anything to help them. The wife did not do her homework, the divorce is final, and she and her children are going to have to live with her mistakes.

Education - the process of learning by reading, studying, or hearing about (and avoiding) others mistakes and experiences.

Experience - the process of learning by getting knocked on your rear-end a few dozen times.

The law is a complex field subject to the whims of changing statutes, capricious case precedents, and the whim of judges. ***You will always do better if you hire a good divorce attorney!!!*** However, it is hoped by educating you about some of the more typical situations you see in divorce court and what tools are at your disposal to get what you need, you will be able to work *with* an attorney to get what is rightfully yours without unnecessary stress or breaking the bank. This book is only a general overview, but if you use it as a reference guide *before* you call your attorney, you can save hundreds or even thousands of dollars off your legal bill simply by not paying to get simple questions answered.

There are numerous books out there which you can get at your local library or go to the law library to read and learn more about specific areas of concern. I hope you follow up on some of the resources recommended in this manual or do your own research into other materials which may be available in *your* home state.

Remember that I was once in your shoes. *Don't* make the same mistakes that I made as a small woodland creature with a limited education, few resources, and little familial or societal support. Educate thyself … and then go kick the Evil Trapper's butt!

Best wishes and good luck!

Rosie the Riveter by J. Howard Miller

A

Abuse
  Defined, 21
Alimony
  Alimony Income, *103*
  Alimony Need, *103*
  Alimony Reform, *112*
  Defined, *97*
  Effect of Remarriage, *109*
  Estimating, *98*
  Four Types Of, *103*
  Gender Neutrality, *107*
  General Term Alimony, *101*
  Income from Assets Already Divided, *103*
  Interplay with Child Support, *104*
  Life Insurance and, *108*
  Rehabilitative Alimony, *102*
  Reimbursement Alimony, *102*
  Swapping Out Marital Assets for, *110*
  Tax Issues, 132
  Temporary Solution, *97*
  Termination, *107*
  Transitional Alimony, *103*
  Types of, *100*
Appeals, 511
Appreciating Asset, 136
Attorney
  Getting Your Spouse to Help Pay, 165
  How to Save Money On, 160
Attorneys
  How to Find, 158
  Lawyer Of The Day Programs, 170
  Saving Money on Legal Bills, 181
  State Self-Help Website List, 176
Automatic Restraining Order, 187, 353
Automatic stay
  Exceptions - attorney fees, 7
Automatic Stay, 168

B

Best Interests of the Child, 375
bifurcate, 388
Burden of Proof, 119
  Income, *77*
  Sympathy for the Self-Employed, *78*
Business Property
  Defined, 116

C

CASA, 390

Case Law Citation, 179
Child Abduction, 16
Child Custody
  Best Interests of the Child Standard, 375
  Custody Defects, 376
  Guardian Ad Litem, 390
  Joint Legal Custody, 376
  Motion to Appoint a GAL, 391
  Parenting Plans, 389
  Primary Caretaker, 376
  Relocation Out of State, 393
  Shared Physical Custody, 376
  Sole Physical Custody, 376
  Types of Custody, 375
Child Support
  Calculating, 70
  Child Support Enforcement Division, *93*
  Children from Prior Relationships, 71
  Court Orders For, *93*
  Defined, 65
  Emancipation, 68
  Spouses Hiding Money, 72
  States Where Ends at H.S., 69
  States Where Through College, 69
  Who is Obligated to Pay, 65
Choice of Forum Clause, 229
Choice of Law Clause, 228
Closing Argument, 503
Community Property
  Defined, 115
Complaint
  Complaint for Divorce, 348
Complaints
  Complaint for Contempt, 515
Contempt, 513
Contested Divorce
  Defined, 185
Contested Divorces
  Checklist, 343
court appointed special advocate, 390
Credit Rating
  Credit Reports, 196
  Steps to Protect, 192
Cross-Examination, 488

D

de minimus
  defined, 129
Dear Judge Letter, *457*
Debt
  Credit card bills, 6
  Credit Card Debt, 141

Credit Counseling Agencies, 153
List of Resources, 154
Medical and Dental Debts, 141
Secured Debt, 139
Solutions to, 150
Student Loans, 141
Depositions, *438*
Depreciating Asset, 136
Direct Examination, *478*
Direct Examination Questions, *479*
Discovery
Answering Discovery Requests, 417, *424*, *430*, *437*
Attorney Trade Manuals, 401
Defined, 40, 399
Deposition - Motion to Quash, *441*
Deposition Subpoena, *439*
Depositions, *438*
Depositions - Type Of, *438*
Document Requests, 413
Expert Interrogatories, *435*
Interrogatories, *425*
Interrogatories - Limit of 30, *425*
Interrogatories - Sample, *426*
Mandatory Self-Disclosure, 409
Motion to Compel, *447*
Motion to Compel Financial Statement, 407
Request for Financial Statement, 405
Request for the Production of Documents, 414
Requests for Admissions of Fact, 422
Sample Expert Interrogatories, *436*
Sanctions, *445*
Domestic Violence
Children, 20, 26
Hotline, 19
Dress
How to Dress for Court, 364
Dress, for court, 30

E

Emancipation
Defined, 68
Equitable Distribution
Defined, 116
Equity
defined, 42
Evidence, *476*
Evidentiary Issues
Hearsay, 478
'truly and accurately depict', 30
Expert Interrogatories, *435*

F

Father's Rights movement, 387

Father's Rights Movement, 27
Financial Statement
Certification under Oath, 64
Gross Weekly Income Calculator, 57
Salary v. Wage, 56
Financial Statements
Dissected, 54
Save $50, 52
Tax Fraud, 55
Where to Find, 53
Forum Shopping, 202
Four-Way Conference, *459*

G

Gifted Property, 119
gifts, 117
Guardian Ad Litem, 390

H

Health Insurance
issues, 35
Hearsay
defined, 30
Hiding Money
B.S. in Financial Statement, *79*
Child Support, *72*
Scrutinizing the Schedule C, *84*
Using Quicken to Document Expenses, *83*
High Maintenance Asset, 136

I

Identification of the Parties, 224
Immigration Issues, 17, 31
Impeach, *479*
Incorporate and Merge, 206
Indemnification, 233
Inheritances or gifts, 117
Inherited Property, 119
Interrogatories, *425*

J

Judgment of Divorce, 508
Jurisdiction, 202, 350
Forum Shopping, 202

K

Keeper of the Records, *438*

L

Legal Resources

Attorney Trade Manuals, 178
Legal Services, 169
Liquidation of Assets, 17

M

Mandatory Self-Disclosure, 33, 409
Mediation, 167
    Advantages, 186
    Court Connected, 169
    Disadvantages, 187
    Mediation Clauses, 237
    When Not a Good Fit, 167
Merger v. Survival, 206
    Merger and Survival Clauses, 228
Motion for Attorney Fees, 516
Motion for Attorney Fees Pendente Lite, 165

O

Opening Statement, 499

P

Parental Alienation Syndrome:, 387
Personal Property
    Defined, 116
Pre-Trial Conference, *453*
    Four-Way Conference, *459*
    Pre-Trial Conference Order, *455*
Pre-Trial Memorandum, *460*
Privelege, *442*
    Clergyman/communicant, *443*
Privilege, *392*
    Attorney/Client, *443*
    Husband/Wife, *443*
    Physician/Patient, *442*
    Psychotherapist/Patient, *442*
Property division
    Effect of child custody, 10
Property Division
    Buying Out the Marital Home, 128
    Gifted or Inherited Property, 119
    Property Division Factors, *457*
    Tax Issues, 131
    Who Will Stay in Marital Home, 198
Property, type of
    Commingled Property, 117
Property, types of
    Marital Property, 117
    Separate Property, 117

R

Real Property
    Defined, 116

Reasonably Prudent Person Standard, 22
Rehabilitative Witness, *486*
Request for the Production of Documents, 413
Requests for Admission, 422
Restraining Orders
    criteria to get, 21
    Evidence of Abuse, 28
    talking points, 28
Retirement Assets
    Defined Benefit Plan, 44
    Defined Contribution Plan, 43
    Pension Valuation Services, 44
    Vested, 44

S

Same sex marriage, 13
Separation Agreement
    Blank Example - With Children, 277
    Blank Example - Without Without Children, 311
    Defined, 186
Separation Agreements
    Permanancy, 217
    Preamble, 224
    Temporary Separation Agreement, 201
Social Media Hazards, 48
Social Security, 36
Stable Value Asset, 136
Stipulations
    Sample Family Services Stipulation, 368
Subpoenas, 492
Survive as a Separate Contract, 206

T

Tax Issues
    Alimony, 132
    Marital Home, 132
    Pensions and Retirement Accounts, 132
    Property Division, 131
    Stocks and Bonds, 132
    Tax Evasion, *77, 84*
Temporary Orders, 356
    Affidavit in Support Of, 359
    Counter Claim, 362
Trial
    Closing Argument, 503
    Cross-Examination, 488
    Direct Examination, *478*
    Opening Statement, 499
Trial Preparation, *470*
    Attorney Trade Manuals, *471*
    Theory of the Case, *471*

U

Uncontested Divorce
    Defined, 185

V

Valuation, 40
    Acorns Checklist, 39
    Asset Valuation Notebook, 38
    Business Equipment, 45
    Business Records, 36

    Expense Notebook, 38
    Hobby Supplies, 45
    Motor Vehicles, 42
    Pensions and Retirement Benefits, 43
    Personal Property, 46
    Real Property (house, land), 42
    Valuation Worksheet, 40

W

Waiver of Liability Clause, 233
Warranty of Free Will, 229

ABOUT THE AUTHOR

Anna T. Merrill practices family law, intellectual property law, and municipal 'green' zoning law on Cape Cod, Massachusetts. She is passionate about providing affordable, sensible legal services for 'real' people who the mainstream legal system has forgotten. She serves men and women equally, but volunteers her legal services to various agencies to help low- and moderate-income people access the legal system.

She has worked with agencies such as the Committee for Public Counsel Services Children and Family Law Project, and also pro bono legal work for women's services agencies such as WE CAN, Inc., and the Women's Bar Foundation Family Law Project for Battered Women. She is also trained in corporate law with a specialty in business continuity services (i.e., disaster planning) and worked five years in the business continuity field helping Fortune 500 companies draft and implement continuity (disaster) plans.

She is a graduate of Massachusetts School of Law, with an undergraduate degree in Psychology from Lesley University and an Associate's Degree in Business from Fisher College.

In addition to volunteering her legal expertise, she also volunteers on the Barnstable County CERT (Community Emergency Response Team) and also the Cape Cod Amateur Radio Emergency Service (ARES). She is a licensed ham radio operator, a frugal living zealot, and studies Urban Goju karate. In addition to writing alone or in collaboration with others numerous corporate business continuity plans, zoning by-laws, policies and procedures manuals and other trade publications, she has written several frugal living self-help guides and also publishes fiction under a pen name.

SERAPHIM PRESS

CAPE COD, MA

DIVORCE BOOTCAMP FOR LOW- AND MODERATE-INCOME WOMEN

Made in the USA
Middletown, DE
27 July 2017